# MEMORY, HISTORY, FORGETTING

# Memory, History, Forgetting

## PAUL RICOEUR

Translated by Kathleen Blamey and David Pellauer

THE UNIVERSITY OF CHICAGO PRESS
Chicago & London

PAUL RICOEUR is the John Nuveen Professor Emeritus in the Divinity School, the Department of Philosophy, and the Committee on Social Thought at the University of Chicago. Among his many books are the three-volume *Time and Narrative*, *Oneself as Another*, and *The Just*, all published by the University of Chicago Press.

Kathleen Blamey has taught philosophy at California State University, Hayward, and the American University in Paris. David Pellauer is professor of philosophy at DePaul University.

The University of Chicago Press, Chicago 60637
The University of Chicago Press, Ltd., London
© 2004 by The University of Chicago
All rights reserved. Published 2004
Printed in the United States of America
13 12 11 10 09 08 07 06 05          3 4 5

ISBN: 0-226-71341-5 (cloth)

Frontispiece: D. H. Herberger, *History and Chronos*, ca. 1750, Wiblingen Monastery, Ulm, Germany. Photo © Atelier Juliane Zitzlsperger.

Library of Congress Cataloging-in-Publication Data

Ricoeur, Paul.
  [Mémoire, l'histoire, l'oubli. English]
  Memory, history, forgetting / Paul Ricoeur ; translated by Kathleen Blamey and David Pellauer.
    p.  cm.
  Includes bibliographical references and index.
  ISBN 0-226-71341-5 (hardcover : alk. paper)
  1. Memory (Philosophy)   2. History—Philosophy.   I. Title.
  B2430.R553M4613   2004
  128'.3—dc22

                                        2004001269

⊗ The paper used in this publication meets the minimum requirements of the American National Standard for Information Sciences—Permanence of Paper for Printed Library Materials, ANSI Z39.48-1992.

*Dans la mémoire de Simone Ricoeur*

*He who has been, from then on cannot not have been:*
*henceforth this mysterious and profoundly obscure fact of*
*having been is his viaticum for all eternity.*

§ Vladimir Jankélévitch

*In a special place in the library of the monastery there stands a superb baroque sculpture. It is the dual figure of history. In the foreground, Kronos, the winged god. An old man with wreathed brow: his left hand grips a large book, his right hand attempts to tear out a page. Behind and above, stands history itself. The gaze is grave and searching; one foot topples a horn of plenty from which spills a cascade of gold and silver, sign of instability; the left hand checks the act of the god, while the right displays history's instruments: the book, the inkpot, and the stylus.*

§ Wiblingen Monastery, Ulm

Entre la DÉCHIRURE par le temps ailé

et l'ÉCRITURE de l'histoire et son stylet

Paul Ricœur

# CONTENTS

# PREFACE

The present investigation has grown out of several preoccupations, some private, some professional, and others, finally, that I would call public.

Private preoccupation: to say nothing of my gaze directed back now over a long life—*Réflexion faite* (looking back)—it is a question here of returning to a lacuna in the problematic of *Time and Narrative* and in *Oneself as Another*, where temporal experience and the narrative operation are directly placed in contact, at the price of an impasse with respect to memory and, worse yet, of an impasse with respect to forgetting, the median levels between time and narrative.

Professional consideration: this investigation reflects the frequenting of works, seminars, and symposia in the company of professional historians who have been confronting the same problems regarding the ties between memory and history. This book is a prolongation of this uninterrupted conversation.

Public preoccupation: I continue to be troubled by the unsettling spectacle offered by an excess of memory here, and an excess of forgetting elsewhere, to say nothing of the influence of commemorations and abuses of memory—and of forgetting. The idea of a policy of the just allotment of memory is in this respect one of my avowed civic themes.

§

The work contains three clearly defined parts, distinguished by their theme and their method. The first part, devoted to memory and to mnemonic phenomena, is placed under the aegis of phenomenology in the Husserlian sense of the term. The second part, dedicated to history, comes under the scope of an epistemology of the historical sciences. The third part, culminating in a meditation on forgetting, is framed within a hermeneutics of the historical condition of the human beings that we are.

Each of these three parts unfolds along a planned course marked in each case by a threefold rhythm. In this way, the phenomenology of memory begins deliberately with an analysis turned toward the object of memory, the memory (*souvenir*) that one has before the mind; it then passes through the stage of the search for a given memory, the stage of anamnesis, of recollection; we then finally move from memory as it is given and exercised to reflective memory, to memory of oneself.

The epistemological course embraces the three phases of the historiographical operation; from the stage of witnessing and of the archives, it passes through the usages of "because" in the figures of explanation and understanding; it ends on the scriptural level of the historian's representation of the past.

The hermeneutics of the historical condition also embodies three stages; the first is that of a critical philosophy of history, of a critical hermeneutics, attentive to the limits of historical knowledge that a certain hubris of historical science transgresses again and again; the second stage is that of an ontological hermeneutics intent on exploring the modalities of temporalization that together constitute the existential condition of historical knowledge; buried under the footprints of memory and history then opens the empire of forgetting, an empire divided against itself, torn between the threat of the definitive effacement of traces and the assurance that the resources of anamnesis are placed in reserve.

These three parts, however, do not constitute three books. Although the three masts carry interlocking but distinct sails, they belong to the same ship setting off for a single itinerary. A common problematic, in fact, flows through the phenomenology of memory, the epistemology of history, and the hermeneutics of the historical condition: the problematic of the representation of the past. The question is posed in its radicality as early as the investigation of the object-side of memory: what is there to say of the enigma of an image, of an *eikōn*—to speak Greek with Plato and Aristotle—that offers itself as the presence of an absent thing stamped with the seal of the anterior? The same question crosses through the epistemology of testimony, then through that of social representations taken as the privileged object of explanation/understanding, to unfold on the plane of the scriptural representation of events, conjunctures, and structures that punctuate the historical past. The initial enigma of the *eikōn* will continue to grow from chapter to chapter. Transferred from the sphere of memory to that of history, it reaches its height in the hermeneutics of the historical condition, where the representation of the past is found to be exposed to the dangers of forgetting, but is also entrusted to its protection.

§

A few remarks addressed to the reader.

In this book I am trying out a form of presentation I have never used before: in an effort to rid the text of the most burdensome didactic considerations—introducing each theme, recalling the links with the preceding line of arguments, anticipating subsequent developments—I have placed guidelines to the reader at the main strategic points of the work that will tell the reader at what point I am in the investigation. I hope that this manner of negotiating with the reader's patience will be well received.

Another remark: I frequently mention and quote authors belonging to different epochs, but I do not present a history of the problem. I summon this or that author according to the requirements of the argument, without concerning myself with the epoch. This seems to me to be the right of every reader, before whom all the books are open simultaneously.

Shall I confess, finally, that I have no fixed rule in the use of "I" and "we," excluding the "we" of authority and majesty? I prefer to say "I" when I assume an argument as my own and "we" when I hope to draw my reader along with me.

So let our three-masted ship set sail!

§

Allow me, now that the work is over, to express my gratitude to those among my close relations who have accompanied and, if I may venture to say, have approved of my undertaking. I will not name them here.

I set apart the names of those who, in addition to their friendship, have shared their competence with me: François Dosse who advised me in my exploration of the historian's workshop; Thérèse Duflot who, thanks to her typing skills, became my first reader, always vigilant and at times merciless; and, finally, Emmanuel Macron to whom I am indebted for a pertinent critique of the writing and the elaboration of the critical apparatus of this work. A final word of thanks to the president and director of the Éditions du Seuil and to the directors of the collection "L'ordre philosophique," who have, once again, accorded me their trust and their patience.

# PART I

## *On Memory and Recollection*

*The phenomenology* of memory proposed here is structured around two questions: *Of what* are there memories? *Whose* memory is it?

These two questions are asked in the spirit of Husserlian phenomenology. Within this heritage, priority has been given to the assertion expressed by the well-known adage that all consciousness is consciousness of something. This "object-oriented" approach poses a specific problem on the plane of memory. Is not memory fundamentally reflexive, as the pronominal form which predominates in French would lead us to believe: to remember (*se souvenir de*) something is at the same time to remember oneself (*se souvenir de soi*)? We were determined, nevertheless, to pose the question "What?" before the question "Who?" despite the philosophical tradition that tends to favor the egological side of mnemonic experience. The primacy long accorded to the question "Who?" has had the negative effect of leading the analysis of mnemonic phenomena to an impasse, when the notion of collective memory was to be taken into account. If the "I" in the first person singular is too hastily declared the subject of memory, the notion of collective memory can take shape only as an analogical concept, even as a foreign body in the phenomenology of memory. If one wishes to avoid being stymied by a fruitless aporia, then one must hold in abeyance the question of attributing to someone—hence, to any of the grammatical persons—the act of remembering and begin with the question "What?" In accordance with solid phenomenological doctrine, the egological question—whatever the *ego* may signify—should come after the intentional question, which is imperatively that of the correlation between the act (the noesis) and the intentional correlate (the noema). The wager made in this first part devoted to memory, without regard to its fate over the course of the historiographical stage of the relation to the past, thus hinges on our ability to carry out a phenomenology of memory, the objective moment of memory, as far as possible.

The time to move from the question "What?" to the question "Who?" will be delayed even further by a significant split within the initial question between a properly cognitive side and a pragmatic side. The history of the notions and the words is instructive in this regard: the Greeks had two words *mnēmē* and *anamnēsis* to designate, on the one hand, memory as appearing, ultimately passively, to the point of characterizing as an affection—*pathos*—the popping into mind of a memory; and, on the other, the memory as an object of a search ordinarily named recall, recollection. Memories, by turns found and sought, are therefore situated at the crossroads of semantics and pragmatics. To remember is to have a memory or to set off in search of a memory. In this sense, the question "How?" posed by *anamnēsis* tends to separate itself from the question "What?" more narrowly posed by *mnēmē*. This split into the cognitive and pragmatic approaches has a major influence on the claim of memory to be faithful to the past: this claim defines the truthful status of memory, which will later have to be confronted with the truth claim of history. In the meantime, the interference of the pragmatics of memory, by virtue of which remembering is doing something, has a jamming effect on the entire problematic of veracity: possibilities of abuse are ineluctably grafted onto the resources of usage, of use, of memory apprehended along its pragmatic axis. The typology of uses and abuses proposed in chapter 2 will be superimposed on the typology of the mnemonic phenomena of chapter 1.

At the same time, the pragmatic approach of *anamnēsis* will provide an appropriate transition from the question "What?" taken in the strict sense of an investigation into the cognitive resources of memory, to the question "Who?" centered on the appropriation of memory by a subject capable of self-recollection.

This will be our path: from "What?" to "Who?" passing by way of "How?" From memories to reflective memory, passing by way of recollection.

# CHAPTER 1

## *Memory and Imagination*

### READING GUIDELINES

By submitting to the primacy of the question "What?" the phenomenology of memory finds itself at the outset confronting a formidable aporia present in ordinary language: the presence in which the representation of the past seems to consist does indeed appear to be that of an image. We say interchangeably that we represent a past event to ourselves or that we have an image of it, an image that can be either quasi visual or auditory. In addition to ordinary language, a long philosophical tradition, which surprisingly combines the influence of English-language empiricism with the rationalism of a Cartesian stamp, considers memory the province of the imagination, the latter having long been treated with suspicion, as we see in Montaigne and Pascal. This continues to be the case, most significantly, in Spinoza. We read in proposition 18 of the second part of the *Ethics: On the Nature and the Origin of the Soul*: "If the human Body has once been affected by two or more bodies at the same time, then when the Mind subsequently imagines one of them, it will immediately recollect the others also."[1] This sort of short-circuit between memory and imagination is placed under the sign of the association of ideas: if these two affections are tied by contiguity, to evoke one—to imagine it—is to evoke the other—to remember it. Memory, reduced to recall, thus operates in the wake of the imagination. Imagination, considered in itself, is located at the lowest rung of the ladder of modes of knowledge, belonging to the affections that are subject to the connection governing things external to the human body, as underscored by the scholia that follows: "this connection happens according to the order and connection of the affections of the human Body in order to distinguish it from the connection of ideas which happens according to the order of the intellect"

(466). This declaration is all the more remarkable in that we read in Spinoza a magnificent definition of time, or rather of duration, as "continuation of existence." What is surprising is that memory is not related to this apprehension of time. And as memory, considered, moreover, as a mode of learning, in terms of the memorization of traditional texts, has a bad reputation—see Descartes's *Discourse on Method*—nothing comes to the aid of memory as the specific function of accessing the past.

As a countercurrent to this tradition of devaluing memory, in the margins of a critique of imagination, there has to be an uncoupling of imagination from memory, as far as this operation can be extended. The guiding idea in this regard is the eidetic difference, so to speak, between two aims, two intentionalities: the first, that of imagination, directed toward the fantastic, the fictional, the unreal, the possible, the utopian, and the other, that of memory, directed toward prior reality, priority constituting the temporal mark par excellence of the "thing remembered," of the "remembered" as such.

The difficulties inherent in this operation of uncoupling hearken back to the Greek origin of the problematic (section 1: "The Greek Heritage"). On the one hand, the Platonic theory of the *eikōn* places the main emphasis on the phenomenon of the presence of an absent thing, the reference to past time remaining implicit. This problematic of the *eikōn* has its own relevance and its own proper instance, as our subsequent investigations will confirm. Nevertheless, it has become an obstacle to recognizing the specificity of the properly *temporalizing* function of memory. We must turn to Aristotle to find an acknowledgment of this specificity. The proud declaration that we read in the magnificent little text of the *Parva naturalia: On Memory and Recollection*—"All memory is of the past"—will become our lodestar for the rest of our exploration.

The central part of this study, "A Phenomenological Sketch of Memory," will be devoted to an effort to form a typology of mnemonic phenomena. Despite its apparent dispersion, this study aims at determining the original experience of temporal distance, of the depth of time past, through a series of approximations. I will not conceal the fact that this plea on behalf of memory's mark of distinction has to be paired with a parallel revision of the thematic of the imaginary, similar to what Sartre undertook to do in his two books, *L'Imagination* and *L'Imaginaire*, a revision that would tend to dislodge the image from its alleged place "in" consciousness. The critique of the picture-image would then become one document in the file common to imagination and to memory, a file that begins with the Platonic theme of the presence of the absent.

However, I do not think that one can be content with this twofold operation of specifying the imaginary, on one hand, and memories, on the other. There must be an irreducible feature in the living experience of memory that explains the persistence of the confusion conveyed by the expression "memory-image." It does appear that the return of a memory can only take place in the mode of becoming-an-image. The parallel revision of the phenomenology of memories and the phenomenology of images will encounter its limit in this image-making process of memories (section 3: "Memories and Images").

The constant danger of confusing remembering and imagining, resulting from memories becoming images in this way, affects the goal of faithfulness corresponding to the truth claim of memory. And yet . . .

And yet, we have nothing better than memory to guarantee that something has taken place before we call to mind a memory of it. Historiography itself, let us already say, will not succeed in setting aside the continually derided and continually reasserted conviction that the final referent of memory remains the past, whatever the pastness of the past may signify.

§

## THE GREEK HERITAGE
The problem posed by the entanglement of memory and imagination is as old as Western philosophy. Socratic philosophy bequeathed to us two rival and complementary *topoi* on this subject, one Platonic, the other Aristotelian. The first, centered on the theme of the *eikōn*, speaks of the present representation of an absent thing; it argues implicitly for enclosing the problematic of memory within that of imagination. The second, centered on the theme of the representation of a thing formerly perceived, acquired, or learned, argues for including the problematic of the image within that of remembering. These are the two versions of the aporia of imagination and memory from which we can never completely extricate ourselves.

### Plato: The Present Representation of an Absent Thing
It is important to note from the start that it is within the framework of the dialogues on the sophist and, through this person, on sophistry itself and the properly ontological possibility of error, that the notion of the *eikōn* is encountered, either alone or paired with that of the *phantasma*. In this way,

from the very outset, the image but also by implication memory are cast under a cloud of suspicion due to the philosophical environment in which they are examined. How, asks Socrates, is the sophist possible and, with him, the false-speaking and, finally, the non-being implied by the non-true? It is within this framework that the two dialogues bearing the titles *Theaetetus* and *Sophist* pose the problem. To complicate matters further, the problematic of the *eikōn* is, in addition, from the outset associated with the imprint, the *tupos*, through the metaphor of the slab of wax, error being assimilated either to an erasing of marks, *semeia*, or to a mistake akin to that of someone placing his feet in the wrong footprints. We see by this how from the beginning the problem of forgetting is posed, and even twice posed, as the effacement of traces and as a defect in the adjustment of the present image to the imprint left as if by a seal in wax. It is noteworthy that memory and imagination already share the same fate in these founding texts. This initial formulation of the problem makes all the more remarkable Aristotle's statement that "all memory is of the past."

Let us reread the *Theaetetus*, beginning at 163d.[2] We are at the heart of a discussion centered around the possibility of false judgment, which concludes with a reference to the thesis that "knowledge is simply perception" (151e–187b).[3] Socrates proposes the following "attack": "Supposing you were asked, 'If a man has once come to know a certain thing, and continues to preserve the memory of it, is it possible that, at the moment when he remembers it, he doesn't know this thing that he is remembering?' But I am being long-winded, I'm afraid. What I am trying to ask is, 'Can a man who has learned something not know it when he is remembering it?'" (163d). The strong tie of the entire problematic to eristic is immediately obvious. Indeed, it is only after having crossed through the lengthy apology of Protagoras, and his open pleading in favor of the measure of man, that a solution begins to dawn, but, before that, an even more pointed question is raised: "Now, to begin, do you expect someone to grant you that a man's present memory of something which he has experienced in the past but is no longer experiencing is the same sort of experience as he then had? This is very far from being true" (166b). An insidious question, which leads the entire problematic into what will appear to us to be a trap, namely, resorting to the category of similarity to resolve the enigma of the presence of the absent, an enigma common to imagination and memory. Protagoras tried to enclose the authentic aporia of memories, namely, the presence of the absent, in the eristic of the (present) non-knowledge of (past) knowledge. Armed with a new confidence in thinking, likened to a dialogue of the soul with itself, Socrates develops a sort of phenomenology of mistakes, where one thing is taken for another. To resolve this paradox he proposes the metaphor of the block of wax: "Now I want you to suppose, for the sake of the argument, that we have in our souls a block of wax, larger in one person, smaller in another, and of pure wax in one case, dirtier in another; in some men rather hard, in others rather soft, while in some it is of just the proper consistency." Theaetetus: "All right, I'm supposing that." Socrates: "We may look upon it, then, as a gift of Memory [*Mnemosyne*], the mother of the Muses. We make impressions upon this of everything we wish to remember [*mnēmoneusai*] among the things we have seen or heard or thought of ourselves; we hold the wax under our perceptions and thoughts and take a stamp from them, in the way in which we take the imprints [marks, *sēmeia*] of signet rings. Whatever is impressed upon the wax we remember and know so long as the image [*eidōlon*] remains in the wax; whatever is obliterated or cannot be impressed, we forget [*epilelēsthai*] and do not know" (191d). Let us note that the metaphor of the wax conjoins the problematics of memory and forgetting. There follows a subtle typology of all the possible combinations between the moment of knowledge and the moment of the acquisition of the imprint. Among these, let us note the following pairs: "that a thing which you both know and are perceiving, and the record of which you are keeping in its true line [*ekhōn to mnēmeion orthōs*] is another thing which you know . . . that a thing you both know and are perceiving and of which you have the record correctly in line as before, is another thing you are perceiving" (192b–c). It is in an effort to identify this veridical characteristic of faithfulness that we will later reorient the entire discussion. Pursuing the analogy of the imprint, Socrates assimilates true opinion to an exact fit and false opinion to a bad match: "Now, when perception is *present* to one of the imprints but not to the other; when (in other words) the mind applies the *imprint* of the absent perception to the perception that is *present*; the mind is deceived in every such instance" (194a).[4] We need not linger over the enumeration of the different kinds of wax, intended as a guide to the typology of good or bad memories. But let me not fail to mention, however, for our reading pleasure, the ironic reference (194e–195a) to "those whose wax is shaggy" (*Iliad* II!) and "soft." Let us retain the more substantive idea that false opinion resides "not in the relations of perceptions to one another, or of thoughts to one another, but in the connecting [*sunapsis*] of perception with thought" (195c–d). The reference to time we might expect from the use of the verb "to preserve in memory" is not relevant in the framework of an epistemic theory that is concerned with the status of false opinion, hence with judgment and not with memory as such. Its strength is to embrace in full, from the perspective of a phenomenology of mistakes, the aporia of the presence of absence.[5]

With regard to its impact on the theory of imagination and of memory, it is the same overarching problematic that is responsible for the shift in metaphor with the allegory of the dovecote.[6] Following this new model ("the model of the aviary" in the words of Burnyeat), we are asked to accept the identification between possessing knowledge and actively using it, in the manner in which holding a bird in the hand differs from keeping it in a cage. In this way, we have moved from the apparently passive metaphor of the imprint left by a seal to a metaphor that stresses power or capacity in the definition of knowledge. The epistemic question is this: does the distinction between a capacity and its exercise make it conceivable that one can judge that something one has learned and whose knowledge one possesses (the birds that someone keeps) is something that one knows (the bird one grabs in the cage) (197b–c)? The question touches our discussion inasmuch as a faulty memorization of the rules leads to an error in counting. At first glance, we are far from the instances of errors of fit corresponding to the model of the block of wax. Were these not, nevertheless, comparable to the erroneous use of a capacity and, by this, to a mistake? Had not the imprints to be memorized in order to enter into use in the case of acquired knowledge? In this way the problem of memory is indirectly concerned by what could be considered a phenomenology of mistakes. The failed fit and the faulty grasp are two figures of mistakes. The "model of the aviary" is especially well-suited to our investigation inasmuch as grasping is in every case comparable to a possession (*hexis* or *ktēsis*), and above all to hunting, and in which every memory search is also a hunt. Let us again follow Socrates, when, as a true sophist, he surpasses himself in subtleties, mixing ring doves with doves but also non-doves with real doves. Confusion is rampant not only at the moment of capture but also with respect to the state of possession.[7]

By these unexpected divisions and duplications, the analogy of the dovecote (or the model of the aviary) reveals a richness comparable to that of the foot mistakenly placed in the wrong print. To the mis-fit is added the erroneous grasp, the mis-take. However, the fate of the *eikōn* has been lost from sight. The *Sophist* will lead us back to it.

The problematic of the *eikōn* developed in the *Sophist* comes directly to the aid of the enigma of the presence of absence concentrated in the passage in *Theaetetus* 194 related above.[8] What is at stake is the status of the moment of recollection, treated as the recognition of an imprint. The possibility of falsehood is inscribed in this paradox.[9]

Let us focus on the key passage in the *Sophist* in which Plato distinguishes veracity from trickery in the order of imitation (234ff.).[10] The framework of the discussion resembles that of the *Theaetatus*: how are sophistry and its art of illusion possible? The Stranger and Theaetatus are in agreement in saying that the sophist—him again!—is principally an imitator of being and of truth, someone who manufactures "imitations" (*mimēmata*) and "homonyms" (*homōnuma*) of beings (234b). Here we change metaphors. We pass from the imprint in wax to the portrait, the metaphor extending in its turn from graphic arts to language arts (*eidōla legomena*, "spoken copies of everything" capable of making us believe "the words are true" [234c]). We are thus in the midst of technique, of mimetic technique, in which imitation and magic ("a kind of magician" [235b5]) are indistinguishable. Within this assigned framework Plato practices his favored method of *division*: "We'll divide the craft of copymaking [*eidōlopoiikēn tekhnēn*] as quickly as we can" (235b). On one side we have *tekhnē eikastikē* ("the art of likeness-making. That's the one we have whenever someone produces an imitation by keeping to the proportions of length, breadth, and depth of his model, and also by keeping to the appropriate colors of its parts" [235d–e]). On the other side we have the simulacrum or appearance, for which Plato reserves the term *phantasma*. So here we have *eikōn* opposed to *phantasma*, "eikastic" art to "fantastic" art, the making of likenesses to the making of appearances (236c). With regard to its specific character, the problem of memory has disappeared, overwhelmed by the dominant problematic, namely, the question of knowing in what compartment the Sophist can be placed. The Stranger confesses his bafflement. The entire problem of mimetics is, by the same stroke, dragged into the aporia. To get out of it, it will be necessary to move higher in the hierarchy of concepts and assume nonbeing.

The idea of "faithful resemblance" belonging to the eikastic art will at least have served as a relay. Plato seems to have noted the threshold of the impasse, when he asks himself: "what in the world do we mean by a 'copy' [*eidōlon*]?" (239d). We lose our way in the enumeration of examples that seem to escape the art of orderly division and, first of all, that of generic definition: "What in the world would we say a copy is, sir, except something that's made similar (*heteron*) to a true thing and is another thing that's like it?" (240a). But what is the meaning of "a true thing"? And "another thing"? And "like it"? Now we are at sea: "So you're saying that which is like [*eikōna*] is not really that which is, if you speak of it as not real existence, if you are going to call it not true?" (240b). To say this, we recognize that we have been forced "to agree unwillingly that that which is not in a way is" (240c). The phenomenological difference, as it were, between eikastic and fantastic is caught up in the whirl-wind in which eristic and dialectic are scarcely distinguishable. All of this is perhaps due to the fact that the sophist's question of being has swamped the discussion, and the battle against Parmenides—against "what our Father says" (241d)—has expended all the intellectual energy. We even see the three terms, *eidōlon*, *eikōn*, and *phantasia*, reunited under the ignominious charge of deception (*apatō*, 260c), and a bit later: "copy-making and appearance-making [*eidōlopoiikēn kai phantastikēn*]" (260d). It is simply recommended that "we have to search around for the nature of speech [*logos*], belief [*doxa*], and appearance [*phantasia*]" (260e) from the viewpoint of their "association with *that which is not*" (ibid.).

Let us take stock of the aporetic results of our passage through the Platonic texts on memory. We can lay out the difficulties in the following order. The first has to do with the absence (noted in passing) of explicit reference to the distinctive feature of memory, namely, the anteriority of "marks," *sēmeia*, in which the affections of the body and the soul to which memory is attached are signified. It is true that on many occasions past verb tenses are explicitly employed, but there is no separate reflection devoted to these indisputable deictic forms. It is on this point that Aristotle's analyses will mark a clear break.

The second difficulty concerns the sort of relation that exists between the *eikōn* and the first mark, as this is sketched out within the framework of the imitative arts. To be sure, the distinction made in the *Sophist* between eikastic art and fantastic art is vigorously affirmed. And we can consider this distinc-tion to be the starting point for a full recognition of the problematic at the center of this study, namely, the truthful dimension of memory and, let us add in anticipation, of history. Moreover, throughout the debate over sophistry, the epistemological and ontological status given to falsity presupposes the possibility of wresting true discourse away from the vertigo of falsity and its real nonbeing. The chances of a true icon are, therefore, preserved. But if the problem is recognized in its specificity, the question arises whether the requirement of faithfulness, of veracity, contained in the notion of an eikastic art finds an appropriate framework within the notion of a mimetic art. The result of this classification is that the relation to the signifying marks can only be a relation of similarity. In *Time and Narrative*, vol. 1, I explored the resources of the concept of *mimēsis* and attempted to give it a wider scope at the cost of deepening the split between *mimēsis* and imitation as copy. The question nevertheless remains whether the problematic of similarity does not constitute a diriment impediment to recognizing the specific features that distinguish memory from imagination. Can the relation to the past be only a variety of *mimēsis*? This difficulty will continue to hound us. If our doubt is well founded, the idea of "faithful resemblance," proper to the eikastic art, will likely turn out to be a mask rather than a way station in the exploration of the truthful dimension of memory.

We have not yet reached the end of the impasse. We saw the *Theaetetus* link the study of the *eikōn* closely to the assumption of a mark comparable to the imprint of a seal upon a block of wax. We recall the terms in which the *Theaetetus* made the connection between *eikōn* and *tupos*: "Suppose, for the sake of argument, that we have in our souls a block of wax ... " (191c). This assumption is supposed to allow us to solve the puzzle of confusing or mistaking, not to mention the puzzle of the persistence of the marks or, again, that of their effacement in the case of forgetting. This gives an indication of the burden the hypothesis bears. In this regard, Plato does not hesitate to place the hypothesis under the sign of Mnemosyne, the mother of all the Muses, thereby lending a tone of solemnity to the hypothesis. The alleged conjunction of *eikōn* and imprint is thus held to be more primitive than the relation of resemblance that sets the mimetic art into play. Or, to say this in other words, there can be a truthful or deceitful mimetic because there is between the *eikōn* and the imprint a dialectic of accommodation, harmonization, or *adjustment* that can succeed or fail. With the problematic of the imprint and that of the relation between *eikōn* and imprint, we have reached the end-point of the entire regressive analysis. This hypothesis—or better, admission—of the imprint has, over the course of the history of ideas, produced a procession of difficulties that have continued to overwhelm not only the theory of memory, but also the theory of history, under another name—the "trace." History, according to Marc Bloch, aspires to be a science of traces. It is now possible to lift some of the confusion relative to the use of the word "trace" in the wake of the term "imprint." Applying the Platonic method of division recommended—and practiced—by Plato in the *Sophist*, I distinguish three major uses of the word "trace."

I provisionally set aside the traces on which historians work: these are traces that are written and eventually archived. These are the ones Plato has in mind in the myth of the *Phaedrus* that recounts the invention of writing. We shall return to them in the prelude to part 2. A dividing line will thus be drawn between the "external" marks of writing properly speaking, of written discourse, and the graphic component inseparable from the eikastic component of the image by virtue of the metaphor of the wax impression.

The myth of the *Phaedrus* will tip the typographical model, upon which David Farrell Krell constructs his interpretation of the *Theaetetus*, from the intimacy of the soul to the exteriority of the public writing of discourse. The origin of written traces will become for all that more mysterious.

Quite another matter is the impression as an affection resulting from the shock of an event that can be said to be striking, marking. This impression is essentially undergone, experienced. It is tacitly presupposed in the very metaphor of the *tupos* at the moment the seal is pressed into the wax, inasmuch as it is the soul that receives the imprint (*Theaetetus* 194c). It is explicitly invoked in the third Platonic text which we will now consider. This text is found in the *Philebus* 38a–39c.[11] Once again, it is opinion, sometimes true, sometimes false, that is at issue here, in this case in its relation to pleasure and pain, initial candidates in the competition among rival goods presented at the beginning of the dialogue. Socrates proposes: "And is it not memory and perception that lead to judgment or the attempt to come to a definite judgment as the case may be?" (38b). Protarchus acquiesces. Then comes the example of someone who wants to "distinguish" (*krinein*) what appears to him from afar to be a man. What happens when it is to himself that he addresses his questions? Socrates proposes: "That our soul in such a situation is comparable to a book" (38e). "How so?" asks Protarchus. The explanation follows: "If memory and perceptions concur with other impressions [*pathēmata*] at a particular occasion, then they seem to inscribe [*graphein*] words in our soul, as it were. And if what [the experience, *pathēma*] is written is true, then we form a true judgment and a true account of the matter. But if what our scribe [*grammateus*] writes is false, then the result will be the opposite of the truth" (39a).[12] And Socrates then proposes another comparison, this time with painting, a variant of graphism: "Do you also accept that there is another craftsman [*dēmiourgos*] at work in our soul at the same time?" Who? "A painter [*zōgraphos*], who follows the scribe and provides illustrations [*graphei*] to his words" (39b). This takes place as a result of a separation between, on the one hand, opinions and discourses accompanied by sensation and, on the other hand, "the images he has formed inside himself" (39b). Such is the inscription in the soul to which the *Phaedrus* will oppose the external marks with which written discourse is constructed. The question posed by this affection-impression is therefore twofold: on the one hand, how is it preserved, how does it persist, whether or not it is recalled? On the other, what meaningful relation does it maintain in relation to the marking event (what Plato calls *eidōlon* to avoid confusion with the present *eikōn* of the absent mark that poses a problem of resemblance with the initial mark). A phenomenology (or a hermeneutics) of this sign-impression is possible at the limit of what Husserl terms a hyletic discipline.

The third use of the mark: the corporeal, cerebral, cortical imprint, as discussed by neuroscience. For the phenomenology of the affection-impression, these corporeal imprints are the object of a presupposition concerning external causation, a presupposition whose status is extremely difficult to establish. We shall speak in this instance of a substratum, to indicate the connection of a particular sort between the impressions stemming from the world of experience and the material imprints in the brain belonging to the neurosciences.[13] I shall say nothing more about this here but only point out the differences among these three uses of the indistinct idea of trace: trace written on a material support; affection-impression "in the soul"; corporeal, cerebral, cortical imprint. This is, to my mind, the ineluctable difficulty attached to the status of the "imprint in the soul" *as* in a block of wax. It is no longer possible today to avoid the problem of the relations between the cerebral imprint and the experienced impression, between the preservation-storage and the perseverance of the initial affection. I hope to show that this problem, inherited from the old debate over the relations between the soul and the body, and a problem audaciously assumed by Bergson in *Matter and Memory*, can be posed in terms other than those opposing materialism to spiritualism. Are we not dealing with two different readings of the body, of corporeality—the body as object confronting the body as lived—the parallel now shifting from the ontological plane to the linguistic or semantic plane?

### Aristotle: "Memory Is of the Past"

Aristotle's treatise *Peri mnemēs kai anamnēsēos*, which has come down to us under the Latin title *De memoria et reminiscentia*, part of a collection of nine small treatises the tradition has named *Parva naturalia*, can be placed against the eristic and dialectic backdrop inherited from Plato.[14] Why a double title? To distinguish, not the persistence of memories in relation to their recall, but their simple presence to mind (which I shall later call simple evocation in my phenomenological sketch) in relation to recollection as a search.

Memory, in this particular sense, is directly characterized as affection (*pathos*), which distinguishes it precisely from recollection.[15]

The first question raised is that of the "thing" remembered; it is here that the key phrase that will accompany my entire investigation is announced: "But memory is of the past" (449b15).[16] It is the contrast with the future of conjecture and expectation and with the present of sensation (or perception) that imposes this major characterization. And it is under the authority

of ordinary language ("No one would say.... Rather he says simply ...")
that the distinction is made. Even more forcefully: it is "in one's soul"[17] that
one has heard, or perceived, or thought this before (*proteron*) (449b23).
This temporal mark raised to the level of language belongs to what below
I shall call declarative memory. This mark is repeatedly stressed: just as it
is true that we remember "without actually exercising (knowledge and perception)" (449b19), so it must also be emphasized that there is memory
"when time has elapsed" (449b26).[18] In this regard, humans share simple
memory with certain animals, but all do not have the perception (*aisthēsis*)
of time (449b29). This perception consists in the fact that the mark of anteriority implies the distinction between before and after, earlier and later.
Now "earlier and later are in time [*en chrono*]" (450a21). This is in complete
agreement with the analysis of time in *Physics* 4.11, according to which it is
in perceiving movement that we perceive time; but time is perceived as other
than movement only if we determine (*horizomen*) it (*Physics* 218b30),[19] that
is to say, if we distinguish two instants, one as earlier, the other as later.[20] On
this point, the analysis of time and the analysis of memory overlap. The second question concerns the relation between memory and imagination. They
are tied together as a result of belonging to the same part of the soul, the
sensible soul, following a method of division previously practiced by Plato.[21]
But the difficulty lies elsewhere: the proximity between the two problematics
gives new strength to the old aporia concerning the mode of presence of the
absent: "One might be puzzled how, when the affection is present but the
thing is absent, what is not present is ever remembered" (450a25–26).

Aristotle responds to this aporia with what appears evident (*dēlon*) to
him, namely, that the affection produced "by means of perception in the
soul and in that part of the body which contains [it]" (450a26–27)[22] should
be considered a sort of picture (*zōgraphema*), "the having of which we say
is memory" (450a30). Here, expressed in new terms that will interest us
below, we find saddled up again the well-known problematic of the *eikōn*
and, with it, the imprint (*tupos*), which is linked to the metaphor of the
stamp and the seal. Nevertheless, in contrast to the *Theaetetus*, which places
the imprint "in the souls"—even if it means treating them as impregnable—
Aristotle connects the body to the soul and develops on this dual basis a rapid
typology of the various effects of imprints (450b1–11). But our author has
not finished with this metaphor. A new aporia arises: if this is the case, he asks,
what is it that we remember? Is it the affection or the thing that produced
it? If it is the affection, then it is not something absent one remembers; if it
is the thing, then how, while perceiving the impression, could we remember

the absent thing that we are not at present perceiving? In other words, while perceiving an image, how can we remember something distinct from it?

The solution to this aporia resides in the introduction of the category of otherness, inherited from the Platonic dialectic. The addition of the notion of imprint to that of drawing, of inscription (*graphē*)[23] we would say today, sets us on the path toward a solution. It belongs to the notion of inscription that it contain a reference to the other; the other-than-affection as such. Absence, as the other of presence! Let us, Aristotle says, consider an example: a drawing of an animal. We can read this drawing in two ways: either we can consider it in itself, as a simple image drawn on a support, or as an *eikōn* ("a copy," both of our translators write). We can do this because the inscription consists in both things at once: it is itself and the representation of something else (*allou phantasma*). Here, Aristotle's vocabulary is precise: he reserves the term *phantasma* for the inscription itself and that of *eikōn* for the reference to the inscription's other.[24]

The solution is clever but it has its own difficulties. The metaphor of the imprint, of which that of inscription is held to be a variant, invokes "movement" (*kinēsis*), from which the imprint results. This movement invokes an external cause (someone, something has made the imprint), while the double reading of the drawing, of the inscription, implies a division within the mental image, today we would say a double intentionality. This new difficulty seems to me to result from the competition between the two models, the impression and the inscription. The *Theaetetus* had paved the way for their confrontation by treating the imprint itself as a signifying mark, a *sēmeion*. It was then in the *sēmeion* itself that the external causation of the blow (*kinēsis*) and the actual meaning of the mark (*sēmeion*) were merged. The secret discordance between the two models emerges in Aristotle's text when the production of the affection is set over against the iconic signification which both translators interpret as copy, hence as resemblance. This conjunction between (external) stimulation and (internal) resemblance will remain, for us, the crux of the entire problematic of memory.

The contrast between the two chapters of Aristotle's treatise—*mnēmē* and *anamnēsis*—is more apparent than their belonging to one and the same problematic. The distinction between *mnēmē* and *anamnēsis* rests on two things: on the one hand, the simple memory arises in the manner of an affection, while recollection[25] consists in an active search. On the other hand, the simple memory is under the dominion of the agent of the imprint, whereas movements and the entire sequence of changes that will be discussed have their principle in us. Nevertheless, the connection between the two chapters is secured by the role played by temporal distance: the act of remembering (*mnēmoneuein*) is produced when time has elapsed (*prin khronisthēnai*) (451a30). And it is this interval of time, between the initial impression and its return, that recollection traverses. In this sense, time indeed remains the factor common to memory as passion and to recollection as action. This factor, it is true, is almost lost from sight in the details of the analysis of recollection. The reason for this is the emphasis placed from here on, on the "how," on the method of effective recollection.

In a general sense, "acts of recollection happen because one change [*kinēsis*] is of a nature to occur after another" (451b10).[26] Now this succession can take place by necessity or out of habit; a certain margin of variation, a matter we shall return to below, is thereby preserved. Having said this, the priority given to the methodical side of the search (a term dear to all the Socratics) explains the insistence on the choice of a starting point for the course of the recollection. The initiative of the search thus stems from our "capacity for searching." The starting point remains under the command of the explorer of the past, whether the connection that follows is the result of necessity or of habit. What is more, along this course, several paths remain open leading from this same starting point. The metaphor of making one's way is thus induced by that of change. This is why the quest can mistakenly take the wrong track, and luck can always play a role. But the question of time is not lost from sight during these exercises of methodical remembering: "the main thing is that one must know the time" (452b7). This knowledge has to do with the measurement of the intervals elapsed, whether precise or indeterminate. In both cases, the estimation of more or less is part and parcel of this knowledge. And this estimation depends on the power to distinguish and compare magnitudes, whether of greater or smaller distances or dimensions. This estimation extends to the notion of proportion. Aristotle's words confirm the thesis that the notion of temporal distance is inherent in the essence of memory and assures the distinction in principle between memory and imagination. Moreover, the role played by the estimation of lapses of time underscores the rational side of recollection: this "search" constitutes "a sort of reasoning [*sullogismos*]" (453a13–14). This does not prevent the body's being involved in the sort of affection that is displayed in the hunt for the image (*phantasma*) (453a16).

In contrast to a reductive reading, this approach has produced a number of traditions of interpretation. First, the tradition of *ars memoriae*, which consists, as we shall say in chapter 2, in a form of memory training in which the operation of memorization prevails over the recollection of individual events of the past. Second, the associationism of modern philosophers, which, as Sorabji's commentary underscores, draws solid support from Aristotle's text. The text, however, also leaves room for a third conception, in which the accent is placed on the dynamism, the invention of connections, as in Bergson's analysis of "the effort to recall."

At the end of our reading and interpretation of Aristotle's *De memoria et reminiscentia*, we are in a position to attempt an evaluation of the contribution of this treatise to a phenomenology of memory.

Its major contribution lies in the distinction between *mnēmē* and *anamnēsis*. We will encounter it below in a different vocabulary, with the terms "simple evocation" and "effort to recall." By drawing a line in this way between the simple presence of memories and the act of recollection, Aristotle has preserved for all time a space for discussion worthy of the fundamental aporia brought to light by the *Theaetetus*, namely, the presence of the absent. The results of his contribution to this discussion are mixed. On the one hand, he sharpened the point of the enigma by making the reference to time the distinctive note of memory in the field of the imagination. With memory, the absent bears the temporal mark of the antecedent. On the other hand, by assuming the category of *eikōn* for the framework of the discussion, in connection with the category of *tupos*, he is in danger of pursuing the aporia to the point of impasse. The impasse is even twofold. On the one hand, throughout our investigation there will remain the troublesome question of determining whether the relation between the memory-image and the initial impression is one of resemblance, even of a copy. Plato had approached this difficulty by taking as his target the deceit inherent in this kind of relation, and in the *Sophist* he had even tried to distinguish between two mimetic arts: the fantastic art, deceitful by nature, and the eikastic art, capable of veracity. Aristotle appears to be unaware of the risks of error or illusion attaching to the conception of *eikōn* centered on resemblance. By holding at bay the misfortunes of the imagination and of memory, he may have wanted to shield these phenomena from the quarrels fomented by the sophists, reserving his reply and his attacks on them for his *Metaphysics*, principally in the framework of the problem of the self-identity of *ousia*. However, by not taking into account the degrees of fallibility belonging to memory, he removed the notion of iconic resemblance from the discussion. Another impasse: by taking for granted the tie between *eikōn* and *tupos*, he adds to the difficulties of the image as a copy those belonging to the notion of the imprint. But what of the relation between the external cause—"motion"—producing the imprint and the initial affection targeted by and in memory? To be sure, Aristotle has made great strides in the discussion by introducing the category of otherness into the very heart of the relation between the *eikōn*, reinterpreted as an inscription, and the initial affection. Having done this, he begins to advance the concept of resemblance, which, moreover, had not been challenged. But the paradoxes of the imprint will continue to reemerge, primarily with the question of the material causes of the *anamnēsis* of memory, prior to its recall.

As for *anamnēsis*, Aristotle has presented under this term the first analytical description of the mnemonic phenomenon of recollection, which is contrasted to the simple evocation of a memory that comes to mind. The richness and subtlety of his description place him at the head of a wide range of schools of thought seeking a model of interpretation for modes of connection arising from "necessity" or from "habit." The associationism of the British empiricists is only one of these schools.

The astonishing thing, however, is that Aristotle retained the very term *anamnēsis*—one of the key words of Plato's philosophy, from the *Meno* through the other great dialogues—to describe recollection as it operates under ordinary conditions. How are we to explain this faithful use of terms? Reverence due to his teacher? An appeal to authority suitable for covering an analysis that, nonetheless, naturalizes the grandiose vision of a knowledge lost at birth and recalled by study? Worse: betrayal disguised as faithfulness? Conjectures are endless. But none of those just mentioned goes beyond the level of the psychology of the author. Each draws its plausibility from the presumed thematic tie held to exist between the *anamnēsis* of Plato and that of Aristotle. This thematic tie is twofold: it is, first of all, on the plane of the aporia, the heritage of *eikōn* and of *tupos*, coming from the *Theaetetus* and the *Sophist*. For Plato, these categories were held to account for the possibility of sophistry and for the very existence of the Sophist, and so to stand in the position of counterpoint to the theory of reminiscence, which accounted only for the happy memory of the young slave of the *Meno*. With Aristotle, *eikōn* and *tupos* are the only categories available to account for the functioning of everyday memory; they no longer designate simply an aporia, but the direction in which this aporia has to be resolved. There is, however, an even stronger connection between Plato and Aristotle than that of the aporia on the path toward resolution. This tie has to do with their faithfulness to Socrates in the use of the two emblematic terms: "learning" and "seeking." One must first have "learned" and then painfully "seek." Because of Socrates, Aristotle was unable to, nor did he want to, "forget" Plato's *anamnēsis*.


## A PHENOMENOLOGICAL SKETCH OF MEMORY

Allow me to open the following sketch by making two remarks.

The first is in the guise of a warning against the tendency of many authors to approach memory on the basis of its deficiencies, even its dysfunctions, tendencies whose legitimate place we will indicate later.[27] It is important, in my opinion, to approach the description of mnemonic phenomena from the standpoint of the *capacities*, of which they are the "happy" realization.[28] In order to do this, I shall present in the least scholarly manner possible the phenomena that, in the ordinary language of everyday life, are placed under the heading of memory. What, in the final analysis, will justify taking this position in favor of "good" memory is my conviction, which the remainder of this study will seek to establish, that we have no other resource, concerning our reference to the past, except memory itself. To memory is tied an ambition, a claim—that of being faithful to the past. In this respect, the deficiencies stemming from forgetting, which we shall discuss in good time, should not be treated straight away as pathological forms, as dysfunctions, but as the shadowy underside of the bright region of memory, which binds us to what has passed before we remember it. If we can reproach memory with being unreliable, it is precisely because it is our one and only resource for signifying the past-character of what we declare we remember. No one would dream of addressing the same reproach to imagination, inasmuch as it has as its paradigm the unreal, the fictional, the possible, and other nonpositional features. The truthful ambition of memory has its own merits, which deserve to be recognized before any consideration is given to the pathological deficiencies and the nonpathological weaknesses of memory, some of which will be examined in the next section of this study, even before the confrontation with the deficiencies examined in the following study under the heading, abuses of memory. To put it bluntly, we have nothing better than memory to signify that something has taken place, has occurred, has happened *before* we declare that we remember it. False testimonies, which we shall discuss in the second part, can be unmasked only by a critical agency that can do nothing better than to oppose those accounts reputed to be more reliable to the testimony under suspicion. For, as will be shown, testimony constitutes the fundamental transitional structure between memory and history.

Second remark. Contrary to the polysemy, which, at first sight, seems sufficient to discourage even the most modest attempt at ordering the semantic field encompassed by the term "memory," it is possible to *sketch* a splintered, but not radically dispersed, phenomenology in which the relation to time remains the ultimate and sole guideline. But this guideline can be held with a firm hand only if we succeed in showing that the relation to time of the various mnemonic modes encountered by our description is itself susceptible to a relatively well-ordered typology that is not exhausted, for example, by the case of the memory of a one-time event that occurred in the past. This second wager of our undertaking builds upon the minimal coherence of the assertion borrowed from Aristotle at the beginning of this study, according to which memory "is of the past." But the being of the past can be said in many ways (in keeping with the famous passage from Aristotle's *Metaphysics* that "being is said in many ways").

The first expression of the splintered nature of this phenomenology stems from the object-oriented character of memory: we remember something. In this sense a distinction must be made in language between memory (*la mémoire*) as intention and memory (*le souvenir*) as the thing intended. We say memory (*la mémoire*) and memories (*les souvenirs*). Fundamentally, what is at issue here is a phenomenology of memories. In this regard, Latin and Greek use the preterite forms (*genomenou, praeterita*). It is in this sense that I speak of past "things." Indeed once the past has been distinguished from the present in the memory of memories, then it is easy for reflection to distinguish at the heart of remembering the question "What?" from "How?" and from "Who?" following the rhythm of our three phenomenological chapters. In Husserlian terminology this is the distinction between the noesis of remembering and the noema of memories.

The first feature characterizing the domain of memories is their multiplicity and their varying degrees of distinctness. Memory in the singular is a capacity, an effectuation; memories are in the plural: we have memories (it is even said, unkindly, that the old have more memories than the young but less memory!). Later we shall evoke Augustine's brilliant description of memories that spill over the threshold of memory, presenting themselves one by one or in bunches according to the complex relations of their themes or circumstances, or in sequences more or less amenable to being put into narrative form. In this regard, memories can be treated as discrete forms with more or less discernible borders, set off against what could be called a memorial backdrop, which can be a source of pleasant occupation in states of *anamnēsis*.

The most important feature, however, is the following: it has to do with the privilege spontaneously accorded to events among all the "things" we remember. In terms of the analysis we shall later borrow from Bergson, the "thing" remembered is plainly identified with a singular, unrepeatable event, for example a given reading of a memorized text. Is this always the case? To be sure, as we shall say in conclusion, the memory-event is in a way paradigmatic, to the extent that it is the phenomenal equivalent of a physical event. The event is simply what happens. It takes place. It passes and occurs (*se passe*). It happens, it comes about. It constitutes what is at stake in the third cosmological antinomy of the Kantian dialectic: either it results from something prior in accord with necessary causation or else it proceeds from freedom, in accord with spontaneous causation. On the phenomenological level, on which we have situated ourselves here, we say that we remember what we have done, experienced, or learned in a particular instance. But a range of typical cases unfolds between the two extremes of singular events and generalities, which can be termed "states of affairs." Still closely resembling a unique event, we find discrete appearances (a certain sunset one particular summer evening), the singular faces of our loved ones, words heard according to their manner of utterance each time new, more or less memorable meetings (which we shall divide up again below following other criteria of variation). Things and people do not simply appear, they reappear as being the same, and it is in accordance with this sameness of reappearing that we remember them. In the same way, we recall names, addresses, and telephone numbers. Memorable meetings offer themselves to be remembered due less to their unrepeatable singularity than to their typical resemblance, even their emblematic character: a composite image of waking up in the morning in the house in Combray permeates the opening pages of Proust's *Remembrance of Things Past*. Next comes the case of "things" we have learned and so acquired. In this way, we say that we still remember the table of Greek and Latin declensions and conjugations, or German and English irregular verbs. Not to have forgotten them is to be able to recite them without learning them all over again. These examples link up with the opposite pole, that of "states of affairs," which, in the Platonic and Neoplatonic tradition to which Augustine still belongs, constitute the paradigmatic examples of Reminiscence. The canonical text for this tradition remains Plato's *Meno* and the famous episode of the young slave's rediscovery of certain noteworthy geometrical propositions. At this level, remembering and knowing completely coincide with one another. But states of affairs do not consist only in abstract generalities, in notions. Made the target of critique, as we shall say later, the events considered by documentary history display a propositional form that gives them the status of fact. It is then a matter of the "fact that ..." things happened this way and not some other way. These facts can be said to be acquired; even, in the design of Thucydides, elevated to the rank of an "everlasting possession." In this way, within the framework of historical knowledge, events tend to link up with "states of affairs."

Given this diversity of past "things," by what features are these "things"— these *praeterita*—recognized as being "of the past"? A new series of modes of dispersion characterize this "being of the past" common to all our memories. To guide our passage through the polysemic field of memory, I propose a series of oppositional pairs, constituting something like a rule-governed typology. This will obey an organizing principle capable of justification apart from its implementation, as is the case with Max Weber's ideal types. If I were to seek terms of comparison, I would first think of analogy in Aristotle, halfway between simple homonymy, relegated to the dispersion of meaning, and polysemy, structured by a semantic core that would be identified by a genuine semiotic reduction. I would also think of Wittgenstein's "family resemblance." The reason for the relative indeterminacy of the epistemological status of the classification proposed has to do with the interconnection between preverbal experience—what I call lived experience, translating the *Erlebnis* of Husserlian phenomenology—and the work of language that ineluctably places phenomenology on the path of interpretation, hence of hermeneutics. Now the "working" concepts that prime the interpretation and direct the ordering of the "thematic" concepts proposed here, escape the mastery of meaning that a total reflection would want to command. More than others, the phenomena of memory, so closely connected to what we are, oppose the most obstinate of resistances to the *hubris* of total reflection.[29]

The first pair of oppositions is formed by *habit* and *memory*. It is illustrated in contemporary philosophy by the famous distinction between *mémoire-habitude* (memory as habit) and *mémoire-souvenir* (memory as distinct recollection) proposed by Bergson. We shall temporarily bracket the reasons why Bergson presents this opposition as a dichotomy. We shall instead follow the counsel of the experience least charged with metaphysical presupposition, for which habit and memory form two poles of a continuous range of mnemonic phenomena. What forms the unity of this spectrum is the common feature of the relation to time. In each of the opposing cases an experience acquired earlier is presupposed; however, in the case of habit what is acquired is incorporated into the living present, unmarked, unremarked as past. In the other case, a reference is made to the anteriority of the prior acquisition. In both cases, then, it remains true that memory "is of the past," but according to two distinct modes—unmarked and marked—of reference to the place in time of the initial experience.

If I place the pair habit/memory at the start of my phenomenological sketch, this is because it provides the first opportunity to apply to the problem of memory what, since the introduction, I have called the conquest of temporal distance, a conquest relying on a criterion that can be described as a gradient of distantiation. The descriptive operation then consists in arranging experiences relative to temporal depth, beginning with those in which the past adheres, so to speak, to the present and continuing on to those in which the past is recognized in its pastness as over and done with. Let me refer, as so many others have done, to the famous pages in chapter 2 of *Matter and Memory* devoted to the distinction between "two forms of memory."[30] Like Augustine and the ancient rhetoricians, Bergson places himself in the situation of reciting a lesson learned by heart. Habit-memory is then the one we employ when we recite the lesson without evoking one by one each of the successive readings of the period of learning. In this case, the lesson learned "is part of my present, exactly like my habit of walking or of writing; it is lived and acted, rather than represented" (91). On the other hand, the memory of a particular reading, of a given phase of memorization, presents "*none* of the marks of a habit": "It is like an event in my life; its essence is to bear a date, and consequently to be unable to occur again" (90). "The image, regarded in itself, was necessarily at the outset what it always will be" (90). And again: "Spontaneous recollection is perfect from the outset; time can add nothing to its image without disfiguring it; it retains its memory in place and date" (95). In short: "The memory of a given reading is a representation, and only a representation" (91); whereas the lesson learned is, as just said, "acted" rather than represented, it is the privilege of representation-memory to allow us "in the search for a particular image [to] remount the slope of our past" (92). To memory that repeats is opposed memory that imagines: "To call up the past in the form of an image, we must be able to withdraw ourselves from the action of the moment, we must have the power to value the useless, we must have the will to dream. Man alone is capable of such an effort" (94).

This is a text of great richness. In its crystalline sobriety, it posits the more extensive problem of the relation between action and representation, of which the exercise of memorization is only one aspect, as I will state in the next chapter. In doing this, Bergson underscores the kinship between the lesson learned by heart and "my habit of walking or of writing." What is stressed in this way is the set to which recitation belongs, that of *knowing-how*, which includes in an array of different modes the common feature of being ready to . . . , without having to repeat the effort of learning again, of re-learning; as such, these modes are able to be mobilized in a range of different occasions, just as they are open to a degree of variability. It is to these instances of knowing-how that, among the vast panoply of uses of the word "memory," we apply one of its accepted senses. In this way, the phenomenologist will be able to distinguish "remembering how . . . " and "remembering that . . . " (an expression that will lend itself to further distinctions). This vast empire covers forms of know-how on very different levels: we encounter first corporeal capacities and all the modalities of "I can" which are considered in my own phenomenology of the "capable human being": being able to speak, being able to intervene in the course of affairs, being able to recount, being able to ascribe an action to oneself by making oneself its actual author. To this must be added social customs, mores, all the *habitus* of life in common, part of which is involved in the social rituals belonging to phenomena of commemoration, which we will later contrast to the phenomena of rememoration, assigned to private memory alone. Several polarities intersect in this way. We will encounter others equally significant in the framework of the present consideration, where the accent falls on the application of the criterion of temporal distantiation.

The fact that, on the phenomenological plane, we are considering a polarity and not a dichotomy is confirmed by the eminent role held by phenomena situated between the two poles that Bergson opposes following his customary method of division.

The second set of opposites is constituted by the pair *evocation/search*. By evocation let us understand the unexpected appearance of a memory. Aristotle reserved for this the term *mnēmē*, reserving *anamnēsis* for what we shall later call search or recall. And he defined *mnēmē* as a *pathos*, as an affection: it happens that we remember this or that, on such and such an occasion; we then experience a memory. Evocation is an affection, therefore, in contrast to the search. In other words, abstracting from this polarity, evocation as such bears the weight of the enigma that set in motion the investigations of Plato and Aristotle, namely, the presence now of the absent that was earlier perceived, experienced, learned. This enigma must be provisionally disassociated from the question raised by the perseverance of the first affection, illustrated by the famous metaphor of the imprint of the seal and, consequently, from the question of whether the faithfulness of a memory consists in the resemblance of the *eikōn* to the first imprint. Neuroscience has taken up this problem under the title of mnestic traces. This problem must not monopolize our attention: phenomenologically speaking, we know nothing of the corporeal, and more precisely cortical, substratum of evocation, nor are we clear about the epistemological status of the correlation between the formation, conservation, and activation of these mnestic traces and the phenomena that fall under the phenomenological gaze. This problem belonging to the category of material causation should be bracketed as long as possible. I shall wait until the third part of this work before confronting it. However, what must be brought to the fore, following Aristotle, is the reference to the anteriority of the "thing" remembered in relation to its present evocation. The cognitive dimension of memory, its character of knowing, lies in this reference. It is by virtue of this feature that memory can be held to be trustworthy or not and that properly cognitive deficiencies are to be accounted for, without our rushing to construe them according to a pathological model, under the heading of this or that form of amnesia.

Let us move to the other pole of the pair evocation/search. This is what was designated by the Greek term *anamnēsis*. Plato had turned it into myth by tying it to a prenatal knowledge from which we are said to have been separated by a forgetting that occurs when the life of the soul is infused into a body—described, moreover, as a tomb (*soma-sēma*)—a forgetting from birth, which is held to make the search a relearning of what has been forgotten. In the second chapter of the treatise analyzed above, Aristotle naturalizes *anamnēsis*, so to speak, bringing it closer to what in everyday experience we term recollection. Along with all the Socratics, I designate recollection by means of the enigmatic term of searching (*zētēsis*). The break with Platonic *anamnēsis* is nevertheless not complete, to the extent that the *ana* of *anamnēsis* signifies returning to, retaking, recovering what had earlier been seen, experienced, or learned, hence signifies, in a sense, repetition. Forgetting is thus designated obliquely as that against which the operation of recollecting is directed. The work of *anamnēsis* moves against the current of the river *Lēthē*. One searches for what one fears having forgotten temporarily or for good, without being able to decide, on the basis of the everyday experience of recollection, between two hypotheses concerning the origin of forgetting. Is it a definitive erasing of the traces of what was learned earlier, or is it a temporary obstacle—eventually surmountable—preventing their reawakening? This uncertainty regarding the essential nature of forgetting gives the search its unsettling character.[31] Searching is not necessarily finding. The effort to recall can succeed or fail. Successful recollection is one of the figures of what we term "happy" memory.

With regard to the mechanism of recollection, I mentioned, within the framework of my commentary on Aristotle's treatise, the range of procedures employed, from quasi-mechanical association to the work of reconstruction which Aristotle compares to *sullogismos*, to argumentation.

I would like to give a modern echo here to the ancient texts. Once again I shall refer to Bergson, reserving for later a thorough examination of the fundamental theory of *Matter and Memory*, which will encompass the borrowings made here from Bergson's analyses. I am thinking in this regard of the essay titled "Intellectual Effort" in *Mind-Energy*,[32] principally those pages devoted to "the effort of memory."

The primary distinction is between laborious recollection and spontaneous recollection (188–203), where spontaneous recollection can be considered the zero-degree of searching and laborious recollection its purposeful form. The major interest of Bergson's essay lies in the struggle against the reduction performed by associationism of all the forms of searching to the most mechanical among these. The distinction between the two forms of recollection is set within a more extensive inquiry, placed under a single question: "What is the intellectual characteristic of intellectual effort?" (187). Whence the title of the essay. The scope and the precision of the question deserve to be underscored in turn. On the one hand, the recollection of a memory belongs to a vast family of mental facts: "When we call to mind past deeds, interpret present actions, understand a discourse, follow someone's train of thought, attend to our own thinking, whenever, in fact, our mind is occupied with a complex system of ideas, we feel we can take up two different attitudes, one of tension, the other of relaxation, and they are mainly distinguished by the feeling of effort which is present in the one and absent from the other" (186). On the other hand, the precise question is this: "Is the play of ideas the same in each case? Are the intellectual elements of the same kind, and have they the same relations among themselves?" (186). The question, we see, cannot fail to interest contemporary cognitive science.

If the question of recollection comes first in the study applied to the various types of intellectual labor, this is because the gradation "starting with the easiest, which is reproduction, and ending up with the most difficult, which is production and invention" (188) is most marked here. What is more, the essay can use as a basis the distinction made in *Matter and Memory* between "a series of different 'planes of consciousness,' beginning with the plane of 'pure memory' not yet translated into distinct images, and going down to the plane where the same memory is actualized in nascent sensations and incipient movements" (188). The voluntary evocation of a memory consists precisely in this traversal of planes of consciousness. A model is then proposed for distinguishing the role of automatic, mechanical recall from that of reflection, of intelligent reconstruction, intimately mingled in ordinary experience. It is true that the example chosen is recalling a text learned by heart. It is, therefore, at the time of learning that the split occurs between the two types of reading; in the analytical reading, there is a hierarchy between the dominant idea and the subordinate ideas, to which Bergson relates the famous concept of a *dynamic scheme*: "I mean by this, that the idea does not contain the images themselves so much as the indication of what we must do to reconstruct them" (196). Exemplary in this regard is the chess-player, who can play several games at once without looking at the board: "What is present to the mind of the player is a composition of forces, or rather a relation between allied or hostile forces" (198). Each game is thus memorized as a whole following its own profile. It is, therefore, in the method of learning that we must seek the key to the phenomenon of recollection, for example, that of the troublesome search for a recalcitrant name: "an impression of strangeness, but not of strangeness in general" (199). The dynamic scheme acts as a guide "indicating a certain *direction of effort*" (200). In this example, as in many others, "the effort of memory appears to have as its essence the evolving of a scheme, if not simple at least concentrated, into an image with distinct elements more or less independent of one another" (201). Such is the manner of traversing the planes of consciousness, "a descent of the scheme towards the image" (202). We can then say that "the effort of recall consists in converting a schematic idea, whose elements interpenetrate, into an imaged idea, the parts of which are juxtaposed" (203). It is in this that the effort of recall constitutes a case of intellectual effort and is associated with the effort of intellection examined in chapter 2 of *Matter and Memory*: "Whether we are following an argument, reading a book or listening to a discourse" (205), the "feeling of effort, in intellection, is produced on the passage from the scheme to the image" (211). What remains to be examined is what makes the work of memory, intellection, or invention an effort, namely, the *difficulty* signaled by the discomfort experienced or the obstacle encountered, finally the properly temporal aspect of slowing down or of delay. Longstanding combinations resist the reworking required by the dynamic scheme, as do the images themselves in which the schema seeks to be inscribed. Habit resists invention: "In this peculiar kind of hesitation is likely to be found intellectual effort" (215). And "we may conceive that this indecision of the mind is continued in a disquietude of the body" (222). Arduousness thus has its own affectively experienced temporal mark. There is *pathos* in *zētēsis*, "affection" in "searching." In this way, the intellectual and the affective dimensions of the effort to recall intersect with one another, as they do in every other form of intellectual effort.

At the end of this study of recollection, I would like to make a brief allusion to the relation between the effort to recall and forgetting (before we have the opportunity in the third part of this work to engage in a proper discussion of the problems concerning forgetting, problems we encounter here in random order).

It is, in fact, the effort to recall that offers the major opportunity to "remember forgetting," to anticipate the words of Augustine. Searching for a memory indeed attests to one of the major finalities of the act of remembering, namely, struggling against forgetting, wresting a few scraps of memory from the "rapacity" of time (Augustine *dixit*), from "sinking" into oblivion (*oubli*). It is not only the arduousness of the effort of memory that confers this unsettling character upon the relation, but the fear of having forgotten, of continuing to forget, of forgetting tomorrow to fulfill some task or other; for tomorrow, one must not forget... to remember. In the next chapter, what I will call the duty of memory consists essentially in a duty not to forget. In this way, a good share of the search for the past is placed under the sign of the task not to forget. More generally, the obsession of forgetting, past, present, and future, accompanies the light of happy memory with the shadow cast by an unhappy memory. For meditating memory—*Gedächtnis*—forgetting remains both a paradox and an enigma. A paradox, as it is unfolded by Augustine the rhetorician: how can we *speak* of forgetting except in terms of the memory of forgetting, as this is authorized and sanctioned by the return and the recognition of the "thing" forgotten? Otherwise, we would not know that we have forgotten. An enigma, because we do not know, in a phenomenological sense, whether forgetting is only an impediment to evoking and recovering the "lost time," or whether it results from the unavoidable wearing away "by" time of the traces left in us by past events in the form of original affections. To solve the enigma, we would have not only to uncover and to free the absolute ground of forgetting against which the memories "saved from oblivion" stand out, but also to articulate this non-knowledge concerning the absolute ground of forgetting on the basis of *external* knowledge—in particular, that of the neurological and cognitive sciences—of mnestic traces. We shall not fail to return, at the appropriate time, to this difficult correlation between phenomenological knowledge and scientific knowledge.[33]

A separate and prominent place must be given to the distinction introduced by Husserl in *The Phenomenology of the Consciousness of Internal Time* between retention or primary memory and reproduction or secondary memory.[34] We read of this distinction in the second section of the 1905 "Lectures on the Phenomenology of the Consciousness of Internal Time," which form the first part of the work, supplemented by additions and complements from the years 1905–10. I have separated out those analyses that concern the object-side of memory, as the translation of *Erinnerung* by "memory" (*souvenir*) confirms, and, in the remainder of the present chapter, added to them Husserl's reflections on the relation between memory and image. By separating this section out from the main context of the 1905 lectures, I remove it from the province of the subjective idealism that is grafted onto the reflexive side of memory (which I will examine later in the concluding chapter of this phenomenology of memory). I confess that this liberation cuts against the grain of the overall dynamic of the 1905 lectures, which, from the first to the third section, traverse a series of "levels of constitution" (Husserl, §34), gradually erasing the objective character of the constitution to the benefit of the self-constitution of the flow of consciousness. The "temporal objects"— in other words, the things that endure—then appear as "constituted unities" (Husserl, §37) in the pure reflexivity of the consciousness of internal time. My argument here is that the famous *epoché* with which the work opens and that results in bracketing objective time—the time that cosmology, psychology, and the other human sciences take as a reality, formal to be sure, yet of a piece with the realist status of the phenomena it frames—does not begin by laying bare a pure flow, but rather a temporal experience (*Erfahrung*) that has an object-oriented side in memory. The constitution at the first level is that of a thing that endures, however minimal this objectivity may be, first following the model of a sound that continues to resonate, then of a melody that one remembers after the fact. However, in each case, "something" endures. The *epoché*, to be sure, does expose pure experiences, "*experiences* of time" (Husserl, §2, 10). But in these experiences, "data 'in objective time' are *meant*" (ibid.). They are termed "objectivity" (ibid.) and contain "*a priori* truths that pertain to the different constitutive moments of the objectivity" (ibid.). If from the start of our reading, the reference to this "objective" aspect appears provisional, this is because a radical question is raised, that of the "origin of time" (11), which is intended to be kept out of the realm of

psychology, without thereby slipping into the orbit of Kantian transcendentalism. The question posed by the experience of a sound that continues and
of a melody that returns concerns the sort of persistence by which "what we
perceive remains present to us for a time, but not without undergoing modification" (Husserl, §3, 11). The question is: what is it for something that
endures to remain? What is temporal duration? This question is no different than those posed by William James and Henri Bergson in similar terms:
endure, persist, remain. What modification is this? Is it a sort of association
(Brentano)? Is it a sort of recapitulative comparison with the last sound (W.
Stern)? These solutions can be discarded but not the problem, namely, "the
apprehension of transcendent temporal objects that are extended over a duration" (§7, 23). Let us call these objects "temporal objects" (*Zeitobjekten*)
on the basis of which the question of the constitution of time will later be
posed, when it will be considered to be a duration undifferentiated by the
objects that endure. The analysis will then shift from the perception of the
duration of something to a study of the duration of perception as such. It
will then no longer be the sound, the melody that will be thematized but
rather their unobjectifiable duration. Just before this change of emphasis,
the noteworthy distinction between immediate memory or retention and
secondary memory (recollection) or reproduction will become meaningful.

The experience described has a pivotal point, the present, the present of
the sound that resonates now: "When it begins to sound, I hear it as now;
but while it continues to sound it has an ever new now, and the now that
immediately precedes it changes into a past" (§7, 25). It is this modification
that constitutes the theme of the description. There is an "ever new" now.
The situation described is in this regard no different from that considered by
Augustine in book 11 of the *Confessions*: the modification is of the present.
Of course, Augustine is unaware of the bracketing of every transcendent thesis and the reduction of the sound to a pure "hyletic datum" (§8, 25). But
the idea that something begins and ceases, begins and "recedes" after it ends
into the most distant past, is common. What is then proposed is the idea of
"retention": "In this sinking back, I still 'hold onto it,' have it in a 'retention.' And as long as the retention lasts, the tone has its own temporality"
(25). At this stage of the analysis the two propositions coincide: the sound
is the same, its duration is the same. Later, the second one will assimilate the
first one. We will then pass from the phenomenology of memory to that of
the consciousness of internal time. The transition is prepared by the remark
that "I can direct my attention to the way in which it is given" (25). Then
the "modes" and their continuity, in a "continual flow," will move to the

forefront. This, however, will not eliminate the reference to the now that, at the start of the analysis with which we are concerned here, is the phase of a sound, that phase termed "consciousness of the commencing tone" (ibid.): "The tone is given; that is, I am conscious of it as now" (25–26). At a later stage of the analysis, this stubborn reference to the present will attest to the reign of what Heidegger and those influenced by him denounce as a "metaphysics of presence."[35] On the level to which I am confining the analysis here, the reference to the present links up with the everyday experience that we have of things that begin, continue, and cease to appear. Beginning constitutes an undeniable experience. Without it, we could not understand the meaning of continuing, enduring, remaining, stopping. And always, there is something that begins and ceases. Moreover, the present is not to be identified with presence—in any metaphysical sense. The phenomenology of perception does not even have any exclusive right regarding the description of the present. The present is also the present of enjoyment and suffering and, more significantly for an investigation of historical knowledge, the present of initiative. The reproach that can legitimately be made to Husserl, at this preliminary stage of his analysis, is to have enclosed the phenomenology of the present within perceived objectivity at the expense of affective and practical objectivity. Within these limits, his thesis is simply that perception is not instantaneous, that retention is not a form of imagination, but consists in a modification of perception. The perception of something has a duration. The distance "from the actually present now-point" (§9, 27) is still a phenomenon of perception and not of imagination. It is with regard to something that we say it endures: "The 'consciousness,' the 'experience,' is related to its object by means of an appearance in which precisely the 'object in its way of appearing' stands before us" (§9, 28). The phenomenology of memory is initially that of memories, if by this is understood "the object in its way of appearing." What is called present, past, are its "running-off characters" (§10, 29), eminently immanent phenomena (in the sense of a transcendence reduced to its hyletic status).

If a tension is observable in the analysis, before the appearance of the distinction between retention and remembering, it is between fixing on the actual now and the indivisibility into fragments of the phenomenon of running-off. But Husserl should not be reproached for this tension, as though it were the inconsequential result of a metaphysical complacency: it is constitutive of the phenomena described. We can indeed pass without stopping, like time itself, from one phase to the other of the duration of the same object, or stop at one phase: the beginning is simply the most remarkable of these stopping points; but cessation is just as remarkable. In this way, we begin doing something and we stop doing it. Acting, in particular, has its knots and its swells, its fits and its starts; acting is muscular. And in the smoother succession of perception, the distinction between beginning, continuing, and stopping is perfectly reasonable. It is as a beginning that the present makes sense and that duration amounts to a modification: "Since a new now is always entering on the scene, the now changes into a past; and as it does so the whole running-off continuity of pasts belonging to the preceding point moves 'downwards' uniformly into the depths of the past" (§10, 30). Is the term "source-point" used here (§11, 30)? This is within the framework of the relation beginning-continuing-ceasing. The impression is primal, in a nonmetaphysicial sense, in the sense of something that simply begins and by reason of which there is a before and an after. The present is continually changing, but it is also continually arising: what we call happening. On this basis, running-off is only "a retention of retention" (§11, 31). But the distinction beginning/continuing never ceases to signify, so that "this continuity itself is again an actually present point that is retentionally adumbrated," which Husserl likens to the tail of a comet. We then speak of a duration that "is finished" (31). This end-point can indeed be analyzed in terms of a continuity of retentions; but as an end, it presents itself as a "now-apprehension," as "the head attached to the comet's tail" (32).[36]

What then of the eventual end of the attenuation that would be its disappearance? In evoking this, Husserl speaks of imperceptibility (32), thereby suggesting the limited character of the temporal field as a field of visibility. This remark is also valid for the diagram in §10: "No ending of retention is foreseen there" (Husserl's note, 32), which, according to certain authors, would allow for both an admission that forgetting is unavoidable and that there is an unconscious persistence of the past.

In summary, to term "primal" the past instant proper to retention is to deny that this is a figuration in terms of images. It is this distinction that we will take up anew on the basis of the unpublished texts and in relation to a different cycle of analyses tied to the positional/nonpositional opposition. In the 1905 lectures the opposition between impressional and retentional predominates. This distinction suffices to separate the now of consciousness from the "just past" that gives a temporal extension to perception. An opposition to the imaginary is nevertheless already in place: in truth, it existed as early as the critique of Brentano in the first section. As for the distinction between impression and retention, the focus of our discussion here, it derives, according to Husserl, from an eidetic necessity. This is not given *de facto*: "we teach the *a priori* necessity that a corresponding perception, or a corresponding primal impression, precede the retention" (§13, 35). In other words, for something that endures, continuing presupposes beginning. One might raise certain "Bergsonian" reservations about the equivalence between the now and the point, but not about the distinction between beginning and continuing. This distinction is constitutive of the phenomenology of memory—of that memory of which it is said, "givenness of the past is memory" (§13, 36). And this givenness necessarily includes a moment of negativity: the retention is not the impression; the continuity is not a beginning. In this sense, retention is "not now": "'Past' and 'now' exclude one another" (36). To endure is in a certain way to go beyond this exclusion. To endure is to remain the same. This is what is signified by the word "modification."

It is in relation to this exclusion—to this primordial not-now—of the past nevertheless retained that a new kind of polarity is suggested within the not-now of memory itself. This is the polarity of primary memory and secondary memory, of retention and reproduction.

Reproduction assumes that the primary memory of a temporal object such as melody has "disappeared" and that it comes back. Retention still hangs onto the perception of the moment. Secondary memory is no longer presentation at all; it is re-presentation. It is the same melody but heard "as it were" (§14, 37). The melody heard earlier "in person" is now re-membered, re-presented. The memory itself can in turn be retained in the mode of having just been remembered, re-presented, re-produced. All the distinctions suggested elsewhere between spontaneous and laborious evocation as well as those concerning degrees of clarity can be applied to this modality of secondary memory. The essential thing is that the reproduced temporal object has no longer a foot, so to speak, in perception. It has removed itself. It is really past. And yet it links up with, it follows after the present and its comet's tail. The interval is what we name a lapse of time. At the time of the 1905 lectures and the 1905–10 supplements, reproduction is classified among the modes of imagination (Appendix II, 107–9). The distinction remains to be made between thematizing and de-thematizing imagination, the sole tie between them being absence, a major bifurcation recognized by Plato, in terms of mimetic art, in the distinction between the fantastic and the iconic. Speaking here of the "reproduction" of duration, Husserl implicitly evokes the differential thetic character of memory.[37] The fact that reproduction is also imagination, is Brentano's limited truth (§19): in negative terms, to reproduce is not to give in person. To be given once again is not to have just been given. The difference is no longer continuous, but discontinuous. The formidable question is then posed, that of knowing under what conditions "reproduction" is reproduction of the past. The difference between imagination and recollection depends on the answer to this question. It is then the positional dimension of recollection that makes the difference: "Recollection, on the other hand, posits what is reproduced and in this positing gives it a position in relation to the actually present now and to the sphere of the original temporal field to which the recollection itself belongs" (§23, 53). Husserl refers here to Appendix III: "The Nexus-Intentions of Perception and Memory—The Modes of Time-Consciousness." At this price, the reproduced now can be said to "coincide" with a past now. This "double intentionality" corresponds to what Bergson and others have called recognition—the conclusion to a happy quest.

At this point, a meticulous analysis devoted to the distinction between *Erinnerung* and *Vorstellung*, collected in volume 23 of *Husserliana*, picks up from that of the second section of *The Phenomenology of the Consciousness of Internal Time*. I will return to it in the final section of this chapter in the context of the confrontation between memories and images.

I would like to complete this review of the polarities by considering one pair of opposed yet complementary terms, the importance of which will be fully revealed at the time of the transition from memory to history.

I am speaking of the polarity between *reflexivity* and *worldliness*. One does not simply remember oneself, seeing, experiencing, learning; rather one recalls the situations in the world in which one has seen, experienced, learned. These situations imply one's own body and the bodies of others, lived space, and, finally, the horizon of the world and worlds, within which something has occurred. Reflexivity and worldliness are indeed related as opposite poles, to the extent that reflexivity is an undeniable feature of memory in its declarative phase: someone says "in his heart" that he formerly saw, experienced, learned. In this regard, nothing should be stripped from the assertion that memory belongs to the sphere of interiority—to the cycle of inwardness, to borrow Charles Taylor's vocabulary in *Sources of the Self*.[38] Nothing should be removed except the interpretive surplus of subjectivist idealism that prevents this moment of reflexivity from entering into a dialectical relation with the pole of worldliness. To my mind, it is this "presupposition" that burdens the Husserlian phenomenology of time, despite its ambition to be constituted without presuppositions, listening only to the teaching of the "things themselves." This is a questionable effect of the *epoché*, which, under the guise of objectification, strikes worldliness. Actually, in defense of Husserl, it must be said that the phenomenology of the *Lebenswelt,* developed in Husserl's last great book, partially eliminates the equivocation by restoring its primordial character to what we globally term the situation in the world, without, however, breaking with the transcendental idealism that marks the works of the middle period, culminating in *Ideen I* but already foreshadowed in *The Phenomenology of the Consciousness of Internal Time.*

The considerations which follow owe an immense debt to Edward Casey's magisterial work, *Remembering.*[39] The sole point of divergence separating me from Casey concerns the interpretation he draws from the phenomena he so marvelously describes: he thinks he must step outside the region permeated by the theme of intentionality and, along with it, by Husserlian phenomenology, under the sway of the existential ontology inaugurated by Heidegger in *Sein und Zeit.* Whence the opposition that guides his description of mnemonic phenomena, separating them into two great masses signaled by the titles "Keeping Memory in Mind" and "Pursuing Memory beyond Mind." But what does "mind" (an English term so difficult to translate into French) signify? Does not this term refer to the idealist interpretation of phenomenology and to its major theme, intentionality? As a matter of fact, Casey accounts for the complementarity between these two great ensembles by inserting between them what he calls "mnemonic Modes," namely, *Reminding, Reminiscing, Recognizing.* What is more, he makes no bones about calling his great work *A Phenomenological Study.* Allow me to add a word to confirm my profound agreement with Casey's undertaking: above all, I admire the general orientation of the work, aimed at protecting memory itself from forgetfulness (whence the title of the introduction "Remembering Forgotten: The *Amnesia* of *Anamnesis*"—to which part four, "Remembering Re-membered," provides a response). In this regard, the book is a plea for what I call "happy" memory, in contrast to descriptions motivated by suspicion or by the excessive primacy accorded to phenomena of deficiency, even to the pathology of memory.

I have nothing really new to say here concerning the reflexive pole of the pair considered here, to the extent that this title encompasses phenomena that have already appeared in the other pairs of opposites. One would have to trace them back to the polarity between one's own memory and the collective memory of our next study. Moreover, it is with the latter, under the title of "Commemoration," that Casey completes his "pursuit" of memory "beyond mind." One would then have to collect under the heading of reflexivity the "right hand" term of each of the preceding pairs. In this way, in the opposition between habit and memory, the habitual side is less marked with regard to reflexivity: one exercises know-how without noticing it, without paying attention to it, without being *mindful* of it. When a performance is flubbed, then one is called to attention: *mind your step!* As for the pair evocation/recollection, reflexivity is at its height in the effort to recall; it is underscored by the feeling of arduousness tied to the effort. Simple evocation can, in this regard, be considered neutral or unmarked, inasmuch as the memory is said to arise as the presence of the absent. It can be said to be marked negatively in the case of spontaneous, involuntary evocation, well known to the readers of Proust's *Remembrance of Things Past*, and even more so in the case of the obsessional irruptions considered in the next chapter. Evocation is no longer simply experienced (*pathos*) but suffered. "Repetition" in the Freudian sense is then the inverse of remembering, which can perhaps be compared, as the work of memory, to the effort of recollection described above.

The three "mnemonic modes" that Casey interposes between the intentional analysis of memory held captive, as he says, "in Mind" and the pursuit of memory "beyond Mind" constitute, in fact, transitional phenomena in memory, between the pole of reflexivity and the pole of worldliness.

What does the word *reminding* convey? There is no appropriate term in French, if not one of the uses of the word *rappeler*: this reminds me (*me rappelle*) of that, makes me think of that. Might we say memento, memory-aid, *pense-bête*, or in the experimental sciences, points of reference, reminders? Indeed, it stands for clues that guard against forgetting. They are distributed on either side of the dividing line between the inner and the outer; they are found, first, on the side of recollection, either in the frozen form of the more or less mechanical association by which one thing is recalled by means of another associated with it through a learning process, or as one of the "living" relays of the work of recollection. They are found a second time in the form of external points of reference for recall: photographs, postcards, diaries, receipts, mementos (the famous knot in the handkerchief!). In this way, these signposts guard against forgetting in the future: by reminding us what is to be done, they admonish us not to forget to do it (feed the cat!).

As for *reminiscing*, this is a phenomenon more strongly marked by activity than *reminding*; it consists in making the past live again by evoking it together with others, each helping the other to remember shared events or knowledge, the memories of one person serving as a reminder for the memories of the other. This memorial process can, of course, be internalized in the form of meditative memory, an expression that best translates the German *Gedächtnis*, with the help of a diary, memoirs or anti-memoirs, autobiographies, in which the support of writing provides materiality to the traces preserved, reanimated, and further enriched with unpublished materials. In this way, provisions of memories are stored up for days to come, for the time devoted to memories . . . The canonical form of reminiscing, however, is conversation in the province of the spoken word: "Say, do you remember . . . , when . . . you . . . we . . . ?" The mode of reminiscing thus unfolds along the same line of discursivity as simple evocation in its declarative stage.

There remains the third mnemonic mode, which Casey terms one of transition: *recognizing*. Recognizing appears at first as an important complement to recollection, its sanction one might say. We recognize as being the same the present memory and the first impression intended as other.[40] In this way, we are referred back by the phenomenon of recognition to the enigma of memory as presence of the absent encountered previously. And the "thing" recognized is doubly other: as absent (other than presence) and as earlier (other than the present). And it is as other, emanating from a past as other that it is recognized as being the same as. This complex otherness itself presents degrees corresponding to the degrees of differentiation and distantiation of the past in relation to the present. The otherness is close to zero in the feeling of familiarity: one finds one's bearings, one feels at ease, at home (*heimlich*) in the enjoyment of the past revived. The otherness is, in contrast, at its height in the feeling of strangeness (the famous *Unheimlichkeit* of Freud's essay, the "uncanny"). It is maintained at its median degree when the event recalled is, as Casey says, traced "back there where it was" (125). This median degree announces, on the plane of the phenomenology of memory, the critical operation by which historical knowledge restores its object to the kingdom of the expired past, making of it what Michel de Certeau called "the absent of history."

The small miracle of recognition, however, is to coat with presence the otherness of that which is over and gone. In this, memory is re-presentation, in the twofold sense of re-: turning back, anew. This small miracle is at the same time a large snare for phenomenological analysis, to the extent that this representation threatens to shut reflection up once again within the invisible enclosure of representation, locking it within our head, in the mind.

Nor is this all: the fact also remains that the recognized past tends to pass itself off as a perceived past, whence the strange fate of recognition to be able to be treated within the framework of the phenomenology of memory and within the framework of perception. There is no forgetting Kant's famous description of the threefold subjective synthesis: apprehension, reproduction, recognition. Thus recognition assures the cohesion of the perceived itself. It is in similar terms that Bergson speaks of the unfolding of the dynamic scheme in images as a return to perception. We will come back to this in the third section of this chapter when we consider memories in the form of images.

Once we have run through the "mnemonic modes" that Casey's typology places half-way between the phenomena that the phenomenology of intentionality (overburdened, in my opinion, by subjective idealism) is held to situate *in Mind* and those it seeks *beyond Mind*, we are faced with a series of mnemonic phenomena implying the body, space, the horizon of the world or of a world.

In my opinion, these phenomena do not take us out of the sphere of intentionality but reveal its nonreflexive dimension. I remember having experienced pleasure and pain in my body at one time or another in my past life; I remember having lived for a long time in a certain house in a certain town, to have traveled in a certain part of the world, and it is from here that I evoke all those elsewheres. I remember the expanse of a certain seascape that gave me the feeling of the vastness of the world. And, during a visit to an archeological site, I evoked the cultural world gone by to which these ruins sadly referred. Like the witness in a police investigation, I can say of these places, "I was there."

Beginning with corporeal memory, let us recognize that it too is capable of being divided along the first axis of oppositions: from the body-as-habit to the body-as-event, so to speak. The present polarity of reflexivity/worldliness partially coincides with the former one. Corporeal memory can be "enacted" in the same manner as all the other modalities of habit, such as driving a car when I am at the wheel. It is modulated in accordance with all the variations of feelings of familiarity or of strangeness. But the ordeals, illnesses, wounds, and traumas of the past invite corporeal memory to target precise instances that call in particular upon secondary memory, upon recollection, and invite a recounting. In this regard, happy memories, especially erotic ones, leave no less a mark of their singular place in the elapsed past, without forgetting the promise of repetition that they contain. Corporeal memory is thus peopled with memories affected with varying degrees of temporal distantiation: the magnitude of the interval of time elapsed can itself be perceived, felt, in the mode of regret, of nostalgia. The moment of awakening, so magnificently described by Proust at the beginning of *Remembrance of Things Past*, is especially favorable for returning things and beings to the place assigned to them in space and in time the previous evening. The moment of recollection is then the moment of recognition. The latter, in its turn, can span all the degrees from tacit remembering to declarative memory, ready for narration once again.

The transition from corporeal memory to the memory of places is assured by acts as important as orienting oneself, moving from place to place, and above all inhabiting. It is on the surface of the habitable earth that we remember having traveled and visited memorable sites. In this way, the "things" remembered are intrinsically associated with places. And it is not by chance that we say of what has occurred that it took place. It is indeed at this primordial level that the phenomenon of "memory places" is constituted, before they become a reference for historical knowledge. These memory places function for the most part after the manner of reminders, offering in turn a support for failing memory, a struggle in the war against forgetting, even the silent plea of dead memory. These places "remain" as inscriptions, monuments, potentially as documents,[41] whereas memories transmitted only along the oral path fly away as do the words themselves. It is also due to this kinship between memories and places that the sort of *ars memoriae* that we will discuss at the beginning of the next study was able to be constructed as a method of "*loci.*"

This tie between memory and place results in a difficult problem that takes shape at the crossroads of memory and history, which is also geography. This is the problem of the degree of originality of the phenomenon of dating, in parallel with localization. Dating and localization constitute in this respect solidary phenomena, testifying to the inseparable tie between the problematics of time and space. The problem is the following: up to what point can a phenomenology of dating and localization be constituted without borrowing from the objective knowledge of geometrical—let us say, Euclidian and Cartesian—space and from the objective knowledge of chronological time, itself articulated in terms of physical movement? This is the question posed by all the attempts to recover an earlier *Lebenswelt*—conceptually, if not historically—in the world (re)constructed by the sciences of nature. Bergson himself, so vigilant regarding the threats of contamination of the pure experience of duration by spatial categories, did not refrain from characterizing recollection-memory by the phenomenon of dating in contrast to habit-memory. Concerning particular readings, whose evocation interrupts the recitation of a lesson, he says: "It is like an event in my life; its essence is to bear a date, and consequently to be unable to occur again"

(*Matter and Memory*, 90); and a little later, "confronted by two different memories theoretically independent," he notes: "The first records, in the form of memory-images, all the events of our daily life as they occur in time; it neglects no detail; it leaves to each fact, to each gesture, its place and date" (92). The date, as a place in time, thus appears to contribute to the first polarization of mnemonic phenomena divided between habit and memory properly speaking. It is equally constitutive of the reflective phase, or as we have called it, the declarative phase of remembering; the effort of memory is in large part an effort of dating: When? How long ago? How long did it last? Nor did Husserl escape this question, long before the period of the *Krisis*, as early as *The Phenomenology of the Consciousness of Internal Time*. I cannot say that a sound begins, continues, stops, without saying how long it lasts. What is more, to say that B follows A is to recognize a primordial character in the succession of two distinct phenomena: "The *consciousness of succession* is consciousness that gives its object originally: it is 'perception' of this succession" (§18, 44). We are not far from Aristotle, for whom the distinction of before and after is the distinguishing factor of time in relation to movement. The consciousness of internal time as original already possesses, according to Husserl, the a priori that governs its apprehension.

Returning to the memory of places, we can attempt, following Casey, to recover the sense of spatiality on the basis of the abstract conception of geometrical space. For the latter, he employs the term "site" and reserves "place" for lived spatiality. The place, he says, is not indifferent with regard to the "thing" that occupies it or rather fills it, in the manner in which, according to Aristotle, the place constitutes what is contained within a specific volume. Some of these remarkable places are said to be memorable. The act of inhabiting, mentioned above, constitutes in this respect the strongest human tie between the date and the place. Places inhabited are memorable par excellence. Declarative memory enjoys evoking them and recounting them, so attached to them is memory. As for our movements, the successive places we have passed through serve as reminders of the episodes that have taken place there. They appear to us after the fact as hospitable or inhospitable, in a word, as habitable.

The question will, nevertheless, arise at the beginning of the second part, at the turning point from memory to history, regarding whether a historical time, a geographical space can be conceived without the help of the mixed categories that join lived time and lived space to objective time and geometrical space, which the *epoché* has methodically bracketed to the benefit of a "pure" phenomenology.

The question already encountered several times as to whether the Husserlian *epoché* is ultimately tenable arises again here. Regardless of the ultimate destiny of the memory of dates and places on the level of historical knowledge, what primordially legitimizes the disengagement of space and time from their objectified forms is the tie linking corporeal memory to the memory of places. In this regard, the body constitutes the primordial place, the here in relation to which all other places are there. The symmetry is complete in this respect between spatiality and temporality: "here" and "now" occupy the same rank, alongside "me," "you," "he," and "she," among the deictic forms that punctuate our language. Here and now, in truth, constitute absolute places and dates. But how long can we maintain this bracketing of objectified time and space? Can I avoid relating my here to the there delimited by the body of the other without having recourse to a system of neutral places? The phenomenology of the memory of places seems to be caught, from the outset, in an insurmountable dialectical movement of disinvolvement of lived space with regard to geometrical space and of reinvolvement of each by the other in every process by which what is one's own is related to what is foreign. Could I consider myself as someone's neighbor without a topographical sketch? And could the here and the there stand out against the horizon of a common world, if the chain of concrete neighborhoods was not set within the grid of a great cadastre in which places are more than sites? The most memorable places would not seem to be capable of exercising their memorial function if they were not also notable sites at the intersection point of landscape and geography. In short, would the places of memory be the guardians of personal and collective memory if they did not remain "in their place," in the twofold sense of place and of site?

The difficulty referred to here becomes especially troublesome when, following Casey, we place the mnemonic phenomena tied to commemoration at the end of the path held to lead memory away from its "mentalist" core. To be sure, it is perfectly legitimate to place commemoration back within the framework of the reflexivity/worldliness polarity.[42] But then the price to pay for inserting commemoration within the context of worldliness is particularly high: once the emphasis has been placed on corporeal gestures and on the spatiality of the rituals that accompany the temporal rhythms of celebration, then the question of the nature of the space and the time in which these festive figures of memory unfold cannot be avoided. Could the public space at the heart of which the celebrants are gathered together and the calendar of feasts that mark the high points of ecclesiastical liturgies and patriotic celebrations be said to fulfill their functions of assembling the community (*religio* equivalent to *religare?*) without the articulation of phenomenological space and time onto cosmological space and time? More particularly, are not the founding events and actions, ordinarily situated in a far distant time, tied to calendar time, to the extent that they sometimes determine the zero point of the official system of dating?[43] An even more radical question: does not the sort of perennialization resulting from the series of ritual reenactments, continuing beyond the deaths one by one of the co-celebrants, make our commemorations the most wildly desperate act to resist forgetfulness in its most surreptitious form of erasing traces, of grinding into dust? Now this forgetfulness seems to operate at the point of intersection of time and physical movement, at the point where, Aristotle notes in *Physics* 4.12, time "wastes things away." It is on this note of hesitation that I interrupt, rather than complete, this sketch of a phenomenology of memory.

## MEMORIES AND IMAGES

Under this title "Memories and Images" we reach the critical point of the entire phenomenology of memory. It is no longer a question of a polarity capable of being embraced by a generic concept such as memory, even when it is split into the simple presence of a memory—Greek *mnēmē*—and recall, recollection—Greek *anamnēsis*. The troublesome question is the following: is a memory a sort of image, and if so, what sort? And if it should prove possible through appropriate eidetic analysis to account for the essential difference between images and memories, how could their interconnectedness, even their confusion, be explained not only on the level of language but on the level of actual experience: Do we not speak of what we remember, even of memory as an image we have of the past? The problem is not new: Western philosophy inherited it from the Greeks and from their variations on the term *eikōn*. To be sure, we have stated repeatedly that imagination and memory have as a common trait the presence of the absent and as a differential trait, on the one hand, the bracketing of any positing of reality and the vision of something unreal and, on the other, the positing of an earlier reality. And yet our most difficult analyses will be devoted to reestablishing the lines of transference from one problematic to the other. After having uncoupled imagination from memory, what necessity compels us to reassociate them for a reason other than that which presided over their dissociation? In a word: what is the eidetic necessity attested by the expression memory-image that continues to haunt our phenomenology of memory and that will return in full force on the epistemological level in the historiographical operation that constitutes the historian's representation of the past?[44]

We will take Husserl as our first guide in the investigation of the eidetic differences between image and memory. Husserl's contribution to this discussion is considerable, although his fragmentary analyses scattered over more than twenty-five years did not result in a finished work. Several of these analyses, however, have been collected in volume 23 of *Husserliana* under the title *Phantasie, Bildbewusstein, Erinnerung 1898–1925*,[45] employing a vocabulary imposed by the state of the discussion at the end of the nineteenth century around thinkers as important as Brentano. For my part, I salute in these analyses, with their combined patience and intellectual honesty, the second major contribution of descriptive phenomenology to the problematic of memory, alongside the analyses devoted to retention and recollection in the first two sections of the 1905 "Lectures on the Phenomenology of the Consciousness of Internal Time." It is indeed to the correlation between these two parallel series that I wish to draw the reader's attention: each of them has to do with the "objective" side of *Erinnerung* which is appropriately designated in French by the substantive *souvenir* (memory).

These laborious texts explore the specific differences that distinguish by means of their "objective" (*Gegenständlichen*) correlates a variety of acts of consciousness characterized by their specific intentionality. The difficulty of the description comes not only from the interweaving of these correlates but from the linguistic burdens of prior usages, some highly traditional ones such as the use of the term *Vorstellung*, imperatively but unhappily translated in French (as in English) by "representation," some others imposed by the discussions of that period. Hence the word *Vorstellung*, unavoidable since Kant, includes all the correlates of sensory, intuitive acts, distinct from judgment: a phenomenology of reason, which Husserl continually projected, could not do without it. But the comparison with perception and all the other intuitive sensory acts offered a more promising entry. And this is what Husserl obstinately pursued: it forced him to distinguish among a variety of "the modes of presentation" of something, perception constituting "presentation pure and simple," *Gegenwärtigung*, all the other acts being classified under the heading of presentification, *Vergegenwärtigung* (a term also translated by "re-presentation," at the risk of confusing re-presentation and representation, *Vorstellung*).

The title of Husserl's volume covers the field of a phenomenology of intuitive presentifications. We see where the overlap can be made with the phenomenology of memory: the latter is a sort of intuitive presentification having to do with time. Husserl often places his program under the aegis of a "phenomenology of perception, of *Bild*, of *Phantasie*, of time, of the thing [*Ding*]," a phenomenology that has yet to be realized. The fact that perception and its mode of presentation are taken as guidelines should not prematurely give rise to a suspicion of some sort of "metaphysics of presence"—it is a matter of the presentation of something with its distinctive character of intuitivity. All the manuscripts in the volume have to do, therefore, with objective modes that share in intuitivity but differ from perception by the non-presentation of their object. This is their common feature. Their differences come later. As concerns the place of memories on this palette, it remains incompletely determined as long as its tie with the consciousness of time has not been established; but this tie can be made on the level of the analyses of retention and of reproduction that remain within the objective dimension. We must then compare, as Husserl requests, the manuscripts collected in *Husserliana*, vol. 10, "The Consciousness of Internal Time," and those of volume 23. In the latter collection, what matters is the kinship with the other modalities of presentification. The stakes of the analysis at this stage concern the relation between memory and image, our word "image" occupying the same ground as Husserl's *Vergegenwärtigung*. But was this not already the case with the Greek *eikōn* and its run-ins with *phantasia*? We will return to this with *Bild* and *Phantasie*. In fact, memories are involved in these two modalities, as their enumeration in Husserl's preferred title reminds us, and to them should be added expectation (*Erwartung*), placed on the same side as memory but at the opposite end of the palette of temporal presentifications, as we also see in the manuscripts on time.

When Husserl speaks of *Bild*, he is thinking of presentifications that depict something in an indirect manner: portraits, paintings, statues, photographs, and so on. Aristotle had begun this phenomenology by noting that a picture, a painting could be read as a present image or as an image designating something unreal or absent.[46] Everyday language, quite imprecise, speaks in this situation of image as well as representation; but it sometimes specifies by asking what a particular picture represents, of what it is the image. One could then translate *Bild* as depiction, based on the model of the verb to depict.

When Husserl speaks of *Phantasie*, he is thinking of fairies, angels, and devils in stories: it is indeed a matter of fiction (some texts state *Fiktum*). Husserl is, moreover, interested in this by reason of the ties to spontaneity, which is a feature of belief (a term he uses often in accordance with the usage of the English-language tradition). The phenomenology of memory is implied in these distinctions and these ramifications. But the examples proposed by no means eliminate the need for an essential, eidetic, analysis. And Husserl's interminable analyses attest to the difficulty of stabilizing meanings that continue to tread one upon another.

It is the distinction between *Bild* and *Phantasie* that proved troublesome for him from the beginning (1898–1906), hence at the time of the *Logical Investigations*, in the context of a theory of judgment and of the new theory of meanings that pushes to the forefront the question of intuition in terms of *Erfühlung*, of the "fulfillment" of signifying intentions. Later, during the period of the *Ideen*, it is the modality of neutrality specific to *Phantasie* that will move to the fore, confronting the positional character of perception. Intervening as well, though obliquely, will be the question of the individuation of something, performed by the different types of presentations, as if periodically it was intuition that reasserted itself at the top of the scale of knowledge. At other times, it is the extreme distancing of *Phantasie* in relation to presentation in the flesh that intrigues him. *Phantasia* then tends to occupy the entire place held by the English word "idea" as it is opposed to "impression" in the British empiricists. It is no longer simply a matter of devilish intrigues but also of poetic or other fictions. It is non-presenting intuition that delimits the field. Should we venture to speak tranquilly of fantasy, of the fantastic in the manner of the Greeks? (The graphism "phantasy" or "fantasy" then remains open.) What matters to the phenomenology of memory is that the temporal note of retention can be linked up with fantasy considered provisionally as a genus common to all non-presentations. However, the vocabulary of *Vorstellung* is retained when the emphasis falls on the intuition common to presentation and to presentification in the field of a phenomenological logic of meanings. Is it then on *Phantasie* alone that the temporal marks of retention and reproduction are to be grafted? Yes, if the emphasis falls on non-presentation. No, if it falls, in the case of secondary remembering, on reproduction: then the kinship with *Bild* is imposed, which, beyond the examples mentioned above, covers the entire field of the "depicted" (*das Abgebildete*), that is to say, of an indirect presentification based on a thing itself presented. And if the emphasis falls on "the belief of being attached to the memory" (*Seinsglaube an das Erinnerte*), then the opposition between memory and fantasy is complete: the latter lacks the present "as it were" of the reproduced past. On the other hand, the kinship with the "depicted" seems more direct, as when one recognizes a loved one in a photograph. The "remembered" then draws upon the "depicted." It is with this play of attractions and repulsions that Husserl continues to struggle.[47] The sole fixed point remains the theme of intuitive presentifications, taking into account their own entanglement with the conceptual modalities of representation in general, a theme that covers presentations and non-presentations, hence the totality of objectifying "apprehensions," leaving out only practical and affective lived experiences, which, in truth, were presumed to be constructed on the basis of these apprehensions.

The field thus continues at times to widen to include all *Auffassungen* ("apprehensions"), at times to narrow to the innumerable ramifications of presentifications or representations. The interplay between the remembered, the fictive (*Fiktum*) and the depicted (*Abgebildete*) is then invoked against the backdrop of the global opposition to perception, whose object presents itself directly (*Selbstgegenwärtige*); the depicted advancing over the pretended by its indirect character, a physical image (*Bild*) offering support. The split then passes between the image (*Bild*) and the thing (*Sache* in the sense of *res*, *pragmata*), the thing in question, not the thing (*Ding*) in space.

If a memory is an image in this sense, it contains a positional dimension that, from this point of view, brings it closer to perception. In another vocabulary, which I am adopting, one speaks of the having-been of the remembered past, the ultimate referent of the memory in action. What will then pass to the forefront, from the phenomenological point of view, will be the split between the unreal and the real (whether it be present, past, or future). While imagination can play with fictional entities, when it does not depict but cuts itself off from the real, memories posit past things; whereas the depicted still has one foot in presentation as indirect presentation, fiction and the pretend are situated radically outside of presentation. However, considering the diversity of viewpoints under which phenomena are described and the variable scope recognized concerning these phenomenological types, "consciousness of *Bild*" and "consciousness of *Phantasie*" can, in turn, be distinguished from one another on the same plane, then set in opposition to one another, or made to include one another in one sense or in the other, depending on the place that is given to them in the field of intuitive presentifications: the entire place or part of it. (It happens that Husserl reserves the substantive *Phantasma* for these supports for the operation of depicting, pulling *Phantasie* itself in this way into the field of depicting the *Bild*.)[48]

It is this inclusive problematic of presentification that will be upset in the third section of *The Phenomenology of the Consciousness of Internal Time*. The opposition between presentation and presentification continues, nonetheless, to function within the objective field of the correlates of intentional consciousness, as does the distinction between primary memory and secondary memory, considered as temporal varieties of presentification, of "making present" that which does not give itself as present in the sense of presenting. The same analyses made on the basis of memories and no longer concerning *Bild* or *Phantasie* add to the complexity. As past, the thing remembered would be a pure *Phantasie*,[49] but, as given once more, it imposes memory as a modification sui generis applied to perception;[50] under this second aspect *Phantasie* would place a memory in "suspension" (*aufgehoben*),[51] which would make the memory simpler than the fiction. We would then have the sequence: perception, memory, fiction. A threshold of inactuality is crossed between memory and fiction. The phenomenology of memory therefore has to free itself from the tutelage of fantasy, of the fantastic, marked with the seal of inactuality, of neutrality. Yet to evoke neutrality, as was done in *Ideen I*, §111, in order to situate the fantastic in relation to the remembered, is to invoke belief: to the certainty common to the series: perception, memory, expectation is opposed a mode of uncertainty such as admission (*Aufnahme*), presentiment (*Ahnung*). These modalities belong to the same cycle as do all "positings" (*Stellungnahmungen*), the genus common to all the modalities of the inactual, the neutral.

The dividing line thus runs all along the break between presentation and presentification. Memories are a specific modification of presentation, at least as primary memory or retention, as confirmed by the first section of the 1905 lectures. Here *Husserliana*, vol. 23 and *Husserliana*, vol. 10 coincide, their primary emphasis bearing on the operative mode (or performance) (*Vollzug*), which distinguishes reproduction from production, inactuality from actuality, non-positing from positing. Any possibility of confusing a memory with an image in the sense of the term *Bild* is henceforth eliminated. Everything is played out on the scene of the "objective" correlate of the experiences interrogated.

*Ideen I*, despite the idealist turn taken by the philosophy of consciousness, will not speak a different language concerning the "manner of fulfillment" of the intuitive modalities included within the scope of presentification.[52] The criterion of positionality will continue to be strengthened in the texts coming after *Ideen I*: memories belong to the "world of experience" in contrast to the "worlds of fantasy," of irreality. The former is a common world (without, as yet, any mention of the manner of intersubjective mediation), the latter are totally "free," their horizon completely "undetermined." In principle, then, they cannot be confused or mistaken one for the other, whatever may be said regarding the complex relations between *Fiktum* and possibility, even their irreducibility to one another. A phenomenology attentive to eidetic differences never finishes making distinctions.

If one had to define the difference in approach between the applications in *Husserliana*, vol. 10 (which themselves repeat those of the first section of the 1905 "Lectures on the Phenomenology of the Consciousness of Internal

Time") and the applications concerning the sequence *Phantasie, Bild, Erin-nerung,* one could say that with regard to the latter the emphasis is placed on the differences between members of the family of presentifications, hence on the modifications affecting the presentations of the "objective" correlate, while in the 1905 lectures, the emphasis falls on the temporal modalities specific to the sort of presentification characterizing memories. In this respect, it is noteworthy that in the analyses in *Husserliana,* vol. 23 the key notion of presentation (*Gegenwärtigung*) is still distinguished from the temporal present, just as the theme of the now (*Jetzt*) is still absent from the objective analysis of memories, without producing any negative effects. Must we not conclude that the present—the now, a notion by which the series of indicators of temporality are to be governed—is not to be separated from the idea of presentation, to which the various types of presentification are themselves referred? And if this hypothesis has merit, is it not then the kinship between memories and images within the great family of presentifications that authorizes, retrospectively, the break I made when I stopped the movement that carries the entire work of the 1905 lectures toward the self-constitution of the flow of consciousness at the objective moment? The transition will turn on the return to the self, from intentionality *ad extra*—transversal, as it is called—still at work in the phenomenology of memory, to intentionality *ad intra*, or longitudinal, which predominates in the self-constitution of the flow. We will retie this broken thread in the third chapter of the phenomenology of memory.

At the end of this voyage in the company of Husserl through the labyrinth of entanglements that make this peregrination a difficult one, I must confess that only half of the route has been covered when we account for the confusion that hampers the comparison between image and memory. How are we to explain that memories return in the form of images and that the imagination mobilized in this way comes to take on forms that escape the function of the unreal? It is this double imbroglio that we must now untangle.

I am adopting here as my working hypothesis the Bergsonian conception of the passage from "pure memory" to memory-image. I am speaking of a working hypothesis, not to separate myself from his fine analysis but from the outset to indicate my concern with distinguishing in the text of *Matter and Memory,* as far as this is possible, the psychological description from the metaphysical (in the strong and noble sense of the word) thesis concerning the role assigned to the body and to the brain and, consequently, asserting the immateriality of memory. This bracketing of the metaphysical thesis amounts to dissociating, in the heritage received from the Greeks, the notion of *eikōn* from that of *tupos*, of the imprint, which was associated with it from the start. From the phenomenological point of view, the two notions belong to two distinct orders: the *eikōn* contains within itself the other of the original affection, while the *tupos* involves the external causality of an impetus (*kinēsis*), which is itself at the origin of pressing the seal into the wax. The entire modern problematic of "mnemonic traces" is, in fact, heir to this ancient alliance between *eikōn* and *tupos*. The metaphysics of *Matter and Memory* proposes, precisely, to link systematically the relation between the action, the center of which is the brain, and the pure representation which is self-sufficient as a result of the persistence, in principle, of the memory of the initial impressions. It is this presumed relation that I am bracketing in the analysis that follows.[53]

The distinction Bergson makes between "pure memory" and memory-image radicalizes the thesis of the two memories with which we began the preceding phenomenological sketch. And it is, therefore, this thesis that is made even more radical in its turn by the metaphysical thesis upon which *Matter and Memory* is constructed. It is within this intermediary location, with regard to the strategy of the work as a whole, that we will carry through our description of the passage from "pure memory" to memory-image.

Let us start the analysis by accepting that there does exist something like a "pure memory" that has not yet been put into images. We will say a little further on in what way it is possible to speak of this and how important it is to be able to speak convincingly of it. Let us start at the furthest point reached by the theory of the two memories: "To call up the past in the form of an image, we must be able to withdraw ourselves from the action of the moment, we must have the power to value the useless, we must have the will to dream. Man alone is capable of such an effort. But even in him the past to which he returns is fugitive, ever on the point of escaping him, as though his backward turning memory were thwarted by the other, more natural, memory, of which the forward movement bears him on to action and to life" (Bergson, *Matter and Memory*, 94). At this stage of the analysis, we have available to us in speaking of "pure memory" only the example of a lesson learned by heart. And it is by a sort of passage to the limit that we write, following Bergson: "Spontaneous recollection is perfect from the outset; time can add nothing to its image without disfiguring it; it retains in memory its place and date" (95). The distinction between a "memory which recalls" and a "memory which repeats" was the fruit of a method of division that consisted in distinguishing "two extreme forms of memory in their *pure* state," then in reconstructing the memory-image as an intermediary form, as a "mixed phenomenon which results from their coalescence" (103). And it was in the act of recognition that this fusion occurred, signaled by the feeling of déjà vu. It is also then in the work of recollection that this operation of putting the "pure memory" into images can be grasped in its origin. We can speak of this operation only as a movement from the virtual to the actual, or again as the condensation of a cloud or as the materialization of an ethereal phenomenon. Other metaphors suggest themselves: movement from the depths to the surface, from shadows to the light, from tension to relaxation, from the heights to the lower levels of psychical life. Such is the "movement of memory at work" (171). It carries memory back so to speak into a region of presence similar to that of perception. But—and here we reach the other side of the difficulty—it is not just any sort of imagination that is mobilized. In contrast to the function of derealization, culminating in a fiction exiled to the margins of reality considered in its totality, what is celebrated here is instead the visualizing function of imagination, its manner of giving something to be seen. On this point, what unavoidably comes to mind is the final component of the *muthos* that, according to Aristotle's *Poetics*, structures the configuration of tragedy and epic, namely, the *opsis*, held to consist in "placing before the eyes," showing, making visible.[54] This is also the case when "pure memory" is put into images: "Essentially virtual, it cannot be known as something past unless we follow and adopt the movement by which it expands into a present image, thus emerging from obscurity into the light of day" (173). The strength of Bergson's analysis is to keep the two extremities of the spectrum separate and yet connected. At one end: "*To imagine* is not *to remember*. No doubt a recollection, as it becomes actual, tends to live in an image; but the converse is not true, and the image, pure and simple, will not be referred to the past unless, indeed, it was in the past that I sought it, thus following the continuous progress which brought it from darkness into light" (173–74, trans. modified).

If we follow this thought to the other extreme, descending from "pure memory" to memory-image—and, as we shall see, far beyond that—we witness a complete reversal of the imaging function, whose shadow also extends from the far pole of fiction to the opposite pole of hallucination.

It was the fiction-pole of the imagination that I considered in *Time and Narrative* when I opposed fictional narrative to historical narrative. It is in relation to the other pole, the hallucination-pole, that we now have to situate ourselves. Just as Bergson dramatized the problem of memory by his method of division and the shift to opposing poles, it is important to dramatize the thematic of the imagination in the same way by organizing it in relation to the two poles of fiction and hallucination. By moving to the pole of hallucination, we uncover the *pitfall of the imaginary* for memory. It is, in fact, just this sort of memory that is a common target of the rationalist critiques of memory.

In order to account for this trap, I thought it might be appropriate to summon, alongside Bergson, another witness, Jean-Paul Sartre in *The Psychology of Imagination*.[55] This astonishing book sets off along the path of just such a reversal of the problematic of memory, even though this is not its purpose. I called this book astonishing. It begins, in fact, with a plea for a phenomenology of the unreal, approaching from the other side the effort of uncoupling imagination and memory, which we attempted earlier. As is firmly asserted in the conclusion, despite the drift we will discuss: "the hypothesis of the imaginative consciousness is radically different from the hypothesis of a consciousness of the real. This means that the type of existence of the object of the image, *as long as it is imagined*, differs in nature from the hypothesis of existence of the object of the real.... This essential nothingness of the imagined object is enough to distinguish it from the object of perception" (261). Memory is on the side of perception, as concerns its thesis of reality: "there is . . . an essential difference between the theme of a recollection and that of an image. If I recall an incident of my past life I do not imagine it, I *recall* it. That is, I do not posit it as *given-in-its-absence* but as *given-now-in-the-past* in the past" (263). This is exactly the interpretation proposed at the beginning of this study. But now here is the reversal. It takes place on the terrain of the imaginary. It results from what can be called the hallucinatory seduction of the imaginary. The fourth part of *The Psychology of Imagination* is devoted to this seduction under the title "The Imaginary Life": "The act of imagination . . . magic alone. It is an incantation destined to produce the object of one's thought, the thing one desires, in a manner that one can take possession of it" (177). The incantation is equivalent to the voiding of absence and distance. "This is a way of *playing at* satisfying my desire" (179). The imagined object's "not-being-there" is covered over by the quasi presence induced by the magical operation. Its unreality is warded off by this sort of "dance before the unreal" (205). In truth, this voiding was nascent in "placing before the eyes" considered as "putting into images," the putting-on-stage constitutive of the memory-image. In this text, Sartre did not foresee the rebound effect on the theory of memory. But he paves the way for this understanding in his description of what is soon to become a "pathology of the imagination" (213ff.). It is centered on the hallucination and its distinctive feature, obsession, namely, "that sort of vertigo inspired in particular by flight in the face of that which is forbidden." Every effort "not to think about it anymore" is spontaneously transformed into "obsessive thinking." Confronting the phenomenon of fascination with the forbidden object, how can we help but leap to the plane of collective memory and evoke the sort of hauntedness, described by historians of the present day, which stigmatizes this "past that does not pass"? Hauntedness is to collective memory what hallucination is to private memory, a pathological modality of the incrustation of the past at the heart of the present, which acts as a counterweight to the innocent habit-memory, which also inhabits the present, but in order to "act it" as Bergson says, not to haunt it or torment it.

From Sartre's description of the reversal of the imagination's function of derealization into a function of hallucination, a curious parallel results between the phenomenology of memory and the phenomenology of imagination. It seems as though the form that Bergson calls intermediary or mixed memory—namely, memory-image, half-way between "pure memory" and memory reinscribed in perception, at the stage where recognition blossoms in the feeling of déjà-vu—corresponded to an intermediary form of imagination, half-way between fiction and hallucination, namely, the "image" component of the memory-image. So it is also as a mixed form that we must speak of the function of the imagination consisting in "placing before the eyes," a function that can be termed ostensive: this is an imagination that shows, gives to be seen, makes visible.

A phenomenology of memory cannot fail to recognize what we have just called the pitfall of the imaginary, inasmuch as this putting-into-images, bordering on the hallucinatory function of imagination, constitutes a sort of weakness, a discredit, a loss of reliability for memory. We will return to this when we consider a certain way of writing history, after the manner of Michelet, we might say, in which the "resurrection" of the past also tends to take on quasi-hallucinatory forms. In this way, writing history shares the adventures of memories put-into-images under the aegis of the ostensive function of imagination.

I do not want to conclude on this note of perplexity, but instead with the provisional response than can be given to the question of trust that the theory of memory passes on to the theory of history. This is the question of the reliability of memory and, in this sense, of its truth. This question stood in the background of our entire investigation concerning the differential feature that separates memory from imagination. At the end of our investigation, and in spite of the traps that imagination lays for memory, it can be affirmed that a specific search for truth is implied in the intending of the past "thing," of *what* was formerly seen, heard, experienced, learned. This search for truth determines memory as a cognitive issue. More precisely, in the moment of recognition, in which the effort of recollection is completed, this search for truth declares itself. We then feel and indeed know that something has happened, something has taken place, which implicated us as agents, as patients, as witnesses. Let us call this search for truth, faithfulness. From now on, we will speak of the faithfulness of memories, of memories being true to . . . , in order to express this search, this demand, this claim, which constitutes the veridical-epistemic dimension of the *orthos logos* of memory. The study that follows will have the task of showing how the epistemic, *veridical* dimension of memory is united with the *practical* dimension tied to the idea of the *exercise* of memory.

# CHAPTER 2

## *The Exercise of Memory: Uses and Abuses*

### READING GUIDELINES

The cognitive approach to memory developed in the preceding chapter from the "objective" angle does not exhaust the description of memory. A pragmatic approach is also required. This new consideration is joined to the earlier one in the following manner: remembering is not only welcoming, receiving an image of the past, it is also searching for it, "doing" something. The verb "to remember" stands in for the substantive "memory." What the verb designates is the fact that memory is "exercised." Now the notion of exercise, applied to memory, is no less ancient than that of *eikōn*, of representation. Joined to that of "searching" (*zētēsis*), it shines in the firmament of Socratic concepts. Following Socrates, Plato does not hesitate to shift his discourse on the *eikōn* to the arena of "imitative techniques" and to distinguish a "fantastic" mimetics, fated to be deceitful, and an "iconic" mimetics, reputed to be "upright" (*orthos*) and "truthful" (*alēthinos*). Aristotle, in his turn, in the chapter "*Anamnēsis*" in his short treatise bearing a double title, describes recollection as a "search," whereas *mnēmē* was characterized in the first chapter as an "affection" (*pathos*). Both of our Greek masters thus anticipated what will be called the effort of memory by Bergson and the work of remembering by Freud, as we shall soon see.

The remarkable fact is that these cognitive and practical approaches overlap in the operation of recollection; recognition, which crowns the successful search, designates the cognitive side of the recollection, while effort and work are inscribed in the practical field. Henceforth, we will reserve the term "remembering" (*remémoration*) to signify this superposition of the two problematics—cognitive and pragmatic—in one and the same operation of *anamnēsis*, of recollection, of recall.

This split into cognitive and pragmatic dimensions accentuates the specificity of memory among the phenomena classified under the heading of the psychical. In this regard, the act of exercising memory comes to be inscribed within the list of powers, capacities, belonging to the category "I can," to take up the expression dear to Merleau-Ponty.[1] But it seems that this act of exercising memory itself presents the most complete superimposition in a single act, with respect to its description, of the cognitive aim and the practical operation—the act of remembering, direct heir to the Aristotelian *anamnesis* and indirect heir to Platonic *anamnēsis*.

This originality of the mnemonic phenomenon is of considerable importance for all that follows in our investigations. Indeed, it also defines the historiographical operation as a theoretical practice. The historian undertakes to "do history" (*faire de l'histoire*) just as each of us attempts to "remember" (*faire mémoire*). For the most part, the confrontation between memory and history will play itself out on the level of these two, inseparably cognitive and practical, operations.

The ultimate stakes of the investigation that follows concern the fate of the desire for faithfulness that we have seen linked to the intention of memory as the guardian of the depth of time and of temporal distance. In what way, with respect to these stakes, are the vicissitudes of the exercise of memory likely to affect memory's ambition to be truthful? In a word, the exercise of memory is its use; yet use includes the possibility of abuse. Between use and abuse slips the specter of the bad "mimetics." It is from the angle of abuse that memory's aim of truthfulness is seriously threatened.

The pages that follow aim at sketching out a loosely knit typology of these abuses of memory. They are in each case correlated with an aspect of the exercise of memory.

The feats of *ars memoriae*, the art celebrated by Frances Yates, will be set out separately;[2] the excesses it has occasioned are those of an artificial memory that methodically exploits the resources of the operation of memorization, which we want carefully to distinguish, already on the level of natural memory, from remembering in the limited sense of the evocation of singular facts, of events. The longest section of this chapter will, thus, be devoted to the abuses of natural memory. These will be divided into three levels: on the pathological, therapeutic level, the disturbances of blocked memory will emerge; on the properly practical level, those of manipulated memory; and on the ethico political level, those of a memory abusively summoned, when commemoration rhymes with rememoration. These multiple forms of abuse expose the fundamental vulnerability of memory, which results from the relation between the absence of the thing remembered and its presence in the mode of representation. The highly problematical character of this representative relation to the past is laid bare in its essence by all the abuses of memory.

§

## THE ABUSES OF ARTIFICIAL MEMORY: THE FEATS OF MEMORIZATION

There is one modality of the act of exercising memory that presents itself as practice par excellence, namely, the memorization that has to be rigorously distinguished from remembering.

With remembering, the emphasis is placed on the return to awakened consciousness of an event recognized as having occurred before the moment when consciousness declares having experienced, perceived, learned it. The temporal mark of the before thus constitutes the distinctive feature of remembering, under the double form of simple evocation and of the recognition that concludes the process of recall. Memorization, on the other hand, consists in the ways of learning relating to forms of knowledge, know-how, capacities marked from a phenomenological point of view by a feeling of facility, ease, spontaneity, in such a way that these are fixed and remain available for activation. This feature constitutes the pragmatic counterpoint to the recognition in which recall terminates on the epistemological plane. In negative terms, this is an economy of effort, as the subject is dispensed from learning all over again in order to perform a task appropriate to specific circumstances. The feeling of ease then represents the positive side of this successful actualization of a memory, which Bergson would say is "acted" rather than "represented." In this regard, memorization can be held to be a form of habit-memory. But the process of memorization is specified by the methodical character of the ways of learning aiming at an easy actualization, the privileged form of happy memory.

It thus becomes a legitimate project to describe the methods of learning directed to this easy actualization from the perspective of the techniques of acquisition and to attempt to spot the weaknesses that allow abuse to infect use. We will follow an order of increasing complexity in which the opportunities for misuse grow along with the ambition of mastery exerted over the entire process of memorization. For it is indeed in this ambition of mastery that the possibility to slip from use to abuse resides.

At the lowest level, we find the techniques belonging to what is called *learning* (*apprentissage*) in experimental psychology. I am speaking in general and broad terms of "ways of learning" in order carefully to mark out the field. Learning, openly associated with memory in specialized works, belongs to a biology of memory.[3] This learning, in fact, consists in the acquisition by a living being of new behaviors that are not part of inherited, genetically programmed repertoires of abilities or know-how, nor do they stem from cortical epigenesis. What is important for our investigation is that the control over the learning process belongs to the experimenter who directs the manipulation. He or she determines the task, defines the criteria of success, organizes punishments and rewards, and, in this way, "conditions" the learning. This situation constitutes the form most in opposition to that of the *ars memoriae*, which we will discover at the end of our survey and which will be the fruit of discipline, of an "ascetic"—the *askēsis* of the Socratics, meaning "exercise"—of which the apprentice will himself be the master. Speaking of manipulation, we are certainly not denouncing an abuse but only intend to characterize the type of mastery that presides over experimentation. Only manipulation in the human milieu, as will be discussed below in connection with ideology, will deserve to be marked with the seal of infamy. Nevertheless, already at this level, and without leaving the psycho-biological plane on which these experiments are conducted, one can level an appropriate critique at the conditions controlling the manipulation of the living beings undergoing these tests. During the period of behaviorism, such tests were supposed to provide an experimental basis for verification using "models" based on stimulus-response type hypotheses. Criticisms raised by authors such as Kurt Goldstein, echoed by Merleau-Ponty in *The Structure of Behaviour*[4] and Canguilhem in *La Connaissance de la vie*,[5] relate essentially to the artificial character of the situations in which an animal, even a human subject, is placed under the control of the experimenter, in contrast to the spontaneous relations of the living being with its environment, as these are apprehended by ethological science in an open setting. The conditions of experimentation are not neutral with respect to the meaning of observed behavior. They contribute to masking the living being's resources of exploration, anticipation, and negotiation, through which this being is engaged in an *Umwelt* that belongs to it in its own right and that it helps to construct.

This discussion matters to us inasmuch as the forms of learning that we are now going to consider have the capacity, in their turn, to oscillate between manipulation, the mastery of the teacher, and the discipline expected of the disciple.

And so, it is to the dialectic of the teacher and the disciple that the exercises of memorization as part of a program of education, of *paideia*, belong. The classical model is well known: it consists in the *recitation* of the lesson learned *by heart*. Augustine, the rhetorician, likes to derive his analysis of the threefold present—present of the past or memory, present of the future or expectation, present of the present or intuition—from an examination of the act of reciting a poem or a biblical verse. Reciting from memory, we say, without hesitation or mistake, constitutes a small feat that prefigures larger ones, as we will say later. Now, before unleashing our critique of the abuses of learning "by heart," we must first recall the justification for its beneficial use. Within the framework of teaching, which, as we will soon see, is only one part of *paideia*, recitation has long constituted the preferred mode of transmission, under the direction of educators, of texts considered, if not as founding works of the culture of instruction, at least as prestigious, in the sense of texts that are authoritative. For it is indeed authority that is at issue in the final analysis, more precisely enunciative authority, to distinguish it from institutional authority.[6] Here, we reach a political concept in the most fundamental sense, concerning the establishment of the social bond. We can hardly conceive of a society in which the horizontal bond of living together would not intersect with the vertical bond of the authority of the Ancients, following an old adage cited by Hannah Arendt: *potestas in populo, auctoritas in senatu*. The eminently political question is knowing what the "Senate" is, who the "Ancients" are, and where their authority comes from. Education takes place short of this problem and as though sheltered from the questioning of its own legitimacy. Whatever the effect of this enigma of authority—the heart of what Rousseau called the "labyrinth of politics"— every society has the burden of transmitting from one generation to the next what it holds to be its cultural acquisitions. For each generation, the learning process, as we suggested above, can dispense with the exhausting effort to reacquire everything each time all over again. In this way, people in Christian communities have long learned to recite the catechism. But it is also in this way that the rules of correct spelling were learned—Oh, those dictations!—then the rules of grammar and of mathematics. And it is yet again in the same manner that we learn the rudiments of a dead language or a foreign language—Oh, those Greek and Latin declensions and conjugations! As young children, we learned rhymes and rounds, then fables and poems; in this regard, have we not gone too far in the war against learning "by heart?" Happy, indeed, are those who, like Jorge Semprun, can whisper in the ear of a dying man—Maurice Halbwachs, helas!—Baudelaire's verses: "Ô mort, vieux capitaine, il est temps, levons l'ancre . . . nos coeurs que tu connais sont remplis de rayons . . . " But learning "by heart" is not the perquisite only of the schooling of the past. Many professionals—doctors, lawyers, scientists, engineers, teachers—have recourse over the entire course of their lives to the copious memorization of information resting on repertories, lists of items, protocols that are kept available for actualization at the appropriate time. All must have at their disposal a well-trained memory.

This is not all: neither the pedagogical nor the professional use of memorization exhausts the treasury of the ways of learning countenanced by a faultless recitation without hesitation. We must mention in this connection all the arts that Henri Gouhier places under the generic title of the arts in two measures—dance, theater, music—in which the execution is distinct from the composition of the work, found in a libretto, a score, or some other form of inscription.[7] These arts require of their practitioners a laborious training of the memory, based upon a stubborn and patient repetition, until an execution, at once faithful and innovative, is obtained, one in which the prior labor is forgotten under the appearance of a happy improvisation. How can one fail to admire the dancers, actors, musicians who have recorded extensive repertories, which they "execute" for our pleasure. They are the true athletes of memory. Perhaps, in this, they represent the only indisputable witnesses to a use without abuse of memory, obedience to the injunctions of the work inspiring in them the humility capable of tempering their legitimate pride in the exploit accomplished.

At the third stage of our journey through the forms of learning, I would like to mention the long-standing tradition that raised memorization to the level of an *ars memoriae*, worthy indeed of the name of art, of technique. Under the title *The Art of Memory*, Frances A. Yates has devoted a work to this tradition, one that remains a classic on this subject.[8] The Latin name is not a mere convention: originally, it refers to the mnemotechnic procedures recommended and practiced by the Latin rhetoricians—the unknown author of the *Ad Herennium* (mistakenly attributed to Cicero by the Medieval tradition), Cicero himself frequently called *Tullius* and Quintilian. The founding myth, however, is not Roman but Greek. It refers to a famous episode, situated around the year 500 B.C. at the fatal end of a banquet given by a rich benefactor in honor of a well-known athlete. The poet, Simonides of Ceos—who, moreover, is mentioned favorably by Plato—had been hired to give a panegyric in honor of the victorious athlete. Opportunely summoned outside the banquet hall to meet two benevolent demi-gods, Castor and Pollux, he escapes the catastrophe that befalls the athlete and the other guests, who are buried under the ruins of the collapsed roof. This happy fate suffices for the Greek myth in which the poet is held to be blessed by the gods. But the Latins are acquainted with a sequel better suited to their culture of eloquence. The poet is supposed to have been able to indicate from memory the place of each guest and, so, according to Weinrich, "to identify the dead according to their location in space." A fabulous victory over forgetfulness— the catastrophe symbolized by sudden death—is the meaning of the exploit. But this is at the price of a hard schooling that annexes the art of memory to rhetoric. This art consists essentially in associating *images* with *places* (*topoi*, *loci*) organized in rigorous systems corresponding to a house, a public place, an architectural setting. The rules of this art are of two sorts: the first govern the selection of the places, the second govern the mental images of the things one wishes to remember and which the art assigns to the places selected. The images stored in this way are supposed to be easy to recall at the appropriate moment, the order of the places preserving the order of the things. From the treatise *Ad Herennium*—the earlier Greek treatises having been lost— comes the lapidary definition that will be repeated from age to age: "The artificial (*artificiosa*) memory is established from places and images." As for the "things" that are depicted by the images and the places, these are objects, persons, events, facts relating to a cause to be argued. What matters is that the ideas be attached to images and that the items be stored in places. We thus meet up again here with the old metaphor of inscription, with places now in the role of the wax tablet and images in that of the letters inscribed on it. And, from beneath this metaphor, reemerges the genuinely founding metaphor, coming from the *Theaetetus*, of the wax, the seal, and the imprint. But the novelty consists in the fact that the body—eventually, the brain—or the soul joined to the body is no longer the support for this imprint, but rather the imagination considered as a spiritual power. The mnemotechnics applied to it are all to the glory of the imagination, of which memory becomes an annex. In the same stroke, spatialization obliterates temporalization. Not the spatiality of the lived body and its environing world, but that of the mind. The notion of place has chased away the mark of the past which had characterized memory since Aristotle's *De memoria et reminiscentia*. Memory no longer consists in recalling the past but in actualizing what has been learned and stored in a mental space. In Bergsonian terms, we have crossed over to the side of habit-memory. But this habit-memory is a memory that, according to certain texts, is exercised, cultivated, trained, sculpted. These are genuine exploits performed by the fabulous memory of true athletes of memorization. Cicero calls such performances "almost divine."

The tradition that stems from this "oratorical institution," to borrow the title of Quintilian's treatise, is so rich that our contemporary discussion concerning the places of memory—real places inscribed in geography—can be considered the most recent heir to this art of artificial memory coming from the Greeks and the Latins, for whom the places were the sites of a mental script. If, before *Ad Herennium*, the tradition was most certainly a long and varied one, leading back not only to the *Theaetetus* and its apologue of the seal in the wax, but also to the *Phaedrus* and its famous condemnation of memory bound by external "marks," how much richer it has proven from "Tullius" to Giordano Bruno, in whom Frances Yates sees the culmination of the *ars memoriae*! What a journey from one end to the other and what twists and turns! At least three turning points have punctuated this strange epic of memorizing memory.

First comes the reinscription by Augustine of Latin rhetoric in a decidedly Platonic interpretation of a memory more closely related to the essential than to the order of events. From the beginning of the present work, we have alluded to the *De memoria* of book 10 of the *Confessions*: in addition to the famous exordium on the "palaces" and "storehouses" of memory, we find there the apologue of the stamp in the wax, extended by the theme of the "effigies." What is more, the act of reciting is taken as the basis for the analysis of recall. We retain in particular, though, the exclamation: "How great is the power of memory!" For it is indeed the power exerted in the act of remembering that is at issue in the entire tradition of the *ars memoriae*. But Augustine still fears forgetfulness, which will, clearly, be forgotten at the apogee of the *ars memoriae*.

With the second turning point, the *ars memoriae* undergoes a thorough moralization on the part of the Medieval Scholastics; this happens through a surprising union of the already moralized rhetoric of Cicero—"Tullius"[9]—and the Aristotelian psychology of *De anima* and *De memoria et reminiscentia*.[10] The latter text, in particular, considered an appendix to *De anima*, was highly esteemed by medieval thinkers; Saint Thomas wrote a detailed commentary on it. Memory, then, is found inscribed on several lists: it is one of the five parts of rhetoric, alongside *intelligensia* and *providentia*, where rhetoric itself is one of the seven liberal arts (grammar, rhetoric, dialectic, arithmetic, geometry, music, astronomy); but memory is also one part of the virtue of prudence, which figures among the major virtues, along with courage, justice, and temperance. Framed in all these different ways, and as such submitted to a second-order memorization, the medieval memory is the object of praise and of particular attentions, as we would expect from a culture that knows writing, of course, but not printing, and that, in addition, carried enunciative and scriptural authority to its pinnacle: Greek and Latin masters figure as *auctoritates*, alongside Holy Scripture, the texts of the councils, and the works of the doctors of the church. At the dawn of the Middle Ages, Alcuin, whom Charlemagne entrusted with restoring the educational system of antiquity in the Carolingian empire, declared to his emperor that memory is the "treasure-house of all things"; all things: articles of faith, paths of virtue leading to heaven, paths of iniquity leading to hell. Through memorization, on the basis of "memory notes," are *inculcated* all systems of knowledge, know-how, belief, ways of living that mark the progress toward beatitude. The Secunda Secundae of Saint Thomas's *Summa Theologica* constitutes, in this respect, the major document of this instruction of reason and faith for which the *ars memoriae* became the repository and the *organon*. Along with reason and faith, devotion receives its share with eloquent images of Hell, Purgatory, and Paradise, themselves considered as the places in which vices and virtues are inscribed, memory places, in the strong sense of the word. It is then not surprising that this path of memorization leads far beyond the feats of individual memory to Dante's *Divine Comedy*. The places visited under Virgil's and then Beatrice's guidance form so many way-stations for a meditating memory, which unites the recollection of exemplary figures, the memorization of the major teachings of the tradition, and the commemoration of the founding events of Christian culture.[11] Compared to this superb metaphor of spiritual places, the exploits of artificial memory prove to be paltry indeed. In fact, a poetic memory was required to transcend the opposition between natural memory and artificial memory, to grind to dust the opposition between use and abuse.[12] This will no longer be the case at the conclusion of the third turning point.

The third turning point affecting the fate of artificial memory is marked by the union of mnemotechnics and *hermetic secrets*. Giordano Bruno, toward whom all of Frances Yates's analyses converge, is the emblematic figure of this new and almost final phase of the incredible progress of the *ars memoriae*. The art in question has become a magic, an occult art. Presiding over this metamorphosis is the conception of a system of correspondences between the stars and the lower world, presented as a revelation, as a secret that has been pierced. The art consists in placing on concentric circles of a "wheel"—the "wheel of memory"—following the principle of a one-to-one correspondence, the position of the stars, the table of virtues, the collection of expressive images of life, lists of concepts, the series of heroic or saintly human figures, all the conceivable archetypal images, in short, everything that can be enumerated and put into systematic order. What is entrusted to memory in this way is a divine power, conferring the absolute mastery of a combinatory art that links the astral order to the earthly one. It is still a matter of "placing" images onto places, but these places are stars and these images, "shadows" (the first book on memory published by Bruno in 1582 was called *De umbris idearum*), in which the objects and events of the lower world consist. This true "alchemy of the imagination," as Frances Yates calls it (224), presides over a magical mnemotechnics which gives limitless power to the one who possesses it. The revenge of Platonic, and especially Neoplatonic, reminiscence over the Aristotelian psychology of memory and recollection is complete, but at the price of the transformation of reasoned speculation into mystagogy. Yes, "great is the power of memory," to borrow Augustine's words; but the Christian rhetorician did not know to what eccentricity this praise of happy memory could lead. And Cicero might have called the exploits of trained memory "almost divine"; but he, too, could not have predicted the excesses produced by the occult memory of a man of the Renaissance, the one whom Yates calls the "Magus of Memory" (293).

To conclude this rapid overview of the *ars memoriae*, I would like to refer to the questions posed by Frances Yates at the end of her own study, before she writes the sort of post-scriptum that composes her final chapter, titled "The Art of Memory and the Growth of Scientific Method" (368ff.). I quote Yates: "The question to which I can give no clear or satisfactory answer is: What was the occult memory? Did the change from forming corporeal similitudes of the intelligible world to the effort to grasp the intelligible world through the tremendous imaginative exercises such as those to which Giordano Bruno devoted his life really stimulate the human psyche to a wider range of creative imaginative achievement than ever before? Was this the secret of the Renaissance and does the occult memory represent that secret? I bequeath this problem to others" (367).

How to answer Yates? We cannot be content to simply record the fact that the history of ideas has not produced a sequel to this extravagant cultivation of memory and that a new chapter was opened with the notion of method, with Francis Bacon's *Novum Organon* and Descartes's *Discourse on Method*.

After all, the *ars memoriae*, with its cult of order on the levels of both images and places, was in its own way an exercise of method. It is at the heart of the enterprise that the reason for its eclipse must be sought. Francis Bacon goes straight to the critical point when he denounces the prodigious ostentation that lies at the base of the culture of artificial memory. From the start, this art was vaunted as an exploit, as a marvel. A sort of inebriation—Kant will speak of *Schwärmerei* in the sense at once of enthusiasm and drunkenness—insinuated itself at the point of intersection of natural memory and artificial memory. An inebriation that transformed into its opposite the modesty of a hard schooling begun within the limits of natural memory, with regard to which it had always been legitimate to try to reinforce its powers, that is to say, at once its scope and its exactness. For it is indeed the notion of limit that is at issue here. With Giordano Bruno the transgression of limits is carried to its furthest point. But what limits? Basically, this is the limit suggested by the relation of memory to forgetfulness.[13] The *ars memoriae* is an outrageous denial of forgetfulness and, following this, of the weaknesses inherent in both the preservation of traces and their evocation. Correlatively, the *ars memoriae* is unaware of the constraints of traces. As was suggested above in the context of our discussion concerning the Platonic metaphor of the *tupos*, of the imprint, the phenomenological notion of trace, distinct from the material, corporeal, cortical condition of the imprint, is constructed on the basis of *being-affected* by an event, becoming its witness after-the-fact through narration. For the artificial memory, all is action, nothing is passion. The places are sovereignly chosen, their order hides the arbitrariness of their selection; and the images are no less manipulated than are the places to which they are assigned. A twofold denial is then posed: of forgetting and of being-affected. The seed of the deadly infatuation lies in this original denial. Great indeed is the power of memory, Augustine exclaims. But, as we have noted in the opening pages of this book, he was not unaware of forgetfulness; with fright, he took the measure of its danger and its ravages. Moreover, from this denial of forgetting and of being-affected results the preeminence accorded to memorization at the expense of remembering (*remémoration*). The overemphasis on images and places by the *ars memoriae* has as its price the neglect of events that astonish and surprise. By breaking the pact of memory with the past in this way to the benefit of private writing in an imaginary space, the *ars memoriae* passed from the athletic exploits of a trained memory to what Yates rightly calls an "alchemy of the imagination." The imagination, freed from its service to the past, has taken the place of memory. The past, the absent with respect to the history that recounts it, constitutes the other limit of this ambitious mnemotechnics, along with forgetfulness, which we will discuss below in terms of its solidarity with the pastness of the past.[14]

There are two ways to follow up on these primary considerations that reintroduce the idea of limit into a project that excludes it. The first is to restore measure to a culture of memorization within the limits of natural memory; the second is to take into consideration the abuses that are grafted onto its use, once this use becomes a form of manipulation under the guise of artificial memory.

The final considerations of this section are devoted to the modalities of an art of memorization contained within the bounds of natural memory. We will, therefore, retreat from the magic of memory in the direction of a pedagogy of memory—framing the cultivation of memory within an educational project. In this way, we are led back to the discussion initiated above concerning the use and abuse of memory in education. We return to it, however, mindful of the principal episodes of the fabulous history of artificial memory. It is not, truly speaking, the power of an imagination carried to extreme that serves as the target in the process of reciting by heart, during the very period of the Renaissance that witnessed the feats of artificial memory, but rather the authority of the cultural heritage transmitted by texts. For these critics, the beast of burden is readily labeled the animal emblematic of silly memory plodding under the weight of imposed knowledge: "You simply," says Montaigne, "produce donkeys laden with books" (*Essays*, I, 25).[15] It is noteworthy that the critique of memorizing memory coincided with the praise of *ingenium*—genius, spirit—in the sense given to this word by Helvétius in *De l'esprit*.[16] In this way, there was a fusion between the plea for method, harkening back to Ramus, and the plea for *ingenium*, which contained the seed of the cultivation of the creative imagination. This fusion occurs in the notion of judgment, dear to the champions of the Enlightenment. But at the very heart of judgment, the rational understanding does not succeed in restraining *ingenium*. Witness Rousseau's revolt against the Enlightenment thinkers. It is in the name of an untamed *ingenium* that Rousseau attacks the cultivation of even natural memory, pounding it with the strongest blows: "Émile will never learn anything by heart, not even the fables, not even those of La Fontaine, as innocent, as charming as they are."[17]

We might wonder if, at this point, the critique of memorizing memory has not outstripped its goal. To the abuse of excess in Giordano Bruno responds the abuse of deficiency in Jean-Jacques Rousseau. It is true that it is not the same memory celebrated by one and struck down by the other. The excess of the first affects the *memoria artificiosa*, the abuse by deficiency of the second wrongs natural memory, which also demands its due. We return, then, to the mind, beyond the scholastic use of memorization, to the admirable feats of professional memory, to the memories of doctors, judges, teachers, and so on, and to those of the artists of dance, theater, and music. We have, in truth, never finished with memorization.

Before turning the page on the *ars memoriae*, I would like to take a brief excursus with Harald Weinrich into the region of forgetting. We stated above that the *ars memoriae* was inspired by the exorbitant desire "not to forget anything." Does not a measured use of memorization also imply a measured use of forgetting? Can we not, following Descartes, speak of a "methodical forgetting"? If, in fact, methodical doubt produces a reflective rejection of the entire memory-based pedagogy, and in this sense implies a certain strategy of forgetting, does not the rule of recapitulation of the *Discourse on Method* constitute a methodical use of memory, but of a natural memory freed from mnemotechnics? In the same way, can we not speak of "enlightened forgetting," in the spirit of the Enlightenment? Enlightened forgetting, which would serve as a guardrail (*garde-fou*, in the strict sense of the term) to protect against the frenzied cultivation of memorizing memory? We will have to return to this at the appropriate time, when we will attempt to give to the *ars memoriae* the symmetry that would come from the *ars oblivionis*, as this is expressed by Weinrich in *Lethe*.[18] In the meantime, these suggestions converge toward the plea for a measured use of remembering (*rémemoration*)—under the heading of a *just memory*, an idea that will take shape when the time comes through our reflection on the abuses of a memory manipulated by ideology. In a sense, the poetic surpassing of artificial memory by Dante and methodical forgetting after the manner of Descartes lead back, each in its own way, to the rich problematic of natural memory.

## THE ABUSES OF NATURAL MEMORY: BLOCKED MEMORY, MANIPULATED MEMORY, ABUSIVELY CONTROLLED MEMORY

The present study will be devoted to a typology of the *uses* and *abuses* of natural memory. The path in this direction has been cleared by Nietzsche in his *Unfashionable Observations*, the second of which bears the eloquent title, "On the Utility and Liability of History for Life."[19] The manner of questioning, inaugurated by this text, unites in a complex semiology the medical treatment of symptoms and the philological treatment of texts. To be sure, the polemic raised here concerns history above all, more precisely, the philosophy of history and its place in culture. But the tone is set for a similar treatment of memory, in particular, collective memory, which, as I will repeat at the beginning of the next study, constitutes the soil in which historiography is rooted. As was stated at the beginning of the present study, it is as *exercised* that memory falls under this perspective.

I propose the following reading grid, in an effort to avoid a broad and indiscriminate use of the notion of the abuse of memory. I will first distinguish a clearly pathological approach, employing clinical, and eventually therapeutic, categories, borrowed principally from psychoanalysis. I will attempt to restore breadth and density to this pathology by relating it to some of the most basic human experiences. Then I will make room for concerted forms of the manipulation or instrumentalization of memory, within the framework of a critique of ideology. It is at this median level that notions of the abuse are the most relevant. Finally, I would like to reserve for a normative, explicitly ethico-political viewpoint the question of the duty of memory; this normative viewpoint must be carefully distinguished from the preceding viewpoint with which it is too often confused. In this way, the path from one level to the next will become a path from one figure to the next characterizing the uses and abuses of memory, from *blocked* memory to *forced* memory, passing through *manipulated* memory.

### The Pathological-Therapeutic Level: Blocked Memory

It is on this level and from this viewpoint that we can legitimately speak of *wounded*, even of *sick* memory. Common expressions such as traumatism, wound, scar, and so forth, attest to this. The use of these words, themselves expressions of pathos, cannot but give rise to certain serious difficulties. Up to what point, we will first ask, are we authorized to apply to collective memory categories forged in the analytical colloquy, hence at the interpersonal level, marked principally by the mediation of transference? This first difficulty will be definitively resolved only at the end of the following chapter. We will acknowledge here, provisionally, the operative value of the concept of collective memory; moreover, the use it will be put to will later contribute to legitimizing this problematical concept. There is another difficulty to be resolved here: one can wonder to what extent a pathology of memory, and so the treatment of memory as *pathos*, fits into an inquiry into the exercise of memory, the memorial *tekhnē*. The difficulty is a new one: what is at issue are the individual and collective alterations due to the use, to the practice of memory.

To situate us with regard to this twofold difficulty, I thought it appropriate to turn to two remarkable essays by Freud and to compare them to each other, which their author seems not to have done. The first of these texts, dating from 1914, is titled, "Remembering, Repeating, and Working-Through."[20] Note right away that the German title contains only verbs, stressing the fact that these are three processes belonging to the play of psychical forces with which the psychoanalyst "works."

The starting point for Freud's reflection lies in identifying the main obstacle encountered by the work of interpretation (*Deutungsarbeit*) along the path of recalling traumatic memories. This obstacle, attributed to "resistances due to repression" (*Verdrängungswiderstände*), is designated by the term "compulsion to repeat" (*Wiederholungszwang*); it is characterized among other things by a tendency to act out (*Agieren*), which Freud says is substituted for the memory. The patient "reproduces it not as a memory but as an action; he *repeats* it, without, of course, knowing that he is repeating it" (*S.E.*, 12:150; *G.W.*, 10:129). We are not far from the phenomenon of obsession mentioned above. Let us leave aside the implications of the phenomenon as they concern forgetting. We shall return to them in the chapter on forgetting in part 3. Then the emphasis is on acting out and on the place this takes, without the knowledge of the patient. What matters to us is the tie between the compulsion to repeat and resistance, as well as the substitution of this twofold phenomenon for the memory itself. This forms the obstacle to continuation of the analysis. Beyond this clinical aspect, Freud offers two therapeutic proposals that will be of the greatest importance for us, when we transpose the clinical analysis to the level of collective memory, as we consider ourselves authorized to do at that stage of the discussion. The first proposal concerns the analyst, the second, the analysand. The analyst is advised to be very patient with regard to the repetitions occurring under the cover of transference. Transference, Freud notes, creates something like an intermediary domain between illness and real life; one can speak of it as a "playground," in which the compulsion is authorized to manifest itself in almost total freedom, offering an opportunity for the pathogenic background of the subject to manifest itself openly. But something is also asked of the patient: ceasing to lament or to hide his true state from himself, "he must find the courage to direct his attention to the phenomenon of his illness. His illness itself must no longer seem to him contemptible, but must become an enemy worthy of his mettle, a piece of his personality, which has solid ground for its existence and out of which things of value for his future life have to be derived" (*S.E.*, 12:152; *G.W.*, 10:132). Otherwise, there will be no "reconciliation" (*Versöhnung*) of the patient with the repressed material. Let us hold in reserve this term of reconciliation, which will return to the fore in our subsequent reflections on forgiveness. Let us stop for a moment with the twofold handling of resistances by the patient and the analyst, to which Freud gives the name of *Durcharbeiten* (*S.E.*, 12:155; *G.W.*, 10:136), "working through" in the English translation, *perlaboration* in the French, or, as I prefer to say, *remaniement* (reworking). The important word here is work— or rather, "working"—which underscores not only the dynamic character of the entire process, but the collaboration of the analysand in this work. It is in relation to this notion of work, stated in the form of a verb, that it becomes possible to speak of memory itself, freed in this way, as a work—the "work of remembering" (*Erinnerungsarbeit*) (*S.E.*, 12:153; *G.W.*, 10:133). Work is thus the word repeated several times and symmetrically opposed to compulsion: the work of remembering against the compulsion to repeat, thus could be summed up the theme of this precious little essay. Belonging to this work are both the patience of the analyst with respect to the repetition channeled by the transference and the courage required on the part of the analysand to recognize himself as ill, in search of a truthful relation to his past.

Before examining the transpositions that might be made between the analytic relation and the public plane of collective memory and of history, and taking into consideration the reservation in principle mentioned above, let us turn to the second essay, titled "Mourning and Melancholia" ("Trauer und Melancholie") (*S.E.*, 14; *G.W.*, 10).[21] This essay, no doubt, offers greater resistance than the preceding one to a transposition to the plane of collective memory, insofar as mourning is treated less in its own right, precisely as work, than as a term of comparison in order better to pierce the enigmas of melancholia. It is the pairing with the preceding essay that can help to draw some positive information from the comparison itself concerning the work of mourning.[22] But especially, this essay awakens resounding echoes of a millenary experience, which has had melancholia itself as a theme of meditation and as a source of torment.

These initial reservations do not prevent us from noting that it is mourning—the work of mourning—that is first taken as a term of comparison assumed to be directly accessible, at least initially. Furthermore, the pair mourning and melancholia is to be taken as one block, and it is the tendency of mourning to become melancholia and its difficulty in extracting itself from this terrible neurosis that will give rise to my subsequent reflections on the pathology of collective memory and the therapeutic perspectives this opens.

"Mourning," it is stated, "is regularly the reaction to the loss of a loved person, or to the loss of some abstraction which has taken the place of one, such as one's country, liberty, an ideal, and so on" (*S.E.*, 14:243). An opening is thus made from the outset in the direction that we shall take below. And the first question that the analyst poses is to know why, in the case of certain patients, "the same influences produce melancholia *instead of mourning*" (my emphasis). The expression "instead of . . . " directly indicates the kinship, from the viewpoint of my strategy of argumentation, between the two essays we are comparing: instead of remembering, acting out; instead of mourning, melancholia. So in a certain sense it is the opposition between mourning and melancholia that is at issue here, the bifurcation on the "economic" level between different affective investments, and in this sense, of a bifurcation between two sorts of work. The first opposition noted by Freud is the dissimulation of "self-regard" (*Selbstgefühl*) in melancholia, whereas "the disturbance of self-regard is absent in mourning" (244). Whence the question: what is the work supplied in mourning? Answer: "Reality-testing has shown that the loved object no longer exists, and it proceeds to demand that all libido shall be withdrawn from its attachment to that object. This demand arouses understandable opposition" (244). There follows a careful description of the "great expense of time and cathetic energy" (245) required for the obedience of the libido to the commands of reality. Why is the cost so high? Because "the existence of the lost object is psychically prolonged." The heavy price to pay for this liquidation is, therefore, due to the hypercathexis of the memories and expectations by which the libido remains attached to the lost object: "this compromise by which the command of reality is carried out piecemeal . . . [is] extraordinarily painful."

But why then is mourning not melancholia? And what is it that makes mourning tend toward melancholia? What makes mourning a normal, albeit painful, phenomenon is that "when the work of mourning is completed the ego becomes free and uninhibited again" (245). It is from this angle that the work of mourning can be compared to the work of remembering. If the work of melancholia occupies a strategic position in the present essay parallel to that occupied by the compulsion to repeat in the previous one, this suggests that it is as a work of remembering that the work of mourning proves to be liberating, although at a certain cost, and that this relation is reciprocal. The work of mourning is the cost of the work of remembering, but the work of remembering is the benefit of the work of mourning.

Before drawing the consequences I have in mind, let us look at some complementary lessons that the work of melancholia contributes to the preceding picture of the work of mourning. Starting again from the opening remark concerning the diminution of *Ichgefühl* in melancholia, we must say that unlike mourning, in which it is the universe that seems impoverished and empty, in melancholia it is the ego that finds itself in desolation: it succumbs to the blows of its own devaluation, its own accusation, its own condemnation, its own abasement. But this is not all, not even the essential point: do not the reproaches addressed to the self serve to mask reproaches aimed at the love object? As Freud audaciously puts it: "Their complaints are really 'plaints' in the old sense of the word [*Ihre Klagen sind Anklagen*]" (248). These "plaints" or accusations can even defame the loved one, reaching into the deepest recesses of mourning. Freud proposes the hypothesis that the accusation, by weakening the object-cathexis, facilitates the retreat into the ego, while transforming the discord with the other into self-laceration. We will not follow Freud any further in his properly psychoanalytic investigations concerning the regression from object-love to original narcissism, even to the oral phase of the libido—including the element of sadism incorporated into narcissism—or the investigations concerning the tendency of melancholia to invert itself into the symptomatically inverse state of mania. Freud himself, moreover, is very circumspect in his explorations. We will limit our remarks to this citation: "Melancholia, therefore, borrows some of its features from mourning, and the others from the process of regression from narcissistic object-choice to narcissism" (250).

If we now ask what melancholia teaches about mourning, we must return to the *Ichgefühl*, considered well established and which Freud once characterized as "recognition of oneself." To it belongs shame before others, something the melancholic is unaware of, so occupied is he with himself. Self-esteem and shame would then seem to be joint components of mourning. Freud remarks on this: "the censorship of consciousness"—the expression of the agency generally termed conscience—goes together with "reality-testing, among the major institutions of the ego" (247). This remark links up with what was said in the preceding essay concerning the responsibility of the analysand in forgoing acting out and in pursuing the work of memory. Another observation: if in melancholia complaints are accusations, mourning also contains the mark of this uncanny similarity, under the condition of a certain measure proper to mourning, a measure that limits the accusation as well as the self-reproach under which it is concealed. Finally—and this is perhaps the most important thing—does not the proximity between *Klage* and *Anklage*, between complaint and reproach, which is exhibited in melancholia, stem from the ambivalence of amorous relations in which love and hate are side by side, even in mourning?

However, it is on the positive outcome of mourning, in contrast to the disaster of melancholia, that I would like to conclude this brief incursion into one of Freud's most famous essays: "Melancholia confronts us with yet other problems, the answer to which in part eludes us. The fact that it passes off after a certain time has elapsed without leaving traces of any gross changes is a feature it shares with mourning. We found by way of explanation that in mourning time is needed for the command of reality-testing to be carried out in detail, and that when this work has been accomplished the ego will have succeeded in freeing its libido from the lost object. We may imagine that the ego is occupied with analogous work during the course of melancholia; in neither case have we any insight into the economics of the course of events" (252–53). Let us set aside Freud's admission concerning the explanation and retain only his clinical lesson: the time of mourning is not unrelated to the patience required by analysis in the passage from repetition to memory. Memory does not only bear on time: it also requires time—a time of mourning.

I do not want to end this confrontation between mourning and melancholia on Freud's statement of perplexity: "in neither case have we any insight into the economics of the course of events." If the last word on mourning and on the work of mourning in psychoanalysis has not been uttered, this is because it has also not been uttered on melancholia. Must melancholia be left to the physicians, psychiatrists, and psychoanalysts? Is it solely a mental illness? For anyone who has read *Saturn and Melancholy* by Raymond Klibansky, Erwin Panofsky, and Fritz Saxl,[23] the nosological reduction of melancholia, begun by E. Kraepelin and redirected by Ludwig Binswanger, is unacceptable. How indeed could we fail to mention the place held by melancholia in the ancient system of four humors in Greek medicine, in which the melancholic humor—black bile (*altra bilis*)—takes its place alongside the sanguine, choleric, and phlegmatic humors? Here is one more list to memorize, taking into account the network of correspondences with the cosmic elements, divisions of time, ages of life: Melancholia, state medieval texts of the twelfth century, imitates the earth, grows in autumn, reigns in maturity. Physiology, psychology, cosmology are thus found to be joined, following a threefold principle: the search for primary elements common to the microcosm and the macrocosm, the establishment of a numerical expression for these complex structures, and the law of harmony or proportionality among the elements. In this, we recognize the spirit of Pythagoras, followed by Empedocles. What is important in the sort of excursus that I am making, beyond—or perhaps, short of—Freud, is that the concept of humor has continued to oscillate between the idea of illness and the idea of character or temperament, the scale showing the degree of harmony or disharmony among the elements. It is precisely in melancholia that the ambivalence culminates, and this becomes the critical point of the entire system. This privilege, so to speak, accorded to melancholia has become more pointed as the theory of the four humors has been transformed into a theory of temperaments and mental types. Depression and anxiety (or fear) become the characteristic symptoms of melancholia. Melancholia then becomes synonymous with insanity, madness. The intersection between melancholia and humoreal theory and the madness of tragic heroes—Ajax, Hercules, Bellerophone—raised by Plato to the level of a philosopheme, is completed with the most famous of the "Problems" attributed to Aristotle, book 30, problem 1—a monograph on black bile, according to our sources. "Why," asks the author of problem 1, "is it that all those who have become eminent in philosophy or politics or poetry or the arts are clearly melancholics?" And the text adds the names of Empedocles, Plato, and Socrates to the list of troubled spirits. How, then, can we not call to mind the theory of the multiple figures of *mania* in Plato himself and the comparison made in so many dialogues between exaltation, ecstacy, inebriation, and other "divine" states? For all these states are the work of black bile! Here the normal and the pathological rub shoulders, melancholia being passed from the physician to the pedagogue and vice versa. The melancholic is the "exceptional" individual. The Romantic theory of "genius" is contained in germ in this ambiguous description of "fury" (to borrow Cicero's translation of the Greek *mania*). The Stoics alone resist, clearly opting before the fact for the psychoanalytic reading.

It is the thinkers of the Renaissance, who, beyond the medieval transmission of the divided heritage received from the Greek physicians and philosophers of nature, redirected the meditation on melancholia toward the modern doctrine of genius.[24] The astral theme, which scholars trace back to Arab astrology, stands ready to emerge in our impassioned Renaissance figures.[25] The Renaissance man—represented by an Erasmus, a Marsilio Ficino, a Pico della Mirandola, a Nicholas of Cusa, a Dürer—is in pursuit less of individual salvation than of the unfettered development of individual spontaneity; it is in this *élan*, which announces the fire of Romantic genius, that the troubling contrast between exaltation and depression is to be found. The negative pole is nothing other than what Lessing will call "voluptuous melancholia," heir to medieval *acedia*, that perfidious temptation hesitating between sin and illness. The Renaissance man, however, also makes the wager that melancholia can be *melancholia generosa* (Klibansky et al., 241).[26]

It is, however, in Dürer's engraving, *Melencolia I*, that all the attempts at rehabilitating Saturn and melancholia are crystallized. And it is over this engraving that the commentaries of Klibansky, Panowsky, and Saxl linger. Let us "read" this engraving. A woman is seated, her gaze plunging into empty space, her face indistinct, her chin resting on a clenched fist; at her waist hang some keys, symbols of power, and a purse, symbol of wealth—two forms of vanity, in short. Melancholia remains forever this hunched, pensive figure. Fatigue? Grief? Sorrow? Meditation? The question returns: is this the posture of declining health or of reflective genius? The response is not to be sought in the human figure alone; the environment is also tacitly eloquent: unused instruments lie scattered across the immobile scene—a three-dimensional geometrical figure depicting geometry, the fifth of the "liberal arts." The vanity of knowledge is thus incorporated in the idle figure. This fusion of geometry giving way to melancholia and melancholia lost in a dreamlike geometry gives to *Melencolia I* its enigmatic power:[27] Might not truth itself be gloomy, following the adage of Ecclesiastes?

The question then arises: what shadowy light is cast on Freud's text by this backward turn? It seems to me that to make sense of it we must extend the inquiry into melancholia to one of the sources of the theme buried under medicine, psychology, literature, and iconography: behind the lament of an Alain Chartier invoking "Dame Merencolye" or of Roi René celebrating "Dame Tristesse" is silhouetted *acedia*, named already above, in which the spiritual leaders of the Middle Ages saw the worst of temptations, beyond even sanguine "luxury," choleric "discord," namely, complaisance toward sadness. *Acedia* is this sort of laziness, lassitude, disgust, to which the member of a religious order who is not praying or working is in danger of succumbing. Do we not touch here upon the moral ground of melancholia, barely alluded to by Freud in the vocable, *Selbstgefühl*? That toward which *acedia* is complaisant, is it not the sadness of meditative memory, the specific "mood" of finitude rendered conscious of itself? This *sadness without a cause*, is it not akin to Kierkegaard's sickness-unto-death, that relative of despair, or rather, following Gabriel Marcel's suggestion, of no hope (*inespoir*)?[28] By moving back in this way to the *acedia* of the religious, have we not provided a worthy vis-à-vis for the work of mourning? Someone may object that the work of mourning has no antecedent in the literature of melancholia. In this sense, it would indeed be a creation of Freud. But the work of mourning also has antecedents in the antidotes by which the medical, psychological, moral, literary, and spiritual tradition has attacked melancholia. Among these remedies, we find gaiety, humor, hope, trust, and also . . . work. The authors of *Saturn and Melancholy* are not wrong to seek in lyrical poetry dating from the end of the Middle Ages and from the Renaissance, in particular, the

English Renaissance, from Milton and the Shakespeare of the Sonnets to Keats, the praise of a contrasting and, if I may call it so, a dialectical humor, in which Delight responds to Melancholia under the auspices of beauty. This review of the poeticized figures of melancholia would have to be followed as far as Baudelaire, to restore to melancholia its enigmatic profoundness, which no nosology could never exhaust. This is the direction in which Jean Starobinsky pulls us in *La Mélancolie au miroir: Trois lectures de Baudelaire*.[29] Does not the opening poem, "To the Reader," in *The Flowers of Evil* term the "saturnine book" the book of Ennui? The lost gaze of Melancholia is reflected in the mirror of reflective consciousness, whose reflections are modulated by poetry. A path of memory is opened in this way by "Spleen": "Je suis le sinistre miroir." "J'ai plus de souvenirs que si j'avais mille ans...." It is, in fact, figures of the historical past that haunt the famous poem "Le Cygne" ("The Swan") which we will approach from a different angle, at the point where the memorization of history intersects with the historization of memory:[30]

> Andromaque—my thoughts are turned to you! ...
> This lying Simois swelled by your tears,
> Has suddenly enriched my fertile memory ...
> Thus in the forest where my mind is exiled
> An old Memory blows mightily into its horn![31]

And why should we not refer *in fine* to Beethoven's last quartets and sonatas and to their powerful evocation of a sublime sadness? There, the word has been uttered: sublimation. This missing piece in the panoply of Freud's metapsychology might perhaps have provided him with the secret of the reversal from the complaisance toward sadness to sadness sublimated—into joy.[32] Yes, grief is that sadness that has not completed the work of mourning. Yes, joy is the reward for giving up the lost object and a token of the reconciliation with its internalized object. And, inasmuch as the work of mourning is the required path for the work of remembering (*souvenir*), joy can also crown with its grace the work of memory (*mémoire*). On the horizon of this work: a "happy" memory, when the poetic image completes the work of mourning. But this horizon recedes behind the work of history, the theory of which has yet to be established beyond the phenomenology of memory.

Having said this, I return to the question left in abeyance, namely, to what extent it is legitimate to transpose to the plane of collective memory and to history the psychological categories proposed by Freud in the two essays we have just read. A provisional justification can be found on both sides—on the side of Freud and on the side of the phenomenology of wounded memory.

On the side of Freud, one will have noted the various allusions to situations that go far beyond the psychoanalytic scene, in terms of both the work of remembering and the work of mourning. This extension is all the more anticipated as all of the situations referred to in the psychoanalytic treatment have to do with *the other*, not only the other of the "familial novel," but the psychosocial other and the other, as it were, of the historical situation. Furthermore, Freud did not hesitate to make similar extrapolations in *Totem and Taboo*, in *Moses and Monotheism*, in *The Future of an Illusion*, or in *Civilization and Its Discontents*. And even certain of his private psychoanalyses, we may venture to say, were psychoanalyses in absentia, the most famous of these being the case of Dr. Schreber. And what are we to say of "Michelangelo's Moses" or of *A Childhood Memory of Leonardo da Vinci*? No scruples should hamper us, then, on this score. The transposition has been rendered easier by certain reinterpretations of psychoanalysis close to hermeneutics, as we see in some of the earlier works of Jürgen Habermas, in which psychoanalysis is reformulated in terms of desymbolization and resymbolization, and in which the emphasis is placed on the role of systematic distortions of communication on the plane of the social sciences. The sole objection that has not been answered in the hermeneutical interpretations of psychoanalysis concerns the absence of recognized therapists in interhuman relations. But could we not say that, in this case, the public space of discussion constitutes the equivalent of what above was called the "playground" as the intermediary region between the therapist and the analysand?

Regardless of this genuinely formidable difficulty, it is more important for our purpose to look to collective memory and to discover there the equivalent of the pathological situations with which psychoanalysis is concerned. It is the bipolar constitution of personal and community identity that, ultimately, justifies extending the Freudian analysis of mourning to the traumatism of collective identity. We can speak not only in an analogical sense but in terms of a direct analysis of collective traumatisms, of wounds to collective memory. The notion of the lost object finds a direct application in the "losses" that affect the power, territory, and populations that constitute the substance of a state. Mourning behaviors, from the expression of affliction to complete reconciliation with the lost object, are directly illustrated by the great funeral celebrations around which an entire people is assembled. In this way, we can say that such mourning behaviors constitute a privileged example of the intersecting relations between private and public expression. It is in this way that our concept of a sick historical memory finds justification a posteriori in this bipolar structure of mourning behaviors.

The transposition of pathological categories to the historical plane would be more completely justified if we were able to show that it applies not only to the exceptional situations just mentioned, but that these depend on a fundamental structure of collective existence. What I refer to here is the fundamental relation of history to violence. Hobbes was not wrong in making political philosophy arise out of an original situation in which the fear of violent death pushes man out of the "state of nature" into the bonds of a contractual pact that, first of all, guarantees him security; moreover, there exists no historical community that has not been born out of a relation that can, without hesitation, best be likened to war. What we celebrate under the title of founding events are, essentially, acts of violence legitimated after the fact by a precarious state of right. What was glory for some was humiliation for others. To celebration on one side corresponds execration on the other. In this way, symbolic wounds calling for healing are stored in the archives of the collective memory. More precisely, what, in historical experience, takes the form of paradox—namely, *too much* memory here, *not enough* memory there—can be reinterpreted in terms of the categories of resistance and compulsion to repeat, and, finally, can be found to undergo the ordeal of the difficult work of remembering. Too much memory recalls especially the compulsion to repeat, which, Freud said, leads us to substitute acting out for the true recollection by which the present would be reconciled with the past: how much violence in the world stands as acting out "in place of" remembering! We can, if we like, speak of repetition-memory for these funeral celebrations. But then it must immediately be added that this repetition-memory resists criticism and that recollection-memory is fundamentally a critical memory.

If this be the case, then too little memory belongs to the same reinterpretation. What some cultivate with morose delectation, and what others flee with bad conscience, is the same repetition-memory. The former love to lose themselves in it, the latter are afraid of being engulfed by it. But both suffer from the same lack of criticism. They do not attain what Freud termed the work of remembering.

We can take one further step and suggest that it is on the level of collective memory, even more perhaps than on that of individual memory, that the overlapping of the work of mourning and the work of recollection acquires its full meaning. When it is a matter of national self-love, we can properly speak of a lost love-object. It is always in terms of its losses that the wounded memory is forced to confront itself. What it does not know how to do is the work imposed on it by reality-testing: giving up the investments (cathexes) by which the libido continues to be bound to the lost object, as long as the loss has not been definitively internalized. But this is also the place to underscore that this submission to reality-testing, constituting the true work of mourning, is also an integral part of the work of recollection. The suggestion made above concerning the exchanges of meaning between the work of recollection and the work of mourning finds its full justification here.

A transition from the pathological level to the properly practical level is provided by notations concerning the appropriate therapy for these troubles. Freud continuously calls upon the cooperation of the analysand, placing the analytical experience, in this way, entirely at the point of intersection between the passive, pathic side of memory and the active side of the exercise of memory. In this respect, the notion of work—the work of remembering, the work of mourning—occupies a strategic position in reflection on the failures of memory. This notion supposes that the difficulties in question are not only undergone, but that we are responsible for them, as witnessed by the therapeutic advice that accompanies the working-through. In one sense, the abuses of memory, which we will now discuss, can appear as perverse diversions of this work, in which mourning is joined to remembering.

### The Practical Level: Manipulated Memory

Whatever may be the validity of the pathological interpretations of the excesses and deficiencies of collective memory, I would not want them to occupy all of the territory. A distinct place must be set aside, next to the more or less passive modes of these "abuses," undergone, suffered—even taking into account the correction made by Freud himself to this unilateral treatment of passivity—for abuses, in the strong sense of the term, resulting from a concerted manipulation of memory and of forgetting by those who hold power. Thus I shall be speaking here less of wounded memory than of instrumentalized memory (the Weberian category of rationality in accordance with an end—*Zweckrationalität*—in opposition to the category of rationality in accordance with a value—*Wertrationalität*—has a place here; as does the category employed by Habermas of "strategic reason" in opposition to "communicational reason"). It is on this plane that we can more legitimately speak of the abuses of memory, which are also abuses of forgetting.

The specificity of this second approach lies in the intersection of the problematics of memory and of identity, collective as well as personal.

We will linger over this problem of intersection in the next chapter, in the context of Locke's theory in which memory is established as the criterion of identity. The heart of the problem is the mobilization of memory in the service of the quest, the appeal, the demand for identity. In what follows from this, we recognize some disturbing symptoms: too much memory, in a certain region of the world, hence an abuse of memory; not enough memory elsewhere, hence an abuse of forgetting. It is in the problematic of identity that we have to seek the cause of the fragility of memory manipulated in this way. This is in addition to the properly cognitive frailty resulting from the proximity between memory and imagination, which finds in the latter its spur and its helper.

What constitutes the fragility of identity? It is identity's purely presumptive, alleged, reputed character. This "claim," as one would say in English, this *Anspruch* in German, is lodged in the responses to the question, "Who?" "*Who* am I?" Responses in terms of "What?" of the form: this is what we are, we, ourselves. How we are, this way and not otherwise. The fragility of identity consists in the fragility of these responses in terms of what, claiming to give the recipe of the identity proclaimed and reclaimed. The problem is therefore carried back a step, from the fragility of memory to that of identity.

As the primary cause of the fragility of identity we must cite its difficult relation to time; this is a primary difficulty that, precisely, justifies the recourse to memory as the temporal component of identity, in conjunction with the evaluation of the present and the projection of the future. This relation to time is a problem by reason of the equivocal nature of the notion of the same, implicit in the notion of the identical. What, in fact, does it mean to remain the same over time? In the past, I took on the challenge of this enigma, with respect to which I suggested distinguishing two senses of identical: the same as *idem*, *même*, *gleich*, and the same as *ipse*, *self*, *Selbst*. It seemed to me that self-constancy over time rests on a complex interplay of sameness and ipseity, if I may venture these barbarisms; in this equivocal play, the practical and pathetic aspects are more formidable than the conceptual, epistemic ones. I will say that the temptation of identity, of *déraison identitaire*, as Jacques Le Goff calls it, consists in the retreat of *ipse* identity into *idem* identity or, if one prefers, in the slippage, the drift, from the flexibility, proper to self-constancy as manifested in the promise, to the inflexible rigidity of a *character*, in the quasi-typographical sense of the term.

The second cause of fragility lies in the confrontation with others, felt to be a threat. It is a fact that the other, because other, comes to be perceived as a danger for one's own identity, our identity as well as my identity. To be sure, we may find this surprising: is our identity so fragile that we are unable to bear, unable to endure the fact that others have different ways than our own of leading their lives, of understanding themselves, of inscribing their own identity in the web of living together? This is so. There are indeed humiliations, real or imagined attacks on self-esteem, under the blows of poorly tolerated otherness, that turn a welcome into rejection, into exclusion—this is the relation that the same maintains with the other.

Third cause of fragility: the heritage of founding violence. It is a fact that there is no historical community that has not arisen out of what can be termed an original relation to war. What we celebrate under the heading of founding events are, essentially, violent acts legitimated after the fact by a precarious state of right, acts legitimated, at the limit, by their very antiquity, by their age. The same events are thus found to signify glory for some, humiliation for others. To their celebration, on the one hand, corresponds their execration, on the other. It is in this way that real and symbolic wounds are stored in the archives of collective memory. Here, the third cause of the fragility of identity merges with the second. It remains to be shown under what angle the forms of misuse of memory can be grafted onto the demand for identity, whose specific fragility we have just outlined.

The manipulations of memory we are going to discuss below result from the intervention of a disturbing and multiform factor that insinuates itself between the demand for identity and the public expressions of memory. This is the phenomenon of ideology, involving a mechanism I have attempted to demonstrate elsewhere.[33] The ideological process is opaque in two ways. First, it remains hidden; unlike utopia, it is unacknowledged; it masks itself by inverting itself, denouncing its adversaries in the field of competition between ideologies, for it is always the other who stoops to ideology. On the other hand, the process is extremely complex. I have suggested distinguishing three operative levels of the ideological phenomenon, in terms of the effects it exerts on an understanding of the human world of action. Running from top to bottom, from surface to depth, these effects are, in succession, distortions of reality, the legitimation of the system of power, and the integration of the common world by means of symbolic systems immanent in action. At the deepest level, that on which Clifford Geertz works, the ideological phenomenon indeed appears to constitute an unsurpassable structure of action, to the extent that symbolic mediation marks the difference between the motivations of human action and the hereditary structures of genetically programmed behaviors. A remarkable correlation is established at this fundamental level between a symbolic synthesis and a semiotic system, some of this belonging clearly to a system of rhetorical tropes.[34] Considered at this deep level, the analysis of the ideological phenomenon is obviously part of a "semiotics of culture." It is in fact in this role that ideology, as a factor of

integration, can be established as the guardian of identity, offering a symbolic response to the causes affecting the fragility of this identity. At this
level of radicality, that of symbolically mediated action, there is as yet no
manipulation, hence no abuse of memory. One can speak only of the silent
constraint exerted on the mores of a traditional society. This is what makes
the notion of ideology practically ineradicable. But it must be added straight
away that this constitutive function of ideology can scarcely operate outside
of the connection to its second function—the justification of a system of order or power—nor can it operate even potentially apart from the function of
distortion that is grafted onto the preceding one. At the limit, it would only
be in societies without a hierarchical political structure—and, in this sense,
societies without power—that we might have a chance of encountering the
naked phenomenon of ideology as an integrative structure in its, so to speak,
innocent form. Ideology, when all is said and done, revolves around power.[35]

In fact, what ideology aims to legitimize is the authority of order or
power—order, in the sense of an organic relation between the whole and the
part; power, in the sense of a hierarchical relation between governing and
governed. In this regard, the analyses that Max Weber devotes to the notions
of order (*Ordnung*) and domination (*Herrschaft*) are of considerable interest
for our undertaking, even if the author of *Economy and Society* does not treat
ideology and its relation to identity thematically. The entire Weberian analysis
of power revolves around the claim to legitimacy raised by every form of
power, be it charismatic traditional, or bureaucratic.[36] Everything then turns
on the nature of the knot—the *nexus*—that binds the legitimacy claims raised
by the governors to the belief in that authority on the part of the governed.
The paradox of authority resides in this knot. Ideology, we may presume,
arises precisely in the breach between the request for legitimacy emanating
from a system of authority and our response in terms of belief. Ideology is
supposed to add a sort of surplus value to our spontaneous belief, thanks
to which the latter might satisfy the demands of the authority. At this stage,
the function of ideology would be to fill the gap of credibility opened by all
systems of authority, not only the charismatic system—because the chief is
sent from above—and the system based on tradition—because things have
always been done this way—but also the bureaucratic system—because the
experts are supposed to know. Max Weber provides support for the present
hypothesis by defining the types of legitimacy, their imperatives, and their
requirements on the basis of the types of belief "by virtue of which" the order
is legitimized, and power justified. These types of belief constitute, each in
its own way, a reason for obeying. Moreover, it is in this way that authority is

defined as the legitimate power to make (others) obey. *Herrschaft*, according to Weber, consists essentially in a hierarchical relation between commanding and obeying. It is expressly defined by the expectation of obedience and the probability—the likelihood—that this will be fulfilled. It is at this critical point that the symbolic systems and their rhetorical expressions discussed elsewhere by Clifford Geertz are seen to be mobilized. They supply the selling points that elevate ideology to the level of a surplus value added to the belief in the legitimacy of power.[37]

This relation between ideology and the legitimation process of systems of authority seems to me to constitute the central axis in relation to which are organized, on the one hand, the more radical phenomenon of community integration on the basis of the symbolic—even rhetorical—mediations of action, and on the other hand, the more visible phenomenon, easier to deplore and to denounce, of the distortion-effect on which Marx focused his best analyses in *The German Ideology*.[38] We are familiar with the debatable metaphors of the inverted image or of man standing on his head. The mechanism of distortion, itself cast into images in this way, would be plausible only if it were joined to the phenomenon of legitimation, which I placed at the center of the ideological apparatus, and if this mechanism were, in the final analysis, to affect the unavoidable symbolic mediations of action. Brushing aside these mediations, the detractor of ideology assumes he is capable of giving a true, unwarped description of fundamental human reality—namely, *praxis*, transforming activity—hence a description free from any interpretation in terms of meaning, value, or norm. This realism, even ontology, of *praxis*[39] and, more precisely, of living labor[40] are at once the strength and the weakness of the Marxian theory of ideology. If, in fact, *praxis* does not, primordially, incorporate an ideological layer, in the primary sense of the word "ideology," then I cannot see what in this *praxis* could provide the material for distortion. Separated from this original symbolic context, the denunciation of ideology is reduced to a pamphlet against propaganda. This enterprise of purification is not vain; it can possess circumstantial necessity, if it is conducted from the perspective of the reconstruction of a public space of discussion and not from the viewpoint of a merciless struggle, whose horizon would be circumscribed by civil war.[41]

If this analysis is plausible, or even accurate, we easily see which springs are working the various efforts to manipulate memory.

It is easy to trace them back to the respective operative levels of ideology. On the deepest level, that of the symbolic mediation of action, it is through the narrative function that memory is incorporated into the formation of identity. Memory can be ideologized through the resources of the variations offered by the work of narrative configuration. And, as the characters of the narrative are emplotted at the same time the story is told, the narrative configuration contributes to modeling the identity of the protagonists of the action as it molds the contours of the action itself. The narrative, Hannah Arendt reminds us, recounts the "who of action." It is, more precisely, the selective function of the narrative that opens to manipulation the opportunity and the means of a clever strategy, consisting from the outset in a strategy of forgetting as much as in a strategy of remembering. We will account for this in the thematic study reserved for forgetting. However, it is on the level where ideology operates as a discourse justifying power, domination, that the resources of manipulation provided by narrative are mobilized. Domination, we have understood, is not limited to physical constraint. Even the tyrant needs a rhetorician, a sophist, to broadcast his enterprise of seduction and intimidation in the form of words. The narrative imposed in this way then becomes the privileged instrument of this twofold operation. Even the surplus value that ideology adds to the belief offered by the governed in responding to the claim of legitimacy made by the governing body presents a narrative texture: stories of founding events, of glory and humiliation, feed the discourse of flattery or of fear. It thus becomes possible to account for the express abuses of memory on the level of the effect of distortion belonging to the phenomenal level of ideology. At this level of appearance, imposed memory is armed with a history that is itself "authorized," the official history, the history publicly learned and celebrated. A trained memory is, in fact, on the institutional plane an instructed memory; forced memorization is thus enlisted in the service of the remembrance of those events belonging to the common history that are held to be remarkable, even founding, with respect to the common identity. The circumscription of the narrative is thus placed in the service of the circumscription of the identity defining the community. A history taught, a history learned, but also a history celebrated. To this forced memorization are added the customary commemorations. A formidable pact is concluded in this way between remembrance, memorization, and commemoration.

We are touching here upon the precise abuses denounced by Tzvetan Todorov in his essay appropriately titled *Les Abus de la mémoire*,[42] in which we can read a stern indictment of the contemporary frenzy of commemorations, with their parade of rites and myths, ordinarily tied to the founding events referred to above. This grip on memory, Todorov insists, is not a specialty of totalitarian regimes alone; it is the apanage of all those enamored of glory. This denunciation sounds a warning against what the author terms the "unconditional praise of memory" (13). "The stakes of memory," he adds, "are too great to be left to enthusiasm or to anger" (14). I will not dwell upon a further aspect of the problem, namely, the claim of our contemporaries to place themselves in the position of victim, to assume the status of victim: "To have been a victim gives you the right to complain, to protest, and to make demands" (56). This position engenders an exorbitant privilege, which places everyone else in the position of owing a debt. I will retain instead a final remark by Todorov, that will bring us to the difficult question of the duty of memory: "The work of the historian, like every work on the past, never consists solely in establishing the facts but also in choosing certain among them as being more salient and more significant than others, then placing them in relation to one another; now this work of selecting and combining is necessarily guided by the search, not for truth, but for the good" (50). Whatever our reservations may be regarding the alternative suggested here between truth and goodness, we must hold in reserve, in light of our later discussion of the duty of memory, the reorientation of the whole issue of the abuse of memory under the auspices of the search for justice. This concern links up with the preceding discussion thanks to a most judicious piece of advice from Todorov, to extract from traumatic memories the exemplary value that can become pertinent only when memory has been turned into a project. If the trauma refers to the past, the exemplary value is directed toward the future. What the cult of memory for the sake of memory obliterates is, along with the aim of the future, the question of the end, of the moral issue. For the very notion of use, implicit in that of abuse, is unavoidably related to this question of the end. And with the question of the end we have already crossed over the threshold into the third level of our investigation.

### The Ethico-Political Level: Obligated Memory

What about, I will ask in conclusion, the alleged duty of memory? In truth, the question is rather premature in view of the distance our thinking has yet to cover. It projects us well beyond a simple phenomenology of memory, and even beyond an epistemology of history, to the heart of the hermeneutics of the historical condition. We cannot, it is true, abstract from the historical conditions in which the duty of memory is required, namely, those of Western Europe and, in particular, France, several decades after the horrible events of the mid-twentieth century. The injunction is meaningful only in relation to the difficulty experienced by the national community or by the wounded parts of the body politic to remember (*faire mémoire de*) these events calmly. These difficulties cannot be discussed responsibly until we have crossed through the arid plains of the epistemology of historical knowledge and entered the region of conflicts among individual memory, collective memory, and historical memory, at the point where the living memory of survivors confronts the distantiated, critical gaze of the historian, to say nothing of the viewpoint of the judge.

It is at this point of friction that the duty of memory proves to be particularly equivocal. The injunction to remember risks being heard as an invitation addressed to memory to short-circuit the work of history. For my part, I am all the more attentive to this danger as this book is a plea on behalf of memory as the womb of history, inasmuch as memory remains the guardian of the entire problem of the representative relation of the present to the past. The temptation then is great to transform this plea into a claim on behalf of memory in opposition to history. Just as I shall resist, when the time comes, the inverse claim to reduce memory to a simple object of history among its "new objects," at the risk of stripping it of its function of matrix, so too shall I refuse to allow myself to be enlisted into making the inverse plea. It is in this frame of mind that I have chosen to pose the question of the duty of memory for the first time in the context of the uses and abuses of memory, prepared to return to it at greater length in the context of forgetting. To say: you will remember, is also to say: you will not forget. It may even be that the duty of memory constitutes, at one and the same time, the epitome of good use and of abuse in the exercise of memory.

Let us wonder first at the grammatical paradox that is formed by the injunction to remember. How is it possible to say: "you will remember," hence to employ the future tense to speak of this memory that is given as the guardian of the past? More seriously: how can it be permissible to say: "you must remember," hence speak of memory in the imperative mood, although it is characteristic of memory to emerge as a spontaneous evocation, hence as *pathos*, according to Aristotle's *De memoria*? How can this prospective movement of the mind, turned toward memory as a task to be accomplished, be joined to the two dispositions left as though in suspense—the work of memory and the work of mourning, taken in turn separately and as a pair? In a certain manner, it extends their prospective character. But what does it add to this?

It is true that within the precise framework of the therapeutic cure the duty of memory is formulated as a task: it marks the will of the analysand to contribute from then on to the joint undertaking of the analysis as it navigates through the pitfalls of transference. This will even adopts the form of the imperative, allowing the representatives of the unconscious to speak and, in this way, as far as is possible, to "tell all." We should reread in this regard the advice that Freud gives to analyst and to analysand alike in the course of his essay "Remembering, Repeating, and Working-Through." For its part, the work of mourning, since it requires time, projects the artisan of this work ahead of himself: he will have to continue, one by one, to cut the ties that hold him in the grip of the lost objects of his love and his hate; as for reconciliation with the loss itself, this will forever remain an unfinished task. This patience toward oneself even possesses the features of a virtue, if it is contrasted, as we have tried to do, to the vice of giving in to sadness, to the *acedia* of spiritual teachers, that hidden passion that drags melancholia ever downward.

Having said this, what is missing from the work of memory and from the work of mourning that would make them equivalent to the duty of memory? What is missing is the imperative element that is not expressly present in the notion of work: work of memory, work of mourning. More precisely, what is still absent is the twofold aspect of duty, as imposing itself on desire from outside and as exerting a constraint experienced subjectively as obligation. Where are these two features found together, in a form least subject to dispute, if not in the idea of justice, which we have already mentioned above in reply to the abuses of memory on the level of manipulation? Extracting the exemplary value from traumatic memories, it is justice that turns memory into a project; and it is this same project of justice that gives the form of the future and of the imperative to the duty of memory. We can then suggest that the duty of memory considered as the imperative of justice is projected as a third term onto the point of intersection of the work of mourning and the work of memory. In return, the imperative receives from the work of memory and the work of mourning the impetus that integrates it into an economy of drives. This united force of the duty of justice can then extend beyond the memory and mourning pair to the pair formed by the truthful and the pragmatic dimensions of memory; indeed, our own discourse on memory has been conducted up to now along two parallel lines, the line of memory's concern for truth, under the aegis of the epistemic fidelity of memories with respect to what actually took place, and the line of memory use, considered as practice, even as the technique of memorization. This marks the return, therefore, of the past and the exercise of the past, this bi-partition repeating the division of the two chapters of Aristotle's treatise. It is as though the duty of memory were projected ahead of consciousness as a point of convergence between the truth perspective and the pragmatic perspective on memory.

The question then arises as to what gives the idea of justice its federating force with regard to the truthful and pragmatic aims of memory as well as to the work of memory and the work of mourning. It is thus the relation of the duty of memory to the idea of justice that must be interrogated.

First element of a response: it must be recalled, first, that among all the virtues, the virtue of justice is the one that, par excellence and by its very constitution, is turned toward others. We can even say that justice is the component of otherness inherent in all the virtues that it wrests from the closed-circuit of the self with itself. The duty of memory is the duty to do justice, through memories, to an other than the self.[43]

Second element of a response: the time has come to introduce a new concept—debt, which must not be limited to the concept of guilt. The idea of debt is inseparable from the notion of heritage. We are indebted to those who have gone before us for part of what we are. The duty of memory is not restricted to preserving the material trace, whether scriptural or other, of past events, but maintains the feeling of being obligated with respect to these others, of whom we shall later say, not that they are no more, but that they were. Pay the debt, I shall say, but also inventory the heritage.

Third element of a response: among those others to whom we are indebted, the moral priority belongs to the victims. Todorov cautioned above against the tendency to proclaim oneself a victim and endlessly to demand reparation. He was right. The victim at issue here is the other victim, other than ourselves.

This being the legitimation of the duty of memory as a duty of justice, how are abuses grafted upon its proper use? These abuses can occur only through the manner in which the idea of justice is handled. It is here that a certain demand raised by impassioned memories, wounded memories, against the vaster and more critical aim of history, lends a threatening tone to the proclamation of the duty of memory, which finds its most blatant expression in the exhortation to commemorate now and always.

Anticipating further developments that rely upon a more advanced state of the dialectic of memory and history, I want to indicate the existence of two clearly distinct, yet compatible, interpretations of this slippage from use to abuse.

On one side, the emphasis can be placed on the regressive character of the abuse, which carries us back to the first stage of our inquiry into the uses and abuses of memory under the sign of thwarted memory. This is the explanation proposed by Henry Rousso in *The Vichy Syndrome: History and Memory in France since 1944.*[44] This explanation is of value only within the limits of present-day history, so over a relatively short time-span. Rousso makes the best possible use of categories belonging to a pathology of memory—trauma, repression, return of the repressed, obsession, exorcism. Within this conceptual framework, which draws its legitimacy from its heuristic effectiveness, the duty of memory functions like an attempted exorcism in a historical situation marked by the obsession with traumas suffered by the French in the years 1940–45. The extent to which the proclamation of the duty of memory remains captive to the symptom of obsession makes it waver continually between use and abuse. Yes, the way in which the duty of memory is proclaimed can take the form of an abuse of memory in the manner of the abuses denounced earlier under the heading of manipulated memory. To be sure, these are no longer manipulations in the sense defined in terms of the ideological relation of the discourse of power, but in a more subtle manner in the sense of an appeal to conscience that proclaims itself to be speaking for the victims' demand for justice. Inveigling the silent word of the victims in this way makes use turn to abuse. We should not be surprised to find again on this somewhat higher level of obligated memory the same signs of abuse recognized in the preceding section, principally in the form of the frenzy of commemoration. The concept of obsession will be treated in a thematic manner at a later stage of this work in the chapter on forgetting.

Pierre Nora proposes an explanation less centered on the recitative of the history of the present day in the article that concludes the third volume of *Les Lieux de mémoire—Les France*—under the title: "L'Ère de la commémoration."[45] The article is devoted to "obsession with commemoration" (609) and can be understood only in terms of the dialogue the author undertakes with the inaugural text of "the places of memory." I shall, at the appropriate moment, devote a study to Nora's dialogue with himself.[46] If I mention it now, it is to extract a warning from it concerning the assimilation of my own work to an attack on history in the name of memory. Nora himself complains of a similar assimilation of the theme of the "places of memory" by "commemorative bulimia [that] has all but consumed all efforts to control it" (609): "The destiny of these *Lieux de mémoire* has been a strange one. The work was intended, by virtue of its conception, method, and even title, to be a counter-commemorative type of history, but commemoration has overtaken it.... What was forged as a tool for maintaining critical distance became the instrument of commemoration par excellence" (609). There is a historical moment, our own, that now defines itself completely in terms of "the obsession with commemoration": May 1968; the bicentennial of the French Revolution, and so on. The explanation proposed by Nora does not yet concern us, just his diagnosis: "Thus the very dynamics of commemoration have been turned around; the memorial model has triumphed over the historical model and ushered in a new, unpredictable, and capricious use of the past" (618). For what historical model has the memorial model been substituted? For the model of celebrations devoted to the impersonal sovereignty of the nation-state. This model deserved to be called historical because French self-understanding was identified with the history of the establishment of the nation-state. What has been substituted for it are particular, fragmented, local, and cultural memories.[47] What claim is attached to this inversion of the historical into the commemorative? What interests me here has to do with the transition from the phenomenology of memory to the epistemology of scientific history. The latter, Nora tells us, "consisted in the rectification and enrichment of the history of memory. Although it was intended to be 'critical,' it was in fact only a deepening of that tradition. Its ultimate goal was identification through filiation. It was in this sense that history and memory were identical: history was verified memory" (626). The inversion that is at the origin of commemorative obsession is said to consist in the assimilation of defunct traditions, slices of the past from which we have become separated. In short, "commemoration has freed itself from its traditionally assigned place, but the epoch as a whole has become commemorative" (627).

I would like to state at the close of this chapter devoted to the practice of memory that my undertaking is not a part of this "enthusiasm for memorial commemoration" (629). If it is true that "memory's moment" (632) defines an era, our own, my work aspires to escape the criteria that define this era, whether this be in its phenomenological phase, its epistemological phase, or its hermeneutical phase. Rightly or wrongly. For this reason my work is not threatened but reassured by Pierre Nora's conclusion, announcing a time when "the era of commemoration will be over for good" (637). For it is not to "the tyranny of memory" (637) that it will have desired to contribute. This abuse of abuses is among those it denounces with the same vigor with which it resists the substitution of the duty of memory for the work of mourning and the work of memory, and it limits itself to placing both of these labors under the sign of the idea of justice.

The question posed by the duty of memory, therefore, exceeds the limits of a simple phenomenology of memory. It even outstrips the resources of intelligibility of an epistemology of historical knowledge. Finally, as an imperative of justice, the duty of memory belongs to a moral problematic the present work just begins to approach. A second partial evocation of the duty of memory will be proposed within the framework of my meditation on forgetting, in relation to an eventual right of forgetting. We will then be confronted with the delicate connection between the discourse of memory and forgetting and the discourse of guilt and forgiveness.

In this state of suspense, we interrupt our examination of the exercised memory, its exploits, its uses and its abuses.

# CHAPTER 3

## *Personal Memory, Collective Memory*

### READING GUIDELINES

In the contemporary discussion, the question of the actual subject of the operations of memory tends to occupy the forefront. This precipitation is encouraged by a preoccupation peculiar to our field of investigation: it matters to historians to know the nature of their vis-à-vis, whether it is the memory of the protagonists of an action taken one by one or that of the collectivities taken as a body? Despite this twofold urgency, I have resisted the temptation to begin my investigation with this sometimes unwieldy debate. I thought that the venom might be sucked out of it if this issue were demoted from the first rank, where the pedagogy of the discourse presented here would also suggest it be placed, to the third rank, where the coherence of my enterprise requires it to be situated. If one does not know what is meant by the experience of memory in the living presence of an image of things past, nor what is meant by seeking out a memory, lost or rediscovered, how can one legitimately ask oneself to whom this experience or this search is to be attributed? Postponed in this way, the discussion has some chance of being directed to a less abrupt question than the one ordinarily posed in the form of a paralyzing dilemma: is memory primordially personal or collective? This question is the following: to whom is it legitimate to attribute the *pathos* corresponding to the reception of memories and the *praxis* in which the search for memories consists? The response to the question posed in these terms has a chance of escaping the alternatives of either/or. Why should memory be attributed only to me, to you, to her or to him, in the singular of the three grammatical persons capable of referring to themselves, of addressing another as you (in the singular), or of recounting the deeds of a third party in a narrative in the third person singular? And why could the attribution not be made directly to us, to you in the plural, to them? The discussion opened by the alternative summed up in the title of this chapter is not, of course, resolved by this mere displacement of the problem, but at least by first opening up the space of attribution to all of the grammatical persons (and even to nonpersons: one, whoever, each) an appropriate framework is offered for a confrontation between positions that have been made commensurable.

This is my first working hypothesis. The second is the following: the alternatives from which we begin are the relatively late fruit of a double movement that acquired shape and substance long after the development of the two major problematics of the experience of and the search for memory, a development whose origin goes back, as we have seen, to the time of Plato and Aristotle. On one side, it is the emergence of a problematic of a frankly egological mode of subjectivity, on the other, the irruption of sociology in the field of the social sciences and, with it, the appearance of an unprecedented concept of collective consciousness. Neither Plato nor Aristotle, nor any of the Ancients, had held the question to be prior of knowing *who* remembered. They asked themselves what it meant to have or to search for a memory. The attribution to someone capable of saying I or we remained implicit in conjugating the verbs of memory and forgetting in the grammatical persons and in the different verbal tenses. They did not ask themselves this question because they were asking another concerning the practical relation between the individual and the city. They resolved it well or poorly, as is attested by the quarrel initiated by Aristotle in book 2 of the *Politics* against the reform of the city proposed by Plato in the *Republic*, books 2 and 3. At least this problem was safe from any ruinous alternative. In any event, individuals ("each," *tis*, "man"—at least the free men defined by their participation in the government of the city) cultivated on the level of their personal relations the virtue of friendship that rendered their exchanges equal and reciprocal.

It was the emergence of a problematic of subjectivity and, more and more pointedly, of an egological problematic, that gave rise both to problematizing consciousness and to the movement by which consciousness turned back upon itself, to the point of a speculative solipsism. A school of inwardness, to borrow Charles Taylor's expression,[1] was thus gradually established. I shall propose three characteristic examples of this. The price to pay for this subjectivist radicalization is high: any attribution to a collective subject becomes unthinkable, derivative, or even frankly metaphorical. However, an antithetical position arose with the birth of the human sciences— from linguistics to psychology, sociology, and history. Adopting the type of objectivity belonging to the natural sciences as their epistemological model, these sciences put in place models of intelligibility for which social phenomena are indubitable realities. More precisely, to methodological individualism, the Durkheimian school opposed a methodological holism, to which Maurice Halbwachs would adhere. For sociology at the turn of the twentieth century, collective consciousness is thus one of those realities whose ontological status is not in question. Instead, individual memory, as a purportedly original agency, becomes problematic; emerging phenomenology struggled to avoid being dismissed under the more or less infamous label of psychologism, which phenomenology claimed to reject. Private consciousness, stripped of any claim to scientific credibility, no longer lends itself to description and explanation, except along the path of internalization, which has as its final stage the famous introspection lampooned by August Comte. At best it becomes what is to be explained, the *explicandum*, without any privilege of primordiality—the very word "primordiality" possessing, moreover, no meaning within the horizon of the total objectification of human reality.

In this intensely polemical situation, which opposes a younger tradition of objectivity to the ancient tradition of reflexivity, individual memory and collective memory are placed in a position of rivalry. However, they do not oppose one another on the same plane, but occupy universes of discourse that have become estranged from each other.

Having said this, the task of a philosophy concerned with understanding how historiography articulates its discourse in terms of that of the phenomenology of memory is, first, to discern the reasons for this radical misunderstanding through an examination of the internal functioning of the discourses proffered on either side; the task is, then, to throw some lines between the two discourses, in the hope of providing some credibility to the hypothesis of a distinct, yet reciprocal and interconnected, constitution of individual memory and of collective memory. It is at this stage of the discussion that I will propose invoking the concept of attribution as an operative concept capable of establishing a certain commensurability between the theses in opposition. Then will follow an examination of some of the modes of exchange between the self-attribution of mnemonic phenomena and their attribution to others, strangers or neighbors.

The problem of the relations between individual memory and collective memory will not thereby be put to rest. Historiography will again take up this problem. And it will arise once more when history, presenting itself in turn as its own subject, will be tempted to abolish the status of the womb of history commonly accorded to memory, and to consider memory as one of the objects of historical knowledge. It will then be the task of the philosophy of history, with which the third part of this work will open, to cast a final look at both the external relations between memory and history and the internal relations between individual memory and collective memory.

§

## THE TRADITION OF INWARDNESS

### Augustine

The plea for the originary and primordial character of individual memory has ties to the usages of ordinary language and to the popular psychology that sanctions these usages. In no other area of experience, whether it be the cognitive field, the practical field, or the affective field, is there such total adherence of the subject's act of self-designation to the object-oriented intention of experience. In this regard, the use in French and in other languages of the reflexive pronoun "soi" (self) does not seem to be accidental. In remembering something (*se souvenant de quelque chose*), one remembers oneself (*on se souvient de soi*).

Three features are apt to be underscored in favor of the fundamentally private character of memory. First, memory does seem to be radically singular: my memories are not yours. The memories of one person cannot be transferred into the memory of another. As mine, memory is a model of mineness, of private possession, for all the experiences of the subject. Next, it is in memory that the original tie of consciousness to the past appears to reside. We said this with Aristotle, we will say it again more forcefully with Augustine: memory is of the past, and this past is that of my impressions; in this sense, this past is my past. Through this feature, memory assures the temporal continuity of the person and, by this means, assures that identity whose difficulties and snares we confronted above. This continuity allows me to move back without interruption from the living present to the most distant events of my childhood. On the one hand, memories are divided and organized into levels of meaning, into archipelagos, sometimes separated by gulfs; on the other, memory remains that capacity to traverse, to move back through time, without anything, in principle, preventing the pursuit of this movement, without any end to its continuity. It is primarily in narrative that memories in the plural and memory in the singular are articulated, and differentiation joined to continuity. It is in this way that I am carried back to my childhood, with the feeling that those things occurred in another epoch. It is this otherness that, in turn, will serve to anchor the differentiation of the lapses of time made by history on the basis of chronological time. It remains, however, that this factor, which distinguishes between the moments of the remembered past, destroys none of the major characteristics of the relation between the recollected past and the present, namely, the temporal continuity and the mineness of memories. Third and final feature: it is to memory that the sense of orientation in the passage of time is linked; orientation in two senses, from the past to the future, by a push from behind, so to speak, following the arrow of the time of change, but also from the future toward the past, following the inverse movement of transit from expectation toward memory, across the living present. It is on basis of these features collected by common experience and ordinary language that the tradition of inwardness was constructed. It is a tradition whose titles of nobility extend back to late antiquity with a Christian coloration. Augustine is at once the expression of this tradition and its initiator. He can be said to have invented inwardness against the background of the Christian experience of conversion. The novelty of this discovery-creation is heightened by the contrast with the Greek, then Latin, problematic of the individual and the *polis* that initially occupied the space that will be gradually divided between political philosophy and the dialectic of split memory considered here. But if Augustine knows the inner man, he does not know the equating of identity, self, and memory. This is the invention of John Locke at the beginning of the eighteenth century. He is also unaware of the transcendental sense of the word "subject," inaugurated by Kant and bestowed to his post-Kantian and neo-Kantian successors, up to Husserl's transcendental philosophy, which will attempt to distinguish itself from neo-Kantianism and from the psychologizing of the transcendental subject. It is not, however, with Kant that I will linger, inasmuch as the problematic of the "internal sense" presents an extremely arduous reading, taking into account the shattering of the problematic of the subject into the transcendental, the noumenal, and the empirical. What is more, neither his theory nor his practice leaves room for a meaningful examination of memory. It is, therefore, directly toward Husserl that we will turn. In his extensive unpublished work, the problematic of memory links up with that of the subject who remembers, with interiority and reflexivity. With Husserl, the school of inwardness reaches its apex. At the same time, the entire tradition of inwardness is constructed as an impasse in the direction of collective memory.

It is not yet consciousness and the self, nor even the subject, that Augustine describes and honors, but rather already the inner man remembering himself. Augustine's strength is to have tied the analysis of memory to that of time in books 10 and 11 of the *Confessions*. This double analysis is, in fact, inseparable from an absolutely singular context. To begin with, the literary genre of confession is strongly associated with the moment of penitence, which earlier dominated the common usage of the term, and even more so with the initial avowal of the submission of the self to the creative word that has always preceded private language, a properly reflexive moment that directly ties memory and self-presence in the pain of the aporia. In *Time and Narrative* I quoted, following Jean Guitton,[2] this magnificent "confession": "O Lord, I am working hard in this field, and the field of my labours is my own self. I have become a problem to myself, like the land which a farmer works only with difficulty and at the cost of much sweat. For I am not now investigating the tracts of heaven, or measuring the distance of the stars, or trying to discover how the earth hangs in space. I am investigating myself, my memory, my mind" (*Ego sum qui memini, ego animus*).[3] So, no phenomenology of memory apart from the painful quest of interiority. Let us recall a few stages in this quest.

First, to book 10 of the *Confessions*. To be sure, the privilege of interiority is not everything here, inasmuch as the search for God immediately provides a dimension of loftiness, of verticalness, to the meditation on memory. But it is *in* memory that God is first sought. The heights and the depths—these are the same things—are hollowed out within interiority.[4]

The fame this book has enjoyed stems from the well-known metaphor of the "spacious palace" of memory. It provides interiority with a specific kind of spatiality, creating an intimate place. This pivotal metaphor is reinforced by a host of other related figures: the "storehouse" where the variety of memories to be enumerated are "stored away," "entrusted for safekeeping": "All these sensations are retained in the great storehouse of the memory, which in some indescribable way secretes them in its folds. They can be brought out and called back again when they are needed" (10.8, 214–15). The study focuses on the marvel of recollection.[5] Calling up as I please all the things "brought into my memory" bears witness to the fact that "all this goes on inside [*intus*] me, in the vast cloisters of my memory" (10.8, 215). Augustine celebrates a happy memory: "The power of the memory is prodigious, my God. It is a vast immeasurable sanctuary. Who can plumb its depths? And yet it is a faculty of my soul. Although it is part of my nature, I cannot understand all that I am" (10.8, 216). Doubly admirable is memory.

First, by virtue of its scope. Indeed, the "things" collected in memory are not limited to images of sensible impressions that memory saves from dispersion by gathering them together, but also include intellectual notions, which can be said to be learned and, from then on, known. Vast is the treasure that memory is said to "contain": "The memory also contains the innumerable principles and laws of numbers and dimensions" (10.12, 219). To sensible images and to notions is added the memory of passions of the soul: the memory is, in fact, capable of recalling joy without being joyful, and sadness without being sad. Second marvelous operation: concerning notions, it is not simply the images of things that return to the mind but the intelligible ideas themselves. In this, the memory is equated with the *cogito*.[6] Moreover, the memory of "things" and the memory of myself coincide: in them I also encounter myself, I remember myself, what I have done, when and how I did it and what impression I had at that time. Yes, great is the power of memory, so that I even "remember that I have remembered" (10.13, 220). In short, "the mind and the memory are one and the same" (10.14, 220).

A happy memory, then? Certainly. And yet the danger of forgetting continues to haunt this praise of memory and its power: from the beginning of book 10 the inner man is spoken of as the place where "my soul is bathed in light that is not bound by space and where resounds a sound that rapacious time cannot steal [*quod non rapit tempus*]" (10.6, 212; trans. modified). Later, evoking the "great field" and the "spacious palace" of memory, Augustine speaks of memories stored as things not yet "swallowed up and buried in forgetfulness" (10.8, 214). Here, the storehouse resembles the sepulcher ("forgetfulness obliterates [buries] all that we remember" [10.16, 223]). To be sure, recognizing something remembered is experienced as a victory over forgetfulness: "If I had forgotten the thing itself, I should be utterly unable to recognize what the sound implied" (10.16, 222). We must, therefore, "remember forgetfulness" (10.16, 222) in order to be able to speak of recognition. For what indeed is a lost object—the drachma lost by the woman in the gospel parable—if not something that has somehow been retained in the memory? Here, finding is recovering, and recovering is recognizing, and recognizing is accepting, and so judging that the thing recovered is indeed the same as the thing sought, and thus considered after the fact as the thing forgotten. If, then, something other than the object sought comes to mind, we are capable of saying: "That's not it." The object "was only lost to sight, not to the memory" (10.18, 225). Are we completely reassured by this? In truth, only the recognition, in language and after-the-fact, attests that "if we had completely forgotten it, we should not even be able to look for what was lost" (10.19, 226). But is not forgetting something different from what we remember having forgotten because we do remember it and recognize it? To ward off the danger of a more radical forgetfulness, Augustine the rhetorician proposes to add to the memory of memory a memory of forgetting: "If it is true that what we remember we retain in our memory, and if it is also true that unless we remember forget-fulness, we could not possibly recognize the meaning of the word when we heard it, then it is true that forgetfulness is retained in the memory" (10.16, 222). But what can actually be said about true forgetfulness, namely, "ab-sence of memory"? "When it is present, I cannot remember. Then how can it be present in such a way that I can remember it?" On the one hand, we must say that, at the moment the forgotten object is recognized, it is memory that attests to the existence of forgetting; and if this is so, then "forgetfulness is retained in memory" (10.16, 223). On the other hand, how could we speak of the presence of forgetfulness itself when we truly forget? The vice tightens: "What am I to say, when I am quite certain that I can remember forgetfulness? Am I to say that what I remember is not in my memory? Or am I to say that the reason why forgetfulness is in my memory is to prevent me from forgetting? Both suggestions are utterly absurd. There is the third possibility, that I should say that when I remember forgetfulness, it is its image that is retained in my memory, not the thing itself. But how could I say that it is the image of forgetfulness that my memory retains and not forgetfulness itself, when I remember it? How could I say this too?" (10.16, 223; trans. modified). Here, the old eristic pierces through the confession: "Yet, however it may be, and in whatever inexplicable and incomprehensible way it happens, I am certain that I remember forgetfulness, even though forgetfulness obliterates all that we remember" (10.16, 223).

Passing over this enigma, the search for God is pursued in the memory, higher than memory, through the mediation of the quest for the happy life: "I shall go beyond this force that is in me, this force which we call memory, so that I may come to you, my Sweetness and my Light" (10.17, 224). But this movement of surpassing, in turn, is not devoid of the enigmatic: "I must pass beyond memory to find you. . . . But where will the search lead me? Where am I to find you? If I find you beyond my memory, it means that I have no memory of you. How, then, am I to find you, if I have no memory of you?" (10.17, 224). Here we catch a glimpse of a forgetfulness even more fundamental than the destruction of all visible things by time, the forgetting of God.

It is against this backdrop of admiration for memory, an admiration colored with concern about the danger of forgetfulness, that the great declarations of book 11 on time can be placed. However, to the extent that memory is the present of the past, what can be said about time and its relation to interiority can readily be applied to memory.

As I noted in *Time and Narrative*, Augustine enters into the problematic of interiority through the question of the measurement of time. The initial question of measurement is assigned directly to the place of the mind: "It is in my own mind, then, that I measure time" (11.27, 276). It is only the past and future that we say are long or short, whether, for example, the future shortens or the past lengthens. More fundamentally, time is a passage, a transition witnessed by meditating reflection: "we can be aware of time and measure it only while it is passing" (11.16, 266). And later: "we measure time as it passes" (11.21, 269). In this way, the *animus* is considered to be the place in which future things and past things are. It is in the internal place of the soul or the mind that the dialectic between *distension* and *intention*, which provided the guiding thread for my interpretation of book 11 of the *Confessions* in *Time and Narrative*, unfolds. The *distentio* that dissociates the three intentions of the present—the present of the past or memory, the present of the future or expectation, and the present of the present or attention—is *distentio animi*. It stands as the dissimilarity of the self to itself.[7] Moreover, it is of the highest importance to stress that the choice of the reflexive point of view is tied polemically to a rejection of the Aristotelian explanation of the origin of time on the basis of cosmic motion. With respect to our polemic surrounding the private or public character of memory, it is worth noting that, according to Augustine, the authentic and original experience of inner time is not primarily opposed to public time, to the time of commemoration, but to the time of the world. In *Time and Narrative* I raised the question whether historical time could be interpreted in terms of a similar antinomy, or whether it was not constructed instead as a third time, at the point of articulation of lived time, of phenomenological time so to speak, and of cosmological time. A more radical question arises here, namely, whether inserting individual memory into the operations of collective memory does not require a similar conciliation between the time of the soul and the time of the world. For the moment, it is enough to have anchored the question "Who?" in that of the *animus*, the authentic subject of the *ego memini*.

I do not want to abandon these brief remarks concerning the Augustinian phenomenology of time without mentioning a problem that will accompany us up to the final chapter of this work. It is the problem of knowing whether the theory of the threefold present does not accord a preeminence to the living experience of the present such that the otherness of the past is affected and compromised by it. And this despite the notion of *distentio*. The question is posed more directly by the role played by the notion of "passing" in the description of *distentio animi*: "while we are measuring it, where is it coming from [*unde*], what is it passing through [*qua*], and where is it going [*quo*]?" (11.21, 269). The passage (*transire*) of time, Augustine says, consists in "passing from [*ex*] the future, passing through [*per*] the present, and going into [*in*] the past" (ibid.). Let us forget the inevitable spatial character of the metaphor of the place of transit and focus instead on the *diaspora* of this passage. Does this passage—from the future toward the past through the present—signify an irreducible diachrony or a subtle synchronic reduction, to evoke Levinas's terminology in *Otherwise than Being*? This question anticipates, within phenomenology, the question of the pastness of the past, inseparable from the notion of temporal distance. It is to this question that our final reflections will be devoted.[8]

## Locke

The situation of John Locke within the philosophical current of inwardness is utterly singular. The echo of Platonism and Neoplatonism is no longer perceptible, as it was in Augustine and as it continues to resonate forcefully with Cudworth and the Cambridge Platonists, whom Locke knew well and upon whose views he had reflected. Moreover, the kinship with the Christian problem of conversion to inwardness has ceased to be discernible. It is with Descartes that we believe him—wrongly, we shall see—most closely associated, precisely on the question of the *cogito*. However, the critique of innate ideas already served to distance Locke definitively from him, at least on the level of the ideas of perception. It remains that John Locke is the inventor of the following three notions and the sequence that they form together: identity, consciousness, self. Chapter 27 of book 2 of *An Essay concerning Human Understanding*, titled "Of Identity and Diversity," occupies a strategic position in the work beginning with the second edition (1694) of the work first published in 1690. As Étienne Balibar, to whom we owe a new translation, replacing that of Pierre Coste (1700), and a substantial commentary, directly underscores, Locke's invention of consciousness will become the acknowledged or unacknowledged reference for theories of consciousness in Western philosophy from Leibniz and Condillac, passing through Kant and Hegel, to Bergson and Husserl.[9] For it is truly an invention with respect to the terms "consciousness" and "self," an invention that has an impact on the notion of identity that serves to frame them. This assertion may seem surprising if one considers the prestige of the Cartesian *cogito* and the occurrences, if not of the word "consciousness," at least of the adjective *conscius* in the Latin versions of the *Meditations* and *Responses* (a significant detail: *conscius* is commonly rendered in French by other expressions: *en être "connaissants"*—being aware of, knowing; *en avoir "une actuelle connaissance"*—having genuine knowledge of; *"expérimenter"*—experience).[10] But the grammatical subject of the Cartesian *cogito* is not a *self*, but an exemplary *ego* whose gesture the reader is invited to repeat. In Descartes, there is no "consciousness" in the sense of self. What is more, if the *cogito* includes diversity by virtue of the multiple operations of thought enumerated in the *Second Meditation*, this is not the diversity of the places and moments by means of which the Lockean self maintains its personal identity; it is a diversity of functions. The *cogito* is not a person defined by his or her memory and the capacity to give an accounting to himself or herself. It bursts forth in the lightning flash of an instant. Always thinking does not imply remembering having thought. Continual creation alone confers duration upon it. The *cogito* does not possess duration in its own right.

The way is opened by a series of prior operations of reduction. Whereas the philosophy of the *Meditations* is a philosophy of certainty, in which certainty is a victory over doubt, Locke's essay is a victory over diversity, over difference. In addition, whereas in the *Meditations* the certainty of existence is inscribed within a new philosophy of substances, for Locke, the person is identified by consciousness alone, which is the self, to the exclusion of a metaphysics of substance, which, without being radically excluded, is methodologically suspended. This consciousness is also purified in another way, in terms of language and the use of words; this reduction lays bare the mental, the mind—the English version of the Latin *mens*. Signifying without words—tacitly in this sense—is characteristic of mind, capable of reflecting directly on "what passes within itself" (book 2, chap. 21, "Of Power," §1). The final purification: it is not innate ideas that consciousness finds within itself; what it perceives are the "Operations of Our Own Minds" (book 2, chap. 1, §4), sometimes passive, as regards the ideas of perception, sometimes active, as regards the powers of the mind, to which chapter 21 of book 2, "Of Power," is devoted.

Having said this, what about the triad: identity-consciousness-self? As we question the egological character of a philosophy of consciousness and memory, which does not appear to offer a possible transition in the direction of any sort of being-in-common, any dialogical or communal situation, the first remarkable feature we note is the purely reflexive definition of identity with which the discussion (book 2, chap. 27, "Of Identity and Diversity") begins. It is true that identity is opposed to diversity, to difference, by an act of comparison by the mind, as it forms the ideas of identity and difference. The places and the moments in which something exists are different. But it is indeed this thing, and not some other, which is in these different places and moments. Identity is, to be sure, a relation, but the reference to that other thing is also erased: a thing is "the same with itself, and no other" (chap. 27, §1). This surprising expression "the same with itself" poses the equation: identity equals sameness with self. The movement of folding back upon itself, in which reflection initially consists, takes shape in this self-referential relation. Identity is the fold of this folding back. Difference is named only to be suspended, reduced. The expression "and no other" is the mark of this reduction. Proposing to define in new terms the principle of individuation (*principium individuationis*), "so much inquired after" (§3), Locke takes as his first example an atom, "a continued body under one immutable superficies," and reiterates his formula of self-identity: "For being at that instant what it is, and nothing else, it is the same, and so must continue as long as its existence is continued; for so long it will be the same, and no other" (§3).

Difference, excluded as soon as it is posited, returns under the kinds of differentiation belonging to the types of identity: after the identity of particles, which we have just mentioned, comes the identity of plants (the same oak retains the same organization), the identity of animals (a single life continues), the identity of man ("nothing but a participation of the same continued life," §6), and, finally, personal identity. The important break thus passes between man and self. It is consciousness that constitutes the difference between the idea of the same man and that of a self, also termed person: "which, I think, is a thinking intelligent being, that has reason and reflection, and can consider itself as itself, the same thinking thing, in different times and places" (§9). The difference is no longer marked by the repudiated outside of "another thing" but by the displayed inside of times and places. The knowledge of this self-identity, of this "thinking thing" (with a nod to Descartes), is consciousness. The sole negation admitted: "it being impossible for anyone to perceive without perceiving that he does perceive" (§9). This eliminates the classic reduction to substance, whether material or immaterial, one or many, to the source of that consciousness, the same as itself and knowing itself to be such. Has the difference with respect to something other been warded off? Not for a minute: "For ... consciousness always accompanies thinking, and it is that that makes everyone to be what he calls self, and thereby distinguishes himself from all other thinking things" (§9). This identity of the self in consciousness suffices to pose the equation that interests us here between consciousness, self, and memory. In fact, "as far as this consciousness can be extended backwards to any past action or thought, so far reaches the identity of that person; it is the same self now it was then; and it is by the same self with this present one that now reflects on it, that that action was done" (§9). Personal identity is a temporal identity. It is here that the objection drawn from forgetting and from sleep, considered as interruptions of consciousness, suggests the invigorated return of the idea of substance: is not the continuity of a substance required to overcome the intermittence of consciousness? Locke replies bravely that, whatever may be the status of the substantial ground, consciousness alone "makes" personal identity (§10). Identity and consciousness form a circle. As Balibar observes, this circle is not a logical fallacy of the theory: it is Locke's own invention, supported by the reduction of substance: "the same consciousness unit[es] those distant actions into the same person, whatever substances contributed to their production" (§10). And Locke goes to battle on the front of other apparent counterexamples: the little finger cut off and separated from the body is missed not by some corporeal substance but by corporeal consciousness. As for multiple personalities, they are without any assignable link to the same thinking substance, assuming that the same immaterial substance remains unchanged; these are indeed multiple, split consciousnesses, "two distinct persons" (§14). Locke has the courage to maintain his chosen option. The reply to the objection drawn from the alleged preexistence of souls is of the same nature: "The question being what makes the same person; and not whether it be the same identical substance which always thinks in the same person, which, in this case, matters not" (§10). And, further: No one becomes Socrates who has no consciousness "of any of Socrates' actions or thoughts" (§14). The same reasoning applies in the case of the resurrection of a person in a body different from that of the world here below, "the same consciousness going along with the soul that inhabits it" (§15). It is not the soul that makes the man but the same consciousness.

With regard to our inquiry, the matter has been decided: consciousness and memory are one and the same thing, irrespective of any substantial basis. In short, in the matter of personal identity, sameness equals memory.

Having said this, what otherness could then slip into the folds of this sameness to self?

On what is still a formal level, we can observe that identity continues to be a relation of comparison that has opposite it diversity, difference; the idea of something other continues to haunt the self-reference of the same. The expression, "the same with itself, and no other" contains the antonym that is stated only to be crossed out. More precisely, with respect to the principle of individuation, reinterpreted by Locke, others are excluded as soon as they are cited; the stated incommunicability of two things of the same kind implies that, under the heading of "no other," it is other consciousnesses that are obliquely intended. To designate "this" consciousness, must one not hold in reserve an "any," an "everyone," a secretly distributive term? The identity of *this* is not that of *that* person (§9). In the hypothesis of "two distinct incommunicable consciousnesses acting in the same body, the one constantly by day, the other by night," one can legitimately wonder "whether the day- and the night-man would not be two as distinct persons as Socrates and Plato" (§23). To form the hypothesis, we must be able to distinguish between two consciousnesses, hence establish the difference between the consciousnesses. More gravely, what is at issue is the logico-grammatical status of the word "self," at times taken generically: the self, at times in the singular: my self, as permitted by the flexibility of English grammar.[11] There is no discussion concerning the status of the nominalized pronoun, which shifts in this way between the deictic and the common noun. Locke had decided to disconnect ideas from names. Yet, "*Person*, as I take it, is the name for this self" (§26). And the final word of this discussion is left to the name: "For whatever be the composition whereof the complex idea is made, whenever existence makes it one particular thing under any denomination, the same existence continued, preserves it the same individual under the same denomination" (§29).

On a more material plane, difference brings back the two extremes of the palette of meanings attaching to the idea of the identical self. Diversity, formally excluded by the expression, a thing "the same with itself, and no other," offers itself to memory as the diversity, traversed and retained, of places and moments that memory links together. This diversity touches on an aspect of life underlying memory that is nothing other than the very passing of time. Consciousness is consciousness of what is passing, occurring within it. The passage is that of perceptions and operations and, hence, of all of the contents placed under the heading of the "what" of memory in the two preceding chapters. No bridge has been constructed between consciousness folded back upon itself and its powers, which, nevertheless, formed the object of a separate discussion in the long chapter, "Of Power." Not having available to him the category of intentionality, Locke does not distinguish between the memory and its memories, memories of perceptions and of operations. Memory is, I venture to say, without memories. The only perceptible tension is between consciousness and life, despite their identification. It is apparent in the expression "continued existence," made more explicit by the expression "vital union" (§29). The alternation between waking and sleeping, the phases of remembering and forgetting, compels this recourse to the vocabulary of life: continued existence is preserved only so long as there persists "a vital union with that wherein this consciousness then resided" (§25). Were this "vital union" to dissolve, then that part of ourselves could well "become a real part of another person" (§25). Along with the vocabulary of life is thus suggested that of "a part of that same self" (§25). "Continued existence," with its threat of internal division, then tends to outstrip consciousness: now it is continued existence that, in the final analysis, "makes identity" (§29). A philosophy of life is sketched out beneath the philosophy of consciousness at the point of articulation of the identity of the man with the identity of the self. If we add to the relation to the past the relation to the future, the tension between anticipation and remembering gives rise to the uneasiness that affects the use of the powers of the mind. Consciousness and uneasiness then risk being dissociated from one another.

At the other end of the range of synonyms of the self, the ethical vocabulary suggests significant reworking of the sameness of the self to itself. We noted above the forensic character of judicial language to which the word "person" belongs, even though it is "the name for this self" (§26). Concern, ascription, appropriation belong to the same ethico-juridical field, followed by punishment and reward. The key concept is that of an "account of self" (§25). It responds to the admission of intimate diversity just mentioned. This idea of an account leads even further. First of all, in the direction of the future: it is in the future also that "the same self [is] ... continued on" (§25). And this continued existence moving forward as well as retrospectively gathered together, makes consciousness responsible: those who can account for their actions to themselves are "accountable." They can impute these actions to themselves (§26). Other expressions follow suit: being accountable is also being "concerned" (we recognize in this term the Latin *cura*). The "concern for happiness [is] the unavoidable concomitant of consciousness" (§26). The shift to a judicial vocabulary is not far off. The transitional concept is that of "person," the other "name for this *self*" (§26). What makes it a synonym for the self, despite its "forensic" character? The fact that it signifies that the self "reconciles" and "appropriates," that is to say, assigns, allocates to consciousness the ownership of its acts. The vocabulary is extremely dense here: the verb "to appropriate" plays on the possessive and on the verbs signifying to own and to impute to oneself (§26).

We touch here on a domain that is open to a double reading, depending on whether we start with the self or with others. For who assigns? Who appropriates? And, even, who imputes? Does one not also, and perhaps to begin with, give an accounting to others? And who punishes and rewards? And what agency on that last day will pronounce the sentence, regarding which Locke, taking sides in the theological debate, declares that it "shall be justified by the consciousness all persons shall have" (§26).

This double reading is not Locke's. What drew me to his treatise on identity, consciousness, and the self is the intransigence of an uncompromising philosophy that has to be termed a philosophy of "sameness."[12]

We find confirmation of the univocity of this philosophy of sameness in comparing the conceptuality and vocabulary of the *Essay* to the *Second Treatise of Government*.[13] The reader is carried straight to the heart of what Hannah Arendt liked to call human plurality. We are from the outset Adam's heirs, subjected to rulers who are on earth today, and we ask ourselves about the source of their authority: "he that will not give just occasion to think that all government in the world is the product only of force and violence, and that men live together by no other rules but that of beasts, where the strongest carries it, and so lay a foundation for perpetual disorder and mischief, tumult, sedition, and rebellion . . . must of necessity find out another rise of government" (2). We are thrown *in medias res*. When there are already men, rulers, war and violence, threats of discord, a question arises concerning the origin of political power. The state of nature evoked first, along with its privilege of perfect equality, is without roots in the philosophy of the self, even if notions of action, possession, and person are presented from the beginning of the text. There appears to be no visible link to the consciousness, closed upon itself, of the *Essay concerning Human Understanding*. In an unmotivated leap, we pass from personal identity to the state of equality, the "state all men are naturally in" (4). It is indeed a question of power, but it is straightaway "a power over another," and a strange power at that, since it is the power "only to retribute to him so far as calm reason and conscience dictate what is proportionate to his transgression, which is so much as may serve for reparation and restraint" (7). The state of war is, moreover, mentioned soon after in chapter 3. It assumes enmity and destruction; this state confirms "the fundamental law of nature, man being to be preserved as much as possible" (14). Man, not the self. Just as in Hobbes, man fears violent death, this evil done by man to man. The law of nature gives me the right to "kill him, if I can" (16). We always already find ourselves in a world in which the state of nature and the state of war are in conflict. Nothing in the theory of the self allowed us to anticipate this.[14] The *Second Treatise of Government*, thereafter, unfolds on a stage different from that of the self.

## Husserl

Husserl will be our third witness to the tradition of inwardness. He comes after Locke, but by way of Kant and the post-Kantians, especially Fichte, whom he resembles in many respects. Husserl attempts to situate himself in relation to a transcendental philosophy of consciousness, by virtue of a critical return to the Descartes of the *cogito*. However, he distinguishes himself from Descartes no less than did Locke. It is finally with Augustine, frequently mentioned approvingly, that Husserl can best be compared, at least with regard to the manner of tying together the three problematics of interiority, memory, and time. My approach to Husserl in the present context differs noticeably from that proposed in *Time and Narrative*, where the constitution of time was the principal issue. In the perspective of a confrontation between the phenomenology of individual memory and the sociology of memory, the focus is shifted in the direction of the "Fifth Cartesian Meditation," where the problem of the passage from egology to intersubjectivity is tackled directly. I, nevertheless, did not want to confront the difficulty head on. I have preferred the patient path, worthy of the rigor of the eternal "beginner" that Husserl was, passing by way of the problem of memory. It is, in fact, at the center of this problem, as it is treated in the *Phenomenology of the Consciousness of Internal Time*, that there is a change in direction by reason of which the inner gaze shifts from the constitution of memory in its objective relation to an object spread out in time, an object that endures, to the constitution of the temporal flow itself, excluding any object-oriented intention. This shift of gaze seemed to me so fundamental, so radical, that I have taken the risk of treating the question of memory in two different chapters. In the first chapter, I considered what belonged specifically to a phenomenology of memories, on the one hand, from the viewpoint of its relation to a thing that continues (the examples of the sound that continues to resonate and of the melody that one re-presents to oneself anew) and, on the other hand, from the viewpoint of its difference with respect to the image (*Bild, Vorstellung, Phantasie*). I ended the analysis of retention and protention at the point where the reference to an object that endures—the reference constitutive of the memory properly speaking—gives way to a constitution without reference to any given object, that of pure temporal flow. The dividing-line between a phenomenology of memories and a phenomenology of temporal flow is relatively easy to draw as long as the memory, in opposition to the image, preserves its distinctive mark as a positional act. It becomes indiscernible when the notions of impression, retention, protention no longer refer to the constitution of a temporal object but to that of pure temporal flow. The three notions just mentioned thus occupy a strategic position, to the point that they can either be assigned to an analysis of objects, or can be mobilized by a reflection that excludes any objective reference. It is this shift, equivalent to a veritable reversal, that is now taken into account. The question that drives me is this: to what extent does this retreat outside of the objective sphere—where *Erinnerung* means memories (*souvenir*) rather than memory (*mémoire*)—pave the way for the egological thesis of the *Cartesian Meditations*, which blocks the path in the direction of the "foreign" before it determines the means of access?[15] The choice of this guiding question explains why I connect in a kind of short-circuit the *Phenomenology of the Consciousness of Internal Time* and the "Fifth Cartesian Meditation." In the first collection, the reign of egology is prepared; in the second text a heroic exit is attempted in the direction of "higher intersubjective communities."

The *Phenomenology of the Consciousness of Internal Time*[16] shows its colors in its very title: the consciousness of time is declared to be internal. Moreover, consciousness is not taken here in the sense of consciousness of . . . , following the model of *ad extra* intentionality. Better put, it is a question, to speak as Gérard Granel does, of time-consciousness—"of the *immanent time* of the flow of consciousness" (5), as we read in the opening pages of Husserl's text. No gap, therefore, between consciousness and time. It is noteworthy that this perfect immanence is obtained in a single stroke by bracketing, by "reducing" "objective" time, world-time, which common sense considers to be outside of consciousness. This inaugural gesture recalls the one made by Augustine, who separated the time of the soul from the physical time that Aristotle had tied to change, thereby placing it within the domain of physics. We shall have to recall this when we develop the notion of historical time as the time of the calendar, grafted onto the cosmic order. From the outset, a major obstacle is placed across the path of the transition from this consciousness of internal time to historical time. The consciousness of internal time is closed up upon itself from the start. As concerns the nature of the mind's "apprehension" of the flow of consciousness and so of the past, it is a question of whether this *experienced* time is capable of being apprehended and *stated* without borrowing from objective time, in particular with regard to simultaneity, succession, and the sense of temporal distance— notions already encountered in our first chapter, where it was a matter of distinguishing memory, turned toward elapsed time, from imagination, directed toward the unreal, the fantastic, the fictional. Husserl believes that he avoids these difficulties by assuming for the consciousness of internal time a priori truths inhering in the "apprehensions" (*Auffassungen*), themselves inhering in this *experienced* time. It is noteworthy that this problem of the original articulation of the consciousness of time is posed on the level of a "hyletic" in the sense of *hulē*, of "matter" for the Greeks, in opposition to a morphology related to perceived objects, apprehended in accordance with their unity of meaning. This is the level of radicalness claimed by the consciousness of internal time and its self-constitution.

I shall not discuss again here the two phenomenological discoveries that we owe to Husserl, on the one hand, the difference between "retention" of the phase of flow that has "just" elapsed, and that "still" adheres to the present, and the "remembering" of temporal phases that have ceased to adhere to the living present, and, on the other hand, the difference between the positional character of memories and the non-positional character of images. I ventured to evoke these within the framework of an "objective" phenomenology that aims at distinguishing the past reality of memories from the unreal character of the imaginary. I will concentrate here on the presuppositions of an investigation that claims to be part of a phenomenology of *consciousness* and, more precisely, of *internal consciousness*, from the perspective we are adopting in this chapter, namely, the confrontation between private remembering and public commemoration.

The third section of the 1905 lecture links up in the following way with the preceding section in which the analysis of temporality was still based on an "individual object" (§35, 78), on something that endures: a sound or a melody. The identity of this something was constituted in its very duration. From then on, it is the continuity of the flow that takes the place of the temporally constituted identity. Thus §36 carries the title: "The Time-Constituting Flow as Absolute Subjectivity" (79). The effacement of the object, and hence of the individual process and its afferent predicates, does not thereby leave a linguistic void: there remains the pure internal relation to the continuity of appearances between a now and a before, between a current phase and a continuity of pasts. Let us note the difference in usage of the category of the now: it no longer signifies simply the beginning or the ceasing of something that continues, but the pure actuality of the appearing. We continue, of course, to name this flow in accordance with what is constituted "but it is not 'something in objective time'" (§36, 79). "It is *absolute subjectivity* and has the absolute properties of something to be designated *metaphorically* as 'flow'; of something that originates in a point of actuality, in a primal source-point, 'the now,' and so on. In the actuality-experience we have the primal source-point and a continuity of moments of reverberation. For all of this, we lack names" (79).

In truth, names are not absolutely lacking. The metaphorical use of flow, which Husserl shares with William James and Bergson, authorizes that of source: an axis of reference is thereby preserved to express continuity; this axis is that of the primal source-point. Not the beginning of something, but maintaining the surging-forth. We can retain the vocabulary of retention, but without the support of something constituted as enduring. The vocabulary is transferred to the side of appearing as such. Can we still speak of unity? Of a unitary flow? Yes, in the sense that the incessant transformation of "now" into "no longer," and of "not yet" into "now," is equivalent to the constitu-tion of a single flow, if the word "constitution" retains a sense when nothing is constituted beyond the flow itself: "Immanent time is constituted as *one* for all immanent objects and processes. Correlatively, the time-consciousness of what is immanent is an all-inclusive unity" (§38, 81). This all-inclusiveness is nothing other than a "steady continuum of modes of consciousness, of modes of having elapsed" (81). Appearing one after the other or together— all at once—this is what is commonly called succession and coexistence. The necessity, and at the same time the impossibility, of forgoing the reference to things that endure did not leave Husserl unconcerned: "But what does that mean? One can say nothing further here than: 'look'" (82). Look at what? At the continuous transformation of the immanent now ("a tone-now") into the modes of consciousness of the immediate past. Which produces a new now that Husserl terms "a form-now" (82). Let us note this recourse to the notion of form underpinning the language of flow: "The consciousness, in its form as primal sensation-consciousness, is identical" (82). However, unlike Kant, for whom the language of form is that of presupposition, of the a priori and, in this sense, of invisibility,[17] a certain intuitive character is attached to these forms: now, before, at once, one after the other, constantly (*stetig*). This intuitive character is related to the situation of the phase. It is conveyed by the persistence of the vocabulary of intentionality, but divided between two uses of the term "retention," on the one hand to express the duration of something, on the other to express the persistence of the current phase in the unity of the flow: "There is one, unique flow of conscious-ness in which both the unity of the tone in immanent time and the unity of the flow of consciousness itself become constituted at once" (§39, 84). On this point, Husserl declares his puzzlement: "As shocking (when not initially

even absurd) as it may seem to say that the flow of consciousness constitutes its own unity, it is nonetheless the case that it does. And this can be
made intelligible on the basis of the flow's essential constitution" (§39, 84).
The solution to this apparent paradox is the following: on the one hand, the
unity of what endures is constituted *across* its phases; on the other hand, the
gaze is directed *to* the flow. There are, then, two intentionalities: one transverse, targeting the thing that endures (one then speaks of retention of the
tone); the other, aiming only at the "still" as such of the retention and of
the series of retentions of retentions. "Now the flow . . . coincides with itself
intentionally, constituting a unity in the flow" (87). And Husserl continues:
"If I focus on the 'horizontal intentionality' . . . I turn my reflective regard
away from the tone" (87), and consider only the relation of retention to the
primal appearing, in short the continuing newness of the flow itself. But
the two intentionalities remain intertwined. In other words, we can arrive at
the absolute constitution of the flow only correlatively (the word was used
above) with the constitution of something that endures. By virtue of this
correlation between two intentionalities, it is legitimate to write: "The flow
of the consciousness that constitutes immanent time not only *exists* but is so
remarkably and yet intelligibly fashioned that a self-appearance of the flow
necessarily exists in it, and therefore the flow itself must necessarily be ap-
prehensible in the flowing" (§39, 88). A new difficulty is quickly brushed
aside: might it be in a second flow that the self-appearance of the flow would
be given? No: there is no danger of an infinite regression; the constitution
of the flow is final, because it consists in a self-constitution in which the
constituting and the constituted coincide, inasmuch as the constitution of
the immanent contents—namely, of experience in the usual sense—is "the
achievement of the absolute flow of consciousness" (§40, 88). Does this
achievement, nevertheless, possess limits? The question arose earlier with
regard to the flow: "These 'determinate' retentions and protentions have
an obscure horizon; in flowing away, they turn into indeterminate retentions and protentions, related to the past and future course of the stream.
It is through the indeterminate retentions and protentions that the actually
present content is inserted into the unity of the flow" (§40, 89). The question raised concerning the horizon remains open. Neither the question of
birth nor the question of death has a place here, at least outside of the field
of a genetic phenomenology. As for the indubitability accorded to the retention of something that endures, it refers back to the self-constitution that
partakes of the intuitiveness that Kant denied to the a priori forms of sensibility. Such is the double valence of the "impression" in relation to which the

"reproductions"—termed "presentifications"[18] in the joint analysis of fantasies and memories—are organized. The present is to the presentification of something (Husserl speaks here of "impressional consciousness") what the temporal index is to the "objective" content of the memory. Inseparable. The correlation is made in the following manner: "Perceiving is the consciousness of an object. As consciousness, it is also an impression, something immanently present" (§42, 94). "Original consciousness" (94) is the name for this nexus, this center of "objective" presentation and of reflexive present. We can say of this original consciousness what one said of the absolute flow, which requires no other more original flow: "primary consciousness that has no further consciousness behind it in which it would be intended" (94). In this way, it is original in the sense of primary. In relation to this original consciousness, the transverse intentionality, belonging to the consciousness of something, can be considered an "objectivation": "Immanent time becomes objectivated into a time of the objects constituted in the immanent appearances thanks to the fact that an identical physical reality, which in all of its phases constantly presents itself in multiplicities of adumbrations, appears in the multiplicity of adumbrations of the sensation-contents understood as unities belonging to phenomenological time and, correlatively, in the multiplicity of adumbrations of the apprehensions of those contents in phenomenological time" (§43, 97). The relation is therefore inverted with respect to the analyses of the preceding section, in which the transverse intentionality aiming at something that endures serves as a support for the horizontal intentionality brought to the analysis by reflection. Have all the resistances offered by objective phenomenology to the absolutizing of the presence of the present fallen away? How could this unity of the flow be expressed without the support of some constituted objectivity? Husserl obstinately reverses the relation: in order to have something that endures, there must be a flow that is self-constituting. It is in this self-constitution that the enterprise of *pure* phenomenology finds its completion.

The primacy accorded in this way to the self-constitution of the temporal flow does not immediately make apparent the obstacles raised by this extreme subjectivism to the idea of the simultaneous constitution of individual memory and of collective memory. It still remains to be discovered that the transcendental consciousness constituted in this flow designates itself as an *ego* that is itself transcendental, in other words, that the pair *cogito/cogitatum* unfolds within the triad *ego/cogito/cogitatum*. This movement of radicalization, begun in *Ideen I*, is made fully explicit in the "Fourth Cartesian Meditation," precisely in preface to the problem of intersubjectivity. The transcendental consciousness of the flow designates itself there as the consciousness of a solitary I, resulting in the difficulty of passing from the solitary *ego* to the other, capable of becoming, in turn, an us.[19] What seems to be lacking in the egological approach is the recognition of a primordial absence, the absence of a foreign I, of an other who is always already implied in the solitary consciousness of self.

The question now arises whether this seemingly narrowly targeted lack of knowledge regarding absence does not affect the entire phenomenological enterprise, and whether the phenomenology of the consciousness of internal time does not already suffer from an equally intimate absence that would eventually have to be connected to that other absence, the absence of the other in the positing of *ego*.

It is worth noting that the question of absence in relation to presence, posed at the start of our inquiry by the Platonic theory of the *eikōn*, seems to have disappeared from the philosophical horizon of phenomenology. This relation of the present image to an absent thing constituted, as early as the period of the *Theaetetus*, the enigma par excellence of the representation of the past, the mark of anteriority compounding that of absence. We can thus wonder whether the dynamism that leads from one level of constitution to another, going beyond the constitution of the duration of something by means of the self-constitution of the temporal flow, is not equivalent to the progressive reduction of negativity in the very concept of time. A reduction that would find its counterpart in the reduction of the foreign in the constitution of the sphere of ownness.

This reduction of absence commences on the level of the "objective" phenomenology of memories, first with the analysis of the relations between perception, primary memory, and secondary memory, next with the analysis of the relations between memories and the other modalities of presentification. It cannot be said, however, that no hint of negativity is perceptible in one or the other of these eidetic analyses. Secondary memory, we said, is not primary memory, nor is the latter perception. What has just taken place has already begun to fade away, to disappear. To be sure, it is retained, but only what has already disappeared is retained. As for recollection, it no longer has any attachment to perception—it is clearly past; it is no longer, but the "just past" is already cessation; it has ceased appearing. In this sense, we can speak of increasing absence along the length of the memorial chain.

The interpretive hypothesis is then the following: the metacategory that works to obliterate these differences is "modification." Its major operation is to make retention the key concept of the entire temporal analysis at the expense of recollection. In terms of modification, retention is an extended, enduring perception. It "still" participates in the light of perception; its "no longer" is a "still." Whereas an Aristotelian phenomenology of recollection accords to the search for past time a place equal to that accorded to the presence to the soul of mnemonic affection, the Husserlian phenomenology of memory has difficulty proposing an equivalent to *anamnēsis*, to the reappropriation of lost time and hence to recognition as the attestation of identity in difference. We can attribute to the dominance of the metacategory of modification the general tendency of the phenomenology of memories to absorb secondary memory into primary memory, veritable temporal annex to the present. This absorption occurs by means of the idea of the retention of retentions, under which the mediating function of secondary memory is concealed. Secondary memory is finally true memory, if, as I believe, the fundamental temporal experience is that of distance and temporal depth. The result is that every dialectical movement is eliminated from the description, and all the polarities we have used to construct the phenomenology of memory (chapter 1, section 2) are in a sense flattened, dampened under the cloak of the idea of modification.

The second series of phenomenological analyses, concerning the place of memories in the family of presentification, offers greater resistance to the effort to reduce otherness: the entire series *Bild, Phantasie, Erinnerung* is situated on the side of presentification, hence of nonpresence or, more precisely, of nonpresentation (I am stressing once again here the nuance that protects the analysis of representations from being prematurely swallowed up by a hegemonic theory of the present, in the sense of now). In this instance, the opposition between actuality and inactuality appears primitive, irreducible. We can, with Husserl, interweave *Bild, Phantasie, Erinnerung* in a number of different ways: the interplay continues between the members of the great family of presentifications or re-presentations. The negative is present from the very start, with the "fantastic," the "fictional," and the "remembered." Husserlian phenomenology offers all the descriptive means to take account of this feature, but its dynamism pushes it to minimize its own discovery, even to cancel it.

This is the case it seems with the third section of the *Phenomenology of the Consciousness of Internal Time*. By virtue of the shift from the "objective" analysis of memories to the reflexive analysis of memories, negativity is definitively lost from sight, reduced to the character of receptiveness (*récipiscence*). There is one unmistakable sign of this: the undisputed primacy of the problematic of retention that, by means of reduplication, of iteration, absorbs to its own benefit the problematic of memory, to the point that only the retention of retentions will ever be in question.[20] Even more seriously: the problematic of double—transverse and horizontal—intentionality will be tied to retention alone. The problematic of unity can, therefore, be preserved on the level of the flow, despite the dependence of this problematic on the constitution of temporal objects (a tone, one and the same tone). The flow thus benefits from the privilege of self-identity. The residual differences are then relegated to the idea of multiple phases and a "continuity of adumbrations" (§35, 78). The concluding idea of a "continuity of appearance" (§36, 79) thus crowns the initial idea of modification.

The points of resistance to the triumph of presence are to be sought in several places: first, on the ultimate plane of constitution, with the imperious correlation between the horizontal intentionality of the flow in the course of constitution and the transverse intentionality of temporal objects, reflection never ceases to require the support of the "objective" structure of memories. Next, if we climb back up the slope of the *Phenomenology*, the split into primary memory and secondary memory resists the dictatorship of retention. Finally, there is the whole admirable phenomenology of the family of presentifications: fiction, depiction, memories, all attesting to a fundamental split between representation and presentation.

At the end of this appraisal, I return to my earlier suggestion: if we deny the internal negativity of self-consciousness, is this not secretly denying the primordiality of our relation to what is foreign in the egological constitution of self-consciousness? The question remains open.[21]

It is on this note of puzzlement that we leave our reading of the *Phenomenology of the Consciousness of Internal Time* in order to turn our attention toward the problematic that interests us here, namely, the relation between individual memory and collective memory.[22] We now move in one fell swoop to the other side of phenomenology, at the crossroads of the theory of transcendental consciousness and the theory of intersubjectivity. This occurs in the "Fifth Cartesian Meditation," when Husserl attempts to pass from the solitary *ego* to the other capable of becoming, in turn, an us.[23]

The *Phenomenology of the Consciousness of Internal Time* did not allow any projection of the path along which temporal experience could become shared experience. Phenomenology at this stage still shared with "psychologism," which it nonetheless castigated as the objectification of the psychic field, the problematic of a science of solitary consciousness. The question then arises whether the extension of transcendental idealism to intersubjectivity is capable of paving the way for a phenomenology of common memory.

The final paragraphs of the famous "Fifth Cartesian Meditation" do indeed propose the theme of the "communalization" of experience at all its levels of meaning, from the foundation of a common ground of physical nature (§55, 120–28) to the celebrated constitution of "higher intersubjective communities" (still called "personalities of a higher order"), a constitution resulting from a process of "social communalization" (§58, 132). We certainly do not encounter the word "common memory" in this broadened context of transcendental phenomenology, but it would be perfectly in harmony with the concept of "worlds of culture," understood in the sense of "concrete life-worlds in which the relatively or absolutely separate communities live their passive and active lives" (§58, 133).

We must measure the price to be paid for this extension of phenomenology to the domain of shared life. First the idea of transcendental idealism has to be radicalized to the point where solipsism is assumed as a legitimate objection; the "reduction of transcendental experience to the sphere of ownness" (§44, 92) represents in this respect the extreme point of internalizing experience. Temporal experience, so well described forty years earlier, is virtually assigned to this sphere of ownness. Its character of flow and of an infinitely open horizon is even explicitly underscored as early as the title of §46, "Ownness as the Sphere of the Actualities and Potentialities of the Stream of Subjective Processes" (100). This forced passage by way of the sphere of ownness is essential to the interpretation of what follows: the constitution of the other person as foreign will not be a mark of weakness but of the reinforcement of Husserlian transcendentalism, culminating in an egology. It is indeed "in" the sphere of ownness that the experience of the other as foreign is constituted, at the cost of the paradoxes I have presented elsewhere.[24] An intense competition plays out between two readings of the phenomenon that Husserl himself calls by the term *Paarung* ("pairing," §51, 112). On the one hand, it is indeed as foreign, that is as not-me, that the other is constituted, but it is "in" me that he is constituted. An unstable equilibrium is proposed between these two readings by the recourse to the concept of "appresentation," held to be an exceptional mode of analogy.[25] In this regard, we can say that the reduction to the sphere of ownness, and the theory of analogical apperception that follows from it, constitute the two obligatory points of anchorage for a subsequent phenomenology of the "communalization" of experience sketched out at the end of the "Fifth Cartesian Meditation." Sphere of ownness, pairing, and communalization thus form an unbroken conceptual chain, leading to the threshold of what could be called a phenomenological sociology, which I have ventured to link up with the key concepts that Max Weber placed at the start of his great work, *Economy and Society*, in the form of an interpretive sociology.[26]

I will spend no more time dwelling on the difficulties of principle that are related to pairing transcendental idealism with the theory of intersubjectivity. Instead, I would like rather to raise what I consider to be a prior question: in order to reach the notion of common experience, must we begin with the idea of ownness, pass through the the experience of the other, and finally proceed to a third operation, said to be the communalization of subjective experience? Is this chain truly irreversible? Is it not the speculative presupposition of transcendental idealism that imposes this irreversibility, rather than any constraint characteristic of phenomenological description? But is a pure—that is, presuppositionless—phenomenology either conceivable or feasible? I remain puzzled by this. I am not forgetting the distinction and—let's admit it—the leap that Hegel is forced to make when he passes from the theory of the Subjective Spirit to that of the Objective Spirit in the *Encyclopedia*, and, even earlier, in the heart of the *Phenomenology of Spirit*, on the threshold of the chapter on Spirit (chap. 6). There is a moment when one has to move from *I* to *we*. But is this moment not original, in the manner of a new beginning?

Irrespective of these difficulties, if we remain within the framework of the "Fifth Cartesian Meditation," the sociological concept of collective consciousness can result only from a second process of objectification on the level of intersubjective exchanges. We then have only to forget the process of constitution that gave birth to these entities in order to treat them, in turn, as subjects in which predicates can inhere, predicates similar to those we ascribe in the first instance to individual consciousness. We can then extend to these products of the objectification of intersubjective exchanges the analogical character that Husserl ascribes to every *alter ego* in relation to one's own *ego*. By reason of this analogical transfer we are authorized to use the first person in the plural form and ascribe to an us—whomever this may be—all the prerogatives of memory: mineness, continuity, the past-future polarity. With this hypothesis, which makes intersubjectivity bear all the weight of the constitution of collective entities, it is important, however, not to forget that it is only by analogy, and in relation to individual consciousness and its memory, that collective memory is held to be a collection of traces left by the events that have affected the course of history of the groups concerned, and that it is accorded the power to place on stage these common memories, on the occasion of holidays, rites, and public celebrations. Once this analogical transfer is recognized, nothing prevents our considering these higher-order intersubjective communities as the subject in which their memories inhere, or our speaking of their temporality or their historicity; in short, our extending the mineness of memories analogically to the idea of our possessing of our collective memories. This is enough to give written history a point of anchorage in the phenomenological existence of groups. For the phenomenologist, the history of "mentalités," of "cultures," demands no less, but also no more.

## THE EXTERNAL GAZE: MAURICE HALBWACHS

Several decades after the publication of *The Collective Memory*,[27] Maurice Halbwachs has benefited from unexpected public attention.[28] This sort of consecration cannot leave us indifferent to the extent that history's claim to support, correct, critique, even to include memory can only refer to the forms of collective memory. This collective memory constitutes the appropriate counterpart to history.

We owe to Halbwachs the bold intellectual decision to attribute memory directly to a collective entity, which he names a group or society. He had, to be sure, already forged the concept of "the social frameworks of memory" before *The Collective Memory*.[29] Then, it was strictly as a sociologist, in the footsteps of Émile Durkheim, that he employed memory in the third person and endowed it with structures accessible to objective observation. The advance made in *The Collective Memory* was to draw the reference to collective memory out of the very work of personal memory engaged in recalling its memories. The chapter titled "Individual Memory and Collective Memory" is written from start to finish in the first person singular, in quasi-autobiographical style. This text basically says: to remember, we need others. It adds: not only is the type of memory we possess not derivable in any fashion from experience in the first person singular, in fact the order of derivation is the other way around. The objective of my critical reading is to test this extreme consequence. But it must first be said that it is on the basis of a subtle analysis of the individual experience of belonging to a group, and through the instruction received from others, that individual memory takes possession of itself. This being the strategy selected, it is not surprising that the opening theme is an appeal to the testimony of others. It is essentially along the path of recollection and recognition, the two principal mnemonic phenomena of our typology of memories, that we encounter the memory of others. In this context, such testimony is not considered as it is uttered by someone in order to be collected by someone else, but as it is received by me from someone else as information about the past. In this regard, the earliest memories encountered along this path are shared memories, common memories (what Edward Casey places under the title "Reminiscing"). They allow us to affirm that "in reality, we are never alone"; and in this way the thesis of solipsism is set aside, even as a tentative hypothesis. The most remarkable among these memories are those of places visited together with others. They offer the special opportunity of setting oneself mentally back in this or that group. Starting with the role of the testimony of others in recalling memories, we then move step-by-step to memories that we have as members of a group; they require a shift in our viewpoint, which we are well able to perform. In this way, we gain access to events reconstructed for us by others. It is then by their place in an ensemble that others are defined. A school class is, in this respect, a privileged place for this shift in viewpoint in memory. Generally speaking, every group assigns places. And these are retained or formed in memory. Already, earlier in our discussion, memories of trips served as examples of this change of place.[30]

The essay enters its critical phase by attacking what could be called the psychologizing thesis, represented at that time by Charles Blondel, according to which individual memory is held to be the necessary and sufficient condition for the recollection and recognition of memories. In the background the shadow of Bergson is cast and, close by, sounds the clash of competition with historians for preeminence in the field of the human sciences, then in a period of full expansion. The battle is therefore engaged on the very terrain of the central mnemonic phenomenon. Negative argument: when we no longer belong to the group in the memory of which a given recollection is preserved, our own memory is weakened for lack of external supports. Positive argument: "a person remembers only by situating himself within the viewpoint of one or several groups and one or several currents of collective thought" (*The Collective Memory*, 33).[31] In other words, one does not remember alone. Here, Halbwachs directly attacks the sensualist thesis that the origin of a memory lies in a sensible intuition preserved as such and recalled as identical. A memory such as this is not only impossible to find, it is inconceivable. Childhood memories are an excellent reference in this regard. They take place in socially marked places: the garden, the house, the basement, and so on, all places that Bachelard will cherish: "The image is still situated within the framework of the family, because it was initially enacted there and has never left it" (37). And again: "For the child the world is never empty of human beings, of good and evil influences" (41). By this we understand that the social framework ceases to be simply an objective notion and becomes a dimension inherent in the work of recollection. In this regard, adult memories do not differ from childhood memories. They make us travel from group to group, from framework to framework, in both a spatial and a temporal sense. Recognizing a friend from a portrait sends us back to the milieu where we have seen him. What proves to be impossible to find and inconceivable is the idea of a unified "internal series" in which some "internal, or subjective, connection" (*La Mémoire collective*, 82–83) would alone intervene in explaining the reappearance of a memory. In short, it is the connectedness of memory, dear to Dilthey (whom Halbwachs seems not to have known) that has to be abandoned, and so too the idea that "what is held to found the coherence of memories is the internal unity of consciousness" (83). The fact that we think we observe something like this in ourselves is certain; "but we are the victims here of a rather natural illusion" (83). It is explained by the fact that the influence of the social setting has become imperceptible to us. In the chapter on forgetting, we shall have the opportunity to discuss this amnesia characteristic of social action. It is only, Halbwachs notes, when rival influences battle within us that we take notice of them. But even then the originality of the impression or the thoughts that we experience is not explained by our natural spontaneity, but "by the meetings, within us, of currents that have an objective reality outside of us" (83).

The main point of the chapter consists, therefore, in denouncing the illusory attribution of memories to ourselves, when we claim to be their original owners.

But does Halbwachs not cross an invisible line, the line separating the thesis "no one ever remembers alone" from the thesis "we are not an authentic subject of the attribution of memories"? Does not the very act of "placing oneself" in a group and of "displacing" oneself or shifting from group to group presuppose a spontaneity capable of establishing a continuation with itself? If not, society would be without any social actors.[32] If, in the final analysis, the idea of spontaneity in the recollections of an individual subject can be denounced as an illusion, it is because "our perceptions of the external world follow one another in accordance with the very order of succession of facts and material phenomena. It is the order of nature, then, that penetrates our mind and governs the course of its states. How could it be otherwise since our representations are only the reflections of things. A reflection is not explained by an earlier reflection but by what it reproduces in that very moment" (85). There are thus only two principles of connection: that of the "facts and material phenomena" and that of collective memory. Now the former principle is reflected in consciousness only in the present: "Sensible intuition is always in the present" (84). On the side of consciousness, it follows that only "the very divisions presented by reality" govern the sensible order without any possibility of invoking some "spontaneous and mutual attraction among the states of consciousness related in this way" (85). In a word, "a reflection is not explained by an earlier reflection but by what it reproduces in that very moment" (85). So we must turn to the side of collective memory to account for the logics of coherence presiding over the perception of the world. Unexpectedly, we find a Kantian argument made on behalf of social structures. And we slip back into the old use of the notion of framework: it is within the frameworks of collective thought that we find the means of evoking the series and the connection of objects. Collective thought is alone capable of this operation.

It remains to be explained how the sentiment of the unity of self derives from this collective thought. It occurs through the intermediary of the consciousness we have at every instant of belonging at the same time to different milieus; but this consciousness exists only in the present. The only concession that the author makes is providing every consciousness with the power to place itself within the viewpoint of the group and, in addition, to move from one group to another. But the concession is rapidly withdrawn: this ultimate attribution is still an illusion resulting from our habituation to social pressure, which makes us believe that we are the authors of our beliefs: "Therefore most social influences we obey usually remain unperceived" (*The Collective Memory*, 45). This defect in apprehension is the main source of illusion. When social influences are in opposition to one another and when this opposition itself is unperceived, we convince ourselves that our act is independent of all these influences because it is exclusively dependent on no one of them: "We do not perceive that our act really results from their action in concert, that our act is governed by the law of causality" (49).

Is this the final word of this study, so remarkable in other ways, rigidifying itself in the end into in a surprising dogmatism? I do not think so. The starting point for the entire analysis cannot be erased by its conclusion: it was in the personal act of recollection that the mark of the social was initially sought and then found. This act of recollection is in each case ours. To believe this, to attest to it, cannot be denounced as a radical illusion. Yet Halbwachs himself believes that he can place himself in the position of the social bond, when he critiques it and contests it. In fact, we find in Halbwachs's own text the resources for a critique directed against him. This would be the quasi-Leibnizian use of the idea of viewpoint, of perspective: "While The Collective Memory endures and draws strength from its base in a coherent body of people, it is individuals as group members who remember. . . . I would readily acknowledge that each memory is a viewpoint on The Collective Memory, that this viewpoint changes as my position changes, that this position itself changes as my relationships to other milieus change" (48). It is Halbwachs's very use of the notions of place and change of place that defeat a quasi-Kantian use of the idea of framework, unilaterally imposed on every consciousness.[33]

## THREE SUBJECTS OF THE ATTRIBUTION OF MEMORIES: EGO, COLLECTIVES, CLOSE RELATIONS

The two preceding series of discussions suggest the same negative conclusion: whether we consider the sociology of collective memory or the phenomenology of individual memory, neither has any greater success than the other in deriving the apparent legitimacy of the adverse positions from the strong position each, respectively, holds: on one side, the cohesion of the states of consciousness of the individual ego; on the other, the capacity of collective entities to preserve and recall common memories. What is more, the attempts at derivation are not even symmetrical; this is why there appear to be no areas of overlap between a phenomenological derivation of collective memory and a sociological derivation of individual memory.

At the end of this inquiry into a major aporia of the problematic of memory, I propose to explore the complementary resources contained within the two antagonistic approaches, resources masked, on the one hand, by the idealist prejudice of Husserlian phenomenology (at least in the published part of his work) and, on the other, the positivist prejudice of sociology in the glory of its youth. I will seek, first of all, to identify the linguistic region where the two discourses may be made to intersect.

Ordinary language, reworked by means of the tools offered by a semantics and a pragmatics of discourse, offers valuable assistance here with the notion of ascribing psychical operations to someone. Among the features we noted at the start of our analyses is the grammatical use of possessive forms such as "my," "mine," and all the rest, in both the singular and the plural. In this respect, asserting the possession of memories as one's own constitutes in linguistic practice a model of mineness for all psychical phenomena. The text of the *Confessions* is strewn with these indices of appropriation, which the rhetorical mode of confession encouraged. But it was John Locke who, by virtue of the flexibility of the English language, began to theorize the operation by introducing the expression "appropriate" as well as a series of semantic moves with the word "own," taken in its pronominal or verbal form. Locke noted in this connection that juridical language, by reason of its "forensic" character, introduced a certain distance between the property appropriated and the owner. This expression can be associated with a plurality of possessors (e.g., my own self) and even a nominalized self: the self. In addition, to the expression "appropriate" are joined ones such as "impute," "accountable" (take upon one's own account, be accountable, or hold someone else accountable). In fact, a juridical theory of *ascription* has been constructed on this basis, which contributes to elucidating the concepts of imputation and responsibility.[34] However, the use of the term "appropriation" in a juridical context must not limit its semantic scope. In *Oneself as Another* I tried to restore part of this range to appropriation in the context of the relation between action and its agent.[35] Here, I propose to pursue this opening further by extending it to memories, both in the passive form of the presence to mind of a memory and in the active form of the search for memories. These operations, in the broadest sense of the term including *pathos* and *praxis*, are the objects of an attribution, of an appropriation, of an imputation, of taking something into account, in short, of an ascription. This extension of the idea of appropriation from a theory of action to a theory of memory is made possible by a general thesis relating to the totality of the psychical field, a thesis inspired by P. F. Strawson's work, *Individuals*.[36] Among the positions developed by Strawson concerning the general relations between practical predicates in particular and mental predicates in general, there is one that directly interests us: it is a characteristic of these predicates that, whenever they are attributable to oneself, they can be attributed to someone other than oneself. This mobility of attribution implies three distinct propositions: (1) the attribution can be suspended or performed; (2) these predicates retain the same sense in two distinct situations of attribution; (3) this multiple attribution preserves the asymmetry between self-ascribable and other-ascribable.

According to the first presupposition, attribution compensates in a sense for an inverse operation, which consists in suspending the attribution to someone, with the sole aim of providing a stable descriptive status to the mental predicates considered apart from attribution. This is what we in fact did without saying so, when, in the preceding two chapters, we held memories to be a certain sort of image and recollection to be an enterprise of searching, to be crowned—or not—with recognition. Plato, speaking of the *eikōn*, did not ask to whom the memory "happens." Aristotle, investigating the operation of recollection, did not inquire about the one who performs the task. Our own phenomenological investigation, concerning the relations between remembering, memorizing, and commemorating, was conducted in line with this abstention from attribution. Memory is, in this regard, both a particular case and a singular case. A particular case, inasmuch as mnemonic phenomena are mental phenomena among others: we speak of them as affections and as actions, and it is as such that they are attributed to anyone, to each one, and that their sense can be understood apart from any explicit attribution. It is under this form that they also enter into the thesaurus of the mental concepts explored by literature, sometimes in the third person of the novel in he or she, sometimes in the first person of autobiography ("I long went to bed early"), or in the second person, invoking or imploring ("Lord, remember us"). The same suspension of attribution constitutes the condition for the attribution of mental phenomena to fictional characters. This aptitude of mental predicates to be understood in themselves in the suspension of all explicit attribution constitutes what can be called the "psychical," what in English is termed "mind": the psychical, the mind is the repertoire of mental predicates available in a given culture.[37] Having said this, the case of mnemonic phenomena is singular in more than one sense. First, the attribution adheres so closely to the affection constitutive of the presence of a memory and to the action of the mind in finding it that the suspension of the attribution seems particularly abstract. The pronominal form of the verbs of memory attests to this close adherence that makes remembering something (*se souvenir de quelque chose*) remembering oneself (*se souvenir de soi*). This is why the tiny distinction, marked by the difference between the verb "se souvenir" (to remember) and the substantive "souvenir" (a memory, memories) can remain invisible to the point of going unnoticed. The adherence of attribution to the identification and the naming of mnemonic phenomena doubtless explains the ease with which the thinkers of the tradition of inwardness were able to assign memory directly to the sphere of the self.[38] In this regard, the school of inwardness can be characterized by a denial of distantiation by reason of which we can, to use Husserl's expression, distinguish the noema, "what" is remembered, from the noesis, the act of remembering, reflected in its "who." In this way, mineness could be designated as the primary distinctive feature of personal memory. This tenacious adherence of the "who" to the "what" is what makes the transfer of memories from one consciousness to another so difficult.[39] Yet it is the suspension of attribution that permits the phenomenon of multiple attribution, which constitutes the second presupposition underscored by Strawson: if a phenomenon is self-ascribable, it must be other-ascribable. This is how we express ourselves in ordinary language and at a higher reflexive level. Ascription to others is therefore found to be not superimposed upon self-ascription but coextensive with it. We cannot do the one without doing the other. What Husserl called *Paarung*, "pairing," involved in the perception of others, is the silent operation that, on the pre-predicative level, makes possible what linguistic semantics terms other-ascription, attribution to others. What in other contexts is termed *Einfühlung*, that sort of affective imagination through which we project ourselves into the lives of others, is not something different from *Paarung* on the plane of perception, nor from other-ascription on the plane of language.

There remains the third presupposition: the asymmetry between self-ascription and other-ascription, at the very heart of multiple ascription. This asymmetry involves the modalities of the "fulfillment"—or confirmation—of ascription. In the case of the foreign, the confirmation—that is its name—remains conjectural; its rests on the comprehension and interpretation of verbal and nonverbal expressions on the plane of the behavior of others. These indirect operations belong to what Carlo Ginzburg will later call the "evidential method";[40] it is guided by the affective imagination—by the *Einfühlung*—that carries us in the direction of the lived experience of others, in the mode of what Husserl termed "appresentation," and that cannot be equivalent to an actual "re-living." In the case of self-ascription, the "fulfillment"—this is its name—is direct, immediate, certain; it places on my acts the mark of possession, of distantless mineness. A prethematic, prediscursive, antepredicative adherence underlies the judgment of attribution, to the point that it renders imperceptible the distance between the self and its memories, and lends legitimacy to the theses of the school of inwardness. The judgment of attribution becomes explicit only when it replies, on the plane of reflection, to the suspension of the spontaneous self-ascription of mnemonic phenomena. This abstraction is not arbitrary, but is constitutive of the linguistic moment of memory as it is promoted by the practice of ordinary language, as it permits naming and describing distinctly the "mental," mind, as such. It is, moreover, this subtle distantiation that justifies the use of the very term "fulfillment," belonging to a general theory of meaning. It is through these features that the "fulfillment" of the meaning "self-ascribable" is distinguished from the "appresentation" characteristic of the meaning "other-ascribable." It is not conjectural, indirect, but certain, direct. An error can be noticed after the fact in the conjecture concerning others, an illusion in self-ascription. Error and illusion, taken in this sense, stem from corrective procedures themselves just as asymmetrical as the modalities of the judgment of attribution, the expectation of an asymmetrical verification giving in each case a different meaning to attribution: self-ascribable on the one hand, other-ascribable on the other. On this point, Husserl's considerations in the "Fifth Meditation" concerning the asymmetry in fulfillment and those belonging to a theory of the multiple ascription of mental predicates overlap perfectly.

It is true that recognizing this asymmetry at the very heart of the ascription of mnemonic phenomena to someone seems to cast us back to sea. Does not the specter of the discordance between individual memory and collective memory reappear at the very moment we think we have found safe harbor? This is not the case if we do not separate the third presupposition from the other two: asymmetry is an additional feature of the capacity of multiple ascription, which presupposes the suspension of ascription allowing the description of mnemonic phenomena just as with every other mental phenomenon apart from the attribution to anyone. The problem of two memories is not abolished. It is framed. What distinguishes self-ascription is appropriation under the sign of mineness, of what is my own. The appropriate linguistic form is self-designation, which, in the case of action, bears the specific form of imputation. But we saw with Locke that we can speak of imputation wherever there is a self and consciousness. Upon this broadened basis, one can consider appropriation as the self-ascribable modality of attribution. And it is this capacity to designate oneself as the possessor of one's own memories that leads to attributing to others the same mnemonic phenomena as to oneself, whether by the path of *Paarung*, of *Einfühlung*, of other-ascription, or something else.

It is against the backdrop of these linked presuppositions concerning the notion of attributing mental phenomena in general, and mnemonic phenomena in particular, to someone that we can attempt a rapprochement between the phenomenological thesis and the sociological thesis.

A phenomenology of memory, one less subject to what I venture to term an idealist prejudice, can draw from the competition presented to it by the sociology of memory an incitement to develop in the direction of a direct phenomenology applied to social reality, which includes the participation of subjects capable of designating themselves as being, to different degrees of reflective consciousness, the authors of their acts. These developments are encouraged by the existence of features characterizing the exercise of memory that contain the mark of the other. In its declarative phase, memory enters into the region of language; memories spoken of, pronounced are already a kind of discourse that the subject engages in with herself. What is pronounced in this discourse occurs in the common language, most often in the mother tongue, which, it must be said, is the language of others. But this elevation of memory to language is not without difficulties. This is the place to recall the traumatic experiences mentioned above in connection with thwarted memory. Overcoming obstacles through remembering, which makes memory itself a work, can be aided by the intervention of a third party, the psychoanalyst among others. The latter can be said to "authorize" the patient to remember, to borrow an expression from Marie Balmary.[41] This authorization, which Locke termed "forensic," is linked to the work of memory performed by the patient—better called the analysand—who attempts to bring symptoms, phantasms, dreams, and so on, to language in an effort to reconstruct a comprehensible mnemonic chain, acceptable to him or to her. Set on the path of orality in this way, remembering is also set on the path of the narrative, whose public structure is obvious. It is along this line of development that we shall encounter, at the start of the second part, the procedures of testimony presented before a third party, received by this party, and eventually deposited in an archive.

The entry of memory into the public sphere is no less remarkable in the phenomena of identification that we have encountered in an arena close to that of thwarted memory, namely, manipulated memory: the comparison with others then appeared to us as a major source of personal insecurity. Even before taking into account the grounds for fragility related to the confrontation with others, we would have to pay the attention it merits to the gesture consisting in giving a name to one who comes into the world. Each of us bears a name that we have not given to ourselves, but have received from another: in our culture, this is a patronym that situates me along a line of filiation, and a given name that distinguishes me from my siblings. This word of the other, placed upon an entire life, at the price of the difficulties and the conflicts we are familiar with, confers a linguistic support, a decidedly self-referential turn, to all the operations of personal appropriation gravitating around the mnemonic nucleus.

However, it is in making itself directly into a phenomenology of social reality that phenomenology was able to penetrate into the closed field of sociology. These developments drew support from Husserl's last great work, *The Crisis of the European Sciences and Transcendental Philosophy*, in which attention is directed to the prepredicative aspects of the "life-world," which is not identified in any way with a solitary, even less a solipsistic, condition but includes from the outset a communal form.[42] This extension of phenomenology to the social sphere resulted in a remarkable work, that of Alfred Schutz.[43] Schutz does not engage in the laborious stages of the perception of others in the manner of the "Fifth Meditation." For him, the experience of others is a given as primal as the experience of the self. Its immediacy is less that of cognitive evidence than that of practical faith. We believe in the existence of others because we act with them and on them and are affected by their actions. The phenomenology of the social world, in this way, penetrates directly into the order of life in common, of living-together in which acting and suffering subjects are from the outset members of a community or a collectivity. A phenomenology of belonging is then free to provide itself with its own conceptual system without any concern with deriving it from an egological pole. This phenomenology can readily be combined with an interpretive sociology like that of Max Weber, for whom the "orientation toward others" is a basic structure of social action.[44] And, at a later stage, with a political philosophy like that of Hannah Arendt, for whom plurality is a basic principle of practical philosophy. One of the developments of this phenomenology of social reality directly concerns the phenomenology of memory on the plane of social reality: it is addressed to the transgenerational phenomenon that is inscribed in the intermediate zone that we will discuss in conclusion.[45] Alfred Schutz devotes an important study to the connection formed by the periods of contemporaries, predecessors, and successors.[46] The period of contemporaries is the pivot here: it expresses "the simultaneity or quasi-simultaneity of the other self's consciousness with my own" (143); in the character of its experience, it is marked by the phenomenon of "growing old together" (163), which places two unfolding time-spans in a relation of synergy. One temporal flow accompanies another, as long as they both endure. The shared experience of the world rests upon a community of time as well as space. The originality of this phenomenology of shared memory resides principally in the arrangement of degrees of personalization, and inversely of anonymity, between the poles of an authentic "us" and that of "one," of "them." The worlds of predecessors and successors extend in the two directions of the past and the future, of memory and of expectation, those remarkable features of living together, first deciphered in the phenomenon of contemporaneousness.

This extension of phenomenology to the social sphere places it, we have said, alongside sociology. Sociology, in some of its contemporary manifestations, has taken a step in the direction of phenomenology parallel to that taken by phenomenology in the direction of sociology. I will limit myself here to a few brief remarks, inasmuch as it is in the field of historiography that these changes have produced the effects that most matter to me. Three observations can serve as stepping stones. First, it is in the field of action theory that the developments I will echo in the second part of this work have been most noteworthy. With Bernard Lepetit, I emphasize the formation of the social bond within the framework of interactive relations and on the identities constructed on this basis.[47] Initiatives and constraints develop their respective dialectics here. Some distance will thus be taken with respect to a phenomenology too closely tied to perceptual and, in general, cognitive phenomena. Phenomena of representation—among these mnemonic phenomena—will be commonly associated with social practices. Second, the problems posed by the sociology of collective memory will be reformulated by historians in connection with the temporal dimension of social phenomena: the layering of long, middle, and short-term time-spans by Braudel and the historians of the *Annales* school, as well as considerations regarding the relations between structure, conjuncture, and event all belong to this renewed interest on the part of historians in problems faced by sociologists on the level of collective memory. The discussion will thus be resituated on the border between collective memory and history. Finally, my last remark: considerations by historians regarding the "interplay of scales" will provide the opportunity for a redistribution of mnemonic phenomena between the ranks of microhistory and of macrohistory.[48] In this regard, history will offer schemata for mediating between the opposite poles of individual memory and collective memory.

I would like to conclude this chapter and part 1 with a suggestion. Does there not exist an intermediate level of reference between the poles of individual memory and collective memory, where concrete exchanges operate between the living memory of individual persons and the public memory of the communities to which we belong? This is the level of our close relations, to whom we have a right to attribute a memory of a distinct kind. These close relations, these people who count for us and for whom we count, are situated along a range of varying distances in the relation between self and others. Varying distances but also variation in the active and passive modes of the interplay of distantiation and closeness that makes proximity a dynamic relationship ceaselessly in motion: drawing near, feeling close. Proximity would then be the counterpart to friendship, that *philia* celebrated by the ancient Greeks, halfway between the solitary individual and the citizen, defined by his contribution to the *politeia*, to the life and activity of the *polis*. In this manner, these close relations occupy the middle-ground between the self and the "they," from which the relations of contemporaneousness described by Alfred Schutz are derived. Close relations are others as fellow beings, privileged others.

What is the trajectory of memory attribution along which close relations are located? The tie to them cuts crosswise and selectively through filial and conjugal relations as well as through social relations dispersed in accordance with multiple orders of belonging[49] or respective orders of standing.[50] In what sense do they count for me from the viewpoint of shared memory? To the contemporaneousness of "growing old together," they add a special note concerning the two "events" that limit a human life, birth and death. The first escapes my memory, the second cuts short my plans. And both of them interest society only in terms of public records and from the demographic point of view of the replacement of generations. But both events were, or will be, of importance to my close relations. Some of them will deplore my death. But before that, some rejoiced at my birth and celebrated on that occasion the miracle of natality,[51] and the bestowal of the name by which I will call myself my entire life. In the meantime, my close relations are those who approve of my existence and whose existence I approve of in the reciprocity and equality of esteem. This mutual approbation expresses the shared assertion that each one makes regarding his or her powers and lack of powers, what I termed attestation in *Oneself as Another*. What I expect from my close relations is that they approve of what I attest: that I am able to speak, act, recount, impute to myself the responsibility for my actions. Here again, Augustine is the master. I read in book 10 of the *Confessions*: "This is what I wish my true brothers to feel in their hearts [*animus...fraternus*]. I do not speak of strangers or of 'alien foes who make treacherous promises, and lift their hands in perjury.' But my true brothers are those who rejoice for me in their hearts when they find good in me [*qui cum approbat me*], and grieve for me when they find sin. They are my true brothers, because whether they see good in me or evil, they love me still. To such as these, I shall reveal myself [*indicabo me*]" (*Confessions*, 10.4, 209). In my turn, I include among my close relations those who disapprove of my actions, but not of my existence.

It is, therefore, not with the single hypothesis of the polarity between individual memory and collective memory that we enter into the field of history, but with the hypothesis of the threefold attribution of memory: to oneself, to one's close relations, and to others.

# PART II

## *History, Epistemology*

*I, Herodotus of Halicarnassus, am here setting forth
my history [historiē], that time may not draw the color from what man has
brought into being, nor those great and wonderful deeds, manifested by both
Greeks and barbarians, fail of their report, and, together with all this,
the reason why they fought one another.*

*The chroniclers [logioi] among the Persians say that it was the
Phoenicians who were the cause of the falling-out . . .*

§   Herodotus, *The History*[1]

*The second part* of this work is devoted to the epistemology of historical knowledge. Here I want to situate this stage of my inquiry and its principal interconnections.

On one side, I consider the phenomenology of memory to be ended, making reservation for the cultural variations that historical knowledge, when integrated into individual and collective memory, may introduce into self-understanding in the mnemonic mode. A subtle combination of those features of memory we can call transhistorical and its variable expressions over the course of history will have to be taken into account when the time comes. This will be one of the themes of the hermeneutics of the historical condition to be dealt with in part 3, chapter 2. Before that, however, history will have to have attained its fully autonomous status among the human sciences, following the vow that orients this middle section of my work. Then, on a second degree level of reflection, the question of the internal limits of a philosophical project that often remains tacit can be posed. This question has to do not only with the epistemological autonomy of historical research but also with the self-sufficiency of history's own self-awareness, in accord with the favorite expression that presided over the birth of and apology for the German school of history. It is within the framework of this reflection on the limits stemming from a critical philosophy of history that the confrontation between intending the truth of history[2] and the aim of that veracity or, as I shall put it, the intention of being faithful to memory (part 3, chapter 1) can be brought to a good ending. Until then, the status of history as regards memory will be held in suspense without my, for all that, forbidding myself from noting along the way the resurgence of the aporias of memory in their cognitive and practical aspects, principally the aporia of the representation of an absent something that once happened, along with that of the use and abuse to which memory lends itself as actively exercised and practiced. Yet this obstinate return of the aporias of memory at the heart of historical knowledge cannot take the place of a solution of the problem of the relations between knowledge and the practice of history and the experience of lived memory, even if this solution were to present ultimately indecisive features. Nevertheless, these features will have to be painfully won on the field of battle of a reflection carried to its limits.

It remains the case that the autonomy of historical knowledge in relation to the mnemonic phenomenon remains the major presupposition of a coherent epistemology of history both as a scientific discipline and a literary one. At least this is the presupposition assumed in this middle part of this work.

I have adopted the expression the "historical"—or better "historiographical"—operation to define the field traversed by the following epistemological analysis. I owe it to Michel de Certeau in his contribution to the large-scale project edited by Jacques Le Goff and Pierre Nora under the title *Faire de l'histoire*.[3] Beyond this, I have also adopted the broader lines of the triadic structure of Certeau's essay, although I give them different contents on some important points. I first tried out this clear and insightful tripartite approach in an essay requested by the Institut International de Philosophie.[4] Keeping this double influence in mind, I shall call the "documentary phase" the one that runs from the declarations of eyewitnesses to the constituting of archives, which takes as its epistemological program the establishing of documentary proof (chapter 1). Next I shall call the explanation/understanding [*explicative/compréhensive*] phase the one that has to do with the multiple uses of the connective "because" responding to the question "why?": Why did things happen like that and not otherwise? The double term "explanation/understanding" is indicative of my refusing the opposition between explanation and understanding that all too often has prevented grasping the treatment of the historical "because" in its full amplitude and complexity (chapter 2). Finally, I shall call the "representative phase" the putting into literary or written form of discourse offered to the readers of history. If the major epistemological crux occurs in the explanation/understanding phase, it does not exhaust itself there inasmuch as it is the phase of writing that plainly states the historian's intention, which is to represent the past just as it happened—whatever meaning may be assigned to this "just as." It is also at this third phase that the major aporias of memory return in force to the foreground, the aporia of the representation of an absent thing that occurred previously and that of a practice devoted to the active recalling of the past, which history elevates to the level of a reconstruction (chapter 3).

At the beginning of each of these three chapters in part 2 I shall lay out the program belonging to each of these phases. Here I shall confine myself to a more specific statement of the historian's threefold commitment.

I have proposed the word "phase" to characterize the three segments of the historiographical operation. There is no need for any equivocation concerning the use of this term. It is not a question of distinct chronological stages, but of methodological moments, interwoven with one another. As will be repeated, no one consults an archive apart from some project of explanation, without some hypothesis for understanding. And no one undertakes to explain a course of events without making use of some express literary form of a narrative, rhetorical, or imaginative character. Any idea of chronological succession must be banished from our use of the term "operative phase." It is only in the discourse undertaken here on the moments of the unfolding of the historiographical operation that these phases become stages, successive steps in a trajectory that unrolls its linearity. We can completely avoid such equivocation regarding succession if we speak of levels, a term that evokes superposition, stacking things up. But we need to keep an eye out for another equivocation as well, that of a relation between an infra- and a super-structure, much used and abused by vulgar Marxism (which I am not confusing with Marx's major works). Each of the three operations of the historiographical operation stands as a base for the other two, inasmuch as they serve successively as referents for the other two. In the end, I have preferred the term "phase" inasmuch as, in the absence of a chronological order of succession, it underscores the progression of this operation as having do to with the historian's intention of a true reconstruction of the past. It is only in the third phase—as has already been suggested—that the intention to represent the truth of past things openly declares itself, through which the cognitive and practical project of history as it is written by professional historians defines itself over against memory. A third term, which I preferred in my preliminary work, is "program." It works well to characterize the specificity of the immanent project in each step along the way. In this sense, it has an analytic privilege in regard to the other two terms. This is why I have made recourse to it whenever the accent is placed on the nature of the operations undertaken at each level.

The final word of this general orientation will be about the term "historiography." Until recently, it designated by preference the epistemological inquiry such as we are undertaking here following its threefold rhythm. I use it, as does Certeau, to designate the very operation in which historical knowing is grasped at work. This choice of vocabulary has a major advantage that does not appear if we reserve this term for the writing phase of the operation, as suggested by the very composition of the word: historiography or history writing. In order to preserve the amplitude of the term "historiographical," I will not call the third phase the writing of history, but instead the literary or scriptural phase, when it is a question of the exposition, presentation, or exhibiting of the historian's intention taken in terms of the unity of its phases, that is, the present representation of absent, past things. Writing, in effect, is the threshold of language that historical knowing has already crossed, in distancing itself from memory to undertake the threefold adventure of archival research, explanation, and representation. History is writing from one end to another. And in this regard, archives constitute the first writing that confronts history, before it completes itself in the literary mode of "scripturality." Explanation/understanding thus finds itself encased, upstream and downstream, by two writings. It gathers energy from the former and anticipates the energy of the latter.

But it is above all the setting out in writing of the historian's knowledge starting from the upstream side of archives that gives rise to the question of confidence that cannot be answered from inside the epistemology of historical knowledge, the question of what finally becomes of the relation between history and memory. This is the question of confidence that a critical philosophy of history has the task, if not of resolving, at least of articulating and considering. But it is posed in an originary manner by the entry into writing of the historian's knowledge. It floats as the unsaid over the whole undertaking. For me, who knows what follows, this unsaid, which will be taken up in part 3, needs to be left in suspense, in reserve, something like a methodological *epoché*.

To indicate this setting in reserve, in the most decidedly interrogative, skeptical way, I have chosen to place in the position of prelude a kind of parody of the Platonic myth from the *Phaedrus* dedicated to the invention of writing. Inasmuch as the gift of writing is held by this myth to be the antidote to memory, and therefore a kind of challenge opposed by the truth claim of history to memory's vow of trustworthiness, it can be taken as the paradigm for every dream of substituting history for memory, as I shall consider further in the beginning of part 3. Thus, it was in order to underscore the gravity of a cultural choice from which there was no going back, that of writing history, that I have amused myself in my own fashion, with what was first due to Plato, in reinterpreting, if not rewriting, the myth his *Phaedrus* recounts concerning the invention of writing. The question whether the *pharmakon* of history-writing is remedy or poison, to take one of the propositions of the myth in the *Phaedrus*, will continue to accompany our epistemological inquiry as a kind of background music before breaking forth in full force on the reflective plane of the critical philosophy of history.

Why refer to myth, even in the preliminary material of a highly rational epistemological analysis? In order to confront the aporia in which every inquiry bearing on the birth, the beginning, the beginnings of historical knowledge gets lost. This perfectly legitimate inquiry, to which we owe many worthwhile works,[5] rests, insofar as it itself is historical, on a kind of performative contradiction, namely, that the writing of beginnings presupposes itself as already existing in order to think of itself at its birth. We need therefore to distinguish origin from beginning. We can seek to date a beginning in a historical time scanned by chronology. This beginning is perhaps not discoverable, as the antinomies articulated by Kant in the Dialectic of the *Critique of Pure Reason* suggest. We can, of course, indicate something as a start in a critical treatment of testimonies, but this is not a beginning of the mode of historical thinking, if we mean by this a temporalization of common experience in a way irreducible to that of memory, even collective memory. This unassignable anteriority is that of the inscription that, in one form or another, has always accompanied orality, as Jacques Derrida has magisterially demonstrated in his *Of Grammatology*.[6] Human beings have spaced their signs, at the same time—if this has a meaning—that they have woven them together in terms of the temporal continuity of the verbal flow. This is why the beginning of the historian's scripturality is undiscoverable. The circular character of assigning a historical beginning to historical knowledge invites us to distinguish, at the heart of the amphibolous concept of birth, between beginning and origin. The beginning consists in a constellation of dated events, set by the historian at the head of the historical process that will be the history of history. It is toward this beginning or these beginnings that the historian of the birth of history advances by a retrospective movement that produces itself within the already constituted setting of historical knowledge. The origin is something else again: it designates the upsurge of the act of taking a distance that makes possible the whole enterprise and therefore also its beginning in time. This upsurge is always current and always already there. History continues to be born from this taking of a distance which consists in the recourse to the exteriority of the archival trace. This why we find its mark in the innumerable modes of graphism, of inscription that precede the beginnings of historical knowledge and the historian's profession.

The origin, therefore, is not the beginning. And the notion of birth conceals beneath its amphiboly the gap between the two categories of beginning and origin.

It is this aporia of birth that justifies the Platonic use of myth: the beginning is historic, the origin is mythic. It is a question, of course, of a reuse of a form of discourse appropriate to any history of beginnings presupposing themselves, such as the creation of a work, the birth of an institution, or the vocation of a prophet. Reused by the philosopher, myth presents itself as myth, in the guise of an initiation and supplement to dialectic.

# PRELUDE

## *History: Remedy or Poison?*

I shall speak in the manner of Plato's *Phaedrus* of the mythic birth of the writing of history. That this extension of the myth of the origin of writing may sound like a myth of the origin of history, thanks to rewriting, is, if I may put it this way, authorized by the myth itself, inasmuch as what is at stake is the fate of memory, even if the irony is directed in the first place at the "written discourses" of orators such as Lysias. Furthermore, it also has to do with other fabulous inventions: calculation, geometry, but also checkers and dice, which the myth compares to the invention of writing. And does not Plato indirectly include his own writing, he who wrote down and published his dialogues? But it is to true memory, genuine memory, that the invention of writing and its related drugs is opposed as a threat. How then can the debate between memory and history not be affected by this myth?

To get quickly to the point, what fascinates me, as it does Jacques Derrida, is the insurmountable ambiguity attached to the *pharmakon* that the god offers the king.[1] My question: must we not ask whether the writing of history, too, is remedy or poison? This question, no less than that of the amphibology of the notion of birth applied to history, will not let go of us. It will spring up again in another prelude, at the beginning of part 3: Nietzsche's second *Unfashionable Observation*.

Let us take up the myth: "Theuth said: 'O king, here is something that, once learned, will make the Egyptians wiser and will improve their memory [*mnēmonikōterous*]; I have discovered a potion [*pharmakon*] for memory [*mnēmēs*] and wisdom [*sophias*]'" (274e)![2] It is the *grammata* that come to the fore among the potions offered by the one whom Theuth calls "the father of writing," "the father of *grammata*." Is not historiography in a certain way the heir of the *ars memoriae*, that artificial memory that we referred to above as a way of expressing memorization turned into an exploit? And is it not memorization rather than remembering, in the sense of a precise memory of past events, that is at issue in this narrative?[3] The king readily concedes to the god the privilege of engendering the art, but he retains the right to judge what he calls its "benefit" and "harm"—just as Nietzsche will subsequently do as regards history in his second *Unfashionable Observation*. How does he respond to the god's offer? "In fact, it will introduce forgetfulness into the soul of those who learn it: they will not practice using their memory [*mnēmēs*] because they will put their trust in writing [*graphēs*], which is external and depends on signs that belong to others [*tupōn*], instead of trying to remember [*anamimnēskomenous*] from the inside, completely on their own. You have not discovered a potion [*pharmakon*] for remembering, but for reminding [*hupomnēseōs*]; you provide your students with the appearance of wisdom, not with its reality" (275a).[4] The verbs and nouns having to do with memory are important and differ: the god's offer is that of a jointly held capacity—that of being "capable of remembering." But what the king opposes to the alleged potion is instead recollection (*ana-*). And what he sees in the features of the potion is not memory but a *hupomnēsis*, a *memory by default*; that is, a technique offering something "certain" (*saphes*) and "clear" to those naïve people who believe "that words that have been written down [*logous gegrammenous*] can do more than remind [*hupomnēsai*] those who already know what the writing is about" (275c–d). Again it is memory by default (which I am proposing to call memorization) that is at issue here.

The narrative continues: writing is compared with painting (*zōgraphia*), whose works present themselves "as if they are alive [*hōs zōnta*]." We ought not to be surprised by this comparison. It imposed itself during our discussion about the imprint on the wax.[5] In effect, we have passed from the metaphor of imprinting to that of writing, another variety of inscription. Therefore it is really inscription in the generality of its signification that is at issue. But it remains that the kinship with painting is perceived as disturbing (*deinon*, "strange") (275d). We shall speak further of this when we confront narrative and picture at the properly literary level of historiography: the picture makes one believe in the reality through what Roland Barthes calls a "reality effect," which, as is well known, condemns the critic to silence. This is certainly the case with "written discourse": "it continues to signify just that very same thing forever" (275d). Yet, where is the repetitive side more clearly indicated in a nonproblematic way if not in memorized writings, learned by heart? The case turns out to be even more damning: written down once and for all, the discourse is in quest of some interlocutor, whoever it may be—one does not know to whom it is addressed. This is also the case for the historical narrative that gets written and published: it is tossed to the winds, it is addressed, as Gadamer says of *Schriftlichkeit*, to whomever knows how to read. There is a parallel vice: questioned, "it can neither defend itself nor come to its own support" (275e). This is certainly the case for a history book, as for any book. It has cut its ties to its speaker. What I elsewhere have called the semantic autonomy of the text here is presented as a situation of distress. The help this autonomy deprives it of can only come through the interminable work of contextualization and recontextualization that makes up reading.

But then, what quality does that other kind of discourse—"a legitimate brother of this one" (276a)—that of true memory, offer? "It is a discourse that is written down, with knowledge, in the soul of the listener; it can defend itself, and it knows for whom it should speak and for whom it should remain silent" (276a). This discourse that can defend itself before the one to whom it is well fitted is the discourse of true, happy memory, assured of being "timely" and of being capable of being shared. However, the opposition to writing is not total. The two modes of discourse remain akin, like brothers, in spite of their difference as regards legitimacy. Above all, both are written down, inscribed. But it is in the soul that the true discourse is written.[6] It is this underlying kinship that allows us to say that "the written one can be fairly called an image [*eidōlon*]" (276a) of what is "living," "breathing" in memory. The metaphor of life introduced above, with the painting of living beings, can thus be shifted to the fields of the sensible farmer who knows how to plant, grow, and harvest. For true memory, inscription is a kind of sowing, its true words are "seeds" (*spermata*). Thus we are authorized to speak of "living" writing, for this writing in the soul and for these "gardens of letters" (276d). Here, despite the kinship among these *logoi*, lies the gap between a living memory and a dead deposit. This remnant of writing at the very heart of memory authorizes our envisaging writing as a risk to run: "When he [the farmer] writes, it's likely he will sow gardens of letters for the sake of amusing himself, storing up reminders for himself 'when he reaches forgetful old age' and for everyone who wants to follow in his footsteps, and will enjoy seeing them sweetly blooming" (276d). Forgetfulness is named for a second time. Above it was entailed by the alleged gift of writing. Now it is something undergone as a consequence of old age. But it does not lack the promise of amusement. Do we not have then a struggle against forgetfulness that preserves the kinship between "the abusive and the legitimate brother"? And, faced with forgetfulness, playfulness? Playfulness that will be welcomed by those old graybeards Nietzsche will condemn in his second *Unfashionable*

*Observation.* But how serious is the game that animates those discourses that have as their object justice and as their method, dialectic! A game in which one takes pleasure, but equally a game where one is as happy as a human being can be: the just person, in effect, finds himself crowned with beauty (277a)!

The transition in terms of forgetting and games is so essential that the dialogue can elevate itself to another level, that of dialectic, where the opposition between living memory and dead deposit becomes secondary. We have moved beyond the violence of the myth that led to overstatement and entered into philosophy (278a). Discourses, to be sure, are "written in the soul," but they bring aid to the writings that vouch for this memory which is a memory on crutches (*hupomnēsis*).

The case of Lysias, Socrates' target from the beginning of this dialogue, can serve as a touchstone. The case against him is not that he writes down his discourses, but rather that these preach against art, where the art that he lacks is that of definitions, divisions, and the organization of a discourse as colorful as a multicolored soul. So long as one does not know "the truth concerning everything you are speaking or writing about" (277b), one will lack mastery of the how to use "speech artfully [*to logōn genos*]" (277c) considered in terms of its full amplitude, which includes political documents. What is at issue, then, is not just epistemological, in that truth is at stake, but ethical and aesthetical, in that the question is to understand "whether it is noble or shameful [*aiskhron*] to give or write a speech" (277d). Why then does writing not have the "clear knowledge of lasting importance" that the myth had reserved for memory? Is this not the case with laws? The blame does not fall on writing as such but on the relation of the discourse to the just and the unjust, the bad and the good. It is with regard to this criterion that discourses "written in the soul" win out over all others and why one must bid farewell to all these others (278a).

Is this farewell also addressed to the *pharmakon* of the myth? We are not told. We do not learn whether philosophical discourse is capable of conjuring up the equivalent of a potion concerning which we never know whether it is healing or poisonous.

What would be the equivalent of this indecisive situation for our attempt to transpose the myth from the *Phaedrus* to the plane of the relations between living memory and written history? To the outcome of a prudent rehabilitation of writing and the outline of a family reunion between the bastard and the legitimate brother at the end of the *Phaedrus* will correspond, on our side, a stage where, on the one hand, an educated memory, illuminated by historiography, perfectly overlaps, on the other, a scholarly history capable of reanimating a fading memory and thereby, in Collingwood's terms, in "reactualizating," "reliving" the past. But is not this wish condemned to remain unsatisfied? In order to be fulfilled, the suspicion would have to be exorcized that history remains a hindrance to memory, just like the *pharmakon* of the myth, where in the end we do not know whether it is a remedy or a poison, or both at once. We shall have to allow this unavoidable suspicion to express itself again more than one time.

# CHAPTER 1

## *The Documentary Phase: Archived Memory*

### READING GUIDELINES

The initial chapter in this second part is devoted to the documentary phase of the historiographical operation, on the basis of the tripartite division of the tasks proposed above. We shall not forget that within this phase we do not have in mind chronologically distinct stages of the whole enterprise, but rather levels within a research program that are distinguished only by the distantiated epistemological gaze. This phase, taken in isolation, presents itself as a meaningful sequence whose stages lend themselves to discrete analysis. The *terminus a quo* is still memory grasped at its declarative stage. The *terminus ad quem* has the name: documentary proof. Between these two extremes unfolds a quite broad interval that I shall demarcate in the following way. We shall first pinpoint the switch to history from memory on the formal level of space and time. I shall then seek what on this level of the historiographical operation can be the equivalent of a priori forms of experience as they are determined by a transcendental aesthetics in a Kantian style: what is it that makes for a historical time and a geographical space, allowing for the fact that they cannot be articulated separately from each other? (section 1: "Inhabited Space," and section 2: "Historical Time").

Passing from form to content, from historical space-time to things said about the past, I shall follow the movement thanks to which declarative memory externalizes itself in testimony. I shall give all its force to the witness's commitment in his testimony (section 3: "Testimony"). I shall dwell then awhile on the moment of inscription of testimony that is received by another. This moment is the one when things said tip from the oral field to that of writing, which history will not henceforth abandon. It is also the moment of the birth of the archive, collected, preserved, consulted. Passing through the door of archives, testimony enters the critical zone where it is not only submitted to the harsh confrontation among competing testimonies, but absorbed into a mass of documents that are not all testimonies (section 4: "The Archive"). The question will then arise about the validity of documentary proof, the first component of proof in history (section 5: "Documentary Proof").

Considered in light of the myth from the *Phaedrus*, these steps taken together denote a tone of assurance as regards the well-foundedness of the confidence placed in the capacity of historiography to enlarge, correct, and criticize memory, and thereby to compensate for its weaknesses on the cognitive as much as on the pragmatic plane. The idea we shall confront at the beginning of part 3, that memory can be divested of its function of being the birthplace of history to become one of its provinces, one of the objects it studies, certainly finds its greatest backing in the self-confidence of the historian "sitting down to work," the historian in the archives. It is good that it should be so, if only to disarm those who negate great crimes who will find their defeat in the archives. In the following stages of the historiographical operation there will be stronger reasons for not simply celebrating this victory over the arbitrary that is the glory of archival labor.

Yet we must not forget that everything starts, not from the archives, but from testimony, and that, whatever may be our lack of confidence in principle in such testimony, we have nothing better than testimony, in the final analysis, to assure ourselves that something did happen in the past, which someone attests having witnessed in person, and that the principal, and at times our only, recourse, when we lack other types of documentation, remains the confrontation among testimonies.

§

## INHABITED SPACE

The impetus given the present investigation by taking up the myth from the *Phaedrus* leads to our organizing our reflection around the notion of inscription, whose amplitude exceeds that of writing in the precise sense of the fixation of oral expressions of discourse by a material support. The dominant idea is that of external marks adopted as a basis and intermediary for the work of memory. In order to preserve the amplitude of this notion of inscription, I shall first consider its formal conditions, namely, the mutations affecting the spatiality and temporality of living memory, whether collective or private. If historiography is first of all archived memory and if all the subsequent cognitive operations taken up by the epistemology of historical knowledge proceed from this initial gesture of archiving, the historian's mutation of space and time can be taken as the formal condition of possibility for this gesture of archiving.

A parallel situation to the one that lies at the origin of Kant's transcendental aesthetic associating the destiny of space with that of time is recognizable here. In passing from memory to historiography, the space in which the protagonists of a recounted history move and the time in which the told events unfold conjointly change their sign. The explicit declaration of the witness, whose profile we shall take up below, states this clearly: "I was there [*j'y étais*]." The use of the grammatical imperfect tense in French indicates the time, while the adverb marks the space. Together the here and there of the lived space of perception and of action, and the before of the lived time of memory, find themselves framed within a system of places and dates where the reference to the here and absolute now of lived experience is eliminated. That this double mutation can be correlated with the position of writing in relation to orality is confirmed by the parallel constitution of two sciences, geography, on the one hand, seconded by cartography (I think here of the imposing gallery of maps in the Vatican museum!), and historiography, on the other.

Following Kant's transcendental aesthetic, I have chosen to take up the pair space/time starting from the side of space. The moment of exteriority, common to every "external mark" characteristic of writing according to the myth from the *Phaedrus*, then finds itself immediately underscored. What is more, the alternation of continuities and discontinuities that mark the historical mutation of these two a priori forms is then easy to decipher.

At the beginning, we have the corporeal and environmental spatiality inherent to the evocation of a memory. To make sense of this, in part 1 I opposed the worldliness of memory to its reflexive pole. The memory of having inhabited some house in some town or that of having traveled in some part of the world are particularly eloquent and telling. They weave together an intimate memory and one shared by those close to one. In memories of this type, corporeal space is immediately linked with the surrounding space of the environment, some fragment of inhabitable land, with its more or less accessible paths, its more or less easy to cross obstacles. Thinkers in the middle ages would have said that our relation to the space open to practice as well as to perception is "arduous."

From such shared memory, we pass by degrees to collective memory and its commemorations linked to places consecrated by tradition. It is the occurrence of such experiences that first introduced the notion of sites of memory, prior to the expressions and fixations that have subsequently become attached to this expression.

The first milestone along the way of the spatiality that geography sets in parallel with the temporality of history is the one suggested by a phenomenology of "place" or "site." We owe the former to Edward Casey, from whom I have already borrowed important insights having to do precisely with the worldliness of the mnemonic phenomenon.[1] If the title chosen suggests something like a nostalgia desirous of "putting things back in their place," it has to do with the adventure of a being of flesh and bones who, like Ulysses, is in his place as much in the places visited as upon his return to Ithaca. The navigator's wanderings demand their right no less than does the residence of the sedentary person. To be sure, my place is there where my body is. But placing and displacing oneself are primordial activities that make place something to be sought out. And it would be frightening not ever to find it. We ourselves would be devastated. The feeling of uneasiness—*Unheimlichkeit*—joined to the feeling of not being in one's place, of not feeling at home, haunts us and this would be the realm of emptiness. But there is a question of place because space is not yet filled, not saturated. In truth, it is always possible, often urgent, to displace oneself, with the risk of becoming that passerby, that wanderer, that flâneur, that vagabond, stray dog that our fragmented contemporary culture both sets in motion and paralyzes.

Investigation into what "place" signifies finds support in ordinary language, which includes expressions such as emplacement and displacement, expressions that usually come in pairs. They speak of experiences of the lived body that demand being spoken of in a discourse prior to Euclidean or Cartesian space, as Merleau-Ponty emphasized in his *Phenomenology of Perception*. The body, the absolute here, is the landmark for any there, be it near or far, included or excluded, above or below, right or left, in front or behind, as well as those asymmetric dimensions that articulate a corporeal typology that is not without at least implicit ethical overtones, for example, height or the right side. To these corporeal dimensions are added some privileged postures—upright, lying down—weightiness—heavy, light—orientations to front or rear, the side, all determinations capable of opposed values: active man, standing upright, someone sick and also the lover lying down, joy that awakens and arises, sadness and melancholy that lower the spirits, and so on. To these alternatives of rest and movement is grafted the act of inhabiting, which has its own polarities: reside and displace, take shelter under a roof, cross a threshold and go out. One might think here of the exploration of a house, from basement to attic, in Gaston Bachelard's *Poetics of Space*.

In truth, displacements of the body and even its remaining in place cannot be spoken of, nor even thought, nor even at the limit experienced without some, at least allusive, reference to points, lines, surfaces, volumes, distances inscribed on a space detached from the reference to the here and there inherent to the lived body. Between the lived space of the lived body and the environment and public space is intercalated geometric space. In relation to it, there is no longer any privileged place but only different localities. The act of inhabiting is situated at the boundaries of lived space and geometric space. And this act of inhabiting is put in place only by an act of construction. Hence, it is architecture that brings to light the noteworthy composition that brings together geometric space and that space unfolded by our corporeal condition. The correlation between inhabiting and constructing thus takes place in a third space—if we want to adopt a concept parallel to that of the third time that I propose for the time of history, spatial localities corresponding to dates on the calendar. This third space can also be interpreted as a geometrical checkering of lived space, one of "places," like a superimposition of "places" on the grid of localities.

As for the act of constructing, considered as a distinct operation, it brings about a type of intelligibility at the same level as the one that characterizes the configuration of time by emplotment.[2] Between "narrated" time and "constructed" space there are many analogies and overlappings. Neither reduces to the fragments of the universal time and space of geometers. But neither do they oppose a clear alternative to them. The act of configuration takes place at the point of rupture and suture of two levels of apprehension: constructed space is also geometrical, measurable, and calculable space. Its qualification as a lived place superimposes itself upon and is interwoven with its geometrical properties in the same way that narrated time weaves together cosmic and phenomenological time. Whether it be fixed space or space for dwelling, or space to be traversed, constructed space consists in a system of sites for the major interactions of life. Narrative and construction bring about a similar kind of inscription, the one in the endurance of time, the other in the enduringness of materials. Each new building is inscribed in urban space like a narrative within a setting of intertextuality. And narrativity impregnates the architectural act even more directly insofar as it is determined by a relationship to an established tradition wherein it takes the risk of alternating innovation and repetition. It is on the scale of urbanism that we best catch sight of the work of time in space. A city brings together in the same space different ages, offering to our gaze a sedimented history of tastes and cultural forms. The city gives itself as both to be seen and to be read. In it, narrated time and inhabited space are more closely associated than they are in an isolated building. The city also gives rise to more complex passions than does the house, inasmuch as it offers a space for displacement, gathering, and taking a distance. There we may feel astray, rootless, lost, while its public spaces, its named spaces invite commemorations and ritualized gatherings.

It is at this point that Casey's final reflections take on strength.[3] The attraction of wild nature emerges reinforced by the opposition between the constructed and the nonconstructed, between architecture and nature. This latter does not allow itself to be marginalized. The best of civilization cannot abolish the primacy of the wilderness. The experience of the first American colonists, handed over to the two traumatic experiences of uprooting and desolation, which become legendary, returns in force with the dark moods of uprooted city dwellers that the countryside and its landscapes no longer comfort. Only those who, like Casey, aspire to the calmness and stability of house and home, can aspire to going wild in the Land, leaving an escape from the *Unheimlichkeit* of the wilderness, even of such a friendly setting as that envisaged by Thoreau in *Walden*. Even in France we have our Du Bellay and his "petit Liré."

These incidental notes must not cover over the permanent lesson of the *Odyssey*, a narrative that weaves together events and places, an epic that celebrates episodes and stops along the way as much as it does the indefinitely delayed return, the return to Ithaca that is supposed to "return things to their place." Joyce, Casey recalls, wrote in his preparatory drafts to his *Ulysses*: "Topical History: Places Remember Events."[4]

But, to give the time of history a spatial analogue worthy of a human science we must elevate it higher on the scale of the rationalization of places. We have to move from the constructed space of architecture to the inhabited land of geography.

That geography, within the order of the human sciences, constitutes the exact guarantor of history, is still not to say much. In France, geography began by anticipating certain methodological conversions in history that will concern us below.[5] Vidal de La Blache was the first, before Martonne, to react against the positivism of historicizing history and to give meaning to the notions of setting, lifestyle, and everydayness. His science was a geography in the sense that its object was above all one of "places," "countrysides," "of visible effects on the earth's surface that were both natural and human" (Dosse, 15). The geometrical side of the experience of space was visualized by the cartography whose mark we shall rediscover when we consider the interplay of scales below. The human side is marked by the concepts of biological origin, cell, tissue, organism.

What was to influence the history of the *Annales* school was, on the one hand, the accent placed on things that were permanent, represented by the stable structures of the countryside, and, on the other, the preference for description expressed by the flourishing of regional monographs. This attachment to territory, principally rural landscapes, will find more than an echo in the *Annales* school with the promotion of a veritable geopolitics where the stability of landscapes and the quasi-immobility of the long time span are conjoined. Space, Braudel liked to say, was the best means of slowing down history. These spaces were in turn those of regions and those of seas and oceans. "I loved the Mediterranean passionately," he declared in his great book where the Mediterranean was both site and hero. As Lucien Febvre wrote to Braudel: "Between these two protagonists, Philip and the interior ocean, the match is not equal" (quoted in Dosse, 108). As for the question that led to the preceding observations, that of the switch-over from the space of geographers and historians in relation to the space of lived experience, itself anchored in the range of the body and its environment, we must not focus exclusively on the break between them. Above, I referred to the schema of an alternation of ruptures, sutures, and reprises at a higher level of determinations stemming from the existential level. Geography is not geometry insofar as the land surrounded by oceans is an inhabited one. This is why geographers of the school of Vidal de La Blache speak of it as a "milieu." But the milieu, as we learn from Canguilhem, is one pole of a debate—an *Auseinandersetzung*—where the living creature is the other pole.[6] In this respect, the emphasis on possibility of Vidal de La Blache anticipates the dialectics of a von Uexküll and a Kurt Goldstein. And, if in Braudel's geohistory milieu and space are taken as equivalent terms, the milieu remains that of life and civilization. "Any civilization is at bottom a space worked by men and history," we read in *The Mediterranean and the Mediterranean World in the Age of Philip II*.[7] And again: "What is a civilization if not the timeworn placement of a certain humanity in a certain space?" (cited by Dosse, 109). It is this mixture of climate and culture that makes up geohistory, which in turn determines the other levels of civilization, according to modes of interconnectedness that we shall discuss in the following chapter. The geopolitical perspective can be taken as "more spatial and temporal"

(110), but it is so in relation to the level of institutions and events, which is that of layers built upon the geographical soil and in their turn placed under the constraint of structures of a temporal nature. I had earlier noted, in my attempt to re-narrativize Braudel's great work, and to read it in terms of the great plot of *The Mediterranean*, that the first part, where space is said to be the theme, is a peopled space. The Mediterranean itself is the interior sea, a sea between inhabited or uninhabitable, hospitable or inhospitable lands. This space is the setting for the inscription of slower oscillations than those known by history.[8]

Braudel's other great work, *Civilization and Capitalism, 15th–18th Century*, calls for similar considerations.[9] What succeed each other in time are "world economies" inscribed in space but articulated in terms of places qualified by human activities and divided into concentric circles whose centers change over time. This "differential geography" (Dosse, 125) never leaves space without the interaction of exchange that binds an economy to a geography and distinguishes this latter from simple geometry.

In conclusion, from the phenomenology of "places" that beings of flesh and blood occupy, leave, lose, rediscover—in passing through the intelligibility belonging to architecture—up to the geography that describes an inhabited space, the discourse of space too has traced out an itinerary thanks to which lived spaced is turn by turn abolished by geometrical space and reconstructed at the hyper-geometrical level of the *oikoumenē*.[10]

## HISTORICAL TIME

To the dialectic of lived space, geometrical space, and inhabited space corresponds a similar dialectic of lived time, cosmic time, and historical time. To the critical moment of localization within the order of space corresponds that of dating within the order of time.

I shall not repeat my analysis of calendar time from *Time and Narrative*.[11] My focus is different today inasmuch as it is not so much the reconciliation of the phenomenological and cosmological perspectives on time that is at issue as the transition from living memory to the "extrinsic" positing of historical knowledge. Thus it is as one of the formal conditions of possibility of the historiographical operation that the notion of a third-order time reappears.

I will limit myself to the definition that Benveniste gives of "chronicle time," which I am calling third-order for the sake of my argument: (1) the reference of every event to a founding event that defines the axis of time; (2) the possibility of traversing the intervals of time in terms of the two opposed directions of anteriority and posteriority in relation to the zero date; and (3) the constitution of a repertory of units serving to name recurring intervals: day, month, year, and so on.

It is this constitution that we need now to place in relation to the historian's mutation of the time of memory. In one sense, dating, as a phenomenon of inscription, is not without some connections to a capacity for dating, in an originary datability, inherent to lived experience, and singularly to a feeling of being distanced from the past and of having a sense of temporal depth. Aristotle in *De memoria et reminiscentia* takes for granted that simultaneity and succession characterize in a primitive manner the relations between remembered events. Otherwise, there would be no question, in the work of recalling, of choosing a starting point in order to reconstruct the interconnectedness of such events. This primitive character of a sense of intervals results from the relationship time maintains with movement. If time "has something to do with movement," a soul is required, in order to distinguish two instants, to relate them to each other as before and after, and to evaluate their difference (*heteron*) and to measure the intervals (*to metaxu*), operations thanks to which time can be defined as the "number of motion in respect of 'before' and 'after'" (*Physics* 4.219b). As for Augustine, who is hostile to any subordination of time to physical movement, he admires in the rhetorician the power of the soul to measure within itself lengths of time, and thereby to compare long and short syllables on the level of diction. For Kant, the notion of temporal extension makes for no difficulty. It does not result from a possibly unwarranted second-order comparison with spatial extension, but rather precedes it and makes it possible. Husserl takes the relations of time relative to its passage as inseparable a priori from "apprehensions" immanent to the inner experience of time. Finally, even Bergson, the philosopher of the *durée*, does not doubt that in pure memory the evoked event comes with its date. For all of them, extension appears as a primitive fact, as attested in language by questions such as "when," "since how long ago," "for how long," which belong to the same semantic plane as do declarative memory and testimony. To the declaration "I was there" is added the affirmation "this happened 'before,' 'during,' 'after,' 'since,' 'during so much time.'"

Having said this, what calendar time adds consists in a properly temporal mode of inscription, namely, a system of dates extrinsic to the events to which they apply. Just as in geographical space the places referred to the absolute "here" of the lived body and its environment become particular locations that can be inscribed among the sites that cartography maps, so too the present moment with its absolute "now" becomes a particular date among all the ones whose exact calculation is allowed for by the calendar in terms of the framework of some calendar system accepted by a more or less extended part of humanity. As concerns the time of memory in particular, the "another time" of the remembered past is henceforth inscribed within the "before that" or the dated past. Symmetrically, the "later" of expectation becomes the "when that," marking the coincidence of an anticipated event with the grid of dates to come. Every noteworthy coincidence refers in the final analysis to those events, in chronological time, between some social event and an astrally based cosmic configuration. In the pages devoted above to the *ars memoriae*, we had plenty of time to take the measure of the incredible exploitation that subtle minds have given to calculations in service of an insane dream of mastery over human destiny. Those times of such exploits of memorization are no longer our own, but in many ways our lives in common remain governed by such calculation of dated conjunctions. The distinctions familiar to economists, sociologists, and political scientists, to say nothing of historians, between short term, mid-term, long term, cycle, period, and so on—distinctions to which we shall return below—are all inscribed on the same calendar time where the intervals between dated events allow themselves to be measured. The brevity of human life stands out against the immensity of indefinite chronological time.

In turn, calendar time stands out against a rising series of representations of time that cannot be reduced to what phenomenology knows as lived time. Thus Krzysztof Pomian, in *L'Ordre du temps*, distinguishes "four ways of visualizing time, of translating it into signs": chronometry, chronology, chronography, and chronosophy.[12] This order stems essentially from a kind of thinking that overflows that of the knowable (to use the Kantian distinction between *Denken* and *Erkennen*) within whose limits historians' history confines itself. As thinkable, these articulations ignore the distinction between myth and reason, between philosophy and theology, between speculation and symbolic imagination. These considerations from the preface to *L'Ordre du temps* have a lot to say to our inquiry. We ought not to believe, for example, that historical knowledge has only collective memory for its opposite. It has also to conquer its space of description and explanation against the speculative background deployed by the problems of evil, love, and death. This is why the categories closest to the historian's practice that Pomian considers over the course of his book—events, repetitions, ages, structures—stand out against the fourfold frame of the order of time. We can again recognize calendar or chronological time in the times of chronometry and chronology.

The first of these designates the short or long cycles of time that recur, that return in cycles: day, week, month, year. The second designates the linear time of long periods: century, millennium, and so forth, whose scansion is punctuated in diverse ways by founding events and founders; cycles that take place over a number of years, such as, for example, the Greek Olympiads. These are the two kinds of time measured by clocks and calendars, with the reservation that the intervals of chronology—such as eras—have a significa-tion that is as much qualitative as quantitative. Chronology, which is closer to the historian's intention, knows how to order events as a function of a series of dates and names, and to order the sequence of eras and their subdivisions. But it ignores the separation between nature and history. It allows us to speak of cosmic history, of the history of the earth, the history of life where human history is just one segment. With chronography, we come to systems of notation that can go beyond the calendar. The noted episodes are defined by their relations to other episodes: a succession of unique, good or bad, joyful or sorrowful events. This time is neither cyclic nor linear, but amor-phous. It is what relates the presented chronicle to the narrator's position, before narrative detaches the told tale from its author. As for chronosophy, which will take more of our time, it exceeds the project of a critical history that has become our project. It has been cultivated by numerous families of thought that arrange times in terms of rich typologies opposing station-ary time to reversible time, which may be cyclical or linear. The history we may construct of these great schemes is equivalent to a "history of history," from which professional historians may never completely free themselves, once it is a question of assigning a significance to facts: continuity vs. dis-continuity, cycle vs. linearity, the distinction of periods or eras. Once again, it is not principally the phenomenology of lived times or the exercises of popular or scholarly narratives that history confronts here, but an order of thought that ignores the sense of limits. And the categories that come from it have not ceased to construct the temporal "architecture" of "our civiliza-tion" (xiii). In this regard, the time of history proceeds as much by limiting this immense order of what is thinkable as by surpassing the order of lived experience.

It is principally on the basis of such great chronosophies of speculation on time that historical time was conquered at the price of a drastic self-limitation. I will retain from Pomian's rich analyses only what has to do with the persistence of chronosophy on the horizon of the large categories that shape historical discourse in the phase of explanation/understanding and in that of the representation of the past, whether it be a question of "events," "repetitions," "ages," or "structures" (the titles of the first four chapters of his book). These are the same categories that we have come upon more than once in our epistemological inquiry. It is good to know what excess of the thinkable they have conquered before being able to face up to the demand for truth with which history is supposed to confront the trustworthiness of memory. By chronosophy, Pomian means those large-scale periodizations of history such as those of Islam and Christianity (in Daniel and Saint Augustine) and their attempts to make them correspond with chronology. Religious and political chronosophies clash in this field. With the Renaissance appears a periodization in terms of "ages" of art and with the eighteenth century one in terms of "centuries."

One will readily take the notion of event to be the least speculative among these developments and also as the most self-evident one. Michelet as much as Mabillon, Droysen as much as Dilthey profess with confidence the primacy of the individually determined fact. Reduced to the sphere of visibility, the event's coming to perception would be unjustifiable. An aura of invisibility which is the past itself encircles it and hands it over to mediations that are the objects of research and not of perception. Along with the invisible, speculation comes into play and proposes a "historical typology of chronosophies" (26). In the Christian West, it is principally in terms of the opposition between profane and sacred history, on the plane of a theology of history, that the relations between the continuous and the discontinuous were conquered. We must not lost sight of this speculative history when we take up in succession the Braudelian plea for a history not based on events and the "return of the event" in the wake of the return of the political, up to the most sophisticated models pairing up event and structure.[13]

Would one have formed the notion of "repetitions" without the idea of a direction and a signification that were first provided by a typology on the chronosophical level? We owe to this latter the opposition between a stationary time and a nonrepeatable one, whether cyclic or linear, and, in the latter case, either progressive or regressive. It is from these large-scale orientations that the present receives a meaningful place in history as a whole. Then we speak of ages, centuries, periods, stages, epochs. Like the notion of event, that of the architecture of historical time is conquered through the disintegration of the overall time of history, from which emerges the problem of the relationships between different local times. But have we stopped adding to proposals of the type that Bernard of Chartres spoke of in talking about the "visual acuity" of dwarfs in comparison to the "greatness" of the giants upon whose shoulders they were perched? Have we renounced opposing a time of rebirth to one of darkness, spotting oscillations indicated by some cyclical phenomena, watching out for advances and retreats, extolling the return to sources, protecting taste and customs from the corruption of the cumulative effects of history? Are there no more battles between the Ancients and the Moderns? Haven't we read and understood Vico and Turgot? The "struggle of the chronosophy of progress" (58) against the specter of philosophies of regression undoubtedly has not disappeared from our horizons. The plea for or against modernity that I shall refer to below continues to borrow from this panoply of arguments. We do not readily admit the chronosophic status of the idea of a cumulative and irreversible linear time, still familiar to professional historians. The chronosophy of cyclical time at the turn of the twentieth century suffices to recall it. And do not the cycles so dear to economists ever since the takeoff of the history of prices and economic fluctuations, with Ernest Labrousse among others, point us in the direction of a synthesis of cyclical and linear time? Even the piling up of time-spans, in the manner of Braudel, and the attempt joined to it to articulate conjuncture and event in terms of a triadic structure, poorly conceals the chronosophic residue that hides itself behind a scientific façade. In this sense, breaking away from every chronosophy, to the benefit of a certain methodological agnosticism concerning the direction of time, has not been achieved. Perhaps it is not desirable that it should be, if history is to remain interesting, that is, if it is to continue to speak of hope, nostalgia, anxiety.[14]

The concept of ages (Pomian, chap. 3) is perhaps the most troublesome, inasmuch as it seems to be superimposed on chronology in order to cut it into large periods. For example, in the West we continue to divide the teaching of history and even historical research into antiquity, the Middle Ages, early modernity, and the modern world. Here we recall the role that Émile Benveniste assigns to the zero point in the calculation of historical time. The birth of Christ for the Christian West, the Hegira for Islam. Yet periodizations have an even richer history as far back as Daniel's dream as recounted in the Hebrew Bible, leading to the theory of four monarchies according to Augustine. Then we find successive quarrels between Ancients and Moderns, which play on rival periodizations. The comparison of ages of life also has its adepts, as does doubt concerning the historical replica of biological aging: Does history know an old age that does not lead to death? In truth, the concept of periods does not lend itself to a history distinct from that of cyclical or linear, or stationary or regressive conceptions.

Hegel's *Philosophy of History* offers in this regard an impressive synthesis of multiple ways of ordering historical time. And after Hegel, despite my vow to "renounce Hegel," the question arises anew whether every chronosophic residue has disappeared from the use of terms such as "stages" adopted in economic history, on the plane where cycles and linear segments intersect. What is at stake is nothing less than the possibility of a history without direction or continuity. It is here, according to Pomian, that the theme of structure takes over from that of periods.[15]

But can one do history without periodization? I mean, not merely teach history, but produce it? According to Claude Lévi-Strauss, we would have "to spread out in space those forms of civilization which we imagined as spread out in time" (337). Were we to succeed, would this not be to remove from history any horizon of expectation, to us a concept often referred to in this work that I owe to Reinhart Koselleck? Even for Lévi-Strauss history cannot withdraw into an idea of an extended space without any horizon of expectation, inasmuch as "it is only from time to time that history is cumulative—in other words, that the numbers can be added up to form a favorable combination" (338).

The mark of the great chronosophies of the past is less easy to discern at the level of "structures," in which Pomian sees the fourth articulation of time. I want to show its role as one phase of the historiographical operation, where the notion of structure enters into variable compositions along with those of conjuncture and event. But it is worth recalling its birth from large-scale speculations on the movement of global history. The human and social sciences have certainly given it an operative dimension. Yet the mark of its origin in speculation can still be recognized in "the split within each [of these disciplines], setting aside a few rare exceptions, into theory and history" (165). The autonomy of the theoretical in relation to the experimental was first conquered in biology, in conjunction with linguistics and anthropology. Structures are new objects, theoretical objects, endowed with a demonstrable reality or existence, in the same way that one demonstrates the existence of a mathematical object. Within the human sciences, this split between theory and history is due to Saussurian linguistics and "the simultaneous entry of theory and the object-structure into the field of the human and the social sciences" (168). Theory must deal only with atemporal entities, leaving to history the question of beginnings, developments, and genealogical trees. Here the object-structure is *langue*, language as a system, distinguished from *parole*, language as actually used, as speech. More will be said below about the happy and unhappy effects of this transposition from the linguistic domain as it has affected the historiographical incorporation of this linguistic model by those who followed Saussure—in particular, that the notions of diachrony and synchrony lose their phenomenological basis when they enter into a structural system. Conciliation between an approach based on system, as the enemy of the arbitrary, and a historical one, set out in terms of discrete events, itself becomes the object of speculation, as we see in Roman Jakobson (cf. Pomian, 174). And history as a discipline finds itself indirectly caught up in the reintegration of linguistics as a science into the space of theory as well as by the overlapping within this same space of studies of literary, and in particular of poetic language. But it is also the claim to dissolve history into a logical or algebraic combinatrics, in the name of the correlation between process and system, that the theory of history has had to deal with in the last third of the twentieth century, almost as though structuralism had given historiography a perfidious kiss of death.[16] My own recourse to models stemming from the theory of action will inscribe itself within this revolt against the hegemony of structuralist models, but not without retaining something of the imprint they have exercised on the theory of history; for example, the concepts of transition as important as those of competence and performance, taken from Noam Chomsky, retailored to the scale of the relationship among the notions of agent, agency (in Charles Taylor's sense), and structures of action, such as constraints, norms, and institutions. Equally to be rediscovered and rehabilitated are prestructuralist philosophies of language, such as that of Humboldt, which give to the spiritual dynamism of humanity and its productive activity the power to engender gradual changes of configuration. "For spirit," proclaimed Humboldt, "to be is to act." History was recognized in this generative dimension. Yet professional historians, who might take interest in Humboldt, cannot overlook the highly theoretical dimension of his reflections, such as those cited by Pomian: "Taken in its essential reality, language is continually changing and at each instant in the midst of some anticipatory transition.... In itself, language is not a work done (*ergon*) but an activity in the process of happening (*energeia*). Thus its true definition can only be genetic" (cited, 209).[17]

This long excursus devoted to the speculative and highly theoretical past of our notion of historical time has had a single goal, to recall to historians a number of things:

—The historiographical operation proceeds from a double reduction, that of the lived experience of memory, but also that of the multimillenary speculation on the order of time.

—The structuralism that has fascinated several generations of historians stems from a theoretical stance that, through its speculative side, is situated along the prolonging of the great theological and philosophical chronosophies, as a kind of scientific, even scientist chronosophy.

—Historical knowledge perhaps has never, in fact, stopped dealing with these visions of historical time, when it speaks of cyclical or linear time, stationary time, decline or progress. Will it not then be the task of a memory instructed by history to preserve the trace of this speculative history over the centuries and to integrate it into its symbolic universe? This will be the highest destination of memory, not before but after history. The palace of memory, we have read in Augustine's *Confessions*, not only holds the memories of events, the rules of grammar, and rhetorical examples, it also preserves theories, including those that, claiming to embrace it, have threatened to eliminate it.

## TESTIMONY

Testimony takes us with one bound to the formal conditions of the "things of the past" (*praeterita*), the conditions of possibility of the actual process of the historiographical operation. With testimony opens an epistemological process that departs from declared memory, passes through the archive and documents, and finds its fulfillment in documentary proof.

As a first step, I shall take up testimony as such while holding in suspense the moment of inscription that is archived memory. Why this delay? For several reasons. First of all, testimony has several uses: archiving in view of consultation by historians is only one of them, beyond the practice of testimony in daily life and parallel to its judicial use sanctioned by a tribunal's passing judgment. Furthermore, at the very interior of the historical sphere, testimony does not run its course with the constitution of archives; it reappears at the end of the epistemological inquiry at the level of the representation of the past through narrative, rhetorical devices, and images. Moreover, in some contemporary forms of deposition arising from the mass atrocities of the twentieth century, it resists not only explication and representation, but even its being placed into some archival reserve, to the point of maintaining itself at the margins of historiography and of throwing doubt on its intention to be truthful. Which is to say that in this chapter we shall follow only one of the destinies of testimony, the one sealed by its being placed into an archive and sanctioned by documentary proof. Whence the interest and importance of an attempt at an analysis of the essence of testimony as such, while respecting its potentiality for multiple uses. When we shall borrow from one or another of these uses, I shall seek to isolate those features capable of being shared among most of these uses.[18]

It is within the everyday use of testimony that the common core of its juridical and historical use is most easily discerned. This use brings us immediately face to face with the crucial question: to what point is testimony trustworthy? This question balances both confidence and suspicion. Thus it is by bringing to light the conditions in which suspicion is fomented that we have a chance of approaching the core meaning of testimony. In effect, suspicion unfolds itself all along the chain of operations that begin at the level of the perception of an experienced scene, continuing on to that of the retention of its memory, to come to focus in the declarative and narrative phase of the restitution of the features of the event. The untrustworthiness of witnesses has taken on scientific form within the framework of judicial psychology as an experimental discipline. One of the basic tests consists in imposing on a group of subjects the task of producing a verbal restitution of some filmed scene. This test is supposed to allow measurement of the trustworthiness of the human mind with regard to the proposed operations, whether at the moment of perception, or during that of its retention, or finally when it comes to its verbal restitution. The artifice of this test to which it is important to draw our attention is that it is the experimenter who defines the conditions of the test and who validates the reality status of the fact to be attested to. This reality status is taken for granted in the very putting together of the experiment. It is thus the gap between this reality recognized by the experimenter that is taken into consideration and measured. The implicit model of this presupposition is the undisputable trustworthiness of the camera's eye. The results of these experiments are certainly not negligible. They have to do with the flagrant presence of distortions between the reality known in this way and the depositions made by the laboratory subjects. For me, the question is not to criticize the conclusions of these investigations as disqualifying testimony in general, but rather to call into question, on the one hand, what Dulong calls the "paradigm of recording," that is, the video camera, and, on the other, the idea of the "disengaged observer," a prejudice to which the experimental subjects are submitted.

This criticism of the "regulative model" of judicial psychology leads us back to the everyday practice of testimony in ordinary conversation. This approach is profoundly in agreement with the theory of action that will be brought into play in the explanatory and representative phases of the historiographical operation, and with the primacy that will be accorded to the problematic of representation in relation to action on the level of the constitution of the social bond and the identities that stem from it. The activity of testifying, grasped before the bifurcation between its judicial and its historiographical uses, then reveals the same amplitude and the same import as does that of recounting, thanks to the manifest kinship between these two activities, to which we must soon add the act of promising, whose kinship with testimony remains more concealed. Placing into an archive, on the historical side, and a deposition before a tribunal, on the judiciary one, constitute specific uses, governed on the one side by documentary proof and on the other by the passing of a judgment. The use of testimony in ordinary conversation best preserves those essential features of the fact of testifying that Dulong sums up in the following manner: "An autobiographically certified narrative of a past event, whether this narrative be made in informal or formal circumstances" (43).

Let us unpack the essential components of this operation:

1. Two sides are initially distinguished and articulated in terms of one another: on the one side, the assertion of the factual reality of the reported event; on the other, the certification or authentification of the declaration on the basis of its author's experience, what we can call his presumed trustworthiness. The first side finds its verbal expression in the description of the experienced scene in a narration that, if it does not explicitly mention the implication of the narrator, confines itself to conveying information; the scene, so to speak, recounts itself following the distinction proposed by Émile Benveniste between narrative and discourse. There is an important nuance: This information must be taken to be important; the attested-to fact must be significant, something that renders problematic too sharp a distinction between discourse and narrative. Yet it remains the case that the factuality attested to is supposed to trace a clear boundary between reality and fiction. The phenomenology of memory early on confronted us with the always problematic character of this boundary. And the relation between reality and fiction will continue to torment us, right up to the stage of the historian's representation of the past. Which is to say that this first component of testimony is a weighty one. It is over against this articulation that a whole battery of suspicions will take their place.

2. The specificity of testimony consists in the fact that the assertion of reality is inseparable from its being paired with the self-designation of the testifying subject.[19] The typical formulation of testimony proceeds from this pairing: I was there. What is attested to is indivisibly the reality of the past thing and the presence of the narrator at the place of its occurrence. And

it is the witness who first declares himself to be a witness. He names himself. A triple deictic marks this self-designation: the first-person singular, the past tense of the verb, and the mention of there in relation to here. This self-referential character is sometimes underscored by certain introductory remarks that serve as a "preface." These kinds of assertions link point-like testimony to the whole history of a life. At the same time, the self-designation brings to the surface the inextricable opacity of a personal history that itself has been "enmeshed in stories." Which is why the affective imprint of an event capable of striking the witness like a blow does not necessarily coincide with the importance his audience may attach to his testimony.

3. Self-designation gets inscribed in an exchange that sets up a dialogical situation. It is before someone that the witness testifies to the reality of some scene of which he was part of the audience, perhaps as actor or victim, yet, in the moment of testifying, he is in the position of a third-person observer with regard to all the protagonists of the action.[20] This dialogical structure immediately makes clear the dimension of trust involved: the witness asks to be believed. He does not limit himself to saying "I was there," he adds "believe me." Certification of the testimony then is not complete except through the echo response of the one who receives the testimony and accepts it. Then the testimony is not just certified, it is accredited. It is this accreditation, as an ongoing process, that opens the alternative I began with between confidence and suspicion. A questioning argument can be undertaken, which the judicial psychology mentioned above supplies with well-established forms of reasons. This argument may bear on the most common conditions of bad perception, bad memory, or bad restitution. And among these must be taken into account the interval of time so favorable to what Freud in the *Interpretation of Dreams* calls "secondary elaboration." It may bear in a more disturbing way on the personal qualities of the testifying subject to be habitually believed, as indicated by similar earlier occasions and the witness's reputation. In this case, the accreditation comes down to authenticating the witness on personal terms. The result is what we call his trustworthiness, whose evaluation can be assimilated to comparative orders of magnitude.

4. The possibility of suspicion in turn opens a space of controversy within which several testimonies and several witnesses find themselves confronted with one another. In certain general conditions of communication, this space may be qualified as a public space. It is against this background that a critique of testimony is grafted to its practice. The witness anticipates these circumstances in a way by adding a third clause to his declaration: "I was there," he says, "believe me," to which he adds, "If you don't believe me, ask someone

else," said almost like a challenge. The witness is thus the one who accepts being questioned and expected to answer what may turn out to be a criticism of what he says.

5. In this way, a supplementary dimension gets grafted to the moral order meant to reinforce the credibility and trustworthiness of testimony, namely, the availability of the witness to repeat his testimony. The trustworthy witness is the one who can stay steadfast about this testimony over time. This steadfastness makes testimony akin to promise-making, more precisely to the promise that precedes any promise-making, that of keeping one's promise, of keeping one's word. Thus testimony links up with promise-making among those acts of discourse that specify ipseity in its difference from simple sameness, the sameness of character or, better, that of one's genetic make-up, which is immutable from the birth to the death of an individual, the biological basis of his identity.[21] The witness must be capable of answering for what he says before whoever asks him to do so.

6. This stable structure of the willingness to testify makes testimony a security factor in the set of relations constitutive of the social bond. In turn, this contribution of the trustworthiness of an important proportion of social agents to the overall security of society in general makes testimony into an institution.[22] We can speak here of a natural institution, even if the expression seems like an oxymoron. It is useful for distinguishing this common certification of an account in ordinary conversation from technical, "artificial" uses, consisting, in part, in the placing of things in an archive within the framework of specific institutions, and, in part, in the rule-governed taking of testimony as part of the trial process within the courtroom. I have drawn upon a parallel expression to distinguish the ordinary exercise of remembering from the memory tricks cultivated by the *ars memoriae*. In this way, we can oppose natural to artificial memory. What makes it an institution is, first of all, the stability of testimony ready to be reiterated, and next the contribution of the trustworthiness of each testimony to the security of the social bond inasmuch as this rests on confidence in what other people say.[23] More and more, this bond of trustworthiness extends to include every exchange, contract, and agreement, and constitutes assent to others' word, the principle of the social bond, to the point that it becomes a *habitus* of any community considered, even a prudential rule. First, trust the word of others, then doubt if there are good reasons for doing so. In my vocabulary, it is a question of a competence of the capable human being. The credit granted to the word of others makes the social world a shared intersubjective world. This sharing is the major component of what we can call the

"sensus communis." It is what is strongly affected when corrupt political institutions lead to a climate of mutual surveillance, of mistrust, where deceitful practices undercut the basis of confidence in language. We rediscover here, amplified to the scale of the communication structures of a society as a whole, the problematic of manipulated memory referred to above. What confidence in the word of others reinforces is not just the interdependence, but the shared common humanity, of the members of a community. This needs to be said *in fine* to compensate for the excessive accent placed on the theme of difference in many contemporary theories of the social bond. Reciprocity corrects for the unsubstitutability of actors. Reciprocal exchange consolidates the feeling of existing along with other humans—*inter homines esse*, as Hannah Arendt liked to put it. This "betweenness" opens the field to *dissensus* as much as to *consensus*. And it is *dissensus* that the critique of potentially divergent testimonies will introduce on the pathway from testimony to the archive. To conclude, in the final analysis, the middle level of security of language of a society depends on the trustworthiness, hence on the biographical attestation, of each witness taken one by one. It is against this background of assumed confidence that tragically stands out the solitude of those "historical witnesses" whose extraordinary experience stymies the capacity for average, ordinary understanding. But there are also witnesses who never encounter an audience capable of listening to them or hearing what they have to say.[24]

## THE ARCHIVE

The moment of the archive is the moment of the entry into writing of the historiographical operation. Testimony is by origin oral. It is listened to, heard. The archive is written. It is read, consulted. In archives, the professional historian is a reader.

Before the consulted or constituted archive, there is the archiving of things.[25] This brings about a break in a continuous trajectory. Testimony, we have said, gives a narrative follow-up to declarative memory. Yet narrative can be detached from its narrator, as literary criticism informed by structuralism likes to emphasize. But this does not mean that the phenomenologist is left behind. Between the saying and the said of any utterance, a subtle gap opens that allows what is stated, the saying of what is said, to pursue what we can strictly speaking call a literary career. The emplotment of a told story, moreover, reinforces the semantic autonomy of a text, whose composition in the form of a work gives it the visibility of something written.[26]

To these scriptural features that it shares with narrative, testimony adds specific ones having to do with the exchange structure between the one who gives and the one who receives. Thanks to a reiterable character that confers upon it the status of an institution, testimony can be taken down in writing, deposited. This deposition, in turn, is the condition of possibility of specific institutions devoted to the collecting, conserving, and classifying of documentation with an eye to its subsequently being consulted by qualified personnel. The archive thus presents itself as a physical place that shelters the destiny of that kind of trace I have so carefully distinguished from the cerebral trace and the affective trace, namely, the documentary trace. But the archive is not just a physical or spatial place, it is also a social one. It is in terms of this second angle that Michel de Certeau deals with it in the first of three snapshots of what before me he called the historiographical operation.[27] To relate a product to a place constitutes, he says, the first task of an epistemology of historical knowledge: "envisaging history as an operation would be equivalent to understanding it as the relation between a *place* (a recruitment, a milieu, a profession or business, etc.), analytical *procedures* (a discipline), and the construction of a *text* (a literature)" (57). This idea of a social setting of production includes a critical intention aimed against positivism, a critique that Certeau shares with Raymond Aron from the period when he wrote his *Introduction to the Philosophy of History* (1938). But, unlike Aron, who emphasizes the "dissolution of the object," it is not so much the subjectivity of authors or personal decisions that Certeau accentuates as the unsaid of the social status of history as an institution of knowledge. In this way he distinguishes himself as well from Max Weber who, in "Politics as a Vocation," he asserts, "exempted" the power of scholars from the constraints of political society. In confronting this repression of the relation to the society that engenders the unspoken of "place" from which the historian speaks, Certeau, like Habermas, at the time when he was arguing for a "repoliticizing" of the human sciences, denounces the appropriation of language by a subject supposed to "control" history's discourse: "in this way historical discourse takes priority over every particular historical work, and so does the relation of this discourse to a social institution" (63).

However, it does not suffice to set historians back into society if we are to give an account of the process that constitutes a distinct object for epistemology, that is, in Certeau's own terms, the process leading "from collecting documents to writing books" (66). The multileveled architecture of the social units that constitute archives calls for an analysis of the act of placing materials in such archives, their archiving, capable of being situated in a chain of verifying operations, whose provisory end is the establishing of documentary proof.[28] Before explanation, in the precise sense of establishing answers in terms of "because," there is the establishing of sources, which consists, as Certeau puts it so well, "in redistributing space" that had already been marked out by the collectors of "rarities," to speak like Foucault. Certeau calls "place," "what permits, what prohibits" (68) this or that kind of discourse within which cognitive operations properly speaking are enframed.

This gesture of setting things aside, of putting together, of collecting is the object of a distinct discipline, that of the archivist, to which the epistemology of the historiographical operation is indebted for the description of those features by which the archive breaks with the hearsay of oral testimony. To be sure, if writings constitute the principal materials deposited in archives, and if among such writings testimony by past peoples constitutes the core material, all sorts of traces can be archived. In this sense, the notion of the archive restores to the gesture of writing the full scope given to it by the myth in the *Phaedrus*. At the same time, every plea in favor of the archive will remain in suspense, to the degree that we do not know, and perhaps never will know, whether the passage from oral to written testimony, to the document in the archive, is, as regards its utility or its inconvenience for living memory, a remedy or a poison, a *pharmakon*.

I propose to set within the framework of this dialectic between memory and history what I said about the notion of an archive in *Time and Narrative*.[29] The accent will be on those features by which the archive breaks from the hearsay of oral testimony. What first stands out is the initiative of a person or legal entity intending to preserve the traces of his or its activity. This initiative inaugurates the act of doing history. Next comes the more or less systematic organization of the material thus set aside. It consists in physical measures of preservation and in logical operations of classification stemming from the needs of a highly developed technique at the level of the archivist. All these procedures are in service of a third moment, that of consulting the materials within the limits of the rules governing access to them.[30]

If we consider, with all the reservations I shall speak of below, that the essential core of archival materials consists in texts, and if we want to concentrate on those of these texts that are testimonies left by contemporaries having access to this material, the change in status from spoken testimony to being archived constitutes the first historical mutation in living memory that falls under our examination. We can then speak of those written testimonies that the *Phaedrus* calls "written words": "When it has once been written down, every discourse rolls everything about everywhere, reaching indiscriminately those with understanding no less than those who have no business with it, and it doesn't know to whom it should speak and to whom it should not. And when it is faulted and attacked unfairly, it always needs its father's support; alone it can neither defend itself nor come to its own support" (275e). In one sense, this is a good thing: like all writing, a document in an archive is open to whomever knows how to read. Therefore it has no designated addressee, unlike oral testimony addressed to a specific interlocutor. What is more, the document sleeping in the archives is not just silent, it is an orphan. The testimonies it contains are detached from the authors who "gave birth" to them. They are handed over to the care of those who are competent to question them and hence to defend them, by giving them aid and assistance. In our historical culture, the archive has assumed authority over those who consult it. We can speak, as I shall discuss further below, of a documentary revolution. In a period now taken to be outdated in historical research, work in the archives had the reputation of assuring the objectivity of historical knowledge, protected thereby from the historian's subjectivity. For a less passive conception of consulting archives, the change in sign that turns an orphan text into one having authority is tied to the pairing of testimony with a heuristics of evidentiary proof. This pairing is common to testimony before a court and testimony gathered by the professional historian. The testimony is asked to prove itself. Thus it is testimony that brings aid and assistance to the orator or the historian who invokes it. As for what more specifically concerns history, the elevation of testimony to the rank of documentary proof will mark the high point of the reversal in the relationship of assistance that writing exercises in regard to "memory on crutches," that *hupomnēmē*, or artificial memory par excellence, to which myth grants only second place. Whatever may be the shifts in documentary history—positivism or not—the documentary frenzy took hold once and for all. Allow me to mention here from a more advanced phase of contemporary discourse (to be considered below), Yerulshalmi's dread confronted with the archival swamp, and Pierre Nora's exclamation: "Archive as much as you like: something will always be left out." Once freed of its disgrace and allowed arrogance, has the *pharmakon* of the archived document become more a poison than a remedy?

Let us follow the historian into the archives. We shall do so in the company of Marc Bloch, who was the historian who best delineated the place of testimony in the construction of the historical fact.[31] That history should have recourse to testimony is not fortuitous. It is grounded in the very definition of the object of history. This is not the past, nor is it time, it is "men in time." Why not time? First of all, because time is the setting, "the very plasma in which events are immersed, and the field within which, they become intelligible" (27–28). (In other words, as was indicated above, time as such constitutes one of the formal conditions of historical reality.) Next, because it returns as a variable among things with regard to its rhythms, as the Braudelian problematic of social times will verify. Moreover, physical nature develops in time, and in this broad sense has a history. Finally, the fascination for origins—that "idol of origins"—has to do with the direct and exclusive thematization of time. This is why the reference to human beings has to figure in the definition. But history is a matter of "men in time," which implies a fundamental relationship between the present and the past. It is thanks to this dialectic—"understanding the present by the past" and correlatively "understanding the past by the present"—that the category of testimony comes on the scene as the trace of the past in the present. The trace is thus the higher concept under whose aegis Bloch places testimony. It constitutes the operator par excellence of an "indirect" knowledge.

Bloch carries out his examination of the relationship of history to testimony in two chapters. The first is entitled "Historical Observation," the second "Historical Criticism."

If we can speak of observation in history, it is because the trace is to historical knowledge what direct or instrumental observation is to the natural sciences. Here testimony figures as the first subcategory. It immediately bears the mark that distinguishes its use in history from its use in ordinary exchanges where orality predominates. It is a written trace, the one the historian encounters in the documents in an archive. Whereas in ordinary exchanges testimony and its reception are contemporary with each other, in history testimony is inscribed in the relation between past and present, in the movement of understanding the one by the other. Writing is thus the mediation of an essentially retrospective science, of a thinking "backwards."

However, there exist traces that are not "written testimonies" and that are equally open to historical observation, namely, "vestiges of the past" (53), which are the favorite target of archeology: urns, tools, coins, painted or sculpted images, funerary objects, the remains of buildings, and so forth. By extension we can call them "unwritten testimonies," at the risk of some confusion with oral testimonies whose fate I shall return to below.[32] We shall also see testimonies divide into voluntary testimonies, meant for posterity, and those witnesses in spite of themselves, the target of indiscretion and the historian's appetite.[33] This sequence of definitions—science of men in time, knowledge by traces, written and unwritten testimonies, voluntary and involuntary testimonies—assures the status of history as a discipline and of the historian as artisan. Finally, "in the course of its development, historical research has gradually been led to place more and more confidence in the second category of evidence, in the evidence of witnesses in spite of themselves" (61). Indeed, apart from confessions, autobiographies, and other diaries, maps, secret documents, and some confidential reports by military leaders, the documents in archives for the most part come from witnesses in spite of themselves. The variety of different materials to be found in archives is in fact immense. Mastering them calls for an acquired technique, even the practice of specialized auxiliary disciplines and the consultation of different guides in order to assemble the documents necessary to research. The professional historian is someone who keeps in mind the question: "How can I know what I am about to say?" (71).[34] This mental disposition defines history as "research," following the Greek etymology of the word.

At the heart of observation, this relation to "contemporary testimony" (52)—what "others have said" preserved in archives—suffices to draw two dividing lines: the one runs between history and sociology, and the other crosses history itself, which it divides between two opposed methodological attitudes. Sociology, in Durkheim's sense, as indifferent to time, tends to see in change a residue that it condescendingly leaves to historians. A defense of history in this regard will necessarily be a defense of the event, that privileged object of testimony, as I shall say below. (Pierre Nora's plea in favor of a "return of the event" will stand in line with the thought of Marc Bloch.) The battle between sociology and history will be harsh and often merciless, even if Bloch can admit having learned from sociologists "to think less shoddily" (15). The second dividing line is the one that opposes a self-professed reconstructive method, owing to its active relation to traces, to one that Bloch condemns as "positivism," the method of his own teachers, Seignobos and Langlois, whose intellectual laziness he condemns.[35]

The second section continuing the examination of the relationships of history to written and unwritten testimonies is that of "criticism." This term specifies history as a science. To be sure, challenges and confrontations between human beings occur outside juridical procedures and those of historical criticism. However, only the testing of written testimony, joined with that of those other traces, the vestiges, has given rise to criticism in a sense worthy of this name. In fact, it is within the historiographical sphere that the very word criticism appeared with the sense of corroboration of what others say, before assuming the transcendental function that Kant would assign to it as critique on the level of an exploration of the limits of our cognitive faculty.

Historical criticism has had to blaze a difficult trail between spontaneous credulity and Pyrrhonian skepticism in principle. And it is one that goes beyond mere common sense. We can trace the birth of historical criticism back to Lorenzo Valla's critique of the Donation of Constantine.[36] Its golden age is illustrated by three great names: the Jesuit Paperbroeck, of the Bollandists, the founder of scientific hagiography; Mabillon, the Benedictine from Saint-Maur, who founded diplomatic history; and Richard Simon, the Oratorian who marks the beginnings of critical biblical exegesis. To these three names should be added those of Spinoza with his *Theologico-Political Treatise* and Bayle, who posed so many doubts. Ought we also to add Descartes? No, if we emphasize the mathematical turn of the *Discourse on Method*, yes, if we link historians' doubt with Cartesian methodic doubt.[37] The "struggle with the document," as Marc Bloch so well puts it, is henceforth taken as a given. Its major strategy is to examine sources in order to distinguish the true from the false, and, in order to do this, to "make speak" those witnesses who one knows may deceive themselves or lie, not in order to refute them, but "to understand them" (88).

We owe to this criticism a map or typology of "false testimonies," to which we might compare the results of Bentham's *Treatise on Judicial Proofs*, which Marc Bloch may have known, but which historians have largely improved upon.[38]

Bloch's summary is exemplary. Starting from the fact of imposture, as a deliberate fraud, he moves on to the reasons for lying, mystifying, faking, that may be those of wily individuals, self-interested frauds, or those common to an age open to fabrications. Next he considers the more insidious forms of fakery: sly revisions, clever interpolations. There is room for involuntary errors and pathological errors properly speaking arising from the psychology of testimony. (One interesting remark is that the contingencies of events are more propitious for errors than are things drawn from deeply felt feelings about human fate.) Bloch does not hesitate to draw on his own experience as a soldier in the two world wars of the twentieth century in order to compare his experience as a historian, and principally a medieval one, with that of the engaged citizen, attentive to the role of propaganda, censorship, and the pernicious effects of rumor.

To this typology, Bloch grafts his section entitled "Toward a Logic of the Critical Method" (110–37). This opens a vast workspace to which many following him have contributed. At its center lies the work of comparison and its interplay of resemblances and differences. Ordinary controversy finds here an exemplary technical explication. Apart from the elementary pro-hibition of formal contradiction—an event cannot have happened and not have happened—the argument runs from the art of unmasking the blunders of plagiarists, from spotting what seems obviously unlikely to the logic of probabilities.[39] In this regard, Bloch does not make the mistake of confusing the probability of the production of an event—what, in history, would be the equivalent of the initial equality of chances of a toss of dice? In "the criticism of evidence, almost all the dice are loaded" (126)—with the probability of a judgment concerning genuineness made by a reader in the archives. In weighing the pros and cons, doubt is an instrument of knowledge that as-sesses the degree of likeliness of the chosen combination. Perhaps it would be better to speak of plausibility rather than of probability. That argument is plausible that is worthy of being defended when challenged.

As has been suggested, much remains to be done regarding the validation procedures for any proof and as regards the criteria of internal and external coherence, and many have worked on this problem. Here it seems oppor-tune to bring in a comparison drawn from Carlo Ginzburg concerning the "evidential paradigm."[40] Marc Bloch's work, in effect, leaves unexplored the notion of a vestige, introduced with regard to archeology and quickly assim-ilated to the notion of unwritten testimony. But vestiges play a nonnegligible role in the corroboration of testimonies, as police work confirms, but as also does the interpretation of oral or written testimony. Ginzburg speaks here of clues and of the evidential paradigm, courageously opposed to the Galilean paradigm of the natural sciences.

Two questions arise: what are the usages of clues whose convergence authorizes bringing things together in terms of a single paradigm? Further-more, what *in fine* is the relation of clues to testimony?

The answer to the first question is constructed by Ginzburg's text. As a starting point: reference to the clever art lover—the well-known Giovanni Morelli whom Freud draws upon in his "The Moses of Michelangelo"—who made use of the examination of apparently negligible details (the shape of ear lobes) to uncover copies of original paintings. This method of drawing upon clues was the joy of Sherlock Holmes and of every author of detective novels following him. Freud recognized in it one of the sources of psychoanalysis "accustomed to divine secret and concealed things from unconsidered or unnoticed details, from the rubbish heap, as it were, of our observations." Are not slips of the tongue, when control slips and incongruous signs escape, clues in this sense? Bit by bit, the whole of medical semiotics, with its concept of a symptom, falls under this category of a clue. In the background lies the hunter's knowledge from earlier days, which deciphers mute tracks. After them come writings, and writing itself, concerning which Ginzburg says that "like divination, it too designated one thing through another" (104). So the whole of semiotics turns out to be based on clues. What then allows this group of disciplines to form a paradigm? Several features: the singularity of the thing deciphered, the indirect aspect of the deciphering, its conjectural character (where the term comes from divination).[41] And next comes history. "All this explains why history never became a Galileian science.... As with the physician's, historical knowledge is indirect, presumptive, conjectural" (106). Writing, textuality, which dematerializes orality, changes nothing, for it is once again and always individuals that the historian deals with. Ginzburg links the probabilistic character of historical knowledge to this relation to singularity.

The field opened by the evidential paradigm is immense. "Though reality may seem to be opaque, there are privileged zones—signs, clues—which allow us to penetrate it. This idea, which is the crux of the conjectural or semiotic paradigm, has made progress in the most varied cognitive circles and has deeply influenced the humane sciences" (123).

Now comes the second question: that of the place of Ginzburg's evidential paradigm in relation to the criticism of testimony of Marc Bloch and his successors. I do not think there is room to choose between these two analyses. By encompassing historical knowledge within the evidential paradigm, Ginsburg weakens his concept of a clue, which gains in being opposed to that of written testimony. Conversely, Bloch's treatment of vestiges as unwritten testimonies does harm to the specificity of testimony as the intermediary of memory in its declarative phase and narrative expression. The clue is noticed and decrypted; testimony is deposed and criticized. To be sure, it is the same sagacity that presides over both series of operations. But their points of application are distinct. The semiology of clues exercises its role of complement, control, corroboration in regard to oral or written testimony, to the extent that the signs that it decrypts are not verbal: fingerprints, photographic evidence, and today samples of DNA—that biological signature of the living—"testify" through their muteness. Their discourses differ among themselves in different ways than do oral collections.

Thus the benefit of Ginzburg's contribution is to open a dialectic of clue and testimony internal to the notion of a trace and thereby to give the concept of document its full scope. At the same time, the relation of complementarity between testimony and clue comes to be inscribed in the circle of internal-external coherence that structures documentary proof.

On the one side, in effect, the notion of the trace can be taken to be the common root of testimony and clue. In this regard, its origin in hunting is significant. An animal passed by and left its track. This is a clue. But the clue by extension can be taken as a kind of writing inasmuch as the analogy of the imprint adheres originarily to the evocation of striking a letter, not to speak of the equally primitive analogy to the *eikōn*, written and painted, referred to at the beginning of our phenomenology of memory. Furthermore, writing is itself written down and in this way a kind of clue. Thus graphology deals with writing, its *ductus*, its stroke, as a form of clue. Conversely, in this interplay of analogies, clues merit being called unwritten testimonies, in the fashion of Marc Bloch. But these interchanges between clues and testimony must not prevent our preserving their different uses. In sum, the beneficiary of this operation will be the concept of document, made up of clues and testimonies, whose final amplitude rejoins the initial one of the trace.[42]

There remains the limit case of certain fundamentally oral testimonies, even when written in pain, whose being placed into archives raises a question, to the point of soliciting a veritable crisis concerning testimony. Essentially, it is a question of the testimonies of those who survived the extermination camps of the Shoah, called the Holocaust in English-speaking countries. They were preceded by those of the survivors of the First World War, but they alone have raised the problems I am going to discuss next. Renaud Dulong placed them at the critical point of his work, *Le Témoin oculaire*: "Bearing Witness from within a Life of Testimony," this is the label under which he places a work such as Primo Levi's *Drowned and the Saved*.[43] Why does this genre of testimony seem to be an exception to the historiographical process? Because it poses a problem of reception that being placed in an archive does not answer and for which it even seems inappropriate, even provisionally incongruous. This has to do with such literally extraordinary limit experiences—which make for a difficult pathway in encountering the ordinary, limited capacities for reception of auditors educated on the basis of a shared comprehension. This comprehension is built on the basis of a sense of human resemblance at the level of situations, feelings, thoughts, and actions. But the experience to be transmitted is that of an inhumanity with no common measure with the experience of the average person. It is in this sense that it is a question of limit experiences. And in this way is anticipated a problem that will not find its full expression except at the end of our review of historiographical operations, that of historical representation and its limits.[44] But before the limits of explanation and understanding are put to the test, those of inscription and archiving already are. This is why we may speak of a crisis of testimony. To be received, a testimony must be appropriated, that is, divested as much as possible of the absolute foreignness that horror engenders. This drastic condition is not satisfied in the case of survivors' testimonies.[45] A further reason for the difficulty in communicating has to do with the fact that the witness himself had no distance on the events; he was a "participant," without being the agent, the actor; he was their victim. How "relate one's own death?" asks Primo Levi. The barrier of shame is one more factor with all the others. The result is that the expected comprehension must itself be a judgment, a judgment on the fly, a judgment without mediation, absolute blame. What finally brings about the crisis in testimony is that its irruption clashes with the conquest made by Lorenzo Valla in *The Donation of Constantine*. Then it was a matter of struggling against credulity and imposture, now it is one of struggling against incredulity and the will to forget. Is this just a reversal of what is at issue?

Yet even Levi writes. He writes after Robert Antelme, the author of *The Human Race*,[46] after Jean Améry, the author of *Par-delà le crime et le châtiment*.[47] Their writings have even been written about. And I am writing here about stating the impossibility of communicating and about the unbearable imperative to testify to which, however, they do testify. What is more, these direct testimonies find themselves progressively framed, but not absorbed, by the works of historians of the present time and by the publicity of the great criminal trials whose sentences trail slowly through the collective memory at the price of a harsh *dissensus*. This is why in speaking of these "direct narratives," unlike R. Dulong I do not talk of an "allergy to historiography" (*Le Témoin oculaire*, 219). The "allergy to explanation in general" (220), which is certain, provokes instead a kind of short circuit between the moment of testimony, at the threshold of the historiographical operation, and the moment of representation in its written expression, beyond the steps of archiving, of explanation, and even of comprehension. But it is within the same public space as that of historiography that the crisis of testimony after Auschwitz unfolds.

## DOCUMENTARY PROOF

Let us rejoin the historian in the archives. He is their intended receiver inasmuch as the traces were conserved by an institution in view of their being consulted by those trained to do so, following the rules concerning the right of access, any delay in their being consulted varying depending on the category of documents.

At this stage arises the notion of documentary proof, which designates the part of historical truth accessible at this state of the historiographical operation. Two questions: what is proof for a document or a group of documents—and what is proved thereby?

The answer to the first question is tied to the point of articulation of the documentary phase along with the explanatory and comprehending one, and beyond this with the literary phase of representation. If a proof role can be attached to the consulted documents, it is because the historian comes to the archives with questions. The notions of questioning and of a question-naire are thus the first ones to put in place in elaborating documentary proof. The historian undertakes research in the archives armed with questions. Marc Bloch—in his encounter with the theorists he called positivists, who I prefer to call methodologists, such as Langlois and Seignobos[48]—again, was one of the first to call for caution about what he took to be epistemological naïveté, namely, the idea that there could be a first phase where the historian gathered up the documents, read them, and weighed their authenticity and veracity, following which there came a second phase where he wrote them up. Antoine Prost, in his *Douze Leçons sur l'histoire*, following Paul Lacombe, hammers home the strong declaration: no observation without hypotheses, no facts without questions.[49] The documents do not speak unless someone asks them to verify, that is, to make true, some hypothesis. Therefore there is an in-terdependence among facts, documents, and questions. It is the question, writes Prost, "that constructs the historical object through an original carv-ing out from the unlimited universe of possible facts and documents" (79). He thereby rejoins Paul Veyne's assertion characterizing the current work of historians as "an extending of the questionnaire." What gives rise to this ex-tension is the formation of hypotheses bearing on the place of the questioned phenomenon within the interconnections putting into play explanation and understanding. The historian's question, Prost also says, "is not a bare ques-tion, it is an armed question that brings with it a certain idea of possible documentary sources and research procedures" (80). Trace, document, and question thus form the tripod base of historical knowledge. This irruption of the question provides an occasion for throwing a final look at the notion of document elaborated above beginning from that of testimony. Taken up by a bundle of questions, the document continues to distance itself from testimony. Nothing as such is a document, even if every residue of the past is potentially a trace. For the historian, the document is not simply given, as the idea of a trace might suggest. It is sought for and found. What is more, it is circumscribed, and in this sense constituted, instituted as document through questioning. For a historian, everything can become a document, including the debris coming from archeological excavations and other such vestiges, but in a more striking way kinds of information as diverse and mercurial as price curves, parish registers, wills, databases of statistics, and so on. Having become a document in this way, everything can be interrogated by a historian with the idea of finding there some information about the past. Among such documents are many that today are no longer testimonies. The series of homogeneous items we shall speak of in the next chapter are not even assignable to what Marc Bloch called witnesses in spite of themselves. The same characterization of the document through interrogation that applies to them holds for a category of unwritten testimonies, those recorded oral testimonies, which microhistory and the history of present times make so much use of. Their role is considerable in the conflict between the memory of survivors and already written history. These oral testimonies do not constitute documents until they are recorded. Then they leave behind the oral sphere to enter into that of writing and distance themselves in this way from the role of testimony in ordinary conversation. We can then say that memory is archived, documented. Its object ceases being a memory, in the literal sense of the word, that is, retained within a relation of continuity and appropriation in regard to some present conscious awareness.

Second question: What at this stage of the historiographical operation can be held to have been proved? The answer is clear: a fact, facts, capable of being asserted in singular, discrete propositions, most often having to do with the mentioning of dates, places, proper names, verbs that name an action or state. Here we need to be alert for one confusion, that between confirmed facts and past events. A vigilant epistemology will guard here against the illusion of believing that what we call a fact coincides with what really happened, or with the living memory of eyewitnesses, as if the facts lay sleeping in the documents until the historians extracted them. This illusion, which Henri Marrou fought against in his *The Meaning of History*,[50] for a long time underlay the conviction that the historical fact does not differ fundamentally from the empirical fact in the experimental natural sciences. Just as, in dealing below with explanation and representation, we shall need to resist the temptation to dissolve the historical fact into narration and this latter into a literary composition indiscernible from fiction, so too we need to resist this initial confusion between a historical fact and a really remembered event. The fact is not the event, itself given to the conscious life of a witness, but the contents of a statement meant to represent it. In this sense, we should always write: the fact that this occurred. So understood, the fact can be said to be constructed through the procedure that disengages it from a series of documents concerning which we may say in return that they establish it. This reciprocity between construction (through a complex documentary procedure) and the establishing of a fact (on the basis of the document) expresses the specific epistemological status of the historical fact. It is this propositional character of the historical fact (in the sense of "fact that ... ") that governs the mode of truth or falsity attached to the fact. The terms "true" and "false" can legitimately be taken at this level in the Popperian sense of "refutable" and "verifiable." It is true or it is false that gas chambers were used at Auschwitz to kill so many Jews, Poles, gypsies. The refutation of Holocaust deniers takes place at this level. This is why it was important to correctly delimit this level. In fact, this qualification regarding the truthfulness of "documentary proof" will not reoccur at the levels of explanation and representation, where the Popperian characterization of truthfulness will become more and more difficult to apply.

Some may object to the use that historians make of the notion of an event, either to exile it to the margins in reason of its shortness or fleetingness, or even more because of its privileged tie to the political level of social life, while others may salute its return. Whether it is treated as suspect or as a welcome guest following a long absence, it is as the ultimate referent that the event figures in historical discourse. The question it answers is: What is one talking about when one says that something happened? Not only do I not refuse this referential status, but I will tirelessly plead in its favor throughout this work. And it is to preserve this status of the reference of historical discourse that I distinguish the fact as "something said," the "what" of historical discourse, from the event as "what one talks about," the "subject of ... " that makes up historical discourse. In this regard, that assertion of a historical fact indicates the distance between the said (the thing said) and the intended reference, which according to one of Benveniste's expressions turns discourse back toward the world. The world, in history, is past human life as it happened. This is what it is all about. And the first thing that one says is that something took place. As stated? That is the whole question. And it will accompany us to the end of the stage of representation, where it will find at least its exact formulation under the heading of "standing for" [représentance], if not its resolution. To get there, we need to leave undetermined the question of the actual relation between fact and event, and tolerate a certain indiscrimination in the employment by the best historians of these terms as standing for each other.[51]

For my part, I mean to honor the event by taking it as the actual referent of testimony taken as the first category of the archived memory. Whatever specification one may bring or impose subsequently on the event, principally in relation to the notions of structure and conjuncture, placing the event in third place in relation to other conjoined notions, the event in its most primitive sense is that about which someone testifies. It is the emblem of all past things (*praeterita*). But what is said in spoken testimony is a fact, the fact that ... Let me be more precise. The "that" affixed to the assertion of a fact holds in reserve the intentional object that will be thematized at the end of our epistemological review under the sign "standing for." Only a semiotics inappropriate to historical discourse undertakes to deny this referent to the profit of the exclusive pair constituted by the signifier (narrative, rhetorical, imaginative) and the signified (the statement of a fact). To the binary conception of the sign inherited from Saussurean linguistics, and perhaps already mutilated, I oppose the threefold conception of signifier, signified, and referent. Elsewhere I proposed a formula borrowed from Benveniste whereby discourse consists in someone saying something to someone about something following rules.[52] In this schema, the referent is symmetrical to the speaker, that is, the historian, and before him, to the witness present to his testimony.

I would like to take one last look at the relation between the starting point of this chapter—testimony—and its end—documentary proof—in terms of the mixture of light and shade projected over the whole enterprise by the myth from the *Phaedrus* speaking of the invention of writing. If the continuity of the passage from memory to history is assured by the notions of trace and testimony, the discontinuity tied to the effects of distantiation that we have put in place ends up at a general crisis situation within which the crisis specifically linked to the untimely testimony of the survivors of the death camps takes its place. This general crisis gives to the question of the *pharmakon* a precise coloration that haunts this study. What historical criticism puts in question, at the level of documentary proof, is the trustworthiness of spontaneous testimony, that is, the natural movement of having confidence in the heard word, the word of another. A true crisis is thereby opened. A crisis of belief, which authorizes taking historical knowledge for a school of suspicion. It is not just credulity that is here put in the stocks, but the initial trustworthiness of testimony. A crisis of testimony: this is the harsh way documentary history contributes to the healing of memory, of linking the work of remembering to that of mourning. But can we doubt everything? Is it not to the extent that we have confidence in some testimony that we can doubt some other testimony? Is a general crisis of testimony bearable or even thinkable? Can history cut all its lines with declarative memory? The historian no doubt will reply that history, overall, reinforces spontaneous testimony through the criticism of all testimony, that is, through the confrontation between discordant testimonies, in view of establishing a probable, plausible narrative. To be sure, but the question remains: Is documentary proof more remedy than poison for the constitutive weaknesses of testimony? It will be up to explanation and representation to bring some relief to this disarray, through a measured exercise of questioning and a reinforcing of attestation.[53]

# CHAPTER 2

## *Explanation/Understanding*

### READING GUIDELINES

It is at the level of explanation/understanding that the autonomy of history in relation to memory is affirmed most forcefully on the epistemological plane. In truth, this new phase of the historiographical operation was already implied in the preceding one insofar as there is no document without some question, nor some question without an explanatory project. It is in relation to explanation that the document is proof. Nevertheless, what explanation/understanding adds that is new in relation to the documentary treatment of the historical fact has to do with the modes of interconnectedness of the documented facts. To explain, generally speaking, is to answer the question "Why?" through a variety of uses of the connector "because."[1] In this respect, to the degree that we need to hold open the range of such uses, to the same degree we must keep the historiographical operation in the neighborhood of approaches common to every scientific discipline, characterized by recourse in different forms to modeling procedures subject to verification tests. In this way, model and documentary proof go hand in hand. Modeling is the work of the scientific imagination, as has been emphasized by R. G. Collingwood, Max Weber, and Raymond Aron in dealing with singular causal implication.[2] This use of the imagination carries our minds far beyond the sphere of private and public memory into the range of the possible. If the intellect, however, is to remain within the domain of history, and not slip over into that of fiction, this use of the imagination must submit itself to a specific discipline, namely, an appropriate dividing up of its objects of reference.

This dividing up is governed by two guiding principles. According to the first of these, the explanatory models in use by historians have as a common feature that they relate to human reality as a social fact. In this respect, social history is not one sector among others, but rather the point of view from which history takes its stand, that of the social sciences. By privileging along with one school of contemporary history, as I shall do below, the practical issues of the constitution of the social bond and problems of identity attached to it, we lessen the distance that was opened during the first half of the twentieth century between history and the phenomenology of action, but without abolishing it. The human interactions, and in general the kinds of interval, of *inter-esse* as Hannah Arendt liked to put it, that occur between agents and recipients of human action only lend themselves to the modeling processes by which history inscribes itself among the social sciences at the price of a methodological objectification that has the value of an epistemological break in relation to memory and ordinary narration. In this regard, it is helpful to keep history and the phenomenology of action distinct for the greater benefit of their ongoing dialogue.

The second guiding principle concerns history's place within the field of the social sciences. It is through the emphasis that history places on change and on the differences or intervals affecting such changes that it distinguishes itself from the other social sciences and principally from sociology. This distinctive feature is common to every department of history: economic reality, social phenomena in the strict sense of the term, practices and representations. This common feature defines the referent of historical discourse within the common referent of the social sciences as a limit function. Changes and differences or intervals have a clear temporal connotation. This is why we can speak of a long time span, of the short run, of a point-like event. The discourse of history can thus once again move closer to the phenomenology of memory. To be sure. However, the vocabulary of the historian constructing his hierarchy of time spans, like that of Labrousse and Braudel, or breaking them up, as has been done since Labrousse and Braudel, is not that of phenomenology referring to the lived experience of temporal duration, as was the case in the first part of this work. These time spans are constructed. Even when history ingeniously mixes up their order of priority, particularly in the case of reactions against the rigidity of the architecture of spans piled on one another, it is always in terms of multiple spans that the historian models lived time. Even if memory is the test of the variable depth of time and orders its memories in relation to one another, outlining in this way something like a hierarchy among them, it does not spontaneously form the idea of multiple time spans. This is rather the prerogative of what Halbwachs calls "historical memory," a concept we shall return to when the time comes. The historian's handling of this plurality of time spans is commanded by a correlation among three factors: the specific nature of the change considered—economic, institutional, political, cultural, or whatever; the scale with which it is apprehended, described, and explained; and, finally, the temporal rhythm appropriate to that scale. This is why the privilege accorded economic phenomena by Labrousse and Braudel and, following them, the historians of the *Annales* school had as its corollary the choice of the macroeconomic scale and of the long time span as regards its temporal rhythm. This correlation is the most marked epistemological feature of history's treatment of the temporal dimension of social action. It is reinforced by a supplementary correlation between the specific nature of the social phenomenon taken as referent and the type of privileged document. What the long time span structures on the temporal plane is the priority of series of repeatable facts, rather than singular events likely to be remembered in a distinctive way. In this sense, these facts are open to quantification and to being dealt with mathematically. With serial and quantitative history,[3] we distance ourselves as much as possible from Bergson's or Bachelard's temporal duration. We are in a constructed time, made of structured and quantified durations. It is with regard to these audacious structuring operations, which marked the middle of the twentieth century, that the more recent history of practices and representations has elaborated a more qualitative treatment of durations and thus appears to have redirected history back in the direction of the phenomenology of action and the phenomenology of temporal duration united with it. But for all that this history does not deny the objectifying stance that it continues to share with the more notable efforts of the *Annales* school.

Having said this, as regards the referents of historical explanation, it remains to characterize in a more precise way the nature of the operations related to explanation. I have mentioned the eventual diversity of uses of "because" connected to the answers to the question "why?" Here is where we must insist on the variety of types of explanation in history.[4] In this regard, we can say without injustice that there is no one privileged mode of explanation in history.[5] This is a feature that history shares with the theory of action to the degree that the penultimate referent of historical discourse is those interactions capable of engendering the social bond. It is not surprising therefore that history unfolds the full range of modes of explanation likely to make human interactions intelligible. On the one side, the series of repeatable facts of quantitative history lend themselves to a causal analysis and to the establishing of regularities that draw the idea of a cause, in the sense of efficacy, toward that of lawfulness, toward the model of the "if . . . then" relation. On the other side, the behavior of social agents, responding to the pressure of social norms by diverse maneuvers of negotiation, justification, or denunciation, draw the idea of a cause toward the side of explanation in terms of "reasons for . . . "[6] But these are limit cases. The great mass of historical works unfold in a middle region where disparate modes of explanation alternate and sometimes combine in an unpredictable way. I have titled this chapter "Explanation/Understanding" in order to make sense of this variety of historical explanations. In this regard, we can take the quarrel that arose at the beginning of the twentieth century around the terms "explanation" and "understanding," taken as antagonistic to each other, as surpassed. Max Weber, in combining explanation and understanding from the start, was perspicacious in elaborating the leading concepts of his social theory.[7] More recently G. H. von Wright, in *Explanation and Understanding*, constructed a mixed model of explanation for history that made causal (in the sense of law-like regularity) and teleological (in the sense of motivations capable of being rationalized) segments alternate.[8] In this regard, the correlation mentioned above between the type of social fact taken as determining the scale of description and reading, and temporal rhythm can offer a good guide in the exploration of differentiated models of explanation in their relation to understanding. The reader may be surprised not to see the notion of interpretation appear in this context. Did it not stand alongside that of understanding in the great age of the quarrel between *Verstehen* and *Erklären*? Was not interpretation held by Dilthey to be a special form of understanding linked to writing and in general to the phenomenon of inscription? Far from objecting to the importance of the notion of interpretation, I propose to give it a much broader sphere of application than did Dilthey. For me, there is interpretation at all three levels of historical discourse: at the documentary level, at the level of explanation/understanding, and at the level of the literary representation of the past. In this sense, interpretation is a feature of the search for truth in history that runs across these three levels. Interpretation is a component of the very intending of truth in all the historiographical operations. I shall deal with it in part 3 of this work.

A final lexical and semantic comment at the threshold of this chapter: The reader may be more surprised by my silence about the narrative dimension of historical discourse than my silence about the theme of interpretation within the explanation/understanding framework. I have deliberately put off its consideration, leaving it to the framework of the third operation of the historiographical operation, the literary representation of the past, to which I shall accord an importance equal to that of the other two operations. This is not to say that I take back anything learned from the discussion in the three volumes of my *Time and Narrative*. But, in reclassifying narrativity in the way we are going to discuss, I want to leave to the end one misunderstanding suggested by the upholders of the narrativist school and taken for granted by its detractors, the misunderstanding that the configuring act that characterizes emplotment would as such constitute an alternative in principle to causal explanation.[9] Louis O. Mink's convincing argument, which I continue to respect, seems to me compromised by the imposition of this unfortunate disjunction. The cognitive function of narrativity seems to me, taking everything into account, better recognized if it is linked to the phase of historical discourse representative of the past. Our problem will be to understand how the configuring act of emplotment gets articulated through the modes of explanation/understanding placed in service of the representation of the past. To the extent that representation is not a copy, a passive *mimesis*, narrativity will suffer no *diminutio capitis* from being associated with the properly literary moment of the historiographical operation.

This chapter is constructed on the basis of one particular working hypothesis. I propose to examine the kind of intelligibility proper to explanation/understanding in terms of a class of objects of the historiographical operation, namely, representations. This chapter therefore pairs a method and an object. The reason for this is as follows. The notion of representation and its rich polysemy runs through this whole work. It first brought to light the perplexities of the phenomenology of memory starting from the Greek problem of the *eikōn*. And it will reappear in the following chapter in terms of the historiographical operation itself in the form of the written representation of the past (the writing of history in the narrow sense of this term). The notion of representation also figures two times in the epistemological portion of this work: as the privileged object of explanation/understanding, and as the historiographical operation. At end of this chapter I shall propose a confrontation between these two uses that are here made of the notion of representation.

In this chapter, the object-representation thus plays the role of privileged referent, alongside the economic, the social, the political. This referent is picked out from the much vaster field of social change, taken as the overall object of historical discourse. This is the point of this chapter.

But before reaching that stage of the discussion, three steps must be taken.

In the first section, I propose a quick review of the important moments in French historiography during the first two-thirds of the twentieth century, up to the period qualified as that of a crisis by commentators, whether historians or others. Within this chronological framework, which is essentially structured by the great adventure of the French *Annales* school and dominated by the overarching figure of Fernand Braudel, I shall bring to the fore the questions of method and of the promotion of a privileged object, for a long time now known by the name *mentalités*, the term having first been introduced in sociology by Lucien Lévy-Bruhl with the phrase "primitive mentality"[10] (section 1: "Promoting the History of Mentalities").

We shall follow this double inquiry to the point where the crisis in method is matched by a crisis in the history of mentalities, which has continued to suffer from its debatable origin in the sociology of "primitive mentality."

I shall interrupt this double inquiry to consider three authors—Foucault, Certeau, Elias—whom I shall present as "advocates of rigor" from whom I shall seek help in characterizing in a new the way the history of mentalities as a new approach to the total phenomenon and at the same time to a new object of historiography. By way of these considerations, the reader will become accustomed to associating the notion of mentalities with that of representation, as a way of preparing the moment when at the end the latter will be substituted for the former, thanks to its conjunction with the notions of action and of agent (section 2: "Some Advocates of Rigor: Michel Foucault, Michel de Certeau, Norbert Elias").

This substitution will be prepared through a long intermediary section devoted to the notion of scale. Although one does not see the same things in microhistory, this variety of history illustrated by the Italian *microstorie* will provide the occasion for varying the approach to mentalities and representations as a function of an "interplay of scales." Just as macrohistory is attentive to the weight of structural constraints exercised over the long time span, to a similar degree microhistory is attentive to the initiative and capacity for negotiation of historical agents in situations marked by uncertainty.

The step will then be taken from the idea of mentalities to that of representations in the wake of this notion of variations in scale and within the framework of a new overall approach to the history of societies, the one proposed by Bernard Lepetit in *Les Formes de l'expérience*. There the accent will be found to be on social practices and the representations integrated into these practices, the representations figuring as the symbolic component in the structuring of the social bond and the identities that are at stake within it. We shall pay particular attention to the connection between the operation of such representations and the different sorts of scales applicable to social phenomena: a scale of efficacy and coercion; one of standing within public esteem; and one of time spans embedded within one another (section 3: "Variations in Scale").

I shall end with a critical note in which we shall draw further upon the polysemy of the term "representation" to justify the split between represented object [*représentation-objet*] and the operation of representing [*représentation-opération*], to be taken up in the next chapter. The name Louis Marin will appear for the first time in the closing pages of this chapter, where the adventures of explanation/understanding will have been parsed in terms of the history of mentalities become the history of representations (section 4: "From the Idea of Mentality to That of Representation").

§

## PROMOTING THE HISTORY OF MENTALITIES

I have chosen from the immense literature having to do with explanation in history what concerns the emergence, then the consolidation and renewal of what in turn or in an alternative manner has been called cultural history, history of mentalities, and finally history of representations. I shall explain below why, upon reflection, I adopted this latter name. In the present section, I propose to comment upon the choice of this trajectory, not being already able to justify it. The notion of mentality represents, in fact, one that is particularly vulnerable to criticism owing to its lack of clarity and distinctness, or, if one is charitable, its overdetermination. The reasons why it imposed itself on historians are thus all the more worthy of interest.

As for what concerns me, these reasons run as follows.

First, staying as close as possible to professional historians, what interested me was the progressive promotion of one of those new "objects" that recent history has made a fuss about, to the point of becoming what I shall call a pertinent object, in other words, an object of immediate reference for all the discourse that relates to it. With this promotion comes a redistribution of values of importance,[11] of degrees of pertinence, that affect the ranking of economic, social, and political phenomena within the scale of importance and finally the scale adopted by the historical gaze in terms of micro- and macrohistory. This displacement on the plane of objects of reference, of immediate pertinence, goes with a displacement on the plane of methods and of modes of explanation. The concepts of singularity (of individuals or events), repeatability, serial ordering, are particularly affected; even more so are those of a collective constraint and correlatively of reception, passive or otherwise, on the part of social agents. This is why we shall see such new notions as appropriation and negotiation appear at the end of our comments.

Taking a step back in relation to the historian's work, I wanted to verify the thesis that history, as one of the social sciences, does not disregard its discipline of distantiation in relation to lived experience, to collective memory, once it declares itself to have moved away from what is called, most often wrongly, positivism or more equitably "historicizing history" to characterize the age of Seignobos and Langlois at the beginning of the twentieth century. We might think that with this "new object" history moves closer—whether it knows it or not—to phenomenology, in particular to the phenomenology of action or, as I like to put it, to that of the acting and suffering human being. Despite this shrinking of distance, the history of mentalities and of representations nonetheless remains situated on the other side of the epistemological break that separates it from the outcome of the phenomenology practiced in the first part of this work devoted to memory, and especially to collective memory insofar as memory constitutes one of the powers of that being I call the capable human being. The most recent developments in the history of representations do approach this phenomenology in that the objective posture of this history allows for notions akin to that of "can"—can do, can say, can recount, can impute the origin of one's actions to oneself. As a result, the dialogue between the history of representations and the hermeneutics of acting will turn out to be sharper edged owing to the fact that the invisible threshold of historical knowledge will not actually have been crossed.

However, there is a more subtle reason for my interest in the history of mentalities or of representations, a reason that will grow to the point of affecting the end of this investigation. Anticipating the last section of this chapter, I confess that this reason definitively imposed itself at the moment when, for reasons we shall speak of, the notion of representation was preferred to that of mentality. A case then came to the fore no longer of confusion or of indistinctness, but rather of overdetermination. As it turns out—and it will be necessary to show that this is not the result of some semantic contingency, of a regrettable homonymy resulting from a poverty or parsimony of vocabulary—the word "representation" figures in this work in three different contexts. It first designates the great enigma of memory, in relation to the Greek problem of the *eikōn* and its embarrassing doublet of *phantasma* or *phantasia*. We have said and repeated that the mnemonic phenomenon consists in the presence to the mind of an absent thing that, furthermore, no longer is but once was. If it is simply evoked as a presence, and in this sense as *pathos*, or if it is actively sought out in the operation of recalling that concludes in the experience of recognition, what is remembered is a representation, a re-presentation.

This category of representation appears a second time in the framework of the theory of history as the third phase of the historiographical operation, once the historian's labor, begun in the archives, ends in the publication of a book or an article to be read. The writing of history becomes literary writing. An embarrassing question then invades the intellectual space thereby opened: how does the historical operation preserve, even crown at this stage, the ambition for truth by which history distinguishes itself from memory and eventually confronts the latter's avowal of trustworthiness. More precisely: how does history, in its literary writing, succeed in distinguishing itself from fiction? To pose this question is to ask how history remains or rather becomes a representation of the past, something fiction is not, at least in intention, even if it may be so as a kind of added value. In this way, in its last stage historiography repeats the enigma raised by memory in its first one. Historiography repeats and enriches it through all the conquests I have placed globally under the aegis of the myth from the *Phaedrus* under the sign of writing. The question will then be to know whether historical representation of the past will have resolved, or simply transposed, the aporias linked to its mnemonic representation. It is in relation to these two major occurrences that it will be necessary to situate the use of the term "representation" by historians, at least as regards its conceptual aspect. Between the mnemonic representation from the beginning of our discourse and the literary representation situated at the end of the trajectory of the historiographical operation, representation presents itself as an object, a referent, of the historian's discourse. Can it be that the object represented by historians bears the mark of the initial enigma of mnemonic representation and anticipates the final enigma of the historical representation of the past?

I shall limit myself in the remainder of this section to a brief summary of the leading moments of the history of mentalities since the founding of the French *Annales* school up to the period qualified as one of crisis by observers, be they historians or others. We shall deliberately interrupt this rapid overview and consider three major undertakings that, if they cannot be confined within the strict limits of the history of mentalities and of representations, have addressed to the human sciences a demand for rigor concerning which we will have to ask whether subsequent history has given an answer, and, more generally, if a history of representations is capable of doing so.

It is the first generation of the *Annales* school, that of the founders, Lucien Febvre and Marc Bloch, that is worth questioning first of all, not only because the foundation of the journal of the same name in 1929 marks an important date, but because the notion of mentality was clothed in the founders' works with an importance that would not be equaled in the next generation, during the transitional period marked by Ernest Labrousse and more so by Fernand Braudel. This feature is all the more noteworthy in that *Annales d'histoire économique et sociale*—the journal's initial title—was marked by a shift in interest away from politics toward economics and by a strong rejection of history in the fashion of Seignobos and Langlois, improperly called positivist, at the risk of confusing it with the Comtean heritage, and less unjustly called historicizing in virtue of its dependence on the German school of Leopold von Ranke. Singularity, whether of the event or of individuals, was set aside along with chronology marked out by narration and politics as the privileged site of intelligibility. One set out in search of regularity, fixity, permanence, on the model of geography, brought to a high point by Vidal de La Blache, and on that of Claude Bernard's work in experimental medicine. To the supposed passivity of the historian confronted with a collection of facts, one opposed the active intervention of the historian facing the document in an archive.[12] When Lucien Febvre borrowed from Lévy-Bruhl the concept of mentality, it was to give a particular history, having to do with historical biography, the background of what he called "mental tools."[13] In so generalizing the concept of mentality beyond what was still called "primitive mentality," he killed two birds with one stone. He enlarged the sphere of historical inquiry beyond economics and especially beyond politics, and he gave the reply of a history anchored in the social to the history of ideas practiced by philosophers and by most historians of science. In this sense, the history of mentalities for a long time plowed a furrow between economic history and the dehistoricized history of ideas.[14]

In 1929, Febvre had already published his *Luther* (1928) to which he would add his *Rabelais* and his *Amour sacré, amour profane: Autour de l'«Heptameron.»*[15] Beneath their biographical appearance, these three books pose a problem that will spring up again in another form when history comes to question its capacity to represent the past, that is, the problem of the limits of representation. Confronted with the problem of unbelief in the sixteenth century, Febvre established in a convincing manner that the believable available to the period (not Febvre's phrasing), its "mental tools," did not permit professing or even forming an openly atheistic vision of the world. What the history of mentalities proposed to demonstrate, leaving indeterminate the question what one was meant to think of by means of "mental tools," was what a person of the time could and could not think about the world. Was the collective so undifferentiated as the notion of mental tools seems to imply? Here the historian gave credit to the psychology of a C. Blondel and to Lévy-Bruhl's and Durkheim's sociology.

In *The Royal Touch: Sacred Monarchy and Scrofula in England and France* (1924) and *Feudal Society* (1939), Marc Bloch ran into a comparable problem: How could rumor, the false news of the capacity of kings to cure scrofula, spread and impose itself unless with the help of a quasi-religious devotion as regards royalty?[16] What had to be presumed, even while guarding against anachronism, was the force of a specific mental structure, the "feudal mentality." In contrast to the history of ideas, not rooted in any social ground, history had to make a place for a deliberately historical treatment of "ways of feeling and thinking." What was important were the collective, symbolic practices, the unperceived mental representations, of different social groups, to the point that Febvre could worry about the effacing of the individual in Bloch's approach to the problem.

Between society and the individual, the interplay that Norbert Elias calls civilization was not measured by the same yardstick by the two founders of this school. The imprint of Durkheim was deeper on Bloch, while attention to the aspirations toward individuality among Renaissance figures influenced Febvre.[17] But what united them was, on the one hand, the assurance that the facts of civilizations stand out against the background of social history, and, on the other, the attention paid to the relations of interdependence among the spheres of activity of a society, attention that freed them from getting caught up in the impasse of the relations between an infrastructure and a superstructure, as in Marxist approaches. Above all there was the confidence in the federative power of history in regard to the neighboring social sciences: sociology, ethnology, psychology, literary studies, linguistics. "The average man according to the *Annales*," as François Dosse names him, a social human being, is not eternal man, but rather a historically dated, anthropocentric, humanistic figure inherited from the Enlightenment, the same one Michel Foucault will lambaste.[18] But whatever objections one may oppose to this worldview, which stems from the inseparable interpretation of truth in history, we can legitimately inquire, at this stage of our own discourse, what are the internal articulations of these evolving mental structures, and above all how the social pressure they exercise on social agents is received or undergone. The sociological or psychological determinism of the *Annales* school during the period of its dominance will only really be called into question when history reflecting upon itself will have made problematic the dialectic between the top and bottom of societies at the point of the exercising of power.

Following World War I, the *Annales* school (and its journal now subtitled *Économies, sociétés, civilisations*) was best known for its preference for taking the economy as its privileged referent. The use of quantification applied to repeatable facts, to series, treated statistically with the help of the computer, went along with this initial preference. The humanism of the first generation almost seemed repressed by the reverence for social and economic forces. And Claude Lévi-Strauss's structuralism operated both as an encouragement and a competitor.[19] It was then necessary to oppose to the invariants of the dominant sociology those structures that remained historical, that is, changing. This was exemplified by the long time span, placed by Braudel at the base of a pyramid of time spans following a schema that recalled Ernest Labrousse's triad: structure, conjuncture, event. The time thereby given the place of honor was conjoined with the space of the geographers, whose own permanence helped to slow down the flows of time. The horror Braudel felt for the event is too well known to require emphasis here.[20] What remains problematic is the relationship between these temporalities which accumulate and stack up more than they are dialectically related to one another, following an empirical pluralism deliberately removed from any abstract speculation, unlike George Gurvitch's careful reconstruction of the multiplicity of social times. This conceptual weakness of the Braudelian model was only really taken up when the question of the variation in the scales considered by the historian was taken into account. In this regard, the reference to total history, inherited from the founders and forcefully reiterated by their successors, only allows for a prudent recommendation, that of professing interdependence there where others, the Marxists at their head, thought to discern linear, horizontal or vertical dependencies among the components of the social bond. These relations of interdependence could be problematized for themselves only once the preference for the long time span was clearly assigned to a choice, which up to then had remained unmotivated, for macrohistory, on the model of economic relations.

This coalition between the long time span and macrohistory governed the contribution of the second generation of the *Annales* school to the history of mentalities. Here another triad than that of hierarchical time spans has to be taken into account: that of the economic, the social, and the cultural. But the third stage of this three stage rocket, to use the apt phrasing of Pierre Chaunu, the advocate of serial and quantitative history, obeys the rules of the method of correlation governing the choice for the long time span no less than do the first two stages. The same primacy accorded to repeatable, serial, quantifiable facts holds for the mental as for the economic and the social. And it is the same fatalism inspired by the spectacle of the inexorable pressure of economic forces, and confirmed by that of the permanence of geographical inhabited spaces, that leads to a vision of a humanity overwhelmed by greater forces than its own, as can be seen in Braudel's other great work, *Civilization and Capitalism, 15th–18th Century* (1979).[21] Are we so far from Max Weber's iron cage? Did not the focus on economics hinder the unfolding of this third stage, as seems suggested by Braudel's reticence regarding Weber's thesis about the Protestant ethic and the spirit of capitalism? Was not the dream of federating history with regard to the neighboring social sciences realized solely thanks to an anthropology intimidated by structuralism, despite its vow to historicize it? At the very least, up to his retirement and to the time of his death, Braudel continued forcefully to oppose the demand for a total history to its threatened dispersion.

In the review the journal *Annales* made of its first fifty years in 1979, the editors recall that the community gathered around it had wanted to propose "more a program than a theory," but recognized that the multiplicity of objects submitted to an ever more specialized, more technical research risked making reappear "the temptation of a cumulative history, where the acquired results count more than the questions posed."[22] Jacques Revel confronts this risk in his article "Histoire et science sociale, les paradigms des *Annales*," which follows that of A. Burguière.[23] What, he asks, is "the unity of an intellectual movement that has endured for a half century"? "What is there in common between the highly unified program of the first years and the apparent bursting apart of more recent orientations?" Revel prefers to speak of particular paradigms that succeed rather than eliminate one another. The refusal of abstraction, the plea for the concrete against the schematic, makes the formulation of these paradigms difficult. The first thing to impose itself is the relative economic and social dominance of the first years of the journal, without the social ever becoming "the object of a systematic, articulated conceptualization." "It is rather the place for an always open inventory of correspondences, of relations that ground the interdependence of phenomena." It is easier to see the ambition to organize the social sciences, including sociology and psychology, around history, and the resistance to "the sometimes terrorist antihistoricism" fomented by the reading of Claude Lévi-Strauss's *Tristes Tropiques* (1955) and *Structural Anthropology* (1958), than the conceptual structure that undergirds this ambition and this resistance.[24] This is why the interplay of continuities and even more of discontinuities is so difficult to outline. We do not know exactly what "constellation of knowledge has come undone before our eyes over the past twenty years." Is humanity by itself, if we may put it this way, the federating theme "of a particular ordering of scientific discourse," such that we may assign to the effacing of this transitory object the subsequent fragmentation of the field of inquiry? Revel clearly has in mind discourse about the bursting apart of history, maybe even François Dosse's talk of a "history in pieces." He upholds the refusal and the conviction attached to the claim for a global or total history; the refusal of partitions, the conviction of coherence and convergence. But he cannot hide his unease: "It seems as though the program of global history offers only a neutral framework for the addition of particular histories whose ordering is not a problem." Whence the question: "History burst apart or history under construction?" Revel does not answer.

And in this conceptual mishmash what becomes of the history of mentalities, which this summary inventory does not name (any more than it does the other main branches of the tree of history)?

Confronted with these questions and doubts, a few historians have known how to keep their focus on the question of intelligibility within the region of the history of mentalities, even if it means placing it under different patronage. This is the case with Robert Mandrou, all of whose work is placed under the heading of "historical psychology."[25] He is the one assigned in the *Encyclopedia Universalis* with the defense and illustration of the history of mentalities.[26] Mandrou defines its object in the following way: "It takes as its objective the reconstitution of behaviors, expressions, and silences that express conceptions of the world and collective sensibilities; representations and images, myths and values, acknowledged or affecting groups or society as a whole, and that constitute the contents of collective psychology, provide the fundamental elements for this study." (We can see here the equation between mentality for French-speaking authors and what Germans call *Weltanschauung*, which our concept of mentality is meant to translate.) As for method, the historical psychology that Mandrou himself practices is applied to narrowly defined operative concepts: worldviews, structures, conjunctures. On the one side, worldviews have their own kind of coherence; on the other, a certain structural continuity confers on them a noteworthy stability. Finally, short and long rhythms and fluctuations mark their encounters. In this way, Mandrou presents himself as a historian of the collective mind who gives the most credibility to the intelligibility of the history of mentalities, following a conceptuality that recalls that of Ernest Labrousse (structure, conjuncture, event)—and the least credit to a psychoanalytic rewriting of collective psychology, in contrast to Michel de Certeau.

It was also at the margins of the *Annales* school that Jean-Pierre Vernant in 1965 first published his major book *Myth and Thought among the Greeks*, which has been reprinted a number of times, and which he too subtitles a study in historical psychology, placing it under the patronage of the psychologist Ignace Meyerson (to whom the work is dedicated) and associating it with the work of another Hellenist, Louis Gernet.[27] What is at issue are studies devoted to the inner history of Greek man, his mental organization, the changes that from the eighth to fourth century B.C. "affect the entire framework of thought and the whole gamut of psychological functions: the modes of symbolic expression, and the manipulation of signs, ideas of time and space, causality, memory, imagination, the organization of action, will, and personality" (xi). Twenty years later he will acknowledge his kinship with the structural analysis applied to different myths or mythic groupings by other scholars, including Marcel Détienne, with whom he published *Cunning Intelligence in Greek Culture and Society*.[28] And the work he published with Pierre Vidal-Naquet, *Myth and Tragedy in Ancient Greece*, incontestably bears the same imprint.[29] It is worth noting that Vernant does not break with the humanism of the first generation of the *Annales* school. What is important to him in the final analysis is the sinuous trail leading from myth to reason. As in *Myth and Thought*, it is a question of demonstrating "how, by way of the older tragedy of the fifth century, were outlined the first, still hesitant sketches of man as agent, as the master of and responsible for his acts, as the possessor of a will" (7). Vernant emphasizes: "from myth to reason: these were the two poles between which, in a panoramic view, the destiny of Greek thought seemed to play itself out by the end of this book" (7), without the foreignness of this form of thinking being overlooked, as the study on "the avatars of that particular, typically Greek form, crafty thinking, which is made up of cunning, cleverness, craftiness, deceit, and resourcefulness of all kinds," the Greeks' *mētis*, which "stems exclusively neither from myth, nor from reason."

However, the main tendency of the history of mentalities for the *Annales* school was to turn toward a less certain defense of its right to existence, beginning with the second generation, that of Labrousse and Braudel, and even more so at the time of the so-called "new history." On the one hand, we have the spectacle of a loss of focus, which led to the talk of a burst-apart history, even of a history in little pieces; on the other, thanks to this same dispersion, there was a certain upturn. It was in this sense that the history of mentalities figured as a whole among the "new objects" of the "new history," in volume three of the collection edited by Jacques Le Goff and Pierre Nora, *Faire de l'histoire.*[30] Alongside "new problems" (volume 1) and "new approaches" (volume 2), the history of mentalities freed itself at the very moment when the project of total history was fading. For some, a passion for the long time span and quantitative studies coming from the older commitment to economic history remained, at the price of effacing the figure of the human being of the humanism that was still celebrated by Bloch and Febvre. In particular, the history of climate provided its measures and strategies to this "history without men."[31] This tenacious attachment to serial history by contrast makes the conceptual fuzziness of the notion of mentality reappear among those who accept the patronage of this special kind of history. In this regard, Jacques Le Goff's presentation of this "new object" is more discouraging for the rigorous-minded than were the earlier summaries by Duby and Mandrou. The increasing importance of this *topos*, announcing its eventual disappearance, is greeted by a disturbing phrase from Marcel Proust: "I like 'mentality.' There are a lot of new words like that which people suddenly start using, but they never last."[32] That the expression refers to a scientific reality, that it contains a conceptual coherence, remains problematic. The critic would like to believe so; nevertheless, its very imprecision recommends it for speaking of what is "beyond history"—by which we can understand is meant economic and social history. The history of mentalities thus offers a "change of scenery . . . to those intoxicated by economic and social history and above all a vulgar Marxism" by transporting them to this "elsewhere," to what were mentalities. And in this way one satisfies Michelet's expectation of rendering a face to "the resuscitated living-dead." At the same time, one links up again with Bloch and Febvre. One modulates things in terms of epochs, settings, in the manner of ethnologists and sociologists. If one speaks of archeology, it is not in the sense of Foucault, but in terms of the ordinary sense of stratigraphy. As for their operating, mentalities function automatically, without their bearers being aware of them. They are less well-formed, professed thoughts than commonplaces, more or less worn out heritages, worldviews inscribed in what one can risk calling the collective unconscious. If the history of mentalities could for a period of time merit its place among the "new objects," it was owing to an enlarging of the documentary sphere whereby, on the one hand, every trace became the collective witness of an age, and, on the other, every document concerning behavior marked a gap in relation to the common mentality. This oscillation between the common and the marginal, thanks to the discordances denouncing the absence of the contemporaneousness of contemporaries, could seem to justify recourse to the category of mentalities despite its semantic fuzziness. But then it was not the history of mentalities, as such, that was to have been treated as a new object, but the themes thrown together in the third volume of *Faire de l'histoire*: from climate to festivals in passing through the book and the body,[33] and those that are not named, the large-scale affects of private life,[34] without forgetting young women and death.[35]

This inscribing of the notion of mentality among the "new objects" of history at the price of the expansion I have just spoken of was not tenable. The deep reason for the rejection inflicted upon it does not come down to the objection of semantic fuzziness. It has to do with a more serious confusion, namely, the uncertain simultaneous use of the notion as an object of inquiry, as a dimension of the social bond distinct from the economic and the political, and as a means of explanation. This confusion is to be attributed to the heritage of Lucien Lévy-Bruhl and his concept of "primitive mentality." By primitive mentality one explained what were irrational beliefs from the perspective of scientific and logical rationality. One thought to get beyond this prejudice on the part of the observer, which Lévy-Bruhl himself had begun to criticize in his *Notebooks* published in 1949,[36] by applying the notion of mentality to ways of thinking or sets of beliefs belonging to groups or whole societies that were sufficiently distinct so that it could be used both as a descriptive and as an explanatory feature. One thought that what counted as a distinctive feature was not the content of some actual discourse but an implicit note, an underlying system of belief. But, in dealing with the idea of mentality as both a descriptive feature and a principle of explanation, one did not really get out of the orbit of the concept of primitive mentality dating from sociology at the beginning of the twentieth century.

It was this impure mixture that Geoffrey E. R. Lloyd undertook to dissolve in unpitying fashion in a book that had a devastating effect, titled *Demystifying Mentalities*.[37] Lloyd's argument is simple and direct. The concept of mentality is useless and harmful. It is useless at the level of description, harmful at that of explanation. It had served Lévy-Bruhl for describing prelogical and mystical features, such as the idea of participation, assigned to "primitives." It serves contemporary historians for describing and explaining divergent or dissonant modes of belief from an age in which today's observer does not recognize his conception of the world. It is for a logical, coherent, scientific observer that such past beliefs, or even those of the present, seem enigmatic or paradoxical, if not frankly absurd. Everything prescientific and still unscientific falls under this description. It is a construction of the observer projected on the worldview of the actors in question.[38] This is when the concept of mentality shifts from description to explanation and from being useless to being harmful, inasmuch as it dispenses with having to reconstruct the contexts and circumstances that surrounded the appearance of the "explicit categories *we* commonly use in our highly value-laden descriptions—science, myth, magic and the opposition between the literal and the metaphorical" (7). Next Lloyd's work was devoted to a telling reconstruction of the contexts and circumstances for the appearance of the categories of a rational and scientific observer, principally in the age of classical Greece, but also in China. The conquest of the distinction between the prescientific (magic and myth) and the scientific is the object of close analysis, centered principally on the political conditions and the rhetorical resources for the public use of speech in polemical contexts. One will recognize here an attack on problems comparable to that of Jean-Pierre Vernant, Pierre Vidal-Naquet, and Marcel Détienne.[39] The alleged unspoken and implict something that the concept of mentality is supposed to thematize in a global, indiscriminate manner dissolves into a complex network of gradual, circumstantial acquisitions.

For all that, does Lloyd put an end to mentalities? Yes, assuredly, if it is a question of a lazy mode of explanation. But the answer has to be more circumspect if it is a question of a heuristic concept applied to what within a system of beliefs cannot be resolved into the contents of that discourse. Proof of this is the recourse Lloyd himself makes to the concept of a "style of inquiry" in his reconstruction of the Greek mode of rationality.[40] So it is less a question of the "distinctive or striking peculiarities in patterns of discourse or reasoning, or again in the implicit beliefs that are inferred to underlie modes of behaviour [for the observer]" (4), than of what we might call the available belief structure of an era. To be sure, it is in relation to the observer that this belief structure is defined, but it is with regard to the actors that it is available. It was in this sense that Lucien Febvre could affirm that straightforward atheism was not a concept of belief available for a person of the sixteenth century. It is not the irrational, pre-scientific, pre-logical character of a belief that is thereby pointed out, but its differential, distinctive character on the plane of what Lloyd calls precisely a "style of inquiry." The notion of mentality is thus brought back to its status as a "new object" of historical discourse in the space left open by economics, the social, and the political. It is an *explicandum*, not a lazy principle of explanation. If we conclude that the heritage of the inadequate concept of "primitive mentality" remains the original sin of the concept of mentality, then it would be better indeed to give it up and prefer to it that of re-presentation.

I propose a difficult conquest of the right to proceed to this semantic substitution, first by sending it to school with some strict teachers, then by proposing a detour through an intermediary concept, that of scale and of "changes in scale."

## SOME ADVOCATES OF RIGOR: MICHEL FOUCAULT, MICHEL DE CERTEAU, NORBERT ELIAS

I do not want to hand over the Labroussian and Braudelian models of the history of mentalities and representations to the criticism of a more recent historiography without having listened to three voices, two of whom come from outside historiography *stricto sensu*, but all of whom have raised to a pre-viously unheard level the radicality of the discussion taking place throughout the human sciences. These are, on the one side, Michel Foucault's plea for a science said to be without precedent, called the archeology of knowledge, and, on the other, Norbert Elias's plea for a science of social formations that believes itself to be the enemy of history but that unfolds in an imperious fashion in a frankly historical way. Between them is Michel de Certeau, the inside outsider.

It is worth the effort of placing Foucault and Elias together in order to maintain the pressure of a demand for rigor directed against the discourse of professional historians rebelling against the favored model of the *Annales* school.

Foucault's *Archeology of Knowledge* intervenes at the moment where the theory of the archive yields its place to that of archeology.[41] He describes this turning point as an inversion in approach. Following the regressive analysis leading from discursive formations to bare statements comes the moment of turning back toward possible domains of application, without it for all that being a question of a repetition of the starting point.

It is first of all on the occasion of its confrontation with the history of ideas that archeology opens its way. It is against a discipline that has not been able to find its voice that it means to oppose its harsh schooling. Some-times the history of ideas "recounts the by-ways and margins of history"

(136)—alchemy and animal spirits, almanacs and other fluctuating languages; sometimes it is "the reconstitution of developments in the linear form of history" (137). Once again, denials abound: neither interpretation nor reconstruction of continuities, nor focusing on the meaning of works in a psychological, sociological, or anthropological manner. In short, archeology does not seek to reconstitute the past, to repeat what has been. But what does it want and what can it do? "It is nothing more than a rewriting: that is, in the preserved form of exteriority, a regulated transformation of what has already been written" (140). All right, but what does that mean? The descriptive capacity of archeology plays out on four fronts: novelty, contradiction, comparison, and transformation. On the first front, it arbitrates between the original, which is not the origin but a breaking point with the already said, and the regular, which is not the other of what is deviant but the piling up of the already said. The regularity of discursive practices takes its bearings from analogies that assure "enunciative homogeneity" and from hierarchies that structure these utterances and allow establishing derivation trees, as we see in linguistics with Propp and in natural history with Linnaeus.

On the second front, it credits the role of coherence in the history of ideas to the point of holding this as "a heuristic rule, a procedural obligation, almost a moral constraint of research." Of course, this coherence is the result of research, not its presupposition, but it holds as an optimum: "the greatest possible number of contradictions resolved by the simplest means" (149). But it remains that contradictions are objects to be described for themselves, where we find gaps, dissension, defects in discourse. On the third front, archeology becomes interdiscursive, without falling into a confrontation between worldviews. In this regard, the competition among general grammar, natural history, and the analysis of wealth in *The Order of Things* demonstrated this comparison at work, apart from the ideas of expression, reflection, or influence.[42] There is no hermeneutic of intentions and motivations, only a listing of specific forms of articulation. Archeology plays out its destiny on the fourth front, that of changes and transformations. Foucault is not taken in by either the quasi synchrony of immobile thoughts—an indicator of Eleaticism—nor by the linear succession of events—an indicator of historicism! What stands out is the theme of discontinuity, with ruptures, fault lines, gaps, sudden redistributions, which he opposes to "the practice of the historians of ideas" (170) who are overly concerned with continuities, transitions, anticipations, preliminary sketches. Here is the high point of archeology. If there is a paradox to it, it is not that it multiplies differences, but that it refuses to reduce them, in this way inverting the habitual values. "For the history of ideas, the appearance of difference indicates an error, or a trap; instead of examining it, the clever historian must try to reduce it.... Archeology, on the other hand, takes as the object of its description what is usually regarded as an obstacle: its aim is not to overcome differences but to analyze them, to say what exactly they consist of, to *differentiate* them" (171). In truth, it is the very idea of change, too marked by that of an active force, that must be renounced to the benefit of the idea of transformation, perfectly neutral in relation to the great metaphorics of flow. Should we reproach Foucault for having substituted for the ideology of the continuous one of the discontinuous? He readily returns the compliment.[43] But it is the lesson I want to retain and the paradox that below I want to try to put to work.

The theme of archeology calls for the same perplexity in the face of an exercise that we can qualify as an intellectual asceticism. Under the sign of the two culminating ideas of the archive, as the register of discursive formations, and of archeology, as the description of interdiscursive transformations, Foucault has delimited a radically neutral terrain, or rather a costly neutralized one, that of statements without a speaker. Who can take up a position outside it? And how are we to continue to think about the formation and transformations not of discourses neutralized in this way, but of the relation between representations and practices? Moving from the archive to archeology, Foucault invited us to "reverse the procedure" and to "proceed to possible domains of application" (135). It is just this project that needs to be pursued following Foucault, in a field that cuts through the neutrality of the purged domain of statements. For a historiography that takes as the direct referent of its discourse the social bond, and as its rule of relevance the consideration of the relations between representations and social practices, the task is to leave behind the neutral zone of pure statements with an eye to reaching the relations between discursive formations, in the strict sense of the theory of statements, and the nondiscursive formations where language itself resists any reduction to a statement. Foucault, in truth, is not unaware of the problem posed by "institutions, political events, economic practices and processes" (162). Better, when he refers to these examples borrowed from the "non-discursive domain," and does so within the framework of "comparative facts," he takes the task of archeology to be "to define specific forms of articulation" (162). But can it do so without the kind of exit, of displacement I have spoken of?[44] The notions of dependence and autonomy having ceased to function, the word "articulation" remains largely programmatic. But it needs to be made operational at the price of a displacement of Foucault's displacement.

I do not want to leave Foucault without having again referred to the figure of Michel de Certeau, inasmuch as he offers a kind of counterpoint to the archeology of knowledge. There is also a "Certeau moment" on the plane of explanation/understanding. Essentially it corresponds to the second segment of the triad of "social place," "scientific practices," and "writing."[45] It is the high point designated by the term "practice" (69–86), to which must be joined the conclusion of *L'Absent de l'histoire*,[46] without forgetting the pages of the same collection directly addressed to Michel Foucault: "The Dark Sun of Language" (115–32).

It is first of all as research that historiographical practice enters its critical phase, with the beginnings of the production of documents, which are set apart from actual human practice by a gesture of separation that recalls the collection of "rarities" in the form of archives according to Foucault (*The Writing of History*, 83). Certeau puts his own stamp on this inaugural operation by characterizing it as a redistribution of space that makes research a mode of "production of places." But Foucault's imprint is recognizable by the insistence on the notion of deviation that is expressly attached to this model. It is in relation to models that the differences taken as relevant deviate. Thus, in the history of representations characterizing the religious history practiced by Certeau, "sorcery, madness, festival, popular literature, the forgotten world of the peasant, Occitania, etc., all these zones of silence" (79) make for deviations. Each time, the relevant gesture is the means "of bringing forth differences relative to continuities or to elements from which analysis proceeds" (79). It is expressly to the totalizing claim of earlier history that this "research on the borderline" is opposed. But what models are in question? It is not a question of statements as in Foucault's archeology, but of models drawn from other sciences: econometrics, urban studies, biology, as sciences of the homogeneous. Foucault would place these kinds of models among the "discursive formations" referred to right at the beginning of *The Archeology of Knowledge*. Nevertheless, this recourse to borrowed models suffices to justify the audacious extrapolation that makes Certeau say that the position of the particular in history is situated "at the limit of the thinkable," a position that itself calls for a rhetoric of the exceptional whose outlines stem from the subsequent step of representation and literary writing, which we may take as Michel de Certeau's major contribution to the problematic of the historiographical operation.

But before that we must say in what fashion *L'Absent de l'histoire* further expands the semantic space of the idea of a deviation by pairing it with the idea of the absent, which according to Certeau constitutes the distinctive mark of the past per se, as we shall see later in our section devoted to truth in history. History, in this sense, constitutes a vast "heterology" (173), a tracing of the "traces of the other." But wasn't it already the ambition of memory (which is named on the last page of this book) to produce the first discourse about the absent under the figure of the icon (180)? Whatever reservation we may have as regards the reduction of memory and history to one and the same celebration of absence, we can no longer oppose, in Foucault's intransigent manner, the discontinuities linked to historical discourse and the presumed continuity of the discourse of memory. It may be here that Certeau begins to mark his own deviation in relation to Foucault. In the short, incisive essay titled "The Dark Sun of Language: Michel Foucault," he sets out in search of his own difference. Bit by bit, he speaks haphazardly of his astonishment, his resistance, his second-degree assent, his ultimate reservations. It is true that he refers less to the archeology of knowledge than to the trilogy of works ending with *The Order of Things*. The alternating play of the order belonging to the "epistemological basis" of each episteme and the rupture that takes place between successive epistemes is welcomed, but leaves Certeau hungry for more. What "dark sun" is concealed behind this alternation? Is it not death, which is, however, named by Foucault himself? Yet he, Foucault, finally takes refuge in the "narrative" of this alternation between coherence and events. But it is beneath narrative that reason is truly "called into question by its history" (125). As a consequence, archeology does not escape the "equivocation" resulting from this unspoken something. It is in the wake of this suspicion that Certeau takes his distance from Foucault: "who is it that is to know what no one knows?" (161). In Foucault's works, "who speaks and from where?" The question of May 1968 comes up. And a more cutting arrow is launched: "to speak of the death that founds all language is not yet to confront it, but may be to avoid the death that strikes this very discourse" (132). I fear that Certeau goes astray here, without being assured that he any better than Foucault escapes the question posed at the very heart of his work by the relation of historical discourse to death. For a reader who has both *The Archeology of Knowledge* and *The Writing of History* open before him must look on another side for the real gap between Foucault and Certeau, namely, on the side of the idea of production, and more explicitly the production of a place. The archeology of knowledge, we can say as does Certeau, does not speak of the place of its own production.

Certeau therefore distances himself from Foucault by leaving behind the absolute neutrality of a discourse on discourse and by beginning to articulate this discourse in terms of other significant practices, the very task of a history of representations. In so doing, he puts off the difficulty posed by the question of the place of production until that inaugural moment when the gesture of doing history brings about a gap in relation to the practices through which human beings make history. This will be the moment of truth in history, where we shall encounter Certeau a final time. The actual reason for the deviation of Michel de Certeau in relation to Michel Foucault will have to be sought in how Certeau's research is rooted in a philosophical anthropology in which the reference to psychology is fundamental and foundational. It was not an accident of compilation that brought together in *The Writing of History* the important article on "the historiographical operation," which I have been distilling over the course of this work, and the two articles placed under the overarching title "Freudian Writings." It is indeed a question of psychoanalysis and writing, more exactly, of the writing of psychoanalysis in its relation to the writing of history by historians. The first of these essays, "What Freud Makes of History," was published in *Annales* in 1970. The question is what Freud as an analyst does with history. It is not when one undertakes to nibble at the obscure regions of history with supposed Freudian concepts, "such as the name of the father, the Oedipus complex, transference, in short when one makes use of psychoanalysis that one learns from it, but it is rather when one redoes the analyst's work in the face of a case as singular as a pact concluded with the devil that the 'legend' (given to be read) becomes a 'history.' "[47] Here where the issue is Freud, the conclusion is that he is instructive, not because he makes something of the story told by others, and in the first place by historians, but when in his own way he does history. Beyond the fact that an important part of Certeau's work results from this exchange among different ways of doing history, it is this very exchange that justifies the recourse to psychoanalysis in an epistemology of historical knowledge. The second essay is devoted to "The Writing of *Moses and Monotheism*," the subtitle beneath the general heading "The Fiction of History." What Freud makes understood in this controversial text is not some ethnographical truth, following the canons of that discipline, but the relationship of his construction, which he calls a "novel," a "theoretical fiction," with the fable, that is, the "legend" produced within a tradition. A writing, therefore, comparable under this heading to that of historians turns up in an incongruous manner within the territory of the historian. A historical novel takes its place alongside written histories. The lack of decisiveness of this literary genre between history and fiction, which we shall return to in the following chapter, adds to the difficulty and, in truth, constitutes it. What is important for the moment is the question of knowing in relation to what type of writing written history should situate itself. It is the search for this "place" of historical discourse among the ways of doing history that justifies taking psychoanalysis into account as an epistemology that, starting from within historical discourse, becomes external to it in regard to other ways of doing history. It is the very territory of the historian and his mode of explanation/understanding that finds itself expanded thereby. This carefully worked out opening is once again due to Certeau's rigor.

The exemplary work of Norbert Elias proposes another kind of rigor for historians to think about than that practiced principally by Michel Foucault: not the rigor of a discourse on discursive operations apart from the field of practice, but the rigor of discourse on the conceptual apparatus put to work in an actual history bearing in a general way on the growth of political power from the end of the Middle Ages up to the eighteenth century. If this work can be criticized, it is not in terms of its conceptual coherence, but as regards its choice of the macrohistorical scale that remains unproblematic until it is confronted with a different choice, as we shall see in the following section. I must also add that Elias's work is not defenseless in the confrontation with the reading I am going to undertake upon leaving behind the confused zone and semantic fuzziness that we have been considering.

I shall take as my guide part four of *The Civilizing Process*, titled "Towards a Theory of Civilizing Processes."[48] What Elias calls "civilizing processes" directly concerns my preoccupations relative to the establishing of a history of representations. It has to do with an ongoing process that, as Roger Chartier's foreword to the French translation of *The Court Society* points out,[49] is situated at the point of articulation between one noteworthy social formation, the central power of the state, apprehended in its monarchical phase during the Ancien Regime, and the modifications in sensibility and behavior we call civilization or, better, the civilizing process. In contrast to the future microhistory that installs itself straight away at the level of social agents, Elias's sociology consists in a macrohistory comparable to that of the *Annales* school. And this is true in two ways: on the one hand, the civilizing process is correlated with large-scale phenomena at the level of the organization of society into the state, such as the monopolization of force and taxation and other such fees; on the other hand, this process is described as a series of progressively internalized constraints up to the point where they become a phenomenon of permanent self-constraint that Elias names *habi-tus*. The self is in fact what is at stake in civilization, what civilizes itself, under the institutional constraint. The descending course of an analysis from the top to the bottom of the social scale reveals itself to be particularly efficacious in the case of court society, where the social models unfold around a central core, the court, into coordinated and subordinated layers of society. One quite naturally thinks here of the relation between structure and conjuncture in Labrousse or the hierarchy of scales of different time spans in Braudel. In fact, things are more complicated than that, and the category of habitus will come to include all the features that distinguish a dynamic phenomenon of a historical order from a mechanical one in the physical order. It is worth noting that Elias does not speak of determinism—even if he does speak of constraint—but of the interdependence between the modifications affecting the political organization and those affecting human sensibility and behavior.

In this regard, Elias's key concepts have to be carefully respected in their rigorously spelled out specificity: "formation" or "configuration," designating the contours of the organizing phenomena, for example, the court society; "equilibrium of tensions," designating the hidden springs of social dynamics, for example, in the gathering together of the warriors who preside over the court society and in the competition between aristocracy and bourgeois office holders that will contribute to the breaking up of that society;[50] "evolution of formations," designating the rule-governed transformations that simultaneously affect the distribution and the displacements of political power and the psychic economy that governs the distribution of motives, feelings, and representations. If Elias's apparatus for describing and analyzing had to be designated by a single term, it would be interdependence, which leaves an opening to what in an approach more sensitive to the response of social agents would be called appropriation. Elias, to be sure, did not cross this threshold—and its important corollary, uncertainty—but the place for it is clearly designated. It is located on the trajectory from social to self-constraint that the "Outline of a Theory of Civilization" brings to the fore. The category of habitus, as a result, will become a problem. Elias only covers this trajectory in one direction, the return voyage remains to be done. But what is important in Elias's eyes is first of all that the process is not rational in the sense of being willed and directed by individuals. Its rationalization is itself the effect of self-constraint. Next, the social differentiation, resulting from the increased pressure of competition, gives rise to an increasing differentiation, and hence to a more complete, more regular, more controlled articulation of behaviors and representations, something that is well summed

up in the expression "psychic economy," for which the term "habitus" constitutes an exact synonym. Certainly, it is a matter of a constraint, but of a
self-constraint that includes reserves of reaction that express themselves on
the level of the equilibrium of tensions. All the leading terms of Elias's text—
differentiation, stability, permanence, control, predictability—are capable of
dialecticalization. All the described phenomena of self-constraint constitute
formulas of dispersion for the drifting toward the extremes that the process
of civilization undertakes to resolve. Thus habitus consists in a regulation
sanctioned by the equilibrium between these extremes.[51] The phenomenon
of the diffusion of self-constraint is interesting in this regard. It provides the
occasion for introducing, along with the concept of social layer (first with
the pair warrior/courtier, then with aristocrat/bourgeois) that of a psychic
layer, close to some instances from psychoanalytic theory (superego, ego, id),
despite Elias's mistrust regarding what he takes to be the antihistoricism of
Freudian theory. This phenomenon of diffusion from (social and psychic)
layer to layer also brings to light the phenomena of dispersion and recentering, thanks to the phenomenon of diminishing contrasts that makes us
"civilized."

The most noteworthy contribution of *The Civilizing Process* for a history
of mentalities and representations has to be sought in Elias's examination
of two major modes of self-constraint, that of rationalization and that of
shame. It is within the framework of the court, with its quarrels and plots,
that Elias, encouraged by La Bruyère and Saint-Simon, situates one of the
key moments of the conquest of reflection upon and the regularization of
our emotions, of that knowledge of the human heart and the social setting
that can be summed up by the term "rationalization." In this regard, the
trace of the heritage of the court can be followed up to Maupassant and
Proust. Something is at issue here that is more than what the history of ideas
calls reason. There is a close correlation between the social cohabitation of
human beings and what a "historical psychology" (406) will take as a habitus
of the psychic economy considered as an integrated whole. The history of
ideas wants only to consider contents, "ideas," "thoughts," the sociology of
knowledge focuses on ideologies, or even a superstructure, psychoanalysis on
a conflict between competing drives detached from their social history. But
rationalization consists in an internal relation within each human being that
evolves in correlation with human interrelationships. The civilizing process is
nothing other than this correlation among the changes affecting the psychic
structures and those affecting social structures. And habitus lies at the crossroads of these two processes.[52] A sense of shame is the second figure that the

"habitus of the West" brought about. It consists in a regulation of fear in the face of the inner perils that, in a regime of civility, took the place of the external threat of violence. The fear of revealing one's inferiority, which is at the heart of weakness before another's superiority,[53] constitutes a central theme in the conflict that constructs our psychic economy. Here once again, "we can only speak of shame in conjunction with its socio-genesis" (416). Much more could be said concerning the characterization of this sense of shame (Elias associates it with "embarrassment"). Essentially it has do with the process of internalization of fears that within the emotional order corresponds to rationalization within the intellectual one.

I have said enough to indicate the points where Elias's analyses lend themselves to a dialecticalization of the described processes that he describes in a unilinear fashion from the top to the bottom of the social scale.[54] Below, we shall examine in what way the theme of appropriation may balance that of constraint. Elias himself opens the way to a parallel dialecticalization in one passage where, after having emphasized the nonrational character (in the sense indicated earlier) of the formation of habits, he comments: "But it is by no means impossible that we can make out of it [civilization] something more 'reasonable,' something that functions in terms of our needs and purposes. For it is precisely in conjunction with the civilizing process that the blind dynamics of people intertwining in their deeds and aims gradually leads towards greater scope for planned intervention into both the social and individual structures—interventions based on a growing knowledge of the unplanned dynamics of these structures" (367).[55]

## VARIATIONS IN SCALE

> *Diversity.... A town or a landscape from afar off is a town*
> *and a landscape, but as one approaches it becomes houses, trees, tiles,*
> *leaves, grass, ants, ants' legs, and so on ad infinitum. All that is*
> *comprehended in the word "landscape."*
>
> § Pascal, *Pensées*[56]

In the preceding analyses the question of scale, and more precisely of the chosen scale adopted by the historian, was not posed. To be sure, the heuristic models proposed and used by Labrousse and Braudel and by a great part of the *Annales* school clearly stem from a macrohistorical approach, extended from the economic and geographical basis of history to the social and institutional level and to phenomena said to be of the "third type," from which stem the forms of the most stable predominant mentalities. But this macrohistorical perspective was not deliberately chosen, hence not preferred to something that could be taken as an alternative. The sequence "structure, conjuncture, event" in Labrousse and the hierarchy of time spans in Braudel implicitly rest on an interplay of scales, but as the tripartite composition of Braudel's *The Mediterranean* testifies (which remains the model for this genre), the preference accorded to a reading from the top to the bottom of the hierarchies of time spans was not thematized for itself, so that we can envisage changing scale and the very choice of a scale as a power open to the historian's discretion, with all the liberties and constraints that result from such a choice. Access to this mobility in the historian's gaze constitutes an important conquest of history during the last third of the twentieth century. Jacques Revel even adopts the phase "interplay of scales" to greet the exercise of this methodological freedom, which we shall assign to the part of interpretation implied in the search for truth in history when the time comes.[57]

The approach to microhistory adopted by some Italian historians stems from this interplay of scales.[58] By taking a village, a group of families, an individual caught up in the social fabric for their scales of observation, the practitioners of *microhistoria* not only have made clear the relevance of the microhistorical level with which they work, they have also brought up for discussion the very principle of a variation in scale.[59] We shall not focus on the defense and illustration of *microhistoria* as such, but rather on an examination of the very notion of a variation in scale, in order to evaluate the contribution of this original problem to the history of mentalities or representations, which we have seen threatened in turn from within by collapse and intimidated from without by demands for rigor that its use of fuzzy concepts make it incapable of satisfying.

The key idea attached to the idea of a variation in scale is that, when we change scale, what becomes visible are not the same interconnections but rather connections that remained unperceived at the macrohistorical scale. This is the sense of the magnificent aphorism from Pascal's *Pensées* that Louis Marin, whose name will return below, liked to cite.[60]

The notion of scale is borrowed from cartography, architecture, and optics.[61] In cartography, there is an external referent, the territory that the map represents. What is more, the distances measured by maps of different scales are commensurable according to homothetic relations, which authorizes us to speak of the reduction of a terrain to a given scale. However, from one scale to another we observe a change in the level of information as a function of the level of organization. Think of a roadmap. We see the primary axes of circulation in large scale, the distribution of dwellings on a small one. From one map to another, space is continuous, the territory is the same, hence a small change in scale shows the same terrain. This is the positive aspect of a simple change in proportion. There is no room for an opposition between scales. The counterpart is a certain loss of details, of complexity, hence of information in the passage to a larger scale. This double feature—proportionality of dimensions and heterogeneity of information—has to affect geography, which is so dependent on cartography.[62] A discordant geomorphology appears with a change of scale within the same geopolitical setting, as can be verified in detail by rereading the first part of Braudel's *The Mediterranean*. The term "Mediterranean" situates the object of inquiry at the level of what Pascal calls landscape—all that enveloped by the name Mediterranean, we might say at the end our reading!

The role of the idea of scale in architecture and in urban planning is also relevant to our discussion. Proportional relations comparable to those in cartography are posited along with the balance between gain and loss of information depending on the scale chosen. But unlike the relationship between map and territory, the architect's or urban planner's plan has as its referent a building, a town, yet to be constructed. What is more, the building or the town have varying relations with their contexts scaled in terms of nature, the landscape, communication networks, the already constructed parts of the town, and so on. These characters belonging to the notion of scale in architecture and in urban planning concern the historian inasmuch as the historiographical operation is in one sense an architectural one.[63] Historical discourse has to be built up in the form of a set of works. Each work gets inserted into an already existing environment. Rereadings of the past are in this way reconstructions, at the price sometimes of costly demolitions: construct, deconstruct, reconstruct are familiar gestures to the historian.

It is through these two borrowings that reference to the optical metaphor becomes operative in history. Behaviors linked to the accommodating of this gaze are not noted inasmuch as the nature—or even the beauty—of the uncovered spectacle leads to forgetting the focusing procedures of the optical apparatus used at the price of the learned manipulations. History, too, functions in turn as an eyepiece, a microscope, or a telescope.

What the notion of scale includes within itself in the use historians make of it is the absence of commensurability of the dimensions. In changing scale, one does not see the same things as larger or smaller, in capital or lower case letters, as Plato puts it in the *Republic* about the relationship between the soul and the city. One sees different things. One can no longer speak of a reduction of scale. There are different concatenations of configuration and causality. The balance between gains and losses of information applies to the modeling operations that bring into play different heuristic imaginary forms. In this regard, what we can reproach in macrohistory is its failure to notice its dependence on a choice of scale with its macroscopic optical point of view that it borrowed from a more cartographical than historical model. For example, we can observe in Braudel some hesitation in the handling of the hierarchy of time spans. On the one hand, an interlocking relationship is presumed between homogeneous linear time spans thanks to the inclusion of all of them in one unique calendar time, itself indexed in terms of the stellar order, despite a certain mistrust regarding the abuse of chronology committed by the history focused on short-term events. On the other hand, we can also observe a piling up of superimposed time spans with no dialectical relation between them. The history of mentalities incontestably suffered from this methodological deficiency relative to the changes in scale insofar as the mentalities of the masses were presumed to stem from the long time span, without the conditions of their diffusion on smaller scales being taken into account. Even in Norbert Elias, himself a master in his use of the concept, the phenomena of self-constraint were said to hold across clearly identified social layers—the court, the nobles de robe, the city, and so on. But the changes in scale implied in the examination of the diffusion of models of behavior and of feeling from one social layer to another were not acknowledged. In a general way, the history of mentalities, insofar as it had simply extended the macrohistorical models of economic history to social history and to phenomena of the "third type," tended to deal with the concept of social pressure as an irresistible force operating in an unperceived fashion in relation to the reception of messages by social agents. The treatment of the relations between high and popular culture was particularly affected by this presupposition that goes with a reading that runs from the top to the bottom of the social scale. Other pairs stemming from similar binary systems were equally reinforced by this same prejudice: strength vs. weakness, authority vs. resistance, and, in general, domination vs. obedience, following the Weberian schema of domination (*Herrschaft*).[64]

Two leading works from Italian *microhistoria*, accessible in French, have held my attention. Carlo Ginzburg in a short and incisive preface comments that it is thanks to an exception, given "the scarcity of evidence about the behavior and attitudes of the subordinate classes of the past," that it was possible to recount "the story of a miller of the Friuli, Domenico Scandella, called Menocchio, who was burned at the stake by order of the Holy Office after a life passed in almost complete obscurity."[65] On the basis of the dossiers of his two trials, along with other documents relative to his working life, his family, and also his readings, Ginzburg was able to lay out the "rich picture of his thoughts and feelings, of his imaginations and aspirations" (xiii). Therefore this documentation has to do with what is called "'the culture of lower classes' or even 'popular culture'" (xiv). Ginzburg does not talk about scale but about cultural levels, whose existence is taken as a precondition for what become self-defined disciplines. This argument about the self-definition, almost the tautology, of social groups and professionals—such as the bourgeoisie—practiced in social history can be found in other historians unmarked by Italian microhistory, whom we shall return to below. Terms about culture—popular culture, high culture—and by implication those about dominant and subordinate classes implied in ideological quarrels linked to vulgar Marxism and anticolonial protests are reworked. The scarcity of written documents from a largely oral culture serves as the reason why. Even Robert Mandrou, whose place in the history of mentalities we noted above, is not exempt from reproach for having preferred to deal with the culture imposed upon the popular classes—we shall return to this below with regard to Certeau's *Possession at Loudon*—making this an effect of successful acculturation.[66] If literature meant for the people is not to cover over that produced by the people, this latter has still to exist and to be accessible. This was the case with Menocchio's confessions, which, owing to their uniqueness, do not meet the requirements for serial, quantitative history for which number and anonymity are important.

But how are we to avoid falling back upon anecdotes and the history of events? A first answer is that this objection is directed principally against political history. Another, more convincing one is that it is the latent and dispersed properties of an available historical language—which the computer misses—that the historian brings to light and organizes into discourse. What this historian articulates are the readings of a man of the people, meaning almanacs, songs, pious books, lives of saints, and brochures of all kinds that this miller put together in his own unique way. By leaving behind quantitative history, one does not fall into noncommunication. What is more, these reformulations express not only the reorganizing power of a man of the people's reading, they bring to the surface traditions and sleeping heresies that a surviving situation in a way brings back to life. The consequence for our problem of the history of mentalities is that the very concept of mentality has to be set aside inasmuch as this history, on the one hand, emphasizes only "the inert, obscure, unconscious elements in a given world view" (xxiii) and, on the other, retains the "interclass" connotation of a common culture—a presupposition that even Lucien Febvre did not escape in speaking of "men of the sixteenth century." The great French historian nevertheless did resist the presuppositions so strongly attached to the unhappy heritage of the sociological concept of a "collective mentality." Menocchio, for his part, cannot be situated in terms of that illiterate line, coming as he did after the invention of printing and the Reformation, which he must have read about and discussed.[67]

The other book that caught my attention is by Giovanni Levi, *Le Pouvoir au village: Histoire d'un exorciste dans le Piémont du XVIe siècle*,[68] with a preface by Jacques Revel: "L'Histoire au ras du sol." Here we are on the terrain worked on by Norbert Elias. But at the bottom of the scale—in the village. It is not about large numbers or about an individual. Nor does it deal with quantified indicators—prices or earnings, levels of wealth, distributions of professions—first named, then counted; nor with the regularities of a slow moving, almost immobile history, norms or common customs. The appearance and articulation of the phenomena considered are the fruit of a change of scale. Instead of aggregates followed over the long time span, we have a tangle of interrelations that need to be deciphered. But we ought not to expect from this a resurrection of the lived experience of social agents, as if history were to stop being history and link up again with the phenomenology of collective memory. Respect for that subtle boundary is important for my thesis, which never denies the implicit profession of the epistemological break separating history from memory, even collective memory. It is always interactions that are gathered and reconstituted.[69] The important word "reconstruction" is pronounced, which, later, will relaunch the history of mentalities, now better called the history of representations, beyond the limited example of such *microhistoria*. But, before moving on to this more or less well controlled extrapolation, we need to have brought to its critical point history linked to the choice of a microhistorical scale. We have said, at a smaller, even minute scale, we see things we do not see at a higher one. But we need to add that what we do not see and must not expect to see is the lived experience of the protagonists. What we see remains social interactions, at a fine scale, but one already microstructured. I will add, with a slight hesitation, that Levi's attempted reconstruction only partially satisfies Ginzburg's well known "evidential paradigm" from his essay "Roots of an

Evidential Paradigm." The microanalysis practiced by Levi lacks the flair of a detective or of an expert in detecting counterfeit paintings or of any sort of psychomedical semiotics. The same operation of reconstructing the real that distances it from actual lived experience also distances the evidential, bringing it closer to the more classic operations of dividing things up, of articulation, and of confronting testimonies, all of which allows Levi to speak of an "experimental history." But what does one experiment on? On the exercise of power in the village on a microhistorical scale. What we see at this scale are family and individual strategies, faced with economic realities and hierarchical relationships, in a play of exchanges between center and periphery, in short, the interactions that find their place in a village. With the concept of strategy, a noteworthy figure of rationality is brought to light, whose fruitfulness we shall evaluate below in terms of the uncertainty—opposed in turn to the fixity, permanence, and security—in short, the certainty—attached to the functioning of social norms on the larger scale, those quasi invariants of the history of mentalities over the long time span. It will be a legitimate question whether the forms of behavior placed under this term "strategy" have as their secret or admitted end reducing uncertainty or merely coming to terms with it.[70] "The great social and political game that is the real subject of this book," says Revel in his preface to *Le Pouvoir au village*, is, if you will, the same one that Norbert Elias reconstructs in his *The Civilizing Process*, but in the sense of, in Pascal's words, "all that is comprehended in the word 'landscape.'" But can we say that details that, in a way, lay out the landscape lead to recomposing it following specificable rules?

This is the whole question in the passage from microhistory to macrohistory.[71] If one can reproach macrohistory for proceeding from the long time span to subordinate ones in terms of no stated rule, does microhistory have arguments that allow it to say that it can take up again the project of total history, but beginning from the bottom? Concretely, the question comes down to asking whether the village is a favorable place for identifying the intermediary forms of power, through which power in the village articulates the power of the state as it is exercised in that time and that region? Uncertainty is precisely what affects the evaluation of the forces at work. And it is the task of Levi's book to explore these relationships when the hierarchy is viewed from below. Stated in terms of the epistemology of historical knowledge, the question becomes that of how representative is this history of a village and the interactions that take place there? Is the uncertainty of the protagonists also that of the analyst? Does it also weigh on the capacity held in reserve for generalization in what otherwise only would constitute a case history? And is this lesson generalizable to the extent that it can be opposed point by point to what Norbert Elias draws from his study of court society and other comparable societies?[72] In sum, "how representative is a concatenation circumscribed in this way? What can it teach us that should be generalizable?" (Revel, *Jeux d'échelles*, xxx). Edoardo Grendi has proposed one formula that Revel treats as an elegant oxymoron, namely, the idea of the "normal exception." Yet this formula is valuable because of what it sets aside: an interpretation of the concept of exemplarity in statistical terms, following the model of quantitative and serial history. Perhaps it invites us simply to compare worldviews arising from different levels of scale, without these worldviews being totalized. But from what higher mastery would such an overview of different scales stem? It is doubtful that somewhere there is a place from which to take such an overview. Are not Pascal's two fragments first titled "diversity," then "infinity"?

## FROM THE IDEA OF MENTALITY
## TO THAT OF REPRESENTATION

I must now present the conceptual leap that constitutes access to the following section.

At the end of the first section we left the concept of mentalities in a state of great confusion when set against the background of the notion of total history into which that of mentalities is supposed to be integrated. There we were subject to two kinds of appeals: On the one hand, the one emanating from three kinds of discourse, highly divergent among themselves, but each in its way requiring a conceptual rigor held to be the only one possible for presiding over the reassembling of a burst-apart history; on the other hand, that of an original historiography linked to a choice apparently the opposite of the one implicit in the dominant historiography of the golden age of the *Annales* school, the choice of the microhistorical scale. The time has come to prudentially and modestly set out along the way to a reordering of the historical field, one where the history of mentalities will play a federating role on the condition of assuming the title and function of a history of representations and practices.

In order to get beyond the dispersed situation of history during the last third of the twentieth century, I propose to take as my guide a global approach that seems to me to satisfy in large measure the thrice called-for conceptual rigor inasmuch as it carries the notion of a variation in scale to its farthest limits. I shall attempt to show that the often unexplained replacement of the fuzzy concept of mentality by that of representation, when better articulated and more dialectical, is perfectly coherent with the uses I am about to propose concerning the generalized concept of a variation in scale.

The global approach I am referring to finds its most explicit formulation in the collection of essays titled *Les Formes de l'expérience: Une autre histoire sociale*, edited by Bernard Lepetit.[73] The historians in this volume take as their focal reference term in the societies considered—what I would call the pertinent object of historical discourse—the instituting of the social bond and the modes of identity attached to it. The dominant tone is that of a pragmatic approach where the principal accent is on social practices and the representations integrated into these practices.[74] This approach can legitimately draw on a critique of pragmatic reason where it intersects, without becoming confused with, a hermeneutic of action that itself proceeds from the enriching of the phenomenology of Husserl and Merleau-Ponty by semiotics and by the whole blossoming of works devoted to language games (or to discourse). The resolutely historical branch of this critique of practical reason can be recognized from the fact that the social bond and the changes affecting it are taken to be the relevant object of historical language. In this way, the epistemological break brought about by the Labroussian and Braudelian models is not denied. It is deliberately assumed by the new research program that posits "as its first priority the question of identities and social bonds" (13).

The continuity with preceding programs of the *Annales* school can be seen in that the three problems identified in the introduction to this chapter—that of the kind of change taken as most relevant (economic, social, political, cultural, and so on); that of the scale of description; and that of temporal spans—are dealt with as one interdependent block.[75]

Their commitment to a critique of pragmatic reason first made these historians more attentive to the increasingly problematic character of the instituting of the social bond. This is why they speak more readily of structuration than of structure, and regard norms, customs, or legal rules as institutions capable of holding societies together. Next, this spontaneous commitment to a critique of practical reason made them more attentive to the articulation of practices properly speaking and of representations that we can legitimately take as themselves being theoretical or, better, symbolic practices.[76] Finally, their recourse to a critique of practical reason allows justifying the often unreflected-upon shift from the vocabulary of mentality to that of representation. I will now turn to a motivated reason for this substitution.

The semantic fuzziness for which one can legitimately reproach the idea of a mentality is inseparable from the massive, indiscriminate character of the phenomenon, which was readily assimilated to the expression of some time period, even, thinking of Hegel, to the spirit of a people. This happened because the mere juxtaposing of the mental to other components of society as a whole did not allow for the appearance of its innermost dialectic. Better articulated in terms of social practice or practices, the idea of representation will reveal dialectical resources that the idea of mentality does not allow to appear. I am going to show that the generalization of the idea of a play of scales can constitute a privileged way for bringing to light this dialectic hidden in the idea of representation when paired with that of a social practice.[77]

What is important in the play of scales, in effect, is not the privilege granted to the choice of some scale so much as the very principle of a variation in scale, something like what is conveyed by the aphorism from Pascal used as the epigraph to the preceding section. A variety of effects can then be attributed to the exercising of these variations. I have brought together three of them in terms of the theme of identities and the social bond. They each contribute in different ways to the recentering of historiography at the end of the twentieth century. Exercising this variation in scale can draw upon three converging lines. To the first of these, I would attribute the variations affecting the degrees of efficacy and coerciveness of social norms; to the second, those variations modulating the degrees of legitimation at work in the different spheres to which one can belong among which the social bond is distributed; and to the third, the nonquantitative aspects of the scale of social times, something that will lead us to rework the very idea of social change that presided over our whole inquiry concerning the explanation/understanding practiced in history. Following these three routes, we shall keep in mind Pascal when he says that at each scale one sees things one does not see at another scale and that each vision has its own legitimate end. At the end of this threefold consideration we will be able to confront directly the dialectical structure that calls for preferring the idea of representation to that of mentality.

### The Scale of Efficacy or of Coerciveness

As microhistory has already verified, the initial benefit of a variation in scale is that it shifts the accent to individual, familial, or group strategies that call into question the presupposition of submission by social actors on the bottom rank to social pressures of all kinds, and principally those exercised on the symbolic level. This presupposition is not unconnected to the choice of the macrohistorical scale. It is not only time spans in the models stemming from this choice that appear to be hierarchical and interconnected, but also the representations governing behavior and practices. To the degree that a presupposition of submission by social agents goes with a macrohistorical choice of scale, the microhistorical choice leads to the opposite expectation, that of random strategies in which conflicts and negotiations take precedence under the sign of uncertainty.

If we broaden our gaze beyond macrohistory, we see outlined in other societies than those studied by *microhistoria* entanglements of great complexity between the pressure exercised by models of the behavior seen as dominant and the reception, or better the appropriation, of received messages. At the same time, every binary system opposing high to popular culture, along with their associated pairings (force/weakness, authority/resistance), totters. Opposed to them are: circulation, negotiation, appropriation. The whole complexity of social interaction has to be taken into account. Yet for all that the macrohistorical view is not refuted. We can continue to read Norbert Elias as we trace out symbolic orders and their power of coercion from the top to the bottom of societies. It is precisely because the macrohistorical vision is not abolished that we can legitimately pose the question of how representative microhistorical organizations are when considered in regard to the phenomena of power readable on the broad scale. In any case, the notion of deviation we often find in comparable contexts cannot exhaust the combinatory resources of pictures drawn at different scales. It is still higher-order systems that are considered from below.[78] In this regard, the extension of the domain of representations of the models of long-time-span history remains legitimate within the limits of the macrohistorical point of view. There is a long time scale for the features of mentalities. Nothing is lost from the problem Durkheim posed at the beginning of the twentieth century precisely under the title of "collective representations," a term significantly that has reappeared following the long use of "mentality" by those associated with *Annales*. The Durkheimian idea of "basic norms," which goes with those of unperceived agreements and agreement concerning the modes of agreement, retains its problematic and pragmatic force.[79] The task is rather to place these guiding concepts in a dialectical relation to those governing the appropriation of these rules of agreement about agreement. Furthermore, mere consideration of the necessary economy of the creative forces resisting forces tending toward rupture leads to giving some credit to the idea of a customary habitus that can be assimilated to a principle of inertia, even of forgetfulness.

In this spirit, and under the heading of the scale of efficacy or of coercive-ness, the problems of institutions and of norms, which each obey different contextual rules, can be considered jointly.[80]

The major uses of the idea of an institution—as juridical-political; as an organization functioning in a regular manner; as an organization in the broad sense tying together values, norms, models of relations and behaviors, roles—lead to the idea of regularity. A dynamic approach to the constituting of the social bond will then surmount the contingent opposition between institu-tional regularity and social inventiveness, if we speak of institutionalization rather than of institutions.[81] In this regard, the work of institutional sedi-mentation gains, it seems to me, in being compared to the work of archiving things we saw at work at the documentary level of the historiographical op-eration. Might we not speak, in an analogical sense, of an archiving of a social practice? Considered in this way, the process of institutionalization brings to light two faces of the efficacy of representations: on the one hand, in terms of identification—the logical, classificatory function of representations; on the other hand, in terms of coercion, of constraint—the practical function of establishing conformity in behavior. On the path to representation the institution creates identities and constraints. Having said this, we ought to stop opposing the coercive aspect, by preference assigned to the institution, to the presumably subversive side seen in social experience. Considered from a dynamic point of view, the process of institutionalization oscillates be-tween the production of nascent meaning and the production of established constraints. Thus we can formulate the idea of a scale of efficacy of repre-sentations. Norbert Elias's analyses of the relations between physical forces camouflaged as symbolic power, or those of Michel Foucault in *Discipline and Punish*, would need to be placed on a scale of efficacy considered as a scale of coercion. What is important is that "human beings need institutions, which is another way of saying that they make use of them as much as they serve them" (Revel, "L'Institution et le social," 81).

In other contexts, one will prefer adopting as a conceptual device the idea of a norm, where the accent is turn by turn on the process of evaluation that marks out the permitted and the forbidden or on the modes of feelings of obligation sanctioned by punishment. The idea of a norm, too, deployed from the moral to the juridical plane, lends itself to a variation in the scale of efficacy, in the orders of identification and the qualifying of behavior as much as in that of degrees of coercion. It is along such a scale that we may place the opposed manners of approval and disapproval in procedures of legitimatizing and condemning. I shall have more to say about this when we consider the diversity of applications of the idea of a norm in a plurality of realms of interactions among forms of behavior. Here we can already observe the general dialectical structure. The figures of the just and unjust can be taken to be the basis for opposed evaluations. Those of the just mark out the modes of claimed or assumed legitimacy, those of the unjust the modes of condemned illegitimacy. From the point of view of the process as dynamic, the fundamental competence of social agents to negotiate conflicts is added to this basic polarity. This capacity is exercised as much on the plane of the qualifying of contested or assumed behaviors as on that of the levels of refused or accepted coercion.[82] One interesting concept halfway between justification and condemnation would be that of an "adjustment" of action, of an action that "fits."[83]

### The Scale of Degrees of Legitimation

The second line along which the theme of a variation in scale lends itself to an instructive extension is that of the degree of social status that social agents may claim in the order of public esteem. But one is not great or small at no price. One becomes great when, in a context of discord, one feels justified in acting in the way that one does. High status and justification thus go hand in hand. The notion of justification adds a new dimension of intelligibility to those of the institution and the norm. Discord, conflict, disputes, differences of opinion constitute the relevant context. We laid the way for establishing this pair of high status and justification at the moment when we adopted as a general principle for reorganizing the historical field the establishment of the social bond and the search for identity that is attached to it. It is in situations of discord that social agents raise their demands for justification. The same feeling of injustice we saw at work in the stratagems of condemnation is at work in strategies of legitimation. The question is the following: How to justify agreement and manage disagreement, principally by means of compromise, without giving into violence? Here is where the question of status presents itself, which brings into play something other than a need for taxonomic classification, namely, a need for recognition that takes as its basis the scale of evaluations at work in a series of qualifying tests—a notion we also encounter in other contexts, such as heroic folktales. Luc Boltanksi and Laurent Thévenot have added a complementary component of intelligibility to that of status by taking into account the plurality of regimes of justification resulting from the plurality of types of conflict. Someone who has high status in the commercial order may not be so in the political order or in the order of public reputation or in that of aesthetic creation. The principal concept thus becomes that of "economies of standing."[84] What is important for the present investigation is to join to the hierarchical idea of status or standing, which is a variant of the idea of scale, the horizontal line of the pluralization of the social bond. Interweaving these two problematics contributes to breaking with the idea of a common mentality, too readily confused with that of a undifferentiated common good. Certainly the idea of a "common humanity of the members of the city" (*De la justification*, 96) is not to be rejected. It equalizes human beings as human, excluding in particular slavery or treating some as subhuman. But in the absence of differentiation this bond remains nonpolitical. To the axiom of common humanity must be added that of dissimilarity. It is what sets in movement the qualifying tests and sparks off procedures of justification. In turn, these latter are oriented toward setting in place compromises satisfying the model of an "orderly humanity" (99). The enterprise remains risky and in this sense uncertain inasmuch as "there exists no neutral measuring point, external to and superior to each world, from which the plurality of justices could be considered from on high, like a range of equally possible choices" (285).[85] As a result, attempts at justification make sense in distinct "cities," in multiple "worlds." The difficult question raised by this work is that of the criteria of workable justifications in each city. Each criterion is linked to the question of identifying distinct spheres of action.

Two discussions directly applicable to my thesis—which is that of the fruitfulness of the theme of the play of scales for a history of representations—are opened in this way. The first one concerns the finite character of the regressive process that, from elementary justifications to secondary justifications, leads to an ultimate justification in a given sphere. The division among cities or worlds is strictly correlative with the coherence of regimes of action thereby justified. The problem, once again, is not of a taxonomic order, but one of hierarchy in estimation. As in Aristotle's system, we must admit the necessity to stop somewhere. The enumeration of cities—religious, domestic, retail, cultural, civic, industrial—rests on such a postulate of a finite terminal justification. This difficulty calls forth a second one. What discourse authenticates the final justification appropriate to some city? How do we recognize the ultimate argument proper to some city or world? Here our authors adopt an original but costly strategy. To identify the forms of argument at work in ordinary discussions, they place them under the aegis of more articulated, stronger arguments, where the process of justification is brought to its reflective peak. Thus the works of philosophers, theologians, politicians, and writers, backed up by training manuals meant for corporate managers and union representatives, are called upon. And in this way Adam Smith, Augustine, Rousseau, Hobbes, Saint-Simon, and Bossuet provide the founding discourses for actual discourse in everyday disputes. But the question is then of the fit between these founding discourses and the ones they justify. One may be pleased to see philosophy reintroduced within the social sciences as one argumentative tradition, something that provides an indirect justification of philosophy, and for our two authors, who are an economist and a sociologist, acknowledgment that they belong to a history of meaning. But one may also ask in return about the true nature of the tie existing between the texts read by our sociologists and the discourses practiced by social agents inasmuch as the great foundational texts were not meant for this use and, moreover, they are in general unknown to social agents or their representatives on the plane of public discussion. This objection, which one might direct against our authors' whole enterprise, is not unanswerable in that the social space itself makes a place for another type of scale, that of levels of reading between archetypical texts and the least organized kinds of discourse. Both kinds, as written, were given to be read to a multiplicity of readers forming a chain. After all the sixteenth century Italian miller from the Friuli provided himself with arguments for his clever negotiations on the basis of his contingent readings. Yes, reading also has its scales, which get interwoven with those of writing. In this sense, the great texts that serve to explain and decipher the lesser texts of a lesser caliber of ordinary negotiators stand halfway between those written by historians when they join archetypal texts to the implicit discourses in the cities in question and those sometimes written by social agents themselves about themselves. This chain of writing and reading assures the continuity between the idea of representation as an object of history and that of representation as a tool of history.[86] In its first sense, the idea of representation continues to be part of the problem of explanation/understanding; in the second, it falls under that of the writing of history.

### The Scale of Nonquantitative Aspects of Social Times

I would like to end this brief examination of applications of the notion of a variation in scale with an extension to nonquantitative aspects of the temporal component of social change. The nesting of long, middle, and short time spans, well known to readers of Braudel, rests in the first place on quantitative relations between measurable intervals of centuries for the long time span, decades for conjunctures, down to days and hours for dated events. A common chronology lays out dates and indexed intervals in terms of calendar time. Owing to this, measurable spans of time are correlated with repetitive, quantifiable aspects submitted to a statistical treatment of noted facts. However, within this same well-delimited framework of what is measurable, the time spans considered present intensive aspects oftentimes disguised in extensive measures such as the speed of or acceleration in the changes considered. To these two notions, which are measurable only in appearance, are added values of intensity such as rhythm, cumulativeness, recurrence, persistence, and even forgetting, inasmuch as the reservoir of real capacities of social agents adds a dimension of latency to that of temporal actuality. We can speak in this regard of a scale of available competencies of social agents.[87]

Having said this, we can apply the notions of scale and variation in scale to these intensive modes of historical time. There is no reason to abandon the field of scales of time spans opened by *Annales*. There is also a long time span of the features of mentalities. This holds for global society, but also for those cities and worlds whose plurality structures social space. In this regard, it is necessary to learn to cross the plurality of worlds of action not just with the scales of efficacy, as said above, but with the scale of temporal regimes, as we are now attempting to do. Here too the accent has to be placed on the variation in scale and not on the presumed privilege of one or another scale.

Approached in terms of intensive, not extensive size, the time span Durkheim attached to the notion of successful agreement is worth reexamining. "A successful agreement," observes Bernard Lepetit, "precisely because it is successful makes itself a norm through the regularity of its imitative repetitions" (*Les Formes de l'expérience*, 19). The very notion of regularity is what stops being taken for granted. Paired with that of reiteration, it calls for the counterpart of behaviors that are forms of appropriation, stemming from the actors' competence. A scale of temporalities is thereby opened to intersecting traversals. To the linearity of a slow descent from top to bottom corresponds the reordering continually at work in different uses over the course of the time span. This revision of the temporal concepts used in historiography has to be pushed quite far. It must not leave out, in the opposite direction, certain concepts that were highly privileged in the encounter with an emphasis on supposedly quasi-immobile structures under the influence of structuralism, and also Marxism. The categories of a leap, of deviation, of fracture, crisis, revolution, typically found in historical work during the last third of the twentieth century, all need to be reconsidered. The plea in their favor certainly does not lack relevance. By privileging deviation rather than structure, does not the historian reinforce his discipline over against sociology, which focuses on stable features whereas history concentrates on the instable ones? To be sure. But the categories of stability and instability, of continuity and discontinuity, along with other akin pairs of oppositions, which add a note of radicalness to the categories just enumerated, must, in my opinion, be dealt with in terms of a framework of polarities themselves relative to the idea of social change.[88] This hypercategory is not at the same conceptual level as are the opposed pairs just named. It coheres with the relevant features of the basic referent of historical knowledge, namely, the past as a societal phenomenon. And it is from this same referential level that arise the dynamic aspects of the constituting of the social bond, with its play of identities, of readability, of intelligibility. In relation to the metacategory of social change, the categories of continuity and discontinuity, of stability and instability, have to be treated as opposite poles of a single spectrum. In this regard, there is no reason to leave to the sociologist the question of stability, which seems to me as worthy of reexamination as do those of continuity and discontinuity, which under the helpful influence of Michel Foucault's archeology of knowledge have occupied the foreground of recent discussion. The category of stability is one of the more interesting ones among those stemming from the nonmetric aspects of the passing of time. It is a way of enduring that consists in dwelling. Accumulation, reiteration, permanence are nearby characteristics of this major feature. These features of stability contribute to increasing the degrees of efficacy of institutions and of norms considered above. They can be inscribed on a scale of modes of temporality parallel to the scale of degrees of efficacy and of constraint. Pierre Bourdieu's category of habitus, which has a long history behind it going back to Aristotelean *hexis*, its medieval reinterpretations, and its being taken up by Panofsky and above all by Norbert Elias, needs to be placed on this scale. Below, I shall demonstrate the fruitfulness of this category within the dialectical framework of the pair memory/forgetting. But we can already say that it gains from being paired with the temporal aspects of the highly antihistorical categories used by Norbert Elias in *The Court Society*.

Stability as a mode of social change is to be paired with security, which relates to the political level. These are, in effect, two neighboring categories on the scale of temporal modes. They both have to do with the aspect of the enduring and permanence of the social bond, considered sometimes from the point of view of its truth force, sometimes from that of its authority. The force of ideas has multiple modes of temporalization.

When placed within a dynamic polarized field, these categories call for a counterpart on the side of the appropriation of values stemming from the field of norms. This counterpart, this counter image, may belong to the order of chance, of mistrust, of suspicion, of defection, of denunciation. The category of uncertainty, upon which microhistory sets a premium, is inscribed within this same register. It has to do with the aspect of the trustworthiness of representations on the way to stabilization. It is the most polemic category, oscillating between tearing apart and weaving together the fabric of the social bond. Strategies aimed at reducing uncertainty testify eloquently that it must not become in turn a nondialectical category, as could that of the invariant.[89] "Over time," says the author of *Le Pouvoir au village*, "every personal and familial strategy tends, perhaps, to become blunted enough to blend in with a common outcome of relative equilibrium" (xiii). "The strategic utilization of social rules" by the actors seems to imply a noteworthy use of the causal relation that would be the tendency toward optimization over the course of action. It plays out on both the horizontal axis of living together and on the vertical one of scales of efficacy and temporalization inasmuch as the social game affects the whole framework of relations between center and periphery, between capital and local community; in short, the power relation whose hierarchized structure is unsurpassable.[90] That this strategic logic can in the final analysis be inscribed in the interplay of scales of appropriation is the most important conclusion benefiting a history of representations. The search for equilibrium can even be assigned to one precise temporal category, as Bernard Lepetit proposes, namely, the present of the social agents.[91] By the present in history we are to understand something other than the short time of the hierarchies of nested time spans, a state of equilibrium. "The ravages of defection, or even of defiance and generalized imitation are contained in it through the existence of conventions that delimit in advance the field of possibilities, in this framework assuring the diversity of opinions and behaviors, and allowing for their coordination" (*Les Formes de l'expérience*, 277). Hence we can say: "The adjustment between the individual will and the collective norm, between the intended project and the characteristics of the situation at that moment, take place in the present" (279).[92] Of course, not everything historical can be included within situations of conflict or denunciation. Nor do they all come down to situations of the restoration of confidence through the creation of new rules, through the establishment of new uses, or the renovation of old ones. These situations only illustrate the successful appropriation of the past. Inadaptation contrary to the fitting act, too, stems from the present of history, in the sense of the present of the agents of history. Appropriation and denial of relevance are there to attest that the present of history does include a dialectical structure. Still, it was not unprofitable to emphasize that an investigation into scales of time spans is not complete until we take into account the historical present.[93]

## THE DIALECTIC OF REPRESENTATION

At the end of this journey through the adventures of the "mental" in the historical field, it is possible to explain, even to justify, the slow shifting from the term "mentalities" to that of "representations" in the vocabulary of historiography during the last third of the twentieth century.

The threefold development I have proposed for the notion of a variation in scale—beyond scales of observation and analysis—already sets us on the way of what will reveal itself to be the dialectic of representation. With regard to the variations in efficacy and constraint, the old notion of mentalities appears to be unilateral due to lack of a corresponding term on the side of the receivers of social messages; with regard to the variations in the process of justification at work across the plurality of cities and worlds, the notion of mentality appears undifferentiated, due to the lack of a plural articulation in social space; and finally with regard to the variety equally affecting the least quantifiable modes of temporalization of social rhythms, the notion of mentality seems to operate in a heavy-handed fashion, like the quasi-immobile structures of the long time span, or of cyclic conjunctures, the event being reduced to a function that indicates a break. Therefore, over against the unilateral, undifferentiated, massive idea of mentality, that of representation expresses better the plurivocity, the differentiation, and the multiple temporalization of social phenomena.

In this respect, the political field offers favorable terrain for a rule-governed exploration of phenomena falling under the category of representation. Under this term, or that of opinion, and sometimes ideology, these phenomena lend themselves to operations of denomination and definition in some cases accessible through the method of quantifying the data. René Rémond's *Les Droites en France* offers a noteworthy example of such a systematic explanation combining structure, conjuncture, and events.[94] And a counterexample is thereby brought against the heavy-handed accusation of unscientific conceptual vagueness directed against the notion of representation.[95]

With this threefold impetus, the notion of representation develops in turn a distinct polysemy that risks threatening its semantic relevance. In fact, we can make it in turn assume a taxonomic function—it will contain the inventory of social practices governing the bonds of belonging to places, territories, fragments of the social space of communities of affiliation; and a regulative function—where it will be the measure for evaluating or judging socially shared schemes and values, at the same time that it will mark the fault lines that sanction the fragility of the multiple allegiances of social agents. The idea of representation then runs the risk of signifying too much. It will designate the multiple trajectories of recognition between individuals and between the group and the individual. Thus it will rejoin the notion of "worldviews" that, after all, figures among the antecedents of the idea of a mentality.[96]

Given the threat of this hemorrhaging of meaning, it seemed to me opportune to narrow the gap between the notion of representation as an object of the historian's discourse and two other uses of the same word in the context of the present work. In the following chapter, we shall be confronted with the notion of representation as the terminal phase of the historiographical operation itself. It will be a question not only of the writing of history, as is too often said—history is through and through writing, from archives to history books—but also of the transferring of explanation/understanding to written words, to literature, to a book offered for reading by an interested public. If this phase—which, let me repeat, does not constitute one step in a sequence of operations, but a moment that only didactic exposition places at the end—merits the name of representation, it is because, in this moment of literary expression, the historian's discourse declares its ambition, its claim to represent the past *in truth*. Below we shall consider in greater detail the components of this ambition to be truthful. The historian in this way finds himself confronted with what appears at first to be a regrettable ambiguity of the term "representation," which depending on context designates as a rebellious heir of the idea of mentality the historian's represented object, and as a phase of the historiographical operation, the operation of representing.

In this regard, the history of reading gives the history of representations the echo of their reception. As Roger Chartier has amply demonstrated in his works on the history of reading and of readers, the modes of public and private reading have affected the sense of the understanding of texts. For example, new modes of transmitting texts in the age of the "electronic representation"—the revolution in the reproduction and in the medium of a text—lead to a revolution in the practice of reading and, through this, in the very practice of writing.[97] In this way the loop of representations closes in on itself.

A hypothesis then comes to mind: Does the historian, insofar as he does history by bringing it to the level of scholarly discourse, not mime in a creative way the interpretive gesture by which those who make history attempt to understand themselves and their world? This hypothesis is particularly plausible for a pragmatic conception of historiography that tries not to separate representations from the practices by which social agents set up the social bond and include multiple identities within it. If so, there would indeed be a mimetic relation between the operation of representing as the moment of doing history, and the represented object as the moment of making history.

Furthermore, historians, little habituated to situating their historical discourse in terms of the critical prolonging of personal and collective memory, are not led to bringing together these two uses of the term "representation" in relation to what I have called a more primitive one, unless it is in the order of thematic reflection, at least as regards the constitution of the relation to time, that is, in terms of the act of remembering. This too has its ambition, its claim, that of representing the past *faithfully*. The phenomenology of memory, from the time of Plato and Aristotle, has proposed one key for the interpretation of the mnemonic phenomenon, namely, the power of memory to make present an absent thing that happened previously. Presence, absence, anteriority, and representation thus form the first conceptual chain of discourse about memory. The ambition of the faithfulness of memory would thus precede that of truth by history, whose theory remains to be worked out.

Can this hermeneutic key open the secret of the represented object, before penetrating that of the operation of representing?[98]

Some historians have thought about this, without leaving behind the framework of the history of representations. For them, what is important is actualizing the reflective resources of social agents in their attempts to understand themselves and their world. This is the approach recommended and practiced by Clifford Geertz in *The Interpretation of Cultures*, where as a sociologist he confines himself to conceptualizing the outlines of self-understanding immanent to a culture.[99] The historian can also undertake to do this. But can he do so without providing the analytic instrument that this spontaneous self-understanding lacks? The answer can only be negative. Yet the work thus applied to the idea of representation does not surpass the privilege of conceptualization that the historian exercises from one end to the other of the historiographical operation, hence from reading the archives to writing the book, in passing through explanation/understanding and its literary organization. Therefore there is nothing shocking in introducing into the discourse on the represented object fragments of analysis and of definition borrowed from another discursive domain than history. This is what Louis Marin, Carlo Ginzburg, and Roger Chartier authorize themselves to do.

Chartier, in examining Furetière's *Dictionnaire universel* (1727), discovers in it the outlines of the bipolar structure of representation in general, namely, on the one hand, the evocation of an absent thing through the intervention of a substituted thing that is its representative by default; on the other hand, the exhibiting of a presence offered to the eyes, the visibility of the thing present tending to overshadow the operation of substitution that is equivalent to an actual replacement of what is absent. What is astonishing about this analysis is that it is strictly homogeneous with the one proposed by the Greeks for the mnemonic image, the *eikōn*. However, to the extent that it takes place on the terrain of the image, it ignores the temporal dimension, the reference to the earlier, essential to the definition of memory. On the other hand, it lends itself to a unlimited expansion on the side of a general theory of the sign. This is the direction developed by Louis Marin, the great exegete of the *Port Royal Logic*.[100] Here the relation of representation is submitted to a labor of discrimination, of differentiation, accompanied by an effort at identification applied to the conditions of intelligibility likely to avert mistakes, misunderstandings, as Schleiermacher will later also do in his hermeneutics of the symbol. It is in terms of this critical reflection that we can understand the use and abuse resulting from the priority accorded to the visibility belonging to the image over its oblique designating of the absent. With this point, conceptual analysis turns out to be useful for exploring the illusions resulting from the cooperation that weak belief grants to strong images, as we find in Montaigne, Pascal, and Spinoza. The historian finds aid in these authors for exploring the social force of the representations attached to power, and can thus enter into critical rapport with Norbert Elias's sociology of power. The dialectic of representation adds a new dimension to the phenomena discussed above in terms of scales of efficacy. It is this efficacy per se that benefits from a supplementary degree of intelligibility applied to the idea of the absence of physical violence once it is both signified and replaced by symbolic violence.

Carlo Ginzburg, in responding to Chartier's article in "Représentation: Le mot, l'idée, la chose," fleshes out the dialectic of substitution and visibility pointed out by Furetière through a wide-ranging deployment of examples resulting from his erudite researches.[101] Essentially, it is a question of ritual practices linked to the exercise and manifestation of power, such as the use of a royal mannequin in royal funerals in England, or the empty coffin in France. Ginzburg sees in these manipulations of symbolic objects the simultaneous illustration of substitution in relation to some absent thing—the dead person—and the visibility of the present thing—the effigy. Little by little, voyaging in time and space, he evokes the funerals of images in the form of incinerated wax figurines in Roman funerary rites. From there, he passes to the modes of relationship as much toward death—absence par excellence— as toward the dead, those absent ones who threaten to return or who are endlessly in quest of a definitive resting place, by way of effigies, mummies, "idols of a colossus," and other statutes.[102] Unable, as a historian, to give an overall interpretation of this "changing and often ambiguous status of the images of a given society" ("Représentation: Le mot, l'idée, la chose," 1221), Ginzburg prefers to respect the heterogeneity of his examples, aside from ending his essay with an unanswered question regarding the very status of his own research project: "Do we have to do with the universal status (if there is one) of a sign or image? Or rather with a specific cultural domain— and, in this case, which one?" (1225). To conclude, I want to discuss this hesitation on the historian's part.

One of the reasons for his prudence has to do with his recognition of one troubling fact: "In the case of the status of the image, there was, between the Greeks and us, a deep rupture, which I am going to analyze" (1226). This rupture was a result of the triumph of Christianity, which opened between the Greeks, the Roman emperors, and us the break signified by the cult of martyrs' relics. One can to be sure speak in general terms of the close association between images and the beyond, but the opposition remains strong between forbidden idols, to which Christian polemics reduced the images of the ancient gods and deified persons, and the relics proposed to the faithful for devotion. The heritage of medieval Christianity concerning the cult of images has in turn to be taken into account, and, thanks to a detour through an absorbing history of iconography, a distinct place must be reserved for the practice and theology of the Eucharist, where presence, that major component of representation, is charged with signifying not only something absent, the Jesus of history, but the real presence of the body of the dead and resurrected Christ, beyond its memorial function as regards a unique sacrificial event. Ginsburg does not dwell on this complicated history, but rather ends his inquiry into the Eucharist at the first third of the thirteenth century. Nevertheless, in ending he sets up a narrow bridge between his exegesis of the effigy of the king and the real presence of Christ in the sacrament.[103]

Here is where Louis Marin takes over.[104] He is the irreplaceable exegete for what he takes to be the theological model of the Eucharist in terms of a theory of the sign at the heart of a Christian society. Port Royal was the elect place where a semiotics or logic of the statement—"this is my body"—and a metaphysics of real presence were constructed and exchanged values.[105] But Marin's contribution to the vast problem of the image is so considerable that I am resolved to take it up in a more complete way in the following chapter, inasmuch as it clarifies the use of representation in historiographical discourse in a brighter light than the self-understanding that social agents have of their own practice of representation.

We can observe in the works that precede Marin's last book, *Des pouvoirs de l'image*, a hesitation between two uses of a general theory of representation.[106] The double definition of representation he proposes would fit as well with a theory of the represented object as with that of the representing operation. This definition recalls that of Furetière: on the one hand, "presentation of the absent or the dead" and, on the other hand, "self-presentation instituting affect and meaning in the subject of gaze" (18). This proposition fits equally well with the literary expression of historiography, concerning which I shall say more below, and the social phenomena that previously were put under the heading of a history of mentalities. One can say in the first place that the historian seeks to represent to himself the past in the same way social agents represent the social bond and their contribution to this bond to themselves, in this way making themselves readers of their existing and their acting in society, and in this sense historians of their own present. However, it is the efficacy of the social image that prevails in *Des pouvoirs de l'image*: "The image is both the instrument of force, the means of strength, and its foundation as powerful" (18). But in linking the problematic of power to that of the image, as was already evident in *Portrait of the King*, Marin clearly tips the theory of representation toward the side of examining its social efficacy.[107] We are back in a region visited in another way by Norbert Elias, that of symbolic struggles where the belief in the force of signs has been substituted for the external manifestation of force in a fight to the death. Pascal can again be recalled here, no longer in terms of the aura of the semiotics of the Eucharist and the real presence, but in the wake of a denunciation of the "apparatus" of the powerful. In this regard, the sketch of a theory of imagination in the *Pensées* was already that of a theory of symbolic domination. It is here that the theory of the reception of written messages, with its episodes of rebellious and subversive readings, could allow the theory of symbolic violence laid out in *Des pouvoirs de l'image* to rejoin the investigations proposed above on the responses of social agents to the pressure of injunctions projected in their direction by different instances of authority. In this regard, does not the kind of forgetting linked to the replacing of brute force by the force of images metonymically attached to the exercise of such authority not constitute the implacable corollary to this "power of the image"? Marin's last book opens another way, where the competition between text and image comes to the fore. The theory of representation tips once again toward the side of the literary expression of the historiographical operation.

I want to interrupt, rather than to conclude, this section by expressing a perplexity: Can a history of representations by itself attain an acceptable degree of intelligibility without openly anticipating the study of representation as a phase of the historiographical operation? We have seen Ginzburg's own perplexity, caught between a general definition of representation and the heterogeneity of examples that illustrate the competition between the evoking of absence and the exhibiting of presence. This confession is perhaps what fits best with a treatment of the represented object, if it is true as I am supposing here that it is the historian's actual reflection on the moment of representation included within the historiographical operation that leads to the explicit expression of the understanding that social agents have of themselves and of the "world as representation."

# CHAPTER 3

## *The Historian's Representation*

### READING GUIDELINES

With the historian's representation we come to the third phase of the historiographical operation. It would be an error to apply to it the title of writing history or historiography. One constant thesis in this work is that history is writing through and through—from archives to historians' texts, written, published, given for reading. The seal of writing is thus transferred from the first to the third phase, from an initial to a final inscription. The documents had their reader, the historian in his "mine." The history book has its readers, potentially anyone who knows how to read, in fact, the educated public. By falling in this way into public space, the history book crowns the "making of histories," leading its author back into the heart of "making history." Pulled by the archive out of the world of action, the historian reenters that world by inscribing his work in the world of his readers. In turn, the history book becomes a document, open to the sequence of reinscriptions that submit historical knowledge to an unending process of revisions.

To underscore this phase of the historiographical operation's dependence on some material support onto which the book is inscribed, we can speak with Michel de Certeau of scriptural representation.[1] Or instead, to mark the addition of signs of literariness to the scientific criteria, we can speak of literary representation. Indeed, it is thanks to this final inscription that history indicates that it belongs to the domain of literature. This allegiance was, in fact, implicit already on the documentary plane. It becomes manifest with the coming to be of the history text. We must forget, therefore, that it is not a question of some lowering of standards through which a shift to aesthetics gets substituted for the ambition of epistemological rigor. The three phases of the historiographical operation, let us recall, do not constitute successive phases, but rather intermingled levels where only our didactic concern gives them the appearance of chronological succession.

One final word concerning vocabulary and the semantic choices that govern it. Someone may ask why I do not call this third level "interpretation," as it might seem legitimate to do. Does not the representation of the past consist in an interpretation of the stated facts? To be sure. But, in an apparent paradox, we do not do justice to the idea of interpretation by assigning it solely to the representative level of the historiographical operation. I shall reserve for the following chapter devoted to truth in history the task of showing that the concept of interpretation has the same amplitude of application as that of truth—more precisely, that it designates a noteworthy dimension of history's intending truth. In this sense, there is interpretation at all levels of the historiographical operation; for example, at the documentary level with the selection of sources, at the explanation/understanding level with the choice among competing explanatory models, and, in a more spectacular fashion, with variations in scale. But this will not prevent our talking of representation as interpretation when the time comes.

As for my choice of the noun "representation," it is justified in several ways. First, it indicates the continuity of a single problematic from the explanatory to the scriptural or literary phase. In the preceding chapter we ran into the notion of representation as the privileged object of explanation/ understanding, on the plane of the formation of social bonds and the identities at stake in them. We presumed that the way in which social agents understand themselves has an affinity with the way in which historians represent to themselves this connection between their represented object and social action. I even suggested that the dialectic between referring to absence and to visibility, already perceivable in the represented object, is to be deciphered in terms of the operation of representation. In a more radical fashion, the same choice of terminology allows a deep-lying connection to appear, no longer between two phases of the historiographical operation, but on the plane of the relations between history and memory. It is in terms of representation that the phenomenology of memory, following Plato and Aristotle, described the mnemonic phenomenon in that what is remembered is given as an image of what previously was seen, heard, experienced, learned, acquired. Furthermore, it is in terms of representation that what memory intends can be formulated insofar as it is said to be about the past. It is this same problematic of the icon of the past, posed at the beginning of our inquiry, that comes back in force at the end of our discussion. Historical representation follows mnemonic representation in our discourse. This is the most profound reason for choosing the term "representation" to designate the last phase of our epistemological review. Yet this fundamental correlation imposes on our examination one decisive modification in terminology: literary or scriptural representation must in the final analysis allow itself to be understood as "standing for" [*représentance*], the proposed variation placing the accent not only on the active character of the historical operation, but on the intended something that makes history the learned heir of memory and its foundational aporia. In this way, the fact is forcefully underscored that representation on the historical plane is not confined to conferring some verbal costume on a discourse whose coherence was complete before its entry into literature, but rather that representation constitutes a fully legitimate operation that has the privilege of bringing to light the intended reference of historical discourse.

So we have the target of this chapter. But it will be attained only with the last developments in this chapter. Before that, I shall unfold the specific resources of representation. We shall consider first the narrative forms ("Representation and Narration").[2] I explained above why it may seem as though I have put off any examination of the contribution of narrative to historical discourse. It was because I wanted to move the discussion beyond the impasse into which both the partisans and adversaries of history as narrative have led it. For the former, whom I shall call narrativists, the use of a narrative configuration is an alternative explanatory mode opposed to causal explanation; for the latter, problem-oriented history has replaced narrative history. But for all of them, narrating is equivalent to explaining. By reintroducing narrativity at the third stage of the narrative operation, we remove it not only from an inappropriate demand, but at the same time we free up its representative power.[3] We shall not linger over the equation between representation and narration. And the more precisely rhetorical aspect of staging a narrative will be set aside for a distinct discussion ("Representation and Rhetoric"). The selective role for figures of style and thought in the choice of plots, the mobilizing of probable arguments within the frame of the narrative, and the writer's concern to convince by persuading are the rhetorical resources of staging a narrative. To these solicitations by rhetorical means from the narrator correspond specific postures on the part of the reader in the reception of the text.[4]

A decisive step in the direction of our projected problematic will be made at the end of this chapter with the question of the relation of historical discourse to fiction ("The Historian's Representation and the Prestige of the Image"). The confrontation between historical and fictional narrative is well known when it comes to literary forms. What is less well known is the scope of what Louis Marin, a tutelary figure in these pages, calls the "powers of the image," which outline the contours of an immense realm which is that of the other than the real. How can that absent from present time that is the passed past not be touched by the wing of this angel of absence? Yet was not the difficulty of distinguishing the remembered from an image already the torment of the phenomenology of memory? With this specific problematic of the setting of things said about the past into images comes a distinction unnoticed until now that affects the work of representation, namely, the addition of a concern for visibility in the search for a readability proper to narration. Narrative coherence confers readability; the evoking of the referred to past gives rise to sight. From here on this whole interplay, glimpsed a first time with the represented object, will unfold itself in an explicit manner on the plane of the representation-operation that takes place between the image's referring back to the absent thing and its self-assertion in terms of its own visibility.

This rapid overview of the major themes of this chapter allows us to see that a double effect is expected from the proposed distinctions. On the one hand, it is a question of a properly analytic undertaking aimed at distinguishing the multiple facets of the idea of historical representation in its scriptural and literary aspects; in this way we shall lay bare and unfold the diverse resources of such representation. On the other hand, it is a question of anticipating at each step along the way the major stake of this chapter, which is to discern historical discourse's capacity for representing the past, a capacity I have named "standing for." Under this title we shall find a designating of the very intentionality of historical knowledge that is grafted to that of mnemonic knowledge inasmuch as memory is *of* the past. The detailed analyses devoted to the relationship between representation and narration, between representation and rhetoric, and between representation and fiction will mark out not only a progression in the recognition of this intentional aim of historical knowledge but also a progression in the resistance to this recognition. For example, representation as narration does not simply turn naïvely toward things that happened. The narrative form as such interposes its complexity and its opacity on what I like to call the referential impulse of the historical narrative. The narrative structure tends to form a circle with itself and to exclude as outside the text, as an illegitimate extralinguistic presupposition, the referential moment of the narration. The same suspicion about the referential irrelevance of representation receives a new form under the headings of tropology and of rhetoric. Do not such figures too form a screen between the discourse and what is claimed to have happened? Do not they entrap the discursive energy within the net of the turns of discourse and thought? And is not this suspicion brought to its peak by the kinship between representation and fiction? It is at this stage that the aporia in which memory seemed to have imprisoned us, insofar as what is remembered is given as a kind of image, an icon, springs up again. How are we to preserve the difference in principle between the image of the absent as unreal and the image of the absent as prior? The entanglement of historical representation with fiction at the end of this sequence repeats the same aporia that seemed to have overwhelmed the phenomenology of memory.

Therefore it is under the sign of a progressive dramatization that the unfolding of this chapter will unfold. Challenges will continue to accompany our attestation of the intentional aim of history; this attestation will bear the indelible imprint of a protest against such suspicion, expressed by a difficulty: "And yet . . ."

§

## REPRESENTATION AND NARRATION

My hypothesis governing the following analyses has to do with the place of narrativity in the architecture of historical knowledge. It has two sides. On the one hand, it is taken for granted that narrativity does not constitute an alternative solution to explanation/understanding, despite what the adversaries and advocates of a thesis that, to be brief, I have proposed calling narrativist curiously agree on in saying. On the other, it is affirmed that emplotment nevertheless constitutes a genuine component of the historiographical operation, but on another plane than the one concerned with explanation/understanding, where it does not enter into competition with uses of "because" in the causal or even the teleological sense. In short, it is not a question of downgrading, of relegating narrativity to a lower rank once the operation of narrative configuration enters into play with all the modes of explanation/understanding. In this sense, representation in its narrative aspect, as in the others I shall speak of, does not add something coming from the outside to the documentary and explanatory phases, but rather accompanies and supports them.

Therefore I shall first speak of what we ought not to expect from narrativity: that it fill some lacuna in explanation/understanding. French historians who have expressed their grievances through the opposition between narrative history and problem-oriented history[5] and English-speaking authors who have raised the configuring act of emplotment to the rank of an explanation exclusive of causal and even teleological explanations thus in a curious way join us regarding this struggle that I propose to surpass. For in this way an alternative is created that makes narrativity sometimes an obstacle to, sometimes a substitute for explanation.

For Braudel and those close to him in the *Annales* school, everything turns on the sequence "event, narrative, primacy of the political" when the accent falls on decisions made by leading individuals. To be sure, no one ignores the fact that before becoming an object of historical knowledge, the event is the object of some narrative. In particular, the narratives left by contemporaries occupy a prime place among documentary sources. In this respect, Marc Bloch's lesson has never been forgotten. The question has rather been to know whether the historical knowledge resulting from the critique of these first-order narratives in its scholarly forms is still clothed with features that belong to the narratives of every kind that nourish the art of narrating. The negative answer can be explained in two ways. On the one hand, by a highly restrictive concept of the event that the narrative is supposed to convey, which has been taken to be a minor, even marginal component of historical knowledge. The case against narrative is thus that against the event. On the other hand, before the development of narratology in the linguistic and semiotic sphere, narrative was taken to be a primitive form of discourse, both tied up with tradition, legend, folklore, and finally myth, and too little elaborated to be worthy of passing the multiple tests that mark the epistemological break between traditional and modern history. In truth, these two orders of consideration go hand in hand—an impoverished concept of event goes along with an impoverished concept of narrative. Hence the trial of the event renders superfluous a distinct trial of narrative. In fact, this trial of event-oriented history has distant antecedents. Krzysztof Pomian, for example, recalls the criticism that Mabillon and Voltaire made of a history that, they said, only taught those events that met the conditions of memory and that prevented any turn to causes and principles, hence to making known the underlying nature of human beings. However, if a worked-out writing of event-oriented history had to wait for the second third of the twentieth century, it was because in the meantime political history had occupied the foreground with its cult of what Croce called "individually determined" facts. Ranke and Michelet remain the unsurpassed masters of this style of history, where the event is held to be singular and unrepeatable. It was this conjunction between the primacy of political history and the prejudice in favor of the unique, unrepeatable event that the *Annales* school attacked head on. To the characteristic of unrepeatable singularity Braudel was to add the brevity that allowed him to oppose the "long time span" to the history of events. It was this fugacity of the event that, he held, characterizes individual action, principally that of political decision makers, who it had been claimed were those who made events happen. In the final analysis, the two characteristics of the singularity and brevity of the event go together with the major presupposition of so-called event-oriented history, namely, that the individual is the ultimate bearer of historical change. As for narrative history, it was taken as a mere synonym for such history. In this way, the narrative status of history did not become the object of a distinct discussion. As for the rejection of the event in the point-like sense, it is the direct consequence of the displacing of the principal axis of historical investigation from political history toward social history. In a word, it is in political, military, diplomatic, ecclesiastical history that individuals—heads of state, generals, ministers, prelates—are supposed to make history. There too reigns the event that can be assimilated to an explosion. The denunciation of the history of battles and the history of events thus constitutes the polemical underside of a plea for a history of the total human phenomenon, with however a strong accent on economic and social conditions. It was within this critical context that was born the concept of the long time span opposed to that of the event, understood in the sense of a brief duration, which I have dealt with above. The dominant intuition, we have said, was that of a fierce opposition at the heart of social reality between the instant and "time that takes a long time to unfold." Pushing this axiom to the point of paradox, Braudel went so far as to say that "social science has something like a horror of the event." This head-on attack against the sequence of "event, narrative, primacy of the political" found strong reinforcement with the massive introduction into history of quantitative procedures borrowed from economics and extended to demographic, social, cultural, and even spiritual history. With this development, a major presupposition concerning the nature of the historical event was called into question, namely, that as unique no event repeats itself. Quantitative history, in effect, is fundamentally a "serial history."[6]

If, according to the *Annales* perspective, narrative as a collection of point-like events and the traditional form of cultural transmission is an obstacle to problem-oriented history, according to the narrativist school across the Atlantic, it is worthy to enter into competition with the models of explanation the human sciences share in common with the natural sciences. Far from being an obstacle to the scientific nature of history, narrative becomes its substitute. It was as confronted by an extreme demand represented by the nomological model of historical knowledge that this school of thought undertook to reevaluate narrative's resources of intelligibility.[7] This effort owed little to narratology and its claim to reconstruct the surface effects of narrative on the basis of its deep structures. The work of the narrativist school took place instead in the wake of inquiries devoted to ordinary language, and to its grammar and its logic as these function in natural languages. In this way the configuring character of narrative was brought to the fore at the expense of its episodic character, which was the only thing the *Annales* historians took into account. In relation to the conflict between explanation and understanding, narrativist interpretations tend to deny the relevance of this distinction insofar as to understand a narrative is thereby to explain the events that it integrates and the facts it reports. The question thus will be to know at what point the narrativist interpretation accounts for the epistemological break that has occurred between told stories and history built on documentary traces.

In *Time and Narrative* I summarized the successive theses of the narrativist school.[8] A special place had to be given to the work of Louis O. Mink, which for a long time remained scattered in different articles before being gathered together in a posthumous book titled *Historical Understanding*.[9] This title, which is a good statement of the central thesis of Mink's different essays, must not mislead us. In no way is it a question of opposing explanation and understanding as in Dilthey. On the contrary, it is a question of characterizing historical explanation, as a "gathering together," through a configuring, synoptic, synthetic act, endowed with the same sort of intelligibility as is judgment in Kant's *Critique of the Faculty of Judgment*. Therefore it is not the intersubjective features of *Verstehen* that are emphasized here, but the function of "colligation" exercised by the narrative taken as a whole in relation to the reported events. The idea that the form of the narrative as such should be a "cognitive instrument" follows at the end of a series of increasingly precise approaches—at the price of the discovery of aporias concerning historical knowledge, aporias that only such narrativist interpretation allows to be discovered. With the passage of time, we can today praise Mink for the rigor and honesty with which he summed up these aporias. The problem is posed that will be the torment of any literary philosophy of history: what difference separates history from fiction, if both narrate? The classic answer that history alone retraces what actually happened does not seem to be contained in the idea that the narrative form has within itself a cognitive function. This aporia, which we can call that of the truth in history, becomes apparent through the fact that historians frequently construct different and opposed narratives about the same events. Should we say that some omit events and considerations that others focus on and vice versa? The aporia would be warded off if we could add rival versions to one another, allowing for submitting the proposed narratives to the appropriate corrections. Shall we say that it is life, presumed to have the form of a history, that confers the force of truth on this narrative? But life is not a history and only wears this form insofar as we confer it upon it. How, then, can we still claim that we found this form in life, our own life and by extension that of others, of institutions, groups, societies, nations? This claim is solidly entrenched in the very project of writing history. The result is that it is no longer possible to take refuge in the idea of "universal history as lived." Indeed, what relationship could exist between this presumed unique and determined kingdom of universal history as lived and the histories we construct, when each one has its own beginning, middle, and end, and draws its intelligibility from its internal structure alone? This dilemma strikes narrative not only at its configuring level, but strikes the very notion of an event. Beyond the fact that we can question the rules governing the use of the term (was the Renaissance an event?), we can also ask if there is any meaning in saying that two historians give different narratives of the same events. If the event is a fragment of a narrative, it depends on the outcome of the narrative, and there is no underlying, basic event that escapes narrativization. Yet we cannot do without the notion of the "same event," if we are to be able to compare two narratives dealing, as we say, with the same subject. But what is an event purged of every narrative connection? Must we identify it with an occurrence in the physical sense of this term? But then a new abyss opens between event and narrative, comparable to the one that isolates written history from history as it actually happened. If Mink undertook to preserve the commonsense belief that history is distinguished from fiction by its truth claim, this was, it seems, because he did not give up the idea of historical knowledge. In this regard, the last essay he published, "Narrative Form as a Cognitive Instrument,"[10] sums up the state of perplexity in which he found himself when his work was cut off by his death. Dealing for a last time with the difference between history and fiction, he limits himself to taking as disastrous the possibility that common sense should be dislodged from its entrenched position. If the contrast between history and fiction were to disappear, both would lose their specific mark, namely, the claim to truth on the side of history and the "voluntary suspension of disbelief" on that of fiction. But Mink does not say how the distinction is to be preserved. In renouncing any resolution to the dilemma, he preferred to hold on to it as belonging to the historical enterprise per se.

Rather than playing off the adversaries and the partisans of the explanatory relevance of narrative as a configuring act against each other, it seemed to me more useful to ask about the way in which two types of intelligibility could go together, narrative intelligibility and explanatory intelligibility.[11]

As regards narrative intelligibility, it would be necessary to bring together the still too intuitive considerations of the narrative school and the more analytic work of narratology on the plane of the semiotics of discourse. The result is a complex notion of "narrative coherence" that must be distinguished, on the one hand, from what Dilthey called the "cohesion of a life," in which we can recognize prenarrative features, and on the other hand, from the notion of a "causal or teleological connection (or connectedness)," arising from explanation/understanding. Narrative coherence is rooted in the former and articulated through the latter. What it itself brings is what I have called a synthesis of the heterogeneous, in order to speak of the coordination between multiple events, or between causes, intentions, and also accidents within a single meaningful unity. The plot is the literary form of this coordination. It consists in guiding a complex action from an initial situation to a terminal one by means of rule-governed transformations that lend themselves to an appropriate formulation within the framework of narratology. A logical content can be assigned to these transformations, what Aristotle characterized in his *Poetics* as the probable or the reasonable, the reasonable constituting the face that the probable turns toward the readers in order to persuade them; that is, to induce them to believe precisely in the narrative coherence of the told story or history.[12]

I want to draw on two implications of this concept of narrative coherence.

First, a properly narrative definition of the event, which subsequently will have to be connected to the definitions given it on the plane of explanation. On the narrative plane, the event is what, in happening, advances the action—it is a variable of the plot. Events that give rise to an unexpected turn are said to be sudden—"against expectation" (*para doxan*), says Aristotle, thinking of "theatrical effects" (*peripeteiai*) and "violent effects" (*pathē*).[13] In a general way, any discordance entering into competition with concordance counts as an event. This conjunction of plot and event is open to noteworthy transpositions on the historiographical plane, which go far beyond what is called event-oriented history, which only retains one of the possibilities of the narrative event, namely, brevity combined with suddenness. There are, if we may put it this way, long time span events, indicated by the amplitude, the scope of the history recounted—the Renaissance, the Reformation, the French Revolution make up such events in relation to a period that can extend over several hundred years.

Second implication: inasmuch as the actors in a narrative—the characters—are emplotted along with the story, the notion of narrative identification, correlative to that of narrative coherence, too is open to noteworthy transpositions on the historical plane. The notion of a character constitutes a narrative operator of the same amplitude as that of an event. The characters perform and suffer from the action recounted. For example, the Mediterranean in Braudel's great work can be taken as a quasi character of the quasi plot of the rise to power and the decline of what was "our sea" in the age of Philip II. In this regard, the death of Philip was not an event on the same scale as the plot about the Mediterranean.[14]

A third implication suggested by Aristotle's *Poetics* would have to do with the moral evaluation of the characters, better than us in tragedy, lower or equal to us in virtue in comedy. I shall reserve this discussion for the following chapter in terms of a broader framework having to do with the relationship between the historian and the judge. We shall not, however, avoid some anticipation of this discussion when in speaking about the rhetorical categories applied to plots we shall be confronted with the question of the limits imposed on representation by events taken to be horrible, even morally unacceptable.[15]

I want now to propose two examples of the connecting of "narrative coherence" to "causal or teleological explanation," corresponding to the two types of intelligibility referred to above. The solution of Mink's dilemma and more generally of the aporia whose progression we shall follow in the remainder of this chapter hangs on the plausibility of this analysis. It would be futile to seek a direct tie between the narrative form and the events as they actually occurred; the tie can only be indirect by way of explanation and, short of this, by way of the documentary phase, which refers back in turn to testimony and the trust placed in the word of another.

My first example is suggested by the use made in the preceding chapter of the notion of an interplay of scales. Among all the kinds of syntheses of the heterogeneous that constitute emplotment, must we not take into account the narrativized course of changing scales? In fact, neither microhistory nor macrohistory work continually with a single scale. To be sure, microhistory privileges the level on interactions on the scale of a village, of a group of individuals or families. This is the level where the negotiations and conflicts unfold and the situation of uncertainly reveals itself that history makes evident. But this history does not fail also to read from bottom to top the power relations that play themselves out on another scale. The discussion about the exemplariness of these local histories played out on the lowest level presupposes the interweaving of a small-scale history with a larger-scale one. In this sense, microhistory situates itself on a sequence of changing scales that it narrativizes as it goes. The same can be said about macrohistory. In some forms, it situates itself at one determined level and does not quit it. This is the case with those operations of periodization that scan the time of history in terms of long sequences indicated by large-scale narratives. One important narrative concept proposes itself here that we have already encountered above, that of "scope," which F. R. Ankersmit has elaborated in the context of a narrative logic whose implications concerning the relation between representation and standing for we shall discuss further below.[16] The scope of an event speaks of the persistence of its effects far beyond its origin. It is correlative to the scope of the narrative itself, whose meaningful unity perdures. If we stop at this homogeneous level of a "period," some important aspects of narrativization can be noted, among them the personalization indicated by the use of proper names (or of quasi proper names): Renaissance, French Revolution, Cold War, and so forth. The relationship of these proper names to the descriptions that in a way constitute their predicates poses the problem of a narrative logic appropriate to these strange high-level singularities, to which Ankersmit gives the name *narratio*. However all the narrative resources of macrohistory do not allow themselves to be reduced to effects on a single level. As Norbert Elias's work illustrates, the effects of a system of power, such as that of the monarchical court, unfold along a descending scale down to the forms of behavior of self-control at the level of the individual psyche. In this regard, the concept of habitus can be taken as a concept of narrative transition operating all along this descending way from the higher plane of the production of meaning to the lower one of its concrete actualization, thanks to the forgetting of the cause concealed among its effects.

The second example has to do with the notion of an event. Above we recalled the narrative function as an operator on the plane of the recounted action. However, among all the attempts to define the event on the plane of explanation, we placed the accent on the one that coordinates the event with the structure and with the conjuncture, associating it with the two ideas of deviation and difference. But is it not possible to cross the logical abyss that seems to lie between these two definitions of the event? One hypothesis proposes itself: if we give its full extension to the idea of the plot as the synthesis of the heterogeneous embracing intentions, causes, and accidents, is it not up to the narrative to bring about a kind of narrative integration of the three moments—structure, conjuncture, event—that epistemology dissociates? The just-proposed idea of a narrativization of the interplay of scales suggests this, inasmuch as the three moments refer to different scales having to do as much with the level of efficacy as with that of temporal rhythms. I have found helpful support for working out this hypothesis in the work of Reinhart Koselleck in an essay titled "Representation, Event, and Structure" in his *Futures Past*.[17] Having stated that, as separately identifiable temporal strata, structures stem in fact from description and events from the narrative, he suggests that the dynamic that interweaves them lends itself to a narrativization that makes narrative a switching point between structure and event. This integrative function of the narrative form results from the distance it takes in regard to mere chronological succession in terms of before and after, of the type *veni, vidi, vici*. As a meaningful unity, the plot is capable of articulating structures and events within one and the same configuration. Thus, to cite an example, the evocation of a structure of domination can be incorporated into the narrative of an event such as a battle. The structure as a phenomenon of the long time span through the narrative becomes the condition of possibility of the event. We can speak here of structures *in eventu* whose significance is only grasped *post eventum*. The description of structures in the course of the narrative contributes in this way to clarifying and elucidating the events as causes independent of their chronology. What is more, the relation is reversible. Some events are taken as significant insofar that they serve as indices of social phenomena of the long time span and even seem determined by them—a trial about the right to work can illustrate in dramatic fashion social, juridical, or economic phenomena of the long time span.[18] The narrative integration between structure and event thus fits with the narrative integration between phenomena situated at the different levels of the scales of endurance and efficacy. The distinction between description and narration is not thereby effaced, but if description preserves the stratification of layers, it is up to the narrative to tie them together. The cognitive relation between the two concepts is of the order of a distinction—it finds a didactic complement in their referring to each other thanks to the narrative configuration. Here the relation between structure and event is like that between the layers of time spans. Every stratification can be narratively mediated in this way.[19]

These two examples of the narrativization of explanatory modes at work in the historiographical operation contain two lessons. On the one hand, they show how the written forms of this operation get articulated in terms of the explanatory forms. On the other hand, they show how the intentional aim of narrative beyond its closure runs across such explanation in the direction of the reality attested to. The resistances to this passage have still to be considered.

However I do not want to leave behind the question of narrativity and its contribution to the third phase of the historiographical operation without having dealt with certain aspects of emplotment that, when joined to similar effects of other moments of the written expression of history, render the solution of the problem posed by the historical narrative's claim to represent the past paradoxically more difficult. Along the way from representation to re-presentation, narrative has to deal with obstacles having to do precisely with the structure of the act of configuration.

The challenge in the name of a disjunction between the internal structure of a text and any extratextual reality comes from literary theory. To the extent that the fictional and the historical narrative participate in the same narrative structures, the rejection of a referential dimension by structuralist orthodoxy extends to the whole of literary textuality. This rejection is motivated by an expansion of the Saussurean model from the plane of isolated signs—like those collected into systems of a lexical type—to that of sentences and finally to that of longer textual sequences. According to this model, the relation between signifier and signified gives rise to an entity with two faces, the sign properly speaking, whose apprehension can make an exception of any relation to a referent. This exception is the work of the theoretical gaze that sets up the sign as the homogeneous theme of linguistic science. It is this bipolar model of signifier and signified, excluding any referent, that spread into every region of language accessible to a semiotic treatment. And it was in this way that a Saussurean type of narratology could apply to long textual sequences the bracketing of the referent required by the model. While the effects for fictional narrative seem discussible without being disastrous (something I discussed in *The Rule of Metaphor*), they have been devastating for historical narrative, whose difference from fictional narrative rests on the referential intention that runs through it and that is nothing other than the meaning of its representation. Hence I tried at the time to reconquer the referential dimension by starting from the level of the sentence as the initial unit of discourse, following the analyses of Émile Benveniste and Roman Jakobson. With the sentence, I said, someone says something to someone about something on the basis of a hierarchy of codes: phonological, lexical, syntactical, and stylistic. Saying something about something seemed to me to constitute the virtue of discourse and by extension of the text as a enchaining of sentences.[20] However the problem of the referentiality of historical discourse seemed to me to need to be posed in a distinct way inasmuch as the tendency toward closure inherent in the act of emplotment is an obstacle to the extralinguistic, extratextual impulse of all referential speech through which representation becomes re-presenting.[21] But, before we come to the attestation-protestation that constitutes the soul of what I call the standing for of the past,[22] it will first be necessary to push as far as possible our examination of the other components of the literary phase of the historiographical operation. These add their own denying of the referential impulse of historical discourse to that emanating from the narrative configuration per se.[23]

## REPRESENTATION AND RHETORIC

It is worth the effort of granting distinct attention to the properly rhetorical dimension of the discourse of history, despite entanglement of the figures of this domain with the structures of narrative. Here we touch on a tradition that goes back to Vico and its double heritage: the plane of the description of figures of thought and discourse, called tropes—principally metaphor, metonymy, synecdoche, and irony—and that of the plea in favor of the modes of argumentation that rhetoric opposes to the hegemonic claims of logic.

The stakes in this new step of our investigation do not consist solely in broadening the field of procedures of scriptural representation, but also take into account the resistances that narrative and rhetorical configurations oppose to the referential impulse that turns historical narrative toward the past. Perhaps we shall also come upon the outlines of a counteroffensive by a certain critical realism in regard to the aestheticizing temptation that the advocates of narrative rhetoric risk surrendering to. This is what happened when the protagonists in this discussion found themselves confronted in the last decades of the twentieth century with the problem of the figuration of events that, because of their monstrosity, pushed the "limits of representation." A part of this discussion took place in France, but it was in America that it became the occasion for the confrontation I shall allude to.

The French contribution to the debate dates from the golden age of structuralism. The methodological revolution that the French school following Ferdinand de Saussure claimed to follow brought to light aspects of the narrative code that present a close kinship with the general structural properties of the system of language, distinguished from its use in speech. The basic postulate is that the structures of narrative are homologous with those of the elementary units of language.[24] The result is an extending of linguistics to the semiotics of narrative. The principal effect on the theory of narrative was an exclusion of every consideration borrowed from the literary history of a genre, uprooting the achrony of structures from the diachrony of the practice of discourse to the benefit of a logicization and a dechronologization whose steps I traced in the volume 2 of *Time and Narrative*.[25] The implications for the historical field might never have seen the light of day in that the semiotics of narrative were applied to fiction in the wake of Vladimir Propp. All that one might deplore was the loss of the sense of the marvelous, but this was not a negligible result once the kinship of this emotion *a contrario* to the more frightful one that the history of the twentieth century was to unleash was taken into account. A threat directed against the referential claim of history was, however, already contained in the choice of the Saussurean model on the plane of general semiotics. Above, I referred to the consequences for the treatment of historical discourse of the excluding of the referent required by the binary constitution of the sign as signifier and signified. But for structuralism really to hit history hard it was necessary that the concern for what we can call the scientific aim of its advocates should be joined to a more polemical and ideological concern directed against the presumed humanism of a whole set of representative practices. Historical narrative found itself in the same dock with the realist novel inherited from nineteenth-century European history. Suspicion then was intermingled with curiosity, narrative history being accused particularly of producing subjects adapted to a system of power that gave them a sense of mastery over themselves, nature, and history.[26] For Roland Barthes, the "discourse of history" constitutes the privileged target of this genre of criticism based on suspicion. Taking his stand on the exclusion of the referent in the linguistic field, he held against historical narrative its placing a referential illusion at the very heart of historiography. This illusion consisted in the claim that the supposed external, founding referent—that is, the time of the *res gestae*—was hypostatized at the expense of the signified, that is, the meaning that the historian gives to the reported facts. In this way a short-circuit was produced between the referent and the signifier, and "the discourse, meant only to *express* the real, believes it elides the fundamental term of imaginary structures, which is the signified" (138–39). This fusing of the referent and the signified to the benefit of the referent engenders a "reality effect" in virtue of which the referent, surreptitiously transformed into a disgraceful signifier, is clothed with the privileges of "that's what happened." History thus gives the illusion of finding the real that it represents. In reality, its discourse is only "a fake performative discourse in which the apparent constative (descriptive) is in fact only the signifier of the speech act as an act of authority" (139). At the end of his article, Barthes can applaud the decline of narrative history and the rise of structural history. This, in his eyes, is a veritable ideological revolution more than a change of schools: "Historical narration is dying because the sign of History is henceforth not so much *the real as the intelligible*" (140). It remained to spell out the mechanism of this eviction of the signified, expelled by the presumed referent. This is what a second essay, titled precisely "The Reality Effect," undertakes to do. The key to the riddle is sought on the side of the role exercised by the notations in the realist novel and in history from the same period, that is, those "superfluous" details that contribute nothing to the structure of the narrative, to its thread of meaning. These are "insignificant intervals" in relation to the meaning imposed over the course of the narrative. To account for the reality effect, we have to begin from this insignificance. Prior to the realist novel, such notations contributed to a verisimilitude of a purely aesthetic and in no way referential character. The referential illusion consists in transforming the notation's "resistance to meaning" into a "supposed real." In this, there is a break between the older verisimilitude and modern realism. But, also in this, a new verisimilitude is born that is precisely this realism, by which we can understand "discourse which accepts 'speech-acts' justified by their referent alone" (147). This is in fact what happens in history where "'concrete reality' becomes the sufficient justification for speaking" (146). This argument boils down to transferring one noteworthy feature of the nineteenth-century realist novel to all historical narrative.

Here is the place to ask whether such suspicion is not wholly forged on the basis of a linguistic model that is inappropriate to historical discourse, which would be better understood in terms of alternative models for which the referent, whatever it might be, constitutes a irreducible dimension of discourse addressed by someone to someone about something. It would remain to give an account of the specificity of referentiality in the historiographical domain. My thesis is that this cannot be discerned solely on the plane of the functioning that historical discourse assumes, but that it must pass through the documentary proof, the causal and teleological explanation, and the literary emplotment. This threefold frame remains the secret of historical knowledge.[27]

The major contribution to the exploring of the properly rhetorical resources of historical representation remains that of Hayden White.[28] It is valuable as much for the criticism it has elicited as for the relevance of this thinker's analyses meant to expand his readers' awareness. The discussion he stirred up about literature about the Shoah has given his propositions a dramatic dimension unattained by the French structuralists' theses. This had to do not with a contribution to the epistemology of historical knowledge, but with a poetics that takes the imagination, more precisely, the historical imagination, as its theme. It is in this sense that it shows itself faithful to the spirit of the times and to what has been called the "linguistic turn," inasmuch as it is through the structures of discourse that this imagination is apprehended. Therefore it is verbal artifacts that will be at issue. This detail takes nothing away from the scope of what is intended. In effect, two roadblocks get lifted. The first one has to do with the relation of history to fiction. Seen from the angle of language, historical and fictional narrative both belong to a single class, that of "verbal fictions." All the problems tied to the referential dimension of historical discourse will be taken up starting from this classification. The second roadblock has to do with the distinction between professional historiography and the philosophy of history, at least that part of the philosophy of history that clothes itself in the form of large world-scale narratives. In this way, Michelet, Ranke, Tocqueville, Burckhardt, Hegel, Marx, Nietzsche, and Croce are set within the same framework. What is common to them is bringing the historical imagination to discourse through a form that comes from rhetoric and more precisely from the rhetoric of tropes. This verbal form of the historical imagination is the emplotment.

In *Metahistory* the scope of White's gaze is made manifest in that the operation of emplotment is grasped through considering a sequence of typologies that give the enterprise the allure of a well-ordered taxonomy. But we must never lose sight of the fact that this taxonomy operates at the level of the deep structures of the imagination. This opposition between deep and surface structures was not unknown to semioticians, or to psychoanalysts. In the specific situation of verbal fictions, it allows a hierarchy of typologies rather than simply piling them on top of one another or juxtaposing them. The four typologies we are about to consider and the compositions that result from their being associated with one another must therefore be taken for matrices of possible combinations on the plane of the actual historical imagination.

White's carrying through of this program is methodical. The major typology, which places White in Vico's wake, the typology of plot types, crowns a hierarchy of three typologies. The first one stems from aesthetic perception. It is the dimension of the plot's "story." In a way somewhat like that of Mink, the organization of the story as told exceeds the simple chronology that still prevailed in chronicles and adds to the "storyline" an organization in terms of motifs that we may call inaugural, transitional, or terminal. What is important is that, as with the defenders of narrativism discussed above, the story has an "explanatory effect" in virtue of its structural apparatus alone. Here rhetoric first enters into competition with the epistemology of historical knowledge. The seriousness of the conflict is increased by two considerations. Concerning the form, as White's recent work emphasizes, we have to say that the plot tends to make the contours of the story prevail over the distinct meanings of the events recounted, inasmuch as the accent is placed on the identifying of the configuring class in which a plot is inscribed. As for what is supposed to precede the setting into form, the rhetorician finds nothing prior to the first sketches of narrativization, other than perhaps an unorganized background, an "unprocessed historical record." The question of the status of the factual data in relation to the initial *mise en forme* of the story told is left open.

The second typology has more to do with the cognitive aspects of the narrative. But, as with rhetoricians, the notion of argument is taken in terms of its persuasive capacity rather than as a purely logical demonstration.[29] That there is a manner of arguing proper to narrative and historical discourse, and that this lends itself to a specific typology, constitutes an original idea, whatever may have been borrowed from disciplines other than history concerning the distinction between formalist, organic, mechanical, and contextual arguments.[30]

The third typology, that of ideological implications, stems rather from modes of moral and political commitment and therefore from the insertion in present practice. In this sense, it arises from what Bernard Lepetit calls the present of history. Below we shall return to the problem posed by this typology, in terms of the implication of the protagonists in events that cannot be separated from their moral charge.

Next comes the emplotment, which White takes to be the explanatory mode par excellence. He borrows his typology of four terms—romance, tragedy, comedy, satire—from Northrop Frye's *Anatomy of Criticism*, in this way linking up with Vico's rhetoric.

If we had to characterize White's enterprise in a single word, we would have to speak as he himself does of a theory of style. Each combination among elements belonging to one or another typology defines the style of a work that one can then characterize by the dominant category.[31]

It is not a question of denying the importance of White's pioneering work. With Roger Chartier, we may even regret White's "missed encounter" with Paul Veyne and Michel Foucault, his contemporaries during the 1970s. But the idea of a deep structure of the imagination owes its indisputable fruitfulness to the tie it establishes between creativity and codification. This dynamic structuralism is perfectly plausible. Separated from the imaginary, these paradigms would only be the inert classes of a more or less refined taxonomy. Instead they are generating matrices meant to engender an un-limited number of manifest structures. In this regard, the criticism that White did not choose between determinism and free choice seems to me easily re-futed. It belongs precisely to these formal matrices to open a limited space for choice. We can speak in this way of a rule-governed production, a no-tion that recalls the Kantian concept of the schematism, that "method for producing images." The consequence is that the alternative objections of taxonomic rigidity and restless wandering within the space of imaginative variations miss the originality of the project, whatever hesitations or weak-nesses characterize its execution. The idea that White appears to have drawn back in panic before an unlimited disorder seems to me not only inadequate but unfair, in light of the personal character of the attack that it assumes.[32] The overly dramatic expression "the bedrock of order" ought not to turn our attention from the relevance of the problem posed by the idea of an encoding that functions both as a constraint and a space for invention. A place is made in this way for exploring the mediations proposed by stylistic practice over the course of the history of literary traditions. This connecting of formalism and historicity remains to be done. It belongs to a system of rules, both found and invented, to present original features of traditionality that transcend this alternative. This is what is tied up in what we call style. On the other hand, I regret the impasse that White gets caught up in in dealing with the operations of emplotment as explanatory models, held to be at best indifferent as regards the scientific procedures of historical knowledge, at worst as substitutable for them. There is a true category mistake here that engenders a legitimate suspicion regarding the capacity of this rhetorical the-ory to draw a clear line between historical and fictional narrative. While it is legitimate to treat the deep structures of the imaginary as common generat-ing matrices for the creation of the plots of novels and those of historians, as is attested to by their interweaving in the history of genres during the nine-teenth century, it also becomes urgent to specify the referential moment that distinguishes history from fiction. And this discrimination cannot be carried out if we remain within the confines of literary forms. Nothing is gained by outlining a desperate escape by way of a simple-minded recourse to common sense and the most traditional assertions concerning truth in history. What is required is patient articulating of the modes of representation in terms of those of explanation/understanding and, through these, of the documentary moment and its generating matrix of presumed truth—that is, the testimony of those who declare their having been there where things happened. We shall never find in the narrative form per se the reason for this quest for referentiality. The work of reconstructing historical discourse taken in terms of the complexity of its operative phases is totally absent from Hayden White's preoccupations.

It is with regard to these aporias of the referentiality of historical discourse that the calling into question of the propositions of White's narrative rhetoric by the horrible events placed under the sign of the "final solution" constitutes an exemplary challenge that goes beyond any textbook exercise.

This challenge has found strong expression in the notion of a "limit to representation" such as gives its title to the volume edited by Saul Friedlander, *Probing the Limits of Representation*.[33] This phrase can designate two kinds of limits: on the one hand, a kind of exhaustion in our culture of the available forms of representation for giving readability and visibility to the event known as the "final solution"; on the other hand, a request, a demand to be spoken of, represented, arising from the very heart of the event, hence proceeding from that origin of discourse that one rhetorical tradition takes to be extralinguistic, and forbidden any sojourn in the land of semiotics. In the first case, it would be a question of an internal limit, in the second, of an external one. The problem therefore will be that of the precise articulation between these two limits. The Shoah, which is how we really should name it, at this stage of our discussion proposes for reflection both the singularity of a phenomenon at the limit of experience and discourse, and the exemplarity of a situation where not only the limits of representation in its narrative and rhetorical forms, but the whole enterprise of writing history, are open to discovery.

White's tropology could not fail to get caught up in this.[34] And in Germany itself a vast quarrel between 1986 and 1988 known as the *Historikerstreit* involved respected historians of the Nazi period as well as a philosopher as well known as Jürgen Habermas, over such problems as the uniqueness of Nazism and the relevance of any comparison with Stalinism, with the consistency of Hannah Arendt's concept of totalitarianism as one of the stakes, and finally over the question of the continuity of the German nation with and beyond this catastrophe.[35]

It was against this charged background of questions and passions concerning the very possibility of "historicizing" (*Historiserung*) National Socialism and singularly "Auschwitz" that the American colloquium on the theme "History, Event, and Discourse" took place, during which Hayden White and Carlo Ginzburg set forth their opposing views about the notion of historical truth. In this way the question of the limits of representation in narrative and rhetorical form could take on the proportions of a test—a probing—of the limits of the very project of representing to oneself an event of such magnitude. Historicization and figuration—the same struggle and the same test.

In his introduction to *Probing the Limits*, Saul Friedlander proposes a schema whereby it is necessary to begin from the external limits of discourse in order to form the idea of the internal limits of representation. In this, he deliberately steps out of the circle that representation forms with itself. At the heart of Europe occurred an "event at the limits" (3). This event reached down to the deepest layers of solidarity among human beings: "Auschwitz has changed the basis for the continuation, the basis for the continuity of the conditions of life within history" (3). Life-within-history, not "discourse-about-history." A truth claim arises from behind the mirror that places its exigencies on representation, which reveal the internal limits of literary genres: "There are limits to representation which *should not be* but can easily be transgressed" (3, his emphasis). There can be something wrong with certain representations of events (above all when the transgression is as glaring as Holocaust denial), even if we cannot formulate the nature of the transgression and are condemned to remain in a state of uneasiness. The idea of transgression in this way confers an unexpected intensity on a discussion that began on an inoffensive, if not innocent level, that of semiotics, of narratology, of tropology. The event "at the limits" brings its own opacity along with its morally "unacceptable" character (the word takes on the force of an extreme understatement)—its character of "moral offense." Then it is the opacity of events that reveals and denounces that of language. What is more, this denunciation takes on an unexpected character at one moment of the theoretical discussion marked by what we call by convention "postmodernism," a moment where the critique of naïve realism is at its apogee in the name of the polysemy *en abîme* of discourse, of the self-referentiality of linguistic constructions, which make impossible the identification of any stable reality whatsoever. What plausible response, then, can this so-called postmodernism give to the accusation of having disarmed thought in the face of the seductions of negationism?[36]

Confronted with Friedlander's scheme, which proceeds from the event at its limits in the direction of the internal limits of the operation of representation, Haydon White undertakes, with an extreme honesty, to go as far as possible in the direction of the event by speaking of the rhetorical resources of verbal representation.[37] But can a tropology of historical discourse link up with something like a "demand," in the strong sense of the word in English, a truth claim, proceeding from the events themselves?

White's essay exhibits a kind of quartering of its own discourse. On the one hand, the author increases his claim for the "inexpugnable relativity" of every representation of historical phenomena. This relativity has to be assigned to language itself, insofar as it does not constitute a transparent medium, like a mirror reflecting some presumed reality. The pair plot/trope is once again taken as the site of resistance to any return to a naïve realism. On the other hand, a suspicion grows over the course of his essay that there could be something in the event itself so monstrous as to put to flight all the modes available to representation. This something would have no name in any known class of plot types, be they tragic, comic, or whatever. Following the first direction of his thesis, White points to the roadblocks on the path to the event. It is impossible, he declares, to distinguish between a "factual statement" (singular existential propositions and arguments), on the one hand, and narrative reports, on the other. These latter will always transform lists of facts into stories. But these stories bring with them their plot types, tropes, and typologies. All we are left with is "competitive narratives," which no argument can decide among and for which no criterion drawn from factual statements can arbitrate, once the facts are already facts of language. The principle of a distinction between interpretation and fact is thereby undermined, and the boundary between "true" and "false," "imaginary" and "factual," "figurative" and "literal" story falls. Applied to the events designated by the expression "final solution," these considerations lead to the impossibility of making sense on the narrative plane of the idea of an unacceptable mode of emplotment. None of the known modes of emplotment is unacceptable a priori; nor is any one more appropriate than another.[38] The distinction between acceptable and unacceptable does not stem from tropology, but proceeds from another region of our receptive capacity than that educated by our narrative culture. And, if we say with George Steiner, that "the world of Auschwitz lies outside discourse just as it lies outside reason" (cited by White, 43), whence comes the sense of the unspeakable and unrepresentable? We will not resolve the difficulty by forbidding any mode other than the literal chronicle, which would be equivalent to demanding the denarrativization of the events in question. This is only a despairing manner of setting aside every figurative addition to a literal representation of the events. This solution is despairing in the sense that it falls back on the illusions of a naïve realism that were common to the principal current of the nineteenth-century novel and to the positivist school of historiography. It is an illusion to believe that factual statements can satisfy the idea of the unrepresentable, as though facts could through the virtue of their literal presentation be dissociated from their representation in the form of events in a history; events, history, plot all go together on the plane of figuration. White pushes his argument to the point of striking with suspicion the whole enterprise of the realistic representation of reality by which Erich Auerbach characterized Western culture.[39] At the end of his essay, White attempts a kind of heroic escape, by suggesting that certain modes of writing that make use of postmodernism—which he persists in calling modernist—may have a certain affinity with the opacity of the event. For example, "intransitive" writing, a notion borrowed from Roland Barthes, who compares it in turn with the "middle voice" of ancient Greek grammar. White thinks he can see this in certain of Derrida's comments about "differance." But, if the style of "middle-voicedness" effectively breaks with realism, what assures that it has any affinity with the "new actuality"? Was not totalitarianism modernist? Does it suffice to break with realist representation to bring language close to not only the opacity but also the inadmissible character of the "final solution"? Everything happens as though, at the end of the essay, the critique without any concession of naïve realism paradoxically contributes to reinforcing the truth claim coming from elsewhere than discourse, in such a way as to render derisory the outlines of a compromise with a realism that has become undiscoverable.

Over against White, Carlo Ginzburg makes an impassioned plea in favor not of realism but of historical reality itself as what is intended by testimony. He recalls the declaration from Deuteronomy 19:15 (which he cites in Latin): *non stabit testis unus contra aliquem* ("A single witness shall not suffice to convict a person of any crime or wrongdoing in connection with any offense that may be committed" [NRSV])—and compares it to the Code of Justinian: *testis unus, testis nullus.* With this, the title "just one witness" sounds a despairing note, as though the accumulated documents remain below the threshold of double testimony, unless by antiphrasis we point to the excess of such testimonies in regard to the capacity of plots to produce a coherent and acceptable discourse.[40] His plea in favor of the reality of the historical past, akin to that of Pierre Vidal-Naquet in *The Jews: History, Memory, and the Present* and *Assassins of Memory*,[41] thus bears the double aspect of an uncontestable attestation and of a moral protest that prolongs the violence of the impulse that pushed a survivor like Primo Levi to bear witness.[42] It is this interweaving of attestation and protest in the case of literature about the Shoah that we need to reflect upon. If we do not want to allow this mixed status, we will not understand why and how representation must integrate into its formulation the "inadmissible" dimension of the event. But then, it is the citizen as much as the historian who is summoned by the event. And he is summoned at the level of his participation in collective memory, before which the historian is called upon to give account. But he does not do so by leaving behind the critical resources stemming from his professional competence as a historian. The historian's task faced with events "at the limits" is not confined to the habitual hunt for falsehood that, ever since the *Donation of Constantine*, has become the great specialty of the discipline of history. His task extends to the discrimination among testimonies as a function of their origin: those of the survivors, the executioners,[43] the spectators implied in different ways in the mass atrocities, differ. So it comes down to historical criticism to explain why we cannot write an all-encompassing history that would annul the insurmountable differences among these perspectives. This critical consideration can in particular lead to dissipating useless quarrels like the ones that contrapose the history of the everyday life of the German people, the history of the economic, social, cultural, and ideological constraints, and the history of the decision making at the summit level of the state. The notions of scale, of a choice of scale, of changes in scale can be usefully invoked here in the encounter with the confrontation between what are called "functionalist" and an "intentionalist" interpretations. As we have learned above, the very notions of fact and interpretation vary depending on the scale considered. Nor must the historian of the Shoah allow himself to be intimidated by the postulate that to explain is to excuse, to understand is to pardon. The moral judgment interwoven with historical judgment stems from another layer of historical meaning than that of description and explanation. Therefore it must not intimidate the historian to the point of leading him to censor himself.

Is it possible to be more precise about the way in which the moral judgment, signified by the expression "unacceptable," addressed by Friedlander to forms of figuration of the event, is to be articulated on the basis of the critical vigilance of which we have just given some examples? This is the question Adorno posed when he asked, "What does coming to terms with [*Aufarbeitung*] the past mean?"[44] We can find some help in a prudent recourse to such psychoanalytic categories as trauma, repetition, the work of memory, understood as "working through," and, above all, in that of transference applied not to a person but to situations in which the agents of history were diversely "cathected." Thus above I risked speaking of the use and abuse of memory and singularly of the difficulties of blocked memory. It is a comparable situation that history is confronted with in the face of events at the limit. We need to begin again here from the diversity of situations of the summoned witnesses, as was said above. It is not just a question of different points of view, but of heterogeneous investments. This is the way explored by Dominick La Capra in his contribution to *Probing the Limits*: aged Nazis, young Jews or Germans, and so on, are implied in different transference situations. The question thus arises whether a criterion of acceptability may be disengaged in a such a way that this or that attempted historical treatment of supremely traumatic events is capable of accompanying and facilitating the process of working through.[45] The criterion in this sense is more therapeutic than epistemological. It is difficult to work with inasmuch as the historian in turn is in an indirect transference relation to the trauma by way of the testimonies that he privileges. The historian too has a problem of identification at the moment of choosing his target. This split in the transference relation confirms the hybrid position of the historian confronted with the Holocaust. As a professional scholar, he speaks in the third person, and, as a critical intellectual, in the first person. But we cannot fix once and for all the distinction between the expert and the one Raymond Aron would have called the engaged spectator.

If now we turn in the direction of the source of the demand for truth and therefore the place of the initial trauma, we need to say that this source is not in the representation but rather in the lived experience of "making history" as it is confronted in different ways by the protagonists. Following Habermas, we have said that this means "reaching a deeper level of solidarity with those bearing a human form."[46] It is in this sense that the event called Auschwitz is an event at the limits. It lies in individual and collective memory before being in the discourse of the historian. And it is from this source that the attestation-protestation arises that places the historian-citizen in a situation of responsibility as regards the past.

Must we continue to call this limit imposed on the claims to self-sufficiency of the rhetorical forms of representation external? No, if we consider the true nature of the relation of history to memory, which is that of a critical reprise, one that is internal as much as external. Yes, if we consider the origin of this claim, which is less tied to the actual use of rhetorical forms than to literary theory—whether structuralist or not—which proclaims the closure in on themselves of narrative and rhetorical configurations and announces the exclusion of any extralinguistic referent. Having said this, external and/or internal, the inherent limit of the event said to be "at the limits" prolongs its effects at the core of the representation whose limits it makes appear; that is, the impossible adequation of the available forms of figuration to the demand for truth arising from the heart of lived history. Must we then conclude the exhaustion of these forms, above all of those inherited from the naturalist and realist tradition of the nineteenth-century novel and history text? Undoubtedly, yes. But this assertion must stimulate rather than preclude the exploration of alternative modes of expression, eventually connected to other supports than just that of the printed book: drama, film, the plastic arts. We are not forbidden an ongoing search for a way to fill the gap between the representative capacity of discourse and what the event demands, even while guarding ourselves against nourishing an illusion in favor of those styles of writing Hayden White calls "modernist," parallel to the one he condemns on the side of the realist tradition.

It follows from these considerations that to attempt to write the history of the "final solution" is not a hopeless undertaking, if we do not forget the origin of the limits in principle that affect it. It is rather the occasion to recall the trajectory that critical thought has to carry out, leading back from representation to explanation/understanding and from there to documentary work, up to the ultimate testimonies whose collection we know is broken up among the side of the executioners and that of the victims, that of the survivors, that of the different involved spectators.[47]

Someone may ask how the problems posed by the writing of the event "at the limits" called Auschwitz are exemplary for a general reflection on historiography. They are so insofar as they themselves are, as such, problems "at the limit." Along our way we have encountered several illustrations of this extreme problematization: the impossibility of neutralizing the differences in position of witnesses in the interplay of scales; the impossibility of summing up in one all-encompassing history the reconstructions backed up by heterogeneous affective investments; the unsurpassable dialectic between uniqueness and incomparability at the very heart of the idea of singularity. Perhaps every singularity—turn by turn, unique and/or incomparable—is a sign of exemplarity in this double sense.

## THE HISTORIAN'S REPRESENTATION
## AND THE PRESTIGE OF THE IMAGE

As a first approximation, referring to the iconic dimension of the historian's representation should not introduce any large-scale adjustments to my analysis. Either it is only a question of opposing two fully constituted literary genres, or it is only a matter of accentuating certain features of narrativity I have already noted and amply commented on under the heading of the rhetorical effects that go along with emplotment.

What I want to show, however, is that with this term "image" an aporia comes to the fore that has its place of origin in the iconic constitution of memory itself.

Let us linger a moment at the level of what I have called a first approximation. The pair historical narrative and fictional narrative, as they appear as already constituted at the level of literary genres, is clearly antinomical. A novel, even a realist novel, is something other an a history book. They are distinguished from each other by the nature of the implicit contract between the writer and the reader. Even when not clearly stated, this contract sets up different expectations on the side of the reader and different promises on that of the author. In opening a novel, the reader is prepared to enter an unreal universe concerning which the question where and when these things took place is incongruous. In return, the reader is disposed to carry out what Coleridge called a "willful suspension of disbelief," with the reservation that the story told is an interesting one. The reader willingly suspends his disbelief, his incredulity, and he accepts playing along as if—as if the things recounted did happen. In opening a history book, the reader expects, under the guidance of a mass of archives, to reenter a world of events that actually occurred. What is more, in crossing the threshold of what is written, he stays on guard, casts a critical eye, and demands if not a true discourse comparable to that of a physics text, at least a plausible one, one that is admissible, probable, and in any case honest and truthful. Having been taught to look out for falsehoods, he does not want to have to deal with a liar.[48]

So long as we remain in this way on the plane of constituted literary genres, no confusion is admissible, at least in principle, between the two kinds of narratives. Unreality and reality are taken as heterogeneous modes of reference. Historical intentionality implies that the historian's constructions have the ambition of being reconstructions that more or less approach what one day was "real," whatever the difficulties may be that are taken as resolved by what I continue to call standing for, to which the closing discussion of this chapter will be devoted. Nevertheless, despite the distinction in principle between "real" past and "unreal" fiction, a dialectical treatment of this elementary dichotomy imposes itself through the fact of the interweaving of the effects exercised by fictions and true narratives at the level of what we can call the "world of the text," the keystone to a theory of reading.[49]

What I previously called the "fictionalization of historical discourse" can be reformulated as the interweaving of readability and visibility at the threshold of the historian's representation. One is then tempted to look for the key to this imaginary structure of a new kind on the side of the rhetorical effects referred to above. Do we not call tropes those figures that not only ornament but articulate historical discourse in its literary phase? The suggestion is a good one, but it leads further than anticipated. What must be unrolled, as in examining the back side of a tapestry, is precisely the interwoven connection of readability and visibility at the level of the reception of the literary text. In fact, narrative gives itself to be understood and seen. Dissociation of the two interwoven effects is facilitated when the picture and the sequence, the descriptive stasis and the properly narrative advance, itself precipitated by what Aristotle's *Poetics* calls peripeteia, particularly when it occurs through theatrical or violent effects, are separated. The historian is well aware of this alternation.[50] Often it is through a set of pictures that he depicts the situation wherein the beginning of his narrative is implanted. He can end his work in the same way, unless he should choose to leave it in suspense, like Thomas Mann deliberately losing sight of his hero at the end of *The Magic Mountain*. The historian is not unaware of these strategies for closing a narrative, which only make sense to the eye of an educated reader thanks to an expert game of frustrating one's usual expectations. But it is with the portrait of characters in narratives, whether they be stories from everyday life, narrative fictions, or historical fictions, that visibility decisively carries the day over readability. Here we have a constant thesis of this book: the characters in a narrative are emplotted along with the events that, taken together, make up the story told. With the portrait, distinguished from the warp of the narrative, the pairing of readability and visibility stands out most clearly.

It turns out that this pairing gives rise to noteworthy exchanges that are the sources of meaning effects comparable to those that get produced between fiction and historical narrative. We can say that an art lover reads a painting[51] and that a narrator depicts a battle scene. How are such exchanges possible? Is it only when the narrative unfolds a space, a landscape, places, or when it lingers over a face, a posture, a position that a whole character gives itself as to be seen? In short, is there readability only in a polar relation to visibility—a distinction that superimposing the two extremes does not abolish? Or should we go so far as to say that in every case the narrative sets something before our eyes, gives something to be seen? This is what Aristotle had already suggested in his remarks on metaphor in Book III of his *Rhetoric*. Considering the "virtues of *lexis*" (locution, elocution), he says that this virtue consists in "setting the scene before our eyes" (1410b33). This power of the figure to set the scene before our eyes has to be linked to a more fundamental power that defines the rhetorical project considered as a whole, namely, "the faculty to discover speculatively what, in each case, is likely to persuade" (1356b25–26 and 1356a19–20). The *pithanon*, the "persuasive as such," is the recurrent theme of rhetoric. To be sure, persuasion is not seduction—and Aristotle's whole ambition was to stabilize rhetoric halfway between logic and sophistry, thanks to the connection between the persuasive and the reasonable in the sense of the probable (*to eikos*). This definition of rhetoric as the *tekhnē* of discourse likely to persuade lies at the origin of every prestige that the imagination is capable of grafting to the visibility of figures of language.[52]

Guided by the perplexity of the ancients, we shall take up again the broken thread of our reflections on the dialectic of presence and absence begun within the framework of a history of social representations. There we admitted that the functioning of this dialectic in the representative practice of social agents was not really made clear until it was taken up and rendered explicit through the very discourse of the historian representing to himself the representation of such social agents. The representing operation, at the level of which from here on we want to keep ourselves, will constitute not only a complement with regard to the represented object of history but also a surplus, inasmuch as the representing operation can be taken as the reflective phase of the represented object.

I propose taking as my guide here the works that Louis Marin has devoted to the prestige of the image, as he finds it lucidly fomented by the great writers of the seventeenth century to the glory of monarchical power and its incarnate figure, the king. I shall keep in reserve during the course of my reading of the *Portrait of the King* the question whether some instruction, concerning the relations between the justification of power and the prestige of the image, persists for the citizens of a democracy who believe themselves to have broken with singing the king's praises, beyond what has become for them a kind of slightly exotic case.[53]

Marin immediately puts the accent on the force, the power, of the image substituted for something present elsewhere. It is the transitive dimension of the image that is thereby underscored in what we can call a "theory of effects" that finds strong echoes in Pascal (7). "The power-effect of representation is the representation itself." This power-effect finds its privileged field of exercise in the political sphere, inasmuch as there power is animated by the desire for the absolute. It is the mark of the absolute imposed on power that in a way stirs up the imaginary, leading it in a fantastic direction: lacking an actual infinity, what takes its place is "the imaginary absolute of the monarch." The king is not really king, that is, monarch, except through the images that confer upon him a reputedly real presence. Here Marin comes up with a seductive hypothesis according to which "the political imaginary and symbolism of the absolute monarch" had rediscovered the "eucharistic motif" whose central role Marin's earlier study on the *Logique de Port-Royal* had demonstrated. The utterance "this is my body" governs not just the whole semiotics of the attributive proposition on the logical plane, but the discourse of power on the political one.[54]

The phrase "L'État c'est moi" is the political doublet of the one that consecrates the Eucharistic host.[55] That this political "transposition" stems from the order of the "lure," in line with the "fantastic" referred to by Plato in the *Sophist*, is known only on the basis of an external, ironic, critical discourse, which Marin sees formulated in the famous *Pensées*, where Pascal mercilessly demonstrates the hidden play of exchanges between the discourse of force and that of justice. Three levels of discourse are set up and practiced in this way: the implicit one in the representation at work at the heart of social practice, the explicit one of the representation articulated by the praise of power, and the one that brings to light power as representation and representation as power. Will the third discourse, which gives an anthropological dimension to the interplay of representation and power, have the virtue of setting in motion another inquiry that would bear on a comparable interplay occurring beyond the fall of the monarchy, in new projections of the king's power? This is a question I shall reserve for later.

Whatever may be said about the political resonance of the theology of transubstantiation and the potentially blasphemous turn in such an operation, it is worth noting that the discourse of power, once it is made explicit on the plane of the historian's representation, simultaneously assumes the two forms of narrative (evocative of some absence) and icon (the bearer of some real presence). Yet, taken together, absence and presence produce the representation of power in "the fantastic representation of the absolute monarch in his portrait and in his name" (12). "There is a dimension of narrative and of recitation in the royal portrait that is also the celebration of the king's historical body, his monumental tomb in and through the representation of history" (12).[56] Marin offers two illustrations of this double function of the representation of power. First, with the commentary on the "Projet de l'histoire de Louis XIV" addressed to Colbert by the court historian Pellisson-Fontainier,[57] it is the readability of the narrative that generates visibility in a quasi "portraiture." Second, with the treatment of the "historic medal" struck with the effigy of Louis XIV as "royal host," it is the visibility of the portrait that generates the readability of a quasi recitative of glory.[58]

The "Project for a History of Louis XIV" in effect is a quite extraordinary text in that it presents to its reader's eyes the stratagems of a yet to be written history, along with the barely concealed plan of enticing its ultimate addressee, the king, to fall into the trap of providing a royal subvention for it. The stratagem for writing history thereby laid bare comes down to a cunning use of the prestige of the image used in service of rendering praise. Another rhetoric than that of figures is made use of here, the rhetoric with an Aristotelian origin of the three genres of public discourse: the judicial genre governing pleas for judgments, the deliberative one governing political decisions, and the epideictic one (elsewhere called demonstrative) illustrated by speeches of praise and blame, the funeral oration constituting its most eloquent expression. This classification, governed less by the differences in style than by the distinction among the addressees of the discourse, vigorously takes up the rule-governed exploitation of praise discourse that, in the age of absolute monarchical power, occupies the wide-open space left vacant by the deliberative genre's having been relegated to the back burner, it having been sacrificed to the king's secret cabinet. Where does such praise point within the order of political power? To greatness, and to the flash of such greatness, glory. The prestige of the image made use of by the "Project for a History of Louis XIV" is put to the service of such greatness and glory. The historian's cunning in offering such a service is first of all to anticipate the way in which power that desires to be absolute thinks: "What is the phantasmatic in and through which the politics of this desire is rationalized? What is the imaginary of absolutism, and what are the role and function of the historiographer in constituting this phantasmatic and in constructing this imaginary?" (48). The trap, if we can put it this way, lies wholly in the role played in this proposal by the eulogist: "The king must be praised everywhere but, so to speak, without praise, by a narrative of all that he has been seen to do, say, and think." The ruse succeeds if the adulator succeeds in "enabling [the reader] to conceive of his [the king's] greatness in all sorts of ways" (53). It is not up to the writer to speak of greatness and glory, it is up to the reader under the helpful guidance of the narrative. Among the narrative resources to be brought into play in seeking this effect within the overall field of forces are abbreviation in the narration of exploits, the *brevitas* so dear to Tacitus in making use of litotes, the depiction of actors and scenes, and all the simulacra of presence likely to give rise to pleasure in reading. A place of honor is to be assigned to narrative hypotyposis, that "animated and striking description" (*Robert* dictionary),[59] which, more than any other rhetorical procedure, sets things before the eyes[60] and thereby sets up the character, the event, the scene as instructive examples: "[History] puts all the great things it encounters in a better light through a noble and a more composed style, which encloses a lot in a little space with no wasted words" (*Pensées*, bundle V, cited in *Portrait of the King*, 82). This concern to show in telling is even more strongly marked in the *Éloge historique du roi sur ses conquêtes depuis l'année 1672 jusqu'en 1678* by Racine and Boileau. Marin quotes these eloquent phrases from it: "Some people more particularly zealous for his glory wanted to have in their studies *a précis in pictures* of the prince's *greatest actions*, which prompted this little work that encloses so many marvels in a very small space, so as at any time to put *before their eyes at all times* that which is the dearest occupation of their thoughts" (122). The monarch's greatness stands forth before the eye as soon as the strategy of the narrative succeeds in making it appear like the archactor of the gesture.

Such in brief is the historian's cunning, worthy of the Greek *mētis* described by Jean-Pierre Vernant. It consists in concealing the very panegyric project that, like the repressed, has to return in the reader's mouth. Thus we can speak of a "simulation of history" (74) to designate of this power of representation "that the absolute needs in order to constitute *itself* absolutely" (75), a power targeted on extorting the panegyric from the moment of reading. What is surprising is that the author of this historical project dared to spring the trap by stating it—to the great happiness of the contemporary historiographer. Our question will be whether, with the end of the monarchy of the Ancien Regime and the transfer of sovereignty and its attributes to the people, historiography has been able to eliminate from its representation every trace of the discourse of praise. At the same time, this will be to ask whether the category of greatness and what is connected to it, glory, can disappear without leaving some trace on the horizon of the history of power. Was it reserved only to the "absolutist manner of writing the absolute history of absolutism" (88) to extract from the readability of narrative the visibility of a narrative description that would succeed in "depicting rather than recounting, in making the imagination see everything that was put on paper," following the confession by which the author ends the "Project for a History of Louis XIV"? Has modern democracy put an end to praise of the king and the phantasmatic placed in service of this praise?[61]

The relation between readability and visibility is inverted by the portrait medal of the king. Or rather the exchange between readability and visibility starts from the other pole. Louis Marin can say at the beginning of his study of "The Royal Host: The Historic Medal": "To tell the king's history in a narrative is to show it. To show the king's history in his icon is to tell it" (121). A chiasmus is established that makes the picture speak and the narrative show, each mode of representation finding its most specific, its ownmost effect in the domain of the other. Thus we ourselves say that one reads a painting. The medal is the most remarkable procedure of iconic representation capable of telling by showing. Unlike the drawing that illustrates a text, or even a tapestry, which most often only represents one moment of history, the medal is a portrait that, like hypotyposis, offers an abbreviation of a picture. By presenting something to be seen, the medal—a specific inscription of the king's portrait, a metal engraving—thanks to its gold and its brilliance depicts the flash of glory. What is more, the medal, like a coin, can be shown, touched, exchanged. But above all, thanks to its hardness and the fact that it lasts, it grounds a permanence of memory by transforming the passing flash of the exploit into perpetual glory. A connection to narrative is assured by the motto inscribed on the reverse side of the figure of the king's effigy, and in his name. It assures the potentially universal exemplarity of the virtues engraved in gold. At the center stands the name. Praise comes to the name by way of the exploits and virtues. In this way the historic medal could in its day be called a monument, like those funerary sepulchers that warn and admonish all those who had been absent from the place and time of the commemorated event. The historical medal of the king was par excellence "the monumental sign of absolute political power in the infinity of its representation" (123).

Has the time of the medal run its course, at least in the West, with the fall of absolute monarchy? Did it vanish along with the praise conveyed through the king's narrative? Yes, undoubtedly, if we put the accent on the theological connotation that authorizes calling the medal a "royal host," a "sacramental Host of the power of the State" (134). No, perhaps, if we grant the theme of greatness a kind of transhistorical permanence that would allow it to survive the dead glory of an absolute monarch. Do not a bit of flash, a bit of glory continue to surround the contemporary figure of the prince, even when his portrait is reduced to that of a postage stamp? Nor have medals everywhere, and once and for all, disappeared.

I have said that the narrative and iconographic representation brought about by history brings to light the representation practiced by social actors. But what is brought to light by the strategies of representation once these are said to be fomented by a phantasmatic imaginary and denounced as simulacra? Who says this?

Louis Marin's answer in *Portrait of the King* is striking. It is in Pascal's *Pensées*, dealing with force and justice, that the reader sees the glamour of the imagination dismantled. So it is not to the plane of the historiographical operation that the thinker of the *Pensées* brings his lucidity, but to that of a philosophical anthropology whose propositions abstract from every location in geographical space and historical time, even if for a discourse of a still higher degree it would be easy to take this or that *pensée* as having a particular time and place. But this is not how the *Pensées* ask to be read: the contract with the reader is here that of veracity confronted with dissimulation.[62] What the famous *pensées* dealing with force and justice bring to light are the "effects" of the imagination that are summed up by the as yet not referred to expression of leading to belief. This "effect" is one of meaning insofar as it is one of force. Two proposals are stated by Marin:

1. Discourse is the mode of existence of an imaginary of force, an imaginary whose name is "power."
2. Power is the imaginary of force when it is uttered as discourse of justice. (16)

On the one side, therefore, force becomes power by taking hold of the discourse of justice; on the other, the discourse of justice becomes power in standing for the effects of force. Everything takes place within the circular relation between standing for and being taken for. This is the circle of coming to believe. Here the imaginary does not designate merely the visibility of the icon that sets before the eyes the events and characters of a narrative, but a discursive power.

It is not a question here of undertaking an exegesis of those fragments that suggest placing in series the three key words "force, justice, imagination," as though only one ordering were authorized. Sometimes they are commented on separately, sometimes in pairs, sometimes as all three at once. Therefore it is an interpretation, for all that a highly plausible one, that Louis Marin proposes in the magnificent pages that constitute the "overture" of his work under the title "The King, or Force Justified: Pascalian Commentaries." His gathering and ordering of statements taken from the *Fragments* are openly oriented by a concern to dismantle the stratagems of the imagination of power. "One must have deeper motives and judge everything accordingly, but go on talking like an ordinary person" (§91). Only the pair force/justice is made use of by this text, and we could see it as a sediment of the famous assertion that "as men could not make might obey right, they have made right obey might. As they could not fortify justice they have justified force, so that right and might live together and peace reigns, the sovereign good" (§81). The justification of force can be taken as the linchpin of a whole demonstration where one takes up the titles of the just that ought to be followed and those of force that is to be obeyed, then the reversal of the apparent symmetries between force and justice. "Right without might is challenged, because there are always evil men about. Might without right is denounced" (§103). We can leave aside the question of what would be their reconciliation: "We must therefore combine right and might." What is important for our project is the self-justifying discourse of force. At this point it is easy to introduce the no less famous fragment on the imagination.[63] That, in speaking of "this master of error and falsehood," of "the war between the senses and reason" (§44), Pascal had explicitly in mind the effects of political power is disputable. The discourse of philosophical anthropology is placed under the aegis of broader concepts such as impoverishment and vanity. In any case, taken together, fragments 44, 87, and 828 authorize, among several possible readings, treating the imagination as bringing about the process that justifies force. The imagination is itself a power—an "arrogant force" (§44). "It makes us believe, doubt, deny reason." "It dispenses reputation . . . makes us respect and revere persons, works, laws, the great." Other effects: "Love or hate alters the face of justice." Also: "Imagination decides everything; it creates the beauty, justice, and happiness, which is the world's supreme good." What other power than the imagination would be able to clothe judges, physicians, preachers? The most eloquent of the fragments to my eyes is the one among the unclassified papers in series 31 that confronts in a striking way the "bonds of necessity" and the "bonds of the imagination": "The bonds securing men's mutual respect are generally bonds of necessity, for there must be differences of degree, since all men want to be on top, and all cannot be, but some can.... And that is where imagination begins to play its part. Until then, pure power did it, now it is power, maintained by imagination in a certain faction, in France the nobles, in Switzerland commoners, etc. So these bonds securing respect for a particular person are bonds of imagination" (§828). At this point, Pascal's discourse is certainly one of an accusation against force without justice. It hits the "tyranny" of the power of the great, but if it also strikes the vanity of power it is because it aims well beyond politics.[64]

How far can the critical epistemology of the historiographical operation advance along this path pointed out by Louis Marin's "Pascalian commentaries"? Not very far beyond its own region of competence, even if we extend this to include the order of representations linked to social practice. But far enough nevertheless if we are to find a reason, encouragement, a handhold in the supra-political dimension of anthropological discourse at the moment of posing the question whether other figures of power than that of the absolute king are capable of receiving clarification, even laterally, thanks to the enlarging of the problematic of the representation of power that the Pascalian anthropology makes possible.

Over the course of our reflection we have set down several milestones on a path that, without leaving behind the representations of power, leads in the direction of the neighborhood of post-absolutist political configurations where other forms of the prestige of the image are likely to occur, unless these be the same ones in different guise.

One word may crystallize the question: "greatness." In fact, it belongs to the two registers of politics and anthropology. Furthermore, it is in part bound to the problematic of representation by way of the rhetoric of praise. Let us return one last time to Pascal. On the one side, greatness belongs to the same constellation as does the impoverishment for which it is the other pole in the order of contrarieties and disproportion in human beings, and as does the vanity that builds on such impoverishment: "Man's greatness comes from knowing he is wretched: a tree does not know it is wretched. Thus it is wretched to know that one is wretched, but there is greatness in knowing one is wretched" (§114). On another side, greatness touches politics: "All these examples of wretchedness prove his greatness. It is the wretchedness of a great lord, the wretchedness of a dispossessed king" (§116). Pascal continues: "Who indeed would think himself unhappy not to be king except one who had been dispossessed?" (§117). This figure of a dispossessed king is not simple: man in general can be seen as a dispossessed king. And it is this dispossessed king that, in an astonishing fable meant for the young prince, Pascal sees "tossed up by a storm on some unknown island, where the inhabitants were having difficulty in finding their king who had been lost." This man who finds himself resembling the lost king is "taken for him, recognized as such by all the people." And what did he do? "He received all the respect that they wished to render to him and allowed himself to be treated as king."[65] Therefore it is a "portrait effect," an "effect of representation" that makes the king. And in turn it is the image, dedicated to the prince, of this "drowned king," become the "legitimate usurper," that gives the instructive force to the epistle. Politics and anthropology conjoin in this image. At the same time, the secret is revealed of the simulative representations that underlie those greatnesses in the flesh to whom the king belongs and all those we call or that are called great.

If greatness can in this way belong to the two registers of anthropology ("man") and politics (the "king"), it is because it contains in principle (in its known truth, like all principles, "not only through our reason but also through our heart" [§110]) an ordering and hierarchical rule. The fragment is well known about the "orders of greatness": the greatness of the flesh, of the mind, of charity (§308). Each greatness has its degree of visibility, its luster, its flash—kings are joined with the rich and the captains among the "greatness of the flesh."[66]

From these considerations comes the question by which I will end our inquiry into the prestige of the image entangled with the historian's representation. What remains of the theme of greatness in the narration of power after the elimination of the figure of the absolute king? To ask about the possible permanence of the theme of power is at the same time to ask about the persistence of the rhetoric of praise that is its literary correlate, with its cortege of prestigious images. Has greatness abandoned the political field? And must and can historians renounce the discourse of praise with its vanities?

I will answer the first question by two comments that I shall place in no special order, in that I am concerned not to treat a problem of political philosophy with an air of expertise that I lack, a problem moreover that exceeds the competence of an epistemology of the historical operation. However the question cannot be avoided inasmuch as the nation state remains the organizing center for the ordinary referents of historical discourse, given the lack of access to a cosmopolitan point of view. In order to remain such an organizing center, must the nation state continue to be celebrated as great? This reformulation of the question leads to my first comment. I borrow it from Hegel's philosophy of the state in the *Philosophy of Right*. In considering the power of the prince (§275), Hegel distinguishes three elements that stem from the constitution as a rational totality: to the universality of the constitution and the laws, and to the process of deliberation, gets added "the moment of ultimate decision, as self-determination." In it lies "the distinctive principle of the power of the crown." This moment is incarnated in an individual who, in monarchical regimes, is destined to the dignity of the throne by birth. However contingent this moment may be, a contingency taken up into hereditary right, it is irreducibly constitutive of state sovereignty. Someone may object that Hegel's political thought does not get beyond the orb of the monarchical principle and in this sense from the space of absolute politics, despite his sympathies for a liberal monarchy. But Hegel is already the thinker of the modern post-revolutionary state, that is, the constitutional state in contrast to the aristocratic one. It is within these limits that the question is posed whether in a constitutional regime politics can be exempted from the moment of ultimate decision and, to put it in a word, whether it can escape entirely from the personification of power. Contemporary history seems to ratify this question. Eric Weil, in his *Philosophie politique*, proposes a rational framework with which to discuss this. He defines the state in formal terms: "The State is the organization of a historical community. Organized into a State, the community is capable of making decisions."[67] It is along this trajectory that a decision, within the framework of the constitution, on the basis of an administration during the stage of deliberation and execution, and by means of parliament for discussing and passing laws, poses *in fine* the problem of the exercise of political authority, in particular in tragic situations where the physical existence and moral integrity of the state are in danger. This is when the true *homme d'État* reveals himself. With this notion of a *homme d'État*, in a fully constitutional system, comes the Hegelian question of the prince as the incarnation *hic et nunc* of the "moment of ultimate decision, as self-determination." This moment is also the moment of greatness.

Someone may object that under the figure of the *homme d'État* we are fraudulently reintroducing the portrait of the king. So I will offer my second comment, which will redistribute the figures of greatness in a broader social space, worthy of a Pascalian consideration of the orders of greatness because of its breadth. It was possible during the last decade of the twentieth century for a book to bear the subtitle "Economies of Greatness" and to open a new career for the idea of greatness in liaison not with the greatness of political power but with the greatness of the widest sense of justification, the demand for justice.[68] In disputed situations, debates that appeal to people's opinions must appeal to argumentative strategies meant to justify the action or to sustain the criticisms at the heart of the dispute. What is remarkable is not just that the idea of greatness should return to the sociology of action and therefore also to the history of representations, but that it does so in a pluralistic way. There are economies of greatness. For example, the legitimate forms of the common good are called great in typical situations of differences of opinion once these are legitimated by typical forms of argument. It doesn't really matter here how the arguments are selected on the basis of some canonical text of political philosophy. Their irreducible plurality means that one is great in different ways depending on the qualifying tests that take place in the religious city, the domestic city, the city of popular opinion, the civic city, or the industrial city. For my thesis, what is important is that greatness should be taken into account by practical philosophy and in the social sciences in connection with the idea of justification as one of the ways of apprehending the common good at the heart of being-with-others. It is still very much a question of "political forms of greatness" (see *Portrait of the King*, 89–93), but in such an expanded sense of the term "political" that the prestige of the king in his portrait finds itself entirely exorcised by the substitution of the people and their claims to justice for the figure of the king. The return of the theme of greatness is all the more striking because of this.

This double resistance to elimination of the theme of greatness in a political philosophy centered in turn on the state and in a sociology that takes into account justified action authorizes our posing the question that will cap our inquiry concerning the prestige of the image in the praise of greatness. If the theme of greatness is inexpugnable, does this also apply to the rhetoric of praise, which, in the age of absolute monarchy, was shamelessly taken to the point of crossing the subtle line that distinguishes praise from flattery? History written by such "great" names as Ranke and Michelet cannot escape this indiscreet question. To be sure, it is not in order to judge past actions, hence to esteem them as great or not, that Ranke states that he will limit himself to events "as they actually occurred." This principle, in which I readily read a claim to trustworthiness, was above all else the expression of a restraint, a withdrawal from the region of subjective preferences and a renouncing of selective praise. But does praise not take refuge in the vow that we read in Ranke's *Nachlass*: "Every epoch is directly under God, and its value depends not on what comes from it, but its very existence itself, in its own self.... All generations of mankind are equally justified in the sight of God, and so

must the historian view the thing."[69] The ideas of an epoch and a generation are more diffuse than those of historical individuals, yet they constitute
meaningful units to which the historian's esteem is directed, justification in
God's sight adding the seal of theology to the discretion of praise.

The case of Michelet is even more striking. Few historians have expressed
admiration for the great figures among those who built France with as much
freedom and jubilation. France itself never so merited being designated by
its proper name as in the successive prefaces to his *History of France*.[70] Have
historians of the French Revolution, from Guizot to Furet, escaped this circle
of praise? And does not being a declared thurifer suffice to exempt one?[71]
Is not the discreet charm of the nation state, the usual turning point to the
modern era for history as made and for history as it is told, the coil spring for a
restricted praise that, setting aside any trickery, repeats the admitted strategy
of the "Project for a History of Louis XIV": "The king is everywhere to be
praised, but so to speak without praise, by a narrative of everything what we
have seen him do, say, and think"? And does not the same vow "to draw [the
epithets and magnificent praises that the king merits] from the mouth of
the reader by the things themselves" continue?

This question will seem less incongruous if, in place of praise, we put
blame, its contrary in the class of epideictic discourses, following the classification scheme coming down to us from the rhetorics of antiquity. Is it not
extreme blame, under the litotes of the unacceptable, that stamps the "final
solution" as infamous and that above led to my reflections on the "limits of
representation"? Do not the events "at the limits" referred to there occupy
in our own discourse the pole opposed to that of the signs of greatness used
by praise? In truth, this is a disturbing symmetry that sets back to back the
absolute blame inflicted on Nazi politics by our moral conscience and the
absolute praise addressed by his subjects to the king in his portrait.


## STANDING FOR

This concluding section is meant both to present a recapitulation of the path
covered in this chapter and to open a question that surpasses the resources of
the epistemology of historiography and reaches the threshold of an ontology
of existence in history, for which I shall make use of the phrase "our historical
condition."

"Standing for" condenses within itself all the expectations, the exigencies, and the aporias linked to what I have elsewhere spoken of as the historian's intention or intentionality. It indicates the expectation attached to the

historical knowledge of constructions constituting reconstructions of the course of past events. Above, I introduced this relation in terms of the features of a contract between the writer and the reader. Unlike the contract between an author and a reader of fiction that rests on the double convention of suspending the expectation of any description of some extralinguistic reality and, in return, of holding the reader's interest, the author and reader of a historical text agree that it will deal with situations, events, connections, and characters who once really existed, that is, before the narrative of them is put together, the interest or pleasure in reading coming as a kind of added surplus. The question now posed is whether, how, and to what degree the historian satisfies the expectation and promise conveyed by this contract.

I want to emphasize two complementary replies. First answer: the suspicion that the promise has not and cannot be kept is at its height in the phase of representation, at the moment when, paradoxically, the historian seemed best equipped to honor the intention of representing the past. Is not this intention the soul of all the operations placed under the heading of the historian's representation? The second answer is that the reply to the suspicion of betrayal does not lie only in the moment of literary representation but rather in its articulation in terms of the two prior moments of explanation/understanding and of documentation, and, if we move back even further, in the articulation of history on the basis of memory.

Expectation seems at its height, with regard to the capacity of historiography to keep its contract about reading, with the phase of the historian's representation. This representation means to be a representation *of* . . . If the constructions of the explanation/understanding phase aim at constituting re-constructions of the past, this intention seems to be stated and demonstrated in the representative phase. Is it not in recounting, in submitting the narrative to the turns of a style, and, crowning everything, in setting before the eyes, that one ratifies or, to take up again one of Roger Chartier's expressions, accredits historical discourse?[72] We can put it this way. What in *Time and Narrative* I called the "robust conviction" that animates the historian's work is itself brought before the reader's eyes by the literary writing that both signs and fills the contract in the three ways that run through in turn the narration, the rhetoric, and the imaginative aspect. How can historical intentionality not be at its height with the modes of writing that do not limit themselves to giving a linguistic covering to an understanding of the past that would already be wholly constituted and ready made before being invested in literary forms? Things would be much simpler if the written form of historiography were not to contribute its cognitive value, if the explanation/understanding were complete before being communicated through writing to a public of readers. But, now that we have renounced taking expression for a neutral, transparent garment thrown over a signification complete in its meaning, as Husserl maintained at the beginning of his *Logical Investigations*, now therefore that we are accustomed to taking thought and language as inseparable, we are prepared to listen to declarations diametrically opposed to such a setting out of play of language—that is, that in the case of the literary writing of history, narrativity adds its modes of intelligibility to those of explanation/understanding; in turn, these figures of style can be recognized to be figures of thought capable of adding a specific dimension of exhibition to the readability belonging to narratives. In short, the whole movement that carried explanation/understanding toward literary representation, and the whole internal movement of representation that displaced readability toward visibility, are both clearly meant to remain in the service of the transitive energy of the historian's representation. Yes, the historian's representation as such ought to testify to the historian's ability to keep the pact with the reader.

And yet . . .

And yet we have seen the resistance that the literary form opposes to externalization in the extratextual grow with the same rhythm as does the realist impulse. The narrative form, in giving the narrative a closure internal to the plot, tends to produce a sense of an ending, even when the narrator, in misleading the readers' expectation, undertakes to deceive them through strategies aimed at a kind of non-ending. In this way the very act of recounting comes to split off from that "real" thereby put in parentheses. An effect of the same order proceeds, we have seen, from the interplay of figures of style, to the point of rendering unclear the boundary between fiction and reality, in that these figures claim to be common to everything that is presented as a discursive tale. The paradox is at its height with the strategies meant to set things before our eyes. To the very degree that they give rise to resemblance, they are capable of supporting Roland Barthes's criticism aimed at the "reality effect." In this regard, in thinking of microhistory, we may congratulate the credibility effect these narratives "close to the people" engender by means of such proximity, but then, upon reflection, we may be surprised by the exoticism these descriptions give rise to which their very precision renders alien, even foreign to us. The reader finds himself in the situation of Fabrice at the Battle of Waterloo, incapable of giving any form to the very idea of a battle, still less of giving it a name under which it will be celebrated by those who will set out to place the "details" in some picture whose visibility will cloud our vision to the point of blindness. In the words of Jacques Revel, "read too closely, the image in the carpet is not easy to decipher."[73] There is another way of setting things before our eyes whose effect is to distance and at the limit to exile them. Writing on the broad scale, that which depicts historical periods, creates an effect that we can still call visual, that is, the picture of a synoptic vision. The scale of the gaze is then defined by its magnifying power, as is said of a telescope. An inverse problematic from the preceding one thereby arises from history presented in terms of large-scale features. A new kind of closure threatens, that of those grand narratives that tend to link up with sagas and foundational legends. A logic of a new kind silently is set in place, which Frank R. Ankersmit has attempted to close in on itself: the logic of *narratios* capable of covering vast ranges of history.[74] Use of a proper name—French Revolution, "Final Solution," and so on—is one of the distinctive signs of the circular logic in virtue of which the proper name functions as the logical subject for a whole series of attributes that develop it in terms of events, structures, persons, and institutions. These *narratios*, Ankersmit tells us, tend toward self-referentiality, the meaning of the proper name being given nowhere else than through this series of attributes. The result, on the one hand, is the incommensurability among *narratios* said to deal with the same theme and, on the other hand, the transfer to individual authors of the great controversial *narratios* opened by rival histories. Do we not speak of Michelet's, Mathiez's, Furet's history of the French Revolution? The epistemological discussion thus finds itself carried into the field of what in the next chapter I shall call interpretation, in a limited sense, where the accent is placed on the commitment of the historian's subjectivity. There is, after all, only one Michelet, one Furet, confronted with the unique French Revolution.[75]

In this way, in an unanticipated fashion, the suspicion about closure applied to small-scale narrative and that applied to larger-scale ones overlap. In one case the suspicion sets up an invisible barrier between the signifier/signified pair and the referent; in the second it opens a logical abyss between the presumed real and the cycle formed by the quasi-personified subject and the cortege of events that qualify it. In this way the literary modes said to persuade the reader of the reality, conjunctures, structures, and events set on stage become suspect of abusing the reader's confidence by abolishing the boundary between persuasion and making believe. This slap in the face can then only give rise to a vehement reply that transforms into a protest the spontaneous attestation that the good-faith historian attaches to a well-done work. This protest rejoins in an unexpected way Ranke's peaceable declaration whereby he proposes to report events "as they really [*eigentlich*] happened."

But, then, how are we to avoid the naïveté of such a protest?

The answer seems to me to lie in the following assertion: once the representative modes supposed to give a literary form to the historical intentionality are called into question, the only responsible way to make the attestation of reality prevail over the suspicion of nonpertinence is to put the scriptural phase back in its place in relation to the preliminary ones of comprehensive explanation and documentary proof. In other words, it is together that scripturality, comprehensive explanation, and documentary proof are capable of accrediting the truth claim of historical discourse.[76] Only the movement that moves back from the art of writing to the "research techniques" and "critical procedures" is capable of raising the protest to the rank of what has become a critical attestation.

Do we not nevertheless relaunch the suspicious gesture if we cite Barthes's phrase used as an epigram by White in *The Content of the Form*: "Le fait n'a jamais qu'une existence linguistique"? And have I not myself in dealing with the historical fact proposed to distinguish the proposition stating "the fact that . . . " from the event itself? The critical realism professed here is forced to take another step beyond the factual proposition and to invoke the testimonial dimension of the document. Indeed, it is the force of testimony that presents itself at the very heart of the documentary proof. And I do not see that we can go beyond the witness's triple declaration: (1) I was there; (2) believe me; (3) if you don't believe me, ask someone else. Ought we to make fun of the naïve realism of testimony? It can be done. But this would be to forget that the seed of criticism is implanted in actual testimony,[77] the critique of testimony bit by bit taking over the whole sphere of documents, up to the ultimate enigma of what presents itself under the name "trace," as the sign-effect of its cause. I have said that we have nothing better than our memory to assure ourselves of the reality of our memories—we have nothing better than testimony and criticism of testimony to accredit the historian's representation of the past.

I have rarely to this point pronounced the word "truth," nor have I risked any affirmation concerning the truth in history, even though at the beginning of this work I promised to compare the presumed truth of the historical representation of the past with the presumed trustworthiness of mnemonic representation.

What does the word "truth" add to the word "representation"? A risky assertion that commits the discourse of history not only to a relationship to memory, but to one with the other sciences, both the human sciences and the natural sciences. It is in relation to the truth claims of these other sciences that history's claim to truth makes sense. Thus the criteria qualifying this claim need to be made clear. And it is quite evidently the past itself that is the referential stake of this claim. Is it possible to define this referential stake in other terms than those of correspondence, of adequation? Or to call "real" what would correspond to the assertion of some representation? It would seem not, under the threat of renouncing the very question of truth. Representation has a vis-à-vis, a *Gegenüber*, to use an expression from *Time and Narrative* that I borrowed from Karl Heussi.[78] I also took the risk of speaking of a "taking the place of" to make more precise the mode of truth proper to "standing for," to the point of taking these two expressions as synonyms.[79] But we see better what senses of the notion of correspondence are excluded when we see how this notion is made specific in relation to other uses of the term "correspondence" in other disciplines of knowledge. The so-called picture theory, which would come down to a imitation-copy, is manifestly excluded. It must be said that one is never fully free of this ghost, inasmuch as the idea of resemblance seems difficult to disengage from it without remainder. Did not Plato place the whole discussion about the *eikōn* in terms of an internal distinction about the mimetic arts when he distinguished between two mimetics, a properly iconic mimetic and a fantastical one? But, if the mimetic also includes the fantastical it has quite clearly to distinguish itself from repetition of the same in the form of a copy. Imitation has to incorporate a minimal heterology if it is to cover such a vast country. In any case, a narrative does not resemble the event it recounts; this has been said often enough by the most convincing narrativists. It is this minimal heterology that the Aristotelian use of *mimēsis* in the *Poetics* already satisfies. Following Aristotle, in the past I myself tried to modulate the mimetic resources of narrative discourse with the yardstick of threefold *mimēsis*: prefiguration, configuration, refiguration. I must admit that the notions of vis-à-vis and taking the place of or standing for constitute the name of a problem rather than that of a solution. In *Time and Narrative* I limited myself to proposing a "conceptual articulation" to the enigma that adequation by taking the place of constitutes.[80] Through this highly metahistorical effort, I attempted to save the point of Ranke's formula that it is not the task of history to judge the past but to show events "as they really happened." The "as" of Ranke's formula then designates nothing other than what I call the function of standing for. The "really" past remains then inseparable from the "as" really happened.

I have nothing to change today about this attempt to explicate the concept of taking the place of or standing for. I wish instead to apply myself to another enigma that seems to me to reside at the very heart of the relation of presumed adequation between the historian's representation and the past. Recall that Aristotle, in his theory of memory, distinguishes the recollection (*mnēmē*) from the image in general (*eikōn*) by the mark of the formerly (*proteron*). We can then ask what happens to the dialectic of presence and absence constitutive of the icon when in the realm of history it is applied to the condition of the anteriority of the past in relation to the narrative that is told about it.

We can say this: the historian's representation is indeed a present image of an absent thing; but the absent thing itself gets split into disappearance into and existence in the past. Past things are abolished, but no one can make it be that they should not have been. It is this twofold status of the past that many languages express by a subtle play of verb tenses and adverbs of time. In French we say that something no longer is (*n'est plus*), but has been (*a été*). It is not unacceptable to suggest that "avoir été" (having been) constitutes the ultimate referent intended across the "n'être plus" (being no longer). Absence thus would be split between absence as intended by the present image and the absence of past things as past in relation to their "having been." It is in this sense that "formerly" would signify reality, but the reality of the past. At this point the epistemology of history borders on the ontology of being-in-the-world. I will call our "historical condition" this realm of existence placed under the sign of a past as being no longer and having been. And the assertive vehemence of the historian's representation as standing for the past is authorized by nothing other than the positivity of the "having been" intended across the negativity of the "being no longer." Here, we have to admit, the epistemology of historiographical operation reaches its internal limit in running up against the borders of an ontology of historical being.[81]

# PART III

*The Historical Condition*

*Our examination* of the historiographical operation on the epistemological plane is concluded: it was conducted across the three moments formed by the archive, explanation/understanding, and historical representation. We now open a second-order reflection on the conditions of the possibility of this discourse. It is intended to occupy the place of a speculative philosophy of history, in the twofold sense of the history of the world and the history of reason. The set of considerations belonging to this reflection is placed under the heading of hermeneutics, taken in the most general sense of examining the modes of understanding involved in forms of knowledge whose aim is objectivity. What is it to understand in the historical mode? This is the most inclusive question opening this new cycle of analyses.

It gives rise to two sorts of investigations; these are divided into two areas, the critical and the ontological.

On the side of critique, reflection consists in imposing limits on any totalizing claim attaching to historical knowledge; it takes as its target several forms of the speculative *hubris* that leads history's discourse about itself to set itself up as the discourse of History in-itself knowing itself. To the extent that it carries out this task, critical examination provides the validation of the objectifying operations (coming under the heading of epistemology) that preside over the writing of history (chapter 1, "The Critical Philosophy of History").

On the side of ontology, hermeneutics assigns itself the task of exploring the presuppositions that can be termed existential, both those of actual historiographical knowledge and those of the preceding critical discourse. They are existential in the sense that they structure the characteristic manner of existing, of being in the world, of that being that each of us is. They concern in the first place the insurmountable historical condition of that being. To characterize this historical condition, one could have used, emblematically, the term "historicity." If I, however, do not propose to use this term, it is because of the equivocations resulting from its relatively long history and which I will attempt to clarify. A more fundamental reason leads me to prefer the expression "historical condition." By condition, I mean two things: on the one hand, a situation in which each person is in each case implicated, Pascal would say, "enclosed" (*enfermé*); on the other hand, a conditionality, in the sense of a condition of possibility on the order of the ontological, or, as we have said, the existential, in particular in relation to the categories of critical hermeneutics. We make history, and we make histories (*nous faisons l'histoire et nous faisons de l'histoire*) because we are historical (chapter 2, "History and Time").

The coherence of this enterprise then rests on the necessity of the twofold passage from historical knowledge to critical hermeneutics and from the latter to ontological hermeneutics. This necessity cannot be demonstrated a priori: it is confirmed only through its enactment, which also serves as its test. Up to the end, the presumed connection will remain a working hypothesis.

I decided to conclude the third part of this work with an exploration of the phenomenon of forgetting. The word figures in the title of this work, on an equal footing with memory and history. The phenomenon indeed has the same scope as the two great classes of phenomena relating to the past: it is the past, in its twofold mnemonic and historical dimension, that is lost in forgetting; the destruction of archives, of museums, of cities—those witnesses of past history—is the equivalent of forgetting. There is forgetting wherever there had been a trace. But forgetting is not only the enemy of memory and of history. One of the theses to which I am most attached is that there also exists a reserve of forgetting, which can be a resource for memory and for history, although there is no way to draw up a score sheet for this battle of the giants. This double valence of forgetting is comprehensible only if the entire problematic of forgetting is carried to the level of the historical condition that underlies the totality of our relations to time. Forgetting is the emblem of the vulnerability of the historical condition taken as a whole. This consideration justifies placing the chapter on forgetting in the hermeneutical part of this work following ontological hermeneutics. The transition from one problematic to the other will have been prepared by the general review of the relations between memory and history in the final section of the chapter that will precede it. In this way, the triad placed at the head of this book will come full circle with the chapter on forgetting (chapter 3, "Forgetting").

One party to this inquiry is missing, however: forgiveness. In this sense, forgiveness pairs up with forgetting: is it not a sort of happy forgetting? Even more fundamentally, is it not the figure of reconciled memory? Surely. Nevertheless, there are two reasons that prompted me to examine it outside of the text, so to speak, in the form of an epilogue.

On the one hand, forgiveness refers to guilt and to punishment; yet, the whole of our analyses evaded this issue. The problem of memory basically concerned faithfulness to the past; yet guilt appears as an additional component with respect to the recognition of images of the past. It, therefore, would have been necessary to hold it in suspension, as I did in the case of the fault at the time of the *Philosophy of the Will*. History is a different matter: here, truth in its critical relation to the faithfulness of memory would be at stake; to be sure, we could not have failed to discuss the great crimes of the twentieth century. But it is not the historian who terms them such: the reprobation cast on them and the judgment considering them unacceptable—what an understatement!—is uttered by the citizen, which the historian, it is true, never ceases to be. The difficulty, however, is precisely to exercise historical judgment in a spirit of impartiality under the sign of moral condemnation. As for the inquiry into the historical condition, it also borders on the phenomenon of guilt and hence on that of forgiveness; but it is incumbent on this inquiry not to step beyond the threshold framing the idea of being indebted, in the sense of depending on a transmitted heritage, apart from any sort of accusation.

Another reason: if, on one hand, guilt adds its weight to that of indebtedness, on the other, forgiveness offers itself as the eschatological horizon of the entire problematic of memory, history, and forgetting. This original heterogeneity does not exclude the possibility that forgiveness imprints the mark of its signs on all the instances of the past: it is in this sense that it offers itself as their common horizon of completion. But this approximation of *eskhaton* guarantees no happy ending for our enterprise as a whole: this is why it will be a question only of a difficult forgiveness (epilogue).

# PRELUDE

## The Burden of History and the Nonhistorical

I wanted to set apart, in the margins of the epistemology and the ontology of history, Nietzsche's contribution to the discussion. The second in the series of *Unfashionable Observations* (*Unzeitgemässe Betrachtungen*), published in 1872 by Nietzsche, then professor of classical philology at the University of Basel, contributes nothing to the critical examination of the historical operation; nothing, as well, to the examination of pre- or post-Hegelian philosophy of history. It is unfashionable (*intempestive*, untimely) in the sense that, in the face of the difficulties of an overwhelmingly historical culture, it offers an exit from the historical only under the enigmatic sign of the nonhistorical. On the flag of this fireship waves the programmatic emblem: "On the Utility and Liability of History [*Historie*] for Life."[1] The reading I propose of the second of Nietzsche's *Unfashionable Observations* is based upon the very style of this essay: excessive in its tone, suited as it is to the theme of excess, the excess of history. For this reason, at the threshold of part 3, it deserves to parallel and to echo the myth of the *Phaedrus*, which was placed in prelude to part 2. A loop is thus formed: the reading of the Platonic myth that I proposed itself already constituted an excess, to the extent that it overtly placed historiography on the same side as the *grammata* literally intended by the myth. The free interpretation I now offer of Nietzsche's text ventures to situate the excess of historical culture on the same side as the incriminated *grammata*, and to treat the plea on behalf of the nonhistorical as a post-historiographical and post-historicizing equivalent, so to speak, placing it on the same side as the praise offered by Plato on behalf of a memory that would precede the entry into writing. Everything, including Nietzsche's hesitation regarding the cure of the "historical malady," echoes the ambiguity of the *pharmakon*, oscillating between poison and remedy in the text of the *Phaedrus*. I hope the reader will allow me license regarding the same sort of "play" that Plato requested, not only for his own fable but for the highly serious dialectic that marks the exit from the myth through the great gate of philosophical discourse.

Two remarks before entering into the quick of interpretation: on the one hand, we must not lose sight of the fact that the abuse Plato was protesting was that of written discourse, extending across the entire expanse of rhetoric. In Nietzsche's essay it is the historical culture established in writing of we moderns that occupies a place comparable to that of rhetoric for the ancients. The two contexts, to be sure, are considerably different, so that it would be unreasonable to superimpose term-by-term *anamnēsis* confounded by *grammata* and the protean life-force that the Nietzschean essay wishes to protect from the damage caused by historical culture. My interpretation contains, therefore, the customary limits of an analogical reading. On the other hand, Nietzsche's target is not the historical-critical method, historiography properly speaking, but historical culture. And, what this culture confronts, in terms of utility and liability, is life and not memory. A second reason, then, not to confuse analogy and equivalence.

The question raised by Nietzsche's unfashionable temperament is simple: how to survive a triumphant historical culture? The essay does not come up with a univocal answer. But neither did Plato say in the *Phaedrus* what *anamnēsis* would consist of beyond the crisis of written rhetoric, even if he does say what argumentative dialectic should be. The plea for the ahistorical and the suprahistorical is in this respect in the same programmatic situation as the dialectic celebrated at the end of the *Phaedrus*. The principal thrust of both texts is denunciation: in Nietzsche, the denunciatory tone is already evident in the title: the observations are termed *Unzeitgemässe*—untimely, unmodern, unfashionable, in line with *Unhistorisches* and *Suprahistorisches* summoned to save German culture from historical sickness.[2] The theme of "infirmity" is also planted as early as the preface.[3] And, from the outset, it is an equally unfashionable medication that is sought from classical philology.[4]

I leave for a later discussion the commentary relating to the provocative comparison proposed at the start of the essay between the forgetting of bovines living "*ahistorically*" (88) and the "power to forget" (89) necessary to all action, that very power that allows the one possessing memory and history "to heal wounds, to replace what has been lost, to recreate broken forms out of itself alone" (89). I wish instead to stress here the connection maintained throughout the essay between historical culture and modernity. This connection, firmly underscored in the text by Koselleck discussed earlier, is so strong that it makes the untimely observation a plea at one and the same time antihistoricist and antimodern. The "Second Unfashionable Observation" is also categorically antihistoricist and antimodern in its theme as well as in its tone. From the first section, a suspense is created, an ambiguity preserved: "*The ahistorical and the historical are equally necessary for the health of an individual, a people, and a culture*" (90). The main accent, to be sure, is placed on the ahistorical:[5] "in an excess of history the human being ceases once again" (91). Alone, the "ahistorical, antihistorical through and through—is not only the womb of the unjust deed, but of every just act as well" (92). The no speaks the loudest: in this, the "Second Unfashionable Observation" is, as we have said, excessive. And the author recognizes and admits it: "that life requires the service of history must be comprehended, however, just as clearly as the proposition that will subsequently be proved—that an excess of history is harmful to life" (96).

I propose to illustrate the ambiguity that compensates for the vehemence of the attack by means of the treatment at the beginning of the essay of the "three kinds of history," frequently remarked upon by commentators, and which I will investigate through the lens of poison and remedy. Measured analyses are in fact devoted, in turn, to monumental history, antiquarian history, and critical history. It is important, first, to specify the level of reflection on which these three categories are established: these are not epistemological categories, like those we set in place above—documentary proof, explanation, representation. Neither, however, do they belong to the level of complete reflexivity where the concept of "process," the preferred target of the blows directed against the historicist illusion, is located: "These historical beings," as Nietzsche proposes calling them, "believe that the meaning of existence will come ever more to light in the course of a *process*; they look backward only to understand the present by observation of the prior process and to learn to desire the future even more keenly; they have no idea how ahistorically they think and act despite all their history, nor that their concern with history stands in the service, not of pure knowledge, but of life" (93). The level on which this preliminary investigation is situated is expressly pragmatic, to the extent that what is expressed there is basically the relation of *Historie* to life and not to knowledge: in each case it is the "active and powerful" (96) human being who is the measure of utility for life.

Having said this, it is worthwhile to focus on the work of discrimination applied to each of the three levels distinguished by Nietzsche, as it concerns the equivocation planted at the heart of the essay.

Thus, monumental or exemplary history is not defined in the first instance in terms of excess, but by the usefulness of models to "emulate and improve" (96); through this history, "great moments...form links in one single chain" (97). Now, it is precisely greatness that historical sickness levels into insignificance. It is therefore onto utility that the excess is grafted: it consists in the abuse of analogies that result in "entire large parts of [history being] forgotten, scorned, and washed away as if by a gray, unremitting tide, and only a few embellished facts arise as islands above it" (100). This is how the past is damaged. But the present is as well: the unbounded admiration of the great and powerful figures of the past becomes the travesty behind which the hatred of the great and powerful of the present is concealed.

There is no less ambiguity in traditionalist or antiquarian history. Conserving and venerating customs and traditions is useful to life: without roots, there would be neither flowers nor fruit; but, once again, the past itself suffers, all past things end up covered by a uniform veil of venerability, and "whatever is new and in the process of becoming...is met with hostility and rejected" (105). This history knows only how to conserve, not how to create.

As for critical history, it is not identified with the historicist illusion. It constitutes only one moment, that of judgment, inasmuch as "every past deserves to be condemned" (102); in this sense, critical history indicates the moment of deserved forgetting. Here, the danger for life coincides with its usefulness.

There is, then, a genuine need for history, be it exemplary, antiquarian, or critical. The residual ambiguity, which I compare to that of the *pharmakon* of the *Phaedrus*, results from the fact that history contains non-excess at each of the three levels considered; in short, in the fact of the uncontested usefulness of history for life in terms of the imitation of greatness, the veneration of past traditions, and the critical exercise of judgment. In truth, Nietzsche has not really formed a balance in this text between the utility and the liabilities, inasmuch as excess is posited at the very heart of the historical. The point of equilibrium itself remains problematical: "Insofar as it stands in the service of life," Nietzsche suggests, "history also stands in the service of an ahistorical power; and because of this subordinate position, it neither could nor should become a pure science on the order of mathematics, for example. But the question about the degree to which life needs the service of history at all is one of the supreme questions and worries that impinges on the health of a human being, a people, or a culture. For at the point of a certain excess of history, life crumbles and degenerates—as does, ultimately, as a result of this degeneration, history itself, as well" (95–96). But can the scorecard demanded by the title be drawn up? This is the question that is still posed at the end of the essay.

The attack against modernity, stripped of the preceding nuances, is introduced by the idea of an interpolation between history and life of a "powerfully hostile star," namely, "*the demand that history be a science*" (109). This demand characterizes the "modern human being" (109). And it consists in violence done to memory, amounting to an inundation, an invasion. The first symptom of the sickness is "the remarkable antithesis between an interior that corresponds to no exterior and exterior that corresponds to no interior—an antithesis unknown to the peoples of the ancient world" (109). We are not far from the stigmatized "external marks" of the *Phaedrus*, which alienate memory. But the reproach takes on a modern allure insofar as the distinction between the categories of interior and exterior is itself a modern conquest, one made above all by the Germans: "a people notorious for its inwardness" (113). And yet we have become "walking encyclopedias," on each of which is stamped the title "Handbook of Inward Cultivation for Outward Barbarians" (111).

This all-out attack, as it proceeds, sweeps away the embankments within which Nietzsche planned to direct its flow (the five viewpoints at the beginning of section 5!): eradication of instincts, concealment behind masks, chattering of gray, old men (did not the *Phaedrus* reserve the pleasure of *grammata* for the old?), the neutrality of eunuchs, the incessant reduplication of critique by critique, and the loss of the thirst for justice,[6] to the benefit of an indifferent benevolence regarding "objectivity,"[7] a lazy effacement before the onward march of things, and taking refuge in melancholic indifference.[8] Then sounds the major declaration of the essay ("*Only from the highest power of the present can you interpret the past*" [129]) and the final prophecy ("only those who build the future have a right to sit in judgment of the past" [130]). The path is cleared for the idea of "historical justice" whose judgment "always undermines and destroys living things" (131). Such is the price to pay for the rebirth of the constructive urge destined to release the celebration of art and even religious devotion from the grip of pure scientific knowledge. Then, without any safety net, the praise of illusion is uttered, in strict opposition to the self-realization of the concept in accordance with the grand Hegelian philosophy of history.[9] Plato himself, in book 3 of the *Republic* sided with the "powerful necessary lie" (161), at the expense of the alleged necessary truth. The contradiction is thus carried to the very heart of the idea of modernity: the new times it invokes are placed by historical culture under the sign of old age.

At the end of this all-out attack, it is difficult indeed to say what the ahistorical and the suprahistorical are. One theme, however, connects these limit concepts and makes a plea on behalf of life: the theme of youth. It resonates at the end of the essay, just as the theme of natality will at the end of Hannah Arendt's *The Human Condition*. The exclamation—"Thinking of *youth* at this point I cry out, 'Land ho!'" (158)—may seem a little like pandering, but it takes its meaning in the context of the pair youth/old age, which forms the underlying organization of the essay, to the benefit of a general reflection on aging that the meditation on the historical condition cannot escape. Youth is not an age of life but a metaphor for the plastic force of life.

It is within the aura of the invocation to youth that the recurrent term of historical sickness is re-situated *in fine*; this term evokes, in its turn, the notion of remedy, regarding which we still do not know whether it is actually a poison, by reason of its secret alliance with the justice that condemns. Everything indeed comes together in the final pages of the essay which, until then, seemed to drag on and on: "Well, don't be surprised that [these remedies] are the names of poisons [*Giften*]: the antidotes to history are—*the ahistorical and the suprahistorical*" (163). In truth, Nietzsche is stingy with language in distinguishing between the ahistorical and the suprahistorical. "Ahistorical" is associated with "the art and power to be able to *forget*" and the ability "to enclose oneself in a limited *horizon*" (163). A bridge is cast back toward the considerations regarding the two kinds of forgetting with which the essay opens, that of the ruminant and that of historical man. We now know that this forgetting is not historical but unhistorical. As for the "suprahistorical," it directs the gaze away from the future and carries it toward the eternity-dispensing powers of art and religion. Henceforth, science will speak of poison in this connection, its hatred for these powers matched by its hatred of forgetting in which its sees only the death of knowledge.[10] The ahistorical and the suprahistorical thus constitute the natural antidote (*Gegenmittel*) to the stifling of life by history, to the historical sickness. "It is likely that we, the historically sick, will also have to suffer from these antidotes. But the fact that we suffer from them provides no evidence that could call the correctness of the chosen therapy [*Heilverfahren*] in question" (164).

Youth is the herald of this therapy: it "will suffer simultaneously from the illness and the cure [*Gegenmittel*]" (164).

Youth confronting graying epigone: "This is a parable [*Gleichnis*] for every individual among us" (167).

# CHAPTER 1

## *The Critical Philosophy of History*

READING GUIDELINES
With the critical philosophy of history, we set out along the hermeneutical route. It would be a mistake to think that for lack of a speculative philosophy of history, there is room only for an epistemology of the historiographical operation. There still remains a space of meaning for metahistorical concepts relating to a philosophical critique resembling that conducted by Kant in the *Critique of Judgment*, and which would be worthy of the name of a "critique of historical judgment." I consider it to be the first branch of hermeneutics, in the sense that it asks about the nature of the understanding that passes through the three moments of the historiographical operation. This first hermeneutics approaches a second-order reflection from the perspective of critique, in the twofold sense of a delegitimation of claims made on behalf of the self-knowledge of history, setting itself up as absolute knowledge, and of the legitimation of historical knowledge striving for objectivity.

The epistemology of part 2 began to appeal to this sort of reflection, primarily with respect to the examination of the chronological models the discipline has developed. It lacked, however, a distinct elaboration of the conditions of the possibility of temporal conditions meriting the designation of the time of history. The vocabulary of models—the famous "temporal models" of history of the *Annales*—was not up to the task of this critical enterprise. I owe the identification of the gap between the models employed in the historiographical operation and the temporal categories of history to Reinhart Koselleck. The "history of concepts"—*Begriffsgeschichte*—to which a large part of his work is devoted, concerns the categories governing the historical treatment of time and the generalized "historicizing" of the forms of knowledge relating to the entire practical field. The following chapter will show that this analysis in turn points in the direction of an ontological hermeneutics of the historical condition, to the extent that this historicizing is related to an experience in the full sense of the term, to an "experience of history," following the title of a collection of Koselleck's essays. The present chapter will be confined to the limits of a critique directed to the claim of the self-knowledge of history to be constituted as absolute knowledge, as total reflection.

The two principal meanings of history will be explored in turn. In the first two sections, the negative thrust of critique will be highlighted; in the last two, we shall consider the external and internal dialectics of the self-knowledge of history that attest positively to the presumed self-limitation of this knowledge. We shall then measure the highest ambition assigned to the self-knowledge of history by Romantic and post-Romantic German philosophy. I will conduct this investigation under the guidance of Koselleck's great article "Geschichte," devoted to the constitution of history as a collective singular, binding together the set of special histories. The semantics of historical concepts will serve to bring to our attention the dream of self-sufficiency expressed by the formula "history itself" (*Geschichte selber*) claimed by the authors concerned. This dream will be pursued to the point where it turns the arm of "total history" against itself (section 1: "*Die Geschichte Selber*," "History Itself").

This critique applied to the most extreme and the most widely uttered ambition of the self-knowledge of history will then be applied to the claim, in appearance diametrically opposed to the preceding one, that the present age is considered not only different but preferable to any other. This self-celebration, joined to self-designation, is characteristic of the apology of modernity. In my opinion, the expression "our" modernity leads to an aporia similar to that contained in the expression "history itself." It is first of all the "historical recurrence" of the plea for modernity, from the Renaissance and the Enlightenment up to today, that sows the confusion. But it is most obviously the competition between several pleas mixing values and chronology, coming, for example, from Condorcet and from Baudelaire, that most effectively destablizes the self-preference assumed by a period. It is then a question of knowing whether an argumentation purely in terms of values can avoid the equivocation of a discourse that claims at one and the same time to be universal and to be situated in the historical present. And it is another question to know whether the discourse of postmodernity escapes this internal contradiction. In one way or other, historical singularity reflecting on itself gives rise to an aporia symmetrical to that of the historical totality knowing itself absolutely (section 2: "'Our' Modernity").

The resources of critical hermeneutics are not exhausted in denouncing the open or hidden forms of the claim to total reflection coming from the self-knowledge of history. It is attentive to the tensions, to the dialectics by reason of which this knowledge takes the positive measure of its limitations.

The polarity between judicial judgment and historical judgment forms one of these remarkable dialectics, while, at the same time, remaining an external limitation on history: the vow of impartiality common to both forms of judgment is subjected in its actual exercise to opposite constraints. The impossibility of occupying the position of a third party is already evident in the comparison between the two paths of decision-making: trials, on the one hand, archives, on the other. A particular use of testimony and of proof in one instance and in the other; a particular finality in the final sentence on one side and on the other. The main emphasis falls on the focus in judicial judgment on individual responsibility in opposition to the expansion of historical judgment to contexts more open to collective actions. These considerations regarding the professions of historian and judge serve to introduce the test offered by the example of the great crimes of the twentieth century, subject in turn to the penal justice of the great trials and to the judgment of historians. One of the theoretical stakes of the comparison concerns the status of singularity, at once moral and historical, assigned to the crimes of the last century. On the practical level, the public exercise of both forms of judgment is the occasion to underscore the therapeutic and pedagogical role of *civis dissensus* raised by controversies animating the public space of discussion at the points of interference of history in the arena of collective memory. The citizen is also himself or herself a third party between the judge and the historian (section 3: "The Historian and the Judge").

One last polarity underscores the internal limitation to which the self-knowledge of history is subjected. It is no longer the polarity between history and its other, as in the case of judicial judgment; it lies at the very heart of the historiographical operation, in the form of the types of correlation between the project of truth and the interpretive component belonging to the historiographical operation itself. This concerns much more than the subjective involvement of the historian in the formation of historical objectivity: the set of options that arise at every phase of the operation, from the archive to the representation of the historian. The interpretation proves in this way to possess the same scope as the project of truth. This consideration justifies its placement at the end of the path of reflection traversed in this chapter (section 4: "Interpretation in History").

§

### "*DIE GESCHICHTE SELBER,*" "HISTORY ITSELF"

Along with Reinhart Koselleck, we retrace the journey back to the sources of the grandiose ambition of historical self-knowledge to arrive at total reflection, the eminent form of absolute knowledge. To him, we owe the acknowledgment of the gap between the temporal models employed in the historiographical operation and the temporal categories of history.

To be sure, in volume 3 of *Time and Narrative* I had taken into account Koselleck's celebrated essay, "'Space of Experience' and 'Horizon of Expectation': Two Historical Categories," reprinted in *Futures Past*;[1] but I had not perceived the tie between this essay and the set of investigations belonging to a type of discourse hierarchically superior to the epistemology of the historiographical operation.[2] In the case of notions such as space of experience and horizon of expectation, we are concerned, Koselleck notes, with "epistemological categories which assist in the foundation of the possibility of a history" (*Futures Past*, 269). More radically, it is a matter of defining "historical time," a task characterized in the preface as one of "those questions which historical science has the most difficulty answering" (xxi). In fact, if it is a question of the contents of history, a trustworthy system of dating is enough; as for the temporal rhythms of the ensembles that are sectioned off by historical discourse, they stand out against the backdrop of a "historical time" that punctuates history pure and simple, history as such.

Koselleck has good reason to characterize these categories as metahistorical. This evaluation of their status is confirmed by the homologous constitution linking the categories of historical time in Koselleck and those of internal time in Augustine's *Confessions*. The parallel is striking between the pair: horizon of expectation and space of experience, and the pair: present of the future and present of the past. The two pairs belong to the same level of discourse. What is more, they lend mutual assistance to each other: the structures of historical time are not limited to providing a greater scope to the structures of mnemonic time; they open a critical space in which history can exercise its corrective function with regard to memory. In turn, the Augustinian dialectic of the threefold present opens the past of history onto a present of initiative and a future of expectation, which, when the time comes, must be shown to leave its mark at the heart of the historian's enterprise. Koselleck, however, is justified in holding that neither Augustine nor Heidegger directed their interrogation to the time of history—which is less true of Gadamer, as I admit in *Time and Narrative*. The contribution of Koselleck's analyses consists in his treatment of these categories as conditions for discerning the changes affecting historical time itself, and, in particular, the differential traits of the vision of the moderns regarding historical change.[3] Modernity is itself—we will return to this later—a global historical phenomenon, to the extent that it apprehends modern times as new times; this apprehension can be reflected only in terms of the ever-increasing distancing of expectations with respect to all experiences up to today. This was not the case with the eschatological expectations of historical Christianity, which, given their ultra-worldly status, could not be coordinated with common experience within a single historical process. The opening of a horizon of expectation designated by the term "progress" is the prior condition for the conception of modern times as new, which constitutes the tautological definition of modernity, at least in German. In this regard, one can speak of the "temporalization of the experience of history" as the process of continual and increasing perfection. A variety of experiences can be enumerated both in the order of expectation and in that of remembered experience; unequal rates of progress can even be distinguished, but a global newness widens the distance between the space of experience and the horizon of expectation.[4] Notions such as the acceleration and the open-endedness of history belong to the same cycle. Acceleration is the unfailing indication that the gap is maintained only by continually being modified; acceleration is a metacategory of the temporal rhythms that tie improvement to the shortening of intervals; it gives a historical touch to the notion of speed; it permits *a contrario* speaking of delay, advance, marching in place, regressing. As for the availability of history, its makeability, this designates a capacity that belongs at once to the agents of history and to the historians who make history available by writing it up.[5] That someone makes history is a modern expression unthinkable before the end of the eighteenth century, one ratified, so to speak, by the French Revolution and Napoleon. The metahistorical level of the concept is evident in the fact that it was able to survive the belief in progress, as is attested, outside of the German sphere,[6] by the proud motto borrowed from Michel de Certeau, under the banner of which Jacques Le Goff and Pierre Nora assembled French historians in the 1960s.[7] If the notion of the makeability of history is so tenacious, this is doubtless because it aims at aligning our twofold relation to history—making history and the making of histories (*faire l'histoire et faire de l'histoire*)—with the competence constitutive of the practical field belonging to the one I designate by the inclusive term "capable being."

Nothing better underscores the unilateral character of the concept of the makeability of history than its close tie with the metacategory par excellence formed by the very concept of history as a collective singular. This is the master category, the condition under which the time of history can be thought. There is a time of history insofar as there is one single history. This is Koselleck's master concept, in a seminal article published in the historical lexicon of political-social language in Germany under the simple title, "Geschichte."[8] In this regard, it would be an illusion to think that the noisy repudiation of the Hegelian philosophy of history and, less costly, the high-minded elimination of the risky speculations of a Spengler or a Toynbee, or even of more recent emulators with planetary ambitions, exonerates historians from the task of explaining why the same word "history" designates, without easily deniable amphibology, the collective singular comprising a series of events and the ensemble of discourses pronounced regarding this collective singular. The question belongs to the transcendental level of a critical discourse on history. Koselleck places in its service the remarkable tool of conceptual semantics, a sort of selective lexicography of the basic vocabulary of the historical sciences. However, in contrast to a lexicographical work limited to an examination of concepts under the condition of bracketing the referent, the metacategories brought to light by this undertaking are, like Kantian categories, the conditions of the possibility of a specific experience. The lexicon thus rests on a triangular relation: guiding concept, linguistic functioning, and experience. The field of application of these guiding concepts is constituted by what Koselleck calls the "experience of history,"[9] namely, something more than an epistemological territory, an authentic relation to the world, comparable to that which underlies physical experience. Now this experience is peculiar to the modern period. He speaks of a "new space of experience." This reference to modernity, to which we will return at greater length later, marks from the outset the epochal character of conceptual semantics itself. This epochal mark unavoidably places the enterprise under the heading of historicism, a result it did not seek but to which its own course has led it.

At the start of this history a naïve expectation is affirmed, whose subsequent course will reveal its growing complexity. Koselleck attaches this expectation to "two long-range events that will end by merging together and, through this, will open a space of experience that formerly could not have been formulated" ("Geschichte," 10). This concerns, on the one hand, the birth of the concept of history as a *collective singular* linking together the special histories under a common concept; and, on the other hand, this involves "the mutual contamination" of the concepts *Geschichte*, considered a complex of events, and *Historie*, considered as knowledge, narrative, and historical science, a contamination that ends with the absorption of the latter by the former. The two conceptual events, so to speak, finally amount to only one, namely, the production of the concept of "history as such," of "history itself" (*Geschichte selber*).

The birth of the concept of history as a collective singular, under which the collection of particular histories is placed, marks the bridging of the greatest gap imaginable between unitary history and the unlimited multiplicity of individual memories and the plurality of collective memories underscored by Halbwachs. This conquest is sanctioned by the idea that history itself becomes its own subject. If there is a new experience, it is surely that of the self-designation of a new subject of attribution named "history."

It is understandable that the second "event" signaled by Koselleck—namely, the absorption of *Historie* by *Geschichte*—might have been confused with the formation of the concept of history as a collective singular. The autonomy of history as its own subject ultimately directs the organization of its representation. In producing itself, history articulates its own discourse. This absorption has occurred despite the sporadic resistance of authors, such as Niebuhr, enamored of methodological precision. The old definition harkening back to Cicero ("History is a true account of past things") as well as the assignment to *historia* in antiquity of the role of instruction (*historia magistra vitae*) are seen to be reappropriated by the new experience of history, reflecting upon itself as it comes to pass. Out of the reflexivity of history derives a specific concept of historical time, a properly historical temporalization.[10]

At this stage, which can be called one of naïveté or innocence, the term "history" displays a realist tenor that assures for history as such its own claim to truth.[11]

Before proceeding further, the expression "experience of history," given by Koselleck as the title of the work as a whole, within which the article in question is placed, deserves some thought. "A new space of experience," he says has been opened up, which "has nourished the historical school ever since" (51). This space of experience coincides with modernity. One can then speak, in short, of the modern experience of history. In this regard, the reader will note an important change in Koselleck's vocabulary after *Futures Past*, in which the space of experience was opposed to the horizon of expectation (cf. *Time and Narrative* 3:208–16). Henceforth applied to history as such, the concept of experience, defined by modernity, now covers the three forms of time. It links together the past that has occurred, the anticipated future, and the present as it is being lived and acted. What is held to be modern par excellence is this omnitemporal character of history. In the same stroke, the concept of history includes, in addition to its renewed temporal meaning, a new anthropological meaning: history is the history of humanity, and in this worldwide sense, the world history of peoples. Humanity becomes both the total object and the unique subject of history, at the same time as history becomes a collective singular.

The appearance of notions such as the "philosophy of history" with Voltaire, the "Idea of universal history from a cosmopolitan point of view" with Kant, the "philosophy of the history of humanity" with Herder, and "world philosophy" (*Weltgeschichte*) erected by Schiller as "world tribunal" must be placed back against this backdrop of presuppositions. With this final development, a moralizing reflection on the very meaning of history, universal in scope, is added to the expansion of the narrative territory of history.[12]

All that is lacking is the speculative dimension announced by Novalis, proclaiming that "history produces itself" (quoted in "Geschichte," 48). Hegel's text on "Reason in History" (the introduction to his lectures on the *Philosophy of History*) crowns this conceptual epic. It is under the aegis of the dialectic of the objective spirit that the pact between the rational and the real is sealed, the pact that is said to be an expression of the highest idea of philosophy.[13] The connection in which this identity is manifested is history itself. At the same time, a certain distance is taken with respect to the ordinary historical discipline, which is reproached for dwelling in the house of the dead. In this, we must recognize our debt to Hegel for his critique of the abstract idea of a world that is no longer the power of life carried by the Spirit into the heart of the present. Something is announced here that will find a vehement outcome in Nietzsche's praise of life, and also in Heidegger's opposition between the having-been of the authentic past and the elapsed past that escapes our grasp. But neither can we allow to pass in silence, under the cover of Hegelian philosophy (in this, heir to the antitheological orientation of the Enlightenment thinkers rather than to the Romantics), the birth of a secular religion resulting from the equation between history and reason. History *is* the development of spirit at the heart of humanity. If Koselleck can speak of the experience of history, this is also to the extent that the concept of history can claim to fill the space previously occupied by religion. It is by virtue of this kinship, and this substitution, that the idealist philosophy of history was able to rise above simple causal analyses, integrate multiple temporalities, open itself to the future, or better, open a new future, and in this way reinterpret the ancient *topos* of history, teacher of life, following the promises of redemption spilling out upon humanity to come by the French Revolution, the mother of all ruptures.

But with the word "rupture" a finger is pointed in the direction of a fault-line fissuring from within the presumed encompassing, totalizing idea of world history.

We can follow the trace of the more and more devastating effects of this fault-line.

The first slight crack in the idea of a unified history of humanity is to be ascribed to the various resistances of what in a broad sense can be termed, following Hannah Arendt, *human plurality*. This plurality chips away from within the very concept of history as a collective singular. It is always the special histories that universal history or world history claims to encompass. Now these histories can be listed according to a variety of criteria: be it geographical distribution, periodization of the course of history, thematic distinctions (political and diplomatic history, economic and social history, history of cultures and *mentalités*). These diverse figures of human plurality cannot be reduced to an effect of professional specialization within the profession of historian. They belong to a primary fact, the fragmentation, even the dispersal, of the human phenomenon. There is such a thing as humanity, but there are also peoples (many nineteenth-century philosophers spoke, in this way, of the "spirit of peoples"), that is to say, languages, mores, cultures, religions, and, on the properly political level, nations framed by states. Reference to the nation has been so strong that representatives of the great German historical school continually wrote history from the viewpoint of the German nation. Things were no different in France, with Michelet in particular. The paradox is great: history is proclaimed to be a world phenomenon by historian-patriots. It is then a point of discussion to determine whether history can be *written* from a cosmopolitan point of view.

The resistance of special histories to globalization is not the most threatening aspect: it can be seen to be related either to the limitations of competence belonging to the profession of historian, the historical-critical method requiring an ever narrower specialization regarding research, or to a feature of the condition of the historian, which makes the historian as a person both a scholar and a citizen, a scholar who makes history in writing it, a citizen who makes history in association with the other actors on the public stage. There is nevertheless a certain ambiguity that results concerning the epistemological status of the idea of world or universal history. Is it a *regulative* idea in the Kantian sense, requiring the unification of multiple forms of knowledge on the theoretical plane and proposing on the practical and political plane a task that could be termed cosmopolitan, aiming at establishing peace among the nation-states and at the worldwide dissemination of democratic ideals?[14] Or is it a constitutive, *determinant* idea, after the manner of the Hegelian *Idea* in which the rational and the real coincide? According to the first acceptation, history *has to* become universal, worldwide; according to the second, it *is* worldwide, universal, as the actual becoming of its own production. In both cases, the resistance of human plurality constitutes a paradox and, ultimately, even a scandal. The concept of collective singular would truly be honored only if one managed to renew the Leibnizian principle of sufficient reason, for which the diversity, variety, and complexity of phenomena constitute welcome components of the idea of the whole. This interpretation midway between regulative and constitutive ideas does not seem to me to be beyond the reach of a properly dialectical conception of history.

The idea of universal or world history seems to me to be more severely tested on the very plane of the *temporalization* of the march of history. Modernity makes apparent new and unseen diachronic features that give a new physiognomy to the old tripartite Augustinian division into past, present, and future, and above all to the idea related to a "distention of the soul." In *Futures Past*, Koselleck had already underscored the effects of the *topos* of progress on the representation of the time of history. But the idea of progress is not confined to suggesting an a priori superiority of the future— or, more precisely, of things to come—over things of the past. The idea of *novelty* attached to that of modernity (modernity in German is "new time"—*neuen Zeit,* then *Neuzeit*) implies at the minimum a depreciation of earlier times struck with obsolescence, at the maximum a denial amounting to a rupture. We have already mentioned the rupture effect ascribed to the French Revolution by the European intelligentsia of the nineteenth century. Even then, the lights of reason made Medieval times appear shadowy, dark; following them, the revolutionary impulse made past times appear dead. The paradox is formidable with regard to the idea of universal, world history: can the unity of history be produced by the very thing that ruptures it?[15] To surmount this paradox, the force of integration set free by the energy of novelty would have to be greater than the force of rupture emanating from the event held to found new times. The most recent course of history far from satisfies this wish. The growth of multiculturalism is a source of great puzzlement in this regard.

The phenomenon of depreciation with regard to the past presents several remarkable corollaries. Let us note first the increase in the feeling of distantiation which, on the scale of several successive generations, tends to obliterate the feeling of the debt owed by contemporaries to predecessors, to borrow the language of Alfred Schutz; what is worse, contemporaries, who themselves belong to several generations living simultaneously, suffer the experience of the noncontemporaneousness of contemporaries. Next, one notes the feeling of the acceleration of history, which Koselleck interprets as an effect of the dissolution of the tie between expectation and experience, a large number of phenomena perceived as significant changes occurring in the same lapse of time.

These profound alterations in the unity of history on the plane of its temporalization signal a victory of Augustine's *distentio animi* as it imperils the unity of the *intentio* of the historical process. On the plane of memory, however, there was still a possible recourse, in the form of repetition consisting in the recognition of a remembered past within the present. What could history offer equivalent to this recognition, if it were condemned by the newness of the times to reconstruct a dead past, without affording us the hope of recognizing it as ours? Here we see the emergence of a theme which will take shape only at the end of the following chapter, the theme of the "uncanniness" of history.

The depreciation of the past would not be enough to undermine from within the affirmation of history as a self-sufficient totality if a more devastating effect had not also been added, namely, the *historicization* of all human experience. The value accorded to the future would have remained a source of certainty if it had not been accompanied by the relativizing of the contents of belief held to be immutable. Perhaps the two effects are potentially antagonistic to one another, inasmuch as the second—relativization—contributes to undermining the first—historicization, up until then paired with a self-assured expectation. It is at this point that the concept of history results in an ambiguity which the crisis of historicism will carry to the forefront, but which appears as a perverse effect of what Koselleck calls the historicization of time.

Its devastating effect was particularly apparent in the theological version of the *topos* of progress, namely, the idea of *Heilsgeschichte*—"salvation history"—stemming from Christian eschatology. In truth, the *topos* of progress had first benefited from an impetus coming from theology and the schema of the "promise" and its "realization," which had formed the original matrix of the *Heilsgeschichte* within the Göttingen school as early as the eighteenth century. Now this schema continued to nourish the theology of history up to the middle of the twentieth century. The rebound effect of the theme of historical relativism on the *Heilgeschichte* was severe indeed. If Revelation is itself progressive, then the reciprocal truth imposes itself: the advent of the Kingdom of God is itself a historical development, and Christian eschatology is dissolved into a process. The very idea of eternal salvation loses its immutable referent. In this way, the concept of *Heilgeschichte*, first proposed as an alternative to historization only to function as a theological double for the profane concept of progress, is inverted into a factor of complete historicization.

One by one, all domains of experience are affected by historical relativism. The triumph of the ideas of point of view and perspective attests to this. To be sure, one can assign a Leibnizian origin to this idea, but this is at the price of abandoning the strong reference to an integral of viewpoints. The idea of a plurality of viewpoints, once stripped of any overview, is proposed as the antidogmatic view par excellence. But the question then arises whether the thesis affirming the relativity of every assertion does not self-destruct through self-reference. Stated in the radical form given to it by skepticism— "Every affirmation, every estimation is relative to the historical conditions of its utterance"—it is in danger of falling prey to the charge of "performative contradiction" addressed by Karl-Otto Apel to the partisans of skepticism in the face of the ethical-juridical notion of validity.[16] One can wonder if the idea of truth, but also the ideas of the good and the just, can be radically historicized without disappearing. The relativity resulting from the temporalization of history can nourish for a while the charge of ideology addressed by a protagonist to an adversary—in the form of the peremptory question, "Where are you speaking from?"—but it finally turns against the one making it and becomes internalized as paralyzing suspicion.[17]

At the end of this remarkable essay, "Geschichte," Koselleck freely admits his qualms. After presenting Ranke's scruples concerning the historian's suspension of judgment regarding taking a position on the combats of the present, he notes: "In the same way as these positions tied to the former controversy (and perhaps even more to the point), the ambivalence of the expression 'history itself' [*Geschichte selber*] has the characteristic of delivering all at once all the objections that can be formulated against it" (80). The contradictions undermining the notion have revealed the untenable nature of this claim to absolute knowledge and of the *hubris* that inspired it. It will be another question to determine whether what Koselleck calls "the experience of history" goes beyond the limits of a conceptual history, which I assign to the level of a critical hermeneutics, and whether it involves categories that can be termed existential, belonging to an ontological hermeneutics. This is what the twofold sense of the word "history," considered as the set of events that have occurred and the set of reports on these events, leads us to understand.

## "OUR" MODERNITY

The main task of critical philosophy applied to history is, as we have said, to reflect upon the limits that a self-knowledge of history, taking itself to be absolute, would attempt to transgress. The treatment of history as a collective singular erected as its own subject—History—is the most obvious expression of this claim. But this manifestation is not the only one. A second, more hidden form of the same claim is symmetrically opposed to it: this consists in elevating as an absolute the historical present established as an observation point, even a tribunal, for all the formations, especially cultural formations, that have preceded it. This claim is concealed under the seductive features of a concept that at first sight seems free of any tendency to transgress limits: the concept of modernity. The impossible claim attaching to this concept is laid bare only when its full and precise formulation has been restored to it, when one says and writes "our" modernity. This involves nothing less than "the idea that our time has of itself, in its difference, its 'novelty' in relation to the past."[18] "Our," "our" time, "our" epoch, "our" present—are so many equivalent expressions for the idea of modernity. The question is this: how could "our" time think itself absolutely? The question is rigorously symmetrical to the one that concerned us above: it was then a matter of the whole of History considered a collective singular, attempting to posit itself absolutely as its own subject: "history itself." Dislodged from this untenable position, the claim to absolute reflection switches to the exact opposite of this collective singular, namely, the singular historical moment, the now of this historical present. This claim is thriving today, while the opposite claim has mostly been abandoned. Doubtless, the demand it conveys is unavoidable, as is, most probably, despite criticism, the stubborn reference to total History, under the vocables of world history or universal history, forming the backdrop against which the historical eras marked out by historians stand out. A rigorous agnosticism in relation to the idea of modernity is perhaps impracticable. How indeed could we not be tempted to say in what times we live? Or to express our difference and novelty in relation to every other time? The only result expected from critique would then be an admission of the controversial, polemical, inconclusive nature of all discussions on the "true" sense of "our" modernity.

I will begin by tracing out the argument of what Hans Robert Jauss calls the "historical recurrences" of the word, in contrast to the claim of "our" modernity to stand as the exception to this recurrence and to think itself absolutely.[19] This "historical recurrence" is attested by a discourse that is contained perfectly within a theory of representation belonging, as is shown in the second part of this work, to the historiographical operation. The sole difference that can be noted, although a considerable one, is that this is not one representation among others but the representation that this operation gives of itself, in which both figures—the object-representation and the operation-representation—coincide with one another. This self-representation claims to testify for the entire epoch in which its own discourse is inscribed. Several epochs have defined themselves as modern. Out of this repetition arises the paradox attaching to the very theme "*our* epoch."

We can follow the narrative of the historian retracing the successive occurrences of the terms relating to the same semantic field and repeating the terminological choices that have led to "our" own modernity, we the agents of present history. And we can identify the moment when the implicit or explicit ascription of value confers a normative sense on the expression.

Jacques Le Goff traces this path in *History and Memory*.[20] He links these distinctions in the following way. First, on what is still a formal level, he proposes the distinction between before and after, implied in the related notions of simultaneity and succession. Upon this he constructs the opposition between past and present governing the distinctions that follow, which the historian develops on the level of the "historical social consciousness" (2). The decisive distinction leading up to the idea of modernity is constituted by the opposition "ancient" versus "modern."[21] This distinction, it is stated, "developed in an equivocal and complex context" (21). The term "modern" has indeed changed partners several times (ancient, but also old, traditional), while at the same time binding its fate to different synonyms (recent, new). What is more, the paired terms continue to be accompanied by favorable, pejorative, or neutral connotations. The original use of "modern" in low Latin (the adverb *modo* signifying "recently") and of "ancient" (in the sense of what belongs to the past) was neutral. Less neutral were subsequent usages, when "ancient" designated the earlier Greco-Roman world preceding the triumph of Christianity, a world henceforth designated by the word "Antiquity."[22] Neutrality is out of place when the term "modern" adds to itself the epithet "new," the praiseworthy term par excellence, beginning in the sixteenth century, when it will no longer have as its opposite simply the ancient, but also the medieval, in accordance with the division of history into three periods: ancient, medieval, and modern (*neuere* in German). The ambiguity grows when Antiquity, after being chronologically superseded, becomes once again exemplary during the great Renaissance of the sixteenth century.[23]

This is the period when historical narration intersects with the pejorative or favorable evaluations that have been superimposed on one another at the decline of periods in the style of the chronosophies studied by Pomian (reign, age, era, period, even century, as in the expressions Great Century, century of Louis XIV, century of the Enlightenment). The historian is a witness to this surplus of meaning that makes the superiority of "our epoch" fighting words. This threshold is crossed when the contrary of the idea of novelty is the idea of tradition, which, from the simple transmission of a heritage, becomes synonymous with the resistance to new ideas and mores. Things become even more complicated with the cyclical conception of the Renaissance, in which praise is directed to a rediscovered past—pagan Greco-Roman antiquity— beyond the rupture-effect produced by the eruption of novelty. It is at this crossroads of the linear and the cyclical that the fate of the concept of imitation was played out, a concept itself inherited from the *mimēsis* of the Greeks: is imitating repeating in the sense of copying, or repeating in the sense of calling back to life? The famous quarrel of the Ancients and the Moderns in the French and English seventeenth century revolved around these ascriptions of opposing values to the alleged exemplarity of ancient models.[24] Linearity will definitively prevail in the idea of progress, which merits the title of *topos*, as in this "commonplace" the alliance between the modern and the new is concluded, in contrast to the decrepitude of tradition.

The sequence "modern," "novelty," "progress" functions like a syntagma in two revered texts, which will serve to orient what follows in our discussion: Turgot's *Réfléxions sur l'histoire des progrès de l'esprit humain* (1749), and Condorcet's *Esquisse d'un tableau des progrès de l'esprit humain* (1794). History or tableau, this is the balance sheet of the accomplishment of Western consciousness, presented as a guide for humanity as a whole. On the metahistorical plane, the praise of the modern fuses together the presumed total reflection of history upon itself and the reflection of the privileged historical moment. What matters is that the projection of the future is, henceforth, of a piece with the retrospection on past times. From then on, the century can be seen with the eyes of the future. It is in this sense that the future of past generations, with regard to which our own modernity distinguishes itself, appears as an outmoded future, to borrow Koselleck's beautiful title, *Die vergangene Zukunft* (*Futures Past*), which evokes the future such as it is no longer, understanding in this expression: such as it is no longer ours. But the history of the idea of modernity continues beyond the European Enlightenment, and the hesitations in the vocabulary continue to accumulate. Replacing "old" by "ancient" has already marked the historical distance between modern times and antiquity. The substitution of "modern" by "romantic" is accompanied by the symmetrical substitution of "ancient" by "classical" in the sense of ineffaceable, exemplary, even perfect. With Romanticism, the modern rediscovers a twofold past, "Gothic" and "ancient," while the superiority of our time is tempered by the idea dear to Montesquieu that every epoch and every nation has its own genius. The most surprising element of this history is perhaps the fortune of the words *roman* (novel, romance) and "romanticism":[25] as in the novels of chivalry—those poems in popular language—fiction permeates the image of the world, the fantastic capturing the poetry of life beyond the picturesque, confirming what Aristotle suggested in the famous text of the *Poetics* when he pronounced the superior nature of the epic and the tragic over mere history in the order of truth. But then it is no longer the agreement with the ideas of time that predominates in the idea of modernity, but dissatisfaction and disagreement with the present time. Modernity has gone a long way in defining itself in opposition to itself. Along this trajectory, Germany and France occupy very different positions, the great break occasioned by the French Revolution prolonging itself in a rupture on the level of mores and taste. Stendhal, without whom Baudelaire would be incomprehensible, no longer requires a contrast with antiquity to ascribe an incomparable prestige to the very actuality of the present.[26]

At this point, our discourse on modernity makes an abrupt change of register. Leaving aside the history of the past uses of the term "modern," conducted along the lines of a history of representations, the discussion turns toward the meanings attaching to "our" modernity, we who speak of it today. We are thus attempting to distinguish "our" modernity from that of "others," from that of those who, before us, declared themselves to be modern. From a repetitive, iterative concept, the concept of modernity now becomes the indicator within our discourse of a singularity comparable to that of the here and the now of our corporeal condition. In other words, the possessive adjective "our" functions as a deictic extended to the dimension of an entire period: it is a matter of "our" time. This time is distinguished from other times just as the "here" and the "now" of actual experience are opposed to "long ago" and "elsewhere." An absolute in a nonrelative sense is thereby posited and designated. Vincent Descombes begins an essay dealing with the contemporary uses of the term "modern" with these words: "In other times, words as charged as those of 'present time,' 'modern world,' 'modernity' would have evoked phenomena of innovation and rupture."[27] "In other times"? The expression no longer belongs to an objective history of representations; it signifies times that are no longer ours. The essay continues this way: "For the last twenty years [counted from the present of the writing of the essay], these same themes of the modern and the present are an occasion for philosophers to turn toward their own past. What is designated as modern seems to be behind us" (43). We are no longer speaking as mere observers, as simple chroniclers of past representations. We are speaking as their heirs. It is indeed the heritage of the Enlightenment that is at stake, for we who speak of it today. The tone of controversy is quickly engaged: "The presupposition is then that there is a single heritage of the Enlightenment" (44). Presupposed by whom? They are not named, those who, in the words of the author of the essay, summon us in the second person: "You cannot divide this heritage" (44). The reflection has cast off the tone of retrospection and has become combative. At the same time, it has become more local: "The French Enlightenment thinkers are, for us, inseparable from the French Revolution and its historical sequels. Our reflection on the philosophy of the Enlightenment cannot be exactly the same as the reflection of those who have the American Revolution as a point of reference, or those for whom the Enlightenment is an *Aufklärung* without a direct political translation" (44–45). This is why we do not even know how to translate into French the English "modernity," used, for example, by Leo Strauss, who ascribed to Jean-Jacques Rousseau "the first crisis of modernity," playing at once upon chronology and upon the argument opposing reactionary to radical. In truth, the modernity that is not ours is inscribed in a chronology that has ceased to be neutral, indifferent to what it orders: "Now it is not an indifferent chronology drawn up by the philosophers [of the past twenty years], but a chronology in which the date of thoughts and of facts corresponds to their signification, not to the calendar" (48). This qualified chronology, this "philosophical chronology" (50), is itself a matter of dispute, inasmuch as the thinkers of the Enlightenment pinned their own claims to the superiority of a philosophy of history, worthy of the chronosophies of the past studied by Pomian. This was the case with the "epochs" of Condorcet's tableau, mentioned above, in the register of objective historiography. They satisfy the concept of philosophical chronology proposed here: the modern epoch does not designate only the present epoch, but also the epoch of the triumph of reason. The periodization is philosophical. Can one still call it a chronology? In fact, modernity is at one and the same time self-valorizing and self-referential. It characterizes itself as a superior epoch by designating itself as present and by this quality alone. In the same stroke, notes Descombes, other uses of the term "modernity" remain foreign to Condorcet, for example, the use that would take into account the gap between abstraction and practice, with its cortège of traditions and prejudices, and, even more so, a use of the term that would bring out the historical relativity of the models proposed to people and that would, as a result, see in the masterpieces of Antiquity not failures but masterpieces of another epoch.[28] Has the relativity signaled by the historian suddenly become the modernity of today? In any case, the modern according to Condorcet can no longer be ours.

And why not? Because of Baudelaire, he through whom the word "modernity" entered into the French language with a different accent than the word "modern," inasmuch as "modern" continues to be marked by a normative conception of abstract reason. Modernity now designates "a historical self-consciousness." "Modernity does not exist, *our* modernity exists" (62). At the root of a purely temporal indication that determines the difference of position in time of the modern and the ancient, there is the act of extracting from the present what is worthy of being retained and of becoming ancient, namely, the vitality, individuality, and variety of the world—the "beauty of life," according to the expression we can read in *The Painter of Modern Life*. It is from social mores, more precisely from this new social space of the street and the salon, that the painter will draw his subjects. This reference to mores, echoing Montesquieu by way of Stendhal—and perhaps even more so by way of Herder, for whom all cultures are on an equal footing—permits this admission on the part of the critic: "Every century and every people has had its beauty, we inevitably have our own" (quoted by Descombes, 69). And again: "There are as many forms of beauty as there are customary ways to seek happiness" (69). One can speak of the "morality of the century" (69) in a non-chronological sense of the term, Descombes insists, following a chronology drawn from the contents of what is arranged in accordance with the Ancient and the Modern. A time, an epoch, means "a manner of understanding morality, love, religion, etc." (72). One can well see how a certain cosmopolitanism can result from this, since all the uses are legitimate and even possess a peculiar coherence that articulates "the reasons of usages" (73), which are as diverse as languages. But what is signified by Baudelaire's reference to an "ineffable transcendence" (74), which can be read in his essay on "The Universal Exposition of 1855" dealing with cosmopolitanism?

The critic, presenting "the comparison of nations and their respective products," asserts "their equal utility in the eyes of Him who is indefinable." Can diversity be celebrated without the recourse to an indefinable present?

At the end of this route, we see why Baudelaire's modernity is already no longer that of the moderns of the Enlightenment.[29] But is it still our modernity? Or instead has the latter taken its distances with respect to the former modernity too?

If, then, the concept of modernity is for the history of representations a repetitive concept, what we call "our time" distinguishes itself from other times, to the point that we are able to distinguish our modernity from earlier modernities. There is then a competition between two uses of the term "modernity," depending on whether it designates the iterative phenomenon covered by a history of representations or the self-understanding of our difference, our own, as such and such, under the sway of the deictic "us" which henceforth stands out against the descriptive "them."

The discourse of modernity changes registers once again when it loses sight of the paradox inherent in the claim that our epoch is characterized by its difference with respect to every other, and directs itself instead to values that our modernity is supposed to defend and illustrate. Absent any prior reflection on the conditions of an evaluation such as this, praise and blame are left to alternate in endless controversy. Nor is there any concern with distinguishing, as Vincent Descombes does, between a chronology in terms of content and a chronology in terms of dates. The possibility of characterizing our epoch in a meaningful way in terms of its difference with regard to every other epoch is taken for granted as self-evident. Its merits and defects are directly pointed out. And if this discussion is conducted well, as is the case, in my opinion, in Charles Taylor's small book, *The Malaise of Modernity*, republished as *The Ethics of Authenticity*,[30] the strangeness of a discourse on "our" modernity is avoided by the prudent decision to identify the modern with the contemporary. Taylor's work begins with these words: "I want to write here about some of the malaises of modernity. I mean by this features of our contemporary culture and society that people experience as a loss or a decline, even as our civilization 'develops'" (1). It is understood, and probably legitimately so, that the quarrel would not be taking place if the evolution of mores, ideas, practices, feelings were not irreversible. And it is despite this irreversibility that the question of advancing or falling behind, of improvement or decline, held to mark our epoch is posed. What has to be brought into the discussion are the "features" which are not determined by their temporal situation—today—but by their place on a moral scale. The neutralization of all chronology is quickly made. If "the whole modern era from the seventeenth century is frequently seen as the time frame of decline," "although the time scale can vary greatly, there is a certain convergence on the themes of decline," which "are often variations around a few central melodies" (1). It is the theme of decline that matters. Who then are the operators of this evaluation? Those who, throughout the book, are simply called "people." It is not surprising, then, that the controversy has no identifiable advocates. But, at the same time, it moves outside of the field of reflection concerning the limits set regarding considerations of the meaning of the current epoch as it constitutes the *now* of history. In fact, the three themes discussed by Taylor stem from a moral evaluation, which, at first, has no particular temporal characterization, although it is constantly punctuated by features that can be said to be marked by the epoch. This is true of the three "malaises" examined by Taylor. The first concerns the "finest achievement of modern civilization" (2), which is individualism. The stakes of the discussion are clearly moral: the malaise "is about what we might call a loss of meaning, the fading of moral horizons" (10). The second malaise, resulting from technological domination, involves the threats to our freedom from the realm of instrumental reason. The third concerns the "soft" despotism, in Tocqueville's expression, imposed by the modern state on the citizens placed under its tutelage. The examination of these three malaises sets the detractors of modernity in confrontation with its defenders. But the protagonists' position in the present in this confrontation has lost its relevance. In this way, the first malaise, the only one examined in any detail, gives rise to a discussion on "the moral force of the ideal of authenticity" (17). The interest of Taylor's position is that it attempts to avoid the alternative of despising or apologizing—including even the temptation of a compromise—except by means of "a work of retrieval, through which this ideal can help us restore our practice" (23). His examination of the "sources of authenticity" (25ff.) constantly oscillates between historical and antihistorical considerations. He affirms from the outset that "the ethic of authenticity is something relatively new and peculiar to modern culture" (25). In this sense, it is dated: it has its "source" in Romanticism. Here, "source" means "origin" in the historical sense; but the word also means "ground." Moreover, the accent shifts progressively from the question of origins toward a "horizon of important questions" (40), such as the "need for recognition" (43). This extensive discussion of the individualist ideal of self-realization serves as a model for the other two discussions. Nothing is said in all of this regarding the position in the present of the protagonists of the discussion. If what is left unsaid were to be addressed, this would facilitate an elucidation of the relation between the universal and the present. On the one hand, an ethico-political universal is presupposed by the defense and illustration of certain themes attributed to modernity. On the other, the advocate who maintains this discourse recognizes himself or herself at the heart of considerable social changes. If the historical present can claim to think itself by itself, this can only be as a nodal point of the universal and the historical. It is in this direction that a reasonable discussion of the benefits and harms of "modernity" should be oriented.

A fourth stage of the discussion on modernity is reached with the appearance of the term "postmodern," frequently employed by English-language authors as a synonym for modernist. It implies, in its negative form, the denial of any acceptable meaning of modern and of modernity. To the extent that the still recent use of the concept of modernity contains a degree of legitimation not only regarding its difference but also concerning its preference for itself, the rejection of any normative thesis unavoidably strips the positions that claim to be postmodern of any plausible or probable justification.

This situation is lucidly assumed and analyzed by Jean-François Lyotard in *The Postmodern Condition*: "Our working hypothesis is that the status of knowledge is altered as societies enter what is known as the postindustrial age and cultures enter what is known as the postmodern age."[31] But what is the status of the discourse in which this hypothesis is announced? The postindustrial age has its sociological points of reference and lends itself to a precise enumeration of its distinctive features: "The facts speak for themselves (and this list is not exhaustive)" (4). The hegemony of computers and the logic it imposes also fall under an assignable criterion, as do the commodification of knowledge and the computerization of society following from it.

According to Lyotard, the discourses of legitimation have failed, whether the discourse of positivism, whose expression in history was seen in the school whose method preceded the *Annales*, or of hermeneutics with Gadamer and his German and French disciples. The original idea is then to discern, under these discourses of legitimation, the rhetorical force invested in the "grand narratives," such as those proposed by the secularized forms of Christian theology, in twentieth century Marxism in particular. It is these grand narratives that have lost all credibility. We are engaged, whether we like it or not, in a discourse of delegitimation.[32] To Jürgen Habermas, for whom modernity remains an incomplete project,[33] Lyotard opposes a sharp sense of the irreconcilability of the discourses proffered and the powerlessness of the desire for consensus to arbitrate the debates.[34] The only bright spot: the exercise of justice on the basis of local forms of agreement, interlaced with insurmountable differences and sustained by little narratives.

But how can a debate like the one pursued with Habermas be resolved, if the idea of a criterion for agreement is itself a matter of dispute? More fundamentally, how can one even enter into a debate that avoids the preliminary question of the very possibility of characterizing the epoch in which one lives? This difficulty is common to the claim on behalf of "our" modernity and to the self-designation of our epoch—or at least of a contemporary current within it—as postmodern. This concept—if it is one—assuredly contains a strong polemical charge and an incontestable rhetorical force of denunciation. But a hidden form of the performative contradiction mentioned above no doubt condemns it to declare itself to be unthought and unthinkable.[35]

## THE HISTORIAN AND THE JUDGE

A comparison between the task of historian and the task of judge is no doubt indicated. Why bring it in at this point of our investigation, in the framework of a critical reflection on the limits of historical knowledge? The reason is that the respective roles of historian and judge, characterized by their aims of truth and justice, invite them to occupy the position of a third party with respect to the places occupied in the public space by the protagonists of social action. A vow of impartiality is attached to this third-party position. This ambition is no doubt more modest than the two preceding objectives discussed above. Moreover, the fact that this vow is affirmed by two protagonists as different as the historian and the judge already attests to the internal limitation of this shared commitment. In addition, we must consider the fact that other actors besides the historian and the judge can also claim this position of impartiality: the educator who transmits knowledge and values in a democratic state, the state and its administration placed in the role of arbitrator, and, finally and most especially, the citizen who finds himself or herself in a condition similar to that of Rousseau's *Social Contract* and to John Rawls's "veil of ignorance" in his *Theory of Justice*. This vow of impartiality belonging to the third-party position in all of these versions stems from a critical philosophy of history, inasmuch as the aims of truth and justice must be vigilantly protected along the borders marking the limits of legitimacy. The vow of impartiality must thus be considered in light of the impossibility of an absolute third party.

First, a word regarding impartiality as an intellectual and moral virtue common to all those who would claim the function of a third party. Thomas Nagel covers this well in *Equality and Partiality*.[36] In the chapter "Two

Standpoints," he defines the general conditions for impartial judgment in these terms: "Most of our experience of the world, and most of our desires, belong to our individual points of view: We see things *from here*, so to speak. But we are also able to think about the world in abstraction from our particular position in it—in abstraction from who we are. It is possible to abstract much more radically than that from the contingencies of the self. . . . Each of us begins with a set of concerns, desires, and interests of his own, and each of us can recognize that the same is true of others. We can then remove ourselves in thought from our particular position in the world and think simply of all those people, without singling out the *I* as the one we happen to be" (10). This viewpoint, which is a sort of non-viewpoint, can be termed impersonal. It is indivisibly epistemic and moral. It can be termed an instance of intellectual virtue. The epistemic aspect has to do with the internal split in viewpoint, the moral aspect with the implicit assertion of the equal value and dignity of viewpoints, once the other viewpoint is seen to be the viewpoint of the other: "At the first stage, the basic insight that appears from the impersonal standpoint is that everyone's life matters, and no one is more important than anyone else" (11). And again: Nagel refers to the tradition according to which we should live "in effect, as if we were under the direction of an impartial benevolent spectator of the world in which we appear as one among billions" (15). What follows in Nagel's work concerns the contribution of the idea of impartiality to a theory of justice, through the idea of equality. We will echo him in weighing the respective merits of impartiality invoked in turn by the judge and the historian. Both of them share the same professional deontology summed up in the famous adage *nec studio, nec ira*—neither favor, nor anger. Neither complaisance, nor spirit of vengeance.

In what way and to what extent do the historian and the judge satisfy this rule of impartiality inscribed in their respective professional deontologies? And what social and political, what personal and corporative forces, assist them? These questions are the continuation of those raised regarding History's claim to posit itself outside of any specific point of view and link up with the questions concerning the present epoch's claim to judge all prior forms of modernity. The comparison between the role of the historian and the role of the judge constitutes in many respects a *locus classicus*. I would nevertheless like to add to the list of considerations on which broad agreement can be observed between spokespersons of both disciplines, a more controversial presentation of the reflections prompted at the close of the twentieth century by the irruption into history of dramas of extreme violence, cruelty, and injustice. Now these events have given rise to an important malaise in the fields of both professions, which has, in its turn, left documented traces on public opinion susceptible of enriching and renewing a discussion that an easy *consensus* among specialists would tend to curtail.

Since we are concerned with the most general and most stable constraints placed on the respective professions of judge and historian—at least in the geopolitical sphere of the West and of the epochs historians term "modern" and "contemporary," with the addition of "the history of the present day"— the starting point of the comparison is obvious: it consists in the structural difference separating the trial conducted within the confines of the court and the historiographical critique begun within the framework of the archives. In both situations the same linguistic structure is involved, that of testimony, which we examined above, from its rootedness in declarative memory to its oral phase, and continuing up to its inscription in the mass of documents preserved and codified within the institutional framework of the archive by means of which an institution preserves the trace of its past activity with a view to subsequent consultation. At the time of this examination we took account of the bifurcation of the paths followed by testimony when it passes from its use in ordinary conversation to its historical or judicial use. Before underscoring the most obvious oppositions that distinguish the use of testimony in court from its use in the archives, let us pause to examine two features common to both uses: the concern with proof and the critical examination of the credibility of witnesses—these two features going together. Carlo Ginzburg, in a brief book titled, precisely, *The Judge and the Historian*,[37] favorably quotes Luigi Ferajioli: "The trial is, so to speak, the only case of 'historiographical experimentation'—sources are set out *de vivo*, not only because they are heard directly, but also because they are made to confront one another, submitted to cross-examination, and encouraged to reproduce, as in a psychodrama, the affair being judged."[38] Truly speaking, this exemplarity in the use of proof on the judicial plane operates fully only in the phase of preliminary investigation, when, as in some judicial systems, this is distinct from the central phase of the trial. It is within this limited framework that the questions of proof and veracity are posed, primarily at the time of drafting a confession, whose credibility and, even more importantly, whose veracity are not undeniable. To be sure, applying the criteria of concordance and relying upon independent verification of the confession provide perfect illustrations of the theses offered by Ginzburg, the historiographer, on the "evidentiary paradigm": the same complementarity between the oral nature of testimony and the material nature of the evidence authenticated by expert testimony; the same relevance of "small errors," the probable sign of inauthenticity; the same primacy accorded to questioning, to playing with possibilities in imagination; the same perspicacity in uncovering contradictions, incoherencies, unlikelihoods; the same attention to silences, to voluntary or involuntary omissions; the same familiarity, finally, with the resources for falsifying language in terms of error, lying, self-delusion, deception. In this regard, the judge and the historian are both past masters at exposing fakes and, in this sense, both masters in the manipulation of suspicion.[39]

To be sure, the time is ripe to recall, along with Ginzburg, that the word *historia* stems at one and the same time from medical language, from the rhetorical argumentation of the juridical setting, and from the art of persuasion practiced before the court. Does not the historian often behave as a lawyer pleading a case, in the manner of the French historians of the French Revolution pleading by turns, before the *Annales* period, for or against Danton, for or against the Girondins or the Jacobins? But, more than anything else, Ginzburg's quasi-exclusive insistence on evidence, the handling of which he considers to be common to judges and to historians, should be related to the struggle the author conducts against the doubt instilled in the profession of historian by authors like Hayden White, always in pursuit of the rhetorical style of historical discourse: "For me," Ginzburg insists, "as for many others, the notions of evidence and truth are, on the contrary, an integral part of the profession of historian.... The analysis of representations cannot abstract from the principle of reality" (23). "The profession of each of them [historian and judge] is based on the possibility of proving, in line with determined rules, that X did Y; X designating indifferently the protagonist, possibly anonymous, of a historical event or the subject implied in a penal proceeding; and Y any sort of action" (23).

However, the thesis according to which the situation of the trial would present *de vivo* the sources of judgment common to the historian and the judge has its limits on the very plane on which it establishes its arguments: on the properly inquisitory plane of the investigation. Did not the most fantastic hypotheses presiding over the trials for witchcraft long remain irrefutable, before the Roman Congregation of the Holy Office made the judges require proof, "objective confirmation"? And do not certain modern trials for treason, conspiracy, terrorism, share the same perverse spirit that reigned in olden times in the inquisitorial trials? But, in particular, our earlier reflections on the complexities of the representation of the historian should put us on our guard against an overly hasty recourse to the "reality principle."

It is important, therefore, to take up the examination of the model of the trial at its beginning and to carry it beyond the phase of preliminary investigation—of the instruction, if this is the case—and to take it through the adversarial phase in which the trial more properly consists, carrying it to its conclusion, the pronouncement of the verdict.

Let us recall that the trial rests on a network of relations that articulate the situation-type of the trial in different ways—a situation in which interests, rights, and symbolically contested goods are set in opposition. In this regard, trials of treason, subversion, conspiracy, and terrorism are not exemplary inasmuch as they directly involve issues of security, the primary condition of living together. The dispute over the distribution of private goods is more instructive for our present discussion: here, infractions, misdemeanors, even crimes, bring together comparable, commensurable claims—which will no longer be the case with the great criminal trials discussed below. The infraction, then, is a kind of interaction, a violent one to be sure, but one in which several actors are implicated.

The trial begins by putting on stage the alleged facts with a view to representing them outside of their sheer having occurred and to making visible the infraction committed in relation to the rule of law, presumed to be known to all, by an individual perpetrator at the expense of a victim, authorized to demand that his or her plea be pursued and that the presumed damage be rectified or compensated.[40] Past acts are therefore represented solely in terms of the nature of the charges selected prior to the actual trial. They are represented in the present within the horizon of the future social effect of the verdict that will decide the case. The relation to time is particularly noteworthy here: representation in the present consists in a staging, a theatricalization that has provoked the sarcasm of a Pascal and a Molière, and a measured discourse of conscious legitimation of its second-order functionality. This living presence of the scenes replayed solely on the plane of discourse comes under the heading of visibility, which was shown above to be related to expressibility (*dicibilité*) on the plane of the literary representation of the past. It is solemnified by the social ritual governed by the criminal procedure for the purpose of providing the judicial judgment with a public structure and stature. This, in fact, is but a response to time's wearing away of all types of traces—material, affective, social—left by the misdeed. Antoine Garapon mentions the reflections of Jean Améry, who speaks in this regard of "the process of the moral inversion of time," referring to the quasi-biological time that will be more directly discussed in the chapter on forgetting below. The philosopher-judge also quotes Emmanuel Levinas's expression regarding "copresence before a third-party of justice." Along with the additional moral qualification and in direct relation to it, the representation *of* the facts is also the representation *between* the opposing parties, the face-to-face contact of the protagonists, the appearance in court of all the parties, to which can be contrasted the solitude of the reader in the archives, whose muteness is broken only by the historian. In this way, the trial puts on stage a reconstructed time of the past, in which the facts that are targeted have themselves already constituted tests of memory: in addition to the physical harm inflicted on persons defined by their own history, the breaking of contracts, the disputes over the attribution of goods, positions of power and authority, and all the other infractions and crimes constitute so many wounds inflicted on memory that call for a work of memory inseparable from a work of mourning, with a view toward the reappropriation of the infraction, of the crime, by all the parties despite its essential strangeness. It is against this backdrop that we will later have to place the great criminal trials of the second half of the twentieth century and their progress along the unfamiliar paths of *dissensus.*

Such being the scene of the trial, the traits by which it lends itself to a comparison with historiographical investigation are of two sorts. The first ones have to do with the deliberative phase, the second with the concluding phase of passing judgment. In the deliberative phase the trial consists for the most part in a ceremony of language involving a number of protagonists; it rests on an assault of arguments in which the parties in opposition have equal access to speech; by its very conduct, this organized debate is intended to be a model of discussion in which the passions that fed the conflict are transferred into the arena of language. This chain of criss-crossing discourses articulates, one upon the other, the moments of argumentation containing their practical syllogisms and moments of interpretation, which bear simultaneously on the coherence of the narrative sequence of the purported acts and on the appropriateness of the rule of law called upon to define the acts in penal terms.[41] At the point of convergence of these two lines of interpretation, the verdict falls, the well-named *arrêt* (judgment); in this regard, the punitive aspect of the sentence as sanction should not eclipse the major function of the verdict, which is to pronounce the law in a given situation; for this reason, the verdict's function of retribution has to be considered subordinate to its restorative function, both with regard to the public order and to the dignity of the victims to whom justice is rendered.

It remains that the definitive character of the verdict marks the most obvious difference between the juridical approach and the historiographical approach to the same events: what has been judged can be challenged by popular opinion, but not retried; *non bis idem*; as for the review of the decision, it "cuts only one way" (Garapon). *A contrario*, the slow pace of judging or concluding a trial is said to add further harm to that caused by the infraction or the crime. Yet, not to pass judgment on it would leave this harm with the final word, adding a failure of recognition and abandonment to the wrong inflicted on the victim. After the judgment a new temporal era begins for the person convicted, another horizon of expectation, which opens up options that are envisaged later on under the rubrics of forgetting and forgiveness. If this is the case, it is because the verdict, which concluded the sequence of judging with the beneficial effects that have been stated regarding the law, public order, and the self-esteem of the victims, leaves, on the side of the one convicted, especially under the conditions of detention, an unappeased, unpurged memory, and delivers over to his fortune a patient submitted to new potential forms of violence.

What, then, are we to say about the confrontation between the judge's task and the historian's task? As we have seen, the conditions under which the verdict is pronounced within the courtroom have opened a breach in the common front maintained by the historian in the face of error and injustice. The judge has to pass judgment—this is the function of a judge. Judges must come to a conclusion. They must decide. They must set at an appropriate distance the guilty party and the victim, in accordance with an imperiously binary topology. All this, historians do not do, cannot do, do not want to do; and if they were to attempt it, at the risk of setting themselves up as the sole tribunal of history, this would be at the cost of acknowledging the precariousness of a judgment whose partiality, even militancy, is recognized. But then this bold judgment is submitted to the critique of the corporation of historians and to the critique of the enlightened public, and the work subjected to an unending process of revision, which makes the writing of history a perpetual rewriting. This openness to rewriting marks the difference between a provisional historical judgment and a definitive judicial judgment. The breach opened in this way in the united front of the knights of impartiality continues to widen following the final phase of judgment. Penal judgment, governed by the principle of individual guilt, by nature recognizes only defendants who have proper names and who, moreover, are asked to state their identity at the opening of the trial.

And the actions are specific actions, or at least distinct and identifiable contributions of the protagonists implicated in a collective action—and this is so even in the case of infractions committed "together"—which are submitted to the examination of judges, on both the normative and narrative plane; the fit that the judgment establishes between the presumed truth of the narrative sequence and the imputability by reason of which the accused is held accountable—this good fit in which explanation and interpretation come together at the moment the verdict is pronounced—operates only within the limits traced out by the prior selection of the protagonists and of the acts alleged. As for the staging by which we first characterized the public nature of the trial with the appearance of all the protagonists, a visibility is provided to this very delimiting of actions and persons. The legal stage is limited in principle. To be sure, the court does not forbid extending its investigation to the vicinity of the alleged action, broadening it in space and in time and beyond the biography of the accused. Among the circumstances of the action will be included influences, pressures, constraints, and, in the background, the great social disorders with regard to which the criminal action tends to become one symptom among others. After all, it is a judge who wrote the book titled, *In Geschichten verstrickt* (entangled in stories).[42] Everything happens as if the preliminary investigation were opened up again by the public trial that was supposed to bring it to a close. But, for good or for ill, the exonerating effect of the excessive accommodation to circumstances and to their perpetually widening concentric circles will ultimately be averted by the timely reminder of the rule of the trial, which is to judge a given human being and the particular acts for which this person is accountable, allowing the possibility of harmonizing the verdict with attenuating circumstances, the relative weight of which will potentially be retained by the judge at the time of the sentence, if one is handed down. The potentially unlimited circle of explanation inexorably closes with the verdict, which *in fine* can be only conviction or acquittal. It is then that the decisive word of justice resounds.

The circles that the judge closes after having cautiously opened them, the historian pries open again. The circle of actions for which individual authors are held accountable can be placed back only into event-history, which, as we have seen, can itself be considered one level among others in the stacking up of durations and causations. The purported act can then be aligned, as one event among others, with the conjunctures and structures with which it forms a sequence. And even if, after the great period of the *Annales*, historiography proves to be more attentive to the interventions of historical agents, and if it accords a place of honor to representations in connection with the individual and collective actions from which the social bond proceeds, the representations that are then methodically placed back on their scales of efficacy are still of interest to the historian only as collective phenomena. This is the case even on the plane of microhistory, to which could be compared the aforementioned inquiry into personalities conducted by the court. Only the mark left by individual interventions upon the smallest of societies contains any historical significance.

In this way, the discordance between historical judgment and judicial judgment, evident in the final phase, is amplified pursuant to this ultimate point. This affects all the phases of both the judicial operation and the historiographical operation, so that one can wonder whether the judge and the historian hear testimony, that initial structure common to both roles, with the same ear.

The confrontation between the professions of judge and historian might simply fade into the ennui of an academic debate, if we did not listen to the voices of those who, in various capacities, have had to judge crimes committed in a number of places in the world by totalitarian or authoritarian regimes in the middle of the twentieth century. These voices belong to the transitional period which saw the re-establishment or the establishment of constitutional democratic governments. The peal of voices comes from judges and historians whose judgments are an integral part of this new foundation. I will mention, on the one hand, the role played by the great criminal trials held at the end of the Second World War on the scale of several continents, but especially in Europe in the wake of the Shoah, and on the other hand, the controversy among German historians dealing, as responsible historians, with the same events related to this catastrophe. So, on one side we have the courts and the judges penetrating *volens nolens* into the territory of the historian before their verdicts are carved into the flesh of history as it is being made—on the other, historians who are attempting to do their job of historian under the pressure of a moral, legal, and political condemnation, arising from the same judicial agency as the verdict of the criminal court, a verdict they, in their turn, risk reinforcing, attenuating, displacing, even subverting, because they cannot ignore it.

This secretly conflictual situation between the judicial approach and the historical approach to the same facts demands to be, if not untangled, at least made explicit.

To clarify the first side of the debate, I have chosen a work by Mark Osiel, *Mass Atrocity, Collective Memory, and the Law.*[43] The author, who prides himself on bringing together two mindsets which, at least in the United States, are alien to each other—the mindset of the sociologist and the mindset of the lawyer—proposes to determine the influence exerted on the collective memories of the people concerned by the judicial proceedings and the sentences pronounced by the great criminal trials of the second half of the twentieth century in Nuremberg, Tokyo, Argentina, and France. The thematic object of the investigation—first, with respect to the tribunals, then to the sociologist-lawyer—is designated by the term "mass atrocity" (or "administrative massacre"), a term that is neutral in appearance with regard to the presumption of uniqueness belonging to the Holocaust (called the Shoah by French-language authors), but a term precise enough to define the crimes of state committed by regimes as different as the Nazis, the Japanese militarists, the Argentinian generals, and the French collaborators during the Vichy period. The general line of the book is the following: unlike Durkheim, who saw in the unanimous condemnation of ordinary criminality a direct—mechanical—means of reinforcing social *consensus*, Osiel is drawn to the *dissensus* provoked by the trials' public proceedings and to the educational function exerted by this very *dissensus* on the level of public opinion and collective memory, which is expressed and shaped on this level. The trust he places in the benefits expected to follow from this culture of controversy is related to his moral and political credo on behalf of a liberal society—in the political sense that English-speaking authors give to the term "liberal": a liberal society (in a quasi-tautological fashion) is a society that derives its militant legitimacy from public deliberation, from the open character of the debates and residual antagonisms these debates leave in their wake. What is more, inasmuch as the collective memory is the target of this harsh schooling by which a society constructs its own solidarity, the work also offers the occasion for a reflection on memory itself.[44]

Faithful to its theme—the civic education of the collective memory by *dissensus*—Osiel constructs his book upon the series of objections directed against the claim of the tribunals to pronounce a true and just—and as such, exemplary—verdict, despite the extraordinary nature both of the acts in accusation and of the very conduct of the trials. Of the "six obstacles" considered, I shall retain those that directly concern the relations between the judicial approach and the historiographical approach.[45] The judicial approach is mobilized twice over: once in the course of the trials, in the argumentation provided by the prosecution and the defense, and a second time along the path that leads from the court of justice to the public arena. In truth, these two moments are but one, to the extent that, as we have said, the trial gives a visibility to the events that are played out again on a stage accessible to the public. In return, it is indeed the trial itself that penetrates into people's heads and into their homes by reason of the public discussion, transplanting its own *dissensus* there. By approaching the problem from the side of the "obstacles" confronting the claim of judges to write a just history, Osiel devotes himself to a vast inflation of the objections drawn from the specificity of the historiographical approach, inevitably shaken by the legal argumentation. In this way, the discordances too abstractly alluded to above are maliciously amplified and now illustrated by the concrete turns of events in the trials taken one by one. The tensions between the two approaches result from the fact that the judicial accusation rests on the principle of individual guilt: the result is that judges concentrate their attention on a small number of historical actors, those at the top of the state, and on the range of actions that they can exert on the course of events. The historian cannot admit this limitation of vision, but will extend the investigation to a wider number of actors, to the second-level executors, to bystanders, those more or less passive witnesses that are the silent populations in their complicity. The historian will place the specific decisions of the leaders and their interventions into the framework of broader, more complex interconnections. Where the criminal trial wishes to consider only individual protagonists, the historical investigation continually relates persons to crowds, to currents, and anonymous forces. It is noteworthy that the lawyers of the defendants in the great trials have systematically turned this widening of the field of investigation to the advantage of their clients, both on the side of the interconnections between events and on the side of interlocking individual initiatives and interventions.

Second contrast: criminal trials are acts of political justice intended to establish a new, stable version of the alleged acts by means of the definitive nature of the verdict. To be sure, judges know that the important thing is not the punishment but the pronouncement of justice. But this pronouncement closes the debate, "stops" the controversy. This constraint belongs to the short-term goal of the criminal trial: judge now, once and for all. It is at this price that the verdict of criminal trials can claim to educate public opinion by virtue of the uneasy conscience it starts to prick. Pushing the argument to its conclusion, the challenger will denounce the danger attached to the idea of an official version, even of an official history of events. This is where the accusation of "distortion" comes into play. It can be surprising coming from participants in the debate who are incapable, without contradicting themselves, of presenting a truthful version in opposition to an allegedly corrupted version. What alone can be considered a distortion is the project of proposing, even of imposing, a truthful narrative in support of the condemnation of the accused. Following this argument, all memory is already a distortion inasmuch as it is selective. As a result, one can only counter a partial version with another equally fragile version. However, there is one aspect through which, paradoxically, the trial confirms by its very procedure, rather than by its conclusion, the presumed skepticism of historians influenced by the critique of the "rhetoricians" more or less closely affiliated with Hayden White. By distributing the right to speak equally between the advocates on both sides, and by permitting the opposing narrations and arguments to be heard through this procedural rule, does not the court encourage the practice of a historically "balanced" judgment, tilting to the side of moral equivalence and, ultimately, to the side of exoneration? Criminal attorneys have shown they too know how to use this strategy in the famous interjection: *tu quoque!*

Osiel's treatment of this type of objection is interesting. His entire effort is to include it within his "liberal" vision of the public discussion under the heading of educational *dissensus*. But to succeed in this, he has to strip the objection of its venom of skepticism. To do this, he must affirm, first, that the very exercise of controversy by means of which the most disloyal, unscrupulous of lawyers tries to reap a benefit on behalf of proven criminals constitutes a proof-in-action of the ethical superiority of the liberal values under whose banner the trials are conducted. In this sense, the trial bears witness to this superiority, one of the beneficiaries being the freedom of speech of the lawyer representing the criminals. But Osiel also has to admit that all the narratives are not equivalent, that it is possible to provide, at least provisionally, a more plausible, more likely version, which the defense of the accused does not succeed in discrediting. In other words, it is possible to credit an account independently of the fact that this account has an educational scope with respect to the values of a democratic society in a period of transition.

Here I return once again to my plea on behalf of a more meticulous articulation of the three phases of the historiographical operation, namely, documentary proof, explanation/understanding, and the historian's representation. It is not because the court places reconstructed action on stage that it must retain only the "representative" phase of the historiographical operation, so strongly marked by the tropes and figures with which rhetoric works its magic. But then one must admit that when the field of protagonists and of actions recounted is expanded and the levels of analysis are multiplied, the judge's verdict is overtaken by that of the historian. Wisdom lies in saying that the judge should not play at being a historian; she must judge within the limits of her competence—limits which are imperative; she must judge in her mind and conscience. In this sense, Osiel ventures the expression "liberal memory," even "liberal virtue" (238). But neither do historians have the means to write the one history that would include the history of the perpetrators, the history of the victims, and the history of the witnesses. This does not mean that they cannot attempt to arrive at a partial consensus on the partial histories, the limits of which they, unlike the judges, have the possibility and the duty to transgress over and over again. Let each play his or her role!

If I mention at this time "the historian's debate" (*Historikerstreit*) of 1986 and following years in Germany,[46] this is not an attempt to review the totality of the facts relating to this debate; other aspects will be broached later with regard to forgetting and forgiveness. In a reflection on the relations between the judge and the historian, the question is precisely symmetrical and the inverse of that raised by Osiel's book: to what extent, we asked, can historiographical argumentation legitimately contribute to formulating a penal sentence for the great criminals of the twentieth century and thus to nourishing a *dissensus* with an educational purpose? The inverse question is the following: to what extent can a debate be conducted among professional historians under the surveillance of a previously decided guilty verdict, not only on the plane of national and international public opinion, but on the judicial and penal plane? Is some margin left, on the historiographical plane, for a *dissensus* that would not be perceived as exculpatory? This tie between explanation and exculpation—even approbation—has been little studied in its own right, although it continually underlies the controversy, suspicions held by some producing the self-justifying behavior of others in the play between inculpation and exculpation, as though there were situations in which historians themselves could be indicted as historians.

It is not only the relation of the historian to the judge that is inverted in this way; the historian working under the gaze of the people judges the one who has handed down the verdict. In eliminating praise and apologetics in general, this relation to a historiographical tradition has also worked to eliminate blame.

After asking whether praise had survived the dethronement of the figure of the king, we reserved the question of determining whether blame had followed a comparable fate. And we mentioned the difficulty in representing absolute horror within the confines of representation explored by Saul Friedlander, confronting what he terms "the unacceptable." It is precisely this very problem that reemerges now within the framework of the philosophical critique of history. Is a historiographical treatment of the unacceptable possible? The major difficulty lies in the exceptional gravity of the crimes. Whatever their uniqueness and their comparability may be in historiographical terms—this will ultimately form the heart of the debate—there is an ethical uniqueness and incomparability that result from the magnitude of the crime, due to the fact that it was committed by the state itself on one selected part of society that had a right to safety and protection, and to the fact that it was carried out by a soulless administration, tolerated without notable objection by the leaders of the elite, endured without major resistance by an entire population. The extreme limit of the inhumane corresponds to what Jean Nabert designated by the term "unjustifiable," in the sense of action outstripping negative norms. I have spoken elsewhere of the horrible as the contrary of the admirable and the sublime, which Kant said exceeded the limits of the imaginary in quantity and intensity. It is the exceptional character of evil that is designated in this way. It is in these "impossible" conditions that German historians are assigned the task that Christian Meier sums up in the following words: "condemn and comprehend."[47] In other words: comprehend without exonerating, without making oneself an accomplice to flight and denial. Comprehending involves making use of the categories of uniqueness and comparability in other than the strictly moral sense. In what way can these other uses contribute to the reappropriation by the population of what it condemns absolutely? And, furthermore, how can the extraordinary be received with the ordinary means of historical understanding?

I am purposefully separating out the contribution to this debate made by Ernst Nolte, in his essay "A Past That Will Not Go Away," for the reason that it is the most controversial. This expert on the Nazi period starts from an observation: "The Third Reich ended thirty-five years ago, but it is still very much alive" (in Piper, ed., *Devant l'histoire*, 7). And he adds unambiguously: "If the memory of the Third Reich is very much alive today, it is—except for a few on the fringe—with an entirely negative connotation, and this for good reason" (8). Nolte's discourse is thus not intended to be the discourse of a negationist, a denier, and this is indeed not the case. The moral condemnation made by survivors is presupposed: "A negative judgment is quite simply a vital necessity" (8). What worries Nolte, then, is the danger on the level of research of an account that has been elevated to the level of a founding ideology, the negative becoming legend and myth. What is required, then, is that the history of the Third Reich be subjected to a revision that is not a mere reversal of the fundamentally negative judgment: "For the essential, the negative image of the Third Reich calls for no revision and cannot be the object of any revision whatsoever" (11). The revision proposed concerns essentially what Osiel calls the frame of the narrative. Where should it start? he asks. How far should it extend? Where should it end? Nolte does not hesitate to go back to the beginning of the industrial revolution to evoke *in fine* Chaïm Weizmann's declaration calling upon the Jews of the entire world to fight alongside England in September 1939. And so what the gesture of revision demands is a widening of perspective—and at the same time a terrible shortcut. What it allows to appear in the interval is a multitude of exterminationist antecedents, the most recent being the long period of Bolshevism. "The refusal to replace the extermination of the Jews perpetrated under Hitler in this context responds perhaps to highly admirable motives, but it falsifies history" (21). The decisive shift in the discourse of Nolte himself occurs in the passage from comparison to causation: "What is called the extermination of the Jews perpetrated under the Third Reich was a reaction, a distorted copy and not a first or an original" (21). Three processes are added together here: the temporal widening of the context, the comparison with similar contemporary or earlier facts, the relation of causation from an original to a copy. Together, these propositions signify "the revision of perspective" (23). Whence the question: why does this past not pass, disappear? Why does it become ever more alive, vital and active, not, to be sure, as a model but as a foil? Because this past has been shielded from all critical debate by narrowing the field in order to concentrate on the "final solution": "The simplest rules holding for the past of all countries seem to have been abolished here" (31). These are the rules that require, as has been stated, widening the context, comparing, searching for ties of causation. They permit the conclusion that assassination for reasons of state by the Bolsheviks constituted "the logical and factual precedent" (34) for the racial killings by the Nazis, making the archipelago of the Gulag a "more original" event than Auschwitz.

This massive use of comparison settles the fate of singularity or uniqueness, since comparison alone permits the identification of differences—"the sole exception [being] the technique of gassing" (33). Once the critical debate has been widened in this way, Nolte expects it will allow this past "to pass" like any other and to be appropriated. What is not intended to pass in the final analysis is not the Nazi crime, but its unstated origin, the "Asiatic" crime, regarding which Hitler and the Nazis considered themselves to be the real or potential victims.

With respect to the comparison between the judge and the historian, Nolte places the historian at the opposite pole from the judge, who treats individual cases in a singular manner.[48] On another front, Nolte sets off a crisis between historical judgment and moral, juridical, or political judgment. It is at this juncture that the philosopher Habermas has intervened.[49] I will retain in this connection the relations between historiographical judgment and moral, juridical, or political judgment. Denouncing "the apologetic tendencies" of contemporary German history, Habermas questions the distinction between revision and revisionism. The three rules mentioned earlier—extension of the field, comparison, causal tie—are the pretext for "a kind of settling of damages" (207ff.). What he attacks is, therefore, not the historiographical program but the implicit ethical and political presuppositions, those of a neorevisionism affiliated with the tradition of national conservatism. To this core are attached: the retreat into the commonplaces of anthropology, the overly facile assignment by Heideggerian ontology of the specificity of the historical phenomenon to technical modernity, "the dimension of profundity in which all cats are grey" (222). Habermas hits the mark when he denounces the effect of exoneration resulting from the dissolution of the singularity of the Nazi crimes when they are assimilated to a response to the threats of annihilation coming from the Bolsheviks. We might expect, however, from arguments like those of Habermas, that they would include a reflection on the uniqueness of the Holocaust, not only in the order of moral and political judgment but specifically on the plane of historiography. Absent this discussion, the "distancing understanding" of the partisans of revision can be attacked only on the level of its moral connotations, the most tenacious of which is held to be the service of the traditional nation-state, that "conventional form of . . . national identity" (227)—to which Habermas opposes his "constitutional patriotism," which places allegiance to the rules of a state of law above belonging to a people. We then understand why the shame of Auschwitz must be removed from any suspicion of apology, if it is true that "a connection to universalist constitutional principles that was anchored in convictions could be formed only after—and through—Auschwitz" (227). On this point Habermas's plea links up with Osiel's in favor of a "liberal" memory, a "liberal" account, a "liberal" discussion. But then one has to confront, as Osiel does, the opposing arguments drawn from historiographical practice, if one wants to be accorded the right to couple the assumed singularity of Auschwitz and the voluntarist universality of constitutional patriotism.

To speak as a historian about "the uniqueness of the Nazi crimes" requires that one has already submitted the idea of uniqueness—or, as it is also called, of singularity—to analysis, as a critical philosophy of history demands.

To this end, I propose the following theses:

*Thesis 1:* Historical singularity is not moral singularity, which has been identified above with extreme inhumanity; this singularity by its excess with regard to evil, which Nabert calls the unjustifiable and Friedlander the unacceptable, is certainly not separable from identifiable historical traits; but it belongs to a moral judgment that has, so to speak, become unhinged.

It is therefore necessary to make an entire circuit on the historiographical plane to set into place a concept of singularity appropriate to historical judgment.

*Thesis 2:* With regard to historical singularity, in a primary and banally ordinary sense, every event that simply occurs on the plane of history as it is being made, every narrative sequence that is unrepeatable in time and space, and every contingent causal series in Cournot's sense, are singular; a possible tie to moral singularity results from the imputation of action to individualized agents and to every quasi person and quasi event, identified by a proper noun.[50] This initial approach to the concept of singularity on the plane of historical judgment concerns in an elective manner the historical debate surrounding the Holocaust, opposing the intentionalist school, for which what is most important are the acts of the leaders—in particular, the decisions concerning the "final solution"—to the functionalist school, more attentive to the play of institutions, to anonymous forces, to the behaviors of a population. What is at stake in this debate is ascribing responsibility for the crime to a range of subjects: to someone, to a group, to a people.[51] The greatest affinity is certainly to be found between the attention the partisans of the first school pay to acts imputable to individual agents and the criminal approach of the tribunals. The tension is greater between, on the one hand, moral and political judgment and, on the other, the functional explanation, which conforms more closely to the general tendencies of contemporary history. For this very reason, it is more susceptible to exonerating interpretations. We have seen historians relate the idea of singularity to the idea of temporal continuity within the framework of the self-understanding of the German people: the effect of rupture assigned to singularity can then just as easily be used as an exoneration—"The events of the Holocaust do not belong to the historical chain by which we identify ourselves"—or as an accusing argument—"How could a specific people be capable of such aberrations?" Other moral options are opened in this way: be it infinite lamentation and the leap into the abyss of melancholy, or the plunge into civic responsibility: "What must be done so that such things will never happen again?"

*Thesis 3:* In a second sense, singularity signifies incomparability, which is also designated by uniqueness. One moves from the first sense to the second by the use of comparison between events and actions belonging to the same series, to the same historical continuity, to the same identifying tradition; the exceptional character just mentioned stands out in this transitional sense. The presumed incomparability constitutes a distinct category when two heterogeneous historical ensembles are placed in confrontation:

this was already the case with the mass atrocities and exterminations of the past, among these the Terror in France, but mainly with the partially contemporary unfolding of the Bolshevik and Nazi regimes. Before saying anything regarding the causation of one in relation to the other, we have to be clear about the resemblances and differences involving the power structures, the criteria of discrimination, the strategies of elimination, the practices of physical destruction and moral humiliation. The Gulag and Auschwitz are in all these regards both similar and dissimilar. The controversy remains open concerning the proportion of resemblance and dissimilarity; it directly concerns the German *Historikerstreit*, once the alleged causation has been assigned to the model in relation to the copy. The perverse slippage from similarity to exoneration is made possible by assimilating the equivalence of crimes to the compensation of one by the other (we recognize the argument identified by Osiel under the title of the famous apostrophe: *tu quoque!*). The controversy concerns other peoples besides the Germans, inasmuch as the Soviet model served as the norm for the Western communist parties and, more broadly, for many anti-Fascist movements, for which the very idea of similarity between the two systems long remained anathema. Whatever the degree of resemblance between the two systems may be, the question remains regarding the eventual political will to imitation and the degree of constraint exerted by the model to the point that it might have made inevitable the politics of retaliation under the cover of which the Nazi crimes are held to have unfolded. The deviant uses of comparativism are doubtless easy to unmask along the blurred frontier that separates revision from revisionism. However, beyond these circumstantial quarrels, the problem remains regarding the honest use of comparativism on the plane of historiography: the critical point concerns the category of totalitarianism, adopted by Hannah Arendt among others.[52] Nothing prevents constructing under this term a class defined by the notion of mass atrocities (Osiel). Or, as I prefer, along with Antoine Garapon, by that of third-party crime, understanding by third party the state, defined by its primary obligation to assure the safety of anyone residing within the territory marked by its institutional rules which legitimate and bind it. It is then a simple matter to draw up within this framework the table of resemblances and differences between systems. Thus, the idea of incomparability properly carries meaning only as the zero degree of resemblance, hence within the framework of a procedure of comparison. The controversial questions then begin to multiply: Up to what point does a genus of classification constitute a common structure? And what relation exists between the presumed structure and the actual procedures of extermination? What latitude existed between the strategy programed at the top and all the levels of execution? One can argue about this. But, supposing that the thesis of incomparability applied to the Holocaust is plausible on the historiographical plane, the mistake would be to confuse the absolute exceptionality on the moral plane with incomparability relative to the historiographical plane. This confusion most often affects the thesis that the two systems, Bolshevik and Hitlerian, belong to the same genus, namely, to the totalitarian—even the assertion of the mimetic and causal influence of one crime on the other. The same confusion often affects the allegation of the absolute singularity of Nazi crimes. Inversely, it is hard to see how belonging to the same genus, here the totalitarian—even the mimetic and causal influence of one crime on the other—would have the virtue of exoneration for those who inherit the debt ensuing from a particular crime. The second use of the concept of singularity—the incomparable—does not erase the first—the nonrepeatable: the common genus does not prevent specific difference, as this is what matters to moral judgment assessing each crime taken individually. In this respect, I willingly plead for a properly moral singularity, in the sense of an absolute incomparability of the irruptions of horror, as though the figures of evil, by virtue of the symmetry between the admirable and the abominable, were of an absolute moral singularity. There is no scale of the inhuman, because the inhuman is outside of any scale, once it is outside of even negative norms.

Is there then no assignable connection between the moral usage of the ideas of uniqueness and incomparability and their historiographical usage? I do see one, which would be the idea of the exemplarity of the singular. This notion does not depend on moral evaluation as such; it does not belong to historiographical categorization; neither does it involve their superposition, which would be a return to equivocation and confusion. Rather, this idea takes shape along the path of reception on the plane of historical memory. The ultimate question, in fact, is knowing what responsible citizens make of a debate among historians and, beyond this, of the debate between judges and historians. Here, one finds Mark Osiel's idea of educational *dissensus*. In this respect, it is significant that the pieces on the *Historikerstreit* were printed in a widely circulated newspaper. The historians' debate, carried into the public arena, was already a phase of the democracy-producing *dissensus*. The idea of exemplary singularity can only be formed by an enlightened public opinion that transforms the retrospective judgment on the crime into a pledge to prevent its reoccurrence. Placed back in this way within the category of promising, the meditation on evil can be wrested away from infinite lamentation and disarming melancholy and, even more fundamentally, removed from the infernal circle of inculpation and exculpation.

Having set out to find an impartial yet not infallible third party, we end by adding a third partner to the pair formed by the historian and the judge, the citizen. The citizen emerges as a third party in the order of time: with a gaze that is structured on the basis of personal experience, variously instructed by penal judgment and by published historical inquiry. On the other hand, the intervention of citizens is never completed, placing them more on the side of the historian. But the citizen is in search of an assured judgment, intended to be as definitive as that of the judge. In every respect, the citizen remains the ultimate arbiter. It is the citizen who militantly carries the "liberal" values of constitutional democracy. In the final analysis, the conviction of the citizen alone justifies the fairness of the penal procedure in the courts and the intellectual honesty of the historian in the archives. And it is this same conviction that, ultimately, allows us to name the inhuman, retrospectively, as the absolute contrary of "liberal" values.

## INTERPRETATION IN HISTORY

The final internal limitation affecting history's reflection on its own project of truth is related to the notion of interpretation, whose concept we shall clarify below. The tardy acknowledgment of the theme of interpretation in our own discourse may seem surprising: could it not have made an appearance at the time and place we took up the theme of representation and, hence, within the framework of the epistemology of the historiographical operation? Instead we have made a different semantic choice which, it seems, better serves the scope of the concept of interpretation. Indeed, far from constituting, as representation does, a phase—even a nonchronological one—of the historiographical operation, interpretation belongs instead to the second-order reflection on the entire course of this operation. It draws together all the phases, thereby underscoring at one and the same time the impossibility of the total reflection of historical knowledge on itself and the validity of history's project of truth within the limits of its space of validation.

The amplitude of the concept of interpretation is still not fully recognized in a version that I consider to be a weak form of self-reflection, one ordinarily placed under the heading of "subjectivity versus objectivity in history."[53] It is not that this approach lacks justification; but it remains vulnerable to the charge of psychologism or sociologism, when it fails to situate the work of interpretation at the very heart of each of the stages of historiography. What indeed is underscored, in the canonical vocabulary of "subjectivity versus objectivity," is, on the one hand, the historian's personal commitment to the process of knowledge and, on the other hand, the historian's social—and, more precisely, institutional—commitment. The historian's twofold commitment constitutes a simple corollary to the intersubjective dimension of historical knowledge considered one province of the knowledge of others. More precisely, people of the past take on the twofold otherness of foreign and of past being, to which Dilthey adds the additional otherness formed by the mediation of inscription held to characterize interpretation among the modes of understanding: the otherness of the foreign, the otherness of past things, and the otherness of inscription join together to determine historical knowledge within the *Geisteswissenschaften*. The Diltheyan argument, which is also in part that of Max Weber and of Karl Jaspers, has found an echo in professional historians such as Raymond Aron and Henri-Irénée Marrou.

The principle thesis of Raymond Aron's doctoral dissertation, *Introduction to the Philosophy of History*, carried the subtitle *An Essay on the Limits of Historical Objectivity*.[54] It has often been received with suspicion as a result of some of its provocative expressions. The first section dealing with notions of understanding and meaning concludes with the "dissolution of the object" (118). This expression covers a moderate proposal: "No such thing as a *historical reality* exists ready made, so that science merely has to reproduce it faithfully. The historical reality, because it is human, is *ambiguous* and *inexhaustible*" (118). If the personal, social, and institutional commitment of the historian is underscored, "the necessary attempt at detachment, toward objectivity" (119) is no less taken into account: "This dialectic of detachment and appropriation tends to justify much less the uncertainty of the interpretation than the freedom of the mind (in which the historian has a share as well as the creator); it reveals the true goal of the science of history. This science, like all reflection, is, so to speak, as practical as it is theoretical" (119). Returning in the conclusion of the second section to the "limits of understanding" (151), Raymond Aron attempts to go beyond the acceptation of the term "understanding" such as he believes it is found in Jaspers and Weber. He seeks a balance between two other contrary and complementary meanings of the same expression. On the one hand, understanding implies "an objectification of psychological facts"; yet "what sacrifices does this objectification involve?" (152). On the other hand, understanding "always commits the interpreter. He is never like a physicist—he remains a man as well as a student. And he refuses to become a pure scholar because understanding, beyond knowledge, aims at the *appropriation* of the past" (152). The accent is then placed on "imperfect objectification," tied to the concrete conditions of the "communication between minds" (152). The final section, titled "History and Truth," carries the reflection toward the limits of historical relativism in the direction of an ontology of historical being, which would lead beyond the established framework in the direction of a philosophical conception of existence. The limits of objectivity are in fact those of a scientific discourse in relation to a philosophical discussion: "Man is historical" (319)—the final part of the work unceasingly hammers home this point. It is not without interest for the rest of our discussion that the final accent is placed on ridding historical necessity of its fatalism in the name of freedom that is always in project: "History is free because it is not written in advance, or determined as a sector of nature or a fatality; it is unpredictable, as man is for himself" (320). Ultimately, it is the decision-maker, the citizen, committed or detached as a spectator, who pronounces retrospectively the conclusion to a book devoted to the limits of historical objectivity: "Human life is dialectical, that is, dramatic, since it is active in an incoherent world, is committed despite duration, and seeks a fleeting truth, with no other certainty but a fragmentary science and a formal reflection" (347).

The parallel work by Henri-Irénée Marrou, *The Meaning of History*,[55] constituted, subsequent to Raymond Aron, the sole attempt at a reflection on history offered by a professional historian before Le Roy Ladurie in *Les Paysans de Languedoc* and Paul Veyne in *Comment on écrit l'histoire* (1972), and, of course, before Michel de Certeau (at least in the early editions). Defined as "the knowledge of man's past" (33), more precisely, "the scientifically elaborated knowledge of the past" (34), historical knowledge calls for the correlation between subjectivity and objectivity to the extent that it places in relation, through the initiative of the historian, the past of people who lived before and the present of those who live today. The intervention of the historian is not parasitic but constitutive of the mode of historical knowledge. Pointedly antipositivist words targeting Seignobos and his formula were perhaps isolated arbitrarily: "History is compiled with documents" (72). The historian, Marrou protests, is above all the one who puts questions to the documents. This art is born as hermeneutics. It continues as understanding, which consists for the most part in the interpretation of signs. It aims at "the encounter with the other," at "the reciprocity of consciousnesses." The understanding of others therefore becomes the historian's lodestar, at the cost of an *epoché* of the self in a true self-forgetting. In this sense, the subjective implication constitutes at one and the same time the condition and the limit of historical knowledge. The note characteristic of Henri Marrou, in relation to Dilthey and Aron, continues to be the accent placed on the friendship that makes us "connatural with others" (104). No truth without friendship. One recognizes the Augustinian mark in the talent of a great historian. The critical philosophy of history opens in this way onto the ethics of historical knowledge.[56]

If Marrou's work has not always been well received ("For pity's sake, let's not magnify out of proportion the role of the historian," Braudel protested), it is perhaps because the critique of objectivity was not sufficiently seconded by a parallel critique of subjectivity: it is not enough to mention in general terms an *epoché* of the ego, a forgetting of the self; one must bring to light the precise subjective operations capable of defining what I once proposed to call "good subjectivity"[57] in order to distinguish the self of research from the self of pathos.

Contemporary history, also termed history of the present day, constitutes a remarkable observation point for taking the measure of the difficulties arising between interpretation and the quest for truth in history. These difficulties do not stem principally from the inevitable intervention of subjectivity in history but from the temporal relation between the moment of the event and that of the narrative that reports it. With this sort of contemporary history, the archival work is still confronted with the testimony of the living, who themselves are often survivors of the event considered. It is this novel situation that is examined by René Rémond in his "Introduction" to *Notre siècle, 1918–1988*.[58] He says that, in relation to the rest of history, the history of the recent period presents a twofold singularity, which is acquired from the specificity of its object. This involves, first, contemporariness, in the fact "that it [the present] is none of the moments that make it up, the moments lived by the men and women among us who were witnesses to it" (7). The question is then to know if it is possible "to write the history of one's time without confusing two roles it is important to keep separate, the memorialist and the historian" (8). Next, it is the incompleteness of the period studied: there is no final endpoint from which to embrace a slice of duration in its ultimate signification; to objections by contemporaries in the first instance are likely to be added the refutations of events yet to come. Lacking this perspective, the main difficulty of the history of a too recent time is "establishing a hierarchy of importance to evaluate people and events" (11). Now the notion of importance is the place where, as we were saying, interpretation and objectivity intersect. The difficulty of forming a judgment is the corollary of the difficulty of setting things into perspective. The historian, it is true, will have added to her argument an involuntary result of her enterprise: she will have "softened the most severe judgments, nuanced the most admiring evaluation" (12). Can one, then, not reproach her for this "leveling off of differences" (12)?

The difficulties confronting the historian of the recent past rekindle earlier questions concerning the work of memory and, to an even greater extent, the work of mourning. Everything happens as though a history that is too close prevents recollection-memory from detaching itself from retention-memory, and quite simply prevents the past from breaking off from the present, what has elapsed failing to exert its mediating function of "no longer" with respect to "having been." To adopt another vocabulary that I shall adopt below, the difficulty here is that of constructing the sepulcher, the tomb for yesterday's dead.[59]

To speak of interpretation in terms of an operation is to treat it as a complex of language acts—of utterances—incorporated in the objectifying statements of historical discourse. In this complex several components can be discerned: first, the concern with clarifying, specifying, unfolding a set of reputedly obscure significations in view of a better understanding on the part of the interlocutor; next, the recognition of the fact that it is always possible to interpret the same complex in another way, and hence the admission of an inevitable degree of controversy, of conflict between rival interpretations; then, the claim to endow the interpretation assumed with plausible, possibly even probable, arguments offered to the adverse side; finally, the admission that behind the interpretation there always remains an impenetrable, opaque, inexhaustible ground of personal and cultural motivations, which the subject never finishes taking into account. In this complex of components, reflection progresses from utterance as an act of language to the utterer as the who of the acts of interpretation. It is this operating complex that can constitute the subjective side correlative to the objective side of historical knowledge.

This correlation can be detected at every level of the historiographical operation we have examined. Interpretation is indeed operating as early as the stage of the consultation of archives, and even before that, at the stage of their formation. A choice presided over their establishment: as Collingwood liked to say, "Everything in the world is potential evidence for any subject whatever" (quoted by Marrou, *The Meaning of History*, 311). However liberal the operation of collection and preservation of traces that an institution intends to keep of its own activity, this operation is unavoidably selective.

All traces do not become elements of an archive; an exhaustive archive is unthinkable, and every testimony does not figure in the archives. If we now pass from the stage of institution of archives to the consultation by a given historian, new difficulties of interpretation present themselves. However limited the archives may be in terms of the number of entries, at first sight they constitute an unlimited world, if not real chaos. A new factor of selection enters on stage with the play of questions guiding the consultation of the archives. Paul Veyne has spoken in this regard of the "lengthening of the questionnaire"; the questionnaire itself is not infinite and the rule of selecting questions is not transparent to the mind. Why be interested in Greek history rather than in Medieval history? The question remains for the most part without any clear response, unanswerable. With respect to the critique of the testimonies that constitute the hard core of the documentary phase, it assuredly belongs to the logic of the probable alluded to above. A crisis of credibility cannot, however, be completely avoided concerning the reliability of discordant testimony. How can one gauge trust and distrust with regard to the word of others, whose trace is carried in the documents? The work of clarification and argumentation, occasioned by the critique of testimony, is not without the risks proper to a discipline that Carlo Ginzburg defined by the "evidential paradigm." In this sense, the notion of documentary proof must be invoked with moderation; compared to the later stages of the historiographical operation, and taking into account the flexibility and requirements of a probabilistic logic, documentary proof is what, in history, most closely resembles the Popperian criteria of verification and falsification. Under the condition of a broad agreement among specialists, one can say that a factual interpretation has been verified in the sense that it has not been refuted at the present stage of accessible documentation. In this respect it is important to preserve the relative autonomy of the documentary stage on the plane of the discussion provoked by negationist positions concerning the Holocaust. The alleged facts are certainly not brute facts, even less are they doubles of the events themselves; they remain of a propositional nature: the fact that.... It is precisely as such that they are capable of being confirmed or disconfirmed.

The discussion concerning documentary proof thus leads quite naturally to the question of the relation between interpretation and explanation/understanding. It is at this level that the alleged dichotomy between the two terms is the most misleading. Interpretation is one component of explanation, its "subjective" counterpart in the sense we have stated. One first observes in it a concern for clarification, placed at the head of the operations of interpretation. On this plane the operation to be discerned involves the imbrication in the context of ordinary language of logically heterogeneous uses of the syntactical connector "because." Some of these closely resemble a causal connection or a law-like regularity in the domain of the natural sciences; others deserve to be called explanations in terms of reasons. Their indiscriminate juxtaposition has produced unilateral solutions in terms of "either ... or ...": on the one hand, by the proponents of the principle of the unity of science during the period of logical positivism, on the other, by the advocates of the distinction between the science of mind and the science of nature following Wilhelm Dilthey. The plea on behalf of an explicitly mixed model, in Max Weber or Henrik von Wright,[60] is to be understood as a form of clarification, in the sense of making plain, of laying out. It can be shown that the human capacity for acting within closed dynamic systems implies recourse to mixed models of explanation such as these. What remain relatively opaque are the personal preferences directing the preference accorded to this or that explanatory mode. In this regard, the discussion concerning the play of scales is particularly eloquent: Why is the microhistorial approach preferred? Why the interest in the historical movements that call for this approach? Why the preference for negotiation in situations of uncertainty? Or for arguments of justification in situations of conflict? Here, motivation reaches the underlying articulation joining the present of the historian to the past of the events recorded. What is more, this articulation is not entirely transparent to itself. Taking into account the place occupied by the question of the play of scales in the history of representations, it is the subtle connection between personal motivation and public reasoning that is implied in the correlation between (subjective) interpretation and (objective) explanation/understanding.

Having said this, there is little need to focus on the case of scriptural representation. However, it is at this stage that the danger of misunderstanding is the greatest as regards the dialectical nature of the correlation between objectivity and subjectivity. The often undifferentiated use of the terms "representation" and "interpretation" testifies to this. The substitution of one term for the other is not without reason, given all that has been said about the role of narrative, of rhetoric, and of the imaginary on the scriptural plane. Concerning the narrative, no one is unaware that one can always recount in another way, considering the selective nature of all emplotment; and one can play with different types of plot and other rhetorical strategies, just as one can choose to show rather than to recount. All this is well known. The uninterrupted series of rewritings, in particular on the level of narratives of great scope, testify to the untamable dynamics of the work of writing in which the genius of the writer and the talent of the artisan are expressed together. However, by identifying interpretation and representation without qualification, we deprive ourselves of the distinct instrument of analysis, interpretation already functioning at the other stages of historiographical activity. What is more, treating these two words as mere synonyms consecrates the aptly criticized tendency to separate the representative stratum from the other levels of historical discourse in which the dialectic between interpretation and argumentation is easier to decipher. It is the historiographical operation throughout its entire course and in its multiple ramifications that exhibits the correlation between subjectivity and objectivity in history. If this is indeed the case, then we must perhaps give up this equivocal formulation and speak frankly of the correlation between interpretation and truth in history.

This implication of interpretation at every phase of the historiographical operation finally commands the status of truth in history.

We owe to Jacques Rancière, in *The Names of History*,[61] a systematization of the results of his own reflections concerning this status. He places it under the sign of poetics, near to the point of intersection between what I term critical and ontological hermeneutics.[62] Essentially, this is a second-order reflection on Braudel's "new history," but it is also an evocation of Michelet upstream from the *Annales* historians and of Certeau downstream from them. It is a poetics in the sense that it is continually grappling with the polysemy of words, beginning with the homonymy that we have continually run into regarding the term "history" and, more generally, with the impossibility of establishing the place of history within discourse; between science and literature, between scholarly explanation and mendacious fiction, between history-as-science and history-as-narrative. The impossibility for history in particular, according to the *Annales* school, to elevate itself to the level of scientificity alleged to belong to a science of the social is exemplary in this respect. But how is one to go beyond the "either . . . or" that would result from a simple refusal to select one alternative? The scientific response, Rancière suggests, "belongs to a poetic elaboration of the object and the language of knowledge" (*The Names of History*, 7). It is the tie of the object to language that imposes the term "poetics": it is the "language of stories" that "was suited to the scientificity proper to historical science" (7). In relation to the scope assigned here to the problematic of interpretation on the three levels formed by the archive, explanation/understanding, and representation, Rancière's poetics may seem to be restricted to the phase of representation. In fact, this is not the case. The question of names harkens back, so to speak, from representation to the first workshop of history, to the extent that, as we have asserted here, historiography is writing, through and through; written testimonies and all the monuments and documents have to do with denominations, what the professional historian encounters under the heading of nomenclatures and other questionnaires. Already in the archives, the "captured words"[63] ask to be delivered. And the question arises: Will this be narrative or science? Or some unstable discourse between the two? Rancière sees historical discourse caught between the inadequacy of narrative to science and the annulling of this inadequacy, between a requirement and its impossibility.[64] The mode of truth belonging to historical knowledge consists in the play between this indeterminacy and its suppression.[65]

In order to direct this effort in a positive manner, Rancière turns to the concept of pact, which I have also had occasion to employ. He proposes not a double but a triple contract: scientific, which seeks the hidden order of laws and structures; narrative, which provides readability to this order; political, which relates the invisibility of the order and the readability of the narrative "to the contradictory constraints of the age of the masses" (9).[66]

Rancière has chosen to take as the touchstone for his poetics the operation of language by which Braudel, at the end of *The Mediterranean*, elevates the event-narrative of the death of Philip II to the level of the emblem of the death of the royal figure in his portrait of majesty. The entire problematic of representation by the historian is thus mobilized, but so too is that of its place in the great work directed against the primacy of the event. The primacy of the event is, therefore, at one and the same time toppled and restored, under penalty of seeing the historical enterprise itself dissolved into positive scientificity. Rancière completes my own analysis of the hidden narrative structure of the work as a whole by a study of the grammatical use of verb tenses in light of the distinction received from Benveniste between the narrative tense that recounts itself and the discourse tense in which the speaker engages himself. The distinction is perhaps not as operative as one would like in the case of Braudel's text. The conjunction between the royal function and the proper name of the dead king testifies, however, to the meeting of poetics and politics. The delegitimation of kings forming the backdrop to the death of this king does indeed announce the simultaneous rise of republican politics and of the historical discourse of legitimation, whether open or tacit, of this at once political and poetic regime.[67]

The study of the forms assumed by the articulation between historical knowledge and the pairs of figures and words is continued beyond the reflection on the dead king and the delegitimation of kings. History has always given voice not only to the dead but also to all the silent protagonists. In this sense, it ratifies "the excess of words" (24–41) in view of appropriating the words of the other. This is why the controversy over readings of, for example, the French Revolution is inexhaustible, history being destined to revisionism.[68] Here, words prove to be more than tools of classification: means of naming. Hence, one does not know whether "noble," "social," "order," "class" are proper or improper names; the retrospective illusion is the price paid for the ideology of the actors. This naming process is especially troubling when it concerns "the founding narratives" (42–60), in particular, the ones that gave a name to what followed the kings: France, the country, the nation, those "personified abstractions" (43). Event and name go together in this staging. That which is given to be seen is that which speaks. This granting of speech is particularly ineluctable in the case of the "poor," the anonymous, even when grievances, records, lend support. The substituted discourse is basically antimimetic; it does not exist, it produces the hidden: it says what these others might say. On the horizon of the discussion stands the matter of knowing whether the masses have found, in their own age, an appropriate discourse, between legend and scholarly discourse. What then becomes of the threefold contract of the historian? "A heretical history?" (88–103).

# CHAPTER 2

## History and Time

### READING GUIDELINES

The preceding chapter was devoted to the critical side of hermeneutics, a critique consisting, on the one hand, of establishing the limits for any claim to totalization and, on the other hand, of exploring the validity claims of a historiography aware of its limitations. In its negative form, the critique was directed, in turn, against the open declaration of *hubris* related to the absolute knowledge of "history itself" and against the disguised, and ordinarily unrecognized, forms of the same *hubris*; in its positive form, it took into account some of the most fruitful internal oppositions belonging to the self-knowledge of history, such as the pair formed by the judge and the historian, or, yet again, by the tension between interpretation and objectivity on the plane of scientific history.

The chapter that follows marks the passage from critical hermeneutics to an ontological hermeneutics addressed to the historical condition considered an unsurpassable mode of being.[1] The term "hermeneutics" continues to be taken in the sense of a theory of interpretation, as this was specified in the final section of the preceding chapter. As concerns the substantive form of the verb "to be"—"being," to which the term "hermeneutics" has been associated—it remains open to a number of acceptations, as we read in Aristotle's well-known declaration in *Metaphysics* 4.2: "There are many senses in which a thing may be said to be." I have argued elsewhere on the basis of this Aristotelian warning in exploring the resources of the interpretation that, among the various acceptations, privileges that of being as act and as power on the plane of a philosophical anthropology: it is in this way that I propose in the course of the present chapter to hold the "power to remember" (*le pouvoir faire mémoire*) to be one of these powers—along with the power to speak, the power to act, the power to recount, the power to be imputable with respect to one's actions as their genuine author. Nothing more will be said about being *qua* being. However, we shall consider as legitimate any attempt to characterize the mode of being that we are in each case in opposition to the mode of being characterizing beings other than ourselves, whatever the ultimate relation of this being to Being may be. By adopting this manner of entry into the problem, I situate myself *volens nolens* in proximity to Heidegger, with a reading limited by choice to *Being and Time*, one of the great books of the twentieth century.[2] If I accept the declaration with which this book opens: "This question has today been forgotten—although our time considers itself progressive in again affirming 'metaphysics'" (1), it is meant, as is indicated, to set my "investigation" in the wake of those of Plato and Aristotle, as I began to do in the earliest pages of this work. This obedience to the opening objurgation of *Being and Time*, inviting us to "a retrieve of the question of the meaning of being" (2), will not prevent this chapter from being conducted as a debate with Heidegger, which will give the present discussion a very different tone from that, more of complicity than confrontation, which will prevail in the following chapter on forgetting in the context of Henri Bergson's *Matter and Memory*.

Here are a few of the considerations that keep me in the proximity of the analyses of *Being and Time* and, at the same time, progressively involve me in controversy with them.

Let me cite first of all the attempt to distinguish the mode of being that we are in each case from the other modes of being in terms of the different manner of being-in-the-world and the overall characterization of this mode of being as care, considered in its theoretical, practical, and affective determinations. I all the more readily adopt this essential characterization as I have already presupposed it in a way by giving as the close referent to historiography social action performed in situations of uncertainty under the limitation of the production of the social bond and of the identities concerned. In this regard, it is legitimate to accept the ontological concept of ultimate reference, the Heideggerian *Da-sein*, characterized in a differential manner by care, in contrast to the modes of being of things that are simply given (Heidegger says *vorhanden*, "at hand," objectively present) and manipulable (*zuhanden*, "handy"). The metaphor of the hand suggests a type of opposition presupposed by Kant when he declared persons "ends in themselves," those beings that are not to be treated simply as means because they are as such "ends in themselves." The moral characterization is certainly elevated by this formula to an ontological rank. One can term "existentials" the categories that, following the manner of the analytic of Da-sein, specify the mode of being underlying the corresponding mode of apprehension: existence, resoluteness, conscience, self, being with.... Here, we are only following Aristotle's instructions in the *Nichomachean Ethics* that the method is in every instance determined by the nature of the subject to be studied. The existentials are modes of description of this sort. They are so called because they delimit existence, in the strong sense of the word, as a way of springing forth onto the stages of the world. One presupposes that it is possible to speak in a universal manner of being-human in diverse cultural situations, as is the case, for example, when reading Tacitus, Shakespeare, or Dostoyevsky, we say that we find ourselves in them. One also supposes that it is possible to distinguish the existential, as a domain appropriate to the sort of universality that Kant is held to have compared in his *Critique of Judgment* to the communicability of the judgment of taste, which, nevertheless, is lacking in cognitive objectivity, from the existentiell, as a receptive disposition, whether personal or communal, in the theoretical, practical, or affective order. It is sometimes difficult to maintain this distinction, as will be confirmed in the discussions conducted below on death and being-toward-death.

Permit me to express an initial reservation at this very general level of consideration. The Heideggerian discourse of care does not seem to me to make room for the very particular existential that is the flesh, the animate body, my own body, as Husserl had begun to develop this notion in his last works in line with the "Fifth Cartesian Meditation." It seems to me to be implied in the meditation on death, on birth, and on the between, the interval separating birth and death upon which Heidegger constructed his idea of historicity. This category of the flesh implies some way of bridging the logical gulf hollowed out by the hermeneutics of Da-sein between the existentials gravitating around the center of care and the categories in which the modes of being of things objectively present or handy are related. The capacity of the analytic of Da-sein to recognize and surmount this difficulty still remains to be demonstrated.

Second consideration: I am adopting the guiding idea of *Being and Time* that temporality constitutes not only a major characteristic of the being that we are, but the characteristic that, more than any other, signals the relation of this being to being *qua* being. I have all the more reason to embrace this idea as I hold, moreover, the acceptation of being as act and as power as the one most in keeping with a philosophical anthropology of the capable human being. In addition, being and power manifestly have to do with time as it appears in Hegel's *Logic*, to which Heidegger refers in his exordium. In this sense, time figures as a metacategory of the same order as care in *Being and Time*: care is temporal, and time is the time of care. Recognizing this status does not exclude considering many purportedly exemplary discourses in the history of the problem to be basically aporetical.[3] And this, moreover, is what Heidegger does in his critique of the "vulgar" category of time. I will by no means take part in this quarrel, with regard to which I have many reservations, but will focus instead on a single problem, as limited as others inherited from the philosophical tradition, namely, the capacity for an ontology of temporality to make possible, in the existential sense of possibility, the representation of the past by history and, before that, by memory. This manner of posing the problem is framed by the considerations that follow.

Third consideration: Heidegger proposes an analysis of temporality that articulates the three temporal instances of the future, the past, and the present. As in Augustine and, in his own way, Koselleck, the past—the pastness of the past—is understandable in its distinct constitution only when paired with the future quality of the future and the present quality of the present. Positing this is absolutely decisive with respect to a not yet explicit presupposition of our entire undertaking. It is indeed remarkable that the phenomenology of memory and the epistemology of history rest unawares on a form of pseudo-self-evidence, according to which pastness is held to be immediately perceptible, in the absence of the future, in an attitude of pure retrospection. It is recognized that memory bears, not by preference but exclusively, on the past. Aristotle's statement, which I like to repeat: "Memory is of the past," has no need to evoke the future to give meaning and vigor to its affirmation; the present, it is true, is implied in the paradox of the absent, a paradox, we have seen, that is common to the imagination of the unreal and to the memory of the earlier. But the future is in a way bracketed in the formulating of this past. And the present itself is not thematized as such in the targeting of the earlier. Is this not, moreover, what happens when one looks for a memory, when one invests oneself in the work of memory, even in the cult of memory? Husserl, in this way, developed at length a theory of retention and of remembering, while dealing only summarily with protention, as if it were a required symmetry. The culture of memory as *ars memoriae* is constructed on a similar abstracting of the future. But it is especially history that is involved methodologically in this eclipsing of the future. This is why what we shall be led to say later regarding the inclusion of futureness in the apprehension of the historical past will move strongly against the prevailing flow of the clearly retrospective orientation of historical knowledge. It will be objected against this reduction of history to retrospection that the historian, as a citizen and as actor of the history that is being made, must include in his motivation as an artisan of history his own relation to the future of the city. This is true, and we will give notice of this to the historian when the time comes.[4] It remains that the historian does not include this relation to the object of his study, to the theme that he cuts out of the elapsed past. We have observed in this regard that the investigation of the historical past implies only three temporal positions: that of the target-event, that of the events interspersed between this event and the temporal position of the historian, and finally the moment of the writing of history—three dates then, two of which are in the past, one in the present. The definition of history proposed by Marc Bloch, namely, "the science of men in time," must not mask this internal limit of the retrospective viewpoint of history: men in time are in fact men of earlier times, having lived before the historian writes about them. There is thus a provisional legitimacy for posing the question of the referent of memory and history under the condition of abstracting from the future. The question will then be to determine whether a solution to the enigma of pastness can be found within the limits of this abstraction.

To this non-thematized abstraction characterizing the twofold plane on which it operates—that of the phenomenology of memory and that of the epistemology of history—the hermeneutics of historical being opposes placing pastness into perspective in relation to the futureness of the present and the presence of the present. On this plane the temporal constitution of the being that we are proves more fundamental than the simple reference of memory and of history to the past as such. In other words, temporality constitutes the existential precondition for the reference of memory and of history to the past.

The Heideggerian approach is all the more provocative, since, unlike Augustine, the main accent is placed on the future and not on the present. Recall the startling declarations of the author of the *Confessions*: there are three presents, the present of the past which is memory, the present of the future which is expectation, and the present of the present which is intuition (or attention). This threefold present is the main organizer of temporality; in it is declared the internal tear that Augustine names *distentio animi* and that makes of human time the inadequate replica of divine eternity, that eternal present. Under the province of care, in Heidegger, "being ahead of oneself" becomes the pole of reference for the entire analysis of temporality, with its heroic connotation of "anticipatory resoluteness." It is a good working hypothesis to hold the relation to the future to be the one that induces the series of subsequent temporal determinations of historical experience following a unique mode of implication. As a direct result, the pastness that the historiographical operation isolates is placed into dialectical relation with the futureness that ontology promotes to the place of honor. One can, nevertheless, resist the suggestion that the orientation toward the future would be more fundamental, or, as will be stated later, more authentic and more original than the orientation toward the past and toward the present, by reason of the ontological density of being-toward-death, which will be seen to be closely tied to the dimension of the future; symmetrically, one can resist the tendency to reduce the relation to the present to being-busy: astonishment, suffering, and joy, along with initiative are notable magnitudes of the present that a theory of action and, by implication, a theory of history have to take into account.

Fourth consideration: in addition to the new manner of ordering the threefold division of temporal experience, Heidegger proposes an original hierarchical ordering of the modes of temporalization that will open unanticipated perspectives on the confrontation between philosophy and the epistemology of history. Three headings are given in *Being and Time* to the degrees of this internal hierarchy: temporality properly speaking—I would say, fundamental temporality—introduced by the orientation toward the future and which we will see is characterized by being-toward-death; historicity, introduced by the consideration of the interval that extends, or "stretches," between birth and death, and in which prevails in a certain way the reference to the past privileged by history and, before it, by memory; intratemporality—or being in time—in which predominates the preoccupation that makes us dependent in the present on things that are themselves present and manipulable "alongside which" we exist in the world. As we see, a certain correlation is established between the three levels of temporalization and the prevalence, each in its turn, of the three instances of future, past, and present.

By virtue of this correlation, one can expect that the confrontation between the ontology of historical being and the epistemology of history will be concentrated on the second level, as is suggested by the term *Geschichtlichkeit* which is assigned to it: the word is constructed by the substantive *Geschichte*, "history," by way of the adjective *geschichtlich*, "historical." (I will discuss the translation of the key words in due course.) The fact that the announced confrontation can nevertheless occur on the level of fundamental temporality is what I shall confirm in a moment. But before that I want to open the discussion that will cut through all the levels of analysis. It concerns the nature of the mode of derivation that presides over the transition from one level to the next. Heidegger characterizes this mode of derivation in terms of the degree of authenticity and primordiality that he sees decreasing from one level to the next as one approaches the sphere of gravitation of the "vulgar" conception of time. What is termed authenticity here lacks any criterion of intelligibility: the authentic speaks for itself and allows itself to be recognized as such by whomever is drawn into it. It is a self-referential term in the discourse of *Being and Time*. Its impreciseness is unequaled, except for that striking other term of the Heideggerian vocabulary: resoluteness, a term singularly associated with "being ahead of oneself" and which contains no determination, no preferential mark concerning any project of accomplishment whatsoever; conscience as a summons of the self to itself without any indication relative to good or evil, to what is permitted or forbidden, to obligation or interdiction. From start to finish, the philosophical act, permeated with *angst*, emerges from nothingness and is dispersed in the shadows. Authenticity suffers from this kinship with what Merleau-Ponty calls "wild being"; this is why the discourse it produces is constantly threatened with succumbing to what Adorno denounced as the "jargon of authenticity." The pairing of the authentic with the primordial could save it from this peril if primordiality were assigned a function other than that of reduplicating the allegation of authenticity. This would be the case, it seems to me, if by historical condition one were to understand, in accordance with what the expression suggests, an existential condition of the possibility of the entire series of discourses concerning the historical in general, in everyday life, in fiction, and in history. In this way, the twofold use of the word "history" would be justified existentially, as the set of events (facts), past, present, and to come, and as the set of discourses on these events (these facts) in testimony, narrative, explanation, and finally the historians' representation of the past. We make history and we make histories because we are historical. This is the "because" of existential conditionality. And it is upon this notion of existential conditionality that it is important to organize an order of derivation that would not be reduced to a progressive loss of ontological density but that would be marked by increasing determination on the side of epistemology.

This proposal concerning the mode of derivation from one level of temporality to another directs the style of the confrontation proposed here between the ontology of the historical condition and the epistemology of historical knowledge and, through it, with the phenomenology of memory. The order followed will be that upon which the theory of temporality in *Being and Time* is constructed: temporality, historicity, intratemporality. But each section will include two parts, one concerning the analytic of time, the other the historiographical reply.

Opening the debate between philosophy and history on the level of deep temporality may seem unexpected. As we know, Heidegger has not only placed the main emphasis on the future, in contrast to the retrospective orientation of history and memory, he also placed this futureness under the sign of being-toward-death, submitting in this way the indefinite time of nature and of history to the harsh law of mortal finiteness. My thesis here is that the historian is not left speechless by this radical manner of entering into the entire problematic of temporality. For Heidegger, death affects the self in its untransferable and incommunicable solitude: to assume this destiny is to bestow the seal of authenticity on the totality of experience thus placed in the shadow of death; resoluteness, "being-ahead-of-itself," is the figure in which care appears, confronted at the end by Da-sein's ownmost potentiality-of-being. How could the historian have anything to say on this level where authenticity and primordiality coincide? Should the historian be the advocate of "one dies," in which the rhetoric of the inauthentic fritters itself away? Yet it is this path that offers itself for exploration. I humbly suggest an alternative reading of the meaning of mortality, in which the reference to one's own body requires a detour through biology and the return to the self by way of a patient appropriation of a knowledge entirely outside of the mere fact of death. This reading without pretension would pave the way for a multiple attribution of dying: to the self, to close relations, to others; and among all these others, the dead of the past, which the retrospective gaze of history embraces. Would it then not be the privilege of history to offer to these absent ones of history the pity of an offer of burial? The equation between writing and sepulcher would thus be proposed as the reply furnished by the discourse of the historian to the discourse of the philosopher (section 1: "Temporality").

It is around the theme of *Geschichtlichkeit* that the debate between ontology and historiography tightens. Heidegger's use of the term is inscribed within a semantic history inaugurated by Hegel and relayed by Dilthey and his correspondent, Count Yorck. Heidegger enters the debate by way of the critique of the Diltheyan concept of the "connectedness of life," whose lack of ontological foundation he denounces. He marks his difference by placing the phenomenon of the "extension" between birth and death under the aegis of the more authentic experience of being-toward-death. He retains of the historiography of his own time only the ontological indigence of its guiding concepts accredited by neo-Kantianism. By opening the discussion in this way, the occasion is provided to test the sense Heidegger attaches to the derivation of temporalization from one level to another. I propose to supplement the approach in terms of ontological deficit by taking into account the resources of the existential potentiality of the historiographical approach that are contained, in my opinion, in certain strong points of the Heideggerian analysis: the distinction, on the very level of the relation to the past, between the past as what has elapsed, eluding our grasp, and the past as having-been and belonging as such to our existence as care; the idea of generational transmission, which gives to debt at once a carnal and an institutional coloration; and "repetition," the Kierkegaardian theme par excellence, by virtue of which history appears not only as the evocation of the dead but as the theater of the living of other times (section 2: "Historicity").

It is on the level of intratemporality—of being-in-time—that the ontology of Da-sein encounters history, no longer simply in its inaugural gesture and in its epistemic presuppositions, but in the effectivity of its work. This mode is the least authentic, for its reference to the measures of time places it in the gravitational sphere of what Heidegger considers the "vulgar" conception of time, which he credits to all the philosophers of time from Aristotle to Hegel, a conception whereby time is reduced to an anonymous series of discrete moments. Nevertheless, this mode is not stripped of all primordiality, so that Heidegger can declare it to be "co-primordial" with the preceding modes because "reckoning with time" is understood prior to any measurement, developing a remarkable categorial network that structures the relation of preoccupation connecting us to the things with which we busy ourselves. These categories—datability, what is of a public character, the rhythms of life—allow us to engage in an original debate with historical practice. This positive apprehension of the work of the historian affords me the opportunity to reread all the earlier analyses at the point where history and memory intersect. It seems to me that the ontology of the historical being who embraces its temporal condition in its threefold structure—future, past, present—is empowered to arbitrate the rival claims to hegemony in the closed space of retrospection. On the one hand, history would like to reduce memory to the status of one object among others in its field of investigation; on the other hand, collective memory opposes its resources of commemoration to the enterprise of neutralizing lived significations under the distant gaze of the historian. Under conditions of retrospection common to history and to memory the contest of priority is undecidable. It is this very undecidability that is accounted for in an ontology responsible for its epistemic counterpart. By replacing the present relation of history to the past, which once was but is no longer, against the backdrop of the great dialectic that mixes the resolute anticipation of the future, the repetition of the past as having-been, and the preoccupation with initiative and reasonable action, the ontology of our historical condition justifies the undecidable character of the relation of history to memory evoked as early as the prelude to part 2, devoted to the myth of the invention of writing in Plato's *Phaedrus* (section 3: "Within-Timeness: Being-'in'-Time").

The last word will be left to three historians who, joining the existentiell to the existential, testify to the "uncanniness" of history, under the sign of an aporia which, once understood, will cease to be paralyzing (section 4: "The Uncanniness of History").

§

## TEMPORALITY

### *Being-toward-Death*

It is first to Augustine that we owe the theme of the tridimensionality of the temporality assigned to the soul. Two major features, which will be reinterpreted by Heidegger, are underscored by Augustine: the original *diaspora* of the three dimensions, implying their impossible totalization and, corollary to this theme, the equal primordiality of the three instances. The first theme—I formerly spoke of "discordance" to translate *distentio animi* (in which one finds the *diastasis* of the Neoplatonists)[5]—is presented in the *Confessions* in a tone of lamentation: it is out of the "region of dissimilarity" that the soul emits its sighs. The second theme assumes in Augustine a form with which Heidegger will make a decisive break: the equal primordiality of the three temporal instances is distributed around a center which is the present. It is the present that shatters into three directions, in a way reduplicating itself each time: "there are three times, past, present, and future." Now, "the present of past things is memory; the present of present things is direct perception [*contuitus*; later we will find *attentio*]; and the present of future things is expectation" (*Confessions* 11.20).[6] To be sure, Augustine does not lack arguments: we see the past only on the basis of *vestigia*—images or imprints—present to the soul; the same is true for the present anticipations of things to come. It is, therefore, the problematic (and the enigma attached to it) of the presence of the absent that imposes the threefold reference to the present. One may object, however, that the *vestigia*, the traces, even assuming their presence has to be postulated, are not themselves viewed as belonging to the living present; it is not to them that we are attending but rather to the pastness of past things and to the futureness of things to come. It is, therefore, legitimate to suspect, as do the modern and postmodern critics of "representation," some "metaphysics of presence" surreptitiously slipped under the instance of presence in its capacity as the present of the present, this strange reduplicated present.[7] I plead elsewhere for a more poly-semic reading of the notion of the present: the present cannot be reduced to presence in something like the optical, sensorial, or cognitive sense of the term; it is also the present of suffering and enjoyment, and all the more so, the present of initiative, as celebrated at the end of Nietzsche's famous text referred to in the prelude to this third part of the present work.

Augustine must not be asked to solve a problem that is not his, the prob-lem of the possible relations with historical knowledge. On the one hand, his reflections on time place him, for what follows in the history of ideas, in line with what I characterized earlier as the school of inwardness, with the difficulty that results from it of dealing in equal measure with personal memory and collective memory. On the other hand, it is theology that is asked to interpret historical time. It would then be to *The City of God* and to the conception of the two cities that, following Henri Marrou, himself a good historian, one would have to pose the question of a possible relation between the theology of history and historiography.[8] And it is under the sign of what Pomian names chronosophy that the philosophical investigation of this relation between theology and historiography could be attempted. This would go beyond the boundaries of the present study.

The transition from Augustine to Heidegger is, at first glance, an easy one: it is suggested by the now well-known triad of the instances of tem-porality: past, present, and future. However, two major differences having to do with the respective contexts of the two thinkers hold them far apart. Augustine appears against the horizon of Christian Neoplatonism; Heideg-ger against that of German philosophy culminating in the neo-Kantianism of the early twentieth century. It happens that, for the schools belonging to this philosophical line, there is a problem regarding the possibility and the legitimacy of historical knowledge. In this respect, everything hangs on the passage from a critical philosophy of history, such as that offered in the preceding chapter of the present work, to an ontology of historicity or, as I prefer to say, of our historical condition. The very word "historicity" ex-presses the shift from the critical philosophy to the ontological philosophy of history. This change of front will be the culmination of the investigations that follow. But this critical moment is preceded by an analysis of fundamental temporality, held to be even more original; at first sight, historiography does not appear to be concerned at this level of extreme radicality. I shall state later in what unexpected way it stands as a legitimate partner even before the concept of historicity is thematized. Now, not only is this concept placed in a secondary position, but the access to the most radical level is itself interminably deferred in the text of *Being and Time*. First, the full sense of the philosophical place from which the question is asked must be given. This philosophical place is Da-sein, the name given to "this being which we ourselves in each case are" (6). Is it man? No, if by man we designate a being undifferentiated with regard to being; yes, if this being emerges out of its indifference and understands itself as that being who is concerned about its very being (10). This is why, along with Françoise Dastur, I am resolved to leave the term Da-sein untranslated.[9] This manner of entering into the problematic is of the greatest importance for we who pose the question of the referent of historical knowledge: this final referent was, in the view of Bernard Lepetit, acting-in-common in the social world. The temporal scales considered and traced by historians were based upon this final referent. Acting falls from this position along with man, taken in the empirical sense of the agent and patient of this action; understood in this way, man and his action belong to the category of *Vorhandensein*, which signifies the pure and simple objective presence of things. Fundamental ontology proposes a regression back before this objective presence, on the condition of making the question of the meaning of being—which, according to the first sentence of *Being and Time*, has today been forgotten—the ultimate question. This inaugural rupture, paid for by the untranslatability of the word Da-sein, does not exclude the exercise of a function of conditionality with respect to what the human sciences call human action, social action, to the extent that the metacategory of care occupies a central position in the hermeneutical phenomenology for which Da-sein constitutes the ultimate referent.[10] One must wait until chapter 6 of part 1, division 1, titled "The Prepatory Fundamental Analysis of Da-sein," before arriving at the thematization of care as the being of Da-sein. It is noteworthy that it is in terms of an affection, rather than as a theoretical or practical instance, that care offers itself to be understood, namely, as the fundamental affection of *Angst*, invoked here by virtue not of its emotional character but of its potentiality for openness with respect to the ownmost being of Da-sein confronting itself. It is fundamental that this openness be the openness to the totality of what we are, more precisely to the "structural whole" of this being confronting its being. This question of totality will accompany us throughout the remainder of these reflections.

The possibility of fleeing in the face of oneself is contemporaneous with the capacity of openness inherent in *Angst*. Section 41, "The Being of Da-sein as Care," can be considered the matrix of this preparatory fundamental analysis. It is indeed a question here of Da-sein's "structural whole" (*Being and Time*, 178). We find already sketched out here the theme of being-ahead-of-itself that announces the privilege accorded to the future in the constitution of primordial temporality. Ordinary psychology, which is also that of historians as well as of judges, can grasp of this structure of care only the shadow it casts on everydayness in the forms of taking-care-of (with regard to oneself) and of concern (for others); but "even in inauthenticity, Da-sein remains essentially ahead-of-itself, just as the entangled fleeing of Da-sein from itself still shows *the* constitution of a being that *is concerned about its being*" (180). Of importance to us is the following declaration: "For the present fundamental ontological study, which neither aspires to a thematically complete ontology of Da-sein nor even to a concrete anthropology, it must suffice to suggest how these phenomena are existentially based in care" (181). Care is thus posited as the master category of the analytic of Da-sein and endowed with a corresponding scope of meaning.[11]

As the remainder of our analyses will progressively confirm, what is most deeply important to me is the founding capacity of the hermeneutical phenomenology of *Being and Time* with regard to what is called here "concrete anthropology." The touchstone will be, to paraphrase what has just been quoted, "how these phenomena (the history of historians and the memory of ordinary people) are existentially based in care (and in the temporality of care)." My fear, to put it unabashedly, is that the hierarchical ordering of temporal instances in *Being and Time*—fundamental temporality, historicity, intratemporality—in terms of decreasing primordiality and of increasing inauthenticity will be an obstacle to the recognition of the resources of conditionality—and in this sense of legitimacy—that flow from the fundamental to the founded instance. Throughout the present chapter, this will be the guiding thread of my confrontation with the analytic of Da-sein.

It is especially noteworthy that the second section, titled "Da-sein and Temporality" (§45ff.), begins with a chapter that fuses two problematics: totality ("the possible being-a-whole of Da-sein," §46) and mortality ("the existential project of an authentic being-toward-death," §53). Everything is decided around this nexus of the vastness of total possible-being and the finitude of the horizon of mortality. Before having even begun to explore the strata of temporalization of all the registers of existence, we know that the entry into the dialectic of the instances of temporality will be by way of the future and that futureness is structurally barred by the finite horizon of death. This primacy of the future is implied in the theme of being-toward-death; this theme condenses, then, all the fullness of meaning glimpsed in the preparatory analysis of care under the heading of "being-ahead-of-itself." After this, the narrow nexus between the potentiality of being-a-whole and mortality is offered as a sort of summit from which the movement of step-by-step constitution of the derived instances of temporalization will later proceed. It is important to be clear on the two terms of the inaugural correlation as it is formulated in the title of the first chapter of division two: "The Possible Being-a-Whole of Da-sein and Being-toward-Death" (219). It is the structure of care that, by its very openness, imposes the problematic of totality and that confers on it the modality of potentiality, of possible being, as is summed up in the expression *Ganzseinkönnen* (potentiality of being-a-whole, possible being-a-whole): by whole is to be understood not a closed system but integrality, and in this sense, openness. And openness always leaving room for what is "outstanding" (*Ausstand*, §48), hence for unfinishedness. The term "incompleteness" is important to the extent that the "toward" of being-toward-death seems to imply some destination, some course completed. Is there not some clash between opening and closing, unfulfillable integrality and an end in the form of a barrier? Is not the almost unbearable tension that emerges in language in the form of an oxymoron, the completeness of the incomplete, strangely attenuated by the promotion of being-toward-death, which, in the Heideggerian text, appears to occult the earlier theme of the potentiality for being-a-whole? In order to restore the vigor of this last expression, must one not leave to the potentiality for being its openness by not rushing to add: a whole? This apparently anodine addition conceals the possibility of all the ensuing slippages: being-a-whole, being outstanding as being in suspension, being-toward-the-end, being-toward-death; along with these slippages, the backward redefinitions: the "toward" of being-toward-death proposes a sense of possibility—"being toward a possibility" (241)—which projects itself as a possibility closed upon the open possibility of the potentiality-of-being. Care's being-ahead-of-itself is thereby affected by its reformulation as "anticipation of possibility" (242).

So it is that death becomes "the ownmost possibility of Da-sein" (243), the ownmost, absolute, unsurmountable, certain in a nonepistemological kind of certainty, anguishing because of its indetermination. In this respect, the passage by way of the idea of the end, with its well-known polysemy, deserves to be underscored: the end that awaits Da-sein, that keeps a watch on it, precedes it, an end that is always and imminent.[12] I am not concealing my puzzlement at the conclusion of my rereading of this core chapter: have not the resources of the openness of the potentiality-for-being been closed off by the insistence on the theme of death? Is not the tension between opening and closing attenuated by the dominion exercised *in fine* by being-toward-death treated as being toward a possibility? Does not the *Angst* that places its seal upon the always imminent threat of dying mask the joy of the spark of life? In this respect, the silence of *Being and Time* regarding the phenomenon of birth—at least at this opening stage—is surprising. Along with Jean Greisch (*Ontologie et temporalité*, 283), I wish to mention the theme of "natality" (*Gebürtigkeit*) which, according to Hannah Arendt in *The Human Condition*, underlies the categories of the *vita activa*: labor, work, action. Should not this jubilation be opposed to what does indeed seem to be an obsession of metaphysics with the problem of death, as is expressed in Plato's *Phaedo* (64a) praising the "concern for dying" (*meletē tou thanatou*). If it is true that the banalization of dying at the level of the "they" amounts to flight, does not the anguished obsession with death amount to closing off the reserves of openness characterizing the potentiality of being? Must one not then explore the resources of the experience of the potentiality of being before its capture by being-toward-death? Must we not, then, listen to Spinoza: "Free man thinks of nothing less than of death and his wisdom is a meditation not on death but on life" (*Ethics*, part 4, prop. 67)? Does not the jubilation produced by the vow   which I take as my own   to remain alive until . . . and not for death, put into relief by contrast the existentiell, partial, and unavoidably one-sided aspect of Heideggerian resoluteness in the face of dying?

Against the backdrop of these perplexing questions, I propose to explore two paths which, each in its own fashion, prepare the way for what may be seen as a surprising dialogue between the philosopher and the historian on the subject of death.

It is first of all in contrast to the idea of death as the intimate possibility of one's ownmost potentiality of being that I would like to suggest an alternate reading of the potentiality of dying. In place of the short-circuit that Heidegger makes between the potentiality of being and mortality, I would prefer to substitute the long detour that follows. One theme, indeed, that seems to me to be lacking in the Heideggerian analysis of care is any consideration of the relation to one's own body, to the flesh, by virtue of which the potentiality of being adopts the form of desire in the broadest sense of the term, which includes *connatus* in Spinoza, appetite in Leibniz, *libido* in Freud, and the desire to be and the effort to exist in Jean Nabert. How does death come to be inscribed in this relation to the flesh? Here the long detour begins. I learn of death as the ineluctable destiny of the object-body; I learn of it in biology, confirmed by everyday experience; biology tells me that mortality constitutes the other half of a pair, of which sexual reproduction constitutes one half. Is this knowledge to be considered unworthy of ontology by reason of its factuality, its empirical character? Will it be relegated to the domain of *Vorhandenheit* or of *Zuhandenheit*, among the things objectively present or handy? The flesh perturbs this neat separation of modes of being. A separation which could prevail only if this objective and objectivizing knowledge of death were not internalized, appropriated, imprinted in the flesh of the living being, the being of desire that we are. Once the moment of distantiation has been superseded by the moment of appropriation, death is capable of being inscribed within self-understanding as one's own death, as the mortal condition. But at what price? Biology teaches only a general, generic "it must be so": because we are this sort of living being, we must die, there is for us a "having to die." But, even internalized, appropriated, this knowledge remains heterogeneous to the desire to live, to want to live, this carnal figure of care, of the "potentiality of being-a-whole." It is only at the end of a long work on oneself that the entirely factual necessity of dying can be converted, not to be sure into the potentiality-of-dying but into the acceptance of having to die. This is a question of a unique kind of "anticipation," the fruit of wisdom. At the limit, at the horizon, loving death like a sister, after the manner of the *poverello* of Assisi, remains a gift that depends on an economy inaccessible even to an existentiell experience as singular as the apparent stoicism of a Heidegger, the economy placed by the New Testament under the term *agape*. If one persists in distinguishing the primordial existential from the variety of existentiell positions stemming from different cultural traditions or personal experiences, the gap remains at this primordial level between wanting to live and having to die: the latter makes death an interruption, at once ineluctable and random, of the most primordial potentiality of being.[13] Bridging this gap through acceptance remains a task we must all engage in, and one that we face up to more or less successfully.[14] But, even when it is accepted, death remains frightening, anguishing, precisely because of its radical heterogeneity in relation to our desire, and because of the cost that its reception represents. Perhaps, on this first path—the way of externality and of factuality—we have not even reached the center of intimacy from which death proceeds and that will be recognized only by following the second path.

The detour proposed by this second path is no longer the way of externality and factuality but of plurality. What is there to say about death in light of our manner of being among other humans—regarding the *inter-esse* that Heidegger expresses in the vocabulary of *Mitsein*? It is astonishing that for him the death of others is held to be an experience that does not measure up to the demand for radicality rooted in *Angst* and explicated on the level of discourse by the concept of being-toward-death. That inauthenticity haunts the experience of the death of others is not in doubt: the secret admission that the death that has carried off the close relation dearest to us has, in fact, spared us opens the path for a strategy of avoidance by which we hope that it will also spare us the moment of truth in the face of our own death. But the relation of the self to itself is likewise not immune from ruses just as cunning as this. What it is important to plumb instead are the resources of veracity concealed in the experience of losing a loved one, placed back into the perspective of the difficult work of reappropriation of the knowledge about death. Along the road that passes through the death of the other—another figure of the detour—we learn two things in succession: loss and mourning. As for loss, separation as rupture of communication—the deceased, someone who no longer answers—constitutes a genuine amputation of oneself to the extent that the relation with the one who has disappeared forms an integral part of one's self-identity. The loss of the other is in a way the loss of self and as such constitutes a stage along the path of "anticipation." The next step is that of mourning, evoked on several occasions in this book. At the end of the movement of internalization of the love object that has been lost forever, the reconciliation with this loss—in which, precisely, the work of mourning consists—begins to take shape. Are we not able to anticipate, on the horizon of this mourning of the other, the mourning that would crown the anticipated loss of our own life? Along this road of redoubled internalization, the anticipation of mourning that our close relations will have to go through at the time of our disappearance, can help us to accept our own future death as a loss with which we strive to reconcile ourselves in advance.

Must we take one additional step and receive a message of authenticity from the death of all those others who are not close relations? This is the place once again to redeploy the triad of the self, close relations, and others, as we attempted to do above with respect to the problem of the attribution of memory. I count on this redeployment to open for us the problematic of death in history, which is our target here. One moves too fast, in my opinion, when one traces back to the "they" the sum of inauthentic relations. In addition to the fact that the idea of justice, evoked in the context of the presumed duty of memory, refers to the position of a third party in interpersonal relations, the death of all these others contains a lesson that neither the relation of the self to itself nor the relation to those close to us could ever provide. Loss and mourning display, on the reputedly banal level of the "they," unprecedented forms that contribute to our most intimate apprenticeship of death. There is, in fact, one form of death that is never encountered in a pure form, if one may call it so, except in the sphere of public existence: violent death, murder. There is no way of avoiding this new detour, which is already a detour through history, but also a detour through politics. The fear of violent death is, as we know, considered by Hobbes to be a necessary stage in the passage toward a contract to be made by all the members of a historical community in favor of a sovereign, not party to the contract. Violent death cannot be hastily numbered among those things entirely given and at hand. It signifies something essential concerning death in general and, in the final analysis, concerning our own death. The death of those close to us upon which we prefer to meditate is, in fact, an "easy" death, even if it is disfigured by the horror of agony. Even then it comes as a deliverance, an easing of pain, as the face of the deceased gives us to see, in accordance with the secret wish of the survivors. Violent death cannot be tamed so easily. In the same way, suicide, as murder turned against oneself, when it touches us, repeats the hard lesson. What lesson? That, perhaps, every death is a sort of murder. This is the intuition explored by Emmanuel Levinas in some strong pages of *Totality and Infinity*.[15] What murder—raised to the level of a founding paradigm by the murder of Abel by his brother Cain—lays bare and what the simple disappearance, the departure, the cessation of existing in the death of close relations does not express, is the mark of nothingness, made by the intention to annihilate. Alone, the "passion for murder" exhibits this mark.[16] Levinas goes straight to the ethical response that this passion provokes: the moral impossibility of annihilation is henceforth inscribed in every face. The interdiction of murder replies to a frightening possibility and is inscribed in this very possibility. But, in addition to this great lesson that inaugurates the entrance into ethics, murder, which is fundamentally death inflicted on others, is reflected in my relation to my own death. The feeling of imminence, which precedes all knowledge about death, is given to understanding as the imminence of a threat coming from an unknown point of the future. *Ultima latet*, repeats Levinas: "In death I am exposed to absolute violence, to murder in the night" (*Totality and Infinity*, 233). An unsettling malevolence of the Other advances toward me—against me: "as though murder, rather than being one of the occasions of dying, were inseparable from the essence of death, as though the approach of death remained one of the modalities of the relation with the Other" (234). Silent regarding the eventual aftermath of death ("nothingness or...recommencement? I do not know" [234]), Levinas is clear and firm regarding the before, which can only be a being-against-death and not a being-toward-death. Life? A project in suspension against a horizon of a "pure menace, which comes to me from an absolute alterity" (235). Fear, not of nothingness but of violence and, in this sense, "fear of the Other" (235).[17] To Heideggerian being-toward-death, Levinas opposes a despite-death, an against-death, which opens a fragile space of manifestation for "goodness liberated from the egoist gravitation" (236).[18]

In addition to the ethical—and political—teaching that Levinas elicited from this meditation on the violence of death,[19] I would like to evoke one of the figures assumed by mourning that corresponds to the loss sharpened by the "passion for murder." This figure sets us on the path toward the coming reflections on death in history. What indeed could a peaceful, dignified vision of the threat signified by violent death be? Would this not be the presumed banality of the "one dies?" Could not this banality contain its own force of ontological attestation? This would be the case if we were able to contemplate the threat that our desire will be interrupted as an equitable equalization: just as everyone else, before me and after me, I too must die. With death ends the time of privileges. Is this not the message transmitted by the sober narrative of the death of the Patriarchs in the Torah so dear to Levinas: "He died and was gathered to his father's kin"; "breathed his last, and was gathered to his father's kin?"[20]

### Death in History

Is the historian condemned to remain speechless in the face of the solitary discourse of the philosopher?

The thesis of this section is that, despite Heidegger's explicit discussions and, more particularly, despite the radical nature of the theme of fundamental temporality and of its distance from any historiographical thematic, a dialogue between the philosopher and the historian is possible at the very level established by Heidegger, that of being-toward-death.

Besides the redeployment of this theme suggested by the alternative readings proposed just above, the text of Being and Time proposes other openings in the direction of a common space of confrontation.

First opening: the great chapter on being-toward-death is followed by a meditation devoted to the theme of Gewissen (a term translated by "conscience"). This concept is immediately associated in Heidegger with that of attestation (*Bezeugung*). Attestation is the mode in which the concept of the potentiality-of-being-a-whole and that of being-toward-death are given to be understood. One can speak in this regard of attestation of the future, attestation of the very futureness of care in its capacity of "anticipation." However, in truth, attestation has as its full vis-à-vis our historical condition deployed in its three temporal ecstasies. It is, moreover, possible to consider testimony, as we have encountered it in the present work, in its retrospective forms, in everyday life, in the courts or in history, as the correlate of the past of attestation bearing on the potentiality-of-being apprehended in the figure of anticipation. The role of making-possible, assigned to the metacategory of our historical condition, finds the opportunity to be actualized in the correlation between the attestation of the future and the attestation of the past. To this must be joined the attestation of the present as it concerns the "I can," the verbal mode of all the verbs of action and passion that in *Oneself as Another* express the capable being: capable of speech, of action, of narrative, of imputation; this certainty of the present frames the attestation of the future and the witnessing of the past. The force of Heidegger's text is to permit attestation to radiate out from the future of anticipation toward the past of retrospection.

Second opening: the ontology of the potentiality-of-being/potentiality-of-dying does not leave pastness in a relation of externality or of adversarial polarity, as is still the case with the concepts of the horizon of expectation and of the space of experience in Koselleck and in our own analyses; Koselleck, moreover, did not fail to underscore, as we noted earlier, the singular nature, like a de facto structure, of the "experience of history." According to *Being and Time*, "anticipation" implies pastness. But in what sense of the term? Here, a decision is taken whose indirect consequences for history are immense: it is not as already elapsed and beyond reach of our will to mastery that the past is intended after-the-fact as "having been." In this respect, the decision that is apparently merely semantic to prefer *Gewesenheit*—the quality of having been—to *Vergangenheit*—the past that has elapsed and disappeared—to express pastness has a close affinity with the movement that leads the critical philosophy of history back to the ontology of the historical condition. We have many times anticipated this priority of "having been" over the past as elapsed in the following terms: the "no longer" of the past, we have said, should not obscure the intention of historians whose gaze is directed toward the living who existed prior to becoming the "absent of history." It is of the greatest importance that this redefinition of the past be introduced for the first time within the framework of the analysis of fundamental temporality, that of care (*Being and Time*, §65), before taking into account the theme of historicity and the specific problem of history. The tie between futureness and pastness is assured by a bridging concept, that of being-in-debt. Anticipatory resoluteness can only be the assumption of the debt that marks our dependence on the past in terms of heritage.[21] In the chapter on *Gewissen*, the notion of debt (German, *Schuld*) had already been stripped of its sting of indictment, of guilt, which may seem regrettable in the case of a historical judgment on notorious crimes, such as those mentioned earlier in connection with the debates of the German historians, among others. Was Heidegger excessive in removing its moral character from the concept of debt? I think that the idea of fault must take its place at a very specific stage of historical judgment, when historical understanding is confronted with admitted wrongs; the notion of wrongs done to others then preserves the properly ethical dimension of the debt, its dimension of guilt. We shall say as much in my chapter on forgiveness. But before that, it is good to make use of a morally neutral concept of debt, one that does not express more than a heritage transmitted and assumed, and one that does not exclude a critical inventory.

This concept of heritage-debt comes to take its place under that of standing for proposed in the framework of the epistemology of historical knowledge as the guardian of the referential claim of historical discourse: that the constructions of the historian can have the ambition of being tangentially, so to speak, the reconstructions of what actually took place "as though actually having been," according to the words of Leopold von Ranke, is what the concept of standing for means. However, we were not able to conceal the problematical character of this concept on the very level on which it was articulated. It remains as though suspended, after the fashion of a bold claim posited on the horizon of the historiographical operation. In this regard, being-in-debt constitutes the existential possibility of standing for. Whereas the notion of standing for remains dependent, in the structure of its meaning, on the deliberately retrospective perspective of historical knowledge, being-in-debt constitutes the reverse side of anticipatory resoluteness. In the following section we shall say what the historian can retain of this consideration of "anticipation" on the derivative plane of historicity where, precisely, the dialogue between the philosopher and the historian is taken up.

It is, therefore, under the sign of being-in-debt that having-been predominates in terms of ontological density over the being-no-longer of the elapsed past. A dialectic is begun between "having-been" and "elapsed" that is a great resource for the dialogue between the historian and the philosopher, and for the latter's own work. All the same, we have to preserve the legitimacy of each of the two terms of the pair. Here, we can offer resistance to Heidegger's analysis, for which the determination of the past as elapsed must be considered an inauthentic form of temporality, dependent upon the vulgar concept of time, the simple sum of fleeting nows.[22] It is at this point that the treatment of the qualifiers "authentic" and "inauthentic" is revealed to be inadequate to the possibilizing function assigned to ontological conceptuality, rendering the dialogue between the philosopher and the historian difficult if not impossible. In this regard, this dialogue requires that justice be done to the concept of the elapsed past and that the dialectic of "having been" and "no longer" be reestablished in all its dramatic force. Certainly, there is no doubt that the "simply elapsed" bears the mark of the irrevocable and that the irrevocable, in its turn, suggests the powerlessness to change things; in this sense, the elapsed is drawn to the side of the handy and the objectively present (*vorhanden* and *zuhanden*), categories deemed inadequate to the ontological tenor of care. However, the not-at-hand, not objectively present character of the past does indeed seem to correspond in the practical sphere to absence in the cognitive sphere of representation. It is here that the coupling between being-in-debt—an ontological category—and standing for—an epistemological category—proves to be fruitful, to the extent that standing for raises to the epistemological level of the historiographical operation the enigma of the present representation of the absent past, which, as has been sufficiently repeated, constitutes the primary enigma of the mnemonic phenomenon. But *Being and Time* ignores the problem of memory and only touches episodically on the problem of forgetting. Later we shall consider the consequence of this omission on the plane of historicity and of the debate with historiography. One can, however, deplore this absence already in the radical analysis of care, the level on which the decision is made to oppose "having been"—more authentic—to the "elapsed" past—less authentic. The debate between the philosopher and the historian has everything to gain from re-establishing the dialectic of presence and absence, inherent in every representation of the past, whether mnemonic or historical. The intention of the past as having been comes out of this reinforced, once having-been signifies having been present, living, alive.

It is against this dialectical backdrop that the historian makes a specific contribution to the meditation on death.

How, indeed, could one ignore the simple fact that in history one is concerned with practically nothing but the dead of other times? The history of the present day forms a partial exception, inasmuch as it calls the living to its bar. However, they are summoned as surviving witnesses of events that are in the process of slipping away into the absence of time elapsed; often as inaudible witnesses, as the extraordinary events to which they bear witness appear inconceivable when measured in terms of the ordinary understanding of contemporaries. Thus they may seem further "removed" than any distant past. Sometimes the witnesses die as a result of this lack of understanding. It will be objected that this emphasis on death in history is relevant only in a history of great events that takes into account only the decisions and great passions of a few prominent individuals; in addition it will be objected that this coupling of event and structure grinds into anonymity the feature of mortality posited in the case of individuals taken one by one. Yet, to begin with, even in the perspective of a history in which structure prevails over events, the historical narrative causes the features of mortality to re-emerge on the level of entities treated as quasi characters: the death of the Mediterranean as the collective hero of sixteenth century political history confers upon death itself a magnitude proportional to that of a quasi character. In addition, the anonymous death of all these people who do no more than pass across the stage of history silently poses to meditating thought the question of the very sense of this anonymity. It is the question of "one dies" to which we earlier attempted to restore ontological density, under the twofold sign of the cruelty of violent death and the equity of death as it levels all destinies. This is indeed the death at issue in history.

But in what way and in what terms?

There are two ways of replying to this question. The first is to make the relation to death appear as one of the object-representations which the new history has chosen to inventory. There is indeed a history of death—whether in the West or elsewhere—which constitutes one of the most remarkable conquests in the domain of the history of *mentalités* and of representations. But, if this "new object" may seem unworthy of holding the attention of the philosopher, the same is not true of death as it is implied in the very act of doing history. Death is then mingled with representation in its role as historiographical operation. Death marks, so to speak, the absent in history. The absent in historiographical discourse. At first sight, the representation of the past as the kingdom of the dead seems to condemn history to offering to our reading no more than a theater of shadows, stirred by survivors in possession of a suspended sentence of death. One escape remains: considering the historiographical operation to be the scriptural equivalent of the social ritual of entombment, of the act of sepulcher.

Sepulcher, indeed, is not only a place set apart in our cities, the place we call a cemetery and in which we depose the remains of the living who return to dust. It is an act, the act of burying. This gesture is not punctual; it is not limited to the moment of burial. The sepulcher remains because the gesture of burying remains; its path is the very path of mourning that transforms the physical absence of the lost object into an inner presence. The sepulcher as the material place thus becomes the enduring mark of mourning, the memory-aid of the act of sepulcher.

It is this act of sepulcher that historiography transforms into writing. Michel de Certeau is the most eloquent spokesperson in this regard for the transfiguration of death in history into sepulcher by the historian.

In the first instance, as it is apprehended in *L'Absent de l'histoire*, death is that which history misses. We have already mentioned, at the time of the encounter between Certeau and Foucault, the suspicion addressed to the latter that he did not go as far as would have seemed to be required by "outside thinking," "the black sun of language."[23] This is the harsh consequence of a discourse on deviation: "the change of space in which discourse is produced has as its condition the break that the other introduces into the same" (*L'Absent de l'histoire*, 8), the other appearing only "as the trace of what has been" (9). History will then be this "discourse" organized around a "missing present" (9). Can the voices of the living still be heard? No: "A literature is produced on the basis of definitively silent imprints, what happened will never return and the voice is lost forever and it is death that imposes muteness on the trace" (11). This advance in the meditation on absence was necessary to give its full force to the theme of the sepulcher.[24] The sepulcher appears indeed to exhaust its effect in the act that "renders present in language the social act of existing today and provides a cultural point of reference for it" (159). Alone, the self-positing of the social present appears to compensate for the act that relegates the past to its absence. Absence is then no longer a state but the result of a work of history, the true machine for producing gaps, giving rise to heterology, that *logos* of the other. The image of the cemetery devoted to the deceased then flows naturally from the pen. It is, above all, the strong image of the definite absence of the deceased, the response to the denial of death, a denial that masks itself in the fiction of verisimilitude.

In this moment of suspension, Michelet's discourse appears to be that of "the literary hallucination (the return, 'resurrection') of death" (179). The traces, however, are mute and all that is "still speaking" is the narrative of history: "It can speak of the sense of absence made possible when there is no place other than discourse" (170). The theme of the cemetery then simply outstrips that of absence: "The writing of the historian makes room for lack and it hides it; it creates these narratives of the past which are equivalent to cemeteries in cities; it exorcizes and affirms a presence of death in the midst of the living" (103).

The reversal takes place at the very heart of the cemetery theme, under the sign of the equation between writing and sepulcher. This strong tie is pronounced in a few magnificent pages of *The Writing of History*.[25] It is first in terms of place that sepulcher is evoked. This place in discourse has as its counterpart the place of the reader to whom the writing of history is addressed. The passage from sepulcher-place to sepulcher-act is effected by what Certeau calls "a literary inversion of procedures belonging to research" (100). According to him, this gesture has two aspects. On the one hand, writing, like a burial ritual, "exorcizes death by inserting it into discourse" (100), but this is also done to perfection in the portrait gallery. The fantasy of the Dance of Death, thus, seemed to be confirmed: "Writing places a population of the dead on stage—characters, mentalities, or prizes" (99). On the other hand, writing performs a "symbolic function" which "allows a society to situate itself by giving itself a past through language" (100). A dynamic relation is established in this way between two places, the place of the dead and the place of the reader.[26] Sepulcher-as-place becomes sepulcher-as-act: "Where research had brought about a critique of current models, writing constructs a *tombeau* for the dead. . . . Thus it can be said that writing makes the dead so that the living can exist elsewhere" (100–101). This "scriptural conversion" (100) leads further than simple narrativity; it plays the role of performative: "Language allows a practice to be situated in respect to its *other*, the past" (101). It is not merely narrativity as such which is superseded in this way, but along with it the function of alibi, of the realist illusion which pulls "producing history" to the side of "telling stories" (102); performativity assigns a place to the reader, a place that has to be filled, a "something that must be done" (101).

Echoing these strong words, Jacques Rancière analyzes the theme of the "dead king" in *The Names of History*. He first notes that death in history is not directly the indiscriminate death of anonymous people. It is, primarily, the death of those who bear a name; death that is an event. But it is already a death that joins a proper name to a function and lends itself to the metonymous transfer to the institution: the death of the king is, by reason of the "excess of words," the delegitimation of kings. Besides the ordinary death of Philip II, at what could be termed the Hobbesian crossroads of poetics and politics, the "poetics of knowledge" meets up with the violent death of Charles I of England, which metaphorically evokes the peril of death that each man encounters in the natural condition, but also the death of the political body as such. And then, moving further, there is the death of those tortured by the Inquisition: two extreme testimonies of the relation of speaking-being with death are brought together in this way, regicide and the Inquisition (*The Names of History*, 74); death redeemable by history in opposition to death that is unredeemable, the author notes. This is the occasion for him to connect the problematic of place, which will turn out to be the tomb, to that of the discordant and errant discourses that are related in Emmanuel Le Roy Ladurie's *Montaillou* and Certeau's *Mystic Fable*. The historian then appears as the one who, in a variety of ways, makes the dead speak. And the democratic destitution of the figure of the king was necessary in order to recover the silent voices of the poor and the masses, and through them, common death. For the king dies just like everyone else. And it is here that Rancière joins Certeau. Unknown to Braudel, who lets himself into the king's chambers along with the ambassadors, what matters and what Braudel was not concerned with, are "the conditions in which the writing of the knowledgeable historical narrative takes place in the democratic age, of the conditions of articulation of the threefold—scientific, narrative, and political—contract" (21). Henceforth, "the death drive inherent in the scholarly belief in history" (41) emerges not simply from the figure of the dead king alone, but from the death signified by the completed character of the historical past. It is death on a grand scale that Michelet, the Romantic historian, preceding the scientific language of the *Annales*, exorcizes.[27] This mass death attains readability and visibility at the same time as the "Republican-Romantic" paradigm of history. Death in history, I would say, is inherent in what Rancière calls "the founding narrative" (42ff.). It is death on the scale of the past as it is completed, elapsed. It is "the inclusion of death in science, not as residue but as a condition of possibility. . . . There is history because there is a past and a specific passion for the past. And there is history because there is an absence of things in words, of the denominated in names" (63). A twofold absence, then: of "'the thing itself' that is *no longer there*" and of the event that "never was—because it never was *such as it was told*" (63). Here we find our entire problematic of the relation of memory and history to the absence of the before, joined here by the theme of death in history. Without going as far as the distinction dear to me between the elapsed, the completed, and "havingbeen," Rancière, placing himself in the wake of Michelet, ventures to speak of "the supplement of life," contemporaneous with the "excess of words," even "the redemption of absence" (64), which could be a theme taken from Walter Benjamin. In any event, it is the function of discourse as the place of language to offer soil and a tomb to the dead of the past: "The ground is an inscription of meaning, the tomb a passage of voices" (66). Whence we hear the voice of Certeau assigning two symmetrical places to the reader and to the dead. For one and the other, language is "death, calmed down" (74).

In proffering this discourse, the historian gives a response to the philosopher in the process of "having it out with" the Heideggerian theme of being-toward-death. On the one hand, the ontology of historical being contributes its full justification to this scriptural conversion by reason of which a present and a future are opened up prior to the retrospective discourse of history. In return, the historian's own interpretation of this operation in terms of sepulcher helps to reinforce the philosopher's attempt to oppose to the ontology of being-toward-death an ontology of being-in-the-face-of-death, against-death, in which the work of mourning would be taken into account. An ontological version and a historiographical version of the work of mourning would thus join together in a sepulcher-discourse in two voices.

## HISTORICITY

The second level of temporalization in the order of derivation, Heidegger names *Geschichtlichkeit*. This is the level at which the philosopher is held to encounter the epistemological claims of historiography. It is also at this level, as at the following one, that the sense of the derivation of levels invoked by Heidegger is decided. To the derivation in terms of decreasing orders of primordiality and authenticity, I would like to oppose a derivation in terms of the existential condition of possibility with respect to historical knowledge. Now, this different modality of derivation can be interpreted as an increase of intelligibility as much as a diminution of ontological density.

A prior question arises: how should one translate in French (or in English) the German *Geschichtlichkeit*? Most of the French translators of *Being and Time* have opted for "historialité" in order to emphasize Heidegger's thoroughgoing originality in the use of this borrowed term. The drawback is that it conceals Heidegger's dependence with respect to his predecessors and prevents readers from discovering the fact that in German one and the same term can appear in successive contexts. After all, the term *Geschichte*, on which the second-order abstraction is constructed (one moves from *Geschichte* to *Geschichtlichkeit* by the adjective *geschichtlich*, following a manner of terminological definition dear to Germans, and abundantly exploited by Hegel, his contemporaries, and successors)[28] does not lend itself to this skillful decoupling: *Geschichte* is in the final analysis the only word available, despite the attempts to oppose *Geschichte* to *Historie* and despite the ambiguities, which it is precisely philosophy's job to clarify. Heidegger admits as much when, at the beginning of §73, he announces that "our next goal is to find the point of departure for the primordial question of the essence of history [*Geschichte*], that is, for the existential construction of *Geschichtlichkeit*" (*Being and Time*, 346). It is indeed the word and the notion of history that are in question under the concept of *Geschichtlichkeit*: the condition of historical being. This is why it seemed preferable to me to assume the same ambitions as the German language in a French translation; Heidegger's originality can only be strengthened as a result.[29]

### The Trajectory of the Term Geschichtlichkeit

In our effort to understand better the break marked by Heidegger's use of the term *Geschichtlichkeit*, it may be useful to retrace briefly the trajectory of its uses from Hegel, who acclimatized the term to its philosophical surroundings, up to the correspondence between Dilthey and Count Yorck (1877–97). It is at this final stage that Heidegger intervenes.[30]

The word is a creation of the nineteenth century. It was in fact Hegel who imprinted on it its philosophical signification.[31] It is in his *Lectures on the History of Philosophy* that the term first arises in the full force of its meaning: it concerns Ancient Greece, "in whose name alone the cultivated man of Europe (and in particular we Germans) feels at home [*heimlich in seiner Heimat*]." But it was the specific way in which the Greeks inhabited their cosmologies, their mythologies, their history of gods and men, that gave the Greeks themselves "this character of free and beautiful *Geschichtlichkeit*." The name of Mnemosyne is associated with this "seed of reflective freedom": just as the Greeks were "at home," so, following them, philosophy can enjoy the same spirit of "current familiarity [*Heimatlichkeit*]" (quoted by Renthe-Fink, *Geschichtlichkeit*, 21).

Hegel uses the word in a second context, that of the "immense moment in Christianity," with "the knowledge that Christ became a true human being" (in Michelet's second edition of the *Lectures*). We owe to the Fathers of the Church the development of "the true idea of spirit in the determinate form of historicity at the same time" (quoted by Renthe-Fink, 21).

It is remarkable that it is under the twofold auspices of Greece and of Christianity that the term "historicity" made its entrance into the philosophical lexicon. With the first use—and in passing by way of Mnemosyne—we are not far from the praise the *Phenomenology of Spirit* bestows upon the aesthetic religiousness that imprints mnemonic inwardness (*Erinnerung*)—the *Erinnerung* of the Greeks. As for the second use, a comparable transition by memory is part of the most ancient tradition of Christianity and its establishment ("Do this in remembrance of me").[32] It remains that Hegel did not use the term "historicity" outside of these two references to two critical moments of the history of Spirit.[33] In truth, since Herder and the German Romantics, it is the term *Geschichte*—which *Geschichtlichkeit* repeats—that has carried the tone of depth and gravity that the term "historicity" will take on. It is solely the exemplarity of these two founding moments of the history of spirit that permits us retrospectively to credit the Hegelian usage of the term "historicity" with an equal founding capacity. In the final analysis, meaningful history, for Hegel, is that of Spirit. And the problem he transmits to his interpreters and to his successors is that of the tension between truth and history. How is it, the philosopher asks, that Spirit has a history? By the epochal character of the question, philosophical history has already seceded from the history of the historians. Factuality has lost all philosophical interest; it is relegated to mere narrative.

Dilthey's work—immense, diffuse, and incomplete—constitutes the decisive link in the history of the uses of the term *Geschichtlichkeit*. But its occurrences are rare in comparison to the massive usage of *Lebendigkeit*, "living reality." It is his correspondence with Yorck that will bring it back to the fore. On the other hand, the term *Geschichte* is omnipresent. It is at the heart of the project of establishing the *Geisteswissenschaften* (the human sciences) on an equal footing with the natural sciences.[34] Spirit is historical through and through.

The great matter at issue in the *Introduction to the Human Sciences*,[35] the first part of which was published in 1883—the only part completed—is the defense of the autonomy, the complete self-sufficiency, of the human sciences: "Human sciences as an independent whole alongside natural sciences" (*Introduction*, 77).[36] These sciences owe their autonomy to the unified constitution of the mind itself, apprehended in self-reflection (*Selbstbesinnung*). This sense of the indivisible unity of the mind continued to be reinforced as Dilthey's publications grew. In opposition to the mechanistic views tied to the associationism then triumphant in psychology, the notion of psychical "structural coherence" (*Strukturzusammenhang*) is introduced as early as the opening pages of *The Formation of the Historical World in the Human Sciences*.[37] This expression belongs to a rich semantic field assembled around the term *Zusammenhang*, in close connection with the term "life."[38] One cannot more strongly assert the direct rootedness of scientifically oriented concepts in the very depths of life.[39]

It is worth noting that at no point is the idea of "living structural coherence" or of "psychical structural whole"—or other renderings—ever associated in Dilthey, as it will be in Heidegger, with that of the interval between birth and death. Death is not, for him, the reference of finiteness for self-reflection. Any more than birth is. The living unity of the spirit understands itself by itself, without any other conceptual intermediary. A conceptual network is thus set into place, linking *Lebendigkeit, Geschichtlichkeit, Freiheit,* and *Entwicklung* (life, historicity, liberty, development). Now, in this sequence, the moment of historicity has no particular privilege, nor does it appear in the 1883 *Introduction to the Human Sciences.* It makes a furtive appearance in his "Antrittsrede in der Akademie der Wissenschaften" ("Inaugural Address to the Academy of Sciences")[40] in 1887 and again in Dilthey's address on the occasion of his seventieth birthday, "Rede zum 70 Geburtstag" in 1903.[41] It is not by chance that, in the course of his correspondence with Yorck, Dilthey will emerge bearing a halo of religiosity far removed from theological dogmatism and prolonging the Hegelian work of rationalization and secularization (whether intentional or not) of trinitarian Christian theology.

Against this rich backdrop of reflective certainty, the correspondence with Count Paul Yorck von Wartenberg (1886–87)[42] casts a distanced and critical regard on the very attempt to found the autonomous whole of the human sciences on the concept of life. It was left to Yorck to introduce the gap between self-reflection and any empirical project of historical science. The concept of historicity is clearly called for in the neighborhood of concepts such as vitality and inwardness (all these words in -*heit* and -*keit*!). But the preferred term is finally *geschichtliche Lebendigkeit* (Renthe-Fink, *Geschichtlichkeit,* 113). And Yorck pushes his friend even further in denouncing the spiritual poverty of the empirical historical sciences. Referring to Dilthey's recent publication of *Ideas Concerning Descriptive and Analytical Psychology* (1894; *G. W.,* 5:139–240), Yorck denounces the insufficiency of psychology as a human science to contend with the fullness of "historical life." What self-reflection as a primary means of knowledge lacks, Yorck observes, is a "critical analysis" of the ontological deficit of the sciences assembled around psychology, that is to say, essentially a fundamental logic to precede and guide the sciences. Then comes Yorck's famous sentence: Dilthey's investigations "place too little emphasis on the genetic difference between the ontic and the historical [*historisch*]." This difference, foreign to Dilthey's vocabulary, is intended to express the maximum gap between the ontological and the presumedly scientific. It is starting with this opposition that Heidegger will cast off again. Wherever this difference is lacking, historiography remains prisoner to "purely ocular determinations." Wherever it is recognized, it can be strongly affirmed: "As I am nature, I am history."

Yorck's proposals came at a time when his friend was caught up in the second part of his *Life of Schleiermacher*, which he would never finish, and when he was also attempting to provide a sequel to the 1883 *Introduction*, which would remain incomplete as well. This is also the time when Dilthey was undergoing the attacks of his colleague Ebbinghaus, the spokesman for scientific psychology. Yorck calls upon Dilthey to respond by stressing ever more firmly the immediacy of the certainty attaching to self-reflection, which addresses itself directly to the structural connections of life. *Lebendigkeit* could not forgo this "internal coherence of life." This, however, does not prevent the concept of historicity from being drawn to the side of an anti-dogmatic religiousness, itself termed "historical" in a nonchronological sense of the word. Dilthey's final letter (summer 1897) contains one of his rare confessions: "Yes! the term *Geschichtlichkeit* is the most apt to convey the supreme task of the human sciences, which is to stand up, in self-reflection, in the name of 'victorious spontaneous vitality,' to the lack of spirituality of modern times"; to value, he says, "the consciousness of the supra-sensible and supra-rational nature of historicity itself" (Renthe-Fink, *Geschichtlichkeit*, 107). Yorck died on September 12, 1899. This ended the discussion on historicity. The term will no longer appear except in his 1903 seventieth birthday speech and in the 1911 "Vorrede." This is no more than a terminological erasure, as Dilthey will continue to speak of the "historical world" and will claim for the human sciences "the foundation of knowledge of the world, a foundation which makes the world itself possible" ("Vorrede," *Gesammelte Schriften*, 5:3–6).

Heidegger's intervention is grafted quite precisely on this debate opened by Yorck at the very heart of Dilthey's work. Heidegger makes this admission at the start of section 77 of *Being and Time*: "Our analysis of the problem of history grew out of an appropriation of Dilthey's work. It was corroborated, and at the same time strengthened, by Count Yorck's theses that are scattered throughout his letters to Dilthey" (*Being and Time*, 363). From this follows the strange redaction—one of a kind—consisting of a series of paragraphs composed for the most part of an anthology of citations. Heidegger frankly places himself with Yorck on the critical point at which "psychology," destined to comprehend "life," proposes to reveal "the whole fact of man" (363). How can man, in this guise, be at once the object of the human sciences and the root of these sciences? The question goes well beyond the debate concerning the border between the human sciences and the natural sciences, between understanding and explanation, well beyond the promotion of psychology as the science of reference for philosophy. It has as its stakes the understanding of historicity, as the two friends agreed. From Yorck are retained the intervention relating to Dilthey's publication in 1894 of *Ideas Concerning Descriptive and Analytical Psychology* and the famous distinction between "ontic" and "historical."

One may doubt that this interested recourse to Yorck's comments and especially to his terminology—ontic in opposition to historical—facilitates an "appropriation of Dilthey's work." Yorck's ontic is not Heidegger's ontic, which is paired in a unique way with the ontological. However, to clarify this point would only blur the tracks and lead us away from the true center of Dilthey's thought, namely, the tie between Life and History.

It is not upon this equivocation that Heidegger constructs his own interpretation of historicity but upon the lack experienced at the end of the meditation on the "equiprimordial connection of death, debt, and conscience...rooted in care" (341, trans. modified).[43] What is missing is the other "end," namely, the "beginning," "birth," and, between them, the interval that Heidegger says "stretches along [*Ausdehnung*]" (342). And he admits that this in-between, in which Da-sein constantly holds itself, "was overlooked in our analysis of being-a-whole" (342). It is worth noting that Heidegger confronts Dilthey not over the term "historicity," which furnishes the chapter with its title, but over the theme of the "connectedness of life," whose systematic context we reconstructed above. In a few lines he bids farewell to the Diltheyan concept: for one thing, it is supposed to resolve itself into a succession of experiences unfolding "in time," which would relegate it to the next level of derivation, that of within-timeness; for another, more seriously, the "ontological prejudice" guiding the characterization of the interconnection in question localizes it without reservation "in the actual now," in the ontological region of the "objectively present" and, in so doing, places it under the sway of the vulgar concept of time, which propels the descending dialectic of temporality in its downward motion. It is impossible, Heidegger asserts, to conduct upon this basis "a genuine ontological analysis of the way Da-sein *stretches along* between birth and death" (343). His thesis is that the thinking of being-toward-death alone is capable of providing an ontological anchor to the idea of interval (which Dilthey never considered) under the complementary condition that birth, in its turn, be interpreted as another "end," symmetrical to the end par excellence; Da-sein can then be said to exist "as born" just as it is said to exist as "dying." Now what is this interval, if not care? "As care, Da-sein *is* the 'Between'" (343).

Nowhere, perhaps, does one so sorely feel the absence of a reflection on the flesh, which would have allowed the designation of being-born as the condition of already being-there and not simply as an event of birth, in false symmetry to the not-yet event of death.

Despite these initial limits, the notion of stretching-along is rich with harmonics capable of nourishing the debate with the historian. Three notions suggest themselves: motivity, which expresses the qualitative and dynamic mutability of existence; permanence, which adds a temporal touch to the idea of self-constancy (an earlier analysis recognized the determination of the "who" of Da-sein); finally, "occurrence," which reinterprets in an existential manner the previously charged word, *Geschehen*, by placing emphasis on the temporalizing operation attached to the idea of stretching-along. In this way, the place left vacant on the ontological plane by the Diltheyan concept of the connectedness of life is now occupied. "The question of the 'connectedness' of Da-sein is the ontological problem of its occurrence. To expose the *structure of occurrence* and the existential and temporal conditions of its possibility means to gain an *ontological* understanding of *historicity*" (344).

At the same time as a reply is given to Dilthey, "the *place* of the problem of history... [is] decided upon" (344). It is noteworthy that Heidegger does not in any way directly confront the profession of historian, but rather what he calls "the scientific and theoretical kind of treatment of the problem of history" (344). This essentially concerns attempts in the neo-Kantian tradition to conceive of history either on the basis of the place conferred upon it by its method in the architecture of knowledge, after the manner of Simmel and Rickert, both of whom are named (344), or directly on the basis of its object, the historical fact. What Heidegger considers the fundamental phenomenon of history, namely, the historicity of existence, is immediately swept away by the partisans of the dominant neo-Kantianism: Heidegger asks "how [can] history... become a possible *object* for historiography"? (344). But he scarcely moves any further in the direction we will take. The notion of derivation, taken in the sense of descending degrees of authenticity, produces only a recourse from less to more authentic. As to what makes historical knowledge possible, one is limited to the affirmation that history as science moves among the objectified modalities of the "historical" mode of being. A chain of relations of dependency is thus offered to be read backward: the object of history—the historical—historicity—its rootedness in temporality.

It is essentially this regressive process that Heidegger opposes to any effort to think the objectivity of the historical fact within the framework of a theory of knowledge.

To start this return movement from the inauthentic back to the authentic, Heidegger does not balk at beginning with investigations conducted under the banner of "the vulgar concept of history" (344). What is important, with regard to this starting point, is "the exposition of the ontological problem of historicity" (345). And this can be nothing other than the revelation of "what already lies enveloped in the temporalizing of temporality" (345). Heidegger repeats: "The existential interpretation of historiography as a science aims solely at a demonstration of its ontological provenance from the historicity of Da-sein" (345). In other words: "... *this being is not 'temporal,' because it 'is in history,' but because, on the contrary, it exists and can exist historically only because it is temporal in the ground of its being*" (345).

However, we must admit that we have not actually moved any closer to what in the present work we have called the work of history and which Heidegger attributes to "factical Da-sein" (345); the account of the historiographical operation is put off until the next stage of the process of derivation, that of within-timeness. How indeed can history be made without calendar or clock?[44] This means that the fate of actual history is not decided on the level of historicity but on that of within-timeness. On the plane of historicity, the discussion reaches only a second-order reflection on epistemology, such as we assigned this in the preceding chapter to a critical philosophy of history. The forced referral to the following stage of derivation of the modes of temporalization provokes a flustered remark: "But since time as within-timeness also 'stems' from the temporality of Da-sein, historicity and within-timeness turn out to be equiprimordial. The vulgar interpretation of the temporal character of history is thus justified within its limits" (345). A certain competition is therefore underway between derivation—which a few lines earlier is called "deduction" (in quotes)—and equiprimordiality.[45]

## Historicity and Historiography

Taking advantage of this moment of suspension and hesitation, I would like to return to the attempt at a critical dialogue between philosophy and history, begun at the end of the first section of this chapter and broken off with the theme of the writing of history as sepulcher. I would like to draw the attention of the philosopher to the workshop of the historian. Heidegger himself proposes this by opening his discussion on the status of the science of history with a reflection on the ambiguous senses of the word "history," in which the properly historiographical determinations of the concept are not yet in evidence. He enumerates and runs through four current acceptations of the term: the past as unavailable; the past as still acting; history as the sum of things transmitted; the authority of tradition. According to him, one finds under these four guises the *Geschehen*, the "occurrence," but concealed under the appearances of the appearing and transmitted event. Something is stated here that concerns the historian in a highly constructive sense: having-been wins out over what is simply past, characterized by being removed from our grasp in our sighting of the past. We ourselves have on many occasions come into contact with this dialectic of "having-been" and "being-no-longer" and have underscored its rootedness in ordinary language and in mnemonic experience, before it is developed by historiography considered in its representative phase. Heidegger casts a sharp look at this dialectic on the occasion of a critical reflection on the notions of vestige, ruin, antiquities, and museum objects. Employing his categorization of beings, divided between the existentials (such as care, *Angst*, selfhood) and beings "objectively present" or "handy" (let us say, things given and manipulable), he observes that what we assemble under the idea of a trace would contain no mark of the past if we were not able to relate these indices to an environment that, although it has disappeared, nevertheless carries with it its having-been. If one can say of certain things that they come from the past, it is because Da-sein carries within itself the traces of its provenance, in form of debt and heritage: "Evidently, Da-sein can never be past, not because it is imperishable, but because it can essentially *never* be *objectively present*. Rather, if it is, it *exists*" (348). A dialogue with the historian can begin with this point: the philosopher's contribution lies here in the critique directed against a treatment of the past in terms of a tool, an utensil. The limit of this critique results from the fracture established between the modes of being of the existing individual and of the thing, given and manipulable, a fissure that is repeated by the historiographical operation on the basis of the mnemonic act. We have, however, taken the epistemology of the historiographical operation as far as the enigma of the standing for of the past as having-been through the absence of the past as what has elapsed. Behind this enigma of standing for is silhouetted that of the iconic representation of the past in the act of memory. But Heidegger accords no place to memory nor to its prize, the act of recognition, to which Bergson granted the full attention it was due, as will be amply shown in the chapter that follows. It may, however, be suggested that the dialectic of presence and absence, formulated as early as the Greek problematic of the *eikōn*, ought to be confronted with the

Heideggerian analysis of the vestige. Does not Heidegger too hastily reduce the absence characterizing the elapsed past to the unavailability of the manipulable? And in the same way, has he not thereby avoided all the difficulties tied to the representation of what is no longer but once was? Instead, Heidegger offers, to be sure, the strong idea of the subordination of the whole innerworldly historical to the primordial historical that we are as beings of care. He goes so far as to sketch out, around the "historicity" of Da-sein, the primary "historicity," a secondary "historicity," that of "world history": "Tools and works, for example books, have their 'fates'; buildings and institutions have their history. And even nature is historical. It is *not* historical when we speak about 'natural history,' but nature is historical as a countryside, as areas that have been inhabited or exploited as battlefields and cultic sites. These innerworldly beings as such *are* historical, and their history does not signify something 'external' that simply accompanies the 'inner' history of the 'soul.' We shall call these beings *world-historical*" (355).

But the disjunction of modes of being—with the existential on one hand, and things at hand on the other—prevents extending the movement of derivation to the point where the complete validity of the phenomenon of the trace could be recognized. The problematic of standing for, on the historical plane, and, preceding it, that of iconic representation on the mnemonic plane, seems to me to be capable of straddling this ontological discontinuity. The notion of vestige, broadened to that of trace, could then offer an opportunity for a discussion in which the veridical dimension of the mnemonic act and of the historiographical act could be taken into account. In the absence of this confrontation, Heidegger balances the stubborn reintroduction of the dependence of historicity in the context of fundamental temporality[46] only by evoking the features resulting from the dependence of historical being with regard to the world, in line with the notions of heritage and transmission analyzed previously, completed by that of being-together-with. It is in this way that fate and destiny are discussed, thanks to a certain assonance in the German words *Geschichte*, *Schicksal* (fate), and *Geschick* (destiny). Some may be concerned, in this regard, about the heroic overload that is imposed here by the concern with the concrete.[47]

I prefer, however, to continue my search for points in Heidegger's text upon which to begin a constructive debate.

I will retain two substantive terms: the succession of generations, borrowed from Dilthey, and repetition, received from Kierkegaard. Both of these are capable of playing the role of connector between the ontology of historical being and the epistemology of the historiographical operation.

The concept of generation is assuredly among those best suited to provide concrete density to the more general concept of transmission, even of heritage. But, here again, there lacks the carnal dimension that the concept of birth could have provided. On this basis one could have erected the entire symbolism of filiation and the whole juridical apparatus related to the idea of genealogy, through which the living being itself is instituted. "One must remember," Pierre Legendre states directly, "that institutions are a phenomenon of life."[48] To do so, one must also remember that humanity is to be defined as the speaking living being, which makes genealogy a structure irreducible to the functions of reproduction. In line with his concept of the "connectedness of life," Dilthey would not have repudiated Legendre's assertion that "life does not live and that it is a human task to institute the living": "Producing the institutional tie is the work of genealogy, which allows us to hold the thread of life" (10). Sociologists, jurists, and psychoanalysts are not the only ones interested in "the study of the genealogical principle of the West"; historians are as well, to the extent that they consider, along with Bernard Lepetit, that the referent of history is the constitution of the social bond taken in all its dimensions, at the point of intersection of practices and representations. History too is a science of the speaking living being; the juridical normativity that governs the genealogical field is not only one of its objects, not even a "new" object, but instead a presupposition attached to the positing of its object and in this sense an existential presupposition: history encounters only speaking living beings in the process of institution. Genealogy is the institution that makes life human life. In this sense, it is a component of standing for, constitutive of historical intentionality.

The theme of repetition—originating, we have just recalled, in Kierkegaard—is, in its turn, of great fecundity regarding the ontological foundation of the historiographical enterprise in its entirety: "Resoluteness that comes back to itself and hands itself down, then becomes the repetition [*Wiederholung*] of a possibility of existence that has been handed down" (*Being and Time*, 352, trans. modified). Once again, the accent placed by Heidegger falls on the referral to a more profound foundation: "The authentic repetition of a possibility of existence that has been—the possibility that Da-sein may choose its heroes—is existentially grounded in anticipatory resoluteness; for in resoluteness the choice is first chosen that makes one free for the struggle to come, and the loyalty to what can be repeated" (352, trans. modified). One may well consider that the reflections sketched out open a wider field than the choice of one's own heroes, a surprising remark, whose troubling "destiny" we know well through the period of the "historical" realization of the philosophy of the "flesh." Infinitely more promising for us is the assertion that repeating is neither restoring after-the-fact nor re-actualizing: it is "realizing anew." It is a matter of recalling, replying to, retorting, even of revoking heritages. The creative power of repetition is contained entirely in this power of opening up the past again to the future.

Understood in this way, repetition can be considered an ontological re-casting of the gesture of historiography, seized in its most fundamental in-tentionality. Greater still, repetition allows us to complete and to enrich the meditation proposed above under the heading of death in history. This led us to the act of sepulcher by which the historian, providing a place for the dead, makes a place for the living. A meditation on repetition authorizes a further step, following the idea that the dead of the past once were living and that history, in a certain manner, moves closer to their having-been-alive. The dead of today are yesterday's living, who were acting and suffering.

How can the historian take this additional step, beyond entombment, as a person of retrospection?

The attempt at an answer can be placed under the double patronage of Michelet and Collingwood.

Jules Michelet will remain the visionary historian who, having perceived France, wanted to provide it with a history; but the history of France is that of an active and living being. "Before me," he proclaims, "no one had embraced a view of it in the living unity of the natural and geographic events that constituted it. I was the first to see it as a soul and as a person.... To recover historical life, one must patiently follow it along all its paths, all its forms, all its elements. But one must also have an even greater passion, to remake, reconstruct the interplay of all of these, the reciprocal action of these living forces in a powerful movement that will become once again life itself." Here the theme of resurrection emerges: "Even more complicated and frightening was my historical problem, as the resurrection of life in its totality, not in its surfaces but in its internal and profound organisms. No sage would have ever thought of it. Happily, I was not one" (1869 preface to *The History of France*).[49]

A half-century later, Collingwood echoes Michelet with a more somber theme, that of the "reenactment" of the past in the present.[50] Following this concept, the historiographical operation appears as an un-distancing—an identification with what once was. But this is at the cost of extracting out of the physical event its "inner" face, which can be called thought. At the end of a reconstruction which mobilizes the historical imagination, the thought of the historian can be considered a means of rethinking what was once thought. In a sense, Collingwood announces Heidegger: "The past, in a natural process, is a past superseded and dead" (*The Idea of History*, 225). Now, in nature instants die and are replaced by others. However, the same event, known historically, "survives in the present" (225). Its survival lies in the very act of its reenactment in thought. This identity-based conception clearly misses the moment of otherness that the idea of "repetition" includes; more radically, it rests on the dissociation of occurrence and meaning on the plane of the event. Yet it is this mutual belonging as such that "repetition" captures.

One can do justice to the lyrical conception of "resurrection" and to the "idealist" conception of "reenactment" by placing the "recollection" of the horizon of expectation of people of the past under the banner of the idea of repetition. In this regard, the retrospective character of history cannot by itself be equated with the imprisonment of determinism. This would be the case if one held the opinion that the past is no longer subject to change and so, for that reason, appears to be determined. According to this opinion, the future alone can be held to be uncertain, open, and in this sense undetermined. If, in fact, the facts are ineffaceable, if one can no longer undo what has been done, nor make it so that what has happened did not occur, on the other hand, the sense of what has happened is not fixed once and for all. In addition to the fact that events of the past can be recounted and interpreted otherwise, the moral weight tied to the relation of debt with respect to the past can be increased or lightened. We shall say more about this in the epilogue, which is devoted to forgiveness. But we can even now make quite good progress in this direction by virtue of broadening and deepening the notion of debt beyond that of guilt, as Heidegger proposes: to the idea of debt belongs the character of "charge," of "weight," of burden. In it we find the themes of heritage and of transmission, stripped of the idea of moral lapse. To be sure, the idea of debt is not a simple corollary to the idea of trace: the trace has to be followed back; it is a pure referral of the past to the past; it signifies, it does not obligate. Inasmuch as it obligates, the debt does not exhaust itself in the idea of burden either: it relates the being affected by the past to the potentiality-of-being turned toward the future. In Koselleck's vocabulary, it relates the space of experience to the horizon of expectation.

It is on this basis that one can speak of a rebound-effect of the future onto the past even within the retrospective viewpoint of history. The historian has the opportunity to carry herself in imagination back to a given moment of the past as having been present, and so as having been lived by people of the past as the present of their past and as the present of their future, to borrow Augustine's formulations once more. People of the past once were, like us, subjects of initiative, of retrospection, and of prospection. The epistemological consequences of this consideration are substantial. Knowing that people of the past formulated expectations, predictions, desires, fears, and projects is to fracture historical determinism by retrospectively reintroducing contingency into history.

We link up here with one of Raymond Aron's persistent themes in his *Introduction to the Philosophy of History*, namely, his struggle against "the retrospective illusion of fatality" (183). He introduces this theme in connection with the historian's recourse to unreal constructions, thereby joining with the Weberian concept of "singular causal imputation." But he broadens this same theme through a reflection on the tie between contingency and necessity in historical causation: "We understand here by contingency both the possibility of conceiving the other event and the impossibility of deducing the event from the totality of the previous situation" (222). This general consideration on historical causation tends to relate the reaction against the retrospective illusion of fatality to a global conception of history defined by "the effort to resurrect, or more exactly the effort to put oneself back at the moment of the action in order to become the actor's contemporary" (232).

The history of historians is therefore not condemned to the inauthentic historicity that Heidegger declares is "blind toward possibilities" (*Being and Time*, 357), as a historiography confined by a museographical attitude would be. Historiography also understands the past as the "return" of buried possibilities.

The idea of "repetition," understood according to Heidegger's expression as the "power" of the possible (360), would then be the best suited to expressing the ultimate convergence between the discourse on historicity and the discourse of history. It is with this idea that I would like to conclude the present section, according it the additional scope conferred upon it by what Heidegger calls crossing through the "history of transmission," namely, the thickness of the interpretive processes interpolated between the present representation and the having-been of the "repeated" past.[51] The theme of repetition is the point of intersection of the second and third parts of the present work.

## WITHIN-TIMENESS: BEING-"IN"-TIME

### Along the Path of the Inauthentic

The term "within-timeness" (*Innerzeitigkeit*) designates the third modality of temporalization in *Being and Time* (division 2, chapter 6). In truth, this is the level assigned to the history of the historians as it is factually carried out.

It is indeed "in" time that events occur. "Being-in" was recognized in all its ontological legitimacy in the first part of the work. "Being-in-time" (within-timeness) is the temporal manner of being-in-the-world. In this guise, care, that fundamental structure of the being that we are, gives itself as concern. Being-in then signifies being-alongside—alongside things in the world. The way of "reckoning with time," which sums up all our relations to time at this level, fundamentally expresses the temporal manner of being-in-the-world. And it is by an effect of leveling-off that within-timeness is pulled to the side of the vulgar concept of time as a series of separate instants offered to numerical calculation. It is therefore important to remain attentive to the positive features of this relation to time, which is still part of the ontology of historical being. In this regard, ordinary language is a good guide; it expresses our various ways of reckoning with time: having time, taking one's time, giving one's time, etc.[52] The task of hermeneutics is here, according to Heidegger, to elicit the tacit existential implications of these expressions. They can be grouped together around the concern that places us in a state of dependency with regard to the things "alongside" which we live in the living present. Concern thus brings the reference to the present to the center of the analysis in the same way as being-toward-death imposes the reference to the future and historicity the reference to the past. On this point, the analyses of Augustine and Husserl, organizing time around the instance of the present, find their relevance. Concern ratifies this priority. The discourse of concern is above all a discourse centered on the living present. At the heart of the language apparatus presides the "now that . . ." on the basis of which all events are dated. One would still have to extract datability from the assignment of dates in a chronology that specifies the operation of "reckoning with time" by a "calculation" of measured intervals. Datability, in its turn, as the capacity of time to be numbered, evokes the stretching of time, the concrete figure of what above was termed extension. Finally, a feature is added marking the role of being-in-common in the reckoning with time: it is publicness, the public character of datability and of stretching. The calculation of astronomical time and of calendar time is grafted onto these scansions of the time of concern. Before quantification, there are the rhythmic measurements of day and night, of rest and sleep, of work and festivity. One can speak in this regard of a "time we take care of" (*Being and Time*, 380). Final touch of the existential analysis: one time can be said to be opportune, another inopportune; a time to do or not to do something.[53] "Significance" is held to be the most appropriate recapitulative expression from the chain of determinations of within-timeness. It, nonetheless, continues to gravitate around the now: "saying-now" (380) sums up, tacitly, the discourse of concern.

The power of this analysis lies in its not having allowed itself to be confined to traditional oppositions, such as subjective and objective. World time, it is said, is "*more 'objective' than any possible object*" and "*more 'subjective' than any possible subject*" (384).

## Within-Timeness and the Dialectic of Memory and History[54]

Only once is history mentioned in the chapter in *Being and Time* on within-timeness, in the lines of introduction. What matters to Heidegger is the vulnerability of this temporal mode to the effects of leveling off occasioned by the vulgar concept of time. Consequently, the entire effort is focused on preserving the ties of this temporal mode to historicity and, beyond it, to the fundamental temporality of being-toward-death. I propose, nonetheless, to continue to pursue at this level the dialogue between the philosopher and the historian. Actually, in a sense what authorizes Heidegger to speak from the outset of "the incompleteness of the foregoing temporal analysis of Da-sein" is the concern with explicitly restoring its credentials to "the factical, 'ontic-temporal' interpretation of history" (371). Here, the adjective "factical" aims explicitly at the actual practice of history, to the extent that it, like the natural sciences, invokes the "time factor." It is indeed the profession of historian that is at issue here. A new reflection on this profession deserved to be undertaken under the guidance of the existential analysis in which the act of "reckoning with time" is not yet caught up in "calculation."

The basic reference to concern can serve as a beginning for this final conversation with the historian. Following the general orientation of historiography that we have preferred, the final referent of the discourse of history is social action in its capacity to produce the social bond and social identities. In this way, we bring to the fore agents capable of initiative and orientation, in situations of uncertainty, responding to constraints, norms, and institutions. The attention paid to phenomena of scale has reinforced this primacy accorded to acting in common on the twofold plane of behaviors and representations. We are therefore permitted to add to the preceding enumeration concerning, successively, death in history and historicity in history the reference to humans concerned with their acting in common. The vis-à-vis of the historian is not only the dead for whom she constructs a scriptural tomb; the historian does not only strive to resuscitate the living of the past who are no longer but who once were, but also attempts to re-present actions and passions. For my part, I explicitly relate the plea on behalf of the idea that the final referent of the historian's representation are those formerly living, behind today's absent of history, to the change of paradigm that, at the "critical turning point" of the *Annales* in the 1980s, promoted what could be called the "paradox of the actor."[55] What history is concerned with is not only the living of the past, behind today's dead, but the actor of history gone by, once one undertakes to "take the actors themselves seriously." In this regard, the notions of competence and adjustment well express the historiographical equivalent of Heideggerian concern.

This general consideration will serve as an exordium for a penultimate rereading of the overall movement of the present work, not only at the point where the ideas of standing for and repetition intersected at the end of the preceding section, but, more broadly, at the point of suture between a phenomenology of memory and an epistemology of history. As has been stated, Heidegger has not a word to say about memory, although he gives several penetrating features concerning forgetting, to which we will do justice in the following chapter.[56] Now the most stubborn perplexities concerning the "factical" treatment of time by the historian have to do with the articulation of historical knowledge onto the work of memory in the present of history.[57] I would like to show that, in the attitude, in principle retrospective, common to memory and history, the priority between these two intentions of the past is undecidable. The ontology of historical being that embraces the temporal condition in its three-pronged nature—past, present, future—is empowered to legitimate this undecidable character under the condition of abstracting from the present and the future. I propose to proceed to a repetition of this situation of undecidability in view of validating it as legitimate and justified within the limits where it is recognized.

I will consider together two intersecting and competing developments. On the one hand, there is a claim to dissolve the field of memory into that of history in the name of the development of a history of memory, considered one of its privileged objects; on the other, there is a resistance of memory to such a dissolution in the name of its capacity to historicize itself under a variety of cultural figures. A passage to the limit, the opposite of the preceding one, is traced out in the form of the revolt of collective memory against what appears as an attempt to seize its cult of memory.

## MEMORY, JUST A PROVINCE OF HISTORY?

This *diminutio capitis* is encouraged by the belated development of a history of memory. Nothing indeed prevented casting memory among the "new" objects of history, alongside the body, cooking, death, sex, festivals, and, why not more recently, *mentalités*. The work by Le Goff titled *History and Memory* is exemplary in this regard.[58] The history of memory, it is stated, is part of a "history of history" (xix), hence an enterprise with a reflexive turn. The history of memory is the first chapter of this double history, and, as such, memory is still recognized as the "raw material of history," "the living source from which historians can draw" (xi). The historical discipline "nourishes memory in turn, and enters into the great dialectical process of memory and forgetting experienced by individuals and societies" (xi). But the tone continues to be marked by mistrust with regard to an excessive praise of memory: "To privilege memory excessively is to sink into the unconquerable flow of time" (xii). The status of memory in the history of history is inseparable from a reflection on the pair past/present which belongs to a separate issue, inasmuch as the opposition determined by this pair is not neutral but underlies or expresses a system of values, like the pairs ancient/modern and progress/reaction. What is peculiar to a history of memory is the history of the modes of its transmission. The historian's enterprise here is similar to that of Leroy-Gourhan in *Le Geste et la parole*.[59] Thus one passes successively in the periodic divisions of the history of memory from societies without writing where memory takes wing, passing from oral to written cultures, from Prehistory to Antiquity, then to the balance between oral and written in the Medieval period, then to the progress of written memory from the sixteenth century to our own day, concluding with "the contemporary upheavals affecting memory."[60]

In the wake of the history of memory, the temptation to strip memory of its function as matrix with regard to history begins to take shape. This is the sort of risk that Krzysztof Pomian takes, without succumbing to it, in his essay titled "De l'histoire, partie de la mémoire, à la mémoire, objet d'histoire."[61] The title appears to announce a voyage of no return. In fact, what is taken into account here is a specific culture of memory, one stemming from the past of Christian, and more precisely Catholic, Europe. The history of this figure is traced from its apogee to its decline following a well-known narrative mode. It is not, however, the univocal interpretation announced by the title that prevails at the end of the course, but the acceptance of a more dialectical relation between history and collective memory, without recognizing for all this the features of memory and forgetting that remain least sensitive to the variations resulting from a history of the cultural investments of memory.

At the beginning of the article, memory is quickly characterized as event-like in nature. Nothing emerges here of the subtleties of the relation between the absence of the past and its representation in the present, nor of the difficulties tied to the truth claims of memory in its declarative stage. Memory appears to be caught from the outset in the nets of a transcendent authority, where the problems of credibility are held to be already resolved. At this initial stage collective memory "remains imbricated in the totality of representations that concern the beyond" ("De l'histoire," 73). The idea of an "identification of the ancient past with the beyond" (73) thus plays the role of archetype for the stage that is superseded today. In it, the religious sphere holds captive the resources that would serve to problematize testimony. The representations that transport the imaginary toward a beyond, continually presented in the liturgy, have already filled in the gaps of the fiduciary relationship upon which the testimony is established. This is why the history of the relation of history to memory will never be more than the autonomization of history with regard to memory, a "fissure . . . between the past and the beyond and, similarly, between collective memory and religious belief" (75). This autonomization reaps the benefits of the major episodes of communication related to the emergence of writing and, even more dramatically, to the birth of printing, then of the commercial diffusion of printed works. The significant moments of this emancipation of history in the course of the twentieth century are well known: the *Annales* phase, the growing role of a chronology that owes nothing to remembering, the introduction of new rhetorical requirements into discourse, the establishment of a continuous narration, an appeal to the invisibility of motivations capable of being rationalized, in opposition to any recourse to providence, destiny, fortune, or chance. Arguments on behalf of the credibility of written documents henceforth break with the fiduciary status of memory authorized from above. In this way, the apparently diriment opposition between the singularity of events or works, put forward by hermeneutics, and the repetition of items, in accordance with serial history, can be neutralized. In both cases, history deals with "what was not an object of apprehension on the part of contemporaries" (102). Recourse is made on both sides to "extramemorial paths." Their objects alone differ: on the one side, literary and artistic works, on the other, enumerable entities, as we see in economics, in demography, or in sociology. In all of these ways, the notion of source is freed entirely from that of testimony, in the intentional sense of the term. To this variety of documents is added the notion of vestige borrowed from geological stratigraphy; the broadening of the familiar notions of source, document, trace is thus shown to be temporal, spatial, and thematic—the latter determination taking into account the differentiation between political, economic, social, and cultural history. In this way a past is constructed that no one is able to remember. It is for a history such as this, bound up with a "viewpoint free of all egocentrism," that history has ceased to be "part of memory" and that memory has become "part of history."

Once it has been identified with one of the cultural historically dated figures, Pomian's plea for a history liberated from the yoke of memory is not lacking in power, if we accept the unilateral approach of the author: "The relations between memory and history will be approached here from a historical perspective" (60). In the same stroke, the potential resources of memory that would allow one to employ this term in a less culturally determined sense are ignored. This omission seems to me to result from the initial postulation of a kinship in principle between memory and perception, a kinship hinging, it seems, on the phenomenon of eyewitness testimony. The witness is presumed to have seen something. But the problematic of the presence of the absent in the representation of the past, as well as the primarily fiduciary character of even eyewitness testimony (I was there, so believe me or don't believe me) are thus lost from sight from the start. In the matter of the collective character of memory, what is also lost from sight is the fundamental consciousness of belonging to a group capable of designating itself in the first person plural and of fashioning its identity at the price of the illusions and violence we are familiar with. Above all, what permeates the essay is a visceral distrust with regard to the Medieval memory, for which Le Goff has manifested so much sympathy.

The essay, however, does not follow this tendency without correcting its unilateral character by a series of small adjustments. Numerous observations plead in favor of the idea, not of substituting history for memory, but of continuously reworking the relation between history and collective memory. For example, "the redistribution of the memory of the elites" is credited to humanism (83). In the same way, the "collective memory of the literate" is mentioned (85). Printing is said to have given rise to numerous "renewals of collective memory" (88) tied to the elevation of the near and distant past to the level of an object of study. The crisis opened by the Reformation is also said to have produced within the heart of Christianity a "war of memories" (92). Even the "divorce between history and memory" (93) under the double form of a "rupture of literary and artistic memory and of a rupture of juridical and political memory" amounts to the construction of a "new memory" (94). Finally, the cognitive emancipation with respect to memory (93–97) is said to lead to the temporal, spatial, and thematic broadening of "the collective memories of Europeans" (103). What is actually produced in the course outlined by Pomian's essay, besides overturning the relations between history and memory as summed up in the title, is a system of gaps in which the differences between history and memory are "maximum where it is a matter of a very distant past, the past of nature, and reduced to the minimum where the past is close to history in every respect" (107). This play of differences confirms that the fact of becoming an object of history is still something that happens to memory, whose representative constitution, in my opinion, makes these gaps possible in principle. In this regard, the tone of the final pages of the essay becomes more didactic: "Between history and memory, there is no impermeable partition" (109). A "new memory" is mentioned "which is superimposed on an even more ancient oral memory" (108). I interpret this softening of the vigorous thesis that propels the essay in the following way: it is the concern with preserving the formative role of history with regard to the civic sense, and more precisely with regard to the national sense, hence to the identity projected by the collective consciousness, that has reined in the polemical impulse arising from the major opposition between scholarly history and a memory framed by religion in Christian Europe.

## MEMORY, IN CHARGE OF HISTORY?

Let us now listen to the plea from the other side. It is also permissible to conceive of a history that would make use of the imaginative variations coming from a cultural history of memory and forgetting as revelatory of the mnemonic potentialities that everydayness conceals. One could speak in this regard of the "historicizing of memory," the benefit of which would accrue to memory.

I have chosen as an example of this type of historicizing of memory the study proposed by Richard Terdiman, a literary critic, of what he names the "memory crisis" and which he sees arising out of literature over the course of "the long nineteenth century."[62] A correlation is proposed between the epochal consciousness that Baudelaire characterized by the term "modernity" and this "memory crisis." This correlation pairs a concept belonging to the periodization of history ("the long nineteenth century") and specific figures of the mnemonic operation (figures of crisis). It is in this pairing that the historicizing of memory consists. Far from ratifying the thesis criticized above of the subordination of memory to history as its object, this phenomenon reinforces the opposite thesis, according to which memory is found to be revealed to itself in its depth by the movement of history. Moreover, far from holding the crisis of memory to be the mere dissolution of the relation between the past and the present, the works that afford it written expression assign to it at the same time a remarkable intelligibility tied to the very delimitation of these cultural configurations. This is held to be modernity's gift to phenomenology—hermeneutics casting between the historical phenomenon and the mnemonic phenomenon the bridge of a semiotics of the representations of the past. The enigma of the representation of the past in the present would therefore be deepened and elucidated along with its cultural determination.

In choosing to comment on Musset's *Confession d'un enfant du siècle* and on the poem "The Swan" taken from the section "Parisian Tableaux" in Baudelaire's *Flowers of Evil*, Terdiman has taken as his object a textual space appropriate to the correlation between historical crisis and mnemonic crisis. The passage from one crisis to the other is made possible by the fact that, on the one hand, what we term the revolutions of the nineteenth century are at one and the same time events that actually took place and accounts concerning these events, in short transmitted narratives, and that, on the other hand, literature constitutes a verbal, rhetorical, and poetic laboratory with unbelievable power of elucidation, discrimination, even theorization. The historical recounted and the mnemonic experienced intersect in language.

So these are particular cultural configurations of the mnemonic phenomenon that the history of modern times brings to light. And these are the figures of crisis. The paradox is that these figures that seem to favor the dissolution of the tie by virtue of which the past persists in the present are intelligible figures by reason of the opportunities of conceptualization opened by the poetics of crisis. The multiple variations of this discourse of crisis can be referred back to the everywhere prevalent theme of loss. In this regard, the discourse of modernity forms a contrast, in a summarily binary typology, with the discourse of total reminiscence that we read in Hegel's *Phenomenology of Spirit* and to which Goethean calm provided a vibrant echo. In contrast, we find expressed here: the despair of what disappears, the powerlessness to collect memories and to fix memory in the archives, the excess of the presence of a past that continues to haunt the present and, paradoxically, the lack of presence of a past forever irrevocable, the headlong flight of the past and the frozenness of the present, the incapacity to forget and the powerlessness to remember at a distance from the event. In short, the superimposition of the ineffaceable on the irrevocable. Even more subtle is the break in the dialogicality proper to a shared memory, in the poignant experience of solitude. In the face of these literary texts of extreme subtlety, one must learn the docility of reading and the ruses of a sinuous dialectic.

For example, it is not a matter of indifference that it is through a detheologized transgression of the literary theme of confession, received from

Augustine and Rousseau, and through the avowed reversal of its therapeutic project, that a "child of the century" was able to admit the well-named "mal du siècle" and in this way construe the *epochal* in the singular form, which confers a new performative efficacy on confession.[63]

As regards the poem "Le Cyne" ("The Swan"), the homonymy of a single word—*le cyne* and *le signe* (sign)—from the very title, invites the reader to seek out the ruses hidden in the games of representation intended to signify loss. For it is indeed loss that reigns at the heart of what Terdiman calls the "mnemonics of dispossession." The reader will not fail to compare this interpretation of Baudelaire's "Le Cyne," in which the accent is deliberately placed on the phenomenon of the historicization of memory, to that of Jean Starobinski mentioned earlier (in part 1, chap. 2, nn. 29, 31). By means of this comparison, I propose relating Terdiman's "mnemonics of dispossession" to what, according to Starobinski, could be called the mnemonics of melancholy. It is indeed along the fragile line separating mourning from melancholy that the poem targets the memory crisis.

What the literature of the memory crisis produced by the horror of history finally lays bare is the problematical nature of the past's manner of persevering in the present; this feature, we have repeatedly stated, results from the fact that the reference to absence is constitutive of the mode of presence of memories. In this sense, loss can reveal itself to be inherent in the work of remembering. However, this reference to absence would not be a source of puzzlement if absence were always compensated by the sort of presence proper to anamnesis, when the latter culminates in the living experience of recognition, the emblem of happy memory. What in the memory crisis makes this a crisis is the obliteration of the intuitive side of representation and the threat that is joined to it of losing what can be called the attestation of what-has-occurred, without which memory would be indistinguishable from fiction. The nostalgic dimension of the *mal du siècle*, of *spleen*, nevertheless stems from the resistance of this irreducible attestation in the face of its own destruction. Musset and Baudelaire, one after the other, admit to this irreducibility: "To write the story of one's life, one must first have lived; therefore, it is not mine which I write," Musset declares. "I have more memories than if I were a thousand years old," confesses the poet of the "irreparable."

What is it, in the final analysis, that allows us to attribute this process of historicizing memory to memory rather than to history? It is the need to complete the eidetics of memory with an examination of the imaginative variations privileged by the course of history. This eidetics finally reaches only a capacity, a power to do, the power to remember, as is authorized in the approach to memory in its exercise (part 1, chapter 2). In this regard, the mnemonic potentialities are of the same order as those examined in *Oneself as Another* under the headings of "I can"—act, speak, narrate, and hold myself capable of moral imputation. All of these potentialities designate the aptitudes of what I call capable being. Like the other capacities, it belongs to that mode of certainty that deserves the name of attestation, which is at once irrefutable in terms of cognitive proof and subjected to suspicion by virtue of its character of belief. The phenomenology of testimony led the analysis of attestation to the threshold of doing history. Having said this, these potentialities, whose invariant core eidetics claims to reach, remain undetermined with respect to their historical realization. Phenomenology must elevate itself here to the level of a hermeneutics that takes into account the limited cultural figures that constitute as it were the historical text of memory. This mediation by history is made possible in its principle by the declarative character of memory. In addition, it is rendered more urgent by the problematical character of the central mnemonic phenomenon, namely, the enigma of a present representation of the absent past. It becomes legitimate to suppose that it is always in historically limited cultural forms that the capacity to remember (*faire mémoire*) can be apprehended. On the other hand, inasmuch as these cultural determinations are in each case limited, they are conceptually identifiable. The "memory crisis"—as the "mnemonics of dispossession" according to Terdiman—constitutes one of these crystalizations taken into account jointly by literary history and by phenomenology conceived as hermeneutics. The process of historicizing memory, invoked on behalf of a hermeneutical phenomenology of memory, thus proves to be strictly symmetrical to the process by which history exerts its corrective function of truth with respect to a memory that continues to exert its matrical function with regard to history.

The unending debate between the rival claims of history and memory to cover the totality of the field opened up behind the present by the representation of the past does not, therefore, end in a paralyzing aporia. To be sure, in the conditions of retrospection common to memory and to history the conflict remains undecidable. But we know why this is so, once the relation of the past to the present of the historian is set against the backdrop of the great dialectic that mixes resolute anticipation, the repetition of the past, and present concern. Framed in this way, the *history of memory* and the *historicization of memory* can confront one another in an open dialectic that preserves them from that passage to the limit, from that *hubris*, that would result from, on the one hand, history's claim to reduce memory to the level of one of its objects, and on the other hand, the claim of collective memory to subjugate history by means of the abuses of memory that the commemorations imposed by political powers or by pressure groups can turn into.

This open dialectic offers a reasonable response to the ironic question posed as early as the prelude to part 2, whether the *pharmakon* of the invention of history, after the model of the invention of writing, is poison or remedy. The initial question, falsely naïve, is now "repeated" in the mode of *phronesis*, of prudent consciousness.

It is toward the instruction of this prudent consciousness that the testimonies of three historians who have inscribed this dialectic at the heart of the profession of historian will contribute.

## THE UNCANNINESS OF HISTORY

*Unheimlichkeit* is the name Freud gives to the painful feeling experienced in dreams revolving around the theme of pierced eyes, decapitation, and castration. It is the term that is fortuitously translated by the "uncanny" in English and by "inquiétante étrangeté" in French.

I am adopting it at the moment of elevating testimony one last time to the rank of existential weight characterizing the theoretical stakes at issue under the themes articulated in the chapter headings above, successively, of "death in history," "historicity and historiography," and "the dialectic of memory and history."

### Maurice Halbwachs: Memory Fractured by History
Readers of *The Collective Memory* have perhaps not always taken full measure of the rupture that breaks off the development of the work with the unexpected introduction of the distinction between collective memory and historical memory.[64] Did not the principal dividing line for which the author fought above pass between individual memory and collective memory, those "two types of memory"—"remembrances . . . organized in two ways" (50)? And yet the difference is strongly marked: between individual memory and collective memory the connection is intimate, immanent, the two types of memory interpenetrate one another. This is the major thesis of the work. The same thing is not true of history inasmuch as it is not assigned to what is going to become "historical" memory. The author places himself back in the situation of schoolboy learning history. This educational situation is typical.

History is first learned by memorizing dates, facts, names, striking events, important persons, holidays to celebrate. It is essentially a narrative taught within the framework of a nation. At this stage of discovery, itself remembered after the fact, history is perceived, mainly by the student, as "external" and dead. The negative mark placed on the facts mentioned consists in the student's not being able to witness them. It is the province of hearsay and of didactic reading. The feeling of externality is reinforced by the calendrical framework of the events taught: at this age one learns to read the calendar as one learns to read the clock.[65] Insisting on this concept of externality assuredly has a polemical aspect, but it touches on a difficulty that is familiar to us since Plato's *Phaedrus*. The rest of this chapter is devoted to the progressive disappearance of the gap between the history taught in school and the experience of memory, a gap that is itself reconstructed after the fact. "Thus we can link the various phases of our life to national events only after the fact" (54). But, in the beginning, a certain violence coming from outside presses in on memory.[66] The discovery of what is called historical memory consists in a genuine acculturation to externality.[67] This acculturation is that of a gradual familiarization with the unfamiliar, with the uncanniness of the historical past.

This familiarization consists of an initiation process, moving through the concentric circles formed by the family nucleus, school chums, friendships, familial social relationships, and, above all, the discovery of the historical past by means of the memory of ancestors. The transgenerational tie constitutes, in this regard, the backbone of the chapter "Collective Memory and Historical Memory": through the ancestral memory flows "the confused din that is like the backwash of history" (62, trans. modified). As the family elders become uninterested in contemporary events, they interest the succeeding generations in the framework of their own childhood.

I would like to focus once more on this phenomenon of transgenerational memory which secretly structures Maurice Halbwachs's chapter.[68] It is this phenomenon that assures the transition from learned history to living memory. In *Time and Narrative* I referred to this phenomenon under the title of "The Succession of Generations," and I listed it among the procedures for inserting lived time within the vastness of cosmic time.[69] To tell the truth, this is not yet on the order of a historiographical procedure like calendar time and archives. It is instead an intense experience that contributes to widening the circle of close relations by opening it in the direction of a past, which, even while belonging to those of our elders who are still living, places us in communication with the experiences of a generation other than our own. The notion of generation that is key here offers the twofold sense of the contemporaneousness of the "same" generation to which belong beings of different ages, and the succession of generations, in the sense of the replacement of one generation by another. As children we learn how to situate ourselves in this twofold relation, which is well summed up in Alfred Schutz's expression of the threefold reign of predecessors, contemporaries, and successors.[70] This expression signals the transition between an interpersonal bond in the form of "us" and an anonymous relation. The bond of filiation which serves both as a breach and a suture testifies to this. It is at once a carnal tie anchored in biology, the result of sexual reproduction and the constant replacement of the dead by the living, and a social bond highly codified by the system of kinship proper to the society to which we belong. Between the biological and the social is interposed the affective and juridical sentiment of adoption which raises the raw fact of engendering to the symbolic level of filiation, in the strongest sense of the word.[71] It is this multifaceted carnal tie that tends to be erased in the notion of the succession of generations. Maurice Halbwachs, in his quasi-autobiographical text written in the first person, underscores the role of narratives received from the mouth of family elders in widening the temporal horizon, central to the notion of historical memory. Supported by the narrative of ancestors, the bond of filiation comes to be grafted on the immense genealogical tree whose roots are lost in the soil of history. And, when the narrative of ancestors falls silent in its turn, the anonymity of the generational bond wins out over what is still the carnal dimension of the bond of filiation. Nothing then remains except the abstract notion of the succession of generations: anonymity has caused living memory to spill over into history.

One cannot say, however, that the testimony of Maurice Halbwachs ends in a disavowal of collective memory. The very term sanctions the relative success of integrating history into an enlarged individual and collective memory. On the one hand, the history taught in school, made up of memorized dates and facts, is animated by currents of thought and experience, becoming what the same sociologist had earlier considered to be the "social frameworks of memory." On the other, personal as well as collective memory is enriched by the historical past that progressively becomes our own. Taking over from listening to the words of the "old people," reading gives a dimension to the notion of the traces of the past that is at once public and private. The discovery of monuments of the past provides the opportunity for discovering "those islands of the past" (66), while cities visited retain their "original appearance" (66). In this way, little by little, the historical memory is integrated into living memory. The enigmatic character that obscured the narratives of the distant past fades just as the lacunae of our own memories are filled and their darkness dissipates. On the horizon stands out the wish for an integral memory that holds together individual memory, collective memory, and historical memory, a wish that extracts from Halbwachs this exclamation worthy of Bergson (and Freud): "We forget nothing" (75).

Has history finally melted into memory? And has memory broadened itself to the scale of historical memory? Maurice Halbwachs's ultimate reservations are significant in this respect. At first sight, they testify to a malaise on the borders of this historical discipline and to a debate over the objectives of the partitioning of disciplines. This is true, but, more deeply, the crisis reaches the very point where historical memory runs alongside collective memory. In the first place, the primary reference of historical memory continues to be the nation; yet, between the individual and the nation there are many other groups, in particular, professional groups. Next, a secret discordance, which will be amplified by our other two witnesses, persists between collective memory and historical memory, which makes Halbwachs say: "In general history starts only when tradition ends" (78, trans. modified). The role of writing, which has become for us the axis around which the historiographical operation revolves, is considered by the author to be the principle of distancing characterizing "a coherent narrative" in which history is written down. The distancing in time is thus consecrated by the distancing of writing. In this regard, I would like to underscore the recurrent recourse in Halbwachs's text to the adverb "autrefois" (formerly, in the past), which I prefer to oppose to "auparavant" (before, previously) applied to memory.[72] In the final pages of the chapter, the opposition between the procedures of scholarly history and the exercise of collective memory turns into an indictment, a challenge addressed to colleagues as close as Marc Bloch and Lucien Febvre.

Two distinctive features of history are held to be irreducible. To the continuity of living memory is first opposed the discontinuity introduced by the work of periodization proper to historical knowledge—a discontinuity that underscores the past as over and done with, no longer in existence: "History, however, gives the impression that everything . . . is transformed from one period to another" (80). In this way, history concerns itself especially with differences and oppositions. It then belongs to the collective memory, mainly at the time of great upheavals, to support new social institutions "with everything transferrable from tradition" (82). It is quite precisely this wish, this expectation, that the crisis of historical consciousness evoked by our other two authors will question once more. Second distinctive feature:

there are several collective memories. However, "history is unitary, and it can be said that there is only one history" (83). To be sure, the nation remains the major reference of historical memory, as we have said, and historical research continues to distinguish between the history of France, the history of Germany, the history of Italy. But what is sighted by means of "successive summations" is a total tableau, in which "no fact will be subordinated to any other fact, since every fact is as interesting as any other and merits as much to be brought forth and recorded" (83). This tableau, in which "all . . . is on the same level" (84), suggests the view of impartiality, theorized by Thomas Nagel. The manifestation of this on the part of the historian is "the natural orientation of the historical mind" in the direction of universal history, which can be presented as "the universal memory of the human species" (84). Is not Polumnia the muse of history? But there can be no question of reliving a past such as this which has become external to the groups themselves.

In this way, Maurice Halbwachs's text traces a curve: from history taught in school, external to the child's memory, we move to a historical memory that, ideally, melts into the collective memory which, by the exchange, is augmented, and we end *in fine* with a universal history concerned with differences between periods and encompassing differences of *mentalité* under a gaze directed from nowhere. Does history, reconsidered in this way, still merit the name of "historical memory"?[73] Are not memory and history condemned to a forced cohabitation?

### *Yerushalmi: "Historiography and Its Discontents"*

> *If Herodotus was the father of history, the fathers of meaning in history were the Jews.*
>
> §  Yerushalmi, *Zakhor*

Yosef Hayim Yerushalmi's book has the virtue, displayed by many works written by Jewish thinkers, of providing access to a universal problem through the exception constituted by the singularity of Jewish existence.[74] This is the case with the tension that spans the century between Jewish memory and the writing of history, historiography. This book thus arrives at the right time in my own discourse on history, just when the accent is placed on the distancing constitutive of the historical perspective in relation to memory, even—or especially, it would have to be said—in the form of collective memory. In this sense, this book accompanies the step outside of memory discussed by

Maurice Halbwachs, whom Yerushalmi, moreover, invokes with gratitude. Also significant is the use of the term "historiography" to designate historical knowledge, a term which is too often employed in French to designate, according to the French translator of Yerushalmi's book, a reflective discipline, namely, "the analysis of the methods and interpretations of historians of the past" (*Zakhor*, 5, in the French translation).[75] The singularity of the Jewish experience lies in the secular indifference to the historiographical treatment of a culture itself eminently charged with history. It is this singularity that seems to me to be revealing with respect to the resistance that any and all memory can oppose to this treatment. In this sense, it exposes the crisis that, in a general manner, history as historiography produces at the very heart of memory. Whether personal or collective, memory refers back by definition to the past that continues to be living by virtue of the transmission from generation to generation; this is the source of a resistance of memory to its historiographical treatment. The threat of being uprooted lies herein; did not Halbwachs say: "History starts only when tradition ends"? There are several ways in which tradition ends depending on the manner in which the distantiation of the historian affects memory, whether it consolidates it, corrects it, displaces it, contests it, interrupts it, destroys it. The chart of the effects of distantiation is complex. And it is here that cultural specificities are asserted and that the singularity of the Jews appears the most instructive for everyone.[76] The critical point consists in the fact that the declarative memory, the memory that utters itself, in making itself a narrative, charges itself with interpretations immanent to the narrative. One can speak in this regard of a sense of history, which can be conveyed by literary genres unrelated to the concern to explain historical events. So it is at the very heart of verbal, discursive, literary experience that the distantiation of the historian operates. Here too the case of Jewish memory is at once singular and exemplary. It must not, in fact, be thought that, foreign to historiography, memory is reduced to oral tradition. Nothing could be further from the case with respect to "so literate and obstinately bookish a people" (*Zakhor*, xv); the example of Jewish culture, broadly speaking up to the Enlightenment, is that of a memory charged with meaning but not with historiographical meaning. The call to remember—the famous *Zakhor*—hammered home time after time in the Bible (Deut. 6:10–12; 8:11–18) is well known to us, as was said above; but the injunction directed to the transmission of narratives and laws is addressed here, through close relations, to the entire people summoned under the collective name of Israel. The barrier between the close and the distant is abolished; all those summoned are close relations. "Remember,

Israel," says the *Shema*. The result of this injunction is that "even when not commanded, remembrance is always pivotal" (5). The fact is that this injunction by no means designates the obligation to provide "an actual recording of historical events" (5)—this is what has first to be acknowledged and understood. What is surprising is that, unlike the dominant conceptions of history among the Greeks, "it was ancient Israel that first assigned a decisive significance to history" (8).[77] The expression "God of the fathers" is the first to testify to the "historical" character of biblical revelation.[78] If we focus a moment on this admission, we can ask whether the belated recognition of the historical character of biblical faith is not already a reconstruction stemming from historiography seeking its antecedents, better yet, a soil in which it is rooted, which is not only earlier but also foreign. It is through an effect of strangeness such as this that we employ the word history, even more so when we speak of the sense of history in the absence of historiography.[79] To be sure, a close exegesis of the biblical vocabulary of memory, placed within the language of the covenant, an exegesis completed by a careful work of correlation between rites of the great festivals and the narratives,[80] lends to this reconstruction of the Hebraic meaning of history a preciseness and a faithfulness, making it comparable to reenactment, so dear to Collingwood. The place of the narrative alongside the laws—and even before them, its place in the canonical composition of the Torah—attests to this concern for the meaning of history. But, when the difference between, on the one hand, poetry and legend and, on the other, scholarly history is unrecognized, it also happens that the meaning of history ignores historiography. It is we who, equipped with the historio-critical method, ask ourselves whether this or that narrative constitutes "a genuine account of historical events." It is therefore under the guidance of a retrospective gaze that we can say with Yerushalmi: "We have learned, in effect, that meaning in history, memory of the past, and the writing of history are by no means to be equated... [and that] neither meaning nor memory ultimately depends on [historiography]" (14–15). The sealing of the canon, ratified by the public reading in the synagogue of the narratives of the Pentateuch and the passages taken each week from the prophets, have given to the biblical corpus, completed by the Talmud and the Midrash, the authority of Holy Scripture.[81] On the basis of this authority, for which the rabbis have been the guardians and the guarantors, was to result the indifference, even the resistance, of the Jewish communities of the Middle Ages (and beyond) to a historiographical treatment of their own history and of their own sufferings. To this must be added the subsequent speculations of the Sages, who will frankly distance themselves from any attention to a sense of history still immanent in the narratives and rites of the biblical epoch.

It is not our purpose to reconstruct, following Yerushalmi, the stages of this confrontation between memory, the meaning of history, and historiography. However, the author's concluding reflections are of great importance to us, once Jewish singularity is revealed to be exemplary with regard to what the author himself calls "historiography and its discontents" (77), discontents to which the final four lectures that make up the book *Zakhor* are devoted. The discontent proper to the "professional Jewish historian" (81), which Yerushalmi declares himself to be, is exemplary in that the very project of a *Wissenschaft des Judentums*, born in Germany around 1820, is not confined to the emergence of a scientific methodology but implies a radical critique of the theological sense adhering to the Jewish memory and amounts to adopting a historicist ideology that underscores the historicity of all things. The vertical relation between the living eternity of the divine plan and the temporal vicissitudes of the chosen people, which was the very principle of the biblical and Talmudic meaning of history, cedes its place to a horizontal relation of causal connections and validations by history of all the strong convictions of the tradition. More than others, pious Jews resent the "burden of history."[82]

What is exemplary here is the correlation between historiography and secularization, that is to say, for Jews, "assimilation from without and collapse from within" (85). For a providential conception of history is substituted the notion of a secular Jewish history which would unfold on the same plane of reality as any other history.

Thus, in the example of the destiny of the Jewish people, the problem is posed for us concerning the relations between a historiography separated from the collective memory and what remains in it of nonhistoricized traditions. The range of solutions, referred to above, must now be opened. Inasmuch as in the Jewish culture "group memory...never depended on historians in the first place" (94), the question of the rebound effect of history on all memory is posed. Historiography, Yerushalmi notes, reflecting on this for all of us, "represents, not an attempt at a restoration of memory, but a truly new kind of recollection" (94). Extending the argument further, Yerushalmi asks whether it is, in any case, a reasonable project to want to save everything of the past. Does not the very idea of forgetting nothing reflect the madness of the person with total recall, the famous *Funes el memorioso* ("Funes the Memorious") of Borges's *Ficciones*? Paradoxically, the delirium of being exhaustive proves to be contrary to the very project of doing history.[83] Curiously, Yerushalmi joins Nietzsche's exclamation in the "Second Unfashionable Observation": "There is a degree of sleeplessness, of rumination, of 'historical sense,' that injures and finally destroys the living thing" (quoted in *Zakhor*, 145, n. 33). The author's perplexity remains undiminished. On the one hand, he hears the optimistic words of Rosenstock-Huessy regarding the therapeutic function of history.[84] On the other, he lends an ear to the antihistoricist words of Gershom Scholem and Franz Rosenzweig. Caught between two warring sides—"Today Jewry lives a bifurcated life" (99)—Yerushalmi assumes the "discontents" of the "professional Jewish historian." These discontents are perhaps our own, all of us, the bastard children of Jewish memory and of the secularized history of the nineteenth century.

### Pierre Nora: Strange Places of Memory

Pierre Nora is the inventor of the "places of memory."[85] This notion is the cornerstone of the vast collection of articles collected by Nora and published beginning in 1984 under the auspices of this term. In order to discover its uncanniness, one must retrace the entire course of these masterful essays from 1984 up to 1992, the date of publication of volume 3 of *Les Lieux de mémoire*. The assured tone of the first article, titled "Between Memory and History,"[86] is replaced by one of irritation, occasioned by the confiscation of this theme by the passion of commemoration, against which the author had voiced his opposition in the name of national history. This great shift, from the first to the last essay, reveals the element of strangeness that the notion perhaps contained from the beginning.

(a) From the very start, the 1984 article "Between Memory and History" announced at one and the same time a rupture, a loss, and the emergence of a new phenomenon. The rupture is between memory and history. The loss is that of what is called "memory-history." The new phenomenon is the stage of a "memory seized by history." The tone is that of a historian who takes a position with respect to the time in which he articulates this threefold announcement. This concerns not an event but a situation. And it is against the backdrop of this situation that one must speak, for the first time, of places of memory. Let us take up each of these points beginning with the last one, temporarily bracketing the scattered allusions to the theme of places of memory.

The judgment of the historian is likened to that of the philosopher Karl Jaspers ruling on "the spiritual situation of our time." This situation is approached by the historian as something like a confluence of circumstances, the symptoms of which have to be deciphered with a steadiness that justifies the firmness of the position taken. The memory referred to at the beginning is not the general capacity phenomenology investigates, but a cultural configuration of the same order as the one Terdiman discussed above; and history is not the objective operation that epistemology deals with, but the second-order reflection for which the term "historiography" is so often reserved in France, in the sense of the history of history. This is why its place is indeed at the end of a chapter devoted to the historical condition but apprehended within the limits of the historical present.

First theme, then: for an "integrated memory," the past adhered continuously to the present; this was "true memory." Our own, "which is nothing but history, a matter of sifting and sorting" has lost the "close fit between history and memory" (*Realms of Memory*, 1:2). "With the appearance of the 'trace,' of distance and mediation, however, we leave the realm of true memory and enter that of history" (2).[87] Memory is a phenomenon that is always actual, a living tie with the eternal present, "history a representation of the past" (3). "Memory is absolute, while history is always relative" (3). "History divests the lived past of its legitimacy" (3).[88]

Second theme: the loss of memory-history. "Memory is constantly on our lips because it no longer exists" (ibid., 1). Torn away, terminated, completed, a past definitively dead: so many words that express disappearance. The signs: the end of peasants; the end of society-memories (church, school, family, state); the end of ideology-memories linking the projected future to a remembered past—and, on the other hand, the appearance of a "history of history," of a "historiographical consciousness" (3). It "lays bare the subversion from within of memory-history by critical history" in which "history begins to write its own history" (4). In France especially "history is iconoclastic and irreverent." This is the effect of the "lack of identification with memory" (4). A related theme, which will increase its scope in a later article by Nora, becomes more explicit: the loss of reference to the nation, to the nation-state. This was a form of symbiosis characteristic of the spirit of the Third Republic (marked on the professional level by the birth of the *Revue historique* in 1876), which implies a definition of lost memory as itself already opening, beyond its intimateness and its internal continuity, onto the being in common of the nation-state. Whence the strange notion of memory-history, around which gravitates the first part of this article, which bears the heading "The End of Memory-History" (1–7). The memory lost was not an individual memory, nor a simple collective memory, but was already a memory shaped in the mold of the sacred: "History was holy because the nation was holy. The nation became the vehicle that allowed French memory to remain standing on its sanctified foundation" (5).[89] "The memory-nation was thus the last incarnation of memory-history" (6). Through the nation, memory-history therefore covers the same space of meaning as memory.

Third theme: out of the rupture between history and memory, through assuming the loss of memory-history, a new figure emerges, that of "memory grasped by history" (8). Three features of this new figure are sketched out. First the reign of the archive. This new memory is an "archival" memory, a "paper memory," Leibniz would say (8). We recognize in this "obsession with the archive" (8) the great mutation taken to the extreme by the myth of the invention of writing in the *Phaedrus*: the victory of the scriptural at the very heart of the memorial. Superstition and respect of the trace: "The sacred has invested itself in the trace which is its negation" (9, trans. modified). The sentiment of loss, as in the Platonic myth, becomes the counterpart of that institutionalization of memory. "The imperative of the age is ... to fill archives" (9). It is somewhat in a tone of imprecation that Nora exclaims "archive as much as you like: something will always be left out" (9), states that the archive "is no longer a more or less intentional record of actual memory but a deliberate and calculated compilation of lost memory" (10), and writes of the "'terroristic' effect of historicized memory" (10). This is truly the tone of Plato's *Phaedrus*, but also the recovered tone of Halbwachs, so insistently does Nora underscore the constraint imposed from outside on this memory. It is noteworthy that to this materialization of memory is added the praise of patrimony (1980: the year of patrimony), which in Nora's subsequent essays will be shown to produce corrosive effects regarding the idea of places of memory as contemporaneous with memory seized by history and not in rebellion with respect to history. He nevertheless underscores the dilation "to the bounds of the uncertain" ("Entre mémoire et histoire," xxvii) of "property transmitted by the ancestors [of] the cultural patrimony of a country"—in short, "from a very restrictive conception of historical monuments, we have moved, very abruptly, with the convention on sites, to a conception which, in theory, might well leave nothing out" (xxvii–xxviii).[90] As early as 1984, Nora's reader could understand the threat of an inverse reduction of the places of memory to topographical sites delivered over to commemorations. Second feature, second symptom: Nora sees in the "preoccupation with individual psychology" (*Realms of Memory*,

1:10–11) the price to be paid for the historical metamorphosis of memory. This would not involve, according to him, a direct survival of "true memory" but a cultural product compensating for the historicization of memory. To this conversion we owe Bergson, Freud, and Proust. More than anything else, we owe to it the famous duty of memory that in the first place is imposed on each of us: "When memory ceases to be omnipresent, it ceases to be present at all unless some isolated individual decides to assume responsibility for it" (11).[91]

Final sign, final symptom of the metamorphosis of memory seized by history: after memory-archive, memory-distance. This was actually the first theme, the rupture between history and memory; it is now taken up again under the sign of discontinuity: we have moved from "a firmly rooted past to a past that we experience as a radical break in continuity" (12). There is perhaps an echo in this theme of the Foucault of *The Archeology of Knowledge*, militating against the ideology of memorial continuity. Nora calls it: "the cult of continuity" (12).

It is against the backdrop of this new situation that the notion of the places of memory appears. It is understood that this is not solely nor even mainly a matter of topographical places but of external marks, as in Plato's *Phaedrus*, from which social behaviors can draw support for their everyday transactions. Thus, the first places named in this article are the republican calendar—external grid of social time—and the flag—national emblem offered to all. Such are all the symbolic objects of our memory—the Tricolor, the Archives, libraries, dictionaries, museums, just as much as commemorations, holidays, the Pantheon or the Arc of Triumph, the Larousse dictionary, and the Mur des Fédérés. All these symbolic objects of memory are offered as the basic instruments of historical work. The places of memory are, I would say, inscriptions, in the broad sense given to this term in our meditations on writing and space. The openness of this term must be underscored from the start, for its flattening out into territorial localities, by virtue of the patrimonial metamorphosis of national identity, will permit the cooption of this theme by the spirit of commemoration, deplored in the 1992 article. At the beginning, due to its scope, the notion of places of memory is not meant for the service of memory but of history: "*Lieux de mémoire* exist because there are no longer any *milieux de mémoire*, settings in which memory is a real part of everyday experience"—such is the frank declaration welcoming the arrival of this notion (1). To be sure, it is in such places "in which memory is crystalized, in which it finds refuge" (1), but this is a memory in tatters, whose ruin is not, it is true, so complete that the reference to memory can be erased from it.

The sentiment of continuity is simply "residual" there. The places of memory are "fundamentally vestiges" (6).[92] The subsequent shifts in the notion will start from this initial equivocation. The function of the place is drawn from the rupture and loss we have discussed: "If we still dwelled among our memories, there would be no need to consecrate sites employing them" (2).[93] Nevertheless, from the perspective of critical history, the residual character of memory inspires the statement that "ultimately, a society living wholly under the sign of history would not need to attach its memory to specific sites anymore than traditional societies do" (3). Because the places remain places of memory not of history. The moment of the places of history is the moment when "the life has not entirely gone out of [the old symbols]" (7).

Something remains to be said about the places of memory under the new dominion of memory grasped by history. "Realms of Memory: Another History": this is announced in an assured tone in the third section of the 1984 article (14–20). The essay concludes, in fact, on a conciliatory note. The places of memory are granted remarkable efficacity, the capacity to produce "another history." They draw this power from the fact that they partake of the orders of both memory and history. On the one hand, "a will to remember must be present initially. . . . Without an intent to remember, *lieux de mémoire* would be *lieux d'histoire*" (14–15). But it is not stated whether this memory is the lost memory of memory-history, whose loss was initially deplored, or the memory that takes refuge in the arcana of individual psychology and its appeal to duty. On the other hand, history has to present itself as an enlightened, corrected memory. But nothing is said regarding what becomes of the project of desacralizing history.

This ability to place the two factors in interaction, to the point of their "reciprocal overdetermination," results from the complex structure of the places of memory which incorporates three senses of the word: material, symbolic, and functional. The first anchors the places of memory in realities that can be said to be already given and manipulable; the second is the work of the imagination, and it assures the crystalizing of memories and their transmission; the third leads back to ritual, which history nevertheless attempts to dismiss, as we see in the case of founding events or spectacles, and with places of refuge and other sanctuaries. Nora evokes on this occasion the notion of generation, to which a later article will be devoted and which is supposed to contain all three meanings together. The tone becomes almost lyrical in speaking of this spiral of the collective and the individual, of the prosaic and the sacred, of the immutable and the mobile—and of these "Möbius strips, endless rounds," which enclose "the maximum possible meaning with the fewest possible signs" (15). Under the cover of patrimony, favorably mentioned, the evil of patrimonialization is not yet perceived in its tendency to reduce the place of memory to a topographical site and to deliver the cult of memory over to the abuses of commemoration.

(b) The first article of 1984 on the places of memory was to be followed by several other interventions by Nora at strategic points of the great work he was directing. In the essay "La Nation-mémoire,"[94] published in the series of some forty texts dealing with the nation, the recomposition inspired by these punctual clarifications takes as its guiding theme the development of "national memory." Four types are proposed, marking out a broadly drawn chronology: founding memory, contemporaneous with the feudal monarchy and the period of defining and affirming the state; state-memory, "absorbed in the image of its own representation" (the very one Louis Marin characterized above through the "portrait of the king"); national-memory, the memory of the nation becoming conscious of itself as a nation, to which Michelet bears witness—he "who transcends all places of memory because of all of them he is the geometrical center and the common denominator, the soul of these places of memory" (649); citizen-memory, finally, for which Alain is the "quintessential paragon" (650). But it is stated that the fifth type retrospectively gives a sense to what is, after all, a rather disappointing series: the type that is our own, "a patrimony-memory" (650).

For our investigation into the fate of the idea of places of memory in Nora's texts, this moment of analysis is decisive: it marks an internal reversal of the very notion of place of memory. The definition is concise: "By patrimony-memory one must not be satisfied with understanding the sudden widening of the notion and its recent and problematic dilation to include all the objects that testify to the national past but, much more profoundly, the transformation into a common good and a collective heritage of the traditional stakes of memory itself" (650). Much more will be said about this in Nora's final essay, placed at the end of volume 3, *Les France*, of *Les Lieux de mémoire*; only its mark on the dialectic of memory and history is emphasized here. Concerning this patrimonial transformation, it is simply stated that it "carries the renewal that is everywhere underway in the historical approach to France through memory, an approach whose centrality the work comprising *Les Lieux de mémoire* would like to confirm" (651). Henceforth, the feeling of belonging to the nation "in the manner of a renewed sensibility of national singularity" wins out over the mediations and oppositions involved in identifying the nation with the state: "It is the hour of a patrimony-memory and of a new union between France and a nation without nationalism" (652). Erasing the tie between the nation and the state has as its corollary the promotion of memory, to which alone "the nation owes its unitary acceptation, maintains its relevance and its legitimacy" (653). By thus abstaining from a detour by way of the state, memory claims also to abstain from a detour by way of history, a foundation in France of a piece with the constitution of the nation-state: "With regard to this national sedimentation of memory, which is knotted around the state, a history that unfolds entirely within the horizon of the nation-state is no longer able to account for it" (654). Henceforth, "'France' is its own memory or it is not" (655).

At the conclusion of this brief essay a certain acquiescence prevails regarding the emergence of patrimony-memory, held to characterize the fifth type of national memory, and of its corollary, "dropping the nationalistic, gallocentric, imperial, and universalist version of the nation" (657). It is, nevertheless, not certain that the final word has been uttered, so undetermined is the notion of patrimony, and so little recognition has been paid to its harmfulness with respect to the very idea of a place of memory.

(c) The essay "La Génération,"[95] added to the first book, *Conflits et partages*, of the third volume, *Les France*, of *Les Lieux de mémoire* (931–71), in its title and in its theme, hardly seems to announce any progress in the analysis of the idea of the place of memory and, more precisely, in its transformation in contact with the idea of patrimony. However, this is not the case. With the idea of generation, a purely horizontal view of the social bond prevails; one generation replaces another through continuous substitution. In particular, the idea of generation marks the demotion of the descending generation in the name of the ascending generation: "The past is no longer the law: this is the very essence of the phenomenon" ("Generation," *Realms of Memory*, 1:502). This "symbolic rupture" assures the preeminence of horizontal identity over all forms of vertical solidarity. Despite the aporias a theoretical definition of the phenomenon runs into—and which the author surveys— one type of belonging, generational solidarity, imposes itself, and along with it a remarkable question: "As the pace of change increases, how and why has the horizontal identification of individuals of roughly the same age been able to supplant all forms of vertical identification?" (509). It is not enough to retrace the stages of the "historical construction of the model" (511), although the passage from the biologically oriented notion of the replacement of the dead by the living to that of generation understood as a singular historical formation affords the opportunity to highlight the history of memory: "In every country, it seems, one generation has served as a model and pattern for all subsequent generations" (511). In this way, Musset forged the poetic formula of the "children of the century" that we encountered earlier with Terdiman. In France, in particular, the axes of politics and literature, of power and words, have been intertwined in the generational panoply. It is in this atmosphere that history was promoted as a discipline, with its grand cyclical periodicity which May 1968 would come to concelebrate. It remains to be explained why the history of France has lent itself to being governed by the impulse of generations. What is then offered is the notion of the place of memory and its mixture of memory and history, sounding the note of generational subversion: "Generations have always been mixtures of memory and history, but the amount and role of each in the mix appear to have shifted over time" (522). The inversion consists in the fact that the notion of generation, constructed retrospectively and, as such, permeated with history, slips away into its "effect of remembering" (522), as we see in the time of Péguy and Barrès. First imposed from outside, it is then violently internalized (the reader perceives an echo of Halbwachs's considerations here regarding the formation of what he called "historical memory"). What is more, inhabited by history, generational memory finds itself "crushed by history's weight" (524) (it is now the accent of Nietzsche in the 1872 essay placed here as prelude). Remembering, then, quickly veers off into commemoration, with its obsession of a finite, completed history: "At the inception of a generation there is a sense of lack, something in the nature of a mourning" (525) (where we cross paths with Henry Rousso and the obsession with the Vichy syndrome). "It was this intrinsically mythological and commemorative historical celebration that moved the idea of generation out of history and into memory" (525) (this section is titled "Immersed in Memory," 522–31). One is indeed in pure memory here, memory which mocks history and abolishes duration to make itself a present without history: the past is then, according to a remark by François Furet, "immemorialized" in order better to "memorialize" the present.

At this point, Nora the historian resists: the article "Generation" concludes without making any accommodation to the reign of commemoration, with a plea in favor of a "split historical personality" (528)—split into its "memorial rumination" (528) and the evocation of the grand world history within which France is called to situate its moderate power. To the one-dimensional version imposed by generational mythology, the historian—or doubtless rather the citizen in the historian—opposes a "dividing line . . . between that which belongs *exclusively* under the head of generational memory and that which belongs *exclusively* to historical memory" (530).

What has become of the idea of the place of memory in all this? In a sense, despite the efforts of the historian, it has become sacralized, as it were, as a result of commemoration.[96] It has not yet been stated, however, that the tie perceived in the preceding essay between the idea of the place of memory and the patrimonial transformation of national identity announces the subtle perversion of this idea. What indeed remains to be discussed is the patrimonial conquest of the idea of the place of memory—its capture in space after its capture in the present.

(d) The 1992 article "L' Ère de la commémoration," which appeared at the end of volume 3, *Les France*, book 3, *De l'archive à l'emblème* (975–1012),[97] comes full circle six years after the impressive appearance of the article "Between Memory and History." It comes full circle on a tone of deep regret: "The destiny of these *Lieux de mémoire* has been a strange one. The work was intended, by virtue of its conception, method, and even title, to be a counter-commemorative type of history, but commemoration has overtaken it" ("The Era of Commemoration," *Realms of Memory*, 3:609). The intention had been "to make commemoration itself one of [the] primacy specimens for dissection" (609), but the hunger for commemoration assimilated the attempt to master the phenomenon. Everything occurred as though, by virtue of France's exit from the stage of world history, the publication of *Les Lieux de mémoire* had come to reinforce the commemorative obsession. All that is left is for the historian to reply that he is trying to "understand why this co-optation has taken place" (609).

In fact, it is commemoration itself that has been metamorphosized,[98] as is evidenced more by the self-celebration of May 1968 than by the bicentennial of the French Revolution. The Revolution had invented a classical model of national commemoration. It is this model that disintegrated and was subverted: whereas the earlier articles contain scattered remarks on the decline of the model of national identity centered on the nation-state, "the dissolution of the unifying framework of the nation-state has exploded the traditional system that was its concentrated symbolic expression. There is no commemorative super-ego: the canon has vanished" (614). A battle of memories occupies the stage: the cultural and the local, destroyers of the national, saturate the media.[99]

Returning with a vengeance is the theme of the patrimonial touched upon several times in the earlier articles. "From the National to the Patrimonial" (621)—this section heading in "Generation" identifies the secret of the metamorphosis marked by narratives of commemorations in the preceding pages. The end of the peasant world is one occasion for this; the emergence of France from the orbit of the war, the death of the man of the 18th of June are others; then, the success of the year of Patrimony (1980), consecrating the regionalization of collective memory. The metamorphosis is underway that leads from history to the remembered, and then on to the commemorated, making the era of commemoration the culmination of this series of inversions. History has ceased to be "verified memory" (626), in symbiosis with national history. "Commemoration has freed itself from its traditionally assigned place, but the epoch as a whole has become commemorative" (627). Even the publication of the collection *Faire de l'histoire* edited by Jacques Le Goff and Pierre Nora in 1973, elevating memory to the level of a new object of history through the work of Goubert, Duby, and Lacouture, was to contribute against its will to this subversion of history by memory. The surge of memorial commemoration was so strong that even the Left in France was to succumb to it with François Mitterand at the Panthéon in 1981. But it is the promotion of patrimony and its crystallization into the "historical monument" with its spectacular topography and its archeological nostalgia that marks the signature of the epoch as the "era of commemoration": the "patrimonializable" has become infinite (631). The misinterpretation of the very notion of place of memory is now in place: from a symbolic instrument, whose heuristic interest was to render "place" immaterial, the notion has fallen prey to patrimonial-type commemorations: "The meaning of *patrimoine* has shifted from inherited property to the possessions that make us who we are" (635). At the same time, national history and, with it, history as myth have made way for national memory, that recent idea. "Memorial nation" in the place of what was "historical nation" (636)—the subversion is profound. The past is no longer the guarantor of the future: this is the principal reason for promoting memory as a dynamic field and as the sole promise of continuity. In place of the solidarity of the past and the future, the solidarity of the present and memory have been substituted. "A new concern with 'identity' resulted from the emergence of this historicized present" (635). For the former purely administrative or police use of the term has been substituted a memorial use: "France as a person needed a history. France as identity is merely preparing for the future by deciphering its memory" (635). Bitterness.

Was the notion of place of memory in the final analysis, then, poorly chosen? A shadow passes over the term and its "apparent paradox of linking two words, one of which creates distance while the other creates intimacy" (636). The historian does not however wish to succumb to regret or nostalgia, but prefers the proud rejoinder: "By justifying the joining together of objects of different kinds, the term makes it possible to reassemble the shattered national whole. And this perhaps justifies the ambition of these volumes: to define, within the virtually unbroken chain of histories of France, one moment in the French contemplation of France" (636).

By taking up one's pen in this way, by giving a written representation of the subversion of the "historical nation" by "national memory," the citizen-historian engages in resistance. Not without issuing a challenge to one's time: speaking in the future perfect, the historian evokes the moment when "another way of living together" will be set into place and when "the need to exhume these landmarks and explore these *lieux* will have disappeared" (637). Then—the inverse announcement to that with which the introduction to *Les Lieux de mémoire* opened several years earlier—"the era of commemoration will be over for good. The tyranny of memory will have endured for only a moment—but it was our moment" (637).

Until then, let me say, nonetheless, the "uncanniness" of history still prevails, even as it attempts to understand the reasons why it is contested by commemorative memory.

# CHAPTER 3

## *Forgetting*

READING GUIDELINES

Forgetting and forgiveness, separately and together, designate the horizon of our entire investigation. Separately, inasmuch as they each belong to a distinct problematic: for forgetting, the problematic of memory and faithfulness to the past; for forgiveness, guilt and reconciliation with the past. Together, inasmuch as their respective itineraries intersect at a place that is not a place and which is best indicated by the term "horizon": Horizon of a memory appeased, even of a happy forgetting.

In a sense, it is the problematic of forgetting that is the more expansive, since the appeasement of memory in which forgiveness consists seems to constitute the final stage in the progress of forgetting, culminating in that *ars oblivionis* that Harald Weinrich would like to see constructed alongside the *ars memoriae*, examined and celebrated by Frances Yates. Taking notice of this sense, I have chosen to place forgetting in the title of the present work alongside memory and history. Forgetting indeed remains the disturbing threat that lurks in the background of the phenomenology of memory and of the epistemology of history. Forgetting is, in this respect, the emblematic term for the historical condition taken as the theme of our third part, the emblem of the vulnerability of this condition. In another sense, the problem of memory is more extensive to the degree that the eventual *ars oblivionis* is projected as a double of *ars memoriae*, a figure of happy memory. The idea of happy memory, in a certain manner, opened the way for our entire enterprise, once we were careful not to allow the pathology of memory to overtake the phenomenology of ordinary memory considered in its phases of successful realization. It is true that we did not then know what price had to be paid for according its full sense to happy memory, namely, the passage through the dialectic of history and memory and, finally, the dual test of forgetting and forgiveness.

Against this play of horizons, in the very sense in which we earlier spoke of the play of scales, our investigation will come to its end. Horizon does not mean only the fusion of horizons, in the Gadamerian sense I am assuming, but also the receding of horizons, incompletion. This admission is not unexpected in an enterprise placed from the start under the banner of the merciless critique directed against the *hubris* of total reflection.

One can speak at length of forgetting without ever mentioning the problematic of forgiveness. This is what we will do in this chapter. In the first instance and on the whole, forgetting is experienced as an attack on the reliability of memory. An attack, a weakness, a lacuna. In this regard memory defines itself, at least in the first instance, as a struggle against forgetting. Herodotus strives to preserve the glory of the Greeks and the Barbarians from oblivion. And our celebrated duty of memory is proclaimed in the form of an exhortation not to forget. But at the same time and in the same fell swoop, we shun the specter of a memory that would never forget anything. We even consider it to be monstrous. Present in our mind is the fable of Jorge Luis Borges about the man who never forgot anything, in the figure of *Funes el memorioso*.[1] Could there then be a measure in the use of human memory, a "never in excess" in accordance with the dictum of ancient wisdom? Could forgetting then no longer be in every respect an enemy of memory, and could memory have to negotiate with forgetting, groping to find the right measure in its balance with forgetting? And could this appropriate memory have something in common with the renunciation of total reflection? Could a memory lacking forgetting be the ultimate phantasm, the ultimate figure of this total reflection that we have been combatting in all of the ranges of the hermeneutics of the human condition?

We must keep this presentiment—this *Ahnung*—in mind as we pass through the procession of figures that hide the horizon line.

It is not an exaggeration to speak here of a procession of figures to traverse. Whoever attempts to evaluate the evident misfortunes and the presumed benefits of forgetting first runs into the crushing polysemy of the word "forgetting," whose proliferation is attested by its literary history, as it has been written by Harald Weinrich.[2] To protect ourselves from the feeling of helplessness resulting from the addition of this profusion of language to the nostalgic meanderings inherent in the theme of forgetting, I propose a reading grid based on the idea of the degree of the depth of forgetting.

To clarify this distinction, I will relate it to the one that presided over the description of mnemonic phenomena considered from the perspective of "object" (following the use of the term "memory" as a substantive), the distinction between the cognitive approach and the pragmatic approach. In the first approach, memory was apprehended in accordance with its aim of faithfully representing the past, while the second concerned the operative side of memory, its exercise, which was the occasion for the *ars memoriae* but also for the uses and abuses that we attempted to repertory following a scale proper to memory. Forgetting prompts a rereading of the two problematics and of their articulation in light of a new principle of discrimination, that of levels of depth and of manifestation. Indeed, forgetting proposes a new meaning for the idea of depth, which the phenomenology of memory tends to identify with distance, with remoteness, according to a horizontal formulation of depth. Forgetting proposes, on the existential plane, something like an endless abyss, which the metaphor of vertical depth attempts to express.

Remaining for a moment on the plane of depth, I propose to correlate the problematic relating to this level with the cognitive approach to spontaneous memory. What forgetting awakens at this crossroads is, in fact, the very aporia that is at the source of the problematical character of the representation of the past, namely, memory's lack of reliability. Forgetting is the challenge par excellence put to memory's aim of reliability. The trustworthiness of memories hangs on the enigma constitutive of the entire problematic of memory, namely, the dialectic of presence and absence at the heart of the representation of the past, to which is added the feeling of distance proper to memories, unlike the simple absence of the image, which it serves to depict or to simulate. The problematic of forgetting, formulated on the level of greatest depth, intervenes at the most critical point of this problematic of presence, of absence, and of distance, at the opposite pole from that minor miracle of happy memory which is constituted by the actual recognition of past memories.

It is at this critical point that the grand bifurcation that will command the last two sections of this study is proposed—namely, the polarity between two great figures of profound forgetting, which I shall name forgetting through the erasing of traces and a backup forgetting, a sort of forgetting kept in reserve (*oubli de réserve*), an expression I will attempt in a moment to justify. The first and second sections of this chapter are devoted to this grand bifurcation. As the name of the first figure of profound forgetting leads us to understand, the problematic of the trace commands the problematic of forgetting at this radical level. This irruption has nothing surprising about it. From the start of this work we have been confronted with the proposition of Plato's *Theaetatus* to tie the destiny of the *eikōn* to that of the *tupos*, of the imprint, after the model of the mark left by a signet ring on wax. It is this alleged tie between image and imprint that forgetting forces us to explore at greater depth than we have done previously. Our entire problematic of the trace, from antiquity to today, is truly the inheritor of this ancient notion of imprint, which, far from solving the enigma of the presence of absence that encumbers the problematic of the representation of the past, adds to it its own enigma. Which one?

As early as the commentary on the texts of Plato and Aristotle that invoked the metaphor of the wax imprint, I proposed distinguishing three sorts of traces: the written trace, which has become the documentary trace on the plane of the historiographical operation; the psychical trace, which can be termed impression rather than imprint, impression in the sense of an affection left in us by a marking—or as we say, striking—event; finally, the cerebral, cortical trace which the neurosciences deal with. I am leaving aside here the destiny of the documentary trace discussed in part 2, but not without recalling that, like every material trace—and in this respect the cortical trace is on the same side as the documentary trace—it can be physically altered, effaced, destroyed. Among other objectives, the archive is established to combat this threat of effacement. There remains the articulation of these two sorts of traces: psychical trace, cortical trace. The entire problematic of profound forgetting hinges on this articulation.

The difficulty is first of all a difficulty in the approach taken. It is by radically heterogeneous paths that we have access to one or to the other. The cerebral, cortical trace is known to us only from the outside, through scientific knowledge, without there being any corresponding sensed, lived experience as in the case of that part of organic sensibility that makes us say that we see "with" our eyes and that we grasp "with" our hands. We do not say in the same manner that we think "with" our brains. We learn that this brain-object is our brain, located in this cranial cavity that is our head, with its facade of our face, our head, the emblem of the hegemony that we claim to exert over our members. This appropriation of "our" brain is complex— as are the traces that objective knowledge sketches in it. The first section of this chapter will be devoted to discussions concerning the notion of mnestic trace.[3] From this follows the fate of the first form of profound forgetting, forgetting through the effacement of traces. The access to the presumed psychical traces is entirely different. It is much more deeply concealed. One speaks of it only retrospectively on the basis of precise experiences which have as their model the recognition of images of the past. These experiences make us think, after the fact, that many memories, perhaps among the most precious, childhood memories, have not been definitively erased but simply rendered inaccessible, unavailable, which makes us say that one forgets less than one thinks or fears.

However, the difficulty related to the problematic of the two traces is not only one of access to the phenomena concerned. It touches on the very signification that can be given to these two acceptations of the trace, one external, the other intimate. The first section, dealing with the conceptual handling of the idea of mnestic trace in the framework of the neurosciences, is organized into three moments. (1) We will first ask, what is the position in principle of the philosopher who I am in contrast to scientists who speak in general terms of mnestic or nonmnestic traces? (2) What can be said more specifically about mnestic traces? What mutual instruction can the phenomenologist and the neurologist provide to one another? It is at this stage of questioning that the major interrogation will be carried to its highest problematic level. (3) Finally, what place does the question of forgetting occupy in the table of dysfunctions of memory? Is forgetting itself a dysfunction? It is with this third segment of questioning that forgetting through the effacement of traces will best be determined. But the principle of the proposed solution will be contained in the first stage with the ideas of *causa sine qua non*, a substratum, and a correlation between organization and function. The general orientation is that of an epistemological gap between discourse about the neural and discourse about the psychical. This gap will be protected against any spiritualist extrapolation or any materialist reductionism by our unwavering abstention on the ontological plane from the classical debate concerning the question of the so-called union of the body and the soul.

By virtue of this suspension I shall pursue as far as possible in the second section the presupposition on which the recourse to a distinct notion of psychical trace is based, whatever its neural conditioning may be. The key experience, we have just said, is that of recognition. I speak of it as a minor miracle. It is indeed in the moment of recognition that the present image is held to be faithful to the initial affection, to the shock of the event. Where the neurosciences speak simply of reactivating traces, the phenomenologist, being instructed by lived experience, will speak of a persistence of the original impression. It is this discourse that I will try to carry to its highest degree of incandescence in exploring the entirely retrospective presupposition of a birth of the memory at the very moment of the impression, of a "reliving of images" in the moment of recognition, following Bergson in *Matter and Memory*. An "unconscious" existence of memories must then be postulated, in a sense it is possible to attribute to this unconscious. It is this hypothesis of the preservation by the self, constitutive of duration as such, that I will attempt to extend to other phenomena of latency, to the point that this latency can be considered a positive figure of forgetting, which I call the reserve of forgetting. It is indeed out of this treasury of forgetting that I draw when I have the pleasure of recalling what I once saw, heard, felt, learned, acquired. It is upon this perseverance that the historian, after Thucydides, will be able to create the project of "what is acquired for all time."

To be sure, the problem still remains of how to acknowledge together the neural status of mnestic traces and the status of what is discussed in terms of persistence, remanence, reliving, duration. There is perhaps good reason to confine my remarks, at least in the sort of discourse that is my own, to asserting the polysemy of the notion of trace, the idea of psychical trace claiming an equal right with regard to the idea of a neural trace. The two readings of mnemonic phenomena would then be left in competition. The first tends toward the idea of a definitive forgetting: this is forgetting through the erasing of traces. The second tends toward the idea of a reversible forgetting, even toward the idea of the unforgettable: this is the reserve of forgetting. Our ambivalent feelings about forgetting would thus have their origin and their speculative justification in the competition between these two heterogeneous approaches to the enigma of profound forgetting, one moving along the path of the internalization and appropriation of objective knowledge, the other along the path of retrospection on the basis of the experience *princeps* of recognition. On the one hand, forgetting makes us afraid. Are we not condemned to forget everything? On the other, we welcome as a small happiness the return of a sliver of the past, wrestled away, as we say, from oblivion. Both of these readings are pursued throughout our life—with the permission of the brain.

Continuing our progress along the vertical axis marking forgetting's levels of depth, we reach the figures of manifest forgetting. The third section of this chapter will be devoted to their analysis. The correlation proposed above between the major divisions of this chapter and the distinction between the cognitive and the practical approaches to mnemonic phenomena authorizes us to place this section under the heading of the pragmatics of forgetting. Manifest forgetting is also an exercise of forgetting. To assist us in deciphering the phenomena stemming from this pragmatics of forgetting, I will adopt the reading grid applied to the uses and abuses of memory and the analyses they undergo in the second chapter of part one. A similar hierarchy will punctuate the manifestations of the exercise of forgetting. Forgetting will not offer simply a reduplication of the description in which the same usages of memory will be revealed under the new angle of the uses of forgetting; rather, the latter will bring with them a specific problematic, distributing their manifestations along a horizontal axis split between a passive pole and an active pole. Forgetting will then reveal a clever strategy quite specific to itself. In conclusion, I will propose an example of these uses and abuses of forgetting, borrowed from the history of the present day.

At the end of this investigation devoted to the pragmatics of forgetting, the parallel with the hierarchy of the uses and abuses of memory will ineluctably lead to the question of determining what echo, what response, the difficulties and equivocations raised by the presumed duty of memory can expect to encounter on the side of forgetting—and why one absolutely cannot speak of a duty of forgetting.

§

### FORGETTING AND THE EFFACING OF TRACES

It is customary in the neurosciences to directly attack the problem of the mnestic traces in an effort to localize them or to subordinate questions of topography to questions of connectivity, of the hierarchy of synaptic architectures. From this, one passes to the relations between organization and function, and, on the basis of this correlation, one identifies the mental (or psychical) correspondent of the cortical in terms of representations and images, among these mnestic images. Forgetting is then referred to in the context of dysfunctions of mnestic operations, along the uncertain border between the normal and the pathological.

This program and this path of thinking are scientifically irreproachable. And I shall repeat this journey under the neurologist's guidance. The questions of the philosopher—of a philosopher—are of a different order. There is first the prior question, mentioned in the introductory guidelines, concerning the place of the idea of cortical trace in the typology of the uses of this notion. Once the idea of the cortical trace has been framed, the question is knowing how it is that one recognizes that a trace is a mnestic trace, if not, on the plane of function and of psychical expression, by means of the relation to time and to the past. For the phenomenologist, this relation is specified by the central problematic of the memory-image, namely, the dialectic of presence, absence, and distance that inaugurated, accompanied, and tormented our investigation. The role of the philosopher is then to relate the science of mnestic traces to the problematic central to phenomenology, the representation of the past. The rereading of the neurologist's works that follows is governed wholly by this relation established between neurological knowledge and the dialectic of the mnemonic image. This relation excludes a direct attack of the notion of mnestic trace. The patience of a long detour is required, beginning with the clarification of the relation that the sort of philosophy espoused here maintains with neuroscience. Only then can the notion of mnestic trace be tackled head on with respect to its relation to the enigma of the present representation of the absent past. But, even then, we will not yet have said anything specific concerning forgetting: what sort of dysfunction is it? Is it even a dysfunction like the clinical cases of amnesia?

(a) Concerning my position as philosopher facing the neurosciences, I will take the liberty of summing up the reasoning that I set forth in my discussion with Jean-Pierre Changeux in *What Makes Us Think?*[4] I tried not to situate myself on the level of a monistic or dualistic ontology but on that of a semantics of the discourses conducted, on the one hand, by the neurosciences and, on the other, by philosophers claiming the threefold heritage of reflective philosophy (from Maine de Biran and Ravisson to Jean Nabert), phenomenology (from Husserl to Sartre and Merleau-Ponty), and hermeneutics (from Schleiermacher to Dilthey, Heidegger, and Gadamer).[5] I then drew support from the idea that all knowledge, which is by definition limited, refers to what for it is the final referent, recognized as such by the scientific community of the same discipline, this referent being final only in this domain and being defined along with it. A dualism of referents must not be transformed into a dualism of substances. This interdiction concerns the philosopher just as much as the scientist: for the first, the term "mental" is not the equivalent of the term "immaterial," quite the opposite. Mental experience implies the bodily but in a sense of the word "body" irreducible to the objective body as it is known in the natural sciences. To the body-as-object is semantically opposed the lived body, one's own body, my body (whence I speak), your body (you, to whom I am speaking), his or her body (his or hers, those about whom I recount the story). There is but one body that is mine, whereas all the body-objects are before me. The ability to account for the "objectification," as it is called, by which the lived body is apprehended as a "body-object" remains a problem poorly solved by the phenomenologist-hermeneutian.[6] In fact, the distance is great between the body as lived and the body as object. To travel it, one must take the detour by way of the idea of a common nature and, to do that, pass by way of the idea of an intersubjectivity founding a common knowledge, and move all the way back to the attribution of comparable and concordant mental states among a plurality of embodied subjects. In the final analysis, only this plurality is entitled to speak of "my" brain as one of many brains, as one other among all the other brains. I can then say that the other, like me, has a brain. At the end of this long circuit is "the" brain, the object of the neurosciences. They take for granted the process of objectification that remains a considerable problem for hermeneutical phenomenology, one that in many respects has been poorly solved. Indeed, in what sense are the lived body and the body as object the same body?[7] The problem is difficult inasmuch as we do not, at first glance, see any passage from one discourse to the other: either I speak of neurons and so forth, and I confine myself to a certain language, or else I talk about thoughts, actions, feelings, and I tie them to my body, with which I am in a relation of possession, of belonging. We can credit Descartes with having carried the problem of epistemological dualism to its critical point, beyond the complacencies and confusions of medieval hylomorphism, to the threshold of the notion of "man," considered as that being who is not in his body as the pilot in his ship.[8] The brain is remarkable in this respect: whereas I have a dual relationship with certain—sensorial, motor—organs, which allows me, on the one hand, to consider the eyes and hands as part of objective nature and, on the other hand, to say that I see with my eyes, grasp with my hands, I cannot say in the same manner, in accordance with the same sense of belonging, that I think with my brain. I do not know if it is contingent that the brain is insensible, but it is a fact that I neither feel nor move my brain as an organ belonging to me. In this sense, it is entirely objective. I can appropriate it to myself only as something lodged in my cranial cavity, hence in the head which I honor and protect as the site of power, hegemony, in the upright position, in my manner of carrying myself and holding myself in the face of the outside world. The scientist may perhaps venture to say that the human being thinks with his or her brain. For the philosopher there is no parallel between the two sentences: "I grasp with my hands," "I understand with my brain." For the philosopher, the scientist gives himself leave, in his own linguistic contract, to take the preposition "with" as designating something other than the body's lived bond of belonging and possession, namely, the relation between organization and function, about which we will now say a few words.

Transported to the border of the epistemological and the ontological, the philosopher willingly confines himself to Plato's formula in the *Phaedo*: questioned about the reasons why he does not flee but remains sitting there awaiting the death inflicted on him by the city, Socrates gives two answers: he stays in this position because the parts of his body keep him there; the body is then the cause without which—the *causa sine qua non*; but the true cause that makes him stay there is obedience to the laws of the city. Borrowing this formula, I will say that the brain is the cause only on the level of conditionality expressed by the idea of *causa sine qua non*. Along with Aristotle, within the framework of his theory of the forms of causation, we can thus speak of the material cause, or as I prefer to say, of substratum.

The scientist still respects the limits of this causal discourse when he confines himself to speaking of the "contribution" of a given cortical region, of the "role," the "implication," even the "responsibility" of a certain neural sequence, or when he states that the brain is "involved" in the appearance of certain psychical phenomena. But the biologist demands more, independently of the philosophical option, willingly shared by the scientific community, that the body-soul dualism is anathema and that material monism is a self-evident presupposition, an article of faith that underpins the contract governing the scientific community. On his own territory, the neuroscientist calls for a less negative use for the idea of the causation that reigns between structure or organization and function. This relation spans a certain heterogeneity—organization is not function—and as such amounts to a correlation. But this correlation expresses more than the cause *sine qua non*: to the latter is added a positive conditionality, one which authorizes *in fine* the assertion that the brain is the organization that brings it about that I think, or, in brief, that makes me think. Pushing his advantage further, the biologist will derive an argument from the correlation between structure and function and will trace entities that belong for other reasons to mental discourse, such as representations and images, entities that are manifestly bound up with function, back to the cerebral organization. Here the philosopher will flinch, suspecting a semantic amalgamation that, in his opinion, violates the liberties attached to the idea of correlation. But the biologist sees a reason for this the new ambiguity attached to the notion of function: bit by bit, everything noncortical comes down to such a function. The hegemonic tendency of every science is then exercised with respect to closely related sciences, either below the level of the cortical organization of the organism as a whole, on the level of biochemistry, implied in particular in the treatment of synaptic shifters, or, more problematically for the philosopher, above the properly cortical level, in the order of the cognitive sciences (the expression used becomes the neurocognitive sciences), the psychology of behavior, ethnology, social psychology, even to the point of crossing blithely over the gap separating the cortical trace from the cultural trace. Here, the philosopher may or may not be willing to temper his semantic vigilance with respect to such transgressions stipulated by the scientific community in question. In this way, however, the neurologist allows himself to place images in the brain, despite the reservations nourished by the philosopher's desire for semantic rigor. The transgression can appear less flagrant to the philosopher when the neurosciences approach the phenomenology of action on the basis of the idea that the brain is a projective system, where the related ideas of anticipation and of exploration belong to a new mixed domain, as though the boundary between the scientific and the phenomenological discourses was more porous in the practical domain than in the theoretical dimension. On this plane of action, the correlation between neurology and phenomenology is equivalent to a correspondence.[9]

(b) With the question of specifically mnestic traces, we tighten our grasp and come closer to the source of amnesia and forgetting. At the same time, we come closer to the heart of the debate, namely, the relation between the phenomenological signification of the memory-image and the materiality of the trace.

At first sight, phenomenology has little to gain from clinical instruction, extended by anatomo-physiological observation applied to the brain. On several occasions, I have ventured to say that knowledge of what occurs in the brain makes no direct contribution to self-understanding except in the case of dysfunctions, for the reason that behavior is then affected, if only through the recourse to treatment, and more generally by reason of readjustments in behaviors to a "reduced" environment, to use Kurt Goldstein's expression, already borrowed by Canguilhem. But even then, when an illness emerges that directly involves the brain, the readjustment of all behaviors to the "catastrophic situation" so overwhelms the concerns of the patient's family members, to say nothing of the patient's own difficulties, that this upheaval in behavior becomes an obstacle to taking into account information about the brain. One would be tempted to say that the neurosciences in no way contribute directly to the conduct of life. This is why one can develop an ethical and political discourse on memory—and conduct cutting-edge scientific activities in many human sciences—without ever mentioning the brain. The epistemology of historical knowledge itself has had neither the occasion nor the obligation to resort to the neurosciences; its ultimate referent, social action, has not required it. I have no intention, however, of claiming for the phenomenology of memory any sort of right to ignorance with respect to the neurosciences.

The neurosciences that target memory can provide instruction, in the first instance, about the conduct of life on the level of reflective knowledge in which a hermeneutics of life would consist. Beyond this direct utility, there is our curiosity about the things of nature, and among these the brain is doubtless the most marvelous product. This curiosity—which is basically the same one that motivates the epistemology of history—is one of the dispositions that articulates our relation to the world. The causal dependence in which we find ourselves with respect to cerebral functioning, a dependence whose knowledge we owe to such curiosity, continues to instruct us, even in the absence of suffering due to dysfunction. This instruction helps to warn us about the pretentious *hubris* that would make us the masters and possessors of nature. Our entire being-in-the-world is shaken by this. And if there is one point at which the phenomenology of memory is placed in resonance with this general lesson of the neurosciences, it is at the level of our reflections on the worldly character of memory, following the design of Casey's work, *Remembering*. But this breach in the wall of mutual misunderstanding can be widened.

It is striking that the works dealing directly with memory and its distortions[10] devote a great deal of effort to what Pierre Buser calls a taxonomy of memory or rather of memories: how many memories, one wonders, have to be counted?[11] This is the second great lesson received from chemistry. A direct confrontation with the phenomenology of memory proposed above is required at this level. In this regard, the discordances, more superficial than first apparent, should not surprise us. For the most part, they result from differences on the plane of questioning and of methods of approach. Our typology, with its pairs of oppositions, was essentially motivated by the question of time, of distance and temporal depth; in addition, it was oriented by a traditional conceptuality (as we saw in concepts such as representation, fiction, depiction); finally, it was carried by the concern for essential analysis, often running counter to the distinctions of common sense or of the experimental psychology of the times.

On its side, the taxonomy resulting from clinical investigations depends on observation conditions that are frequently quite remote from those of everyday life. Either these are reconstructions of structures that must be pre-supposed in order to account for the selective nature of this or that dysfunc-tion, or they are observations conducted under entirely artificial conditions, the experimenter being in control of the game, in particular with regard to formulating the tasks proposed to the subjects of the experiment. The responses provided to these tasks are, in their turn, interpreted in terms of the range of criteria of success selected, even in relation to the diversity of options provided by the researchers, often shaped by very different exper-imental traditions. Thus, the distinctions proposed by Buser result from a sort of consensus to which, in addition to clinical work as such, cognitive science, behavioral psychology, ethology, and social psychology have con-tributed. These distinctions are no less interesting as a result. This is true of the best-confirmed distinction between short-term memory and long-term memory, and of the further distinctions within each of these. For example, there is immediate memory, a subdivision of short-term memory, whose effectiveness is measured on the scale of a second (we are straightaway in the objective time of chronometers); there is also task memory, whose very name recalls the manner in which it has been apprehended, namely, in the execution of various cognitive tasks defined by the experimenter. Of partic-ular interest is the distinction between declarative memory and procedural memory (activities of movement and motor aptitudes); this distinction recalls Bergson's "two memories" or the theory of *habitus* in Panofsky, Elias, and Bourdieu. It is striking that this compartmentalizing has continually been pushed further, according to the class of activities concerned (learning, rec-ognizing objects, faces, semantic acquisitions, information, and know-how); everything, even spatial memory, is entitled to a separate mention. One is struck both by the amplitude and precision of the information and by a certain narrowness due to the abstract character of the experimental condi-tions in relation to the concrete situations of life, in relation also to other mental functions, and, finally, in relation to the organism's involvement as a whole. In this respect, the efforts to compensate for this compartmentalizing reported by Buser, leading to the fragmentation of specialized memories, de-serves to be taken into account. The notion of consciousness, in the sense of simple vigilance or awareness, thus makes its reappearance in the field of neu-rocognitive disciplines, and with it the notion of levels of consciousness. One thus obtains the interesting distinction between explicit and implicit mem-ory of the infraconscious order. In this regard, the title Buser gives to one chapter—"Consciousness and Infraconsciousness"—perfectly expresses the ambition to reassemble the disintegrated taxonomies on the basis of levels of consciousness and no longer in terms of criteria of success in accomplishing tasks. It is then no longer the "worldly" side of memory that is addressed, as it was earlier, but its modes of reappropriation by subjective consciousness. In this way, our theory of memory attribution is found to be enriched by taking into consideration the degrees of effectiveness of conscious awareness. Later on we shall return to this theme in connection with recollection and the difficulties of recollection that are of interest to an investigation of forgetting.

The reader will probably wonder what has become in all of this of the cerebral localizations or the assignment of a given mnemonic function to a particular circuit, to a particular neural architecture. Here we touch upon the most delicate point of the adventure, not so much on the plane of anatomical-clinical observation as on that of the interpretation of knowledge about mnestic traces.

It is, in fact, at the moment the neurosciences are closest to their target that they reach their most problematic point. The localizations in terms of areas, circuits, and systems are the most remarkable illustration of the correlation between organization and function. What has just been described in terms of the taxonomy of memories concerns the function side for which properly neuroscience seeks a counterpart in terms of organization, the cortical counterpart. We touch on the most remarkable and most admirable aspect of the entire enterprise here; progress in the identifying of functions and the identifying of organizations. In this respect, the work of localization is far from completed.

But what, finally, would be understood, if one were successful in drawing up a table with two columns, the cortical geography on one side, the functional taxonomy on the other? Would one then understand the mnemonic phenomenon in its most intimate constitution?

To tell the truth, what we are supposed to clarify is the very signification of the notion of trace in relation to elapsed time. The difficulty the entire enterprise runs up against is the result of one simple fact: "All traces are present to our minds. There is no hint of something that is absent. It is necessary then to endow the trace with a semiotic dimension, so that it functions as a sign, and to regard the trace as a sign-effect, a sign of the action of the seal in creating the impression" (*What Makes Us Think?* 149). What if one were to pass from the metaphor of the imprint in wax to that of the graphism of the tableau? The aporia is the same: "How is it that such an inscription is itself present and yet also a sign of what is not present, of what existed previously?" (149). What if one were to invoke the stability of traces, in the manner of hieroglyphics? (Jean-Pierre Changeux speaks of "synaptic hieroglyphs," 141). The hieroglyphs would still have to be deciphered, as when the age of a tree is read by counting the concentric circles drawn on the tree stump. In short, "a trace must therefore be conceived at once as a present effect and as the sign of its absent cause. Now, in the trace, there is no otherness, no absence. Everything is positivity and presence" (150).

In this sense, the aporia was complete in its initial formulation in Plato's *Theaetetus*. The metaphor of the imprint does not resolve the enigma of the representation of absence and distance. That is not its role. Its role is to make a function correspond to an organization. As concerns the mnemonic function, it is specified, among all other functions, by the relation of the representation to time and, at the heart of this relation, by the dialectic of presence, absence, and distance that is the mark of the mnemonic phenomenon. Only discourse about the mind can account for this dialectic. The task of the neurosciences is then to express not what makes me think, namely, this dialectic, but what makes it possible for me to think, namely, the neural structure without which I could not think. This is not nothing, but neither is it everything.

(c) Something still has to be said about forgetting! Clinical investigation approaches the precise subject of forgetting only in the context of dysfunctions, or as is said, of "distortions of memory." But is forgetting a dysfunction, a distortion? In certain respects, yes. In the matter of definitive forgetting, indicating an effacement of traces, it is experienced as a threat: it is against this forgetting that we conduct the work of memory (*oeuvre de mémoire*) in order to slow its course, even to hold it at bay. The extraordinary exploits of the *ars memoriae* were designed to ward off the misfortune of forgetting by a kind of exaggerated memorization brought to the assistance of remembering. But artificial memory is the great loser in this unequal battle. In brief, forgetting is lamented in the same way as aging and death: it is one of the figures of the inevitable, the irremediable. And yet forgetting is bound up with memory, as we shall see in the next two sections: its strategies and, under certain conditions, its cultivation worthy of a genuine *ars oblivionis* result in the fact that we cannot simply classify forgetting through the effacement of traces among the dysfunctions of memory alongside amnesia, nor among the distortions of memory affecting its reliability. Certain facts we will discuss later lend credit to the paradoxical idea that forgetting can be so closely tied to memory that it can be considered one of the conditions for it. This imbrication of forgetting in memory explains the silence of neurosciences on the unsettling and ambivalent experience of ordinary forgetting. But the first silence is here that of the organs themselves. In this respect, ordinary forgetting follows the fate of happy memory: it is silent about its neural base. Mnemonic phenomena are experienced in the silence of our organs. Ordinary forgetting is in this respect on the same silent side as ordinary memory. This is the great difference between forgetting and all the types of amnesia with which clinical literature abounds. Even the misfortune of definitive forgetting remains an existential misfortune which beckons us more to poetry and to wisdom than to science. And, if this forgetting has a word to say on the level of knowledge, it would be to question the border between the normal and the pathological. This effect of interference is not the least troubling. In addition to the biological and medical fields, another problematic rises up against this backdrop of silence. It concerns the limit situations where forgetting rejoins aging and mortality. Here, it is not simply the organs that remain silent, but scientific and philosophical discourse, to the extent that this discourse is caught in the nets of epistemology. The critical philosophy of history and memory fails to prove itself equal to the hermeneutics of the historical condition.

## FORGETTING AND THE PERSISTENCE OF TRACES

We have not yet finished with the question of inscription. As has been said, the notion of trace can be reduced neither to the documentary trace nor to the cortical trace. Both consist of "external" marks but in different senses: that of the social institution for the archive, that of biological organization for the brain. There remains the third sort of inscription, the most problematic but the most significant for what follows in our investigation; it consists in the passive persistence of first impressions: an event has struck us, touched us, affected us, and the affective mark remains in our mind.

It is astonishing that this thesis has to be at the level of a presupposition. We shall say why this is so in a moment. But let us first set out the multiple presuppositions implied here. For one thing, and this is the major presupposition, I contend that it is a primordial attribute of affections to survive, to persist, to remain, to endure, while keeping the mark of absence and of distance, the principle of which was sought in vain on the level of cortical traces. In this sense, these inscription-affections would contain the secret of the enigma of the mnemonic trace: they would be the depository of the most hidden but most original meaning of the verb "to remain," synonym of "to endure." This first presupposition places the entire analysis that follows within the compass of Bergson's *Matter and Memory*.[12]

For another thing, this meaning would ordinarily be concealed from us by the obstacles to recollection which we will attempt to inventory in the third section of this chapter. In this regard certain privileged experiences—we shall discuss their central figure in a moment—constitute, despite these obstacles, the beginning of an existentiell verification of this second presupposition.

Third presupposition: there is no contradiction between the assertion concerning the capacity of the inscriptions-affections to remain and to endure and the knowledge of cortical traces; access to these two sorts of traces stems from heterogeneous modes of thought: existentiell on the one hand, objective on the other.

Fourth presupposition: the survival of images, recognized in its specificity by virtue of the last two presuppositions, deserves to be considered a fundamental form of profound forgetting, which I am calling the reserve of forgetting.

The first presupposition will be the object of our main discussion. The second will be examined in the third section of this chapter. The fourth will appear in the conclusion of the present section.

The third presupposition can be discussed now since it directly places in question the difference between the two types of traces confronted here, the cortical trace and the psychical trace. We must forcefully affirm that nothing is retracted regarding the best-established teachings of the neurosciences by this exploration of the affective trace: more or less serious deficits continue to threaten our memory and result in the fact that forgetting due to the effacement of cortical traces remains the common figure of this insidious danger; besides, the cortical basis of our corporeal existence continues to constitute the cause *sine qua non* of our mental activity in the silence of our organs; finally, the correlation between organization and function also continually sustains, without our knowledge, the constant hum of our corporeal condition. It is therefore not in opposition to this basic structure that the working hypothesis we are proposing here presents its forms of proof. There are two heterogeneous types of knowledge with regard to forgetting: an external knowledge and an intimate knowledge. Each possesses its reasons for confidence and its motives for suspicion. On the one hand, I trust the corporeal machine in the exercise of happy memory; but I am suspicious of its poorly mastered resources for harm, worry, and suffering. On the other hand, I trust the primordial capacity of enduring and continuing belonging to inscriptions-affections, a capacity but for which I would have no access to the partial comprehension of what is meant by the presence of absence, anteriority, distance, and temporal depth; but I am also suspicious of the impediments imposed to the work of memory, which become in their turn the opportunity for uses and abuses of forgetting. It is in this way that we manage to contend with potentially reversible obstacles and with intractable effacement. This confusion is no less harmful on the epistemological level than on the existentiell plane. To the hesitation between the threat of definitive forgetting and forbidden memory is added the theoretical incapacity to recognize the specificity of the psychical trace and the irreducibility of the problems tied to the impression-affection. This state of confusion, as much epistemological as existentiell, forces us to return to the first presupposition which the following two only reinforce.

Which experiences can be held to confirm the hypothesis of the survival of impression-affections beyond their emergence? The experience *princeps* in this regard is recognition, that minor miracle of happy memory. An image comes back to me; and I say in my heart: that's really him, that's really her. I recognize him, I recognize her. This recognition can take different forms. It takes place already in the course of perception: a being was presented once; it went away; it came back. Appearing, disappearing, reappearing. In this case the recognition adjusts—fits—the reappearing to the appearing across the disappearing. This small happiness of perception has provided the occasion for many classical descriptions. One thinks of Plato discussing the disappointments of mistaken and the opportunities of successful recognition in the *Theaetetus* and the *Philebus*. One thinks of the vicissitudes of recognition, of the *anagnōrisis*, in Greek tragedy: Oedipus recognizes in his own person the evil initiator of the misfortunes besetting the city. One thinks of Kant reconstructing the objectivity of the phenomenon on the basis of the threefold subjective synthesis, recognition (*Rekognition*) crowning simple apprehension in intuition and the reproduction of representations in the imagination. One also thinks of Husserl equating perception of the spatial object with the sum of its profiles or sketches. Kantian recognition, in its turn, will have a conceptual descendent in *Anerkennung*, Hegelian recognition, the ethical act in which the problematic of intersubjectivity culminates, at the intersection of the subjective spirit and the objective spirit. In many different ways, cognizing is recognizing. Recognition can thus draw support from a material basis, from a figured presentation such as a portrait or photograph, the representation inducing an identification with the thing depicted in its absence: this entanglement was the subject of Husserl's interminable analyses relating *Phantasie*, *Bild*, and *Erinnerung*.

Finally, there is properly mnemonic recognition, ordinarily called recollection, outside of the context of perception and without any necessary support in representation. It consists in the exact superimposition of the image present to the mind and the psychical trace, also called an image, left by the initial impression. It realizes the "fit" mentioned by the *Theaetetus* between the placement of the foot and the prior imprint. This multifaceted minor miracle proposes a solution in the form of action to the first enigma constituted by the present representation of a past thing. In this respect, recognition *is* the mnemonic act par excellence. Without this actual resolution the enigma would remain an aporia pure and simple. Upon this converge the presumptions of reliability or unreliability directed to memories. Perhaps we have placed a foot in the wrong imprint or grabbed the wrong ring dove in the coop. Perhaps we were the victims of a false recognition, as when from afar we take a tree to be a person we know. And yet, who, by casting suspicions from outside, could shake the certainty attached to the pleasure of the sort of recognition we know in our hearts to be indubitable? Who could claim never to have trusted memory's finds in this way? Do not outstanding events like this, the founding events of a solitary existence or of one shared with others, reveal this prime trust? And do we not continue to measure our mistakes and our disappointments against the signals coming from an unshakable recognition?

The enigma of the presence of absence is resolved, we have just said, in the effective reality of the mnemonic act and in the certainty that crowns this reality. But is it not rendered more impenetrable on the speculative plane? Let us return to the conclusion of our first presupposition: the impression-affection, we judged, remains. And because it remains it makes recognition possible. But how did we know this? The speculative enigma persists at the very heart of its effective resolution. The presupposition is, in fact, entirely retrospective. It is pronounced after-the-fact. Perhaps this is even the model for what is after-the-fact. In the narrative that follows it is pronounced only in the future perfect: it will have been true that I recognized this beloved being as having remained the same despite a long absence, a definitive absence. "So late did I recognize you, O Truth!" Augustine painfully cries. So late did I recognize you, is the emblematic admission of all recognition. On the basis of the retrospective presupposition, I construct an argument: something of the original impression has to have remained for me to remember it now. If a memory returns, this is because I had lost it; but if, despite everything, I recover it and recognize it, this is because its image had survived.

This is, in a nutshell, Bergson's argument in *Matter and Memory*. In my eyes, Bergson remains the philosopher who has best understood the close connection between what he calls "the survival of images" and the key phenomenon of recognition. To verify this, let us stop and look at chapters 2 and 3 of *Matter and Memory*, which form the psychological heart of the entire work. Chapter 2 is titled, "Of the Recognition of Images: Memory and Brain." And chapter 3, "On the Survival of Images: Memory and Mind."

To understand the centrality of these two chapters, let us go back in our investigation to the point where we first encountered, separately, the problematic of recognition and that of the survival of images. We first came across the question of recognition in the framework of our phenomenology of memory on the occasion of the distinction between two memories: habit-memory, which is simply acted out and lacks explicit recognition, and recollection-memory, which is not without declared recognition. But at this stage it remained one polarity among others. As concerns the question of survival, we first came upon it, already with Bergson, in connection with the distinction between memories and images; we then postulated the existence of a "pure" memory as a virtual state of the representation of the past, prior to its becoming an image in the mixed form of memory-image. At that time, it was the "realization of memory" that was retained, without clarifying the postulation of the "pure" memory, as though its quotation marks protected it from our curiosity. We left the "pure" memory virtual. It is at this critical point that we must take up our reading again, pushing it to the point of assigning to this "pure" memory unconsciousness and an existence comparable to that we attribute to external things when we do not perceive them, besides virtuality. These audacious equivalences will later authorize us, in turn, to elevate this status of the survival of images to a second paradigm of forgetting, in competition with the paradigm of the effacement of traces (our fourth presupposition).

In order to understand this conceptual chain, we must move back further in *Matter and Memory* to the inaugural thesis of the whole work, namely, that the body is solely an organ of action and not of representation and that the brain is the organizing center of this acting system. This thesis excludes from the start a search to determine the reason for the conservation of memories on the side of the brain. The idea that the brain remembers having received an impression is held to be incomprehensible in itself. This does not prevent the brain from having a role to play in memory. But this role is of a different order than representation. As an organ of action it exercises its effects on the trajectory from the "pure" memory to the image, hence on the trajectory of recollection. Bergson's discussion with the neurosciences of his time consists entirely in assigning the field of action, that is to say, in assigning physical movement, to the brain. It is because one cannot expect the brain to hold the solution to the conservation of the past in terms of representation that one must turn in another direction and assign to the impression the power of surviving, of remaining, of enduring, and make this power not an *explicandum*—as in the neural thesis—but a self-sufficient principle of explanation. In Bergson, the dichotomy between action and representation is the ultimate reason for the dichotomy between the brain and memory. This double dichotomy corresponds to the method of division applied rigorously throughout the work, consisting in moving to extreme cases before reconstructing the mixed categories, the ambiguous and disordered phenomena of everyday experience, whose comprehension is deferred. Recognition is the model of these reconstructed mixtures, and the entanglement of the two memories is the example of the mixed that is easiest to take apart and to put back together. Without this key, our reading was unable to discern in the famous distinction between the "two forms of memory" (*Matter and Memory*, 79ff.) two modes of recognition, the first resulting from action, the second from an effort of the mind "which seeks in the past, in order to apply them to the present, those representations best able to enter into the present situation" (78).

A question is thereby posed, that of determining "how these representations are preserved, and what are their relations with the motor mechanisms. We shall go into this subject thoroughly in our next chapter, after we have considered the unconscious and shown where the fundamental distinction lies between the past and the present" (78). It is worth noting that this difficulty can only be posed on the basis of the phenomenon of recognition in which it is resolved through action. Meanwhile, psychology is in a position to declare "that the past indeed appears to be stored up, as we had surmised, under two extreme forms: on the one hand, motor mechanisms which make use of it; on the other, personal memory-images which picture all the past events with their outline, their color, and their place in time" (88). It can thus be noted that these two extreme forms, "faithful in preserving"—"memory which recalls" and "memory which repeats" (88)—operate sometimes in synergy, sometimes in opposition. We have nevertheless been warned about the privilege accorded by common sense to the mixed phenomena, and priority has been given, by reason of the rule of division,[13] to the extreme forms, putting out of play "the strange hypothesis of recollections stored in the brain, which are supposed to become conscious as though by a miracle and bring us back to the past by a process that is left unexplained" (89). Here again, I encounter my argument that the material trace is completely present and must be supplied with a semiotic dimension in order to indicate that it has to do with the past. In Bergson's vocabulary, the cortical trace has to be placed back at the center of this totality of images that we call the world (this is the theme of the enigmatic and difficult chapter 1) and treated as "one among these images, the last is that which we obtain at any moment by making an instantaneous section in the general stream of becoming. In this section our body occupies the center" (77).[14]

At this stage of the analysis, a precise division of the two memories is all that prepares the path for the thesis of the independence of representation-memory. Nothing has yet been said about the conditions of this independence. At least it can be affirmed that "the concrete act by which we grasp the past in the present is *recognition*" (90). It will be the task of chapter 3 to take on the question left hanging: "how these representations are preserved, and what are their relations with the motor mechanisms?" (78).

Let us open chapter 3: in forty-some extremely dense pages (133–77), Bergson provides the key to what he calls the "survival of images" (133).

We only scratched the surface of the analysis when we followed the phases of the operation by which the "pure" memory moves out of its virtual state and passes into its actual state; at that time, all that retained our attention was the memory's becoming-an-image. The question posed now is more radical: despite its tendency to imitate perception as it realizes itself, Bergson notes, our memory "remains attached to the past by its deepest roots, and if, when once realized, it did not retain something of its original virtuality, if, being a present state, it were not also something which stands out distinct from the present, we should never know it for a memory" (134). Everything is stated in a tone of great elegance: standing out distinct from the present, knowing it for a memory. This is the enigma, reaffirmed in its entirety, of the present of absence and of distance, as it has been stated from the start of the present work![15]

The survival of images is a radical solution to this enigma. It consists in a chain of propositions derived by implication from the phenomenon of recognition. Recognizing a memory is finding it again. And finding it again is assuming that it is in principle available, if not accessible. Available, as though awaiting recall, but not ready-to-hand like the birds in Plato's dovecote which one possesses but does not hold. The experience of recognition, therefore, refers back to the memory of the first impression in a latent state, the image of which must have been constituted at the same time as the original affection. An important corollary to the thesis of the survival of images of the past in a state of latency is, in fact, that any given present is, from the moment of its appearance, its own past. For how could it become past if it were not constituted at the same time it was present? As Gilles Deleuze notes: "There is here, as it were, a fundamental position of time, and also the most profound paradox of memory: The past is 'contemporaneous' with the present that it *has been*. If the past had to wait in order to be no longer, if it was not immediately and now that it had passed, 'past in general,' it could never become what it is, it would never be *that* past.... The past would never be constituted, if it did not coexist with the present whose past it is" (*Bergsonism*, 58–59). Deleuze adds: "Not only does the past coexist with the present that has been, but ... it is the whole, integral past; it is *all* our past, which coexists with each present. The famous metaphor of the cone represents this complete state of coexistence" (59).

The idea of latency, in its turn, calls for the idea of the unconscious, if we term consciousness the disposition to act, the attention to life, by which the relation of our body to action is expressed. Let us stress with Bergson: "Our present is the very materiality of our existence, that is to say, a system of sensations and movements and nothing else" (*Matter and Memory*, 139). As a consequence of this, "by hypothesis" (140) the past is "that which does not act" (141). It is at this crucial moment of his argument that Bergson declares: "This radical powerlessness of pure memory is just what will enable us to understand how it is preserved in a latent state" (141). The word "unconscious" can then be pronounced in connection with "powerlessness." The chain of implications is completed with the addition of a final term: we are free to accord the same sort of existence to memories that have not yet been brought to the light of consciousness through recollection as the existence we grant to the things around us when we are not perceiving them.[16] It is this sense of the verb "to exist" which is implied in the thesis of latency and of the lack of consciousness of memories of the past that are conserved: "But here we come to the capital problem of *existence*, a problem that we can only glance at, for otherwise it would lead us step by step into the heart of metaphysics" (146–47). This thesis remains at the level of presupposition and retrospection. We do not perceive this survival, we presuppose it and we believe it.[17] Recognition authorizes us to believe it: what we have once seen, heard, experienced, or learned is not definitively lost, but survives since we can recall it and recognize it. It survives. But where? This is the tricky question. An inevitable question perhaps inasmuch as it is difficult not to designate the psychical place as a container "whence," as one says, the memory returns. Does not Bergson himself say that one searches for the memory where it is, in the past? But his entire effort consists in replacing the question "where?" by the question "how?": "I shall then only restore to it its character of memory by carrying myself back to the process by which I called it up, as it was virtual, from the depths of my past" (139). This is perhaps the profound truth of Greek *anamnēsis*: seeking is hoping to find. And finding is recognizing what one once—previously—learned. The powerful images of "places" in Augustine's *Confessions*, comparing memory to "vast palaces" and to "storehouses" in which memories are stocked, literally enchant us. And the ancient association of *eikōn* to *tupos* is insidiously restored. To resist its seduction, the conceptual chain must be continually confirmed: survival equals latency equals powerlessness equals unconsciousness equals existence. The tie linking the elements in the chain is the conviction that becoming, under the sign of memory, does not fundamentally signify passage but duration. A becoming that endures, this is the central intuition of *Matter and Memory*.

But restoring this conceptual chain and rising to this central intuition always involves a leap outside the circle traced around us by our attention to life. It requires carrying ourselves into the region of dreams beyond the realm of action: "A human being who should *dream* his life instead of living it would no doubt thus keep before his eyes at each moment the infinite multitude of the details of his past history" (155). Indeed, a leap is necessary to return to the source of "pure" memory, while another slope of the analysis would lead it in the descent from "pure" memory toward the image in which that memory is realized. The schema of the inverted cone (152) by means of which Bergson visualized, as it were, this process of realization for the reader (as Husserl did in his 1905 lectures) is well known. The base of the cone represents all the memories accumulated in memory. The summit opposite it represents the pinpoint contact with the plane of action, at the point of the acting body. This center is in its own manner a place of memory, but this quasi-instantaneous memory is nothing but habit-memory. It is a moving point, the point of the present that constantly passes, in opposition to "true memory" (151) represented by the vast base of the cone. This schema is meant to illustrate both the heterogeneity of different memories and the manner in which they mutually lend support to one another. The schema is enriched if one superimposes on it the representation of the preceding chapter in which the mass of memories was illustrated by concentric circles that spread indefinitely, following their increasing degree of depth, or was focused on a precise memory, "according to the degree of tension which our mind adopts and the height at which it takes its stand" (105–6). The nonnumerical multiplicity of memories lends itself, in this way, to incorporation into the simplified schema of the cone. It is important that we not overlook this schema, especially as it marks the culmination of the Bergsonian method of division: the relation of the past to the present (152ff.), which the schema illustrates, designates *in fine* the reconstruction of a hybrid, mixed experience: "*Practically, we perceive only the past*, the pure present being the invisible progress of the past gnawing into the future" (150). All the subtleness of the Bergsonian method is at play here: the reflexive movement of returning isolates the "pure" memory in the moment of dreamy thinking. One could speak here of meditating memory, in one of the senses of the German *Gedächtnis*, as distinct from *Erinnerung* and related to *Denken* and *Andenken*. There is, in fact, more than just dreams at issue in the evocation of the latency of what remains of the past: something like speculation (Bergson sometimes speaks of "any entirely contemplative memory," 296), in the sense of thinking at the limit, thinking that speculates on the inevitable quotation marks framing the term "pure" memory. This speculation indeed moves counter to the effort to recollect. In truth, it does not progress, it regresses, recedes, moves back. But it is nevertheless in the very movement of recollection, and so in the movement of the "pure memory" in the direction of the memory-image, that reflection strives to undo what recognition has done, namely, to grasp the past again in the present, absence in presence. Bergson admirably describes this operation. Speaking of the passage of memory from the virtual state to the actual state, he observes: "But our recollection still remains virtual; we simply prepare ourselves to receive it by adopting the appropriate attitude. Little by little it comes into view like a condensing cloud; from the virtual state it passes into the actual; and its outlines become more distinct and its surfaces take on color, it tends to imitate perception. But it remains attached to the past by its deepest roots, and if, when once realized, it did not retain something of its original virtuality, if, being a present state, it were not also something which stands out distinct from the present, we should never know it for a memory" (134). Recognizing a memory "for a memory" sums up the entire enigma. To bring it to light one must dream, to be sure, but one must also think. Then we begin to speculate on the significance of the metaphor of depth, and on the meaning of virtual state.[18]

A few critical remarks are necessary before we consider the fourth and final presupposition of the second voyage to the land of oblivion, namely, the right to consider the "survival of images" as a figure of forgetting, worthy of being opposed to forgetting through the effacement of traces.

My remarks bear on two points: first, is it legitimate to isolate the thesis that Bergson himself terms psychological from the metaphysical thesis which gives *Matter and Memory* its complete title? In fact, the two central chapters that we have taken as our guides are framed by an introductory and a concluding chapter which together sketch out the metaphysical envelope of the psychology. The book opens with a metaphysical thesis: it claims that the whole of reality is a world of "images" in a sense of the word that goes beyond any psychology. It involves nothing less than tackling the opposition between realism and idealism in the theory of knowledge. These images, which are no longer images of anything, are, Bergson says, a little less substantive than what realism holds to be independent of all consciousness and a little more substantive than what idealism, at least that of Berkeley—already attacked by Kant under the title of "The Refutation of Idealism" in the *Critique of Pure Reason*—holds to be merely the evanescent content of perception. Next the body and the brain are considered to be types of practical intervention, as it were, in this neutral universe of images; as such, they are at once images and the practical center of this world of images. The dismantling of what we call matter is already underway, inasmuch as materialism constitutes the height of realism. But chapter 1 goes no further. And one must then wait until the end of chapter 4 before formulating the complete metaphysical thesis, which, in Frédéric Worms's words, consists in nothing less than "a metaphysics of matter based upon duration."[19] And it is on the basis of a metaphysics of this sort that a rereading of the classical problem of the union of soul and body (as Bergson prefers to put it in *Matter and Memory*, 180) is possible, a rereading that consists in part in eliminating a false problem and in part in developing a dualism outside the categories of the historical figures of dualism. In this way, phases of monism alternate with phases of dualism according to the type of multiplicities to be divided and of mixed natures to be reconstructed. One is thus surprised to discover that the opposition between duration and matter is not definitive, if it is true that one can form the idea of a multiplicity of more or less extended rhythms of duration. This differentiated monism of durations has nothing in common with any of the dualisms developed since the period of the Cartesians and post-Cartesians.[20]

This is not, however, the final word of this work. The last pages of *Matter and Memory* are devoted to the formulation of three classical oppositions: extended/unextended, quality/quantity, liberty/necessity. *Matter and Memory*, then, has to be read from the first to the last chapter, and to its final pages. I admit as much.

It remains that the psychology founded on the pair recognition/survival is not only perfectly well defined in the course of the work, but can be considered to be the key to the metaphysics that circumscribes it. Everything begins in fact with the thesis that "our body is an instrument of action, and of action only" (225). This is how the pages titled "Summary and Conclusion" (225–49) begin. The opposition between action and representation, in this sense, constitutes an initial thesis which is explicitly psychological and only implicitly metaphysical by virtue of its consequences for the idea of matter. From this, one passes to the thesis of the self-survival of images of the past, through the intermediary of a corollary to the first thesis, namely, that consciousness of the present consists essentially in the attention to life. This is simply the reverse side of the thesis that a "pure" memory is marked by powerlessness and unconsciousness and, in this sense, exists by itself. A psychological antithesis thus presides over the entire undertaking, and the two terms that provide the title for the two central chapters—the recognition of images and the survival of images—are based upon this antithesis.

It is with respect to this psychology that I attempt to situate myself, abstracting from the generalized theory of images of chapter 1 and from the hyperbolic use that is made of the notion of duration at the end of chapter 4 in the name of a hierarchy of the rhythms of tension and contraction of duration. For my part—and this will be the second series of my remarks—I try to reinterpret the opposition *princeps* between the brain as the instrument of action and self-sufficient representation in terms compatible with the distinction I make between mnestic traces, the material substratum, and psychical traces, the pre-representative dimension of living experience. To say that the brain is the instrument of action and of action only is, to my mind, to characterize the neural approach as a whole, an approach that provides access solely to the observation of phenomena that are actions in the purely objective sense of this term. The neurosciences indeed are cognizant only of the correlation of organizations and functions, hence of physical actions, and the traces resulting from these structures are not designated as traces in the semiological sense of sign-effects of their cause. This transposition of Bergson's inaugural thesis concerning the brain as the simple instrument of action does not keep us from restoring to action, in the lived sense of the word, its share in the structuring of lived experience, paired with and not in antithesis to representation. This restitution, however, encounters definite resistance on the part of Bergson. According to him, action is much more than physical movement, that instantaneous sectioning of the world's process of becoming—it is an attitude of life; it is consciousness itself as acting. And it takes a leap to break out of the magical circle of the attention to life in order to surrender oneself to recollection in a sort of dream-like state. In this respect, literature more than everyday experience is on the side of Bergson: the literature of melancholy, of nostalgia, of *spleen*, to say nothing of *The Remembrance of Things Past*, which, more than any other work, stands as the literary monument in symmetry with *Matter and Memory*. But can action and representation be so radically disassociated? The general tendency of the present work is to consider the pair formed by action and representation to be the twofold matrix of the social bond and of the identities that are established by this bond. Is this difference of opinion the sign of a break with Bergson? I do not believe so. Instead we must return to the Bergsonian method of division which invites us to consider the opposite extremes of a spectrum of phenomena before reconstructing the everyday experience whose complexity and disorder hinder clear description as a mixture. I can thus say that I rejoin Bergson along the path of this reconstruction: in fact, the experience *princeps* of recognition, which is paired with that of the survival of images, presents itself as just such a lived experience along the path of the recollection of memories. It is in this lived experience that the synergy between action and representation is confirmed. The moment of "pure" memory, encountered through a leap outside of the practical sphere, was only virtual, and the moment of actual recognition marks the reinsertion of memories within the thickness of lived action. Granted that at the moment of the leap, the recollection does "stand out distinct" from the present, to borrow Bergson's felicitous expression, this movement of retreat, of hesitation, of questioning is part of the concrete dialectic of representation and action. The participants in Plato's *Philebus* never tire asking: What is it? Is it a man or a tree? The place accorded to mistakes is indicated by this *epoché*, this suspension, which is lifted by the declarative statement: It's really him! It's really her!

From these remarks it results that recognition can be placed on a different scale than the degrees of proximity relating representation to practice. Representation can also be approached in terms of modes of "presentation" in the Husserlian manner, and to perceptive presentation can be opposed the table of re-presentations, or better yet, presentifications, as in the Husserlian triad of *Phantasie, Bild, Erinnerung*; an alternative conception of representation is thereby offered to reflection.

If these critical remarks lead us away from a certain indiscriminate use of the concept of action, applied to the brain considered a scientific object as well as to the practice of life, they reinforce, in my opinion, the major thesis of the self-survival of the images of the past. This thesis has no need of the opposition between lived action and representation to be comprehensible. This double affirmation suffices: first, that a cortical trace does not survive in the sense of knowing itself as the trace of . . . —of the expired, past event; next, that, if lived experience were not itself from the start self-surviving, and in this sense a psychical trace, it could never become so. All of *Matter and Memory* can then be summed up as follows in the vocabulary of inscription, which inheres in the polysemy of the notion of the trace: inscription, in the psychical sense of the term, is nothing other than the self-survival of the mnestic image contemporaneous with the original experience.

The moment has come, at the end of our exploration, to consider the last of the presuppositions upon which the present investigation is constructed, namely, that the self-survival of impressions-affections deserves to be considered one of the figures of fundamental forgetting, occupying the same rank as forgetting through the effacement of traces. This, Bergson does not state. It even seems that he never thought of forgetting except in terms of effacement. The final sentence of his third chapter makes explicit reference to a form of forgetting like this. It comes at the end of an argument in which the method of division leads back to the level of mixed phenomena: the brain is then placed back in the position of "an intermediary between sensation and movement" (177). And Bergson notes: "In this sense, the brain contributes to the recall of the useful recollection, but still more to the provisional banishment of all the others." Then falls the judgment: "We cannot see how memory could settle within matter; but we do clearly understand—according to the profound saying of a contemporary philosopher (Ravisson)—materiality begets oblivion" (177). This is the final word of the great chapter on survival.

On what basis, then, would the survival of memories be equivalent to forgetting?

Precisely in the name of the powerlessness, of the unconsciousness, of the existence recognized as belonging to memories as "virtual." It is then no longer oblivion that materiality begets, forgetting by the effacement of traces, but forgetting in terms of a reserve or a resource. Forgetting then designates the *unperceived* character of the perseverance of memories, their removal from the vigilance of consciousness.

What arguments can be mustered in support of this presupposition?

First comes the equivocalness that is worth preserving on the level of our global attitude toward forgetting. On one hand, we have the daily experience of the erosion of memory, and we link this experience to aging, to the approach of death. This erosion contributes to what I once called "the sorrow of finitude."[21] It is defined by the horizon of the definitive loss of memory, the announced death of memories. On the other hand, we are familiar with the small pleasures of the sometimes unexpected return of memories we had thought lost forever. We then have to say, as we did once above, that we forget less than we think or we fear.

A range of experiences then come to mind that give the dimension of a permanent existentiell structure to the still point-like episodes of recognition. These experiences mark out the progressive widening of the field of the "virtual." To be sure, the core of profound memory consists in a mass of marks designating what in one way or another we have seen, heard, felt, learned, acquired. These are the birds in the dovecote of the *Theaetetus* which I "possess" but do not "hold." Around this core are assembled the customary manners of thinking, acting, feeling; habits in sum, *habitus* in the sense of Aristotle, Panofsky, Elias, and Bourdieu. In this respect, the Bergsonian distinction between habit-memory and event-memory, which holds at the moment of the realization of a memory, no longer holds on the deep level of storing in reserve. Iteration, repetition dulls the edges of the punctual mnemonic marks and produces the broad dispositions to action that Ravisson celebrated in earlier days under the rich term "habit." Deep memory and habit-memory then coincide with one another in the encompassing figure of availability (*disponibilité*). The capable human being draws from this thesaurus and relies on the security, the assurance that it provides. Next come general forms of knowledge, such as rules of calculation or grammar, familiar or foreign lexicons, rules of games, and so on. The theorems discovered by the young slave of the *Meno* are of this sort. Alongside these general forms of knowledge come a priori structures of knowledge—the transcendental, let us say—everything about which, in company with the Leibniz of the *New Essays on Human Understanding*, we can say that everything that is in the understanding has first been in the senses, except human understanding itself. To this should be added the meta-structures of speculation and of first philosophy (the one and the many, the same and the other, being, substance, *energeia*). Finally, there would come what I have ventured to call the immemorial: that which was never an event for me and which we have never even actually learned, and which is less formal than ontological. At the very bottom, we would have the forgetting of foundations, of their original provisions, life force, creative force of history, *Ursprung*, "origin," irreducible to the beginning, an origin always already there, like the Creation Franz Rosenzweig speaks of in *The Star of Redemption*, which he calls the perpetual ground, the Donation that provides absolutely for the giver to give, for the recipient to receive, for the gift to be given, according to Jean-Luc Marion in *Reduction and Givenness* and in *Being Given*.[22] We leave behind all narrative linearities; or, if we can still speak of narration, this would be a narrative that has broken with chronology. In this sense, every origin, taken in its originating power, reveals itself to be irreducible to a dated beginning and, as such, participates in the same status of fundamental forgetting. It is important that we enter into the sphere of forgetting under the sign of a primordial equivocalness. This will never leave us as we proceed to the very end of this work, as though, coming from the depths of oblivion, the double valence of destruction and perseverance continued up to the superficial levels of forgetting.

With these two figures of deep, primordial forgetting, we reach a mythical ground of philosophizing: that by reason of which forgetting is *Lethe*. But it also provides the resource to memory to combat forgetting: Platonic reminiscence has to do with these two figures of forgetting. It proceeds from the second form of forgetting, which birth could not erase and which nourishes recollection, reminiscence: it is thus possible to learn what in a certain fashion we have never ceased to know. In opposition to destructive forgetting, the forgetting that preserves. In this perhaps lies the explanation for a little noted paradox in Heidegger's text, namely, that it is forgetting that makes memory possible.[23] "Just as expectation is possible only on the basis of awaiting, *remembering* [*Erinnerung*] is possible only on the basis of forgetting, *and not the other way around*. In the mode of forgottenness, having-been primarily 'discloses' the horizon in which Da-sein, lost in the 'superficiality' of what is taken care of, can remember" (312). Some light is shed on this apparent paradox if we take into account an important terminological decision, mentioned in the preceding chapter. While Heidegger uses an everyday vocabulary to designate the future and the present, he breaks with the custom of naming the past *Vergangenheit*, deciding to designate it instead by means of the compound past tense of the verb to be: *gewesen, Gewesenheit* (having-been). This choice is crucial and decides an ambiguity, or rather a grammatical duplicity: we do indeed say of the past that it is no longer but that it has been. Under the first form, we indicate its disappearance, its absence. But absence to what? To our claim to act on it, to hold it "at hand" (*zuhanden*). Under the second form, we underscore the complete anteriority of the past with respect to every event that is dated, remembered, or forgotten. An anteriority that is not confined to removing it from our grasp, as is the case of the past as expired (*Vergangenheit*), but an anteriority that preserves. No one can make it the case that what is no longer has not been. The forgetting which, according to Heidegger, conditions remembering is related to the past as having-been. We comprehend the apparent paradox if, by forgetting, we understand an immemorial resource and not an inexorable destruction. To confirm this reading hypothesis, one can go back a few lines, to the passage in which Heidegger relates forgetting to repetition ( *Wiederholung*) in the sense of return, "retrieve," consisting in taking over "resolutely the being that it already is" (311). A pairing is thus made between "anticipating" and "returning," like the pairing of horizon of expectation and space of experience in Koselleck, but on the level that Heidegger considers to be derivative with respect to historical consciousness. The chain of related expressions is organized around the "already," the temporal mark common to throwness, to being-in-debt, to falling-prey-to: having-been, forgetting, ownmost potentiality, repetition, retrieve. In summary, forgetting has a positive meaning insofar as having-been prevails over being-no-longer in the meaning attached to the idea of the past. Having-been makes forgetting the immemorial resource offered to the work of remembering.

Finally, the primary equivocalness of destructive forgetting and of founding forgetting remains fundamentally undecidable. In human experience, there is no superior point of view from which one could apprehend the common source of destroying and constructing. In this great dramaturgy of being, there is, for us, no final assessment.


## THE FORGETTING OF RECOLLECTION:
## USES AND ABUSES

We now turn our attention to the second dimension of memory, the reminiscence of the ancients, the recollection or recall of the moderns: what modalities of forgetting are revealed by the conjoined practice of memory and forgetfulness? We now shift our gaze from the deepest layers of existence, where forgetting silently pursues at one and the same time its work of eroding and its work of maintaining, toward the levels of vigilance where the ruses of the attention to daily life are deployed.

This level of manifestation is also the place where the figures of forgetting are scattered, defying typology, as is evident in the quasi-innumerable variety of verbal expressions, the sayings of folk wisdom, proverbs and maxims, but also the literary embellishments whose analytical history is presented by Harald Weinrich. The reasons for this surprising proliferation are to be sought in several places. On the one hand, remarks about forgetting in large part represent the reverse side of expressions about memory; remembering is in large measure not forgetting. On the other hand, individual manifestations of forgetting are inextricably mixed with its collective forms, to the point that the most troubling experiences of forgetting, such as obsession, display their most malevolent effects only on the scale of collective memories. It is also on this scale that the problematic of forgiving intervenes, a problematic we shall set aside for as long as possible.

In order to orient ourselves in this maze, I propose a simple reading grid containing once again a vertical axis of degrees of manifestation and a horizontal axis of modes of activity or passivity. Pierre Buser's comments on the conscious and the infraconscious on the level of mnemonic phenomena pave the way for the first rule of organization; to this we will add the vast contributions of psychoanalysis which will be made apparent directly below. As concerns the modes of passivity and activity that are spread out horizontally, the entire phenomenology of recollection has prepared us to take this into account: the effort of recollection possesses different degrees on a scale of arduousness, as the Medieval scholars would have said. Is this not the final word of Spinoza's *Ethics*: "All things excellent are as difficult as they are rare"? By joining together in this way two rules of classification, from the deepest to the most manifest, from the most passive to the most active, we thereby link up with the typology of the uses and abuses of memory, without an excessive concern with their symmetry: blocked memory, manipulated memory, obligated memory. This, however, will not represent a simple duplication, insofar as the complex phenomena integrated here could not have been anticipated on the level of the phenomenology of memory, phenomena involving not only collective memory but the complicated play between history and memory, without mentioning the intersections between the problematic of forgetting and that of forgiving which will be treated directly in the epilogue.

### Forgetting and Blocked Memory

One of the reasons for believing that forgetting through the effacement of cortical traces does not exhaust the problem of forgetting is that many instances of forgetting are due to impediments blocking access to the treasures buried in memory. The often unexpected recognition of an image of the past has thus constituted up to the present the experience *princeps* of the return of a forgotten past. For didactic reasons related to the distinction between memory and reminiscence, we confined this experience to the trait of suddenness, abstracting from the work of recollection that may have preceded it. Now it is on the path of recollection that obstacles to the image's return are encountered. From the instantaneousness of the image's return and its grasp, we move back to the gradualness of the search and the hunt.

At this stage of our inquiry, we systematically collect, for the second time, the teachings of psychoanalysis most helpful in breaching the impasse of the analytical colloquy. After rereading the two texts examined in light of the theme of blocked memory, we will widen this opening in the direction of phenomena more specifically assignable to the problematic of forgetting and especially significant on the plane of a collective memory steeped in history.

The blocked memory discussed in "Remembering, Repeating, and Working Through" and in "Mourning and Melancholia" is a forgetful memory. We recall Freud's remark at the start of the first text: the patient repeats instead of remembering. "Instead of": repetition amounts to forgetting. And forgetting is itself termed a work to the extent that it is the work of the compulsion to repeat, which prevents the traumatic event from becoming conscious. Here, the first lesson of psychoanalysis is that the trauma remains even though it is inaccessible, unavailable. In its place arise phenomena of substitution, symptoms, which mask the return of the repressed under the various guises offered to the deciphering engaged in together by the analyst and the analysand. The second lesson is that, in particular circumstances, entire sections of the reputedly forgotten past can return. For the philosopher, psychoanalysis is therefore the most trustworthy ally in support of the thesis of the unforgettable. This was even one of Freud's strongest convictions, that the past once experienced is indestructible. This conviction is inseparable from the thesis that the unconscious is *zeitlos*, timeless, when time is understood as the time of consciousness with its before and after, its successions, and coincidences. In this regard, there is a necessary connection between Bergson and Freud, the two advocates of the unforgettable. I see no incompatibility between their respective notions of the unconscious. Bergson's unconscious covers the whole of the past, which present consciousness centered on action closes off behind it. Freud's unconscious seems more limited, if one may say so, to the extent that it covers only the region of memories to which access is forbidden, censured by the bar of repression; in addition, the theory of repression, tied to the compulsion to repeat, appears to confine the discovery within the domain of the pathological. On the other hand, Freud corrects Bergson on an essential point, which at first sight seems to render Bergsonism inadmissible with respect to psychoanalysis. Whereas the Bergsonian unconscious is defined by its powerlessness, the Freudian unconscious, through its tie with instinctual drives, is characterized as energy, which encouraged the "economic" reading of this doctrine. Everything that Bergson appears to place on the side of the attention to life seems here to be related to the dynamism of unconscious libidinal drives. I do not think that one should stop with this apparently glaring discordance. On Bergson's side, the final word has not yet been uttered with his equating of powerlessness, the unconscious, and existence. The pure memory is powerless only with respect to a consciousness that is preoccupied with practical utility. The powerlessness assigned to the mnemonic unconscious is such only by antiphrasis: it is sanctioned by the leap outside of the magic circle of short-term preoccupation and by the retreat into the domain of dreaming consciousness. What is more, the thesis of the revival of images of the past seemed to us to be compatible with a consideration of the pair action/representation, which leaves outside the field of living experience only the sort of action accessible to the objective gaze of the neurosciences, namely, the neural functioning without which we would not think at all. On the side of psychoanalysis, the break that characterizes the unconscious of repression from the unconscious of pure memory does not constitute an unbridgeable gap in relation to the Bergsonian unconscious. Is there not also a suspension of immediate concern required to access the analytical colloquy and its rule of "saying everything"? Is not the entry into psychoanalysis a manner of letting the dream express itself? But, more especially, what we have just called the second lesson of psychoanalysis, namely, the belief in the indestructibility of the experienced past, is accompanied by a third lesson, more apparent in the second essay mentioned in our chapter on blocked memory: the working-through in which the work of remembering consists does not occur without the work of mourning, through which we separate ourselves from the lost objects of love and hate. This integration of loss through the experience of remembering is of considerable significance for all of the metaphorical transpositions of the teachings of psychoanalysis outside of its sphere of operation. The danger here, and one which cannot be expressed in the same conceptual terms as the compulsion to repeat, at least in the first approximation, is the attraction of melancholia, whose ramifications we explored far outside the properly pathological sphere where it was described by Freud. In this way, the clinical tableau of what are termed transference neuroses is composed, through the figures of substitution expressing the symptoms and the forms of self-deprecation belonging to melancholia, the overpowering return of the repressed, and the hollow feeling of the lost self. It is no longer possible to think in terms of drives without also thinking in terms of lost objects.

Do the lessons of psychoanalysis that we have just recalled provide access to the abuses that are encountered as soon as we step outside of the analytical dialogue framed by professional competence and deontology and move away from the clinical setting? Yes, probably. It is a fact that psychoanalysis, for better or for worse, has produced a sort of vulgate that has raised it to the level of a cultural phenomenon, at once subversive and formative. It is also a fact that Freud was the first to take his discovery beyond the bounds of medical confidentiality, not only by publishing his theoretical investigations, but by multiplying his excursions outside of the sphere of pathology. In this regard, his *Psychopathology of Everyday Life* forms a precious reference point along the path leading from the analytical colloquy into the public arena of the world at large.

It is a fact that the *Psychopathology of Everyday Life* deals principally with forgetting, the sphere of activity so close to public space. And the harvest it yields is a rich one. First, by reconnecting the apparently broken threads of the present with a past one might have thought forever erased, the work enriches in its own way the plea of the *Interpretation of Dreams* on behalf of the indestructibility of the past. Next, by revealing the intentions rendered unconscious by the mechanisms of repression, it introduces intelligibility where one ordinarily invokes chance or reflex. Finally, along its path it sketches lines of transposition running from the private sphere to the public sphere.

The case of forgetting proper names, with which the work opens, provides a marvelous illustration of the first purpose. One seeks a name one knows, another pops up in its place. The analysis reveals a subtle substitution motivated by unconscious desires. The example of screen-memories, interposed between our infantile impressions and the narratives we confidently tell about them, adds to the mere substitution of names in forgetting the actual production of false memories which, unbeknown to us, lead us astray. Forgetting impressions and events we have experienced (that is to say, things we know or knew) and forgetting projects, amounting to omissions, to selective ignorance, reveals a sly side of the unconscious when it is placed on the defensive. The cases of forgetting plans—omitting doing something—reveals, in addition, the strategic resources of desire in its relations with others: conscience will draw its arsenal of excuses from it for its strategy of exoneration. Language contributes to this by its slips; body gestures, by mistakes, awkwardness, and other failed actions (the desk key that one uses in the wrong door). The same cleverness, coiled inside unconscious intentions, can be recognized in another aspect of everyday life, in the life of peoples: forgetting things, screen-memories, failed actions take on gigantic proportions on the scale of collective memory, which history alone, and more precisely the history of memory, is capable of bringing to light.

### Forgetting and Manipulated Memory

Pursuing our exploration of the uses and abuses of forgetting beyond the psychopathological level of blocked memory, we encounter forms of forgetting that are at once further removed from the deep levels of forgetting, hence more manifest, but also more widely spread out between the poles of passivity and activity. This was the level of manipulated memory in our parallel study of the practices related to recollection. This was also the level on which the problematic of memory intersected with that of identity to the point of converging with it, as in Locke: everything that compounds the fragility of identity also proves to be an opportunity for the manipulation of memory, mainly through ideology. Why are the abuses of memory directly abuses of forgetting as well? At that time we stated that it was due to the mediating function of the narrative that the abuses of memory were made into abuses of forgetting. In fact, before the abuse, there was the use, that is the unavoidably selective nature of narrative. If one cannot recall everything, neither can one recount everything. The idea of an exhaustive narrative is a performatively impossible idea. The narrative necessarily contains a selective dimension. Here we touch upon the close relation between declarative memory, narrativity, testimony, and the figured representation of the historical past. As we remarked then, the ideologizing of memory is made possible by the resources of variation offered by the work of narrative configuration. The strategies of forgetting are directly grafted upon this work of configuration: one can always recount differently, by eliminating, by shifting the emphasis, by recasting the protagonists of the action in a different light along with the outlines of the action. For anyone who has crossed through all the layers of configuration and of narrative refiguration from the constitution of personal identity up to that of the identities of the communities that structure our ties of belonging, the prime danger, at the end of this path, lies in the handling of authorized, imposed, celebrated, commemorated history— of official history. The resource of narrative then becomes the trap, when higher powers take over this emplotment and impose a canonical narrative by means of intimidation or seduction, fear or flattery. A devious form of forgetting is at work here, resulting from stripping the social actors of their original power to recount their actions themselves. But this dispossession is not without a secret complicity, which makes forgetting a semi-passive, semi-active behavior, as is seen in forgetting by avoidance (*fuite*), the expression of bad faith and its strategy of evasion motivated by an obscure will not to inform oneself, not to investigate the harm done by the citizen's environment, in short by a wanting-not-to-know. Western Europe and indeed all of Europe, after the dismal years of the middle of the twentieth century, has furnished the painful spectacle of this stubborn will. Too little memory, which we discussed elsewhere, can be classified as a passive forgetting, inasmuch as it can appear as a deficit in the work of memory. But, as a strategy of avoidance, of evasion, of flight, it is an ambiguous form of forgetting, active as much as passive. As active, this forgetting entails the same sort of responsibility as that imputed to acts of negligence, omission, imprudence, lack of foresight, in all of the situations of inaction, in which it appears after-the-fact to an enlightened and honest consciousness that one should have and could have known, or at least have tried to know, that one should have and could have intervened. In this way, as social agents remaster their capacity to give an account, one encounters once again along this path all of the obstacles related to the collapse of the forms of assistance that the memory of each person can find in the memory of others as they are capable of authorizing, of helping to give, an account in the most intelligible, acceptable, and responsible manner. But the responsibility of blindness falls on each one. Here the motto of the Enlightenment: *sapere aude!* move out of the state of tutelage! can be rewritten: dare to give an account yourself!

At this level of the manifestation of forgetting, halfway between the disturbances belonging to a psychopathology of everyday life and the disturbances ascribable to a sociology of ideology, historiography can attempt to give an operational efficacy to the categories borrowed from these two disciplines. The history of the present day provides a propitious framework in this regard for such a test, inasmuch as it situates itself on another frontier, on that border where the testimony of witnesses who are still living rubs up against writing, in which the documentary traces of the events considered are already being collected. As has already been stated once in anticipation, the period of the history of France that followed the violence of the period 1940–45—and in particular, the equivocal political situation of the Vichy regime—lends itself in an elective manner to a historicizing transposition of certain psychoanalytic concepts which themselves have slipped into the public domain, such as trauma, repression, return of the repressed, denial, and so forth. Henry Rousso[24] has taken the epistemological—and at times, political—risk of constructing a reading grid for public and private behaviors, from 1940–44 to today, on the basis of the concept of obsession: the "obsession of the past." This concept is related to that of repetition, which we have encountered along the way, in opposition, precisely, to the concept of working-through, of the work of memory. The author is thus able to consider his own contribution to the history of the "Vichy syndrome" as an act of citizenship, destined to help his contemporaries move on from the still unfinished exorcism to the work of memory, which, it must not be forgotten, is also a work of mourning.

The choice of the theme of the obsession of the past provides the opportunity to write along with the history of the Vichy regime "another history, . . . the history of the *memory* of Vichy, of Vichy's remnants and fate *after* 1944" (Rousso, *The Vichy Syndrome*, 1). In this sense, the Vichy syndrome is an outgrowth of the history of memory discussed in the preceding chapter.[25] The category of obsession belongs to this history of memory as the posterity of the event. Another advantage of this theme: it directly targets forgetting along with memory, through the bungled acts, the things left unsaid, the slips of the tongue, and especially the return of the repressed: "For study reveals that, even at the social level, memory is a structuring of forgetfulness" (4). Another reason for privileging this subject: it puts on stage the fractures produced by the controversy itself, and thus merits inclusion in the file of *dissensus* opened by Mark Osiel.[26] Once the choice of the theme has been made, the justification of the use of the psychoanalytic "metaphor"[27] of neurosis and obsession finds its heuristic fruitfulness in its hermeneutical efficacy. This efficacy is demonstrated principally on the level of the "chronological ordering" of the symptoms referring back to the syndromes. This ordering has, according to the author, brought to light a four-stage process (10). A phase of mourning between 1944 and 1955, in the sense of an affliction rather than the work of mourning properly speaking, which precisely did not take place—"unfinished mourning" the author notes (15–59). A phase marked by the sequels of civil war, from purges to amnesty. A phase of repression in the establishment of a dominant myth, that of resistance (*le résistancialisme*), in the orbits of the Communist party and the Gaullist party. A phase of the return of the repressed, when the mirror is shattered and the myth is exploded to bits (Rousso provides his best pages here with his reflections on the admirable film *The Sorrow and the Pity*, the Touvier affair receiving by ricochet an unexpected symbolic dimension). Finally, a phase of obsession in which it seems we are still, marked by the awakening of Jewish memory and the importance of reminiscences of the Occupation in internal political debate.

How does the "structuring of forgetfulness" operate in these different phases?

With regard to the first, the concept of screen memory operates on the scale of collective memory as it does on that of the psychology of everyday life, through the exaltation of the event of Liberation: "In retrospect, however, the hierarchy of representations, in which the positive or negative character of an event is allowed to color its historical importance, has supplanted the hierarchy of facts" (15); a screen memory permits the great liberator to say that "Vichy always was and is null and void" (17). Vichy will thus be bracketed, hiding in this way the specificity of the Nazi occupation. The return of victims from the universe of the concentration camps thus becomes the most hastily repressed event. Commemorations seal the incomplete memory and its lining of forgetfulness.

In the phase of repression, the "Gaullian exorcism" (71) almost succeeds in concealing, but cannot prevent, at the time of the Algerian war, what the historian subtly characterizes as "the old divisions resurfacing" (75)— playing and replaying the aftermath. Everything is there: heritage, nostalgia, phantasy (Maurras), and once again celebrations (the twentieth anniversary of the Liberation, Jean Moulin at the Panthéon).

The pages in the work titled "The Broken Mirror" (98ff.) are richest on the level of the play of representations: it describes the impact of the film *The Sorrow and the Pity* in terms of "Pitiless Sorrow" (100). The repressed past explodes onto the screen, crying out its "Remember this!" through the mouths of witnesses placed on stage, through the things they leave unsaid and their slips of tongue. A dimension had been forgotten: the French tradition of state anti-Semitism. The demystification of *résistancialisme* passes by way of a brutal confrontation of memories, one worthy of the *dissensus* discussed here in the wake of Mark Osiel. The exhortation to forget, joined to the presidential pardon accorded to the militia member Touvier, in the name of social peace, carries to the fore a question whose ramifications we will unfold at the appropriate moment, when memory, forgetting, and forgiveness intersect. Here, the historian allows the voice of the citizen to be heard: "How could Pompidou have hoped to draw a veil over internal dissension at a time when people's consciences were being reawakened, when *The Sorrow and the Pity* was raising new questions, and when the debate was being revived? Was it really possible to ignore the concerns of former resistance fighters and deportees, whose greatest fear was that the past might be forgotten?" (125). The question is all the more urgent as "the proposed reconciliation failed to offer, as de Gaulle had been able to do, a satisfactory interpretation of history to go with it" (126). The result is that the pardon of amnesty has taken on the value of amnesia.

Under the title "Obsession"—characterizing a period, which is still our own and which gives the book its perspective—a phenomenon such as the rebirth of a Jewish memory provides a concrete content to the idea that, when we fix a gaze upon an aspect of the past—the Occupation—we blind ourselves to another—the extermination of the Jews. Obsession is selective, and the dominant narratives consecrate the obliteration of part of the field of vision; here again, the cinematic representation plays a role (as in *Shoah* and *Nuit et Brouillard*); here, too, the penal intersects with the narrative: the Barbie trial, before the Legay, Bousquet, and Papon affairs, projected to the front of the stage a misfortune and a responsibility which had failed to be apprehended in their distinct specificity because of the fascination with collaboration. Seeing one thing is not seeing another. Recounting one drama is forgetting another.

In all of this, the pathological structure, the ideological conjuncture, and the staging in the media have, on a regular basis, compounded their perverse effects, while the passivity of excuses has joined forces with the active ruses of omission, blindness, and negligence. The famous "banalization" of evil is in this regard simply a symptom-effect of this stubborn agglomeration. The historian of the present day, then, cannot escape the major question regarding the transmission of the past: Must one speak of it? How should one speak of it? The question is addressed to the citizen as much as to the historian; at least the latter, in the troubled waters of collective memory divided against itself, contributes the rigorousness of a distanced gaze. On one point, at any rate, his positivity can be unreservedly affirmed: in the factual refutation of negationism. Negationism does not stem from the pathology of forgetting, nor even from ideological manipulation, but from promoting false documents, against which history is well equipped since the time of Valla and his demolishing of the false documents of the *Donation of Constantine*. The limit facing the historian—just as for the film maker, the narrator, and the judge—lies elsewhere: in the untransmissible part of extreme experiences. However, as has been stressed on several occasions in the course of this work, to say untransmissible is not to say inexpressible.[28]

### Commanded Forgetting: Amnesty

Do the abuses of memory placed under the heading of obligated, commanded memory find their parallel and complement in the abuses of forgetting? Yes, in the institutionalized forms of forgetting, which are a short step across the boundary from amnesia: this mainly concerns amnesty and, in a more marginal sense, pardoning, also called amnestying pardon. The boundary between forgetting and forgiving is crossed surreptitiously, to the extent that these two dispositions have to do with judicial proceedings and with handing down a sentence. The question of forgiving arises where there has been an indictment, a finding of guilt, and sentencing; the laws dealing with amnesty thus consider it as a sort of pardon. I will limit myself in this chapter to the discretionary institutional aspect of the measures involved and will leave for the epilogue the question of blurring the boundary with forgiveness that results from blurring the boundary with amnesia.

The right to pardon is a royal privilege which is put into effect only periodically at the discretion of the head of state. This residue of a quasi-divine right is related to the subjective sovereignty of the prince and was justified in the theologico-political epoch by the religious unction that crowned the prince's power of coercion. Kant has stated all the good and the bad that can be thought of it.[29]

The significance of amnesty is quite different. To begin with, it brings to conclusion serious political disorders affecting civil peace—civil wars, revolutionary periods, violent changes of political regimes—violence that the amnesty is supposed to interrupt. In addition to these extraordinary circumstances, amnesty is characterized by the agency that establishes it: in France today, the parliament. With regard to its content, amnesty is directed toward a category of infractions and crimes committed on all sides during the period of sedition. In this respect, it functions as a sort of selective and punctual prescription which leaves outside of its field certain categories of lawbreakers. But amnesty, as institutional forgetting, touches the very roots of the political, and through it, the most profound and most deeply concealed relation to a past that is placed under an interdict. The proximity, which is more than phonetic, or even semantic, between amnesty and amnesia signals the existence of a secret pact with the denial of memory, which, as we shall see later, distances it from forgiving, after first suggesting a close simulation.

Considered in its stated intention, the aim of amnesty is the reconciliation of enemy citizens, civil peace. We have several remarkable examples of this. The most ancient, recalled by Aristotle in *The Athenian Constitution*, is taken from the famous decree promulgated in Athens in 403 B.C. after the victory of the democracy over the oligarchy of the Thirty Tyrants.[30] The formula is worth recalling. In fact, it is twofold. On one hand, the decree properly speaking; on the other, the oath taken one by one by the citizens. On one hand, "it is forbidden to recall the evils (the misfortunes)"; the Greek has a single syntagma (*mnēsikakein*) to express this, which indicates recalling-against; on the other, "I shall not recall the evils (misfortunes)" under pain of maledictions unleashed by this perjury. The negative formulations are striking: not to recall. For the recall would negate something, namely, forgetting. Forgetting against forgetting? The forgetting of discord against the forgetting of harms suffered? We must plunge into these depths when the time comes. Remaining on the surface of things, the expressed aim of the Athenian decree and the oath have to be recognized. The war is over, it is solemnly proclaimed: the present combats, of which tragedy speaks, become the past not to be recalled. The prose of the political now takes over. A civic imaginary is established in which friendship and even the tie between brothers are promoted to the rank of foundation, despite the murders within families. Arbitration is placed above procedural justice, which maintains the conflicts under the pretext of judging them. More radically, the democracy wants to forget that it is power (*kratos*): it wants to be forgotten even in victory, in shared goodwill. Henceforth, the term *politeia*, signifying the constitutional order, will be preferred to democracy, which carries the trace of power, of *kratos*. In short, politics will be founded anew on the forgetfulness of sedition. Later we will measure the price to be paid by the effort not to forget to forget.

In France we have a different model with the Edict of Nantes issued by Henry IV. In it we read the following: "Article 1: Firstly, let the memory of all things that have taken place on both sides from the beginning of the month of March 1585 up to our arrival on the throne, and during the other preceding troubles and on their occasion, remain extinguished and dormant as something that has not occurred. It will not be admitted or permissible for our state attorneys nor any other persons, public or private, at any time or for any reason, to make mention of, or initiate trial or pursuit in any court or jurisdiction whatsoever. —Article 2: We forbid any of our subjects regardless of their state or quality to retain any memory thereof, to attack, resent, insult, or provoke one another as a reproach for what has occurred for any reason or pretext whatsoever, to dispute, challenge, or quarrel, nor to be outraged or offended by any act or word; but to be content to live peacefully together as brothers, friends, and fellow citizens, under penalty, for those who contravene this decree, of being punished as violators of the peace and disturbers of the public tranquility." The expression "something that has not occurred" is astonishing: it underscores the magical side of the operation which consists in acting as though nothing had taken place. Negations abound, as in the epoch of Thrasybulus's Greece. The verbal dimension is stressed, along with the penal scope through the cessation of prosecutions. Finally, the trilogy "brothers, friends, fellow citizens" recalls the Greek policies of reconciliation.

Lacking is the oath that places amnesty under the protection of the gods and the curse, that machine for punishing perjury. Same ambition to "silence the un-forgetting of memory" (Loraux, *La Cité divisée*, 171). The novelty does not lie here but in the agency that forbids and in its motivation: it is the King of France who intervenes in a religious controversy and a civil war between Christian sects, at a time in which those involved in the dispute were incapable of producing a spirit of concord regarding the religious conflicts. The statesman here has the advantage over the theologians, in the name of a prerogative no doubt inherited from the kingly right of clemency, but in the name of a political conception itself marked with the stamp of the theological, as is forcefully affirmed in the preamble: it is a most Christian king who proposes, not to reestablish religion, but to establish the public order on a more healthy religious foundation. In this sense, one should speak in this regard less of an anticipation of the ethics and politics of toleration than of "a shattered dream of the Renaissance," that of a Michel de l'Hospital in particular.[31]

Entirely different is the amnesty so abundantly practiced by the French Republic under all its regimes. Entrusted to the sovereign nation in its representative assemblies, it is a political act that has become traditional.[32] The right of the king, with one exception (the right of pardon) is transferred to the people: the source of positive right, the people are authorized to limit its effects; amnesty brings to an end all of the trials being conducted and suspends all judicial indictments. This is then a limited juridical forgetting, but one of vast scope, inasmuch as stopping the trials amounts to extinguishing memory in its testimonial expression and to saying that nothing has occurred.

It is certainly useful—this is the right word—to recall that everyone has committed crimes, to set a limit to the revenge of the conquerors, and to avoid compounding the excesses of combat with the excesses of justice. More than anything, it is useful, as it was in the time of the Greeks and the Romans, to reaffirm national unity by a liturgy of language, extended by the ceremonies of hymns and public celebrations. But is it not a defect in this imaginary unity that it erases from the official memory the examples of crimes likely to protect the future from the errors of the past and, by depriving public opinion of the benefits of *dissensus*, of condemning competing memories to an unhealthy underground existence?

In rubbing shoulders in this way with amnesia, amnesty places the relation to the past outside of the field in which the problematic of forgiving would find its rightful place along with *dissensus*.

What, then, is there to say about the alleged duty of forgetting? Besides the fact that any projection into the future in the imperative mood is just as incongruous in the case of forgetting as it was for memory, a command of this sort would amount to a commanded amnesia. If this were to happen—and unfortunately nothing stands in the way of crossing the thin line of demarcation separating amnesty from amnesia—private and collective memory would be deprived of the salutary identity crisis that permits a lucid reappropriation of the past and of its traumatic charge. Short of this ordeal, the institution of amnesty can respond only to the need for urgent social therapy, in the name not of truth but utility. I shall say in the epilogue how the boundary between amnesty and amnesia can be preserved in its integrity through the work of memory, which work is completed by the work of mourning and guided by the spirit of forgiveness. If a form of forgetting could then be legitimately invoked, it would not be as a duty to silence evil but to state it in a pacified mode, without anger. This enunciation will no longer be a commandment, an order, but a wish in the optative mood.

# EPILOGUE

## *Difficult Forgiveness*

Forgiveness raises a question that in its principle is distinct from the one that, beginning with the preface to this book, has motivated our entire undertaking, namely, the question of the representation of the past on the plane of memory and of history at risk of forgetting. The question now posed concerns an enigma different from that of the present representation of an absent thing bearing the seal of the anterior. It is twofold: on the one hand, it is the enigma of a fault held to paralyze the power to act of the "capable being" that we are; and it is, in reply, the enigma of the possible lifting of this existential incapacity, designated by the term "forgiveness." This double enigma runs diagonally through that of the representation of the past, once the effects of the fault and those of forgiveness have traversed all the constitutive operations of memory and of history and have placed a distinctive mark on forgetting. But, if fault constitutes the occasion for forgiveness, it is the word forgiveness that gives its tone to this epilogue as a whole. This is the tone of an eschatology of the representation of the past. Forgiveness—if it has a sense, and if it exists—constitutes the horizon common to memory, history, and forgetting. Always in retreat, this horizon slips away from any grasp. It makes forgiving difficult: not easy but not impossible.[1] It places a seal of incompleteness on the entire enterprise. If forgiveness is difficult to give and to receive, it is just as difficult to conceive of. The trajectory of forgiveness has its origin in the disproportion that exists between the poles of fault and forgiveness. I shall speak throughout this chapter of a difference in altitude, of a vertical disparity, between the depth of fault and the height of forgiveness. This polarity is constitutive of the equation of forgiveness: below, the avowal of fault; above, the hymn to forgiveness. Two speech acts are at work here; the first one brings to language an experience of the same order as solitude, failure, struggle, those "givens of experience" (Jean Nabert)—those "boundary situations" (Karl Jaspers)—upon which reflective thinking is grafted. In this way, the place of moral accusation is bared—imputability, that place where agents bind themselves to their action and recognize themselves as accountable. The second can be heard in the great sapiential poetry that in the same breath celebrates love and joy. There is forgiveness, this voice says. The tension between the avowal and the hymn will be carried almost to a breaking point, the impossibility of forgiveness replying to the unpardonable nature of moral evil. In this way the forgiveness equation will be formulated.

Begun in this way, the trajectory of forgiveness will then take the form of an odyssey destined to lead forgiveness step-by-step back from the regions furthest removed from selfhood (the juridical, the political, social morality) to the place of its presumed impossibility, namely, imputability. This odyssey crosses through a series of institutions established for the purpose of public accusation. These institutions themselves appear to exist in several layers depending on the degree of internalization of guilt indicated by the social rule: it is on the judicial level that the formidable question of the imprescriptibility of crimes is raised, which can be considered to be the first major test of the practical problematic of forgiveness. This course will be pursued from the plane of criminal guilt to that of political and moral guilt inherent in the status of shared citizenship. The question then raised concerns the place of forgiveness at the margins of the institutions responsible for punishment. If it is true that justice must be done, under the threat of sanctioning the impunity of the guilty, forgiveness can find refuge only in gestures incapable of being transformed into institutions. These gestures, which would constitute the incognito of forgiveness, designate the ineluctable space of consideration due to every human being, in particular to the guilty.

In the second stage of our odyssey, we take note of a remarkable relation which, for a time, places the request for forgiveness and the offering of forgiveness on a plane of equality and reciprocity, as if there existed a genuine relation of exchange between these two speech acts. Our exploration of this track is encouraged by the kinship found in numerous languages between forgiving and giving. In this regard, the correlation between the gift and the counter-gift (the gift in return) in certain archaic forms of exchange tends to reinforce the hypothesis that the request for and the offer of forgiveness are held to balance one another in a horizontal relation. It seemed to me that, before correcting it, this suggestion deserved to be pushed to its limit, to the point where even the love of one's enemies can appear as a mode of reestablishing the exchange on a nonmarket level. The problem then is to recover, at the heart of the horizontal relation of exchange, the vertical asymmetry inherent in the initial equation of forgiveness.

The realization of this unequal exchange must then be carried back to the heart of selfhood. A final effort of clarification resting once again on a horizontal correlation will therefore be proposed with the pair, forgiveness and promise. In order to be bound by a promise, the subject of an action must also be able to be released from it through forgiveness. The temporal structure of action, namely, the irreversibility and unpredictability of time, calls for the response of a twofold mastery exerted over the carrying out of any action. My thesis here is that a significant asymmetry exists between being able to forgive and being able to promise, as is attested by the impossibility of genuine political institutions of forgiveness. Thus, at the heart of selfhood and at the core of imputability, the paradox of forgiveness is laid bare, sharpened by the dialectic of repentance in the great Abrahamic tradition. What is at issue here is nothing less than the power of the spirit of forgiveness to unbind the agent from his act.

There remains the attempt to recapitulate the entire course traveled in *Memory, History, Forgetting* in light of the spirit of forgiveness. What is at stake is the projection of a sort of eschatology of memory and, in its wake, of history and of forgetting. Formulated in the optative mood, this eschatology is structured starting from and built on the wish for a happy and peaceful memory, something of which would be communicated in the practice of history and even in the heart of the insurmountable uncertainties that preside over our relations to forgetting.

§

## THE FORGIVENESS EQUATION

### Depth: The Fault

The fault is the existentiell presupposition of forgiveness (I am using the term "existentiell" in order to emphasize the impossibility of distinguishing here between a trait that is inseparable from the historical condition of the being that we in each case are and a personal and collective experience shaped by a historical culture whose universal character continues to be alleged).

The experience of fault is given essentially in a feeling. This is the first difficulty, inasmuch as philosophy, and more specifically moral philosophy, has given little consideration to feelings as specific affections, distinct from emotions and passions. The notion of self-affection stemming from Kant remains a difficult one in this regard. Jean Nabert, the rationalist philosopher who has ventured farthest in this direction, places the experience of fault, along with those of failure and of solitude, among the "givens of reflection."[2] He thus joins Karl Jaspers, less dependent on the Kantian tradition, who situates culpability, another name for fault, among the "boundary situations," that is to say, those nonfortuitous determinations of existence that we always find already there, such as death, suffering, struggle.[3] In this sense, culpability, guilt, like the other "boundary situations," is implied in every contingent situation and belongs to what we ourselves have designated by the phrase our "historical condition" on the level of an ontological hermeneutics.

The experience of fault offers itself as a given to reflection. It gives rise to thought. What is first offered to reflection is the designation of the fundamental structure in which this experience comes to be inscribed. This is the structure of the imputability of our actions. There can, in fact, be forgiveness only where we can accuse someone of something, presume him to be or declare him guilty. And one can indict only those acts that are imputable to an agent who holds himself to be their genuine author. In other words, imputability is that capacity, that aptitude, by virtue of which actions can be held to someone's account. This metaphor of an account constitutes an excellent framework for the concept of imputability, one that finds another fitting expression in the syntax common to languages that employ the modal verb "can": I can speak, act, recount, hold myself accountable for my actions—they can be imputed to me. Imputability constitutes in this respect an integral dimension of what I am calling the capable human being. It is in the region of imputability that fault, guilt, is to be sought. This is the region of articulation between the act and the agent, between the "what" of the actions and the "who" of the power to act—of agency. And this articulation, in the experience of fault, is in a sense affected, wounded by a painful affection.

This articulation is not unknown to us: we explored it in the first part of this work at the crossroads of an objective analysis of memories as objects and of a reflexive analysis of memory of oneself (part 1, chap. 3). It was already a question there of a *nexus* between the "what" of memories and the "who" of memory. On that occasion we tested the concept of attribution of memories to a subject in which they inhere and proposed redistributing attribution along a threefold axis of mineness, of the close, and of the distant.

In the third segment of this epilogue we will once more have occasion to apply this tripartite division of attribution to forgiveness. At this initial stage of the present investigation, the radical nature of the experience of fault requires us to confine ourselves within the limits of the self-ascription of fault, to sketch out at this level the conditions for a common recognition of a fundamental guilt. The specific form taken by such attribution of fault to the self is avowal, admission, that speech act by which a subject takes up, assumes the accusation. This act assuredly has something to do with remembering inasmuch as in remembering a power of connection capable of engendering history is confirmed. But remembering is, in principle, innocent. And it is as such that we have described it. Or rather, as I put it in *Freedom and Nature*, based upon the hypothesis of the *epoché* of guilt,[4] it is within the eidetic indetermination of a description that as a consequence of its method does not recognize the distinction between innocence and guilt that the phenomenology of memory has been conducted from start to finish. The *epoché* is now removed and, with respect to this intended lack of distinction, fault belongs to the *parerga*, the "asides" of the phenomenology of memory. The enigma of fault then only becomes greater. The question remains to what extent the fault treated in Nabert's vocabulary as a "given of reflection" constitutes, in another vocabulary—that of Jaspers—a boundary situation of the same nature and of the same order as suffering, failure, death, and solitude. The avowal, in any event, bridges the abyss between innocence and guilt hollowed out by a conscientious doubt as methodical as is Cartesian hyperbolic doubt.

In turn, beyond the abyss separating empirical guilt from an innocence termed methodical, avowal bridges another abyss, the abyss between the act and its agent. It is this abyss, and this one alone, that will interest us here. To be sure, it is legitimate to draw a line between the action and its agent. This is what we do when we morally, legally, or politically condemn an action. On its objective side, fault consists in transgressing a rule, whatever it may be, a duty, including its recognizable consequences, that is, fundamentally, a harm done to others. It is acting badly and, as such, is blameworthy, receiving an evaluation in negative terms. In the vocabulary of the Kantian essay on negative magnitudes, fault is a negative magnitude of practice.[5] In this first sense, fault is as limited as the rule it infringes, even if the consequences are through their repercussions themselves indefinite in nature in terms of the suffering inflicted. It is a different matter in the case of the implication of the agent in his or her act. This amounts to a transfer, in the words of Nabert, "produced from the quality of a particular action to the causality of the self."[6] With regard to avowal, what is at issue is, "behind the quality of the action, the quality of the causality from which its action issued" (6). At this level of depth, self-recognition is indivisibly action and passion, the action of acting badly and the passion of being affected by one's own action. This is why recognizing the tie between action and the agent is never without a surprise for consciousness, astonished, after the action, "no longer being able to dissociate the idea of its own causation from the memory of the particular act which it has performed" (4). In this regard, the representation of the act prevents, as it were, the return of the action to the agent. The fragmentary representations of memory follow the lines of dispersion of memories. Reflection, on the other hand, leads back to the center of the memory of self, which is the place of the affection constitutive of the feeling of fault. The path from the act to the agent retraces the path from the memory-object to reflecting memory. It retraces it and detaches itself from it, in the feeling of the loss of its own wholeness. The lack of limitation is at the same time the feeling of the unfathomable. Consciousness of the past, escaping the feeling of disjointedness and of what is over and done with, becomes the appropriation of the power to act in its state of dereliction. Between the evil that lies in its action and the evil that lies in its causation, the difference is that of an inadequation of the ego to its deepest desire. This desire can hardly be expressed except in terms of the desire for wholeness; the latter is better known through failings in the effort to exist than through the approximations of its ownmost being. We could speak in this regard, if not of an immemorial past, at least of "a past that goes beyond the limits of its memories and of all its empirical history" (11). It is the virtue, as it were, of fault to provide access to this pre-empirical past, but not absent its history, so closely does the experience of fault adhere to this history of desire. So it is with prudence that we speak here of metaphysical experience in order to express the anteriority of defective constitution in relation to the chronology of action. The signification of this anteriority has to remain practical and resist any speculative appropriation.

Is this to say that even speculation that would remain under the control of practice is forbidden? I do not see how we could keep this resolution, since the vocabulary of being and nonbeing is already caught up in it through every expression designating the being that we are, through the categories of the desire to be and the effort to exist: in short, the being proper to desire itself. The very term "causation" applied to the power to act and to the powerlessness that represents the fault attests to what I formerly called the ontological vehemence of discourse about the self. This ontological vehemence, which is that of attestation, seems to me to be marked in language by the characterization of fault as evil, a moral evil to be sure, but evil nonetheless.

In Nabert, the substitution of the term "evil" for the term "fault" in the book titled, precisely, *Essai sur le mal* is indicative and exemplary in this regard.[7] The unsettling proximity of "metaphysical" discourses that have become untenable should not paralyze the mind's curiosity to the point of excluding the use of the verb "to be" in the negative form of nonbeing, as the term "moral evil" suggests. However, this is on the condition of adhering to the acceptation of being as power and act rather than as substance, attribute, and accident. This deepening of the depth, so to speak, is not without advantages on the very plane of the phenomenology of fault. I will enumerate these.

First, under the aegis of the metacategory of nonbeing, the experience of fault is placed in relation to other negative experiences that can also be said to participate in nonbeing. For example, failure as the contrary of success in the dimension of efficacity, of effectiveness as such, has its specific vocabulary in terms of power and act, of project and realization, of dream and accomplishment. In this way, failure continues the experience of fault in line with the metaphysics of being and power, which corresponds to an anthropology of capable being. The experience of solitude is no less rich in ontological harmonics: to be sure, it adheres to the experience of fault inasmuch as the latter is essentially solitary, but at the same time, on the contrary, it assigns value to the experience of being-with and, in the name of this dialectic of solitude and sharing, authorizes our saying "us" in all truth. In another language, that of Hannah Arendt, solitude is the counterpart of the fact of human plurality. Solitude remains fundamentally an interruption in reciprocal communication and an expression of its intermittence. In turn, the boundary situation of conflict, according to Karl Jaspers, adds to the intermittence belonging to solitude the idea of an insurmountable antagonism upon which an agonistics of discourse and action are grafted: an agonistics of discourse that imposes the irreducible character of *dissensus*, referred to on several occasions in this book, on the political and social plane—an agonistics of action, which appears inseparable from the fact that all action is acting on . . . , hence a source of asymmetry between the author of the action and its recipient. Placed back into this array, the negative experience of fault contains the dimension of evil.

Another effect of pairing fault with evil in this way: the reference to evil suggests the idea of an excess, of an unbearable overabundance. This aspect of things is particularly stressed in the opening pages of Jean Nabert's *Essai sur le mal.* The chapter is titled "The Unjustifiable." What is signified by this word, which was not used in the *Elements for an Ethic?* It is noteworthy that it is first on the side of action that the notion of evil enters the field of reflection on the unjustifiable, before being referred back to the subject. Considered from the side of the object, the unjustifiable designates this excess of the non-valid, what goes beyond infractions measured by the yardstick of the rules recognized by conscience: a type of cruelty, of baseness, of extreme inequality in social conditions distresses me without my being able to name the norms violated. It is no longer a matter of a simple contrary that I would understand in opposition to what is valid. These are evils that belong to a more radical contradiction than that of the valid and the non-valid, and that give rise to a demand for justification for which performing one's duty is not enough to satisfy. This excessiveness of the non-valid can be suggested only by crossing through the valid to its limit. According to Jean Nabert, "these are evils, these are wounds of inner being, conflicts, sufferings, without any conceivable alleviation." These evils are then indescribable misfortunes for those who suffer them.[8] The accounts of the survivors of the Shoah, so difficult simply to listen to, have pointed in this direction throughout our text: Saul Friedlander spoke in this sense of the "unacceptable," which is an understatement. Considered from the side of the agent to whom these acts can be imputed, the excess belonging to the unjustifiable constitutes another sort of non-limitation different from that of the unfathomable causality hollowed out behind the actions in the interiority of the subject. It is a non-limitation symmetrical to that of the harm done to others, the possibility of which is always inscribed within the harm par excellence, namely, murder, death not suffered but inflicted on the other, in short "the evil that man does to man."[9] Over and beyond the will to make others suffer and to eliminate them indeed stands the will to humiliate, to deliver the other over to the neglect of abandonment, of self-loathing. The unjustifiable goes further than the experience of fault, when an admission of the complicity of the will on the side of the agent is added to the admission of exceeding what is not valid on the side of actions. Here we reach an intimate impediment, a radical powerlessness to coincide with any model of dignity, at the same time as a frenzy of commitment to action which can scarcely be measured in terms of hatred and which explodes the very idea of the subject's being affected by his or her own actions. Even the notion of "impure causation" proposed by Nabert seems inadequate. The idea of an irremediable fall is hardly any more acceptable. It is therefore the extreme evil done to others, rupturing the human bond, that becomes the index of that other extreme, that of the intimate malevolence of the criminal. It is at this point that notions such as the irreparable on the side of effects, the imprescriptible on the side of criminal justice, and the unpardonable on the side of moral judgment present themselves. The final moment of this epilogue will confront these notions. What extreme form of justification still remains accessible in return?[10]

Final benefit of a connection between the idea of fault and the idea of evil: the conjuncture invites us to search within the great cultural imaginary that has nourished the mythical expressions of thought. No theme outside of death and love has given rise to as many symbolic constructions as evil.[11] What remains philosophically instructive is the narrative treatment of the question of the origin with respect to which purely speculative thought loses itself and proves its failure. With the narrative, as we see in the Adamic myth of the Jewish Torah, comes the idea of a primordial event, the idea, as it were, of a transhistorical contingency. The loss of innocence is something that takes place in a primordial time, without connection to the time of history, and hence as something that ought not to have happened. The idea is suggested of an evil that was always already there in experience and yet is fundamentally contingent in the primordial order. It is philosophically interesting in that a distance is established in this way between the agent and the action. The action is henceforth universally reputed to be evil and as such universally deplorable and deplored. But something of the subject is exempt from this, which might not have been dissipated in the adherence of the will to the evil act committed, an innocence which perhaps is not completely abolished and which could reappear on the occasion of certain experiences of extreme happiness. I have elsewhere argued in favor of the thesis that guilt constitutes a boundary situation different from the finiteness constitutive of the human condition. Discontinuity, I thought, would justify the fact that one could pass from an eidetics of the voluntary and the involuntary in the Husserlian manner to a hermeneutics open to the primary symbols of the fault, such as stain, sin, and guilt, and to the secondary symbols structured by the great myths that have nourished in particular the thought of the West, to say nothing of the rationalized myths, belonging to the various gnoses, including the Christian antignostic gnosis of original sin. For our present investigation, this attention given to the myths of guilt retains its interest, not so much for a speculation on the origin of evil, the vanity of which seems irremediable to me,[12] but for an exploration of the resources of regeneration which have remained intact. We shall have recourse to these at the end of our investigation. A place for forgiveness will be sketched out in the hollows of the narrative and mythical treatment of the origin of evil.

## *Height: Forgiveness*

If a single word had to be uttered at the close of this descent into the depths of the experience of fault, abstracting from any escape into a mythical imaginary, it is the term "unforgivable." The word is applicable not only to those crimes that, by reason of the immensity of the misfortune that crushes its victims, fall under the heading of the unjustifiable, according to Nabert. It is applicable not merely to the actors who are named as perpetrating these crimes. It also applies to the most intimate tie that unites the agent to the action, the guilty, to the crime. Regardless of what may in fact be the pre-empirical contingency of the founding event of the tradition of evil, human action is forever submitted to the experience of fault. Even if guilt is not originary, it is forever radical. It is this adherence of guilt to the human condition that, it seems, renders it not only unforgivable in fact, but unforgivable by right. Stripping guilt from our existence would, it seems, destroy that existence totally.

This consequence was drawn with implacable rigor by Nicolai Hartmann in his *Ethics*.[13] If forgiveness were possible, he says, it would constitute a moral evil, for it would place human freedom at God's disposal and would offend human self-respect. "The being-guilty associated with bad action cannot be suppressed for anyone, because it is inseparable from the guilty party."[14] We are carried back to the starting point of the preceding analysis, to the concept of imputability, the capacity to hold ourselves accountable for our actions as their true agent. The experience of fault adheres so closely to imputability that it becomes its organ and its means of revelation. To be sure, Hartmann concedes, one can lessen the bite of guilt, its sting, in relations between communities, but not guilt itself: "There is indeed a victory over evil on the moral plane . . . but not an abolishment of fault." One can arrive at comprehending the criminal, but one cannot absolve him. Fault in its essence is unforgivable not only in fact but by right.

Like Klaus M. Kodalle, I will take these statements by Nicolai Hartmann as a warning addressed to any discourse on forgiveness by a philosophical ethics that considers itself immunized against the infiltration of theology. The tie between fault and self, guilt and selfhood seems indissoluble.

The proclamation summed up in the simple phrase: "There is forgiveness" resonates like an opposing challenge.

The expression "there is" is intended to protect what Levinas called *illéité* in every proclamation of the same sort. Here, *illéité* is the height from which forgiveness is announced, without this height being too hastily assigned to someone who would be the absolute subject. The origin is, to be sure, no less than a person, in the sense that it is a source of personalization. But the principle, Stanislas Breton reminds us, is none of that which proceeds from it. The "there is" of the voice of forgiveness says this in its own way. This is why I will speak of this voice as a voice from above. It is from above, in the way that the admission of fault proceeds from the unfathomable depths of selfhood. It is a silent voice but not a mute one. Silent, because there is no clamor of what rages; not mute, because not deprived of speech. An appropriate discourse is in fact dedicated to it, the hymn. A discourse of praise and celebration. It says: *il y a*, *es gibt*, there is . . . forgiveness—the form of the universal designating *illéité*. For the hymn has no need to say who forgives and to whom forgiveness is directed. There is forgiveness as there is joy, as there is wisdom, extravagance, love. Love, precisely. Forgiveness belongs to the same family.

How could one not evoke the hymn to love proclaimed by Saint Paul in the First Epistle to the Corinthians? But, attention: what the hymn names is not someone, at least not in the first stage of thinking, but a "spiritual gift"—a "charisma"—granted by the Holy Spirit: "About the gifts of the Spirit, there are some things of which I do not wish you to remain ignorant." Thus begins the hymn (1 Cor. 12:1). And the Introit properly speaking goes further: "The higher gifts are the ones you should aim at. And now I will show you the best way of all" (12:31). There follows the famous litany of the "I may . . . " (I may speak in tongues of men or of angels, I may have the gift of prophecy, I may have faith, I may dole out all I possess or even give my body to be burnt . . . ) and the litany of "if I have no love . . . " (if I have no love, I am nothing; I am a sounding gong or a clanging cymbal). This rhetorical attack that articulates its theme by denouncing a defect, a lack, at the connecting point of having and being, expresses in negative terms the path of eminence—the path of that which goes beyond all other spiritual gifts. The apostle can then unleash an effusive discourse in the present indicative tense: love is this . . . is that . . . is what it does. "Love keeps no score of wrongs; does not gloat over other men's sins, but delights in the truth. There is nothing love cannot face; there is no limit to its faith, its hope, and its endurance." If love keeps no score of wrongs, this is because it descends to the place of accusation, imputability, where one's scores, one's accounts are kept. If love declares itself in the present, this is because its time is that of permanence, of the most encompassing duration, the least distended, one would say in the language of Bergson. And it "will never come to an end," it "endures." And it endures in a more excellent manner that the other gifts: "In a word, there are three things that last forever: faith, hope, and love; but the greatest of them all is love." The greatest: because it is Height itself. Now if love excuses everything, this everything includes the unforgivable. If not it would itself be annihilated. In this regard, Jacques Derrida, whom I meet up with again here, is right: forgiveness is directed to the unforgivable or it does not exist. It is unconditional, it is without exception and without restriction. It does not presuppose a request for forgiveness: "One cannot or should not forgive, there is no forgiveness, if there is any, except where there is the unforgivable."[15] All that ensues in the problematic results from this, from what Pascal called "disproportion," in a vocabulary marked by cosmic geometry and the algebra that opposes two infinities. This disproportion between the depth of the fault and the height of forgiveness will be our torment to the end of this essay. For this infinite exigency, emanating from an unconditional imperative, is in fact masked by two sorts of factors belonging to the actual inscription of the imperative in history.

First of all, the commandment to forgive is transmitted to us by a determinate culture, whose broad scope does not succeed in concealing its limitation. It is, Derrida notes, "to a religious heritage, let us say Abrahamic, to gather under it Judaism and the various forms of Christianity and Islam" ("Le Siècle et le pardon"), that the language we are attempting to fit into the imperative mood belongs. This complex and differentiated, even conflicting, tradition is at once singular and in the process of universalization. It is singular in the sense that it is carried by "the Abrahamic memory of the religions of the Book and in a Jewish, but more especially Christian interpretation of the neighbor and the fellow human being" (ibid.). In this regard, no one is unaware that Saint Paul's hymn to love is inseparable from the kerygma of Jesus Christ, from its inscription in a trinitarian proclamation and a typology of "gifts" within the community of the early church. Its enthronement, however, is universal, or at least in the process of universalization, which amounts, in fact, Derrida notes, to a "Christianization which no longer has need of the Christian Church," as one sees on the Japanese stage and on the occasion of certain expressions of a "global-latinization" of Christian discourse. This simple observation raises the considerable problem of the relations between the fundamental and the historical for any ethical message with a universal intent, including the discourse of human rights. In this regard, one may speak of an alleged universal in the process of formation on a worldwide scale, submitted to the discussion of public opinion. Lacking any such ratification, there is reason for concern about banalizing the test of universalization, feeding the confusion between universalization on the moral plane, internationalization on the political plane, and globalization on the cultural plane. There would be little to say about this banalization, except to call for greater semantic vigilance in public discussions, if a second factor, which Jacques Derrida calls "staging," did not intervene. He is thinking of "all the scenes of repenting, of confessing, of forgiving, or of making excuses that have been multiplying on the geopolitical stage since the last war and which have accelerated in the last few years." And it is by virtue of these that the Abrahamic language of forgiveness has spread in an uncritical manner. What can be said about "the theatrical space" in which "the great scene of repentance" is played? What about this "theatricality"? It seems to me that one may suspect a phenomenon of abuse to be at work here, comparable to those denounced repeatedly in this work, whether it be a matter of the alleged duty of memory or of the era of commemoration: "But the simulacrum, the automatic ritual, the hypocrisy, the calculation or mimicry have often joined in and invited themselves along as parasites to this ceremony of guilt." In fact, this involves one and the same complex of abuses. But the abuse of what? If we say, again with Derrida, that there is "a universal urgency for memory" and that "we must turn toward the past," the question ineluctably arises of inscribing this moral necessity within history. Derrida admits this when he asks, rightly, that this act of memory, of self-accusation, of "repentance," of summons to appear, be carried "at once beyond the political institutions and beyond the nation-state." But it is then a serious question to know whether a margin beyond the legal and the political can be identified at the heart of either order, in a word, whether the simulacrum can mimic authentic gestures, even legitimate institutions. The fact that the notion of a crime against humanity remains in this respect "on the horizon of the entire geopolitics of forgiveness" is doubtless the ultimate test of this vast interrogation. For my part, I will rephrase the problem in these terms: if there is forgiveness, at least on the level of the hymn—of the Abrahamic hymn, if one likes—is there some forgiveness for us? Some forgiveness, in the sense of the French partitive [as in *du pardon*]. Or must one say, with Derrida: "Each time that forgiveness is in the service of a finality, be it noble and spiritual (repurchase or redemption, reconciliation, salvation), each time that it tends to reestablish a normalcy (social, national, political, psychological) through a work of mourning, through some therapy or ecology of memory, then 'forgiveness' is not pure—nor is its concept. Forgiveness is not, and it should not be, either normal, or normative, or normalizing. It should remain exceptional and extraordinary, standing the test of the impossible: as if it interrupted the ordinary course of historical temporality." This "test of the impossible" is what we must now confront.

## THE ODYSSEY OF THE SPIRIT OF FORGIVENESS: THE PASSAGE THROUGH INSTITUTIONS

The situations globally classified under the heading institution—of the distant other—have in common the fact that fault is placed under the social rule of indictment. Here, within an institutional framework that authorizes it, when someone accuses someone else according to the rules in force, that person becomes an accused, someone who is charged, indicted. A connection that has not yet been mentioned is set into place, the connection between forgiveness and punishment. The axiom goes as follows: in this social dimension, one can forgive only where one can punish; and one must punish where there has been an infraction of the common rules. The series of connections is rigorous: where there is a social rule, there is a possibility of infraction; where there is an infraction there is the punishable, punishment aiming at restoring the law by symbolically and effectively negating the harm committed at the expense of the other, of the victim. If forgiveness were possible at this level, it would consist in lifting the punitive sanction, in not punishing when one can and should punish. It is impossible to do this directly; forgiveness creating impunity is a great injustice. In terms of indictment, forgiveness cannot meet fault head-on but can only marginally encounter the guilty party. De jure unforgivability remains. To guide us through the labyrinth of institutional levels, I am adopting a reading grid similar to that proposed by Karl Jaspers in *Die Schuldfrage*—that shocking work of the early postwar period, translated as *The Question of German Guilt*, which, more than a half-century later, should be restored in its full conceptual scope.[16]

Jaspers distinguishes four types of guilt, all bearing on actions and through them on the persons submitted to the judgment of the court. These acts correspond with the following criteria: what is the category of fault? before what court? with what effects? permitting what sort of justification, exoneration, or sanction? Jaspers places criminal guilt at the fore, as we will do here: this has to do with acts in violation of univocal laws; the competent agency is the court within the framework of the trial; the effect produced is the punishment. The question of legitimacy, one should add, shifts from the plane of an international law in the process of formation to the plane of public opinion educated by *dissensus*, following the schema suggested above in our discussion of the relations between the judge and the historian. I will provisionally set aside the three other sorts of guilt: political guilt associated with the citizen by reason of belonging to the same political body as state criminals; moral guilt related to all the individual acts susceptible of having actually contributed, in one way or another, to crimes of state; and, finally, the guilt termed "metaphysical" that arises from the fact of being a human being, in a transhistoric tradition of evil. This final sort of guilt is the one that was considered at the start of this epilogue.

### Criminal Guilt and the Imprescriptible

The twentieth century brought criminal guilt to the forefront on the occasion of the crimes that belong to Nabert's category of the unjustifiable. Some of these were judged at Nuremberg, in Tokyo, in Buenos Aires, in Paris, Lyon, and Bordeaux. Others are being or will be judged at the Hague before the International Criminal Court. Judging these crimes has given rise to special criminal legislation of both international and domestic law defining these crimes as crimes against humanity, distinct from war crimes, and among these, the crime of genocide. This legal provision touches on our problem of forgiveness through the question of imprescriptibility.

The question of imprescriptibility arises because prescription exists in the law for all violations and crimes. On the one hand, the legislation of civil law itself includes a dual form, acquisitive and liberating. Under the first form, it provides that, after a certain period of time, a claim of ownership of property cannot be opposed to the one who has possession of it in fact; it thus becomes a means of acquiring definitive ownership of property. Under the second form, one is freed from an obligation, from a debt, through its liquidation. On the other hand, prescription is a provision of criminal law, where it consists in the termination of legal action. Once a certain period of time has passed, it forbids the plaintiff from bringing a suit before the competent court. Once the court has taken up a matter, it prevents the continuation of legal action (in France, with the exception of the crimes of desertion and insubordination defined by the code of military justice). Under all its forms, prescription is an astonishing institution, which is reluctantly authorized by the presumed effect of time on obligations that are supposed to persist over time. Unlike amnesty, which, as was shown at the end of the chapter on forgetting, tends to erase the psychical or social traces, as if nothing had happened, prescription consists in a prohibition against considering the criminal consequences of the action committed, including the right and even the obligation to begin criminal proceedings. If prescription has to do with time, if it is "an effect of time" as the French Civil Code declares,[17] then it is irreversibility that is at issue: it is refusing, after a lapse of arbitrarily defined years, to move back up the course of time to the act and to its illegal or irregular traces. The traces are not erased: it is the path back to them that is forbidden, and this is the meaning of the word "cessation" applied to debts and to the right of criminal prosecution. How can time of itself—which is already a manner of speaking—result in prescription without there being a tacit consent by the public to inaction? Its justification is strictly utilitarian. It is a matter of public utility to set a term to the possible proceedings involving the taking of property, the recovery of debts, and the public action directed against those who infringe the social rule. The prescription regarding taking serves to consolidate ownership; the liberating form of prescription protects against indefinite indebtedness. The prescription of public action in criminal matters reinforces the conclusive, "definitive," character of criminal verdicts in general, which are supposed to put an end to the condition of legal uncertainty leading to proceedings. In order to terminate proceedings, they must not be reopened or not opened at all. The concept of termination (*extinction*)—termination of debt in civil law, termination of the right to prosecute in criminal law—is significant in this respect. It includes both a phenomenon of passivity, of inertia, of negligence, of social inaction and an arbitrary social gesture that authorizes considering the institution of prescription to be a creation of positive law. The role of social regulation exercised here is of a different order than forgiveness. Prescription has a role in preserving social order over a long time frame. Even if forgiveness has an important social role, as will be demonstrated later in company with promising, its nature and origin are inscribed within the social function, even when it is most deeply affected by the concern with domestic peace.

It is against this backdrop that we must place the legislation that declares the imprescriptibility of crimes against humanity, and among these the crime of genocide.[18] Imprescriptibility signifies that the principle of prescription has no reason to be invoked. It suspends a principle that itself consists in an obstacle to the exercise of public action. By suppressing the statute of limitations, the principle of imprescriptibility authorizes the indefinite pursuit of the authors of these immense crimes. In this sense, it restores to the law its force to persist despite the obstacles to carrying through the effects of the law. The justification for this suspension of a rule which itself is suspensive draws upon several arguments. Fundamentally, it is the extreme gravity of the crimes that justifies tracking down the criminals without any time limit. Confronting the fallacious argument of the wearing away of public outrage through the mechanical effect of time, the presumption is that the reprobation regarding the crimes considered knows no limit in time. Added to this argument is the consideration of the perversity of concerted plans, as seen in the restrictive definition of a crime against humanity in French domestic law. Such circumstances justify a particular zeal in tracking criminals, taking into account the impossibility of a rapid judgment, so good are the guilty at hiding from justice either by fleeing or changing their identity. In the face of these ruses, proofs are needed that resist time's attrition, as is a language that does not recognize the statute of limitations. Having said this, what about the relations between the imprescriptible and the unforgivable? In my opinion, it would be an error to confuse the two notions: crimes against humanity and the crime of genocide can be said (improperly) to be unpardonable only because the question does not arise. As we suggested above: justice must be done. Pardon cannot be substituted for justice. To forgive would be to ratify impunity, which would be a grave injustice committed at the expense of the law and, even more so, of the victims. The confusion has, however, been encouraged by the fact that the enormity of the crimes breaks with the principle of proportionality governing the relations between the scale of infractions or crimes and the scale of punishment. There is no punishment appropriate for a disproportionate crime. In this sense, a crime of this sort constitutes a de facto instance of the unforgivable.[19] What is more, this confusion could have been encouraged by the related concept of expiation. We do speak of an inexpiable crime. But what would expiation be, if not an absolution obtained from the punishment itself, which would have emptied, so to speak, the cup of wickedness? In this sense, the effect of expiation would be to terminate proceedings, as prescription requires. From then on, to call certain crimes inexpiable would amount to declaring them unforgivable. But this problematic is inappropriate for criminal law.

Is this to say that the spirit of forgiveness can give no sign of itself on the level of criminal guilt? I do not think so. It has been noted that this sort of guilt continues to be measured by the yardstick of the infractions of univocal laws. These are crimes that are said to be imprescriptible. But it is individuals who are punished. Inasmuch as guilty signifies punishable, guilt moves from the acts back to the authors. But something is owed to the guilty. One may call it consideration, the opposite of contempt. One can understand the scope of this provision of the spirit only if one leaves the special region of extreme crimes and returns to common crimes. Their authors have the right to consideration because they remain human beings like their judges; as such, they are presumed innocent until they are found guilty. In addition, they are summoned to appear along with their victims on the same stage within the framework of the trial; they too are authorized to be heard and to defend themselves. Finally, they submit to the sentence which, even when it is reduced to a fine and to the deprivation of freedom, remains one form of suffering added to another, especially in the case of lengthy sentences. Consideration, however, is not limited to the framework of the trial, or to the framework in which the sentence is served. It is called upon to permeate all of the operations implied in the treatment of criminality. It involves, to be sure, police operations. But, even more significantly, consideration concerns the spirit in which criminal matters should be approached. If it is true that one of the functions of the trial is to substitute discourse for violence, discourse for murder, it is a fact that everyone does not have the same access to the arms of discussion. There are those who are excluded from speech, who, dragged before the courts, in particular in the case of those apprehended in flagrante delicto, can view their appearance in court as one more instance of what they experience on a daily basis as institutional violence. It is then the judgment on the law made from outside by morality that justifies the adage: *summum jus, summa injuria*. This judgment made by morality on justice is extended to a judgment made within the judicial system, in the form of injunctions addressed to justice, requiring that it be ever more just, that is to say, at once more universal and more singular, more concerned with the concrete conditions of equality before the law and more attentive to the narrative identity of those who appear before it. All of this is implied in the consideration of persons.

The fact that the horror of immense crimes prevents extending this consideration to their authors is the mark of our inability to love absolutely. This is the sense of Jankélévitch's last admission: "Forgiveness is as strong as evil, but evil is as strong as forgiveness." This statement concurs with that of Freud, whose discussion of the battle of the giants in the confrontation between Eros and Thanatos concludes with a similar hesitation.

## Political Guilt

It is important to distinguish, as Karl Jaspers does, the political guilt of citizens and politicians from criminal responsibility under the jurisdiction of a court and hence from the criminal proceedings governing the course of the trial. Political guilt results from the fact that citizens belong to the political body in the name of which the crimes were committed. In this sense, it can be termed collective on the condition of not being criminalized: the notion of a criminal people must be explicitly rejected. But this sort of guilt involves the members of the political community independently of their individual acts or of their degree of acquiescence to state policies. Whoever has taken advantage of the benefits of the public order must in some way answer to the evils created by the state to which he or she belongs. Before whom is this sort of responsibility (*Haftung*) exercised? In 1947 Jaspers answered: before the victor—"to which the very fact of being alive logically forces all to submit" (*The Question of German Guilt*, 43). Today one would say: before the authorities representative of the interests and the rights of the victims and before the new authorities of a democratic state. This is still a matter, however, of power, of domination, if only the power of the majority with respect to the minority. As for the effects, they are parceled between punitive sanctions, pronounced by courts of justice in the name of a policy of purification, and the long-term obligations of reparation assumed by the state produced by the new power relations. But more important than punishment—and even reparation—remains the word of justice that establishes the public responsibilities of each of the protagonists and designates the respective places of aggressor and victim in a relation of appropriate distance.

The limits of this guilt are certain: power relations remain in play. In this regard, we must refrain from casting the history of force as the world tribunal. But, within these limits, conflicts have their place and are of concern to the problematic of forgiveness. We are always in the domain of guilt, of accusation, insofar as we remain within the field of reprobation and condemnation. The strategies of exoneration are then given free reign, acting as an obstacle to the progress of the spirit of forgiveness in the direction of the guilty self. The defense always has arguments: facts can be opposed to facts; rights of individuals can be invoked in opposition to national rights; the self-interested purposes of the judges can be denounced, even the accusation that they have contributed to the scourge (*tu quoque!*); or, yet again, an attempt can be made to submerge the local misfortunes in the vast history of world events. It then becomes the task of enlightened opinion to always bring the examination of conscience back from that vast stage to the small stage of the state in which one grew up. In this regard, a long-honored form of exoneration has to be denounced, the one invoked by the citizen who considers himself not concerned with the life of the body politic. "The ethos of politics," Karl Jaspers recalls, "is the principle of a state in which all participate with their consciousness, their knowledge, their opinions, and their wills" (35). On the other hand, the consideration due to the accused, on the political level, takes the form of moderation in the exercise of power, of self-limitation in the use of violence, even of clemency with respect to the vanquished: *parcere victis!*—clemency, magnanimity, the shadow of forgiveness...

## Moral Guilt

With moral responsibility, we move one step further away from the structure of the trial and we come closer to the center of guilt, the bad will. This concerns the mass of individual acts, small and large, that contributed by their tacit or explicit acquiescence to the criminal guilt of the politicians and to the political guilt of the members of the body politic. Here, the collective responsibility of a political nature ceases and personal responsibility begins: "Jurisdiction rests with my conscience, and in communication with my friends and intimates who are lovingly concerned about my soul" (*The Question of German Guilt*, 32). What is sketched out here is the transition from the accusation to the exchange between request and forgiveness, to which we shall return in a moment. But it is also at this level that the strategies of exoneration run rampant: they draw support from the quibbles over who is right. Nowhere are intellectual honesty and the will to be lucid with regard to oneself more necessary than on this plane of complex motivations. Once again here we find the will not to know, the refuge of blindness, and the tactics of semi-passive, semi-active forgetfulness discussed above. But we must also mention the inverse excesses, those of ostentatious and shameless self-accusation, the sacrifice of personal pride that can quickly turn to aggression against fellow citizens who remain mute.[20] One is reminded of the verbal staging of the "penitent judge" in Camus's work *The Fall*, in which the roles of the accuser and the accused are cleverly combined, without the mediation of an impartial and benevolent third party.[21] The immediate postwar situation was not, however, to focus attention solely on the moral responsibility involved in the relations between individuals and the public powers of the national state and the internal problems posed by totalitarianism. Wars of liberation, colonial and post-colonial wars, and even more so the conflicts and wars produced by the demands of ethnic, cultural, and religious minorities have projected onto the foreground a disturbing question, which Klaus M. Kodalle places at the start of his reflections on the public dimension of forgiveness: are peoples capable of forgiving? The question is addressed, to be sure, to individuals taken one by one. This is why it is indeed a matter of moral responsibility concerning specific behavior. The motivation of the acts, however, is transmitted by the collective memory on the scale of historical communities laden with history. In this regard, the conflicts that are spread out over the entire planet share with the conflicts evoked in the great criminal trials of the twentieth century the same structure of entanglement between the private and the public. Kodalle's question is raised on this final level. The answer, unfortunately, is negative. One must conclude that discourses on "the reconciliation of peoples remains a pious vow." The collectivity has no moral conscience. Confronted in this way with "outside" guilt, peoples slip back into rehashing old hatreds, ancient humiliations. Political thinking runs up against a major phenomenon here, namely, the irreducibility of the friend-foe relationship, upon which Carl Schmitt constructed his political philosophy, to relations of enmity between individuals. This reluctant observation is particularly troublesome for a conception of memory like the one proposed in this work, which is based upon continuity and the reciprocal relation between individual memory and collective memory, itself established as historical memory in Halbwachs's sense. Love and hate operate differently, it seems, on the collective scale of memory.

Confronting this somber result, Kodalle proposes as a remedy for these diseased memories the idea of normalcy in the relations between neighboring enemies. He conceives of normalcy as a sort of *incognito* forgiveness (*Inkognito der Verzeihung*) (*Verzeihung nach Wendezeiten?* 14). Not, he says, fraternization but proper behavior in relations of exchange. And he attaches this idea to a culture of consideration (*Nachsichtlichkeit*) on the civic and cosmopolitan scale. We encountered this notion on the plane of criminal guilt. It has been extended to the plane of political responsibility in the form of moderation, of mansuetude, of clemency. It can also appear, finally, on the level of moral responsibility in the confrontation with "hereditary hatreds" in the form of a stubborn will to understand those others whom history has made our enemies. Applied to oneself, it implies the refusal to indulge in cheap exoneration with regard to the stranger, the enemy, or the former enemy. Goodwill on this level requires, in particular, an attention to founding events that are not my own and to the life stories that belong to the other side; this is the place to repeat the adage: "learn to recount otherwise." It is within the framework of this culture of consideration applied to the relations of foreign policy that gestures that cannot be transformed into institutions, like Chancellor Brandt's kneeling down in Warsaw, take on meaning. What matters is their exceptional character. It is by virtue of their secret alchemy that they are able to act on institutions, by producing a "disposition to consideration," to use Kodalle's expression. As it happens, these gestures are also requests for forgiveness. As such, they signal their membership in two orders of thinking, that of guilt, which is also the unforgivable, and that of the exchange between a request and an offer, in which the unforgivable begins to be chipped away. It is in the direction of this new order that we must now proceed.

## THE ODYSSEY OF THE SPIRIT OF FORGIVENESS: THE STAGE OF EXCHANGE

Let us take a step outside the circle of accusation and punishment, the circle within which there is but a marginal place for forgiveness. This step is suggested by the sort of question raised by Jankélévitch: "Has anyone asked us for forgiveness?" The question presupposes that, if the aggressor had asked for forgiveness, whether to forgive him would have been an acceptable question. Now this very assumption is directly opposed to the primary characteristic of forgiveness, its unconditionality. If there is forgiveness, we said with Derrida, then it has to be able to be granted without the condition of a prior request. And yet we believe, on the level of practice, that there does exist something like a correlation between forgiveness requested and forgiveness granted. This belief shifts fault from the unilateral sphere of guilt and punishment into the sphere of exchange. The gestures of government leaders asking their victims for forgiveness draws attention to the strength of the request for forgiveness in certain exceptional political conditions.

My thesis here is that, if forgiveness's entrance into the circle of exchange signals taking into account the bilateral relation between the request for and the offer of forgiveness, the vertical character of the relation between height and depth, between unconditionality and conditionality, continues to go unnoticed. The dilemmas peculiar to this nevertheless remarkable correlation attest to this. As Olivier Abel notes in the afterword he writes to an inquiry on forgiveness, one can offer, at least at this stage, only a "geography of dilemmas."[22] These dilemmas are grafted onto the face-to-face confrontation of two speech acts, that of the guilty person who speaks of the fault committed, at the price of a formidable work of formulating the wrong, of a painful emplotment, and that of the presumed victim capable of uttering the liberating word of forgiveness. The latter instance perfectly illustrates the force of a speech act that does what it says: "I forgive you." The dilemmas specifically concern the conditions of such an exchange of words and are presented as a string of questions: "Can one forgive someone who does not admit his fault?" "Must the one who pronounces forgiveness himself have been offended?" "Can one forgive oneself?"[23] But even if a given author decides one way rather than the other—and how could the philosopher not be caught up in this, at least if his task goes beyond simply registering the dilemmas—there is always room for objection.

Confronting the first dilemma, it seems to me that it is a matter of respecting the sense of self of the guilty person—showing him the consideration we spoke of earlier—to expect an admission from him. The second dilemma is more disturbing: the circle of victims continues to grow, taking into account relations of filiation, the existence of community ties, cultural proximity, and so on up to a limit that political wisdom has to determine, if only to be in a position to confront the excesses in the contemporary tendency toward victimization. But it is the counterpart to the question raised that remains troublesome: is it only the primary offender who is in a position to ask for forgiveness? Beyond the suspicion of banalization and theatricalization, the public scenes of penitence and contrition, mentioned above, give rise to a question of legitimacy: on what authority can a political leader in office or the current head of a religious community presume to request forgiveness from the victims, with respect to whom he or she was not personally the aggressor and who themselves did not personally suffer the harm in question? This presents the question of representativeness in time and in space along the line of continuity of an uninterrupted tradition. The paradox is that institutions have no moral conscience and that it is their representatives, speaking in their name, that confer on them something like a proper name and, with it, historical guilt. Certain members of the communities involved can, nevertheless, not feel personally concerned by a cultural solidarity that possesses a force different from the political solidarity from which the collective responsibility mentioned above results.[24]

The third dilemma will receive a complete response only in the final stage of our odyssey. The hypothesis of forgiveness accorded by the self to itself poses a twofold problem. On the one hand, the duality of the roles of aggressor and victim resist complete internalization: only another can forgive, the victim. On the other hand, and this reservation is decisive, the difference of height between forgiveness and an admission of fault is no longer recognized in a relation in which the vertical structure is projected onto a horizontal correlation.

It is this misunderstanding that, in my opinion, results in the overhasty assimilation of forgiveness to an exchange defined by reciprocity alone.

### The Economy of the Gift

In order to clarify this equivocalness, I want to consider the particular structure of the dilemmas of forgiveness along with the difficulties that result from extending the problematic of forgiveness to a model of exchange tied to the concept of the gift. The etymology and the semantics of numerous languages encourage this comparison: *don-pardon*, gift-forgiving, *dono-perdono*, *Geben-Vergeben*. Now the idea of gift has its own difficulties, which can be divided into two parts. It is important first to recover the reciprocal dimension of the gift in contrast to an initial characterization of it as unilateral. It is then a matter of restoring, at the heart of the relation of exchange, the difference in altitude that distinguishes forgiving from giving, following the essence of exchange.

Concerning the first confrontation, one must admit that the thesis of the free gift (*le don sans retour*) is forceful indeed and demands significant attention: to give, the *Robert* dictionary says, is "to deliver over to someone in an intention of generosity, or without receiving anything in return, something one possesses or which one enjoys." The emphasis is, in fact, placed here on the absence of reciprocity. There appears to be complete asymmetry between the one who gives and the one who receives. As a first approximation, this is not false. Giving more than one has to does, in fact, constitute a parallel to giving without receiving anything in return. But, on another side, a different logic propels the gift toward reestablishing equivalence on a level other than the one spurned by the logic of superabundance.[25] In this regard, Marcel Mauss's classic book on the gift, the archaic form of exchange, must alert us.[26] Mauss does not oppose gift to exchange, but to the market form of exchange, to calculation and to self-interest: "A gift given always expects a gift in return," reads an old Scandinavian poem. The counterpart to the gift, in fact, is not receiving but giving in return, giving back. What the sociologist intends "to isolate [is] one important set of phenomena: namely, prestations which are in theory voluntary, disinterested, and spontaneous, but are in fact obligatory and interested" (1). The question is this: "What force is there in the thing given which compels the recipient to make a return?" (1). The enigma lies in the connection between three obligations: giving, receiving, giving back. It is the force of this connection that, according to the spokespersons for these populations,[27] underlies the obligation of the gift in return. The obligation to give back stems from the thing received, which is not inert: "In the things exchanged at a potlatch there is a certain power which forces them to circulate, to be given away and repaid" (*The Gift*, 41).[28] The backdrop against which the market school and its notion of individual self-interest, whose triumph is celebrated by Mandeville's *Fable of the Bees* (74), stand out must remain a foundation to which we return:

"Here, we touch bedrock" (68). "Give as much as you receive, and all is for the best," says a lovely Maori proverb.

## Gift and Forgiveness

Does the archaic model revisited in this way offer sufficient support to resolve the dilemmas of forgiveness? The response can be positive at least as concerns the first part of the argument concerning the bilateral and reciprocal dimension of forgiveness. However, an objection arises in the following manner: by purely and simply aligning forgiveness with the circularity of the gift, the model no longer permits us to distinguish between forgiveness and retribution, completely equalizing the partners. We may then be tempted to reverse the matter and leap to the other pole of the dilemma. With what are we then confronted? With the radical commandment to love our enemies unconditionally. This impossible commandment seems to be the only one to match the height of the spirit of forgiveness. The enemy has not asked for forgiveness: he must be loved as he is. This commandment not only turns against the principle of retribution, not only against the *lex talonis* that this principle claims to correct, but, ultimately, even against the Golden Rule that is supposed to break with retaliation. "Don't do to someone else what you would not want him to do to you," says the Golden Rule. There is no point in writing: "Don't do to others what they would not want you to do to them." It is a matter of reciprocity. Little by little, suspicion is directed against private or public actions that claim to be inspired by a spirit of generosity (volunteer work, public collections, responses to poverty), to say nothing of the attacks that are made today against nongovernmental humanitarian organizations. The adversaries argue this way: giving obliges giving back (*do ut des*); giving secretly creates inequality by placing the givers in a position of condescending superiority; giving ties the beneficiary, placing him or her under obligation, the obligation to be grateful; giving crushes the beneficiary under the weight of a debt he cannot repay.

The criticism is not necessarily malicious. The gospel writers place it in the mouth of Jesus, precisely, just after the reminder of the Golden Rule. We read: "If you love only those who love you, what credit is that to you? Even sinners love those who love them. . . . But you must love your enemies and do good; and lend without expecting any return" (Luke 6:32–35). The earlier criticism is thereby radicalized: the absolute measure of the gift is the love of one's enemies. And with this is associated the idea of a loan without any expectation of return. Far from softening, the critique becomes more radical under the pressure of an (almost) impossible commandment.

I would like to suggest that not only is the market exchange attacked by the critique, so too is a higher form of exchange extending all the way to the love of one's enemies. All the objections, in fact, presuppose a form of self-interest hidden behind generosity. They therefore are themselves situated within the space of market goods, which does have its own legitimacy but, precisely, in a domain in which the expectation of reciprocity takes the form of monetary equivalence. The commandment to love one's enemies begins by breaking the rule of reciprocity and requiring the extraordinary. Faithful to the gospel rhetoric of hyperbole, according to this commandment the only gift that is justified is the one given to the enemy, from whom, by hypothesis, one expects nothing in return. But, precisely, the hypothesis is false: what one expects from love is that it will convert the enemy into a friend. The potlatch celebrated by Marcel Mauss breaks up the order of the market from within through munificence—as does in its own fashion the "expense" formulated by Georges Bataille. The Gospels do this by giving to the gift a measure of "extravagance" that ordinary acts of generosity can only approach from afar.[29]

What name should be given to this nonmarket form of gift? This is no longer an exchange between giving and giving in return, but between giving and simply receiving.[30] What was potentially offended in the act of generosity, which was still a part of the market sphere, was the dignity of the recipient. Giving in honoring the beneficiary is the form that consideration takes on the level of exchange discussed above. The reciprocity of giving and receiving puts an end to the horizontal asymmetry of the gift with no expectation of return, under the aegis of the singular figure constituted by consideration. Recognizing the reciprocal dimension of the relation between the request for and the offer of forgiveness constitutes only a first stage in the complete reconstruction of this relation. What remains to be taken into account is the vertical distance between the two poles of forgiveness: this is at issue in the confrontation between the unconditionality of forgiveness and the conditionality of the request for forgiveness. This incessantly reemerging difficulty reappears at the very heart of the model of exchange applied to forgiveness, in the form of a question: what makes the parties capable of entering into the exchange between admission and forgiveness? The question is not an empty one, if we evoke once again the obstacles that impede access to the admission and those, no less great, that block the threshold of the word of forgiveness. Asking for forgiveness is, indeed, also being prepared to receive a negative response: no, I cannot, I cannot forgive. The model of exchange takes for granted the obligation to give, to receive, and to give in return. Mauss, as we saw, attributes the origin of this to the quasi-magical force of the thing exchanged. What about the invisible force that unites the two speech acts of admitting and forgiving? The problematical character of the presumed transaction results from the asymmetry, which can be termed vertical, tending to mask the reciprocity of the exchange: in truth, forgiveness spans an interval between the high and the low, between the great height of the spirit of forgiveness and the abyss of guilt. This asymmetry is constitutive of the forgiveness equation. It accompanies us like an enigma that can never be fully plumbed.

I would like to mention, in light of these puzzles, the specific difficulties courageously assumed by the initiators of the famous Truth and Reconciliation Commission, desired by the president of the new South Africa, Nelson Mandela, and presided over with panache by Bishop Desmond Tutu. The mission of this commission, which met from January 1996 to July 1998 and presented its five-volume report in October 1998, was to "collect testimony, console the injured, indemnify the victims, and amnesty those who confessed to committing political crimes."[31]

"Understanding, not revenge" was the motto here, in contrast to the punitive logic of the great criminal trials of Nuremberg and Tokyo.[32] Neither amnesty nor collective immunity. In this sense, it is indeed under the aegis of the model of exchange that this alternative experience of purging a violent past deserves to be mentioned.

It is certainly too early to measure the effects of this enterprise of reparative justice on the populations involved. But reflection has been carried quite far by the protagonists, and the testimonies of many direct witnesses allow us to make a provisional assessment concerning the obstacles encountered and the limits inherent in an operation that aims not at pardoning but at reconciliation in its explicitly political dimension, as Jaspers defined it under the heading of political guilt.

On the side of the victims, the benefits are undeniable in therapeutic, moral, and political terms, all together. Families who fought for years to know the facts were able to express their pain, vent their hatred in the presence of the offenders and before witnesses. At the price of long hearings, they had an opportunity to tell of tortures and to name the criminals. In this sense, the hearings truly permitted the public exercise of the work of memory and of mourning, guided by an appropriate process of cross-examination. In offering a public space for complaints and the recounting of suffering, the commission certainly gave rise to a shared *katharsis*. In addition, it is important that, beyond the individuals summoned to appear, there were also professionals coming from the world of business, the press, civil society, and the churches, all of whom were invited to search their memories.

This being so, it is perhaps expecting too much from this unprecedented experience to ask to what extent the protagonists progressed along the path toward genuine forgiveness. It is difficult to say. The legitimate concern with distributing indemnities could have been satisfied without carrying the purification of memory to the extinguishing of anger, tied to the sincere request for forgiveness, as this did occur in the case of subjects possessing religious or meditative consciousness or those familiar with the incantations harkening back to ancestral wisdom. Many, on the other hand, publicly rejoiced when amnesty was denied to those responsible for their loss or who refused the apologies of those who injured their close relations. In this way, the amnesty granted by the competent committee did not amount to forgiveness on the part of victims, who were deprived of the satisfaction that ordinarily results from the sanction of a trial.

On the side of the accused, the assessment is more mixed and especially more equivocal: was not public confession more often a stratagem in view of requesting and obtaining amnesty, freeing the individual from judicial proceedings and criminal conviction? Confessing, so as not to end up in court... Not to answer the questions of the victim but to satisfy the legal criteria on which amnesty depends... The spectacle of public repentance leaves one puzzled. In fact, its public use as a mere linguistic convention could not help but be the occasion for efforts aiming simply at political amnesty. Admitting excesses without relinquishing in any way the conviction that one was right was to make the most economical use of the rules of the game of confession. What then is there to say about those among the accused who turned to their advantage the procedures of confessing by informing on their superiors or their accomplices? To be sure, they helped to establish the factual truth, but at the cost of the truth that liberates. The de facto immunity for earlier crimes was transformed for them into de jure impunity in return for admissions without contrition. In contrast, the haughty refusal of some former leaders, who did not let themselves ask for forgiveness, deserves greater respect, although this refusal is politically harmful as it perpetuates the culture of contempt.

These perplexities, arising on both sides of the exchange between admission and forgiveness, invite us to consider the limits inherent in a project of reconciliation like this. The very establishment of the commission resulted from intensely impassioned negotiations between the former leaders and the new power, to say nothing of the confrontations between rival factions forced to share the victory. More profoundly and more enduringly, the violence of apartheid left wounds that a few years of public testimony were unlikely to heal.[33] This leads us, regretfully, to a viewpoint similar to Kodalle's disturbing observation that peoples do not forgive. The initiators and the advocates of the Truth and Reconciliation Commission dared to give the lie to this disillusioned belief and to provide a historic opportunity for a public form of the work of memory and of mourning in the service of public peace. Often, the commission exposed brutal truths that the agencies of political reconciliation between former enemies could not accept, as is shown by the rejection of the commission's report by many people. It is not a sign of despair to recognize the noncircumstantial, but more properly structural, limitations belonging to an enterprise of reconciliation which not only requires a great deal of time but also a work upon the self, in which it is not an exaggeration to see under the figure of a public exercise of political reconciliation something like an *incognito* of forgiveness.

Due to the very perplexities it has raised for its protagonists and its witnesses, the painful experience of the Truth and Reconciliation Commission has taken us back to the point where we interrupted our discussion of the relations between forgiveness, exchange, and gift. As is suggested by the title given to this section of the epilogue, this discussion was no doubt only a stage along the trajectory stretching from the formulation of the equation of forgiveness and its resolution on the most secret level of selfhood. This stage, however, was necessary in order to make apparent the dimension of otherness in an act that is fundamentally a relation. We attached this relational character to the vis-à-vis that confronts two speech acts, that of admission and that of absolution: "I ask you for forgiveness." "I forgive you." These two speech acts do what they say: the wrong is actually admitted; it is actually forgiven. The question is then to understand how this happens, taking into account the terms of the equation of forgiveness, namely, the apparent incommensurability between the unconditionality of forgiveness and the conditionality of the request for forgiveness. Is this abyss not bridged in a certain manner by virtue of a type of exchange that preserves the polarity of the extremes? The model is then proposed of the gift and its dialectic of the gift in return. The disproportion between the word of forgiveness and that of admission returns under the form of a single question: What force makes one capable of asking, of giving, of receiving the word of forgiveness?

## THE RETURN TO THE SELF

It is now to the heart of selfhood that our investigation must be directed. But to what power, to what courage can one appeal in order simply to ask for forgiveness?

### Forgiving and Promising

Before entering into the paradox of repentance, we must test an attempt at clarification that will be the last for us, after that of exchange and the gift. It is from our ability to master the course of time that the courage to ask for forgiveness seems able to be drawn. This is what Hannah Arendt attempts to show in *The Human Condition*,[34] whose reputation is not undeserved. Her argument rests on reestablishing a very ancient symbolism, that of *unbinding/binding*, then on pairing forgiving and promising under this dialectic, one of which would unbind and the other bind us. The virtue of these two capabilities is that they answer in a responsible manner to the temporal constraints on the "continuation of action" on the plane of human affairs.[35]

Action, as we recall, is the third category of a threesome: labor, work, action. This is the basic triad of the *via activa* considered in terms of its anthropological structures, at the union of the fundamental and the historical. It is by its own characteristic temporality that action is distinguished from the other two terms. Labor is consumed in its consumption, the work is intended to outlast its mortal authors, action simply wants to continue. Whereas in Heidegger there is no category of action, properly speaking, that in connection with care would be capable of providing a base for an ethics and a politics, Hannah Arendt has no need to take the road through *Mitsein* to give care, which in *Being and Time* continues to be marked with the seal of incommunicable death, a communal dimension. Right from the start action unfolds in a space of public visibility where it manifests its network, its web of relations and interactions. Speaking and acting take place in the public space of the manifestation of the human, and this is done directly without any transposition from the private to the public, from inwardness to socialness. Human plurality is primary. Why, then, is it necessary to pass by way of the power to forgive and to promise? Because of what Arendt calls the intrinsic "weaknesses" of plurality. The fragility of human affairs is not, in fact, reducible to the perishable, mortal character of undertakings subjected to the merciless order of things, to the physical effacement of traces, that purveyor of oblivion. The danger has to do with the character of uncertainty that attaches to action under the condition of plurality. This uncertainty is to be related, on the one hand, to the irreversibility that destroys the desire for sovereign mastery applied to the consequences of action, to which forgiveness responds, and, on the other hand, to the unpredictability that destroys confidence in an expected course of action, the reliability of human action, to which the promise responds.[36]

The position assumed by Hannah Arendt marks a significant distance with respect to the problematic we have engaged in from the first sequence of the present section, where forgiveness was seen as coming from above: "The remedy against irreversibility and unpredictability of the process started by acting does not arise out of another and possibly higher faculty, but is one of the potentialities of action itself" (*The Human Condition*, 236–37). Using the vocabulary of faculties, she speaks of "the faculty of forgiving" and "the faculty to keep and make promises" (237). Should one say that no one can forgive himself or herself and that left to ourselves we would wander without strength or aim? This is true: "Both faculties, therefore, depend on plurality" (237). Human plurality is the required vis-à-vis on both sides. The faculty of forgiveness and the faculty of promising rest on experiences that no one can have in isolation and which are based entirely on the presence of others. If the origin of these two faculties is inherent in plurality, their area of exercise is eminently political. On this point, Arendt uses to her own advantage the exegesis of the gospel texts most favorable to her interpretation. These texts say that it is only if humans exchange forgiveness among themselves that they can hope to be forgiven by God as well: the power to forgive is a human power.[37] Arendt notes: "Only through this constant mutual release from what they do can men remain free agents" (240). Confirmation is provided, on the one hand, by the opposition between forgiveness and vengeance, these two human manners of reacting to offenses; on the other hand, by the parallel between forgiveness and punishment, each of them cutting short an endless series of wrongs.[38]

It is this precise symmetry between forgiving and promising in terms of power that I would like to question. It did not escape Hannah Arendt that forgiveness has a religious aura that promising does not. Promising responds to the unpredictability resulting from the intermittencies of the heart and from the complexity of the chains of consequences of our actions. The promise opposes to this twofold uncertainty of human affairs a faculty for mastering the future as if it were the present. And this capacity finds immediate political inscription in the conclusion of accords and treaties consisting in the exchange of promises declared inviolable. On this point, Arendt concurs with Nietzsche in the second essay of *On the Genealogy of Morals*, in which the promise is announced as the "memory of the will" victorious over the laziness of forgetting.[39] To this trait, coming from Nietzsche, Arendt adds the inscription of the act of promising in the play of plurality, which, in its turn, marks the entrance of promising into the political field.

It is a different matter for forgiveness, whose relation to love keeps it at a distance from the political.

We find proof of this *ad absurdum* in the sometimes monstrous failure of all efforts to institutionalize forgiveness. Whereas there are reliable institutions of promising, relating in various ways to the order of oaths—there is nothing like this in the case of forgiveness. We mentioned above the caricature of forgiveness found in amnesty, the institutional form of forgetting. One can also think, however, of the perplexities arising in an entirely different dimension from the sacrament of penance in the Catholic Church.[40] And exactly opposite to the exercise of a power to bind and to unbind with the aim of reassuring and forgiving within a well-ordered ecclesiastical community stands the figure of the Grand Inquisitor of Dostoyevsky's *Brothers Karamozov*.[41] The legend of the Grand Inquisitor is the yardstick by which the most benign attempts to win the salvation of men at the price of their freedom must be measured. There is no politics of forgiveness.

This is what Hannah Arendt foresaw. She says this starting from the opposite pole to that represented by the Grand Inquisitor, the pole of love: love, "one of the rarest occurrences in human lives" (*The Human Condition*, 242), proves to be foreign to the world and, for this reason, not only apolitical but antipolitical. This discordance between the levels on which forgiveness and promising operate is of great importance to us. It is simply masked by the symmetry between the two "weaknesses" that human affairs owe to their temporal condition, irreversibility and unpredictability. Yet this symmetry appears to authorize the leap that Arendt makes in these terms: "Yet what love is in its own, narrowly circumscribed sphere, respect is in the larger domain of human affairs" (243). And she evokes here, rather than the *agapē* of the apostle, the *philia politikē* of the philosopher, that sort of friendship without intimacy, without proximity. This last observation carries forgiveness back to the plane of horizontal exchange examined in our preceding section. It is at the heart of human plurality that forgiveness exerts the same power of revealing the "who" contained in action and in speech.

Arendt even seems to suggest that we could forgive ourselves if we were able to perceive ourselves: if we are said to be unable to forgive ourselves, this is because "we are dependent upon others, to whom we appear in a distinctness which we ourselves are unable to perceive" (243).

But does everything occur within the space of visibility of the public sphere? The final pages of the chapter on action in *The Human Condition* abruptly introduce a meditation on mortality and birth that carries over to human action: "If left to themselves, human affairs can only follow the law of mortality, which is the most certain and only reliable law of a life spent between birth and death" (246). If the faculty of acting, joined to that of speaking, can interfere with this law to the point of interrupting its inexorable automatic processes, it is because action and language possess their own resources in the "fact of natality" (247). Must this not be understood as a discreet yet stubborn protest addressed to the Heideggerian philosophy of being-toward-death? Should we not see action as "an ever-present reminder that men, though they must die, are not born in order to die but in order to begin" (246)? In this respect, "action...looks like a miracle" (246).[42]

The evocation of the miracle of action, at the origin of the miracle of forgiveness, seriously calls into question the entire analysis of the faculty of forgiveness. How can the mastery of time be joined to the miracle of natality? It is precisely this question that sets our entire enterprise into motion again and invites us to pursue the odyssey of forgiveness to the center of selfhood In my opinion, what is lacking in the political interpretation of forgiveness, which assures its symmetry with promising on the same level of exchange, is any reflection on the very act of unbinding proposed as the condition for the act of binding.[43] It seems to me that Hannah Arendt remained at the threshold of the enigma by situating the gesture of forgiveness at the point of intersection of the act and its consequences and not of the agent and the act. To be sure, forgiveness has the effect of dissociating the debt from its burden of guilt and in a sense of laying bare the phenomenon of the debt, as a dependence on a received heritage. But forgiveness does more. At least, it should do more: it should release the agent from his act.

### Unbinding the Agent from the Act

Let us be clear about what is at issue here. Our entire inquiry into forgiveness began with the analysis of the admission by which the guilty person assumes his fault, internalizing in this way an accusation, which, then, points to the author behind the act: what the codes disavow are violations of the law—but what the courts punish are persons. This observation leads us to Nicolai

Hartmann's thesis affirming the inseparability of the act and the agent. From this position, held up as a provocation, we reached the de jure unforgivable character of the guilty self. It was then in reply to this de jure unforgivability that we established the requirement of impossible forgiveness. And all of our subsequent analyses have been an exploration of the gap opened between the unforgivable fault and this impossible forgiveness. The exceptional gestures of forgiveness, the precepts concerning the consideration owed to the defendant, and all the behaviors that we ventured to maintain on the planes of criminal, political, and moral guilt, for the *incognitos* of forgiveness—and which are often no more than alibis for forgiveness—were applied, with difficulty, to fill this gap. Everything, finally, hangs on the possibility of separating the agent from the action. This unbinding would mark the inscription, in the field of the horizontal disparity between power and act, of the vertical disparity between the great height of forgiveness and the abyss of guilt. The guilty person, rendered capable of beginning again: this would be the figure of unbinding that commands all the others.

It is the unbinding that governs all the others. But is it itself possible? Here I concur one last time with Derrida's argument: separating the guilty person from his act, in other words forgiving the guilty person while condemning his action, would be to forgive a subject other than the one who committed the act.[44] The argument is serious and the response difficult. It is to be sought, in my opinion, on the side of a more radical uncoupling than that supposed by the argument between a first subject, the one who committed the wrong, and a second subject, the one who is punished, an uncoupling at the heart of our very power to act—of agency—namely, between the effectuation and the capacity that it actualizes. This intimate dissociation signifies that the capacity of commitment belonging to the moral subject is not exhausted by its various inscriptions in the affairs of the world. This dissociation expresses an act of faith, a credit addressed to the resources of self-regeneration.

To account for this ultimate act of trust, there is no recourse but to assume an ultimate paradox proposed by the Religions of the Book and which I find inscribed in the Abrahamic memory. It is stated in the form of a pairing we have not yet mentioned, one that operates on a level of intimacy that was not reached by any of the other pairs mentioned up to now: the pair forgiveness and repentance.

This is something quite different from a transaction.[45] Rather than constituting a dilemma, this paradox suggests the idea of an entirely unique kind of circle by reason of which the existential response to forgiveness is implied, as it were, in the gift itself, while the antecedence of the gift is recognized at the very heart of the inaugural gesture of repentance. To be sure, if there is forgiveness, "it remains," as is said of love in the hymn that celebrates its greatness. If it is the supreme height, then it permits neither before nor after, whereas the response of repentance occurs in time, whether it be sudden as in certain spectacular conversions, or progressive over the course of an entire life. The paradox is precisely that of the circular relation between what "remains" forever and what comes to be in each instance. We are familiar, in this regard, with so many dogmatic modes of thought that have allowed themselves to be caught up in disjunctive forms of logic: grace first of all, even grace alone, or human initiative first. The impasse becomes complete with the arrival of the idea of causation, be it anticipatory, auxiliary, sovereign, or other. Let us therefore leave the paradox in its stage of emergence, far removed from speculative additions, and confine ourselves to saying how it is inscribed in our historical condition: under the various figures of unbinding affecting the relation of the agent to his act.

This act of unbinding is not a philosophical aberration: it conforms to the lines of a philosophy of action in which the emphasis is placed on the powers that together compose the portrait of the capable being. In turn, this philosophical anthropology is based upon a fundamental ontology which, in the vast polysemy of the term "to be" in Aristotle's metaphysics, accords preference to being as act and as power, in contrast to the preference for an understanding in terms of a concept of substance that prevailed in metaphysics up to Kant. This fundamental ontology of power and act, which can be traced in Leibniz, Spinoza, Schelling, Bergson, and Freud, reemerges, in my view, on the borders of moral philosophy, at the point where a philosophy of religion is grafted onto a deontological conception of morality, as we see in Kant himself in the final section of the essay "Of the Radical Evil in Human Nature," placed at the head of the *Religion within the Boundaries of Mere Reason*.[46] As radical as evil may be, Kant states—and it is indeed radical as the first of all the maxims concerning evil—it is not original. Radical is the "propensity" to evil, original is the "predisposition" to good. It was this predisposition to good that was assumed in the famous formula with which the first section of the *Foundations of the Metaphysics of Morals* opens: "Nothing in the world—indeed nothing even beyond the world—can possibly be conceived which could be called good without qualification except a *good will*." This declaration does not only signal the explicit absorption of a teleological ethics into a deontological morality, but also, in the opposite direction, the implicit recognition of the rootedness of the latter in the former. This rootedness is reaffirmed in the formulas of *Religion within the Boundaries of Mere Reason* that mark the link between the propensity to evil and the predisposition to good: the entire discourse on predisposition (*Anlage*) is in fact a teleological discourse that connects together the predispositions to animality, to rationality, and finally to personality. This threesome is summed up in the affirmation that "the original predisposition in [man] is good" (General Observation). Thus the inaugural formula of moral philosophy and the concluding formula in the essay "Of the Radical Evil in Human Nature" precisely correspond to one another.

It is in the "original predisposition to the good" that the possibility of "the restoration to its power" resides. I would say that under this modest heading—"the restoration . . . of the original predisposition to the good" (89)—the entire project of a philosophy of religion centered on the theme of the liberation of the ground of goodness in human beings is veiled and unveiled. Regarding this "incentive for good," Kant declares, "were we ever to lose it, we would also never be able to regain it" (91). This conviction finds a basis in the philosophical rereading of the old myths dealing with the meta- or trans-historical origin of evil. We earlier referred in this regard to the Adamic myth in which the fall is recounted as a primordial event inaugurating a time after innocence. The narrative form thus preserves the radical contingency of a historical status now irremediable but in no way inevitable as to its occurrence. This gap with respect to the state of creation holds in reserve the possibility of another history inaugurated in each case by the act of repentance and punctuated by all the irruptions of goodness and of innocence over the course of time. This existential-existentiell possibility, placed under the protection of the narrative of origin, is echoed by the predisposition to good upon which the Kantian philosophy of *Religion within the Boundaries of Mere Reason* is constructed. What then can be added in the service of this immense project of restoration would be, on the one hand, the symbols—such as that of the suffering servant and of his christological expression—that nourish the Jewish and Christian imagination; and, on the other hand, the metapolitical institutions—such as, in Christianity, the visible forms of the church placed in the dual position of disciple and guardian with respect to this gift to the imagination. In the remainder of *Religion within the Boundaries of Mere Reason*, which is devoted to these symbols and institutions, which Kant develops, it is true, a more and more vehement tone addressing the historical forms espoused by this basic religious spirit which today we would call the Religions of the Book.

Against the backdrop of this philosophical reading of Western religions, the enigma of forgiveness stands out in the sphere of meaning belonging to these religions. Discussing the inscription of the spirit of forgiveness in the operations of the will, Kant confines himself to assuming the "supernatural cooperation" (89) capable of accompanying and of completing the inclusion of moral "incentives in the maxims of our power of choice" (94). This knot is at one and the same time the unbinding of forgiveness and the binding of promising.[47]

What is there to say, then, about the intelligibility of this conjunction? Regardless of the solutions attempted in the course of theological debates on the theme of freedom and grace, from which Kant dissociates himself in the third part of *Religion within the Boundaries of Mere Reason*, it does not seem that the vocabulary of the unconditional and the conditional, inherited from the antinomies of the dialectic of pure reason, is appropriate for the problematic of forgiveness and repentance. To disjunction, to dilemma, one must, it seems, oppose paradox. And regarding this paradox, one must give up any attempt to speak in the speculative or transcendental mode.[48] Possessing an irreducibly practical nature, it can be uttered only in the grammar of the optative mood.

Under the sign of forgiveness, the guilty person is to be considered capable of something other than his offenses and his faults. He is held to be restored to his capacity for acting, and action restored to its capacity for continuing. This capacity is signaled in the small acts of consideration in which we recognized the *incognito* of forgiveness played out on the public stage. And, finally, this restored capacity is enlisted by promising as it projects action toward the future. The formula for this liberating word, reduced to the bareness of its utterance, would be: you are better than your actions.

## LOOKING BACK OVER AN ITINERARY: RECAPITULATION

Once the trajectory of forgiveness has circled back to its starting point and the self has been recognized in its fundamental moral capacity, imputability, the question arises as to what sort of gaze our reflections on the act of forgiving allow us to cast on the whole of the path covered in this book. What is there to say about memory, history, and forgetting, touched by the spirit of forgiveness? The response to this final question constitutes, as it were, an epilogue to this epilogue.

The discourse that suits this recapitulation is no longer that of phenomenology, nor of epistemology, nor of hermeneutics; it is the discourse of the exploration of the horizon of completion of the chain of operations constituting this vast memorial to time which includes memory, history, and forgetting. I venture to speak in this respect of eschatology to underscore the dimension of anticipation and of projection belonging to this ultimate horizon. The most appropriate grammatical mood is that of the optative of desire, at equal distance from the indicative of description and the imperative of prescription.

In truth, I only recently identified this presumed tie between the spirit of forgiveness and the horizon of completion of our entire undertaking. It is clearly a consequence of rereading. Has the presentiment of this tie guided me from the beginning? Perhaps. If this is the case, will I apply to it the distinction proposed at the beginning of *Oneself as Another* between the underlying current of motivation and the mastered development of the argumentation? Or, yet again, the distinction I owe, I believe, to Eugen Fink between operative concepts, never entirely present to the mind, and thematic concepts, displayed as relevant objects of knowledge? I could not say. What I do know, however, is that the object of the entire quest merits the beautiful name of happiness.

## Happy Memory

I can say after the fact that the lodestar of the entire phenomenology of memory has been the idea of happy memory. It was concealed in the definition of the cognitive intention of memory as faithful. Faithfulness to the past is not a given, but a wish. Like all wishes, it can be disappointed, even betrayed. The originality of this wish is that it consists not in an action but in a representation taken up again in a series of speech acts constituting the declarative dimension of memory. Like all speech acts, those of declarative memory can also succeed or fail. For this reason, this wish at first is not seen as a vow but as a claim, saddled with an initial aporia, one which I have repeated over and over in the following words: the aporia that is constituted by the present representation of an absent thing marked with the seal of anteriority, of temporal distance. If this aporia has constituted a genuine difficulty for thought, it has never been cast as an impasse. The typology of mnemonic operations was thus from start to finish a typology of the ways in which the dilemma of presence and of absence can be overcome. The royal theme of the recognition of memory was gradually developed on the basis of this arborescent typology. At the start it was simply one of the figures of the typology of memory, and it is only at the end, in the wake of the Bergsonian analysis of the recognition of images and under the fine name of the survival or revival of images, that the preeminence of the phenomenon of recognition was confirmed. Today, I discern in it the equivalent of what was characterized as the *incognito* of forgiveness in the preceding sections of this epilogue. But only an equivalent, to the extent that guilt is not the discriminating factor here but rather reconciliation, which places its final stamp on the entire series of mnemonic operations. I consider recognition to be the small miracle of memory. And as a miracle, it can also fail to occur. But when it does take place, in thumbing through a photo album, or in the unexpected encounter with a familiar person, or in the silent evocation of a being who is absent or gone forever, the cry escapes: "That is her! That is him!" And the same greeting accompanies step by step, with less lively colors, an event recollected, a know-how retrieved, a state of affairs once again raised to the level of "recognition." Every act of memory (*faire-mémoire*) is thus summed up in recognition.

The rays extending from this lodestar spread beyond the topology of memory to the whole of the phenomenological investigation.

The reference to happy memory allowed me from the start to put off the contribution of the neural sciences to the knowledge of memory until the end of this book. The underlying argument was that the understanding of mnemonic phenomena takes place in the silence of our organs as long as dysfunctions on the plane of actual behavior and of the conduct of life do not require taking into account the forms of knowledge that have the brain as their object.

It was the same presupposition of self-clarity in the phenomenon of recognition that next supplied the blade that cuts between two types of absence— the anterior and the unreal—and so, as a matter of principle, sunders memory from imagination, despite the disturbing incursions of hallucination into the mnemonic field. I believe that most of the time I can distinguish a memory from a fiction, even though it is as an image that the memory returns. Obviously, I would like always to be capable of making this distinction.

It is still the same gesture of confidence that accompanied the exploration into the uses and abuses that flag the reconquest of memory along the paths of recall. Blocked memory, manipulated memory, commanded memory—so many figures of difficult, but not impossible, recollection. The price to be paid was the conjunction between the work of memory and the work of mourning. But I believe that in certain favorable circumstances, such as the right given by another to remember, or better, the help contributed by others in sharing memories, recollection can be said to be successful and mourning to be checked along the fatal slope of melancholy, that attraction to sorrow. If it were so, happy memory would become memory at peace.

Finally, the reflexive moment of memory culminates in the recognition of oneself in the form of a wish. We resisted the fascination with the appearance of immediacy, certainty, and security likely to be found in this reflexive moment. This too is a vow, a claim, a demand. In this respect, the sketch of a theory of attribution, under the threefold figure of the attribution of memory to the self, to close relations, and to distant others deserves to be reconsidered from the perspective of the dialectic of binding and unbinding proposed by the problematic of forgiveness. In return, by extending in this way to the sphere of memory, this dialectic is able to move out of the sphere specific to guilt to attain the scope of a dialectic of reconciliation. Placed back in the light of the dialectic of binding-unbinding, the self-attribution of the set of memories that compose the fragile identity of a singular life is shown to result from the constant mediation between a moment of distantiation and a moment of appropriation. I have to be able to consider from a distance the stage upon which memories of the past are invited to make an appearance if I am to feel authorized to hold their entire series to be mine, my possession. At the same time, the thesis of the threefold attribution of mnemonic phenomena to the self, to close relations, and to distant others invites us to extend the dialectic of binding-unbinding to those other than oneself. What above was presented as the approbation directed to the manner of being and acting of those I consider to be my close relations—and approbation counts as a criterion of proximity—also consists in unbinding-binding: on the one hand, the consideration addressed to another's dignity—and which was credited above with being an *incognito* of forgiveness in situations marked by public accusation—constitutes the moment of unbinding stemming from approbation, while sympathy constitutes the moment of binding. It will be up to historical knowledge to pursue this dialectic of unbinding-binding onto the plane of the attribution of memory to all the others beyond myself and my close relations.

In this way the dialectic of unbinding-binding unfolds along the lines of the attribution of recollections to the multiple subjects of memory: happy memory, peaceful memory, reconciled memory, these would be the figures of happiness that our memory wishes for ourselves and for our close relations.

"Who will teach us to decant the joy of memory?" exclaimed André Breton in *L'Amour fou*,[49] providing a contemporary echo, beyond the Beatitudes of the Gospel, to the apostrophe of the Hebraic psalmist: "Who will make us see happiness?" (Psalm 4:7). Happy memory is one of the responses given to this rhetorical question.

## Unhappy History?

Applied to history, the idea of eschatology is not without equivocalness. Are we not returning to those metaphysical or theological projections that Pomian places under the heading of "chronosophies," in opposition to the chronologies and chronographies of historical science? It must be clearly understood that we are concerned here with the horizon of completion of a historical knowledge aware of its limitations, whose measure we took at the beginning of the third part of this work.

The major fact made apparent by the comparison between history's project of truth and memory's aim of faithfulness is that the small miracle of recognition has no equivalent in history. This gap, which will never be entirely bridged, results from the break—it could be termed epistemological—made by the system of writing imposed on all the historiographical operations. These, we have repeatedly stated, are from start to finish types of writing, from the stage of archives up to literary writing in the form of books and articles offered to reading. In this regard, we were able to reinterpret the myth of the *Phaedrus* concerning the origin of writing—or at least of the writing entrusted to external signs—as the myth of the origin of historiography in all of its states.

This is not to say that every transition between memory and history has been abolished by this scriptural transposition, as is verified by testimony, that founding act of historical discourse: "I was there! Believe me or not. And if you don't believe me, ask someone else!" Entrusted in this way to another's credibility, testimony transmits to history the energy of declarative memory. But the living word of the witness, transmuted into writing, melts away into the mass of archival documents which belong to a new paradigm, the paradigm of the "clue" which includes traces of all kinds. All documents are not testimonies, as are those of "witnesses in spite of themselves." What is more, the facts considered to have been established are also not all point-like events. Numerous reputedly historical events were never anyone's memories.

The chasm between history and memory is hollowed out in the explanatory phase, in which the available uses of the connector "because..." are tested. To be sure, the coupling between explanation and understanding, which we have continued to underscore, preserves the continuity with the capacity for decision-making exercised by social agents in situations of indecision and, by this means, the continuity with self-understanding dependent on memory. Historical knowledge, however, gives the advantage to those architectures of meaning that exceed the resources of even collective memory: the articulation between events, structures, and conjunctures; the multiplication of the scales of duration extended to the scales of norms and evaluations; the distribution of the relevant objects of history on multiple planes—economic, political, social, cultural, religious, and so on. History is not only vaster than memory; its time is layered differently. History's greatest distance from memory was reached with the treatment of the facts of memory as "new objects," of the same order as sex, fashion, death. Mnemonic representation, our vehicle of our bond with the past, itself becomes an object of history. The question was even legitimately raised whether memory, the matrix of history, had not itself become a simple object of history. Having arrived at this extreme point of the historiographical reduction of memory, we allowed a protest to be heard, one in which the power of the attestation of memory concerning the past is lodged. History can expand, complete, correct, even refute the testimony of memory regarding the past; it cannot abolish it. Why? Because, it seemed to us, memory remains the guardian of the ultimate dialectic constitutive of the pastness of the past, namely, the relation between the "no longer," which marks its character of being elapsed, abolished, superseded, and the "having-been," which designates its original and, in this sense, indestructible character. That something did actually happen, this is the pre-predicative—and even pre-narrative—belief upon which rest the recognition of the images of the past and oral testimony. In this regard, events like the Holocaust and the great crimes of the twentieth century, situated at the limits of representation, stand in the name of all the events that have left their traumatic imprint on hearts and bodies: they protest that they were and as such they demand being said, recounted, understood. This protestation, which nourishes attestation, is part of belief: it can be contested but not refuted.

Two corollaries result from this fragile constitution of historical knowledge.

On the one hand, mnemonic representation, lacking the assurance of recognition, has as its sole historical counterpart the concept of standing for, whose precarious nature we have underscored. Only the work of revising and of rewriting engaged in by the historian in his workshop is capable of reinforcing the merit of the presumption that the constructions of the historian can be reconstructions of events that actually occurred.

Second corollary: the competition between memory and history, between the faithfulness of the one and the truth of the other, cannot be resolved on the epistemological plane. In this respect, the suspicion instilled by the myth of the *Phaedrus*—is the *pharmakon* of writing a poison or a remedy?—has never been dispelled on the gnoseological plane. It is reawakened in Nietzsche's attacks against the abuses of historical culture. A final echo resounded in the testimonies of some prominent historians regarding the "uncanniness of history." The debate must then be transferred to another arena, that of the reader of history, which is also that of the educated citizen. It is up to the recipients of the historical text to determine, for themselves and on the plane of public discussion, the balance between history and memory.

Is this the final word on the shadow that the spirit of forgiveness would cast on this history of the historians? The true response to the absence in history of an equivalent to the mnemonic phenomenon of recognition can be read in the pages devoted to death in history. History, we said then, has the responsibility for the dead of the past, whose heirs we are. The historical operation in its entirety can then be considered an act of sepulcher. Not a place, a cemetery, a simple depository of bones, but an act of repeated entombment. This scriptural sepulcher extends the work of memory and the work of mourning on the plane of history. The work of mourning definitively separates the past from the present and makes way for the future. The work of memory would have attained its aim if the reconstruction of the past were to succeed in giving rise to a sort of resurrection of the past. Must we leave to the avowed or unavowed emulators of Michelet alone the responsibility for this romantic wish? Is it not the ambition of every historian to uncover, behind the death mask, the face of those who formerly existed, who acted and suffered, and who were keeping the promises they left unfulfilled? This would be the most deeply hidden wish of historical knowledge. But its continually deferred realization no longer belongs to those who write history; it is in the hands of those who make history.

How could we fail to mention here Klee's figure titled *Angelus Novus*, as it was described by Walter Benjamin in the ninth of his "Theses on the Philosophy of History"?[50] "A Klee painting named *Angelus Novus* shows an angel looking as though he is about to move away from something he is fixedly contemplating. His eyes are staring, his mouth is open, his wings are spread. This is how one pictures the angel of history. His face is turned toward the past. Where we perceive a chain of events, he sees one single catastrophe which keeps piling up wreckage upon wreckage and hurls it in front of his feet. The angel would like to stay, awaken the dead, and make whole what has been smashed.[51] But a storm is blowing from Paradise; it has got caught in his wings with such violence that the angel can no longer close them. This storm irresistibly propels him into the future to which his back is turned, while the pile of debris before him grows skyward. This storm is what we call progress" (257). What, then, is for us this storm that so paralyzes the angel of history? Is it not, under the figure of progress which is contested today, the history that human beings make and that comes crashing into the history that historians write? But then the presumed meaning of history is no longer dependent on the latter but on the citizen who responds to the events of the past. For the professional historian there remains, short of that receding horizon, the uncanniness of history, the unending competition between memory's vow of faithfulness and the search for truth in history.

Should we now speak of unhappy history? I do not know. But I will not say: unfortunate history. Indeed, there is a privilege that cannot be refused to history; it consists not only in expanding collective memory beyond any actual memory but in correcting, criticizing, even refuting the memory of a determined community, when it folds back upon itself and encloses itself within its own sufferings to the point of rendering itself blind and deaf to the suffering of other communities. It is along the path of critical history that memory encounters the sense of justice. What would a happy memory be that was not also an equitable memory?

### Forgiveness and Forgetting

Should we confess *in fine* something like a wish for a happy forgetting? I want to express some of my reservations regarding assigning a "happy ending" to our entire enterprise.

My hesitations begin on the plane of the surface manifestations of forgetting and extend to its deep constitution, on the level where the forgetting due to effacement and the reserve of forgetting intertwine.

The ruses of forgetting are still easy to unmask on the plane where the institutions of forgetting, the paradigm of which is amnesty, provide grist to the abuses of forgetting, counterparts to the abuses of memory. The case of the amnesty of Athens, which concerned us in the final chapter on forgetting, is exemplary in this regard. We saw how the establishment of civil peace was based upon the strategy of the denial of founding violence. The decree, accredited by oath, ordering that "the evils not be recalled" claims to do no less than to hide the reality of *stasis*, of the civil war, the city approving only external war. The body politic is declared to be foreign to conflict in its very being. The question is then posed: is a sensible politics possible without something like a censure of memory? Political prose begins where vengeance ceases, if history is not to remain locked up within the deadly oscillation between eternal hatred and forgetful memory. A society cannot be continually angry with itself. Then, only poetry preserves the force of unforgetting concealed in the affliction that Aeschylus declares "lust of power insatiate" (*Eumenides*, v. 976). Poetry knows that the political rests on forgetting the unforgettable, "that never formulated oxymoron," says Nicole Loraux (*La Cité divisée*, 161). The oath can evoke and articulate it only in the form of the negation of the negation, which decrees the non-arrival of this misfortune, which Electra proclaims to be itself a "sorrow, which . . . cannot be done away with, cannot forget" (*Electra*, v. 1246–47). Such are the spiritual stakes of amnesty: silencing the non-forgetting of memory. This is why the Greek politician is in need of the religious figure to uphold the will to forget the unforgettable, under the form of imprecations verging on false oaths. Lacking the religious and the poetical, we saw that the ambition of the rhetoric of glory, at the time of kings, mentioned in connection with the idea of greatness, was to impose another memory in place of that of Eris, Discord. The oath, this ritual of language—*horkos* conspiring with *lēthē*—has perhaps disappeared from democratic and republican prose, but not from the city's praise of itself, with its euphemisms, its ceremonies, its civic rituals, its commemorations. Here, the philosopher will refrain from condemning the successive amnesties that the French Republic in particular has so often employed, but he will stress their purely utilitarian, therapeutic character. And he will listen to the voice of the unforgetting memory, excluded from the arena of power by the forgetful memory bound to the prosaic refounding of the political. At this price, the thin wall separating amnesty from amnesia can be preserved. The knowledge that the city remains "a divided city" belongs to practical wisdom and to its political exercise. The fortifying use of *dissensus*, the echo of the unforgetting memory of discord, contributes to this.

Our uneasiness concerning the right attitude to take with regard to the uses and abuses of forgetting, mainly in the practice of institutions, is finally the symptom of a stubborn uncertainty affecting the relation between forgetting and forgiveness on the level of its deep structure. The question returns with insistence: if it is possible to speak of happy memory, does there exist something like a happy forgetting? In my opinion, an ultimate indecisiveness strikes what could be presented as an eschatology of forgetting. We anticipated this crisis at the end of the chapter on forgetting by balancing forgetting through the effacement of traces against the forgetting kept in reserve. And it is once again a question of this balance within the horizon of a happy memory.

Why can one not speak of happy forgetting in precisely the same way we were able to speak of happy memory?

An initial reason is that our relation with forgetting is not marked by events of thinking comparable to the event of recognition, which we have called the small miracle of memory—a memory is evoked, it arrives, it returns, we recognize in an instant the thing, the event, the person and we exclaim: "That's her! That's him!" The arrival of a memory is an event. Forgetting is not an event, something that happens or that someone causes to happen. To be sure, we can notice that we have forgotten, and we remark it at a given moment. But what we then recognize is the state of forgetfulness we had been in. This state can, certainly, be termed a "force," as Nietzsche declares at the beginning of the second essay in *On the Genealogy of Morals*. This is, he says, "no mere *vis inertiae*," "it is rather an active and in the strictest sense positive faculty of repression" (57). But how are we made aware of this power that makes forgetting "a doorkeeper, a preserver of psychic order, repose, and etiquette" (58)? We know it thanks to memory, that faculty "with the aid of which forgetfulness is abrogated in certain cases—namely in those cases where promises are made" (58). In these specific cases, one can speak not only of a faculty but of the will not to forget, "a desire for the continuance of something desired once, a real *memory of the will*" (58). It is in binding oneself that one unbinds oneself from what was a force, but not yet a will. It will be objected that the strategies of forgetting, which we spoke of above, consist in more or less active interventions, which can be denounced as responsible for omission, negligence, blindness. But if a moral guilt can be attached to the behaviors resulting from the class of non-action, as Karl Jaspers required in his *Schuldfrage*, this is because what are involved are a large number of punctual acts of non-acting, the precise occasions of which can be recalled after the fact.

A second reason for setting aside the idea of a symmetry between memory and forgetting in terms of success or accomplishment is that, with respect to forgiveness, forgetting has its own dilemmas. They have to do with the fact that, if memory is concerned with events even in the exchanges that give rise to retribution, reparation, absolution, forgetting develops enduring situations, which in this sense can be said to be historical, inasmuch as they are constitutive of the tragic nature of action. In this way action is prevented from continuing by forgetting, either by the intertwining of roles that are impossible to untangle, or by insurmountable conflicts in which the dispute is unresolvable, insuperable, or yet again by irreparable wrongs often extending back to far-distant epochs. If forgiveness has anything to do in these situations of growing tragedy,[52] it can only be a matter of a sort of nonpunctual work bearing on the manner of waiting for and welcoming typical situations: the inextricable, the irreconcilable, the irreparable. This tacit admission has less to do with memory than with mourning as an enduring disposition. The three figures evoked here are in fact three figures of loss. The admission that loss is forever would be the maxim of wisdom worthy of being held to be the *incognito* of forgiveness in the tragedy of action. The patient search for compromise would be its minor coin, but so would the welcoming of *dissensus* in the ethics of discussion. Must one go so far as to say "forget the debt," the figure of loss? Yes, perhaps, inasmuch as debt confines to fault and is enclosed within repetition. No, inasmuch as it signifies the recognition of a heritage. A subtle work of unbinding and binding is to be pursued at the very heart of debt: on one hand, being released from the fault, on the other, binding a debtor who is forever insolvent. Debt without fault. Debt stripped bare. Where one finds the debt to the dead and history as sepulcher.

The most irreducible reason for the asymmetry between forgetting and memory with respect to forgiveness resides in the undecidable character of the polarity that divides the subterranean empire of forgetting against itself: the polarity between forgetting through effacement and forgetting kept in reserve. It is with the admission of this irreducible equivocalness that the most precious and the most secret mark of forgiveness can come to be registered. Admitting that "in human experience there is no superior point of view from which one could perceive the common source of destruction and of construction": such was, above, the verdict of the hermeneutics of the human condition with respect to forgetting. "Of this great drama of being," we said in conclusion, "there is, for us, no possible balance sheet." This is why there cannot be a happy forgetting in the same way as one can dream of a happy memory. What would be the mark of forgiveness on this admission? Negatively, it would consist in inscribing the powerlessness of reflection and speculation at the head of the list of things to be renounced, ahead of the irreparable; and, positively, in incorporating this renouncement of knowledge into the small pleasures of happy memory when the barrier of forgetting is pushed back a few degrees. Could one then speak of an *ars oblivionis*, in the sense in which an *ars memoriae* has been discussed on several occasions? In truth, the paths are difficult to trace out in this unfamiliar territory. I propose three tracks for our exploration. One could, after the manner of Harald Weinrich, to whom I owe the expression,[53] develop this art in strict symmetry with the *ars memoriae* celebrated by Frances Yates. If the latter art was essentially a technique of memorization rather than an abandonment to remembering and to its spontaneous irruptions, the opposite art would be a "lethatechnique" (*Lethe*, 29). If it were, indeed, to follow the treatises on the mnemonic art contemporaneous with the *ars memoriae*, the art of forgetting would have to rest on a rhetoric of extinction: writing to extinguish—the contrary of making an archive. But Weinrich, too tormented by "Auschwitz and impossible forgetfulness" (253ff.), cannot subscribe to this barbarous dream. This sacking, which in another time was called an auto-da-fé, is traced out against the horizon of memory as a threat worse than forgetting through effacement. Is not this reduction to ashes, as a limit-experience, the proof by absurdity that the art of forgetting, if there is one, could not be constructed as a distinct project, alongside the wish for happy memory? What is then proposed in opposition to this ruinous competition between the strategies of memory and forgetting is the possibility of a work of forgetting, interweaving among all the fibers that connect us to time: memory of the past, expectation of the future, and attention to the present. This is the path chosen by Marc Augé in *Les Formes de l'oubli*.[54] A subtle observer and interpreter of African rituals, he sketches three "figures" of forgetting that the rituals raise to the level of emblems. To return to the past, he says, one must forget the present, as in states of possession. To return to the present, one must suspend the ties with the past and the future, as in the games of role reversal. To embrace the future, one must forget the past in a gesture of inauguration, beginning, and rebeginning, as in rituals of initiation. And "it is always in the present, finally, that forgetting is conjugated" (78). As the emblematic figures suggest, the "three daughters" of forgetting (79) reign over communities and individuals. They are at one and the same time institutions and ordeals: "The relation to time is always thought in the singular-plural. This means that there must be at least two people in order to forget, that is to say, to manage time" (84). But, if "nothing is more difficult to succeed than a return" (84), as we have known since the *Odyssey*, and perhaps also than a suspension and a rebeginning, must one not try to forget, at the risk of finding only an interminable memory, like the narrator of *Remembrance of Things Past*? Must not forgetting, outsmarting its own vigilance, as it were, forget itself?

A third track is also offered for exploration: the path of a forgetting that would no longer be a strategy, nor a work, an idle forgetting. It would parallel memory, not as the remembrance of what has occurred, nor the memorization of know-how, not even as the commemoration of the founding events of our identity, but as a concerned disposition established in duration. If memory is in fact a capacity, the power of remembering (*faire-mémoire*), it is more fundamentally a figure of care, that basic anthropological structure of our historical condition. In memory-as-care we hold ourselves open to the past, we remain concerned about it. Would there not then be a supreme form of forgetting, as a disposition and a way of being in the world, which would be insouciance, carefreeness? Cares, care, no more would be said of them, as at the end of a psychoanalysis that Freud would define as "terminable." ... However, under pain of slipping back into the traps of amnesty-amnesia, *ars oblivionis* could not constitute an order distinct from memory, out of complacency with the wearing away of time. It can only arrange itself under the optative mood of happy memory. It would simply add a gracious note to the work of memory and the work of mourning. For it would not be work at all.

How could we not mention—echoing André Breton's apostrophe on the joy of memory and in counterpoint to Walter Benjamin's evocation of the angel of history with its folded wings—Kierkegaard's praise of forgetting as the liberation of care?

It is indeed to those who are full of cares that the Gospel's exhortation to "consider the lilies of the field and the birds of the air" is addressed.[55] Kierkegaard notes, "Yet this is so only if the person in distress actually gives his attention to the lilies and the birds and their life and forgets himself in contemplation of them and their life, while in his absorption in them he, unnoticed, by himself learns something about himself" (161–62). What he will learn from the lilies is that "they do not work." Are we then to understand that the even the work of memory and the work of mourning are to be forgotten? And if they "do not spin" either, their mere existence being their adornment, are we to understand that man too "without working, without spinning, without any meritoriousness, is more glorious than Solomon's glory by being a human being"? And the birds, "sow not and reap not and gather not into barns." But, if "the wood-dove is the human being," how can he manage not to be "worried" and "to break with the worry of comparison" and "to be contented to be a human being" (182)?

What "godly diversion" (184), as Kierkegaard calls "forgetting the worry" to distinguish it from ordinary distractions, would be capable of bringing man "to consider: *how glorious it is to be a human being*" (187)?

Carefree memory on the horizon of concerned memory, the soul common to memory that forgets and does not forget.

Under the sign of this ultimate *incognito* of forgiveness, an echo can be heard of the word of wisdom uttered in the Song of Songs: "Love is as strong as death." The reserve of forgetting, I would then say, is as strong as the forgetting through effacement.

> *Under history, memory and forgetting.*
> *Under memory and forgetting, life.*
> *But writing a life is another story.*
> *Incompletion.*

§ Paul Ricoeur

# NOTES

## PART ONE, CHAPTER ONE

1. Spinoza, *Ethics*, trans. Edwin Curley, in *The Collected Works of Spinoza* (Princeton: Princeton University Press, 1985), 1:465.

2. Plato, *Theaetetus*, trans. M. J. Levett, rev. Myles F. Burnyeat, *Plato: Complete Works*, ed. John M. Cooper (Indianapolis: Hackett, 1997), 181.

3. On all of this, see David Farrell Krell, *Of Memory, Reminiscence, and Writing: On the Verge* (Bloomington: Indiana University Press, 1990). What, the author asks, can be the truth of memory once past things are irrevocably absent? Does not memory seem to place us in contact with them through the present image of their vanished presence? What about the relation of presence to absence that the Greeks explored under the guidance of the metaphor of the imprint (*tupos*)? These are the implications of the tie between typography and iconography that he explores in close proximity to Jacques Derrida's works on writing. Regardless of the fate of this metaphor as it moves into the era of neuroscience, thinking is doomed by the aporia of the presence of absence to remain on the edges, "on the verge."

4. This passage is Krell's alternative translation (with his emphases, 27).

5. A careful discussion in the tradition of English-language analytical philosophy of the strictly epistemic argumentation can be found in Myles Burnyeat, *The Theaetetus of Plato* (Indianapolis: Hackett, 1990). According to the author, all the most important commentaries of the *Theaetetus* are in English. On "false judgment," its possibility and its eventual refutation (65ff.); on the "wax block" (90ff.); on the "aviary" (105ff.).

6. The model of the block of wax had failed in the case of the faulty identification of a number by means of the sum of two numbers; abstract errors like this defy an explanation in terms of a misfit between perceptions.

7. One will note in passing the unexploited allegory of the archer who misses his mark (194a) and recall that *hamartanein* (to be mistaken and, later, to sin) is to miss the target.

8. We are leaving the *Theaetetus* just at the moment when the discussion, which up to now has been centered on false judgment, tightens around the strictly epistemic problem of the relation among these three themes, namely, knowledge, perception, and true judgment (201e). From a strictly epistemic view-point, one passes from the error of identification and description in the *Theaetetus* to pure errors of description in the *Sophist* (Burnyeat, *The Theaetetus of Plato*, 90).

9. In this regard, I would say, in opposition to Krell, that there is no reason to turn the discovery of this paradox against Plato and to discern in it a foretaste of the ontology of presence; the paradox seems to me to constitute the very enigma of memory, which will follow us throughout this book. It is rather the very nature of the problem that this paradox brings to light.

10. *Sophist*, trans. Nicholas P. White in *Plato: Complete Works*, 236–93.

11. *Philebus*, trans. Dorthea Frede in *Plato: Complete Works*, 399–456.

12. Was the French translator, Auguste Diès, right to render *pathēmata* by "reflection," by reason of the comparison made in the *Republic* 511d, between discursive thinking or intuititon, considered states of the soul, and *pathēmata*? It is essential for the argument of the *Philebus* that the writing within the soul be of the order of attention. It will remain for Aristotle to treat the *mnēmē* as presence to the soul and the memory as a *pathos*.

13. My discussion concerning the status of the cortical trace appears in part 3, in the context of the problematic of forgetting.

14. The French translation of *Petits Traités d'histoire naturelle* and of our trea-tise, *De la mémoire et de la réminiscence*, is by René Mugnier (Paris: Éditions les "Belles Lettres," 1965). I want to express here, in unison with so many others, my debt to the English-language translation and commentary offered by Richard Sorabji under the title *Aristotle on Memory* (Providence, R.I.: Brown University Press, 1972). Following his lead, *anamnēsis* could be translated by "recollection" (*rappel*); I have preferred the French *remémoration*, in agreement with the typology that follows this archeology of the problem.

15. Aristotle designates this evocation simultaneously by a substantive *mnēmē* and by a verb *mnēmoneuin* (449b4). Mugnier translates: "La mémoire et le sou-venir," and a little further on, "Faire acte de mémoire," but Sorabji: "Memory and Remembering." The substantive *anamnēsis* will also be paired with a verb, *anamimnēskesthai*. Mugnier: "Reminiscence" and "Souvenir par *réminiscence*"; Sorabji: "Recollection, Recollecting."

16. Mugnier: "La mémoire s'applique au passé"; Sorabji: "Memory is of the past"; the Greek says: "*tou genomenou*," what has occurred, happened.

17. Sorabji: "For whenever someone is actively engaged in remembering, he always says in his soul. . . ."

18. Mugnier: "Tout souvenir s'accompagne de la notion du temps"; Sorabji: "All memory involves time."

19. "'To be in time' means, for movement, that both it and its essence are measured by time (for simultaneously it measures both the movement and its essence), and this is what being in time means for it, that its essence should be measured" (221a5–7). *Physics*, trans. R. P. Hardie and R. K. Gaye, in *The Complete Works of Aristotle*, ed. Jonathan Barnes (Princeton: Princeton University Press, 1984), 1:374.

20. "Now we mark them ('before' and 'after') by judging that A and B are different, and that some third thing is intermediate to them. When we think of [*noēsomen*, distinguish by the intellect] the extremes as different from the middle and the mind pronounces [*eipēi*] that the 'nows' are two, one before and one after, it is then that we say [*phamen*] that there is time, and this that we say is time" (219a25ff.) [371–72].

21. We must then say that "it is the objects of imagination that are remembered in their own right, whereas things that are not grasped without imagination are remembered in virtue of an incidental association" (*De memoria et reminiscentia*, trans. Sorabji, 450a22–25).

22. What? The soul, or perception, sensation? Mugnier: "qui possède la sensation"; Sorabji: "which contains the soul" (450a25).

23. The expression *zōgraphēma* introduced above contains the radical *graphē*.

24. To this vocabulary must be added the term *mnēmoneuma* (451a2), rendered by Sorabji as "reminder," a sort of memory aid, which I will take into account below in the phenomenological section of the present study. For *mnēmoneuma*, Mugnier employs the simple word "souvenir," in the sense of that which makes us think of something else.

25. Mugnier keeps "Réminiscence," Soabji proposes "Recollection." I myself say "rappel" or "rémemoration," in the perspective of the phenomenological sketch that follows these two "textual commentaries" on Plato and Aristotle. The distinction that Aristotle makes between *mnēmē* and *anamnēsis* appears to me to anticipate the one proposed by a phenomenology of memory between simple evocation and the search or the effort to recall.

26. Mugnier translates: "les réminiscences se produisent quand ce mouvement ci vient naturellement après ce mouvement-là" (451b10).

27. See part 3, chapter 3.

28. In this sense, my undertaking is situated along the same line as my exploration of the basic capacities or powers—to speak, act, recount, hold oneself accountable for one's acts—powers which I classify, in *Oneself as Another*, trans. Kathleen Blamey (Chicago: University of Chicago Press, 1992), under the heading of the capable human being.

29. I am anticipating here considerations that will find their proper place in the third part of this work, at the critical turning point between the epistemology of historical knowledge and the hermeneutics of our historical condition.

30. Henri Bergson, *Matter and Memory*, trans. Nancy M. Paul and W. Scott Palmer (London: Allen and Unwin, 1950). A systematic study of the relations between psychology and metaphysics will be offered in the third part of this work within the framework of an investigation devoted to forgetting.

31. Our chapter on forgetting (part 3, chapter 3) will focus at length on this ambiguity.

32. Henri Bergson, "Intellectual Effort," in *Mind-Energy*, trans. H. Wildon Carr (Westport, Conn.: Greenwood, 1975), 186–230.

33. See below, part 3, chapter 3, on forgetting.

34. Edmund Husserl, *On the Phenomenology of the Consciousness of Internal Time (1893–1917)*, *Collected Works*, vol. 4, trans. John Barnett Brough (Dordrecht: Kluwer Academic Publishers, 1991).

35. In chapter 3 I shall consider the important analyses that Rudolf Bernet devotes to the phenomenology of time in Husserl.

36. With regard to this, the figure that accompanies the phenomenon of running-off in §11 should not mislead us: this is a spatial transcription suggested by the equivalence between the present and a point.

37. The word *phantasma* appears in §19, 68–70.

38. Charles Taylor, *Sources of the Self: The Making of the Modern Identity* (Cambridge, Mass.: Harvard University Press, 1989).

39. Edward S. Casey, *Remembering: A Phenomenological Study* (Bloomington: Indiana University Press, 1987).

40. Recognition will be the object of particular attention in my study of forgetting below.

41. On the relation between document and monument, see part 2, chapter 1, below.

42. One can also situate the commemorative act within the pair habit-memory and recollection-memory. The mediation of texts (founding narratives, liturgical manuals) functions in this regard in the manner of the reminders mentioned earlier; there is no practice of ritual without recalling a myth that guides memory toward what is worthy of commemoration. Commemorations are in this way reminders

of a sort, in the sense of reactualizations, of founding events supported by the "call" to remember which solemnizes the ceremony (commemorating, Casey notes, solemnizes by taking the past seriously and celebrating it in appropriate ceremonies [223]). An approach to the public phenomenon of commemoration, which is more critical than descriptive, will be proposed in part 3 within the framework of a critical philosophy of history. First, however, we have to pass through the layer formed by the epistemology of historical knowledge. The first mention of the pitfalls related to the praise of commemorations will be proposed in the following chapter.

43. Commemorative acts should not, of course, be restricted to religious and patriotic celebrations; elegies and funeral services are celebrations as well. I would say that they unfold in the time of the deceased's close relations, halfway between private memory and social memory; but this time of the close relations and the space that is attached to it—the cemetery, the monument to the dead—stand out against the backdrop of public space and social time. Each time that we pronounce or write the phrase "in memory of..." we are inscribing the name of those we remember in the great book of co-memory, which in its turn is inscribed in the most comprehensive time.

44. See part 2, chapter 3.

45. Edmund Husserl, *Phantasie, Bildbewusstsein, Erinnerung 1898–1925*, ed. Eduard Marbach, *Husserliana*, vol. 23 (The Hague: Martinus Nijhoff, 1980).

46. See Edmund Husserl, *Zur Phänomenologie des inneren Zeitbewusstseins (1893–1917)*, *Husserliana*, vol. 10 (The Hague: Martinus Nijhoff, 1966). On the basis of these texts, Rudolf Bernet has edited and introduced the texts completing the 1905 Lectures and their additions under the title, *Texte zur Phänomenologie des innern Zeitbewusstseins (1893–1917)* (Hamburg: Meiner, 1985).

47. One text of Edmund Husserl, *Erste Philosophie (1923–1924)*, ed. and introduced by R. Boehm, *Husserliana*, vol. 8 (The Hague: Martinus Nijhoff, 1959), expresses Husserl's distress confronting the stupefying entanglement of the phenomena considered: "Apparently the memory presentifies in a simple manner a remembered past, expectation an awaited future, depiction (*Abbildung*) an object depicted, fantasy a fiction (*Fiktum*); in the same way as perception bears on a perceived. But in truth it is not like this" (my translation, 130). This is not the only time that Husserl admits his mistake. Raymond Kassis, an excellent scholar of the Husserlian corpus in its entirety, has pointed out pages to me from *Einleitung in die Logik und Erkenntnistheorie: Vorlesungen (1906–1907)*, ed. and introduced by U. Melle, *Husserliana*, vol. 24 (The Hague: Martinus Nijhoff, 1984), devoted to "the distinction between the consciousness of phantasy and primary memory" (255–58) and to the "analogies" between two sorts of presentifications. These continue to be temporal objects implying a "temporal extension."

48. *Beilage XIII*: "Phantasmen und Empfindungen als wahrnehmungs Objekte und als Auffassungsinhalte von Wahrnehmungen," *Phantasie, Bildbewusstsein, Erinnerung*, 166–69.

49. *Phantasie, Bildbewusstsein, Erinnerung*, text no. 4 (1908): "Glaube als Impression," 218–28.

50. *Phantasie, Bildbewusstsein, Erinnerung*, text no. 6 (1909): "Erinnerung und Phantasie," 241–48.

51. Ibid., 245.

52. *Husserliana*, vol. 10, *Zur Phänomenologie des inneren Zeitbewusstseins*, makes a connection between *Ideen I*, 36 and following to text no. 19 of *Phantasie, Bildbewusstsein, Erinnerung* concerning the operation that constitutes phantasy and the distinction between phantasy and memory in terms of fulfillment: "The thetically unmodified intentionality" of memories forms a barrier against any confusion with phantasy: the correlate of the latter is "pure possibility" with regard to its modality ("Reine Möglichkeit und Phantasie" [1922–23], *Husserliana*, 23:559).

53. I am reserving for chapter 2 of part 3, in the framework of a discussion on forgetting, the question of the role of the body and the brain at the point of articulation of a psychology, in the broad sense, and a metaphysics, conceived fundamentally as "the metaphysics of matter based on duration" (F. Worms, *Introduction à «Matière et Mémoire» de Bergson* [Paris: Presses Universitaires de France, 1997]).

54. In *Poetics* 1450a7–9, Aristotle makes the "spectacle" (*opsis*) one of the component parts of the tragic narrative. It designates the external and visible arrangement (*cosmos*) of the poem, the fable, alongside diction (*lexis*) which expresses its readability. *Rhetoric* 3.10.1410b33 says of metaphor that it "sets before our eyes." We will find this same relation between readability and visibility once again on the level of the representation of historians (part 2, chapter 3).

55. Jean-Paul Sartre, *The Psychology of Imagination* (New York: Citadel, 1965).

## PART ONE, CHAPTER TWO

1. I myself attempted in *Oneself as Another* to consider operations traditionally assigned to distinct problematics as the diverse manifestations of the fundamental power of acting. The same pragmatic turning point is taken in each of the three major sections of the work: *I can* speak, *I can* act, *I can* recount (myself), *I can* ascribe my actions to myself as their actual author. I now say: *I can* remember. In this sense, the investigation of mnemonic phenomena proposed here forms a supplementary chapter in a philosophical anthropology of the acting and suffering being who is the capable being.

2. Frances A. Yates, *The Art of Memory* (Chicago: University of Chicago Press, 1966).

3. Georges Chapouthier, *La Biologie de la mémoire* (Paris: Presses Universitaires de France, 1994), 5ff.

4. Maurice Merleau-Ponty, *The Structure of Behavior*, trans. Alden L. Fisher (Boston: Beacon Press, 1963).

5. Georges Canguilhem, *La Connaissance de la vie* (Paris: Vrin, 1965). On Kurt Goldstein, see the chapter, "Le vivant et son milieu" (143–47).

6. Gérard Leclerc, *Histoire de l'autorité: L'Assignation des énoncés culturels et la généalogie de la croyance* (Paris: Presses Universitaires de France, 1986).

7. Henri Gouhier, *Le Théâtre et l'existence* (Paris: Aubier, 1952).

8. In addition to the work of Frances Yates, Harald Weinrich, in *Lethe: Kunst und Kritik des Vergessens* (Munich: Ch. Beck, 1977), seeks an eventual *ars oblivionis*, symmetrical to this "art of memory," which as been well verified historically. He devotes the opening pages of his book to the latter, memorization receiving preference over remembrance as the axis of reference for a literary history of forgetting, whose course meanders no less than does the mythical river that has given its name to his work. We will return to this in part 3, chapter 3.

9. Cicero bequeathed to the Medieval scholars several important writings on rhetoric: *De oratore, De inventione* (the *Ad Herennium* being considered its second part), and the *Disputes Tusculanes* which exerted a decisive influence in the conversion of Augustine (*Confessions*, book 6). He is the first Latin author to have, toward the end of *De inventione*, made memory part of the virtue of *prudentia*, along with *intelligentia* and *providentia*.

10. In truth, the medieval heritage of Aristotle concerning memory is threefold. First, the extension given to the metaphor of the imprint of the seal in the wax (first chapter of *De memoria*); next, the pairing of memory and imagination, of which it is stated in *De anima* that "it is impossible to think without images"; finally, including mnemotechnics among the procedures of the rational recollection of memories in the second chapter of *De memoria* (the choice of a starting point, ascending and descending the series of associations, and so on).

11. Cf. the beautiful pages devoted to Dante by Yates in *The Art of Memory* (95ff.) and by Weinrich in *Lethe* (142ff.). According to Weinrich, the typology of the beyond, which the poet reaches after drinking the waters of oblivion, makes Dante the *Gedächtnismann*, the man of memory (145). Weinrich knows no equal to the *Divine Comedy* except for Marcel Proust's *Remembrance of Things Past*.

12. Yates concludes her chapter on "medieval memory and the formation of imagery" in these terms: "From the point of view of this book, which is mainly concerned with the later history of the art, it is fundamental to emphasize that the art of

memory came out of the Middle Ages. Its profoundest roots were in a most venerable past. From those deep and mysterious origins it flowed out into later centuries, bearing the stamp of religious fervor strangely combined with mnemotechnical detail which was set upon it in the Middle Ages" (104).

13. Weinrich sees this denial of forgetfulness in the Greek episode of the feat of memory attributed to Simonides, who restored each of the deceased guests to his proper place at the banquet. According to Cicero, the poet is said to have suggested to Themistocles, who was exiled from his country, that he teach him the wonderful art of "remembering everything" (*ut omnia meminisset*). The great man is held to have answered that he would have more taste for an art of forgetting which would allow him to avoid the suffering of remembering what he did not want to and of not being able to forget what he did want to (Weinrich, 24). We shall return to this when we discuss forgetting as a magnitude in its own right.

14. Edward Casey mentions at the beginning of his work, *Remembering*, which we have abundantly cited in the preceding study, the wrong done to memory, in the precise sense of remembering, by the critique of the pedagogy that relies on memory, as if the case against memorization extended indiscriminately to the case of remembering, to the benefit of a culture of *forgetting*.

15. Montaigne, *Essays*, I, 25, quoted by Weinrich, who does not fail to mention in this connection Sancho Panza and his donkey, who contrasts with the sad figure of the "ingenious" knight (*Lethe*, 67–71).

16. Weinrich favorably quotes this statement by Helvétius: "The great mind does not in any way presuppose great memory; I would even add that the extreme extension of the one is absolutely exclusive of the other" (ibid., 78).

17. Quoted by Weinrich, 90.

18. See below on forgetting, part 3, chapter 3.

19. "On the Utility and Liability of History for Life," trans. Richard T. Gray, in *Unfashionable Observations*, vol. 2 of *The Complete Works of Friedrich Nietzsche* (Stanford: Stanford University Press, 1995), 83–167.

20. "Erinnern, Wiederholen, Durcharbeiten," in *Gesammelte Werke*, vol. 10 (Frankfurt am Main: S. Fischer Verlag, 1913–17), 126–36. Pagination will be given first for the German edition (when indicated by Ricoeur) and then for the English translation of the *Standard Edition*: "Remembering, Repeating, and Working-Through," in vol. 12 (1911–13), trans. James Strachey (London: Hogarth Press, 1958), 147–56.

21. "Mourning and Melancholia" appears in the *Standard Edition*, vol. 14: 243–58.

22. What may lead us to overlook the instruction we are seeking concerning the kinship between the work of remembering and the work of mourning is the

fact that the term "work" is applied to both melancholia and to mourning within the framework of the "economic" model so fervently evoked by Freud during the period this essay was written. The theme of mourning, Peter Homans notes in *The Ability to Mourn* (Chicago: University of Chicago Press, 1989), is not simply one theme among others in psychoanalytic description and explanation: it is tied to the symptoms of hysteria and to the famous statement: "Psychopaths suffer from memories." In his *Five Lectures on Psycho-analysis*, Freud makes a connection between hysterical symptoms as mnemonic symptoms and the monuments that decorate our cities (Homans, 261). Monuments are responses to loss. What is more, the work of mourning is coextensive with the entire psychoanalytic enterprise, considered as renunciation and resignation culminating in reconciliation with loss. Homans provides a positive extension to this axial theme under the heading of individuation, understood as self-appropriation in relation to *Phantasie* and the capacity for storytelling.

23. Raymond Klibansky, Erwin Panofsky, and Fritz Saxl, *Saturn and Melancholy: Studies in the History of Natural Philosophy, Religion, and Art* (New York: Basic Books, 1964).

24. The reader will not miss the parallel to the *ars memoriae*, discussed above, and the theory of melancholy. Was not Giordano Bruno, the author of *Shadows of Ideas* (*De umbris idearum*), a "madman"?

25. *Saturn and Melancholy*, 125ff. The parallel between the two thematics is held not to be accidental, as is confirmed by the reference to Saturn, "the star of melancholy," in the literary, pictorial, and poetic tradition.

26. More than anyone else, it is Marsilio Ficino "who gives shape to the idea of the melancholy man of genius and revealed it to the rest of Europe—in particular, to the great Englishmen of the sixteenth and seventeenth centuries—in the magic chiaroscuro of Christian Neoplatonic mysticism" (ibid., 255). We are not far from the enthusiastic athletes of the *ars memoriae*, considering the astral connotations found in so many Renaissance thinkers.

27. It is true that the central figure has wings, albeit folded, which the "putti" enliven: a suggestion of sublimation? A crown encircles the head and, in particular, the number Four—the "magic square" of medical mathematics—appears as an antidote.

28. I encountered this problematic of the "sadness without a cause" at the end of the first volume of my Philosophy of Will under the title of the "Sorrow of Finitude." *Freedom and Nature: The Voluntary and the Involuntary*, trans. Erazim V. Kohák (Evanston, Ill.: Northwestern University Press, 1966), 447–48.

29. Jean Starobinski, *La Mélancholie au miroir: Trois lectures de Baudelaire* (Paris: Julliard, 1989).

30. See below, part 3, chapter 3.

31. Starobinski marks in this way the path that, starting in ancient "acedia" and passing through Dürer's *Melencolia*, leads to Baudelaire's *Spleen*, which, in its turn, leads back to memory. See the third study of *La Mélancolie au miroir*. "Les figures perchées: 'Le Cygne.'"

32. Evoking "poetic melancholy in post-medieval poetry" and in the great Elizabethans announcing Keats's "Ode on Melancholy," the authors of *Saturn and Melancholy* depict this aesthetic melancholy as "heightened self-awareness" (Klibansky et al., 228).

33. Paul Ricoeur, *Lectures on Ideology and Utopia*, ed. George H. Taylor (New York: Columbia University Press, 1986). My investigation took up thinkers as diverse as Marx, Althusser, Mannheim, Max Weber, Habermas (first period), and Clifford Geertz.

34. "With no notion of how metaphor, analogy, irony, ambiguity, pun, paradox, hyperbole, rhythm, and all the other elements of what we lamely call 'style' operate ... in casting personal attitudes into public form, sociologists lack the symbolic resources out of which to construct a more incisive formulation." Clifford Geertz, "Ideology as a Cultural System," in *The Interpretation of Cultures* (New York: Basic Books, 1973), 209.

35. Geertz, whose fields of study have been Morocco and Indonesia, readily admits this: "It is through the construction of ideologies, schematic images of social order, that man makes himself for better or worse a political animal" (ibid., 218). "The function of ideology," he continues, "is to make an autonomous politics possible by providing the authoritative concepts that render it meaningful, the suasive images by means of which it can be sensibly grasped" (ibid.).

36. Ricoeur, *Lectures on Ideology and Utopia*, 181–215.

37. By venturing the expression "surplus value," I am suggesting that the Marxist notion of surplus value, focused on the production of values in the market economy, constitutes only one particular form of the general phenomenon of surplus value attached to the exercise of power, economic power in the capitalist form of the market economy being the variant specified by the division of labor between governing and governed.

38. See Ricoeur, *Lectures on Ideology and Utopia*, 68–102.

39. Michel Henry's work on Marx's ontology remains the prime reference for an in-depth understanding of the Marxian analysis of human reality. Michel Henry, *Marx*, trans. Kathleen McLaughlin (Bloomington: Indiana University Press, 1983).

40. Jean-Luc Petit, *Du travail vivant au système de l'action: Une discussion de Marx* (Paris: Seuil, 1980).

41. This was the contribution made by Habermas at the time of *Knowledge and Human Interests*. (See Ricoeur, *Lectures on Ideology and Utopia*, 216–53.) An interest in emancipation, distinct from the interest in control and manipulation corresponding to the empirical sciences and even from the interest in communication belonging to the historical and interpretive sciences, is held to be the basis of the critical social sciences such as psychoanalysis and ideology critique.

42. Tzvetan Todorov, *Les Abus de la mémoire* (Paris: Éditions Arléa, 1995).

43. See Aristotle, *Nichomachean Ethics*, book 5.

44. Henry Rousso, *The Vichy Syndrome: History and Memory in France since 1944*, trans. Arthur Goldhammer (Cambridge, Mass.: Harvard University Press, 1991); see also *Vichy: An Ever-Present Past*, trans. Nathan Bracher (Hanover, N.H.: University Press of New England, 1998); *The Haunting Past: History, Memory, and Justice*, trans. Ralph Schoolcraft (Philadelphia: University of Pennsylvania Press, 2002).

45. Pierre Nora, "L' Ère de la commémoration," *Les Lieux de mémoire*, vol. 3, *Les France*, book 3, *De l'archive à l'emblème* (Paris: Gallimard, 1992), 975–1012. "The Era of Commemoration," *Realms of Memory*, vol. 3, *Symbols*, ed. Lawrence D. Kritzman, trans. Arthur Goldhammer (New York: Columbia University Press, 1998), 609–37.

46. See below, part 3, chap. 2, "The Uncanniness of History: Pierre Nora: Strange Places of Memory."

47. Nora specifies: this "metamorphosis of commemoration" is held, in turn, to be "the effect of a broader metamorphosis: in less than twenty years France has gone from being a country with a unified national consciousness to a country with a patrimonial type of consciousness" ("The Era of Commemoration," 621).

PART ONE, CHAPTER THREE

1. Charles Taylor, *Sources of the Self: The Making of the Modern Identity* (Cambridge, Mass.: Harvard University Press, 1989), 111ff.

2. Jean Guitton, *Le Temps et l'éternité chez Platon et saint Augustin* (Paris: Vrin, 1933; 4th ed., 1971).

3. Augustine, *Confessions* 10.16, trans. R. S. Pine-Coffin (New York: Penguin Books, 1961), 222–23. Quoted in Paul Ricoeur, *Time and Narrative*, trans. Kathleen McLaughlin and David Pellauer (Chicago: University of Chicago Press, 1984), 1:231, note 3. Quotations from the *Confessions* are taken from the Pine-Coffin translation.

4. "My love of you, O Lord, is not some vague feeling: it is positive and certain" (*certa conscientia*, in my consciousness, I am certain). "And yet when I love him, it

is true that I love a light of a certain kind, a voice, a perfume, a food, an embrace; but they are of a kind that I love in my inner self" (ibid., 10.6).

5. "When I use my memory, I ask it to produce whatever it is that I wish to remember. Some things it produces immediately; some are forthcoming only after a long delay, as though they were being brought out from some inner hiding place; others come spilling from the memory, thrusting themselves upon us when what we want is something quite different, as much as to say 'Perhaps we are what you want to remember?' These I brush aside from the picture which my memory presents to me, allowing my mind to pick what it chooses, until finally that which I wish to see stands out clearly and emerges into sight from its hiding place. Some memories present themselves easily and in the correct order just as I require them. They come and give place in their turn to others that follow upon them, and as their place is taken they return to their place of storage, ready to emerge again when I want them. This is what happens when I recite something by heart [*cum aliquid narro memoriter*]" (ibid., 10.8, p. 214).

6. Once notions "have been dispersed, I have to collect them again, and this is the derivation of the word *cogitare*, which means *to think* or *to collect ones thoughts*. For in Latin the word *cogo*, meaning *I assemble* or *I collect*, is related to *cogito*, which means *I think*, in the same way as *ago* is related to *agito* or *facio* to *factito*" (ibid., 10.11, pp. 218–19). Verbs ending in *-ito* are frequentative verbs, which indicate repetition of the activity represented by the simple form of the verb.

7. More precisely, and more dangerously, the *distentio* is not only of the soul but in the soul. Hence, in something like a place of inscription for the traces, the *effigia*, left by past events; in brief, for images.

8. I will also hold in reserve the question of the status of the past as it is the target of memory. Must we say about the past that it is no longer or that it was? Augustine's repeated recourse to expressions of ordinary language, in particular to the adverbial forms: "no longer," "not yet," "for how long," "long-time," "still," "already," as well as the dual treatment of the past as "being and not being" are but so many touchstones with regard to an ontology, which is prevented from unfolding by the thesis that time inheres in the soul.

9. John Locke, *Identité et différence: L'Invention de la conscience*, trans. and commentary by Étienne Balibar (Paris: Seuil, 1998).

10. The Latin *sibi consciere, sibi conscius esse* and the substantive *conscientia*, which translates the Greek *suneidēsis*, do not mean to be self-conscious but to be informed, to be made aware of something; it is a form of judgment. In the "dossier" that Étienne Balibar joins to his commentary one can read passages from Descartes's writings, in particular the Replies to the Second, Third, Fourth, Sixth and Seventh Objections, *The Principles of Philosophy, Conversation with Burman,*

and several letters (Locke, *Identité et différence*, 265–73). Nevertheless, the word "consciousness" is not absent: it is found in the *Principles*. Leibniz preferred "apperception" (*Monadology*, §14). The sole antecedent on the plane of vocabulary, Balibar tells us, is found in Cudworth and the Cambridge Platonists (*Identité et différence*, 57–63).

11. On the variety of the usages of the word "self" allowed by the English language, see the valuable glossary appended to Étienne Balibar's translation (ibid., 249–55).

12. In this regard, my critique in *Oneself as Another*, reproaching Locke with having confused *idem* and *ipse*, is not relevant to the letter of the *Essay*. The category of sameness reigns from one end of it to the other: personal identity does not propose an alternative to sameness; it is simply one variety of it, the most significant, to be sure, but one that remains within the formal unity of the idea of self-identity. Only a reading that draws its arguments from other sources than personal identity can be considered an alternative to sameness. In Locke, the self is not an *ipse* set in opposition to an *idem*; it is a same—and even a selfsame—placed at the summit of the pyramid of sameness.

13. John Locke, *Second Treatise of Government* ([1689] Chicago: Henry Regnery, 1955).

14. The only plausible connection to be sought is found in the chapter on property (Locke, ibid., chapter 5). The earth and everything on it are given to men by God to assure their existence and well-being, but it remains for them to "appropriate them" (chapter 5, §26). Is this the concept of appropriation found in the *Essay*? It would seem to be, inasmuch as "every man has a property in his own person" (chapter 5, §27). But it is in a relation to others who might take it away. So it is in the language of right that it is spoken of and in relation to a genuine other: "this [his own person] nobody has a right to but himself" (ibid.). Moreover, to this bare property is joined labor, a category foreign to the *Essay*: "For this labor being the unquestionable property of the laborer, no man but he can have a right to what that is once joined to" (ibid.).

15. My question does not coincide with that raised by critics as knowledgeable as Rudolf Bernet: for him, the question of confidence, so to speak, concerns the links that the transcendental phenomenology of time, culminating in the instance of the "living present," retains with the "metaphysics of presence" tracked by Heidegger. For this post-Heideggerian reading, strengthened by Jacques Derrida's perspicacious critique, the absence that permeates the presumed presence of the absolute present is infinitely more significant than the absence inscribed in the relation with that other absence, the "foreign" in relation to my sphere of ownness, to the mineness of personal memory.

16. The *Phenomenology of the Consciousness of Internal Time* posed a considerable problem of editing, and then of translation. Around the core of the "Lectures on the Consciousness of Internal Time from the Year 1905" were collected the "addenda and supplements" (1905–10). It is this material that Heidegger published in 1928 in the *Jahrbuch für Philosophie und phaenomenologiche Forschung*. New manuscripts were included in volume 10 of the *Husserliana*, under the title, *Zur Phänomenologie des inneren Zeitbewusstseins (1893–1917)*.

17. Cf. Ricoeur, *Time and Narrative*, 3:44–59.

18. One also encounters the term *Gegenwärtigkeit*, translated here by "presence," alongside *Gegenwärtigung*, translated by "presentation," in juxtaposition with *Präsentation*, whose translation poses no problem.

19. In the time lectures, we read: the flow is "one, unique" (§39, 84).

20. References to recollection are not absent, but connected to retention; §39 talks in this regard of what "in the retaining, is retained of the second degree" (86). In addition, the notion of the retention of retentions is contained in that of "retentional being-all-at-once" (§39, 87) in which otherness is canceled out. It is true, however, that with the return of the opposition between "impression and reproduction" (§42) the break with presence tends to be felt once again. But the affirmation of the two phenomena and their repeated correlation win out over the recognition of their differences.

21. Readers familiar with Husserl's work will have noted the proximity of my analyses to those of the excellent and learned interpreter of Husserl, Rudolf Bernet, whose "Einleitung" accompanies the *Texte zur Phänomenologie des inneren Zeitbewusstseins (1893–1917)* (Hamburg: Felix Meiner, 1985), xi–lxxvii; as well as "Die ungegenwärtige Gegenwart, Anwesenheit und Abwesenheit in Husserls Analysis des Zeitbewusstseins," in E. W. Orth, ed., *Phänomenologische Forschungen* (Freiburg, Munich: Verlag Karl Alber, 1983), 16–57; and "La présence du passé dans l'analyse husserlienne de la conscience du temps," *Revue de métaphysique et de morale* 19 (1983): 178–98. Rudolf Bernet's thesis—that what is unexpressed in Husserlian thinking lies in his unperceived allegiance to the "metaphysics of presence" that Heidegger sees as pervading Western philosophy in the guise of the forgetfulness of Being—is plausible, despite the violence cloaking this interpretation. But this should not preclude all attempts to rectify Husserlian phenomenology on its own terrain of eidetic analysis. In particular, it does not require abandoning the reference of temporal experience to the present. Without the mark of the now, how could one say that something begins or ends? It is sufficient not to confuse the living present with the point-like instant of objective time: the reduction of objective time protects us from this confusion; without the present, there is no before, no after, no temporal distance or depth. It is in

the experienced present itself, as Augustine perceived, that *distentio animi* operates. The evocation of an eternal present does not lead to dissolving the contrasts
and tensions internal to time, but, far from this, serves as a means of contrast,
revealing the tear, the rip, discussed by Bernet ("La presence du passé," 179). At
the limit, the reversal by which a phenomenology of difference would come to
occupy the same territory as the phenomenology of identical self-presence produces its own difficulties. Interpretations other than those inspired by Heidegger
are still possible: did not Husserl breath new life into the presuppositions of
the Fichtean philosophy of identity, without necessarily attaching to this vein of
thought the presumed single phylum of the metaphysics of presence? We might
also ask, along with Emmanuel Levinas in his great text, *Time and the Other*,
trans. Richard A. Cohen (Pittsburgh: Duquesne University Press, 1987), whether
the first denial is not fundamentally an ethical one, and whether it is not the
failure to acknowledge the original otherness of other people that produces the
blindness with regard to all the forms of otherness, taken one by one. But we
can also presuppose that there is no one reason for the multiple forms of blindness to the negative but only a "family resemblance" inaccessible to systematic
unification, which would paradoxically mark the triumph of identity in the very
name of difference. In *The Hospitality of Presence: Problems of Otherness in Husserl's
Phenomenology* (Stockholm: Almqvist and Wicksell, 1998), O. Birnbaum successfully explores the resources of this family resemblance characterizing all the figures
of negativity in Husserl's work. The most remarkable family resemblance in this
regard would belong to two denials, the denial of absence within internal-time and
the denial of the foreign in egology—the foreign(er), the figure without which
egology could never begin. Bernet can be cited again here: "L'Autre du temps,"
in *Emmanuel Levinas: Positivité et Transcendance*, ed. Jean-Luc Marion (Paris:
Presses Universitaires de France, 2000), 143–63. There then remains to take into
account *Phantasie, Bildbewusstsein, Erinnerung*, volume 23 of *Husserliana*, along
with the distinction between memories as intentional objects and memory as the
apprehending of time; it is solely with the latter that the present discussion is concerned.

  22. *Time and Narrative*, vol. 3, gives priority to a different problematic, that
of the intuitive character of time-consciousness in comparison with its invisibility,
which the Kantian transcendental aesthetics would appear to require.

  23. Edmund Husserl, *Cartesianische Meditationen und Pariser Vorträge*, ed.
S. Strasser, *Husserliana*, vol. 1 (The Hague: Nijhoff, 1963); *Cartesian Meditations*, trans. Dorion Cairns (The Hague: Nijhoff, 1969), which I shall cite here.
I proposed an analysis of the *Cartesian Meditations* as a whole, along with a separate study of the "Fifth Cartesian Meditation," in *Husserl: An Analysis of His*

*Phenomenology*, trans. Edward G. Ballard and Lester E. Embree (Evanston, Ill.: Northwestern University Press, 1967), 82–142.

24. Cf. Paul Ricoeur, "Husserl's Fifth Cartesian Meditation," in ibid., 115–42.

25. One speaks, in this way, of analogical "apperception." Hundreds of pages were devoted to this unlocalizable analogical apperception in the long-left unedited manuscripts dealing with intersubjectivity, finally published under the direction of Iso Kern.

26. Max Weber, *Economy and Society: An Outline of Interpretive Sociology*, ed. Günther Roth and Claus Wittich; trans. Ephraim Fischoff et al. (New York: Bedminster Press, 1968; reprinted Berkeley and Los Angeles: University of California Press, 1978).

27. Maurice Halbwachs, *The Collective Memory*, trans. Francis J. Ditter and Vida Yazdi Ditter (New York: Harper Colophon, 1950; reprinted 1980). In French, there is a newer, revised critical edition by Gérard Namer which incorporates numerous passages concerning *The Collective Memory* from previously unpublished writings found in Halbwachs's notebooks: *La Mémoire collective* (Paris: Albin Michel, 1997).

28. See Patrick H. Hutton, "Maurice Halbwachs as Historian of Collective Memory," in *History as an Art of Memory* (Burlington: University of Vermont Press, 1993), 73ff. Hutton gives Halbwachs a place of honor in a sequence which, in addition to Wordsworth and Freud, includes Philippe Aries and Michel Foucault. For her part, Mary Douglas is the author of an important introduction to the English translation of *The Collective Memory* in which she compares Halbwachs's contribution to that of Edward Evans-Pritchard. Her own study, *How Institutions Think* (Syracuse, N.Y.: Syracuse University Press, 1986), finds a basis in Halbwachs for her study of "structural amnesia," to which I shall return in my chapter on forgetting. Numerous, too, are the French historians who recognize in Halbwachs's work more than a simple appendix to Émile Durkheim's sociology, namely, a genuine introduction to the confrontation between collective memory and history. In this regard, we will confine ourselves in this chapter to an analysis of chapter 1, "Individual Memory and Collective Memory" (22–49), of *The Collective Memory*. I will set aside for a discussion that will take place within the framework of the critical philosophy of history, the key chapter titled, "Historical Memory and Collective Memory" (50–87). The distinction between collective memory and historical memory will then be given an importance equal to the sole distinction we are concerned with at this stage of our investigation, the distinction between individual memory and collective memory.

29. Maurice Halbwachs, *Les Cadres sociaux de la mémoire* (Paris: Alcan, 1925; Albin Michel, 1994). There is a partial English translation of this work in Maurice

Halbwachs, *On Collective Memory*, ed. and trans. Lewis A. Coser (Chicago: University of Chicago Press, 1992), 37–189.

30. Later we shall have the opportunity to discuss the tie Halbwachs establishes between memory and space. This is the title of one of the chapters of *The Collective Memory*: "Space and the Collective Memory" (128–57).

31. Note the emphasis on notions of place and displacement.

32. The historians whom we shall consult in part 2 concerning the constitution of the social bond will restore this initiative to social actors, whether this is in situations of justifying or contesting action in the course of life in various "cities." Halbwachs, however, moves beyond the objection that he himself raises, namely, that the movements of situating oneself, relocating and displacing oneself are spontaneous movements that we know, that we can perform. Paradoxically, the response that he opposes to the sense data theory of memory rests on a deep-seated agreement with the latter concerning the status of the original impression, of sensible intuition.

33. What ultimately weakens Maurice Halbwachs's position is his recourse to a sense data based theory of sensible intuition. This recourse will become more difficult after the linguistic turn and, even more so, after the pragmatic turn taken by the epistemology of history. This double turn, however, can already be made on the plane of memory. Remembering, we said, is doing something: it is declaring that one has seen, done, acquired this or that. And this act of memory is inscribed within a network of practical exploration of the world, of the corporeal and mental initiative which make us acting subjects. It is then in a present much richer than that characterizing sensible intuition that memories come back, in a present of initiative. The preceding chapter, devoted to the exercise of memory, authorizes a rereading of mnemonic phenomena from a pragmatic viewpoint before the historical operation itself is placed back in the field of a theory of action.

34. H. L. A. Hart, "The Ascription of Responsibility and Rights," *Proceedings of the Aristotelian Society* 49 (1948): 171–94. The substantive *ascription* and the verb *to ascribe* have been constructed half-way between "description" and "prescription" to designate in particular the attribution of something to someone.

35. Ricoeur, *Oneself as Another*, Fourth Study.

36. P. F. Strawson, *Individuals* (London: Methuen, 1959). I examine the general thesis in the first study of *Oneself as Another*, 27–39, in the framework of a general theory of "identifying reference" (how is it that we recognize that one individual is not another?). I apply it and make it more precise on the level of the theory of action in the Fourth Study, "The Aporias of Ascription" (96–112). It is the latter analysis that I take up again here, applying it to mnemonic phenomena.

37. I tested this theory of attribution in my discussion with Jean-Pierre Changeux, *What Makes Us Think? A Neuroscientist and a Philosopher Argue about Ethics, Human Nature, and the Brain*, trans. M. B. DeBevoise (Princeton: Princeton University Press, 2000), 125–33.

38. The conception proposed here of the self-attribution of the acts of memory finds valuable support in the analysis of the speech act of self-designation of the witness, who attests to his own engagement in the act of bearing witness (cf. below, part 2, chap. 1).

39. This fixity of attribution in the case of memory explains Husserl's shift in his vocabulary of intentionality, which, from intentionality *ad extra*, as in perception, becomes intentionality *ad intra*, horizontal intentionality, proper to the passage of memory along the axis of temporality. This horizontal intentionality is the very consciousness of internal time.

40. Carlo Ginzburg, "Clues: Roots of an Evidential Paradigm," in *Clues, Myths, and the Historical Method*, trans. John and Anne C. Tedeschi (Baltimore: Johns Hopkins University Press, 1989), 96–125.

41. Marie Balmary is a French psychoanalyst, whose works include *Le Sacrifice interdit: Freud et la Bible* (Paris: Grasset, 1986).

42. Edmund Husserl, *The Crisis of European Sciences and Transcendental Philosophy*, trans. David Carr (Evanston, Ill.: Northwestern University Press, 1970).

43. Alfred Schutz, *The Phenomenology of the Social World*, trans. George Walsh and Frederick Lehnert (Evanston, Ill.: Northwestern University Press, 1967). See also by the same author, *Collected Papers*, 3 vols. (The Hague: Nijhoff, 1962–66), and *The Structure of the Life-World* (London: Heinemann, 1974).

44. Weber, *Economy and Society*.

45. In *Time and Narrative*, 3:109–16, I examined the "succession of generations" within the framework of the connectors that assure the transition between phenomenological time and the common time of history, between mortal time and public time. The mere "replacement" of generations is a phenomenon related to human biology. Whereas, the interpretive sociology of Dilthey and Mannheim elucidates the qualitative features of the phenomenon of the "succession" (*Folge*) of the "generational bond."

46. Schutz, *The Phenomenology of the Social World*, 139–214.

47. Bernard Lepetit, ed., *Les Formes de l'expérience: Une autre histoire sociale* (Paris: Albin Michel, 1995).

48. Jacques Revel, ed., *Jeux d'échelles: La Microanalyse à l'expérience* (Paris: EHESS-Gallimard-Seuil, 1996).

49. Jean-Marc Ferry, *Les Puissances de l'expérience: Essai sur l'identité contemporaine*, vol. 2, *Les Ordres de la reconnaissance* (Paris: Éd. du Cerf, 1991).

50. Luc Boltanski and Laurent Thévenot, *De la justification: Les économies de la grandeur* (Paris: Gallimard, 1991).

51. Hannah Arendt, *The Human Condition* (Chicago: University of Chicago Press, 1958), 247.

## PART TWO, INTRODUCTION

1. Herodotus, *The History*, trans. David Grene (Chicago: University of Chicago Press, 1987), 33. Herodotus: the "father of history" (Cicero) or the "father of lies" (Plutarch)?

2. In his book *L'Histoire* (Paris: A. Colin, 2000), François Dosse proposes a sequence of six developments that mark out the history of history. The first of these sets in place "the historian, as a teacher of truth" (8–29). The problematic of truth begins not with Herodotus, the first *histōr*, but with Thucydides and his "cult of the true" (13). It developed through the birth and death of history as erudition. And it reached a peak with the methodological school and Charles Seignobos, before Ferdinand Braudel imposed a structural form on it that will be called into question under the banner of the "crisis of causality" at the end of the second of the major developments presented by Dosse.

3. In an initial, shorter version published in one of the three volumes edited by Le Goff and Nora—*Faire de l'histoire* (Paris: Gallimard, 1974)—Certeau proposed the expression "historic operation." In the longer version, published in his *The Writing of History*, trans. Tom Conley (New York: Columbia University Press, 1988), he adopts once and for all the phrase "historiographical operation."

4. Paul Ricoeur, "Philosophies critiques de l'histoire: Recherche, explication, écriture," in Fløistad Guttorm, ed., *Philosophical Problems Today* (Dordrecht: Kluwer, 1994), 1:139–201.

5. François Châtelet, *La Naissance de l'histoire* (Paris: Seuil, 1996). See also A. D. Momigliano, *Studies in Historiography* (New York: Harper Torchbooks, 1966), esp. "The Place of Herodotus in the History of Historiography," 127–42. François Hartog, in *The Mirror of Herodotus: The Representation of the Other in the Writing of History*, trans. Janet Lloyd (Berkeley: University of California Press, 1988), notes the substitution of *histōr* for bard (iii–viii, 275–85) in the vocabulary of Herodotus's preface. There where Homer invokes his privileged relation to the Muses ("tell me, Muse, the man of a thousand twists . . . " *Odyssey* 1.1), Herodotus speaks of himself in the third person, of himself and his place: Herodotus of Halicarnassus is here setting forth his research. After him, Thucydides will say that he has "written" the narrative of the war between Pelponnesians and Athenians. In this way, the renown (*kleos*) of Greeks and barbarians, once "exposed," then "written" will be a "possession [*ktēma*] forever." In any case, we cannot speak of a clear and definitive

break between the bard and the historian, or, as I shall say below, between orality and writing. The struggle against forgetting and the culture of eulogy, in the face of the violence of history, against the backdrop of tragedy, mobilizes all the energies of diction. As for the break with myth, as an event in thinking, it is still in terms of myth that it can be spoken of, like the birth of writing.

6. Jacques Derrida, *Of Grammatology*, trans. Gayatri Chakravorty Spivak (Baltimore: Johns Hopkins University Press, 1976).

## PART TWO, PRELUDE

1. See his magnificent essay "Plato's Pharmacy," in Jacques Derrida, *Dissemination*, trans. Barbara Johnson (Chicago: University of Chicago Press, 1981), 61–171.

2. *Phaedrus*, trans. Alexander Nehamas and Paul Woodruff, in *Plato: Complete Works*, ed. by John M. Cooper (Indianapolis: Hackett, 1997), 506–56; Greek terms added.

3. On the continuity between historiography and the *ars memoriae*, see Patrick H. Hutton, *History as an Art of Memory* (Burlington: University of Vermont Press, 1993).

4. The context and coherence of ideas here leads me to distance myself from Luc Brisson, who translates *hupomnēsis* by *remémoration*. I prefer translating this word by "memorization" or *aide-mémoire*. In *Theatetus* 142c2–143a5, M. Narcy translates "I put in writing . . . in order to remember," with an interesting note: "*hupomnēmata*: literally, support of memory" (Plato, *Théétète*, trans. Michel Narcy [Paris: Flammarion, 1994], 306). Léon Robin has "notes" (Plato, *Oeuvres complètes*, trans. Léon Robin. 2 vols. [Paris: Gallimard, 1985]).

5. I will recall here my hypothesis concerning the polysemy of the trace: as material imprint, as affective imprint, and as documentary imprint. And, in each case, as exteriority.

6. I can admit this new recourse to inscription without having to call upon Platonic reminiscence, with the idea of the psychic trace, the perseverance of the first impression, the notion of affection, of *pathos*, which the encounter with the event consists in.

## PART TWO, CHAPTER ONE

1. Edward S. Casey, *Getting Back into Place: Toward a Renewed Understanding of the Place-World* (Bloomington: Indiana University Press, 1993). This is the third volume of a trilogy that includes *Remembering: A Phenomenological Study* (Bloomington: Indiana University Press, 1987) and *Imagining: A Phenomenological Study* (Bloomington: Indiana University Press, 1976). "If imagination," notes Casey,

"projects us out *beyond* ourselves while memory takes us back *behind* ourselves, place subtends and enfolds us, lying perpetually *under* and *around* us" (xvii).

2. In "Architecture et narrativité," in *Catalogue de la Mostra "Identità e Differenze"* (Triennale de Milan, 1994), I tried to transpose to the architectural plane the categories linked to threefold mimesis in the first volume of my *Time and Narrative*: prefiguration, configuration, refiguration. I showed in the act of inhabiting the prefiguration of the architectural act, inasmuch as the need for shelter and circulation lays out the interior space of a dwelling and the given intervals to traverse. In turn, the act of construction is given as the spatial equivalent of narrative configuration through emplotment. From narrative to the edifice, it is the same intention of internal coherence that dwells in the narrator's and the builder's mind. Finally, the inhabiting, which results from this act of construction, can be taken for the equivalent of that "refiguration" that, in the order of narrative, takes place through reading. The inhabitant, like the reader, welcomes the construction with his expectations and also his resistance and challenges. I ended this essay with some praise of traveling.

3. Casey does not ignore the problems posed by architecture. Nevertheless, in his section titled "Building Sites and Cultivating Places" (*Getting Back into Place*, 146–81), the accent is more on the penetration of the natural world into the experience of "places built at the margins." The enclosure of the building is considered in relation to its periphery; monuments stand out against the background of their surroundings. The site and the edifice pursue their competition. This approach assures gardens and parks a fair evaluation that attention devoted exclusively to palaces and less prestigious buildings tends to overlook. In return, the specific problems posed by the art of constructing do not receive their due in an approach more dominated by the opposition between place and space than by their interweaving, which for my part I interpret on the model of the interweaving of cosmic and phenomenological time.

4. Casey, *Remembering*, 277.

5. For what follows I draw upon François Dosse, *New History in France: The Triumph of the Annales*, trans. Peter V. Conroy Jr. (Urbana and Chicago: University of Illinois Press, 1994). For the influence of geography, see 15–16, 57–58, and 109–11.

6. Georges Canguilhem, "Le vivant et son milieu," in *La Connaissance de la vie* (Paris: Vrin, 1965), 129–54.

7. Fernand Braudel, *The Mediterranean and the Mediterranean World in the Age of Philip II*, trans. Siân Reynolds, 2 vols. (New York: Harper and Row, 1972–73). This is a translation of the second revised edition. The first edition was published in 1949. There is a fourth French edition (1979).

8. Allow me to recall my earlier comments on the first part of *The Mediterranean*: "Humans are everywhere present and with them a swarm of symptomatic events. The mountains appear as a refuge and a shelter for free people. As for the coastal plains, they are not mentioned without a reference to colonization, to the work of draining them, of improving the soil, the dissemination of populations, displacements of all sorts: migrations, nomadism, invasions. Here, now, are the waters, their coastlines, and their islands, They, too enter into this geohistory on the scale of human beings and their navigation. The waters are there to be discovered, explored, traveled. Even on this first level, it is not possible to speak of them without mentioning relations of economic and political dominance (Venice, Genoa). The great conflicts between the Spanish and Turkish empires already cast their shadows over the seascape. And with these power struggles, events are already taking shape. Thus the second level is not only implied by actually anticipated in the first: geohistory is rapidly transformed into geopolitics." Paul Ricoeur, *Time and Narrative*, trans. Kathleen McLaughlin and David Pellauer (Chicago: University of Chicago Press, 1984), 1:209.

9. Fernand Braudel, *Civilization and Capitalism, 15th–18th Century*, 3 vols., trans. Siân Reynolds (New York: Harper and Row, 1981–84).

10. One could pursue this odyssey of turn by turn lived, constructed, traversed, and inhabited space by an ontology of "place," at the same level as the ontology of historicity that we shall consider in part 3 of this work. Cf. the essays in Pascal Amphoux et al., *Le Sens du lieu* (Paris: Ousia, 1996), and Augustin Berque and P. Nys, eds. *Logique du lieu et oeuvre humaine* (Paris: Ousia, 1997).

11. See Paul Ricoeur, *Time and Narrative*, trans. Kathleen Blamey and David Pellauer (Chicago: University of Chicago Press, 1988), 3:105–9.

12. Krzysztof Pomian, *L'Ordre du temps* (Paris: Gallimard, 1984), ix.

13. On this subject, see Paul Veyne, *L'Inventaire des différences: Leçon inaugurale du Collège de France* (Paris: Seuil, 1976), and Pierre Nora, "Le retour de l'événement," in Jacques Le Goff and Pierre Nora, eds., *Faire de l'histoire*, 3 vols. (Paris: Gallimard, 1974), 1:285–308.

14. Pomian risks stating that the conception of a linear cumulative and irreversible time is partially verified by three major phenomena: the growth in population, available energy, and the amount of information stored in the collective memory (92–99).

15. The key text in this respect is that by Claude Lévi-Strauss in *Race et histoire* (Paris: UNESCO, 1952; Gallimard, 1987). Pomian (149) quotes one highly significant passage from it: "The development of prehistoric and archaeological knowledge tends to *spread out in space* those forms of civilization which we imagined as *spread out in time*. This means two things: First, that 'progress' (if this term

is still suitable to designate a very different reality from the one to which it was first applied) is neither necessary nor continuous; it proceeds by leaps and bounds, or as the biologists would say, by mutations. Secondly, these leaps and bounds do not always go in the same direction; they go together with changes in orientation, a little like a chess knight that can always avail itself of several progressions but never in the same direction. Humanity in progress hardly resembles a man climbing up a flight of stairs, with each of his movements adding a new stop to all those he has passed. It is rather like a player whose luck is resting on several dice and who, each time he throws, sees them scattered on the table, with a variety of combinations. What one wins on one throw is always liable to be lost on another. It is only from time to time that history is cumulative—in other words, that the numbers can be added up to form a favorable combination." Claude Lévi-Strauss, "Race and History," in *Structural Anthropology*, trans. Monique Layton (New York: Basic Books, 1976), 2:337–38.

16. Pomian, along with René Thom, has made a considerable effort to resolve the problem posed by this dissolution of the historical into the systematic, at the price of a "general theory of the morphogenesis which is a structuralist theory" (Pomian, 197). On Thom, see ibid., 196–202.

17. See also Krzysztof Pomian, "L'Histoire des structures," in Jacques Le Goff, Roger Chartier, and Jacques Revel, eds., *La Nouvelle Histoire* (Paris: Retz CEPL, 1978), 528–53; partially reprinted (Brussells: Ed. Complexes, 1988). He emphasizes the shift in the concept of substance in relation to the level of ontology. The result is the definition of the notion of structure proposed in *L'Ordre du temps*: "An ensemble of rational and interdependent relations whose reality is demonstrated and whose description is given by a theory (which constitutes, in other words, a demonstrable object), and that realizes a reconstructible, observable object whose stability and intelligibility it determines" (215). For Pomian, structure as a theoretical object is in line with the divisions that govern his book: visible/invisible, given/constructed, observed/demonstrated. The theoretical/historical divide is another such aspect.

18. I am in debt here to the work of Renaud Dulong, *Le Témoin oculaire: Les Conditions sociales de l'attestation personnelle* (Paris: EHESS, 1988). It allowed me to improve an earlier version of the present analysis, despite some disagreement with his final thesis of an overall antinomy between "historical testimony" and historiography, a thesis resulting from an almost exclusive focusing on the testimony of war veterans and especially survivors of the Shoah. These are testimonies that resist historiographical explanation and representation. And it is entry into an archive that they first of all resist. The problem posed then is that of the meaning of these limit-case testimonies along the trajectory of a historiographical operation that runs

into its own limits at each step along the way, up to the most demanding kind of reflection (see part 3, chap. 1). Yet Dulong's work initially presents a description of the essence of testimony that does not exclude its being set into an archive, even though he does not develop this theory.

19. The speech-act by which the witness attests to his personal engagement brings a striking confirmation to the analysis proposed above of the self-attribution of remembering—it is already a kind of prepredicative self-designation.

20. In his *Indo-European Language and Society*, trans. Elizabeth Palmer (London: Faber, 1973), Émile Benveniste notes that in Roman law the word *testis*, derived from *tertius*, designates the third parties charged with witnessing an oral contract and skilled at certifying such an exchange. The French edition, *Le Vocabulaire des institutions indo-européens* (Paris: Minuit, 1969), is cited by Dulong, *Le Témoin oculaire*, 43.

21. On this distinction between ipseity and sameness, see my *Oneself as Another*, trans. Kathleen Blamey (Chicago: University of Chicago Press, 1992), 140–68. On promises, see G. H. von Wright, "On Promises," in *Philosophical Papers* (Ithaca: Cornell University Press, 1983), 1:83–99. To "assure" that something has happened, to certify it, is equivalent to a "promise bearing on the past."

22. Here I am in complete agreement with Renaud Dulong's treatment of eyewitness testimony as a "natural institution" (*Le Témoin oculaire*, 41–69). Dulong notes that his analyses are close to those of the phenomenological sociologist Alfred Schutz's *The Phenomenology of the Social World*, trans. George Walsh and Frederick Lehnert (Evanston, Ill.: Northwestern University Press, 1967), as well as to Hannah Arendt's theory of public space.

23. It is this use that von Wright calls "institution" in his "On Promises." This use is close to Wittgenstein's notions of language games and "forms of life."

24. The presupposition of a common world is relatively easy to formulate so long as it is a question of common perceptions. This simplified situation is the one postulated by Melvin Pollner in "Événement et monde commun," subtitled "Que s'est-il réellement passé?" in Jean-Luc Petit, ed., *L'Événement en perspective* (Paris: EHESS, 1991), 75–96. The *sensus communis* there is defined by the presupposition of a possible shared world. "We shall call an idiom of mundane reason the ensemble constituted by this presupposition and by the inference operations that it allows" (76). It is this presupposition, taken as "incorrigible," unfalsifiable, that allows him both to inventory the disagreements and to take them as puzzles reducible through procedures of sagacity. In the case of a cultural world, the criteria of agreement are more difficult to establish. It is much more problematic to affirm that disagreements are distortions. This would be the case if we naïvely adopted the two paradigms criticized above of the video recording and the disengagement

of the observer. The assumption of a shared world then becomes one of ideal harmony rather than of like-mindedness. This idea is then that of the presupposition of a shared form of life against the background of a unique perceived world. To the extent that the events that interest historians are taken to be important, significant, they overflow the perceptual sphere and enter that of opinions. The presumed *sensus communis* is a particularly fragile world of belief, which makes room for conflicts based on disagreements, differences in opinion, leading to controversy. It is in terms of this condition that the question of the plausibility of the arguments advanced by the protagonists is posed. A place is made then for the logical argumentation of the historian and the judge. But the difficulty in hearing the testimony of survivors of the concentration camps constitutes perhaps the most disturbing calling into question of the reassuring cohesion of an alleged common meaningful world. They are "extraordinary" testimonies in the sense that they exceed the capacity of "ordinary" understanding," in the sense that Pollner calls mundane reason. In this regard, the disheartened reflections of Primo Levi in *Survival in Auschwitz*, trans. Stuart Woolf (New York: Collier, 1961), and *The Drowned and the Saved*, trans. Raymond Rosenthal (New York: Vintage Books, 1989), are cause for reflection.

25. This moment of archiving testimony is indicated in the history of historiography by the appearance of the figure of the *histōr*, known to us through Herodotus, Thucydides, and other Greek, then Roman historians. I have already referred, following François Hartog, to the break between the bard or rapsode and the *histōr*. In his *The Mirror of Herodotus: The Representation of the Other in the Writing of History*, trans. Janet Lloyd (Berkeley and Los Angeles: University of California Press, 1988), Hartog spells out the relation between the *histōr* and the witness from this perspective. Before him, Émile Benveniste had emphasized the continuity between the judge who settles conflicts and the eyewitness: "For us, the judge is not the witness; this variation prejudices the analysis of the passage. But it is precisely because the *istōr* is the eyewitness, the only one who can settle the dispute, that made it possible for *istōr* to acquire the sense 'one who decides by a judgment on the question of good faith'" (*Indo-European Language and Society*, 441–42, cited by Hartog, *The Mirror of Herodotus*, 271). Undoubtedly, one should have distinguished here between the person who gives a testimony and the one who receives it; this witness becomes a judge. In this respect, Hartog broadens the gap between the *histōr* and the eyewitness by intercalating a chain of "the indicators of enunciation" between the seeing and the "exposition" of an inquiry: I saw, I heard, I say, I write (289). This game of enunciation thus takes place between the eye and the ear (260), between the written and the oral (273–82), wholly in the absence of any sanction by a master of the truth (ibid., xix). Writing, in this sense, constitutes the decisive mark. To it are grafted all the narrative strategies whence proceed "the

narrative's ability to persuade the addressee to believe it" (294). I shall return to this thesis below in my discussion of the concept of historical representation.

26. See Paul Ricoeur, *From Text to Action*, trans. Kathleen Blamey and John B. Thompson (Evanston, Ill.: Northwestern University Press, 1991).

27. "The gesture which attaches ideas to places is precisely the historians' gesture. For them, comprehension is tantamount to analyzing the raw data which every method first establishes according to its own criteria of relevance—in terms of productions whose locality can be determined." Michel de Certeau, "The Historiographical Operation," in *The Writing of History*, trans. Tom Conley (New York: Columbia University Press, 1988), 56–57; a portion of this essay had been previously published in J. Le Goff and P. Nora, eds., *Faire de l'histoire*, 1:3–41, under the title "L'opération historique."

28. Certeau deals with the establishing of "documents" within the framework of the second historiographical operation, which he puts under the heading of "a practice," in a subsection titled "The Establishment of Sources or the Redistribution of Space" (*The Writing of History*, 72–77). "In history, everything begins with the gesture of setting aside, of putting together, of transforming certain classified objects into 'documents.' This new cultural distribution is the first task" (72).

29. *Time and Narrative*, 3:116–17.

30. See Françoise Hildesheimer, *Les Archives de France: Mémoire de l'histoire* (Paris: Honorée Champion, 1997); Jean Favier and Danièle Neirinck, "Les Archives," in François Bedarida, ed., *L'Histoire et le métier d'historien en France, 1945–1995* (Paris: Éd. de la Maison des sciences de l'homme, 1995), 89–110. The latter authors adopt the rather broad definition of archives given by a French law from 1979: "Archives are the set of documents, whatever their date, their form, and their material support, produced or received by any person or legal entity and by any public or private service or organization in the exercise of their activity" (93).

31. Marc Bloch, *The Historian's Craft*, trans. Peter Putnam (New York: Vintage Books, 1964). The writing of this book, in solitude, was cut off by the arrest and execution of this great historian and resistance fighter by the Nazis.

32. Below, I shall propose to reinforce the distinction between these two kinds of testimony, written and unwritten, by adding to the second one the notion of an index and of indexical knowledge as proposed by Carlo Ginsburg.

33. "The good historian is like the giant of the fairy tale. He knows that wherever he catches the scent of human flesh, there his quarry lies" (Bloch, *The Historian's Craft*, 26).

34. Ought we also to acknowledge the physical fragility of the documents in archives, natural and historical catastrophes, human disasters, great and small? I

shall return to this below in part 3 when I speak of forgetting as the effacing of traces, in particular of documentary ones.

35. Did Charles Seignobos really say: "It is useful to ask oneself questions, but very dangerous to answer them"? Bloch, who doubts this thesis, but cites it, hastens to add: "Surely, this is not the remark of a braggart, but where would physics be today if the physicists had shown no greater daring?" (ibid., 17).

36. Lorenzo Valla, *La Donation de Constantin (Sur la «Donation de Constantin», à lui faussement attribuée et mensongère [c. 1440])*, trans. Jean-Baptiste Giard (Paris: Les Belles Lettres, 1993). This founding text of historical criticism poses a problem for reading and interpretation in that it makes "coexist rhetoric and philology, fictive dialogue and the minute discussion of documentary tests in the same work," according to Carlo Ginzburg's introduction to this translation (xv). It is necessary to go back to Aristotle's *Rhetoric* to find a rhetorical model for the proofs (*ta tekmēria*) (1354a) relevant to the rationality belonging to rhetoric, in terms of the notions of the "persuasive" and the "probable." To be sure, Aristotle had in mind the judicial form of rhetoric, as including "human actions" (*ta prattonta*) (1357a) among past actions (1358b), unlike deliberative rhetoric, the more noble form, dealing with future actions, and epideictic rhetoric, having to do with praise and blame of present actions. This model was transmitted to the scholars in the Italian Renaissance by Quintilian, well known to Valla, whose *Institutio oratoria*, book 5, contains an ample development of such proofs, among which are documents (*tabulae*), such as wills and official documents. "Constantine's *Decree*," notes Ginzburg, "can easily fall within his latter category" (xvi). Set against this background, the mixture of genres of Valla's text is less surprising. It is made up of two parts. In the first one, Valla argues that there is nothing plausible about the donation of a good part of the imperial possessions Constantine is supposed to have made to Pope Sylvester. This rhetorical part is organized in terms of a fictive dialogue between Constantine and the pope. In the second part, Valla argues on the basis of logical, stylistic, and "antiquarian" proofs to demonstrate that the document upon which the Donation was based (the alleged *Decree of Constantine*) was counterfeit.

Starting from an admission that the "distance between Valla as polemicist and rhetorician, and Valla as the initiator of modern historical criticism seems impossible to carry through in practice" (ibid., xi), Ginzburg polemicizes against those among our contemporaries who, following Nietzsche, make use of rhetoric as a skeptical instrument of war against the alleged tenacious positivism of historians. To fill this gap and rediscover an appropriate usage of the notion of proof for historiography, Ginzburg proposes to return to that propitious moment when, in the prolongation of Aristotle and Quintilian, rhetoric and proof were not separated.

Rhetoric has its own rationality; as for proof in history, as Ginzburg's important article on the "evidential paradigm," which I shall discuss further below, demonstrates, it does not principally obey the Galilean model from which proceeds the positive or methodological version of documentary proof. This is why historians' debt to Valla is so great. From him follow the Benedictine erudition of the congregation at Saint-Maur and Mabillon's contribution to the study of diplomatic documents. Cf. Blandine Barret-Kriegel, *L'Histoire à l'âge classique* (Paris: Presses Universitaires de France, 1988). This search for documentary veracity is also to be found in the methodological rules for the internal and external criticism of sources in the twentieth century in the school of Monod, Langlois, Seignobos, Lavisse, and Fustel de Coulanges.

37. Recall that we had already encountered Descartes for the first time with the decline of the *ars memoriae* and Giordano Bruno.

38. Jeremy Bentham, *Traité des preuves judiciaries* (Paris, 1822); *A Treatise on Judicial Evidence* (London: J. W. Paget, 1825). See also R. Dulong, *Le Témoin oculaire*, 139–62, and Catherine Audard, ed., *Anthologie historique et critique de l'utilitarisme*, vol. 1: *Bentham et ses précurseurs (1711–1832)* (Paris: Presses Universitaires de France, 1999).

39. "Here the path of historical research, like that of so many other disciplines of the mind, intersects the royal highway of the theory of probabilities" (Bloch, *The Historian's Craft*, 124).

40. Carlo Ginzburg, "Clues: Roots of an Evidential Paradigm," in *Clues, Myths, and the Historical Method*, trans. John and Anne C. Tedeschi (Baltimore: Johns Hopkins University Press, 1989), 96–125.

41. This last feature relates the rapid, subtle, clever grasping of clues to the Greek *mētis* analyzed in Marcel Détienne and Jean-Pierre Vernant, *Cunning Intelligence in Greek Culture and Society*, trans. Janet Lloyd (Chicago: University of Chicago Press, 1991).

42. The notion of document, under which are conjoined those of clue and testimony, gains in precision by being paired in turn with that of the monument. Jacques Le Goff, in an article titled "Documento/monumento" in the *Enciclopedia Einaudi* (Turin: Einaudi, 1978), 5:38–48, which is not translated in his collection of essays, *History and Memory*, trans. Steven Rendall and Elizabeth Claman (New York: Columbia University Press, 1992), retraces the criss-crossing adventure of these two notions. The document, reputedly less concerned to flag the hero's glory, first of all has won the day over the monument when it comes to praise; in any case, for an ideological critique, the document turns out to be no less biased than the monument. Whence the plea for the mixed concept "document-monument." Cf. *Time and Narrative*, 3:117–19.

43. This book, written a year before the author's death, is a long reflection on his earlier work, *Survival in Auschwitz.* See in particular the chapter titled "To Communicate."

44. This is the title of a volume edited by Saul Friedlander, *Probing the Limits of Representation: Nazism and the "Final Solution"* (Cambridge, Mass.: Harvard University Press, 1992).

45. Levi in this regard refers to "the anguish inscribed in everyone of the 'tohu-bohu' of a deserted and empty universe, crushed under the spirit of God but from which the spirit of man is absent: not yet born or already extinguished" (*The Drowned and the Saved*, 85, cited by Dulong, *Le Témoin oculaire*, 95).

46. Robert Antelme, *The Human Race*, trans. Jeffry Haight and Annie Hamler (Marlboro, Vt.: Marlboro Press, 1992).

47. Jean Améry, *Par-delà le crime et le châtiment: Essai pour surmonter l'insurmontable* (Paris: Acts Sud, 1995).

48. For a fairer reading of Charles Victor Langlois and Charles Seignobos, *Introduction to the Study of History*, trans. G. G. Perry (Westport, Conn.: Greenwood, 1979 [French original, 1898]), see Antoine Prost, "Seignobos revisité," *Vingtième Siècle, revue d'histoire*, no. 43 (July-September 1994): 100–18.

49. Antoine Prost, *Douze Leçons sur l'histoire* (Paris: Seuil, 1996); Paul Lacombe, *De l'histoire considérée comme science* (Paris: Hachette, 1894).

50. Henri I. Marrou, *The Meaning of History*, trans. Robert J. Olson (Baltimore: Helicon, 1966).

51. In Pierre Nora's "Le retour de l'événement," in J. Le Goff and P. Nora, eds., *Faire de l'histoire*, 1:210–28, it is the status of contemporary history that is primarily in question, and hence of the proximity of the reported past to the historical present, in a time like ours where the present is experienced "as charged with an already 'historic' meaning" (210). It is this weight of the present on "doing history" that authorizes saying that "current affairs, that generalized circulation of historical perception, culminate in a new phenomenon: the event" (211). Its appearance can even be dated to the last third of the nineteenth century. What is at issue is the "rapid accession to prominence of this historical present" (211). Positivists are reproached for having made the past something dead, cut off from the living present, the closed field of historical knowledge. That the term "event" does not designate what happened finds confirmation in the simple fact of speaking of the "production of the event" (212) and of "metamorphoses of the event" (216). What is at issue are passing facts picked up by the mass media. Speaking of important facts like the death of Mao Tse-tung, Nora writes: "The fact that they happened does not make them historical. For there to be an event, it has to be known" (212). History thus competes with the media, movies, popular literature, and all the means

of communication. Something like direct testimony returns here with the cry: I was there. "Modernity secretes the event, unlike traditional societies that tend rather to rarify it," states Nora (220). In my vocabulary, an event would be what Nora calls historical, its having taken place. And I would set aside what he calls an event which with its close tie to "its intellectual significance" brings "close a first form of historical elaboration" (216). The event, he exclaims, "is what is admirable in democratic societies" (217). With this "the paradox of the event" gets denounced (222): when the event springs up the underlying depths of the non-event rise to the surface. "The event has the virtue of bringing together a bunch of scattered meanings" (225). "It is up to the historian to unknot them in order to return from the evidence of the event to the system that produces it. For unity, if it is to be intelligible, always postulates the existence of a series that novelty brings to light" (225). And thus the event—the "contemporary event"—regretfully gets handed over to the dialectic fomented by the enemies of the event, the structuralists.

52. Émile Benveniste, *Problems of General Linguistics*, trans. Mary Elizabeth Meek (Coral Gables, Fla.: University of Miami Press, 1977).

53. There are historians who have known how to find an echo of dead voices in the archives, such as Arlette Farges in *Le Goût de l'archive* (Paris: Seuil, 1989). Unlike the judicial archive that "presents a chopped up world," the historian's archive hears the echo of "those derisory laments over derisory events, where some people dispute over a stolen tool and others over the dirty water poured on them. These tiny facts, signs of a minimum disorder having left traces since they gave rise to reports and interrogations, where almost nothing is said and yet so many things transpire, are places to investigate and for research" (97). These traces are in the strong sense of the term "captured words" (97) It thus follows that the historian is not the one who makes past people speak but someone who allows them to speak. In this, the document leads back to the trace, and the trace to the event.

### PART TWO, CHAPTER TWO

1. G. E. M. Anscombe, *Intention* (Oxford: Basil Blackwell, 1957).

2. See Paul Ricoeur, *Time and Narrative*, trans. Kathleen McLaughlin and David Pellauer (Chicago: University of Chicago Press, 1984), 1:182–92.

3. Pierre Chaunu, *Histoire quantitative, histoire sérielle* (Paris: Armand Colin, 1978).

4. François Dosse, *L'Histoire* (Paris: Armin Colin, 2000), places the second stage of his overview of history under the sign of "causal imputation" (30–64). This new problematic begins with Polybius and "the search for causality." It passes through Jean Bodin, inventor of "the order of probability," then traverses the age of Enlightenment, and reaches its peak with Fernand Braudel and the *Annales* school,

before the consideration of narrative that comes with "the interpretive turn," which leads to the threshold of the third problematic, that of consideration of narrative per se.

5. Paul Veyne, *Writing History: Essay on Epistemology*, trans. Mina Moore-Rinvolucri (Middletown, Conn.: Wesleyan University Press, 1984); Antoine Prost, *Douze leçons sur l'histoire* (Paris: Seuil, 1996).

6. In *Time and Narrative*, I essentially devoted my analysis to this confrontation between causal explanation and explanation in terms of reasons for. See *Time and Narrative*, 1:125–28.

7. Max Weber, *Economy and Society: An Outline of Interpretive Sociology*, ed. Günther Roth and Claus Wittich, trans. Ephraim Fischoff et al. (New York: Bedminster Press, 1968; reprinted Berkeley and Los Angeles: University of California Press, 1978), part 1, chap. 1, §1.

8. G. H. von Wright, *Explanation and Understanding* (Ithaca: Cornell University Press, 1971). I discussed von Wright's model in some detail in *Time and Narrative*, 1:132–43. Since then, I have undertaken in a number of essays to pacify the quarrel between explanation and understanding. The opposition was justified at a time when the human sciences felt the strong attraction of the models then dominant in the natural sciences under the pressure of positivism of a Comptean type. Wilhelm Dilthey remains the hero of the resistance of the so-called *Geisteswissenschaften* to the absorption of the human sciences by the natural sciences. The actual practice of the historical sciences leads to a more measured and more dialectical attitude.

9. In speaking of a configuring act I am adopting the vocabulary of Louis O. Mink, *Historical Understanding*, ed. Brian Fay, Eugene O. Golob, and Richard R. Vann (Ithaca: Cornell University Press, 1987).

10. Lucien Lévy-Bruhl, *Primitive Mentality*, trans. Lilian A. Clare (London: George Allen and Unwin, 1923; rpt. Boston: Beacon Press, 1966).

11. I justify this expression below in taking up the relation between truth and interpretation in history.

12. The first warning shot had been given as early as 1903 by François Simiand in his famous article "Méthode historique et science sociale," *Revue de synthèse historique* 6 (1903): 1–22, 129–57, reprinted in *Annales* (1960). The target was Seignobos' *La Méthode historique appliquée aux sciences socials* (Paris: F. Alcan, 1901). Historicizing history, the object of all these sarcasms, would better be known as the methodological school, following the wishes of Gabriel Monod, the founder of the *Revue historique*, with which *Annales* was meant to compete. A fairer judgment can be found in the article already referred to of Antoine Prost, "Seignobos revisité," *Vingtième Siècle, revue d'histoire*, no. 43 (July–September 1994): 100–18.

13. Lucien Febvre, *Combats pour l'histoire* (Paris: Armand Colin, 1953).

14. A. Burguière, "*Les Annales, 1929–1979*," *Annales* 34 (1979): 1344–59; J. Revel, "Histoire et science sociale, les paradigms des *Annales*," *Annales* 34 (1979): 1360–76.

15. Lucien Febvre, *Martin Luther: A Destiny*, trans. Roberts Tapley (New York: E. P. Dutton and Co., 1929); *The Problem of Unbelief in the Sixteenth Century*, trans. Beatrice Gottlieb (Cambridge, Mass.: Harvard University Press, 1982); *Amour sacré, amour profane: Autour de l' «Heptameron»* (Paris: Gallimard, 1944).

16. Marc Bloch, *The Royal Touch: Sacred Monarchy and Scrofula in England and France*, trans. J. E. Anderson (London: Routledge and Kegan Paul, 1973); *Feudal Society*, trans. L. A. Mauyen (Chicago: University of Chicago Press, 1961).

17. Febvre's *The Problem of Unbelief*, which deals with Rabelais, will later be compared to Mikhail Bakhtin's work on the same figure: *Rabelais and His World*, trans. Hélène Iswolksy (Bloomington: Indiana University Press, 1984).

18. François Dosse, *New History in France: The Triumph of the Annales*, trans. Peter V. Conroy Jr. (Urbana: University of Illinois Press, 1994). The new French edition of 1997 has a preface that takes into account developments that I shall also consider below, drawing upon the historian Bernard Lepetit.

19. See Claude Lévi-Strauss, "History and Anthropology" [1949], which was reprinted as the introduction to *Structural Anthropology*, trans. Claire Jacobson and Brooke Grundfest Schoepf (New York: Basic Books, 1963), 1:1–27, to which Fernand Braudel replied with "History and the Social Sciences: The *Longue Durée*" [1958], *Writings on History*, trans. Sarah Matthews (Chicago: University of Chicago Press, 1980), 25–54.

20. I considered in detail the epistemology at work in Braudel's masterpiece, *The Mediterranean and the Mediterranean World in the Age of Philip II*, in the first volume of *Time and Narrative*, 1:101–6. There I undertook a reconstruction of this work that today I would call narrativist, in which I took the Mediterranean itself as a quasi character within an overarching political plot.

21. Fernand Braudel, *Civilization and Capitalism, 15th–18th Century*, 3 vols., trans. Siân Reynolds (New York: Harper and Row, 1988–90).

22. A. Burguière, "*Les Annales, 1929–1979*"; J. Revel, "Histoire et science sociale, les paradigms des *Annales*."

23. J. Revel, "Histoire et science sociale, les paradigms des *Annales*."

24. Claude Lévi-Strauss, *Tristes Tropiques*, trans. John and Doreen Weightman (New York: Atheneum, 1981).

25. Robert Mandrou, *Introduction to Modern France, 1500–1640: An Essay in Historical Psychology*, trans. R. E. Hallmark (New York: Holmes and Meier, 1975); *De la culture populaire en France aux XVIIe et XVIIIe siècles: La Bibliothèque bleue*

*de Troyes* (Paris: Imago, 1999); *Magistrats et Sorciers en France au XVIIe siècle: Une analyse de psychologie historique* (Paris: Seuil, 1989).

26. Robert Mandrou, "L'Histoire des mentalités," *Encyclopedia Universalis* (1968), 8:436–38.

27. Jean-Pierre Vernant, *Myth and Thought among the Greeks* (London: Routledge and Kegan Paul, 1983).

28. Marcel Détienne and Jean-Pierre Vernant, *Cunning Intelligence in Greek Culture and Society*, trans. Janet Lloyd (Chicago: University of Chicago Press, 1991).

29. Jean-Pierre Vernant and Pierre Vidal-Naquet, *Myth and Tragedy in Ancient Greece*, trans. Janet Lloyd (New York: Zone Books, 1990).

30. Jacques Le Goff and Pierre Nora, eds. *Faire de l'histoire*, 3 vols. (Paris: Gallimard, 1974). Partially translated in English as *Constructing the Past: Essays in Historical Methodology* (New York: Cambridge University Press, 1984).

31. Emmanuel Le Roy Ladurie, *Times of Feast, Times of Famine: A History of Climate since the Year 1000*, trans. Barbara Bray (Garden City, N.Y.: Doubleday, 1971).

32. Jacques Le Goff, "Mentalities: A History of Ambiguities," trans. David Denby, in Jacques Le Goff and Pierra Nora, eds., *Constructing the Past: Essays in Historical Methodology*, 166, quoting Marcel Proust, *In Search of Lost Time*, vol. 3: *The Guermantes Way*, trans. C. K. Scott Montcrieff and Terrence Kilmartin, rev. by D. J. Enright (New York: Modern Library, 1993), 319.

33. Jean Delumeau, *Sin and Fear: The Emergence of a Western Guilt Culture, 13th–18th Centuries*, trans. Eric Nicholson (New York: St. Martin's, 1990); Michel Vovelle, *Piété baroque et déchristianisation en Provence au XVIIIe siècle: Les Attitudes devant la mort d'après les clauses des testaments* (Paris: Plon, 1973).

34. Philippe Ariès and Georges Duby, eds., *A History of Private Life*, 5 vols. (Cambridge, Mass.: Harvard University Press, 1987–91).

35. Philippe Ariès, *The Hour of Our Death*, trans. Helen Weaver (New York: Knopf, 1981); see also the work of Alain Corbin, including *The Foul and the Fragrant: Odor and the French Social Imagination* (Cambridge, Mass.: Harvard University Press, 1986).

36. Lucien Lévy-Bruhl, *The Notebooks on Primitive Mentality*, trans. Peter Rivière (New York: Harper Torchbooks, 1978).

37. Geoffrey E. R. Lloyd, *Demystifying Mentalities* (New York: Cambridge University Press, 1990). A French translation was published in 1996.

38. "The all-important distinction that has scrupulously to be observed is— to put it in the social anthropologists' terms—that between *actors'* and *observers'* categories. In the evaluation of the apparently puzzling or downright paradoxical,

a crucial issue is, I argue, precisely the availability or otherwise of *explicit* concepts of linguistic and other categories" (ibid., 7).

39. Jean-Pierre Vernant, *Origins of Greek Thought* (Ithaca: Cornell University Press, 1982); *Myth and Thought among the Greeks*; Détienne and Vernant, *Cunning Intellgience in Greek Culture and Society*; Pierre Vidal-Naquet, "Greek Rationality and the City," in *The Black Hunter: Forms of Thought and Forms of Society in the Greek World*, trans. Andrew Szegedy-Maszak (Baltimore: Johns Hopkins University Press, 1986), 249–62.

40. Speaking of the distinction between the literal and the metaphorical in the age of classical Greece, Lloyd notes: "It must be seen as an item in, and the product of a hard-hitting polemic in which inquiries fought to distinguish themselves from rivals, notably but not exclusively from traditional claimants to wisdom" (*Demystifying Mentalities*, 35). Later, speaking of the tie between the development of philosophy and Greek science, on the one hand, and political life, on the other, he asks how far this hypothesis "can take us towards an understanding of the distinctive features of the styles of inquiry developed in ancient Greece" (36–37). The expressions "style of inquiry" and "style of argument" recur frequently.

41. Michel Foucault, *The Archeology of Knowledge*, trans. A. M. Sheridan Smith (New York: Harper Torchbooks, 1972).

42. Michel Foucault, *The Order of Things: An Archeology of the Human Sciences* (New York: Pantheon, 1970). See also my earlier discussion of this work in *Time and Narrative*, 3:216–19.

43. "And to those who might be tempted to criticize archeology for concerning itself primarily with the analysis of the discontinuous, to all those agoraphobics of history and time, to all those who confuse rupture and irrationality, I will reply: 'It is you who devalue the continuous by the use that you make of it. You treat it as the support-element to which everything else must be related; you treat it as the primary law, the essential weight of any discursive practice; you would like to analyse every modification in the field of this inertia, as one analyses every movement in the gravitational field. But in according this status to continuity, you are merely neutralizing it, driving it out to the outer limit of time, towards an original passivity. Archeology proposes to invert this arrangement, or rather (for our aim is not to accord to the discontinuous the role formerly accorded to the continuous) to play one off against the other; to show how the continuous is formed in accordance with the same conditions and the same rules as dispersion; and how it enters—neither more nor less than differences, inventions, innovations or deviations—the field of discursive practice'" (*The Archeology of Knowledge*, 174–75).

44. As for example with the clinical medicine considered in *The Birth of the Clinic: An Archaeology of Medical Perception*, trans. A. M. Sheridan Smith (New

Notes to Pages 203–208 · 541

York: Vintage Books, 1975), which appears again in *The Archaeology of Knowledge*. What would an archaeological treatment of its relation with medical and non-medical practices, including political ones, look like? We can see what is set aside: the phenomena of expression, of reflection, of symbolization, of the causal relation transmitted by the consciousness of speaking subjects. But what is the positive relation to nondiscursive practices? Foucault confines himself to assigning to archeology the task of showing how and in what sense "political practice" is part of "its conditions of emergence, insertion, and functioning" (163) for example of medical discourse. But it is not a question of its determining this sense and this form.

45. Michel de Certeau, *The Writing of History*, trans. Tom Conley (New York: Columbia University Press, 1988), 57.

46. Michel de Certeau, *L'Absent de l'histoire* (Paris: Mame, 1973).

47. Certeau's *Possession at Loudon*, trans. Michael B. Smith (Chicago: University of Chicago Press, 2000), would pose a comparable problem when it comes to the composition of a history, beyond the contribution of this work to what would become French microhistory from the point of view of a choice of scale.

48. Norbert Elias, *The Civilizing Process: Sociogenetic and Psychogenetic Investigations*, trans. Edmund Jephcott with some notes and corrections by the author; edited by Eric Dunning, Johan Goudsblom, and Stephen Mennell (Malden, Mass.: Blackwell, 2000). Elias integrates into this book the most important results from his *The Court Society*, trans. Edmund Jephcott (New York: Pantheon, 1983), a work with an unusual history. It was written in 1933 when the author was an assistant to Karl Mannheim at the University of Frankfurt, but not published until 1969, with a preface titled "Sociology and History."

49. Roger Chartier, "Formation sociale et économie psychique: La société de cour dans le process de civilization," in Elias, *La Société de cour*, trans. Pierre Kamnitzer and Jeanne Étoré (Paris: Calmann-Lévy, 1974), i–xxviii.

50. As regards the relation between history and society, the preface written in 1969 is not conclusive inasmuch as it is history in the manner of Ranke that is criticized, that is, a history that privileges the individual, the will of decision makers, and the rational desires of men of power. But the historical character of social formations, such as the court, rules out any identification with presumed unchanging invariants. The concept of social change places Elias after all on the side of historians. Chartier's preface is quite clear in this regard.

51. "In reality the result of the civilizing process is clearly unfavourable or favourable only in a relatively few cases at each end of the scale. The majority of civilized people live midway between these two extremes. Socially positive and negative features, personally gratifying and frustrating tendencies, mingle in them in varying proportions" (*The Civilizing Process*, 378).

52. Rationalization would be a good term to focus on for a discussion confronting the emphasis placed on uncertainty by microhistory and that placed on rationalization as the regulation of drives by Elias.

53. It really is a question of what German calls *Schamangst*, shame combined with anxiety, rather than what another tradition, that of Simmel or of Max Scheler, prefers to oppose to a sense of guilt.

54. Here I come back to what Roger Chartier says in his preface to the French translation of *The Court Society*: "By characterizing each social formation or configuration starting from the specific network of interdependencies that bind individuals to one another, Elias means to comprehend the relations that hold together different groups both in terms of their dynamics and their reciprocity of relationships and, in this way, to avoid overly simple, univocal, fixed representations of social domination or cultural diffusion" (*La Société de cour*, xxv).

55. Norbert Elias's contribution to a history of ideas and of representations finds partial extension on the sociological plane in the work of Pierre Bourdieu. By taking up the notion of habitus, which according to him "accounts for the fact that social agents are neither particles of matter predetermined by external causes nor tiny monads exclusively guided by internal reasons, executing a kind of perfectly rational action program," Bourdieu places himself in the dialectic of the construction of the self and institutional constraints established by Elias. See Pierre Bourdieu, with Loïc J.-D. Wacquant, *Responses* (Paris: Seuil, 1992), 110. He takes up and completes the trajectory from social constraint to self-constraint outlined by Elias by giving a richer import to the notion of habitus: "The habitus is not only a structuring structure, which organizes practices and the perception of practices, but also a structured structure: the principle of division into logical classes which organizes the perception of the social world is itself the product of internalization of the division into social classes." Pierre Bourdieu, *Distinction: A Social Critique of the Judgment of Taste*, trans. Richard Nice (Cambridge, Mass.: Harvard University Press, 1984), 170. Thus, habitus allows, on the one hand, the articulation of representations and behaviors, and, on the other, the linking of these representations and behaviors to what Bourdieu calls "the structure of social space," which allows the grasping of "a point of view on the whole set of points from which ordinary agents (including the sociologist and the reader, in their ordinary behavior) see the social world" (ibid., 169). For individuals, habitus leads to the emergence of a "classification system" that continuously transforms "necessities into strategies, constraints into preferences, and without any mechanical determination . . . generates the set of 'choices' constituting life-styles which correspond to the condition of which it is the product" (175). In this way, the back and forth movement from the "structure of social space" (and from the "fields" that overlay it according to Bourdieu)

to the representations and behaviors of agents is grasped in its complexity. Each "field" has its own logic, which imposes "retranslations" on the "structured products (*opus operatum*) which a structuring structure (*modus operandi*) produces" as "the practices and products of a given agent" (172–73). In studying taste, Bourdieu establishes in this way the correspondence between the social layer and the psychic layer outlined by Elias discussed above: "The different ways of relating to realities and fictions, of believing in fictions and the realities they simulate...are very closely linked to the different possible positions in social space and, consequently, bound up with the systems of dispositions (habitus) characteristic of the different classes and class fractions. Taste classifies, and it classifies the classifier" (6–7). In this way he shows how to explain how representations are necessary for grasping this correspondence, this tangle of "systems of dispositions," and thus imply understanding the relationships of agents to "the structure of social space" in their historical aspect. "The 'eye' is a product of history reproduced by history" (3), writes Bourdieu in his study of taste. Thus the notion of habitus as it has been used allows grasping "the general laws reproducing the laws of production, the *modus operandi*" (173, n. 3) and reestablishes the "unity in practice" by conveying more than the reason for the "products (*opus operatum*)" (172). The heuristic value of the explanation/understanding phase of habitus and the methodological use Bourdieu makes of it is thus justified.

56. Pascal, *Pensées*, trans. A. J. Krailsheimer (Baltimore: Penguin, 1966), no. 65, 48.

57. Jacques Revel, ed., *Jeux d'échelles: La Microanalyse à l'expérience* (Paris: Gallimard, 1996).

58. Revel has associated himself and Bernard Lepetit with some of the most active microhistorians: Alban Bensa, Mauricio Gribandi, Simona Cerutti, Giovanni Levi, Sabina Loriga, Edoardo Grandi. We need to add to these names that of Carlo Ginsburg, to whom we shall make frequent reference.

59. "Let us immediately note that the 'micro' dimension, in this regard, enjoys no particular privilege. It is the principle of variation that counts, not the choice of a particular scale." Jacques Revel, "Microanalyse et construction du social," in *Jeux d'échelles*, 19.

60. Another fragment from Pascal can be cited here: "What is man in the infinite? But, to offer him another prodigy equally astounding, let him look into the tiniest things he knows. Let a mite show him it in its minute body incomparably more minute parts, legs with joints, veins in its legs, blood in the veins, humours in the blood, drops in the humours, vapours in the drops: let him divide these things still further until he has exhausted his powers of imagination, and let the last thing he comes down to now be the subject of our discourse. He will perhaps think

that this is the ultimate minuteness in nature" (*Pensées*, no. 199, 88). See Louis Marin, "Une ville, une campagne de loin...: Paysage Pascalien," *Littérature*, no. 161 (February 1986): 10, cited by Bernard Lepetit, "De l'échelle en histoire," in *Jeux d'échelles*, 93.

61. Bernard Lepetit, "De l'échelle en histoire," 71–94; Maurizion Grimaudi, "Échelles, pertinence, configuration," ibid., 113–39.

62. What was said earlier about the notion of place prepared the way for our saying this now.

63. The Nietzschean notion of monumental history I shall refer to in part 3 will confirm this, as also does the place already referred to several times in our discourse on history of the notion of a monument coupled with that of a document.

64. I was surprised in reading the methodological texts of microhistory to see the well-known anthropologist Clifford Geertz accused by Giovanni Levi and others of having described what he took to be shared beliefs at the level of cultures at a certain geographical breadth in terms of models imposed on their submissive receptors. "I pericoli del Geerzismo," *Quaderni storici*, cited by Jacques Revel, *Jeux d'échelles*, 26, n. 22 and 33, n. 27. On the other hand, one Scandinavian author, Fredrik Barth, draws on Geertz in his study of social agents in his research concerning land and its relation to ethnic identity, *Ethnic Groups and Boundaries* (London: Allen and Unwin, 1969). See also, *Selected Essays of Fredrik Barth*, vol. 1, *Process and Form in Social Life* (London: Routledge and Kegan Paul, 1981). There is an essay introducing his work in *Jeux d'échelles*: Paul André Rosental, "Construire le 'macro' par le 'micro': Fredrik Barth et la *microstoria*," 141–59.

65. Carlo Ginzburg, *The Cheese and the Worms: The Cosmos of a Sixteenth-Century Miller*, trans. John and Anne Tedeschi (Baltimore: Johns Hopkins University Press, 1980), xiii.

66. "It is absurd to equate the 'culture produced by the popular classes' with the 'culture imposed on the masses,' or to identify the features of popular culture exclusively by means of the maxims, the precepts and fables of the *Bibliothèque bleue*. The shortcut taken by Mandrou to circumvent the difficulties inherent in the reconstruction of an oral culture actually only takes us back to the starting point" (ibid., xv–xvi). Geneviève Bollème's use of literature of *colportage* falls under similar objections. On the other hand, Bakhtin escapes this criticism with his groundbreaking book on the relationship of Rabelais to the popular culture of his day, although it remains true that his protagonists speak mainly through Rabelais' own words. Emmanuel Le Roy Ladurie's analysis in *Carnival in Romans*, trans. Mary Feeney (New York: George Braziller, 1979), even though based on a hostile source, is a good one in Ginzburg's eyes. On the other hand, Foucault's insistence on the exclusions and prohibitions through which our culture

is constituted risks making popular culture exist only through "the act that suppresses it," as in his *Madness and Civilization*. If madness can speak only through the available language of reason that excludes it, the protagonists are condemned to silence.

67. Ginzburg's preface ends with an audacious prospective: Menocchio precedes us along the way that Walter Benjamin traces in his "Theses on History," where we read: "Nothing that has taken place should be lost to history... but only to redeemed humanity does the past belong in its entirety." "Redeemed and thus liberated" (xxvi), adds Ginzburg, who thereby indicates his own conviction.

68. Giovanni Levi, *Le Pouvoir au village: Histoire d'un exorciste dans le Piémont du XVIe siècle*, trans. Monique Aymard (Paris: Gallimard, 1989). First published in Italian as *L'eredità immateriale: Carriera di un esorcista nel Piemonte del seicento* (Turin: Einaudi, 1985).

69. "Therefore I tried to study a minuscule fragment of the Piedmont of the sixteenth century, using an intensive technique to reconstruct the biographical events of all the inhabitants of the village of Santena that have left some documentary trace" (cited in Jacques Revel's preface to Levi, *Le Pouvoir au village*, xiii).

70. Revel quotes Levi as saying: "This society, like every other society, is made of individuals aware of the zone of unpredictability within which each one has to try to organize his behavior. And the uncertainty comes not only from the difficulty in foreseeing the future, but also from the permanent awareness of having only limited information about the forces at work in the social setting in which one has to act. It is not a society paralyzed by insecurity, hostile to all risk taking, passive, clinging to unchangeable values for self-protection. To improve predictability in order to increase security is a powerful model of technical, political, and social innovation" (preface to Levi, *Le Pouvoir au village*, xxiii–xxiv).

71. This question of the relationship between and the reciprocal relevance of microhistory and macrohistory poses the fundamental epistemological problem in the human sciences of how to aggregate data. Can we simply pass from the "micro" to the "macro" scale and transpose conclusions from one scale to another without making some difference?

72. Revel seems to doubt it: "Read at ground level, the history of a place is probably different from all other places" (preface to Levi, *Le Pouvoir au village*, xxx).

73. Bernard Lepetit, ed., *Les Formes de l'expérience: Une autre histoire sociale* (Paris: Albin Michel, 1995).

74. See Bernard Lepetit, "Histoire des pratiques, pratique de l'histoire," ibid., 12–16.

75. One can see a progressive opening to this by the editors of *Annales* in two critical articles in the journal: "Histoire et science sociale: Un tournant critique?" (1988): 291–93, and especially "Tentons l'expérience," (1989): 1317–23.

76. Here I want to repeat my debt regarding sociology to Clifford Geertz, to whom I owe the concept of mediated symbolic action used in my *From Text to Action* and *Ideology and Utopia*. This is why the warning against Geertz by the microhistorians of *Quaderni* seems to be a bit unfair.

77. "More than any one scale, it is the variation in scale that seems fundamental here" (Revel, preface to Levi, *Le Pouvoir au village*, xxx).

78. See Paul André Rosental, "Construire le 'macro' par le 'micro': Fredrik Barth et la *microhistoria*," in *Jeux d'échelles*, 141–60.

79. "For Durkheim the notion of a 'basic norm' corresponds to a threefold necessity. Its nature permits society to hold together, without principles external to itself, and without in any particular situation either falling into anomie or having necessarily to again elaborate its solidarity at some cost. It constitutes an ad hoc hypothesis or a tautological proposition equivalent to an explanatory detour that would allow for its detailed specification" (Petit, "Histoire des pratiques, pratique de l'histoire," *Les Formes de l'expérience*, 17–18).

80. See Jacques Revel, "L'institution et le social," in *Les Formes de l'expérience*, 63–85; Simona Cerutti, "Normes et pratiques, ou de la légitimité de leur opposition," ibid., 127–51.

81. One important source for this idea comes from Luc Boltanski's book on middle managers, which presents a remarkable example of a particular historical institution captured in the process of coming into existence: *The Making of a Class: Cadres in French Society*, trans. Arthur Goldhammer (New York: Cambridge University Press, 1987).

82. Regarding the examination of condemnatory behavior, see Luc Boltanski, *L'Amour et la Justice comme compétences: Trois essais de sociologie de l'action* (Paris: Métaillé, 1990), part 1: "Ce dont les gens sont capables."

83. Laurent Thévenot, "L'action qui convient," in Patrick Pharo and Louis Quéré, eds., *Les Formes de l'action* (Paris: EHESS, 1990), 39–69.

84. Luc Boltanski and Laurent Thévenot, *De la justification: Les économies de la grandeur* (Paris: Gallimard, 1991). I discussed this work in my *The Just*, trans. David Pellauer (Chicago: University of Chicago Press, 2000), 81–86, in another context, that of the "plurality of instances of justice," in comparison with Michael Walzer, *Spheres of Justice: In Defense of Pluralism and Equality* (New York: Basic Books, 1982). Compared to Walzer, what is at stake for Boltanski and Thévenot is not the problem of the domination of one sphere over another, hence of fairness, but that of the resolution of conflicts, hence of compromise for the common good.

85. There is room for a comparison here with the tenacious idea of human plurality found throughout the work of Hannah Arendt.

86. Here a sociology of reading adds reinforcement to my argument. See Roger Chartier, *On the Edge of the Cliff: History, Language, Practices*, trans. Lydia G. Cochrane (Baltimore: Johns Hopkins University Press, 1993).

87. A typology of these modes of availability fits easily with my comments concerning the use and abuse of memory, depending on whether it is blocked, manipulated, or commanded.

88. The following observations arise from reading the articles, in *Les Formes de l'expérience*, by André Burguière, "Le changement social" (253–72), and Bernard Lepetit, "Le présent de l'histoire" (273–98).

89. See the discussion on this point by J. Revel at the end of his "Presentation" of the work of Giovanni Levi, in *Le Pouvoir au village*.

90. What Giovanni Levi writes about, at Santena, is "the local modulation of large scale history" (ibid., xxi–xxii). Revel dialectizes this category by writing: "It is the major figure through which the people of Santena learn of their time. They have to come to terms with it and, to the measure possible, reduce it" (ibid.). Levi himself raises the question: "This is not a society paralyzed by insecurity, hostile to every risk, passive, holding onto unchanging values for self-protection. To improve the predictability in order to augment security is a powerful engine of technical, psychological, and social innovation" (xxiv). We see that he himself links together reduction of uncertainty and security. The logic of the idea of a strategy implies this inasmuch as it leads to calculations in terms of gains and losses. We may think that this is sufficient to have refuted a unilateral vision of power exercised from above to below. In fact, it is not a simple contrary of the law tending toward a concentration of power that the careful deciphering of the individual and familial strategies of a village points out. The "immaterial" power, the impalpable capital that a modest local *podesta* draws from the equilibrium among protagonists, can be understood only in light of a strategic logic aiming at reducing uncertainty.

91. Lepetit, "Le présent de l'histoire," *Les Formes de l'expérience*, 273–98. Boltanski and Thévenot make use of the same constellation of temporal modes grouped around the theme of adequacy to the present situation, as Lepetit points out (274).

92. Lepetit refers here to Laurent Thévenot, "L'action qui convient," in *Les Formes d'action*.

93. Bernard Lepetit's comments on the present of history go well with my notion of the present as "practical" initiative rather than as "theoretical" presence (*From Text to Action*). In turn, the category of initiative leads to a more encompassing dialectic, like the one through which Koselleck characterizes the

temporalization of history in his *Futures Past: On the Semantics of Historical Time*, trans. Keith Tribe (Cambridge, Mass.: MIT Press, 1985). Within this broader conceptual framework, the present as initiative must then be understood as the shifter between the horizon of expectation and the space of experience. We shall examine Koselleck's categories in greater detail in part 3.

94. René Rémond, *Les Droites en France* (Paris: Aubier, 1982).

95. The thrust of Rémond's book is twofold: on one hand, the relevance of the binary distribution of political opinions between right and left since the French Revolution; on the other, that of a threefold division among reputedly right-wing opinions (legitimism, Orleanism, Bonapartism). Rémond presupposes the constructed character of what he recognizes as a "system" and presents it as an "attempt to make sense of French political life" (ibid., 15). Neither the numbering nor the definition of the figures that give a rhythm to the tempo of the political history of contemporary France are immediately observable facts; even if their identification is suggested by actual practice, it stems from "propositions," "axioms" that the researcher constructs. "Every social reality presents itself to our gaze as an indistinct, amorphous ensemble. Our mind is what traces out the lines of separation and regroups the infinity of beings and positions into a few categories" (18). On the other hand, René Rémond thinks that this intellectual construction can be verified by "reality," where reality is the evaluations at work in political decisions—that it has an explanatory and predictive value equal to that of astronomy. In this sense, we can say that "the distinction is indeed real" (29): "In politics more than in any other domain, what is taken to be true becomes so and weighs as heavily as did the initial situation" (29). The major presupposition is that of an autonomy of political ideas compatible with the thematic variability of criteria of belonging (liberty, nation, sovereignty). "The system of linked presuppositions" (31), whose combination assures the cohesion of the whole, stands out against this background: relativity of the two major categories in terms of each other; a structural, and more precisely, a topological aspect to this bipolarity and others similar to it; a conjunctural renewal of the criteria of distribution and modulation by a plus or minus factor, excluding the extremes; and sensitivity to circumstances beginning with the spatial distribution of the constitutional Assembly in 1789. Do we not find here our triad of "structure, conjuncture, and event" applied to representations? The primacy granted to the binary structure—"The parties turn about a fixed axis like entwined dancers who describe these ballet-like figures without breaking stride"—is authorized by an audacious speculation on the preference given conjointly by thought and by political action to such binarism: a horizontal axis on one side, practical dilemmas on the other. Rémond can legitimately compare these sorts of "archetypes" (39) to Max Weber's ideal types. However, the primacy given to structure as much as

to the binary opposition between right and left in France runs up against some limits. In the first place, the overall displacement of the left toward the right, which assures the dynamics of the system, continues to appear "mysterious," "strange," given to "paradoxes" (35), so strong is the negative connotation of the label "right wing." Nevertheless it sees that "joining the political game, the apprenticeship of practice, and the gradual acceptance of the operative rules lead to a gradual rallying to the regime" (36). A pragmatic constraint? Rémond's explanation seems to me to rejoin my reflections on the pragmatics of social action and on the conditions of "fitting" action, without for all that going so far as to theorize the interplay of initiatives and expedients of the partners in the game in situations of uncertainty, as in microhistory. In the second place, his argument concerning the threefold division of the right, which is the book's central thesis, is a problem following the brilliant plea for binarism. The proof of the relevance of this distribution in a sense is more historical, inasmuch as it is less systematic. What counts as proof then is the possibility of identifying the same three denominations over a rather long period, hence, "the continuity of each of them over the generations" (10). Here the details count: five hundred pages are required to help the reader in orienting himself in political space.

96. See Jacques Le Goff, "Les mentalités: Une histoire ambiguë," in *Faire de l'histoire*, 3:114; "Mentalities: A History of Ambiguities," in Jacques Le Goff and Pierre Nora, *Constructing the Past: Essays in Historical Methodology* (New York: Cambridge University Press, 1985), 170.

97. See Roger Chartier, *Lecteur et lecteurs dans la France de l'Ancien Régime* (Paris: Seuil, 1987); idem., ed., *Histoire de la lecture: Un bilan des recherches* (Paris: IMEC Éditions and Éd. de la Maison des sciences de l'homme, 1995).

98. To complicate things even further, we could bring in the political dimension of the idea of representation. Its most important components allow it to be brought near to memorial and historiographical representation by passing through the ideas of delegation, substitution, and visible figuration, which we shall encounter below. In truth, this political dimension is not absent from the represented objects taken into account by historians. To the double taxonomic and symbolic function of the idea of representation already referred to, can be added "the institutionalized and objectified forms thanks to which 'representatives' (as collective instances or unique individuals) mark in a visible, perpetuated fashion the existence of a group, a community, or class." Roger Chartier, "Le monde comme representation," in *Au bord de la falaise: L'Histoire entre certitude et inquiétude* (Paris: Albin Michel, 1998), 78

99. See my discussion in *Lectures on Ideology and Utopia*, ed. George H. Taylor (New York: Columbia University Press, 1986), 254–66.

100. Louis Marin, *La Critique du discours: Études sur la «Logique de Port-Royal» et les «Pensées» de Pascal* (Paris: Minuit, 1975).

101. Carlo Ginzburg, "Représentation: Le mot, l'idée, la chose," *Annales* (1991): 1219–34. Ginzburg's article is included in this issue of *Annales* under the rubric "Pratique de le représentation."

102. Ginsburg acknowledges his debt here to E. H. Gombrich and his famous book, *Art and Illusion* (Princeton: Princeton University Press, 1960), as well as to Gombrich's *Meditations on a Hobby Horse and Other Essays on the Theory of Art* (London: Phaidon, 1994).

103. "It is the real, concrete, corporeal presence of Christ in the sacraments that, between the end of the thirteenth and the beginning of the fourteenth century, allowed the crystallization of that extraordinary object from which I began, that concrete symbol of the abstraction of the State: the effigy of the kind called *representation*" (Ginzburg, "Représentation: Le mot, l'idée, la chose," 1230).

104. Along with Roger Chartier, I acknowledge the debt contracted by the epistemology of history in regard to the whole of Marin's oeuvre. See, for example, his "The Powers and Limits of Representation," in *On the Edge of the Cliff*, 90–103.

105. "We have seen in what sense the theological body can be said to be the semiotic function itself. Moreover, we have clarified how it was possible in 1683 for the Port Royal logicians to believe that there existed a perfect adequation between the Catholic dogma [of the real presence] on the one hand and a semiotic theory of meaningful representation on the other" (cited by Chartier, ibid., 93–94).

106. Louis Marin, *Des pouvoirs de l'image* (Paris: Seuil, 1993).

107. Louis Marin, *Portrait of the King*, trans. Martha M. Houle (Minneapolis: University of Minnesota Press, 1988).

## PART TWO, CHAPTER THREE

1. Michel de Certeau places the third phase of "The Historiographical Operation" under the title "A Writing." *The Writing of History*, trans. Tom Conley (New York: Columbia University Press, 1988), 86. I have adopted the same sequence for this book. In this section, he also deals with representation as "literary staging" (86), which he still calls "historical writing" (87). Writing, he says, could be the "inverted image of practice," that is, construction properly speaking. "It creates these narratives of the past which are the equivalent of cemeteries within cities; it exorcises and confesses a presence of death amidst the living" (87). I shall return to this latter theme below.

2. François Dosse places the third section of his book, *L'Histoire* (Paris: Armin Colin, 2000), under the heading "narrative" (65–93). From Titus-Livy and Tacitus the narrative road passes through Froissart and Commynes and reaches its peak with

Michelet, before dividing into different "returns" to narrative and before being incorporated in Michel de Certeau's overall historiographical operation.

3. In this sense, the work marks an advance over my *Time and Narrative*, where the distinction between representation as explanation and narration was not made, on the one hand because the problem of the direct relationship between narrativity and temporality occupied my attention at the expense of the passage through memory, on the other because no detailed analysis of the procedures for explanation/understanding was proposed. But, at bottom, the notion of the plot and of emplotment remain primordial in this work as in *Time and Narrative*.

4. On this point, too, the present work goes beyond *Time and Narrative*, where the resources of rhetoric were not distinguished from those of narrativity. The present effort to disentangle the rhetorical from the properly semiotic aspects of narrative will find an opportune occasion for testing out our hypotheses about reading in a discussion of Hayden White's theses.

5. See François Furet, "From Narrative History to Problem-Oriented History," in *In the Workshop of History*, trans. Jonathan Mandelbaum (Chicago: University of Chicago Press, 1984), 54–67.

6. In the preceding chapter, I have briefly described the coming to predominance of the notion of structure, understood by historians in a twofold sense as static—the relational architecture of a given ensemble—and dynamic—as durably stable, at the expense of the idea of the point-like event—whereas the term "conjuncture" tends to designate midrange time in relation to the long time of structures. In this way, the event found itself removed to third place, following structure and conjuncture; the event was then defined as Pomian puts it "as a discontinuity noted within a model."

7. See *Time and Narrative*, 1:141–55.

8. See ibid., 1: 155–74.

9. Louis O. Mink, *Historical Understanding*, ed. Brian Fay, Eugene O. Golob, and Richard T. Vann (Ithaca: Cornell University Press, 1987).

10. Ibid., 182–203.

11. See also Lawrence Stone, "Retour au récit, réflexions sur une vieille histoire," *Le Débat*, no. 4 (1980): 116–42.

12. Aristotle's *Poetics* explicitly links the grasping of this coherence by the spectator to catharsis. The "purifying" of the passions through fear and pity is in this sense the effect of the intellectual comprehension of the plot (cf. *Time and Narrative*, 1:31–87).

13. The category of recognition—*anagnōrisis*—which designates the narrative moment that permits concordance to compensate for the discordance arising from the surprising event set within the plot also stems from a general theory of the plot.

14. It was in regard to the extending to history of the categories illustrated by traditional and fictional narrative that in *Time and Narrative* I added the phrase "quasi" to the notions of plot, event, and character. There I spoke of a second-order derivation of history with regard to traditional and fictional narrative. Today, I would remove the "quasi" and take the considered narrative categories as operators in the full sense of the term on the historiographical plane, inasmuch as the presumed tie in this work between history and the practical field in which social action unfolds authorizes applying the Aristotelian category of "actors" directly to the domain of history. The problem posed is no longer that of a transposition, of some expression starting from other, less scholarly uses of narrative, but of the articulation between narrative coherence and explanatory connectedness.

15. I am leaving aside examination of one component of the plot that Aristotle held to be marginal, but that he nevertheless includes within the perimeter of the "parts" of the *muthos*, the fable, the plot, namely, the spectacle (*opsis*) (*Poetics* 57 and 62a15). Although it does not contribute to the meaning, it cannot be excluded from consideration. It designates the side of visibility added to that of the readability of the plot. The question arises as to what point in the staging of the written form making it visible becomes important. Here seduction by the pleasurable gets added to persuasion by the probable. I shall have more to say about this with regard to the rhetorical component of representation, and more particularly in connection with the "prestige of the image."

16. F. R. Ankersmit, *Narrative Logic: A Semantic Analysis of the Historian's Language* (The Hague: Nijhoff, 1983).

17. Reinhart Koselleck, *Futures Past: On the Semantics of Historical Time*, trans. Keith Tribe (Cambridge, Mass.: MIT Press, 1985), 105–15. This essay is set within the framework of a broader inquiry aimed at defining what "the question of historical time might be," concerning which Koselleck says that it belongs to "those questions which historical science has the most difficulty answering" (xxi). I shall propose a discussion of the Koselleck's major theses in this collection and in *L'Expérience de l'histoire* (Paris: Gallimard-Seuil-EHESS, 1997) in the next chapter in relation to the notion of truth in history. Thus his essay as considered here has been detached from its broader context.

18. Here we come back again to Ginzburg's evidential paradigm.

19. "The processual character of modern history cannot be comprehended other than through the reciprocal explanation of events through structures, and vice versa" (Koselleck, *Futures Past*, 110). Koselleck, it is true, protests against the amalgamation of event and structure. The temporal strata never fully fuse; succession leaves room for the surprise of the unexpected event. The cognitive relationship of the two concepts, which is one of deviation, is not abolished by the

sort of negotiation the narrative brings about between them. Conceptuality and singularity remain heterogeneous to each other.

20. I tried to rediscover for metaphorical discourse its own mode of referentiality at the point conjoining "seeing as" and "being as." This particular kind of referring seemed to me capable of being transposed to the narrative plane as it applied to fictional narrative. What is more, it seemed to me that its power of refiguration could be assigned to fictional narrative through the intermediary of the reader coming to the text with his own expectations structured by his way of being in the world—it is these ways of being in the world that are refigured by the fictional narrative.

21. François Hartog's *The Mirror of Herodotus: The Representation of the Other in the Writing of History*, trans. Janet Lloyd (Berkeley: University of California Press, 1988) proposes an interesting argument about the idea of historical representation for discussion. It has to do, as his subtitle—*the representation of the other*—indicates, with the barbarian space brought on stage by the narrative of the Median wars. Hartog has chosen to isolate from the overall narrative context the "Scythian *logos*" (3–11). It is not the truth of the statements having the Scythians as their object that interest him. What is said about the Median wars considered in its full historical scope is set aside, suspended, to the profit of a narrative segment that Hartog sees delimited by a set of "narrative constraints" (35–40) that work to pick out the relevant features of the nomad something like the reticulated grid of an artist who paints with watercolors (319): "the Athenian, that imaginary autochthous being, has need of an imaginary nomad. The Scythian conveniently fitted the bill" (11). In this way, the text of *The History* will be treated as a mirror, not just for the *histōr* faced with the test of writing, but for the barbarian whose alterity is reflected in it and for the Greek who deciphers his identity in it. One question arises at the edges: how can one be a nomad? But this question does not lead to any referent. In this sense, one does not "exit" the text. One is confronted with statements from the same context—barbarian others, Greeks. The "representation of the other" stems from the same "rhetoric of otherness" (212). If reading nonetheless leads beyond the text, it is not in the direction of the events that occurred in the setting of the Median wars, but at the level of the Greek intratextual imaginary of the fifth century: "it is a movement outward that takes place through and in language, and on the level of the imaginary" (321). The "effect of the narrative" (321) is what "Herodotus's mirror" is, a mirror for viewing the world.

In that this work admits its limits (*quid* of the Median wars?), it is wholly legitimate. It just makes more difficult the question of speaking the truth in history. The investigation into making something believed constantly puts off the question at the risk of completely losing sight of it. The paradox of the narrative vector is thus powerfully indicated: as a guide toward the referent, the narrative is also its screen. Nevertheless, does not the very thesis of evaluating "the effect of the *Histories* on the Greek's imaginary representation of the work" (356) raise the question of the referent in another way—was that effect of the text reached? A history of reading seems required here that would take as its referent the fifth-century Greek reading Herodotus. Do we really know this better than we do the battle of Salamis?

22. "We shall give the name 'standing-for' [*représentance*] (or 'taking the place of' [*lieutenance*]) to the relations between the constructions of history and their vis-à-vis, that is, a past that is abolished yet preserved in its traces" (*Time and Narrative*, 3:100).

23. See ibid., 1:52–87 for my earlier discussion of the general problem of the relations between configuration and refiguration.

24. See Roland Barthes, "Introduction to the Structural Analysis of Narrative," in *Image, Music, Text*, trans. Stephen Heath (New York: Hill and Wang, 1977), 79–124. There we read: "A narrative is a long sentence, just as every constative sentence is in a way the rough outline of a short narrative" (84); "nor does the homology suggested here have only a heuristic value: it implies an identity between language and literature" (84–85).

25. *Time and Narrative*, "The Semiotic Constraints on Narrativity," 2:29–60.

26. Roland Barthes, "The Discourse of History," in *The Rustle of Language*, trans. Richard Howard (New York: Hill and Wang, 1986), 127–40; see also "The Reality Effect," ibid., 141–48. Here we might also refer to the criticism directed by theorists of the new novel—especially, Jean Ricardou in *Le Nouveau Roman* (Paris: Seuil, 1973)—against the "referential illusion" of the realist novel.

27. A more technical discussion is required concerning the role of "notations" in the formation of the "reality effect." Undoubtedly they constitute a good criterion for characterizing some novels as realist. But do they function in the same way in historical narrative? This is not certain. I suggest that they need to be assigned to the dimension of visibility as much as to that of the readability of the literary structures of historical discourse. But, even then, the notations are not separable from the "annotations" that—set at the bottom of the page, which the realist or naturalist novel does without—indicate the documentary sources that the point-like statements about isolated facts are based upon. Annotations, in this way, are the literary expression of the first-order documentary reference of historical discourse.

28. Hayden White, *Metahistory: The Historical Imagination in Nineteenth-Century Europe* (Baltimore: Johns Hopkins University Press, 1978); *The Content of the Form: Narrative Discourse and Historical Representation* (Baltimore: Johns Hopkins University Press, 1987). For my earlier discussion of White, see *Time and Narrative*, 1:161–68; 3:151–56. See also Roger Chartier, "Figures rhétoriques et

représentation historique," in *Au bord de la falaise* (Paris: Albin Michel, 1998), 108–25.

29. A rhetorical theory of argumentation is not absent from the contemporary discussion. See, for example, Wayne Booth, *Rhetoric of Fiction* (Chicago: University of Chicago Press, 1961); closer to the relation between rhetoric and logic is Stephen E. Toulmin, *The Uses of Argument* (New York: Cambridge University Press, 1958).

30. After all, the idea is not foreign to Aristotle's *Poetics* insofar as a coefficient of probability is attached to the emplotment. What is more, metaphor stems as much from rhetoric, as the theory of probable discourse, as from poetics, as the theory of the production of discourse.

31. What White calls style should be compared with the same notion in the work of G. G. Granger, *Essai d'une philosophie du style* (Paris: Armand Colin, 1968). The difference is that for White style is not the focused production of an appropriate individual response to an equally individual situation, but the expression on the manifest plane of the constraints governing the deep structures of the imagination.

32. Hans Kellner, *Language and Historical Representation: Getting the Story Crooked* (Madison: University of Wisconsin Press, 1989), attacks two targets. On the one hand, there is the belief there is something beyond any history asking to be told; on the other, is the claim that history can be "told straight" by an honest or industrious historian using the "right" method. Only the second charge touches White. There must be something voluntary, finally repressive—as we also read in Foucault—in the imposing of order. The contrary plea for discontinuity begins with consideration of the document, basking in the prestige of the archive. The debris of the past is scattered, as are testimonies about the past. The discipline of documentation adds its own selective destructive effects to every mode of loss of information that mutilates alleged "documentary evidence." Thus, rhetoric is not something added to the documentation, it already is invested in it. We would like the narrative to attenuate the anxiety arising from the lacunae in the documentary evidence. But the narrative in turn gives rise to new anxieties, tied to other discontinuities. Here is where the discussion over the tropology introduced by White comes in. The tropological reading, it is said, becomes upsetting in turn—and therefore a new source of anxiety—if we do not construct a new system on the basis of White's four tropes. The alleged "bedrock of order" itself must be taken as an allegorical play where irony is recognized both as the master trope within the system and a point of view on the system. White is suspected of having drawn back before what at the end of *Tropics of Discourse* he himself calls, in a mixture of sympathy and anxiety, "the absurdist moment." Kellner does not tell us how we should write history, nor how the professional historian negotiates with doubt that would not be "hyperbolic" but truly methodic. We are only told how not to write history.

33. Saul Friedlander, ed., *Probing the Limits of Representation: Nazism and the "Final Solution"* (Cambridge, Mass.: Harvard University Press, 1992).

34. Two of his articles in *The Content of Form*—"The Value of Narrativity in the Representation of Reality" and "The Politics of Historical Interpretation"— have been the target of critiques coming from the camp of professional historians, among them Momigliano, Ginzburg, Spiegel, and Jacoby.

35. The principal pieces of this controversy were published as Ernst Reinhard Piper, ed., *Historikerstreit* (Munich: Piper, 1987), and translated into French as *Devant l'histoire: Les Documents de la controverse sur la singularité de l'extermination des Juifs par le régime nazi*, trans. Brigitte Verne-Cain et al. (Paris: Cerf, 1988). In English, there is a special issue on the *Historikerstreit* in *New German Critique*, no. 44 (Spring, Summer 1988) that focuses on Habermas's arguments with the historians. Ernst Nolte's famous title, "A Past that will not Go Away," has had a wide impact through the Western world. Henry Rousso was to apply it to the case of the French memory of the Vichy regime in modified form as *un passé qui ne passe pas* in *Vichy: An Ever-Present Past*, trans. Nathan Bracher (Hanover, N.H.: University Press of New England, 1998).

36. "The exterminations of the Jews of Europe as the most extreme case of mass criminalities must challenge theoreticians of historical relativism to face the corollaries of positions otherwise too easily dealt with on an abstract level" (*Probing the Limits of Representation*, 2). It is true that Friedlander grants to these critiques that it is not possible to sum up in superhistory the point of view of the executioners, the victims, and the spectators who were part of the events. The difficulty, therefore, is not an invention of postmodernism; it will have served a revelatory role in regard to an inextricable dilemma arising from the "final solution" itself.

37. Hayden White, "Historical Emplotment and the Problem of Truth," in Saul Friedlander, ed., *Probing the Limits of Representation: Nazism and the "Final Solution"* (Cambridge, Mass.: Harvard University Press, 1992), 37–53.

38. Why not the comic genre, practiced in a satirical tone, as in Art Spiegelman, *Maus: A Survivor's Tale* (New York: Pantheon, 1986)? Nor is there any decisive argument to be drawn from the history of literary genres to judge the attempted tragic representation in Andreas Hillgruber's two essays, *Zweierlei Untergang: Die Zerschlagung des Deutschen Reiches und das Ende des Europäischen Judentums* (Berlin: Siedler, 1986). Nothing forbids making heroes of the characters, as the tragic mode requires. Another contributor to Friedlander's volume, Peter Anderson, explores the resources of a literary genre close to the *collatio* of ancient rhetoric practiced by Hillgruber, the procedure consisting in placing two narratives side by side, that of the murder of the Jews and that of the expulsion of Germans from their ancient territories in the east: juxtaposition, it is suggested is not the

same as comparison. But can one avoid exculpating one through the transfer of the emotional charge of the one to the other?

39. Erich Auerbach, *Mimesis: The Representation of Reality in Western Literature*, trans. Willard Trask (Princeton: Princeton University Press, 1953), which I had cited already in *Time and Narrative*, 2:162 n. 8. In his first chapter, Auerbach underscores the depth, the richness in background of biblical figures, such as Abraham, the apostle Paul, in contrast to Homer's characters who lack such depth. He sees in this depth an indication of reality.

40. Ginzburg thinks he can undercut White's argument by bringing to light its suspect roots in the relativism and idealism of the Italian thinkers Croce and Gentile. He follows their trace up to White's *The Content of the Form*.

41. Pierre Vidal-Naquet, *The Jews: History, Memory, and the Present*, trans. David Ames Curtis (New York: Columbia University Press, 1996); *Assassins of Memory: Essays on the Denial of the Holocaust*, trans. Jeffrey Mehlman (New York: Columbia University Press, 1992).

42. This is how Friedlander takes Ginsburg's essay: "Although the criticism of White's position . . . opts for an epistemological approach, Carlo Ginsburg's passionate plea for historical objectivity and truth is as much informed by a profoundly ethical position as by analytic categories" (*Probing the Limits of Representation*, 8).

43. In one of the essays in Friedlander's collection, C. R. Browning summarizes his work in the archives on a German reserve police battalion operating in a Polish village: "German Memory, Judicial Interrogation and Historical Reconstruction: Writing Perpetrator History from Postwar Testimony" (ibid., 22–36).

44. Cited by Dominick La Capra, "Representing the Holocaust: Reflections on the Historians' Debate" (ibid., 108–27).

45. "How should one negotiate transferential relations to the object of study?" asks La Capra (ibid., 110). He then goes on to apply his criterion to the terms of one of the sharpest debates in the controversy among German historians: the question whether the Holocaust (the term chosen by La Capra, who takes care to justify it) ought to be treated as a historical phenomenon as unique or as comparable. This is not my problem here. But it is interesting to note the way in which La Capra applies his criterion, which we can call therapeutic. There is a sense, he says, in which the event has to be taken as unique, both as regards the magnitude of its destructive effects and as regards its origin in the behavior of a criminal state. There is also a sense in which it is comparable inasmuch as uniqueness is linked to difference and difference to comparison, and in that comparing is part of understanding. But it is the way in which the argument for uniqueness and that for comparability are handled that is important. The question in both cases is to know whether, for

example, comparison contributes, through leveling situations, to denial, or whether, in the opposite sense, the vehement assertion of the incomparable uniqueness of the event does not end up, along the way of sacralization and monumentalization, in a fixation on the trauma, which following Freud has to be assimilated to repetition, which, we have seen, constitutes the major resistance to working through and leads to being caught up in acting out. We could say the same about the choice of scales discussed above, where one either immerses oneself in the daily life of the German people or attempts instead to pierce the secret of decisions taken at the peak of power. The question then is no longer that of the primacy of uniqueness or of comparability, or of centrality opposed to marginality; it is knowing in what way each approach contributes to a useful negotiation of the "transferential relations to the object of study." The impasses of working through are no less on one side than on the other.

46. Jürgen Habermas, "Apologetic Tendencies," in *The New Conservatism: Cultural Criticism and the Historians' Debate*, ed. and trans. Shierry Weber Nicholsen (Cambridge, Mass.: MIT Press, 1989), 212–28.

47. Nothing is said here about the beneficial influence on collective memory that can be expected from the great criminal trials of the second half of twentieth century and the publication of their proceedings. That presupposes the penal qualification of mass crimes, hence a connection between moral and legal judgment. The possibility of such a qualification is inscribed in the event itself as a third-person crime; that is, one committee by a state that owes security and protection to whomever resides within its jurisdictional territory. This aspect of the "historization" of traumatic events concerns not only their figuration but also their legal qualification. See Mark Osiel, *Mass Atrocity, Collective Memory, and the Law* (New Brunswick, N.J.: Transaction, 1997). I shall return to this point on the occasion of a discussion having to do with the relationships between the historian and the judge. But we can already observe that such a legal qualification negates the thesis that the events of Auschwitz are unspeakable in every regard. We can speak and must speak about them.

48. I dealt with the "interweaving of history and fiction" on the basis of a counterpoint relation in chapter 8 of the second section in volume 3 of *Time and Narrative*, after having considered separately, on the one hand, "Fiction and Its Imaginary Variations on Time" (chap. 5) and, on the other, "The Reality of the Past" (chap. 6). The purpose of this book was to directly scrutinize the relationship between narrative and time without any regard for memory. It was "the neutralization of historical time" that served as an introductory theme to the great interplay of imaginative variations produced by fiction at the site of the fault line between lived time and the time of the world. The liberation of fictional narrative with

regard to the constraints of calendar time was taken as a cultural fact documented by literary history beginning from Greek epic and tragedy through the modern and contemporary novel. The word "contract" [*pacte*] was cited once in volume 2 (183, n. 65) in referring to Philippe Lejeune's *On Autobiography*, trans. Katherine Leary (Minneapolis: University of Minnesota Press, 1989).

49. The world of the text: "a world we might inhabit and wherein we can unfold our ownmost potentialities" (*Time and Narrative*, 2:101). This theme was introduced in volume 1 of *Time and Narrative* under the heading of threefold mimesis, where refiguration constituted the third stage in the movement of the figure, after configuration, and before that, the prefiguration of time (1:52–87). The theory of the intersecting effects of the fictional and the historical narrative constitutes the central discussion of the means of refiguring time in volume 3 of *Time and Narrative*. The only question allowed, so long as we take as given the difference between wholly constituted literary genres, is that of the "interweaving of history and fiction" on the plane of the effective refiguration of lived time, without regard for the mediation of memory. This interweaving consists in the fact that "history and fiction each concretize their respective intentionalities only by borrowing from the intentionality of the other" (3:181). On the one side, we can speak of the historicization of fiction to the degree that the willing suspension of suspicion rests on a neutralization of "realist" features not only of the most elaborated kind of historical narratives but also of the most spontaneous narratives of everyday life, as well as of all those narratives that stem from what we can call narrative conversations. With Hannah Arendt, I said that narrative tells of the "what" of action. It is action, as a model of actuality, that bears narrative to its proper sphere. In this sense, to recount something is to recount it as though it were past. The "as though it actually happened" is part of the meaning we attach to every narrative. At this level, the immanent sense is inseparable from an external, asserted, negated, or suspended reference. This adherence to a reference *ad extra* to the sense even in fiction seems to be implied by the positing character of the assertion of the past in ordinary discourse. Something that was is affirmed or denied. The result is that the fictional narrative preserves this positing feature in the mode of the "quasi." The quasi events and the quasi characters of fictional plots are quasi past. Moreover, it is thanks to this simulation of existence that fiction can explore aspects of lived temporality that the realist narrative does not reach. The imaginative variations on time explored in volume 2 of *Time and Narrative* draw their explorative force, their force of discovery, of revelation from the deep structures of temporal experience. Whence results the character of verisimilitude that Aristotle attaches to epic and tragic tales. And it is thanks to this relation of verisimilitude that fictional narrative is authorized to detect unactualized potentialities of the historical past, in the mode

of imaginative variations. On the other side, an effect of "fictionalizing history" is produced, assignable to the impact of the imaginary in this regard: the construction of ways of measuring time (from the *gnomon* to the calendar to the timepiece) and of instruments for dating historical time—as products of the scientific imagination. As for those traces that are the documents in the archive, they only become readable under the guidance of interpretive hypotheses engendered by what Collingwood called the historical imagination. Here is where we come to a phenomenon to which our present analysis will apply that goes well beyond the imaginary mediations just enumerated: namely, the power to "depict" attached to the properly representative function of the historical imagination.

50. See Reinhart Koselleck, "Representation, Event, and Structure," in *Futures Past*, 105–15. Among the problems of representation (*Darstellung*), he distinguishes between narrating (*erzählen*) and describing (*beschreiben*), structure falling on the side of description and event on that of narrative.

51. Louis Marin, *Opacité de la peinture: Essais sur la représentation du Quatrocento* (Paris: Usher, 1989), 251–66.

52. For Aristotle himself, a more secret connection is established between the power of metaphor to set before the eyes and the project of persuasion that animates rhetoric, namely, the power of metaphor to "signify things in act" (1411b24–25). When is discourse most likely to signify things in act? The answer is found in the *Poetics*, the science of the production of discourse: It is when the *muthos*, the fable, the plot succeeds in producing a *mimēsis*, an imitation, a representation "of men acting and in act" (*Poetics* 1648a24). A bridge is thereby constructed between visibility in discourse and the energy in human things, between the live metaphor and live existence. The expression "to set before the eyes" will make a considerable impact from Fontainier's rhetoric to Pierce's semiotics. Cf. my *The Rule of Metaphor: Multi-Disciplinary Studies of the Creation of Meaning in Language*, trans. Robert Czerny with Kathleen McLaughlin and John Costello, S.J. (Toronto: University of Toronto Press, 1977), chap. 5, §2, "The 'Iconic' Moment of Metaphor," and §6, "Icon and Image."

53. Louis Marin, *Portrait of the King*, trans. Martha M. Houle (Minneapolis: University of Minnesota Press, 1988).

54. Marin finds a basis for his exegesis of political power in Ernst H. Kantorowicz's great book, *The King's Two Bodies: A Study in Medieval Political Theology* (Princeton: Princeton University Press, 1937), which lays out the function of the juridical and political model played by the Catholic theology of the *corpus mysticum* in the elaboration of the theory of royalty, and of the royal crown and dignity. If only the physical body of the king dies and his mystical body remains, it is because, under the aegis of the theology of the sacrament, the monarchical

institution rests on the "repetition of a sacred mystery of the sign and of the secret" (*Portrait of the King*, 9).

55. Marin speaks here of a parody of the Eucharist: "an insuperable boundary" between "the Eucharistic symbols of Jesus Christ" and "the political signs of the monarch" (ibid., 12) was crossed by power's desire for the absolute, thanks to "the fantastic representation of the absolute monarch in his portrait" (12).

56. The Port Royal logicians provided an analytic instrument for distinguishing narrative and icon in *L'Art de penser* in examining the statement "the portrait of Caesar is Caesar," and by exemplifying with cards and portraits the definition of the sign as a representation grounding the right to give the sign the name of the thing signified (ibid., 9).

57. "The King's Narrative, or How to Write History," ibid., 39–88.

58. "The Royal Host: The Historic Medal," ibid., 121–37.

59. "Vivid description of a scene, event, or situation, bringing it, as it were, before the eyes of the hearer or reader." *Oxford English Dictionary*—trans.

60. The expression "sets before the eyes," which comes directly from Aristotle's *Rhetoric*, is applied by Fontanier to hypotyposis, which, Marin notes, brings narration to the height of style by annulling the fiction of a presence "before their eyes" (*Portrait of the King*, 122).

61. Beyond Pascal, whom I shall return to below, the Grand Siècle does not seem to have pushed its self-critique beyond the fragile distinctions between praise and flattery. Is praise distinguished from flattery only by its moderation, its restraint, and its paralipsis ("praise the king everywhere, but so to speak without praise"), taking into account the authorization granted by the ecclesiastical or political institution? Must the flatterer also be a parasite, as La Fontaine's maxim in the tale of the crow and the fox suggests? Here we need to read again the well-known passage on flattery in Hegel's *Phenomenology of Spirit*, as Marin recommends ("The Fox's Tactics," 94–104). I would add here the pages Norbert Elias devotes to the courtier in his *The Court Society*, trans. Edmund Jephcott (New York: Pantheon Books, 1983).

62. This second-degree critical relation between the mere account of procedures of praise and the Pascalian critique of the imagination is presented in the introduction to the *Portrait of the King* as bringing to light a "counter model" (3) in regard to the theory of language of the Port-Royal philosophers, to whom Marin had devoted an earlier work titled *La Critique du discours: Études sur la «Logique de Port-Royal» et les «Pensées» de Pascal* (Paris: Minuit, 1975). In fact, the political use of the theological model of the Eucharist in which Marin sees the semiotics of the proposition and the theology of the sacrament converge has been characterized as a misappropriation.

63. Marin's comment on the ironic tone of §95 ("The more hands one employs, the more powerful one is. Elegance is a means of showing one's power") introduces the interesting notion of a "surplus value," more exactly of a signifying surplus value, that in my *Lectures on Ideology and Utopia*, ed. George H. Taylor (New York: Columbia University Press, 1986), I made use of in a neighboring context, Max Weber's theory of domination and his typology of legitimating beliefs. I compared what is said there about belief as a "surplus" with the idea of a surplus value in the symbolic order.

64. This is why we must not separate the discourse of the imagination from that of custom, nor from that of madness. "Respect and fear" (§25) make the bridge between the discourse of "weakness" and that of "justified force"—to such an extent that the very theme of the imagination does not exhaust all the effects of force and the effects of meaning in politics. The idea of law also has a place in such an articulation: The law is law and nothing more. "Custom is the whole of equity for the sole reason that it is accepted. That is the mystic basis of its authority" (§60).

65. According to one of Pascal's *Discours sur la condition des Grands*, a great person is property holder, "a rich man whose having determines his being" (*Portrait of the King*, 216).

66. Marin was so seduced by this "image" of a drowned king that he used it to conclude *Portrait of the King*, in a symmetrical position in relation to the "fragments of the *Pensées* on force and justice" that make up the "overture" to the work. What is more, he returns to it in *Des pouvoirs de l'image*, gloses VI, "Le portrait du roi naufragé," 186–95.

67. Eric Weil, *Philosophie politique* (Paris: Vrin, 1956), prop. 31.

68. Luc Boltanski and Laurent Thévenot, *De la justification: Les économies de la grandeur* (Paris: Gallimard, 1991).

69. Quoted by Leonard Krieger, *Ranke: The Meaning of History* (Chicago: University of Chicago Press, 1977), 6. In his *English History*, Ranke sought to "extinguish my own self... to let the things speak and the mighty forces appear which have arisen in the course of the centuries" (ibid., 5).

70. E.g., this from the preface to the 1869 edition: "In these memorable days, a great light appeared, and I glimpsed France.... The first time that I saw it as having a soul and as a person."

71. Braudel echoes Michelet on the opening page of his *Identity of France*, trans. Siân Reynolds (New York: Harper and Row, 1988): "Let me start by saying once and for all that I love France with the same demanding and complicated passion as did Jules Michelet; without distinguishing between its good points and its bad, between what I like and what I find harder to accept. But that passion will hardly intrude up the pages of this book. I shall keep it carefully to one side. It may

play tricks on me, and catch me out, so I shall keep it under close watch" (15). Pierre Nora is no less indebted to Michelet and Braudel in *Les Lieux de mémoire*, especially in the third volume, titled *Les France*. Responding to the charge of nationalism, he places under the quasi name of "Francité" ("Frenchness") the unique organism that together comes together as a kind of secular trinity: the Republic, the Nation, Frances, and he adds, pretending to ask a question: "Have you noticed that all the great histories of France, from Étienne Pasquier in the sixteenth century to Michelet, and from Michelet to Lavisse and Braudel, begin or end with a declaration of love for France, a profession of faith? Love, faith, these are words I have been careful to avoid, replacing them by those called for by our age and the ethnological point of view." "La Nation sans nationalisme," in *Espaces Temps, Les Cahiers*, no. 59–60–61 (1995): 69.

72. Roger Chartier, "History between Narrative and Knowledge," in *On the Edge of the Cliff: History, Language, Practice*, trans. Lydia G. Cochrane (Baltimore: Johns Hopkins University Press, 1997), 13–27.

73. Jacques Revel, "Microhistoire et construction du social," in *Jeux d'échelles: La Microanalyse à l'expérience* (Paris: Gallimard, 1996), 15. "With the microhistorians . . . the search for a form does not stem fundamentally from an aesthetic choice (even if it is not lacking). It seems to me instead to belong to a heuristic order; and this in a double way. It invites the reader to participate in the construction of a research object; it associates him with the elaboration of an interpretation" (ibid., 32–33). The parallel with the novel after Proust, Musil, or Joyce suggests a reflection that surpasses the fixed framework of the realist novel of the nineteenth century: "The relation between a form of exposition and known content has become the object of an explicit interrogation" (34). And to evoke the disorienting effect in relation to the interpretive model of the dominant discourse, he invokes Fabrice at Waterloo who "only perceives disorder" (35).

74. Ankersmit, *Narrative Logic*.

75. I have presented a longer analysis ⌐f Ankersmit's *Narrative Logic* in my "Philosophies critiques de l'histoire: Recherche, explication, écriture," in Fløistad Guttorm, ed., *Philosophical Problems Today* (Dordrecht: Kluwer, 1994), 1:139–201. There I emphasize in succession the refutation of every correspondence theory of truth between a *narratio* and something that one is incapable of showing; of the affirmation of heterogeneity between the narrative form and the reality that supposedly occurred; of the kinship existing between the narrative kernel and the effect that develops its meaning with the relation Leibniz establishes between "substance" and its "predicates" which are held to inhere in the substance; and finally, of the complementary recourse to criteria for maximizing the scope of grand narratives that tempers the author's professed idealism. What remains solid, in my opinion, is

the question of the "reality" over which different *narratios* clash in such a way that we can say that one of them rewrites a preceding one dealing with the same theme. What does "past" mean when one declares that "the past itself does not impose the ways in which it should be represented"? Is not the error here wanting directly to stamp the large scale *narratios* with a truth-coefficient, independently of the partial statements arising from the documentary procedure and the explanations limited to shorter sequences?

76. This is Roger Chartier's thesis at the end of his discussion of Hayden White's work. White, we recall, accepts as unsurpassable a semiological approach that calls into question the soundness of testimonies to events and thus authorizes us "to pass over the question of the text's 'honesty,' its objectivity" (*The Content of the Form*, 192, cited in *On the Edge of the Cliff*, 38). Chartier replies: "Isn't the very object of history to understand how, in each particular historical configuration, historians put into operation research techniques and critical procedures that give their discourses (in an unequalled measure) just such an 'honesty' and 'objectivity'?" (ibid.) Elsewhere, he declares: "Rightly to consider that history belongs to the class of narratives is not for all that to take as illusory its intention to be true, to be a truth understood as an adequate representation of what once was." "Philosophie et histoire: Un dialogue," in François Bedarida, ed., *L'Histoire et le métier d'historien en France, 1945–1995* (Paris: Éd. de la Maison des sciences de l'homme, 1995), 163.

77. We cannot insist too much on the critical turn that the famous quarrel over the Donation of Constantine represents for historiography. Cf. Carlos Ginzburg's preface to Lorenzo Valla, *La Donation de Constantin (Sur la «Donation de Constantin», à lui faussement attribuée et mensongère [c. 1440])*, trans. Jean-Baptiste Giard (Paris: Les Belles Lettres, 1993), ix–xxi.

78. Karl Heussi, *Die Krisis des Historismus* (Tübingen: Mohr, 1932). Cf. *Time and Narrative*, 3:143.

79. German gives a further basis for this with the distinction between *Vertretung* and *Vorstellung*, "taking the place of" [*lieutenance*] serving to translate *Vertretung*. Cf. *Time and Narrative*, 3:143.

80. This conceptual articulation depended on a dialectic transposed from that of the "great kinds" in Plato's late dialogues. I privileged the triad of "Same, Other, Analogous." Under the sign of the Same I placed the idea of a reenactment of the past following Collingwood. Under the sign of the Other, the apology for difference and absence, where I brought together Paul Veyne and his *Inventory of Differences* and Michel de Certeau and his insistence on the past as "absent from history." Under the sign of the Analogous I placed Hayden White's tropological approach. Then I brought together the analysis of the "such that" from Ranke's

formula ("such as it really happened") and the analysis of the "like" in the last study in my *The Rule of Metaphor*, where I linked the "seeing as" of the semantic plane to the "being as" of the ontological one. In this way it became possible to speak of a "metaphorical redescription of the past" by history.

81. Upon rereading this section, the most problematic notion of this whole second part is assuredly that of standing for [*représentance*], first made use of in *Time and Narrative*. Is it only the name of a problem taken as a solution or, worse, an expedient? In any case, it is not the fruit of some improvisation. It has a long lexical and semantic history before historiography:

(a) As a distant ancestor it has the Roman notion of *repraesentatio*, used to speak of the legal substitution exercised by the visible "representatives" of a "represented" authority. The substitute, "taking the place of," exercises his rights, but depends on the person represented. In contact with the Christian concept of Incarnation, the notion acquired a new density, that of a represented presence of the divine, which finds in the liturgy and in sacred theater its sphere of expression.

(b) The word passes from classical Latin to German through the intervention of the term *Vertretung*, the exact doublet of *repraesentatio*. (The French translators of Hans-Georg Gadamer's *Truth and Method* [Paris: Seuil, 1996] translate *Vertretung, repraesentatio* by *représentation-suppléance* [146]. One might also have said *représentation vicaire*. Or one could have preserved the Latin *repraesentatio*.) In the context of hermeneutics applied to works of art, *Vertretung* frees itself from the tutelage of *Vorstellung* in the sense of subjective representation, of appearance (or better, apparition) in and for the mind, as is the case in Kant and in the tradition of transcendental philosophy. Here the "phenomenon" remains opposed to the "thing in itself" that does not appear. Gadamer gives full development to the idea of *Vertretung* by restoring its "ontological valence" to it. *Truth and Method*, 2nd rev. ed., trans. Joel Weinsheimer and Donald G. Marshall (New York: Crossroad, 1991), 134. The word then rejoins the broader problematic of *Darstellung*, which the French translation renders as "représentation" in the sense of exposition, exhibition, monstration of an underlying being. This is the theme to which the Gadamerian hermeneutic of the work of art is devoted. The pair *Darstellung/Vertretung* thus moves from the liturgical to the aesthetic playing field in terms of the core concept of *Bild* (picture image). The two notions for all that are not aestheticized, at least in the restricted sense of a drawing away from *Erlebnis*, lived experience. On the contrary, it is the whole aesthetic field that, under the aegis of *Bild*, regains its ontological dignity with the "mode of being of the work of art" (ibid., 101f.) being what is at stake. The *Bild*, according to Gadamer, is more than a copy (*Abbild*), it is delegated to represent a "model" (*Ur-bild*) taken in the broad sense of a set of ways of being in the world, in the Ur of affective tones, real or fictional characters, actions, plots, and so forth. What is important in this "ontological process" (*Geschehen*) is that the dependence of the image on its model is compensated for by the "surplus" (*Zuwachs*) of being that the image confers in return on the model: "The original acquires an image," Gadamer insists, "only by being imaged, and yet the image is nothing but the appearance of the original" (142).

(c) It is against this background that we should set the attempted transposition of the "representation-supplement" from the aesthetic sphere to that historiography, and with it the whole problematic of *Darstellung/Vertretung*. One step in this direction is the image composing the memory. This certainly belongs, according to Gadamer, to the problematic of the sign and of signification (140). The memory designates the past, but it does so in figuring it. Was this not already the presupposition borne by the Greek *eikōn*? And have we not spoken with Bergson about the memory-image? And did we not grant to narrative and emplotment as an image of this the power to add visibility to the readability of the plot? It thus becomes possible to extend to the memory-image the problematic of the representation-surplus and to add to its credit the idea of a "surplus of being" first granted to the work of art. With the memory too, "by being presented it experiences, as it were, an increase in being" (140). What is thereby augmented by the figured representation is the very belonging of the event to the past.

(d) It remains to complete the rest of this trajectory: from memory to the historian's representation. My thesis here is that its belonging to literature, therefore to the field of writing, does not set a limit to the extension of the problematic of representation-supplement. From *Sprachlichkeit* to *Schriftlichkeit*, the ontological structure of *Darstellung* continues to demand its rights. The whole of textual hermeneutics is thus placed under the theme of the increase in being applied to the work of art. In this regard, we must renounce the at-first seductive idea of a restitution by exegesis of the original thought, an idea that, according to Gadamer, remained Schleiermacher's tacit presupposition (166). Hegel, on the other hand, was fully aware of the impotence of any restoration. We need only to recall the celebrated passage of the *Phenomenology of Spirit* on the decline of the ancient way of life and its "religion of art": "The works of the Muses...are now what they are for us—beautiful fruits torn from the tree; a friendly fate presents them to us, as a girl might offer those fruits. We have not the real life of their being." No restoration can compensate for this loss. In replacing these works in their historical context, we set up with them not a living relationship but one of mere representation (*Vorstellung*). The task of the reflective spirit is something different: that the spirit be represented (*dargestellt*) in a higher way. *Erinnerung*—internalization— begins to carry out this task. Here, concludes Gadamer, "Hegel points beyond the entire dimension in which Schleiermacher conceived the idea of understanding" (168).

(e) Such is the long history of representation-supplement I discern in the background of the notion of standing for in history that I have been advocating. Why, in spite of this brilliant ancestry, does the idea of representation-supplementation, of standing for, remain problematic? A first reason for this uneasiness has to do with the fact that it stands at the turning point from epistemology to ontology. The anticipations of an ontology of the historical condition, such as they shall appear in part 3, may be denounced as intrusions of "metaphysics" into the domain of the human sciences by the practioners of history concerned to banish every suspicion of a return of the "philosophy of history." For my part, I assume this risk from the thought that to refuse to take into account at an opportune moment problems having to do with the hermeneutics of the historical condition condemns us to leave unelucidated the status of what legitimately announces itself as a "critical realism" professed at the boundary of the epistemology of historical knowledge. Beyond the questions of method, a deeper reason has to do with the notion of the representation of the past in history. Why does the notion of representation seem opaque if not because the phenomenon of recognition that distinguishes every other relation of memory to the past is without parallel on the plane of history? This irreducible difference risks being misunderstood with the extending of the notion of the representation-supplement of the work of art to memory and to the writing of history. But this gap will continue to be challenged by our subsequent reflections on the relations between memory and history. The enigma of the past is finally that of a knowledge (*connaissance*) without recognition (*reconnaissance*). Is this to say, however, that the historian's representation remains purely and simply in default in relation to what, in my epilogue to the Epilogue I shall take to be the small miracle of memory? This would be to forget the positive side of the representation-supplement, namely, the surplus that it confers on the very thing that is represented. It is even, I believe, with the historian's representation that this augmentation in meaning is brought to its peak, precisely because of a lack of intuition. This surplus is the fruit of the whole set of historiographical operations. It is thus to be used for the benefit of the critical dimension of history. The idea of standing for is then the least bad way to render homage to a reconstructive effort that is the only one available for the service of truth in history.

## PART THREE, PRELUDE

1. "On the Utility and Liability of History for Life," trans. Richard T. Gray, in *Unfashionable Observations*, vol. 2 of *The Complete Works of Friedrich Nietzsche*, ed. Ernst Behler (Stanford: Stanford University Press, 1995), 83–167.

2. "The observations offered here are also unfashionable because I attempt to understand something in which our age justifiably takes pride—namely, its historical condition—as a detriment, an infirmity, a deficiency of the age, and furthermore, because I am even of the opinion that all of us suffer from a debilitating historical fever and that we at the very least need to recognize that we suffer from it" (ibid., 86).

3. An anthology of medical vocabulary, suited to the thematic of life, could be composed: saturation, nausea, distaste, degeneration, staggering weight, burden, infirmity, loss, break, death. On the other side, cure, health, remedy...

4. "But I have to concede this much to myself as someone who by occupation is a classical philologist, for I have no idea what the significance of classical philology would be in our age, if not to have an unfashionable effect—that is, to work against the time and thereby have an effect upon it, hopefully for the benefit of a future time" (ibid., 86–87).

5. A remark here regarding the French translation: *das Unhistorisches* must not be translated as "non-historicité" under penalty of spilling over into a separate problematic, precisely that of *Geschichtlichkeit*, which is framed by an entirely different philosophical horizon and constitutes a very different attempt to pass beyond the crisis of historicism. We shall return to this later.

6. "Only insofar as the truthful person has the unconditional will to be just is there anything great in that striving for truth that everywhere is so thoughtlessly glorified" (ibid., 123).

7. "Measuring past opinions and deeds according to the widespread opinions of the present moment is what these naïve historians call 'objectivity'" (ibid., 115). And further: "This is how the human being spins his web over the past and subdues it, this is how his artistic urge expresses itself—not, however, his urge to truth or justice. Objectivity and justice have nothing to do with one another" (126).

8. Does not the call to arms "'Division of labor!' 'In rank and file!'" (ibid., 136) find an echo in Pierre Nora's disillusioned admission: "Archive as much as you like: something will always be left out"?

9. Nietzsche cannot resist making the outrageous claim that Hegel identified the "universal process" with his own Berlin existence (ibid., 143–44). All that came after was no more than "only a musical coda of the world-historical rondo—or more precisely, as superfluous" (143). Of course, according to Nietzsche, Hegel "did not say this" (143), but instilled the reason to believe so in the minds of others.

10. Giorgio Colli and Mazzino Montinari, the editors of the standard critical edition of Nietzsche's works, cite an earlier version of this page: "Science views both as poisons; but it is really only a lack of science that lets them be conceived as poisons and not as remedies. A branch of science is lacking; a kind of higher hygiene that

examines the effects of science on life and determines the permitted amount from the standpoint of the health of a people or of a culture. Prescription: The ahistorical teaches forgetting, localizes, creates atmosphere, horizon; the suprahistorical makes more indifferent the allurements of history, has a soothing and diverting effect. Nature philosophy art pity" (ibid., 362).

## PART THREE, CHAPTER ONE

1. Reinhart Koselleck, *Futures Past: On the Semantics of Historical Time*, trans. Keith Tribe (Cambridge, Mass.: MIT Press, 1985).

2. In *Time and Narrative*, 3:208–16, I introduce Koselleck's analyses just after my confrontation with the Hegelian philosophy of history ("Should We Renounce Hegel?" 193–206), and I attempt to place them under the heading of a hermeneutics of historical consciousness, whose primary category is that of being-affected by the past, which I owe to Hans-Georg Gadamer. Koselleck is thus placed between Hegel whom I do renounce and Gadamer, to whose position I adhere. What is then lacking in this arrangement is the recognition of a transcendental dimension of metahistorical categories. This recognition became possible only at the term of a patient reconstruction of the historiographical operation freed from the limitations of a dominant concern with narratology. It is in relation to the *models* of the historiographical operation that the *categories* examined by Koselleck define their metahistorical status. I am not thereby repudiating the hermeneutical approach of *Time and Narrative*: Koselleck himself participates in the research group that publishes under the heading *Poetik und Hermeneutik*, alongside Harald Weinrich and Karl Heinz Stierle. It was in volume 5 of this collection, under the title *Geschichte, Ereignis und Erzählung* (History, Event, Narrative) that the articles reprinted in *Futures Past* were first published: "History, Histories, and Formal Structures of Time" (92–104) and "Representation, Event, and Structure" (104–15).

3. The title *Futures Past* can be understood in the sense of the future as it no longer is, the future over and done with, characteristic of the period in which history as such was thought.

4. If Kant did not write the critique of historical judgment that would form the third part of the *Critique of Judgment*, he did indicate its outlines in *The Conflict of the Faculties*, trans. Mary J. Gregor and Robert Anchor, in *Religion and Rational Theology*, ed. Allen W. Wood and George Di Giovanni (Cambridge: Cambridge University Press, 1996), 233–327. In the second part, section 5 we read: "There must be some experience in the human race which, as an event, points to the disposition and capacity of the human race to be the cause of its own advance toward the better, and (since this should be the act of a being endowed with freedom), toward the human race as being the author of this advance. But from a given

cause an event as an effect can be predicted [only] if the circumstances prevail which contribute to it" (301). This "prophetic history of the human race" (301) is based upon signs that actual history provides of the cosmopolitan destination of the human race. The French Revolution was one of these signs for Kant. He says about it: "Such a phenomenon in human history *will not be forgotten*" (section 7, 304).

5. Koselleck devotes a separate analysis to this notion of disposability (*Futures Past*, 198–212).

6. Treitschke's statement, related by Koselleck, is often cited: "If history were an exact science, then we should be in the position to reveal the futures of states. But we are not able to do this; everywhere, historical science runs up against the puzzle of personality. It is persons, men, who make history; men like Luther, Frederick the Great, and Bismarck. This great heroic truth will remain true forever; and it will always be a puzzle to we mortals how these men appear, the right man at the right time. Genius is formed by the times, but is not created by it" (quoted by Koselleck, ibid., 313–14).

7. In the introduction to *Faire de l'histoire*, the novelty of the undertaking is stressed: "A collective and diverse work, this book claims nonetheless to illustrate and promote a new type of history." The novelty, under three headings: "New Problems," "New Concepts," "New Objects," corresponds to the parceling up of the historical field during that period. In this sense, it is in agreement with the unification of the concept of history that will be at issue below.

8. Reinhart Koselleck, "Geschichte," *Geschichtliche Grundbegriffe* (Stuttgart: Klett-Cotta, 1975), 2:593–717.

9. This is the title given to a collection of articles, including "The Concept of History," in *Geschichtliche Grundbegriffe*.

10. "The uncovering of a naturally historical time in the concept of history coincides with the experience of modern Times" (ibid., 21).

11. "This world of experience has an immanent claim to truth" (ibid., 22). And further: "To express this in the form of an exaggeration, history [*Geschichte*] is a kind of transcendental category concerning the condition of the possibility of histories" (ibid., 27). Droysen will say that "it is itself its own form of knowledge" (quoted in ibid.).

12. In Koselleck's incredibly well-documented essay, one learns of the separate contributions of thinkers as important as Chladenius, Wieland, Humboldt, Schlegel, Schiller, Novalis, and, in particular, Herder, to say nothing of the greats of the German historical school: Ranke, Droysen, Niebuhr, Burckhardt.

13. "The only Thought which Philosophy brings with it to the contemplation of History, is the simple conception of *Reason*; that Reason is the Sovereign

of the World; that the history of the world, therefore, presents us with a rational process. This conviction and intuition is a hypothesis in the domain of history as such. In that of Philosophy it is no hypothesis. It is there proved by speculative cognition, that Reason—and this term may here suffice us, without investigating the relation sustained by the Universe to the Divine Being—is *Substance*, as well as *Infinite Power*; its own *Infinite Material* underlying all the natural and spiritual life which it originates, as also the *Infinite Form*—that which sets this Material in motion. . . . That this 'Idea' or 'Reason' is the *True*, the *Eternal*, the absolutely *powerful* essence; that it reveals itself in the World, and that in the World nothing else is revealed but this and its honor and glory—is the thesis which, as we have said, has been proved in Philosophy, and is here regarded as demonstrated." G. W. F. Hegel, *The Philosophy of History*, trans. J. Sibree (Buffalo, N.Y.: Prometheus Books, 1991), 9–10. Cf. *Time and Narrative*, 3:193–206: "Should We Renounce Hegel?" It is true that *The Philosophy of History* is Hegel's weakest work, of little weight in comparison to the *Encyclopedia* and to his great *Logic*, which remain the Himalayas to climb—and to vanquish.

14. Even within the limits of this prudent formulation, the idea of world history conceived as a leading science seems so uncertain in Kant's eyes that he considers it not yet to have been written nor yet to have found its Kepler or its Newton.

15. Koselleck cites a letter sent to Marx by Ruge, dating from 1843: "We can continue our past only by making a clear break with it" (*L'Expérience de l'histoire*, 85). In *The German Ideology*, Marx holds that the arrival of communism will transform current history into world history but only at the price of downgrading all of previous history to the stage of prehistory.

16. The contradiction is performative in the sense that it concerns not the semantic content of the statement but the act that utters it and holds itself as such to be true and not relative.

17. According to Koselleck, J. M. Chladenius, as early as the eighteenth century, is held to have perceived the destructive effect of the idea of point of view (*L'Expérience de l'histoire*, 75). Koselleck notes that "Chladenius sets us a theoretical framework that has not been surpassed to this day" (76). However, it is F. Schlegel, in *Über die neuere Geschichte: Vorlesungen* (1810–11), who, with complete lucidity, is said to have formulated against Hegel "the aporia that appears between the fact of having aimed at truth and the recognition of its historical relativity" (79 and n. 279). More seriously, he is held to have perceived at the heart of the Hegelian project itself a deadly contradiction between the ambition of embracing "the totality of viewpoints" (an expression that can be read in Hegel himself in the introduction to his lectures on the *Philosophy of History*) and the philosopher's plea on behalf of freedom, reason, right. Between totalizing and taking a position,

between speculative reason and militant judgment, a subtle contradiction is held to have slipped in.

18. Hans Robert Jauss, "La 'Modernité' dans la tradition littéraire et la conscience d'aujourd'hui," in *Pour une esthétique de la réception*, trans. C. Maillard (Paris: Gallimard, 1978), 158–209.

19. The very word "modernity," Jauss notes at the beginning of his essay "presents . . . the paradox of obviously denying at every moment by its historical recurrence the claim that it affirms" (ibid., 158). A relativity comparable to that which infected the claim of "history itself" to reflect upon itself absolutely will also strike with its full force the claim of "our" modernity to absolutely distinguish itself from all the modernities of the past. The unavoidable controversies that will afflict the discourse on modernity will be only briefly mentioned, as they represent a symptom complementary to the incapacity of the consciousness of the present totally to reflect upon itself.

20. Jacques Le Goff, *History and Memory*, trans. Steven Rendall and Elizabeth Claman (New York: Columbia University Press, 1992). The English language edition contains four of ten articles ("Past/Present," "Antique (Ancient)/Modern," "Memory," and "History") published in the *Enciclopedia Einaudi* (Turin, 1977–82); Einaudi later published these ten articles separately under the title *Storia et memoria* (Turin, 1986). In "Past/Present" (1–19), the author interrogates, in succession, psychologists (Piaget, Fraisse), linguists (Weinrich, Benveniste), anthropologists (Lévi-Strauss, Hobsbawm), and historians of history (Châtelet, Dupront, Bloch).

21. Ibid., "Antique (Ancient)/Modern," 21–50.

22. We owe to Ernst Robert Curtius the great erudite investigation, *European Literature and the Latin Middle Ages*, trans. Willard Trask (London: Routledge and Kegan Paul, 1953). Jauss underscores the originality of medieval conceptuality, in contrast to Curtius who saw in it only the repetition of a model coming from antiquity itself ("La 'Modernité,'" 159). In particular, the recourse to a typology constitutes a form of original enchantment. The idea of "typological overflowing" even seems to be the key to the famous equivocation contained in the praise which John of Salisbury attributes to Bernard of Chartres: "We are dwarfs standing on the shoulders of giants." What is more honorable, the solidity of a giant, or the perspicacious view of a dwarf?

23. On the period of the Renaissance, see Jauss, *Pour une esthétique de la réception*, 170–75.

24. Regarding the quarrel of the Ancients and the Moderns, see Jauss, ibid., 175–89. The "quarrel," Jauss notes, allows us to fix the date of the beginning of the century of the Enlightenment in France (175) (as, moreover, Diderot and

d'Alembert will be happy to proclaim in the *Encyclopedia*), the issue being the alleged exemplarity of the Ancient models.

25. Jauss cites the 1798 *Dictionnaire de l'Académie*: romantic "is normally said of places, of landscapes, which remind the imagination of descriptions, poems, and novels" (*Pour une esthétique de la reception*, 187–97). We mentioned earlier, with Edward Casey, the role of landscapes in our consciousness of inhabited space. In the case of the Germans, it is Herder and, following him, German romanticism that elevates the Gothic to the level of poetic truth.

26. With Stendhal, Jauss notes, "romanticism is no longer the attraction of what transcends the present, the polar opposition between everyday reality and the far-off past; it is actuality, the beauty of today, which, becoming that of yesterday, will inevitably lose its vibrant appeal and will no longer be able to offer anything but a historical interest." Romanticism is "the art of presenting to the people the literary works, which, in the present state of their habits and beliefs, are likely to provide them with the greatest possible pleasure. Classicism, on the contrary, presents to them the literature that provided the greatest possible pleasure to their grandparents" (quoted in ibid., 196).

27. Vincent Descombes, "Une question de chronologie," in Jacques Poulain, ed., *Penser au présent* (Paris: l'Harmattan, 1998), 43–79.

28. "Condorcet by no means believed that there were stages of a development of the mind or incommensurable frames of reference. Any idea of relativity is foreign to him" (ibid., 61).

29. Vincent Descombes's essay does not go beyond this conclusion: "I have tried to defend the following thesis: the notion of modernity expresses, on the part of a French writer, a (reluctantly granted) consent to be able to represent only a part of humanity. To speak of our modernity is to accept not incarnating immediately, in our language, in our institutions, in our masterpieces, the highest aspirations of humankind" (ibid., 77). To pursue this reflection further, see his *Philosophie par gros temps* (Paris: Minuit, 1989).

30. Charles Taylor, *The Ethics of Authenticity* (Cambridge, Mass.: Harvard University Press, 1991).

31. Jean-François Lyotard, *The Postmodern Condition*, trans. Geoff Bennington and Brian Massumi (Minneapolis: University of Minnesota Press, 1984), 3.

32. "The grand narrative has lost its credibility, regardless of what mode of unification it uses, regardless of whether it is a speculative narrative or a narrative of emancipation" (ibid., 37).

33. Jürgen Habermas, "Modernity: An Incomplete Project," in Hal Foster, ed. and trans., *The Anti-aesthetic* (Port Townsend, Wash.: Bay Press, 1983), 3–15. This was Habermas's speech delivered on the occasion of the Adorno Prize

awarded by the city of Frankfurt, September 11, 1980. The author denounces the aestheticizing tendency of postmodern discourses and the danger of conservatism and of opportunism related to the abandonment of the great causes of liberal politics.

34. "Consensus is only a particular state of discussion, not its end" (Lyotard, *The Postmodern Condition*, 65).

35. Lyotard's most significant book is in fact *The Differend*, trans. Georges Van Den Abbeele (Minneapolis: University of Minnesota Press, 1988). After an ex-ordium without concession—"As distinguished from a litigation, a differend would be a case of conflict, between (at least) two parties, that cannot be equitably re-solved for lack of a rule of judgment applicable to both arguments" (xi)—follows a long transition through "obligation" (107–27) in a tone reminiscent of Levinas—"Causality through freedom gives signs, never ascertainable effects, nor chains of effects" (127)—before the work concludes with a series of narrative figures placed under the title of the last chapter, "The Sign of History" (151–81). Does not the enigmatic ending of the book bring us back from the differend to litigation? And does not the litigation concern the order of discourse maintained here by the analysis of genres of discourse? The author directs this very objection to himself. "In declaring that there is a litigation, you have already passed judgment from a 'universal' point of view, that of the analysis of genres of discourse. The interests put into play through this point of view are not those of the narrations. You too do them a wrong" (158).

36. Thomas Nagel, *Equality and Partiality* (New York: Oxford University Press, 1991).

37. Carlo Ginzburg, *The Judge and the Historian,* trans. Anthony Shugaar (New York: Verso, 2002).

38. Ibid., 240. The circumstances of this essay are not unrelated to our dis-cussion. The great historian develops a closely knit argument on behalf of a friend sentenced to a lengthy prison term for acts of terrorism going back eighteen years, at the time of the hot fall of 1969. The verdict was based for the most part on the confession of another defendant, who had "repented." The paradox of the essay lies in the fact that it is the historian who strives here to refute the judge, despite the credit in principle granted by both sides in the handling of proof.

39. After quoting Lucien Febvre's "Inaugural Lecture at the Collège de France," based upon his remarks on the role of hypothesis, Ginzburg mentions favorably Marc Bloch's exemplary work, *The Royal Touch: Sacred Monarchy and Scrofula in England and France*, which exposed the mechanism of belief by which the kings were able to be graced with the power to cure by their touch those

suffering from scrofula. Here we encounter the Ginzburg familiar with the trials for witchcraft, in which the inquisitors were able to convince the accused themselves of devilry.

40. I owe the observations that follow to Antoine Garapon, "La Justice et l'inversion morale du temps," in *Pourquoi se souvenir?* (Paris: Grasset, 1999).

41. Paul Ricoeur, "The Act of Judging" and "Interpretation and/or Argumentation," *The Just*, trans. David Pellauer (Chicago: University of Chicago Press, 2000), 109–32.

42. Wilhelm Schapp, *In Geschichten verstrickt* (Wiesbaden: B. Heymann, 1976).

43. Mark Osiel, *Mass Atrocity, Collective Memory, and the Law* (New Brunswick, N.J.: Transaction, 1997).

44. Chapter 2, "Solidarity through Civil Dissensus," provides an excellent summary of these theses (ibid., 36–55). Let us retain the bold expression "poetics of legal storytelling" (3), which covers the entire undertaking.

45. Chapter 4, "Losing Perspective, Distorting History" (ibid., 79–141); chapter 8, "Making Public Memory, Publicly" (ibid., 240–92).

46. Ernst Rienhard Piper, ed., *Devant l'histoire: Les documents de la controverse sur la singularité de l'extermination des Juifs par le régime nazi*, trans. Brigitte Vergne-Cain et al. (Paris: Cerf, 1988). This is the second time that I have broached the historical problems relating to the Holocaust. I did this first within the epistemological framework as it applies to the problem of historical representation; the question then concerned the necessary limits involved in representation both with regard to the exposition of events, through language or otherwise, and with regard to the "realistic" scope of the representation. Here, the same facts are placed under the intersecting spotlights of axiological judgment and historiographical judgment.

47. Ibid., 37ff.

48. Another protagonist in this debate, Michael Stürmer, defined the singularity of Auschwitz by the break in temporal continuity as it affected national identity. This break also has antecedents in the German past: the absence of memory's anchorage in certainties which, in the pre-Hitler period, created "a country without a history." For, is not everything possible in a country without a history? Not only the recent barbarism but also the current reticence to seek "the lost history" (ibid., 27). From this results the task the authors are invited to perform: exit this obsession by restoring continuity. For his part, Andreas Hillgruber, the author of *Zweierlei Untergang: Die Zerschlagung des Deutschen Reiches und das Ende des Europäischen Judentums* (Berlin: Siedler, 1986), juxtaposes the sufferings of the Germans in the eastern part of Germany at the time of the Russian front and that of the Jews at the time of their extermination, without making explicit the "somber interaction" of

the two series of events, the "destruction of the German Reich" and the "end of European Judaism." The author thus creates a suspense that leaves the door open for a definitive judgment which the historian is not expected to formulate.

49. Jürgen Habermas, "A Kind of Settling of Damages: Apologetic Tendencies," *The New Conservatism*, trans. Shierry Weber Nicholsen (Cambridge, Mass.: MIT Press, 1989), 207–48.

50. It is indeed difficult for a narrative to be totally without any moral evaluation of the characters and their actions. Aristotle, in the *Poetics*, speaks of tragic figures as "better than us" and of comic figures as "the same as us" or "worse than us." It is true that he banishes the inhuman from the poetic field. This makes Osiel say that, among all the literary genres, even tragedy is not suitable for the legal narrative, but solely the morality play (*Mass Atrocity*, 283ff.).

51. I refer to my theses on the ascription of memory to a range of subjects (see part 1, chap. 3). Later, I shall encounter a comparable problem concerning the multiple ascription of death and dying.

52. Hannah Arendt, *The Origins of Totalitarianism* (New York: Harcourt, Brace and World, 1968).

53. It is from this angle that I first encountered this problem in my articles of the 1950s, collected in *History and Truth*, trans. Charles A. Kelby (Evanston, Ill.: Northwestern University Press, 1965). In the preface to the first edition, there is a discussion of "the limited truth of the historian's history" (5); but this was in the perspective of a "philosophical history of philosophy" which was at that time the subject of my teaching. The polarity between the critique of historical knowledge and an eschatological sense of the infinitely postponed unity of the true assured the dynamic of this collection of essays, alternating between the "epistemological concern" and the "ethico-cultural concern" (11). The stakes then were metahistorical, namely, "the courage to do the history of philosophy without the philosophy of history" (7). In truth, only the first essay (from 1952), "Objectivity and Subjectivity in History" (21–40), answered to the ambitious title of the first part of the book: "Truth in the Knowledge of History."

54. Raymond Aron, *Introduction to the Philosophy of History: An Essay on the Limits of Historical Objectivity*, trans. George J. Irwin (Boston: Beacon Press, 1961). His complementary thesis was titled *La Philosophie critique de l'histoire: Essai sur une théorie allemande de l'histoire* (Paris: Vrin, 1938). It is therefore to Raymond Aron that I owe the expression "critical philosophy of history." There is a more recent edition of this latter work, revised and annotated by Sylvie Mesure (Paris: Gallimard, 1986).

55. Henri-Irénée Marrou, *The Meaning of History*, trans. Robert J. Olson (Baltimore: Helicon, 1966).

56. In an appendix to the French edition, written in 1975, Marrou favorably salutes Certeau's work, *The Writing of History*, and confronts, on the side of the skeptical school, the suspicions of Roland Barthes expressed in the theme of the "reality effect."

57. "Like every scientific subjectivity, the historian's subjectivity represents the triumph of a good subjectivity over a bad one" (*History and Truth*, 30). "The historian's craft makes history *and* the historian" (ibid., 31). At that time I emphasized in succession the judgment regarding what was important, the historian's membership in the same history, the same humanity as men of the past, and the transference into another subjectivity adopted as a sort of perspective.

58. René Rémond (in collaboration with J.-F. Sirinelli), *Notre siècle, 1918–1988*, the final volume of the series *Histoire de France*, whose overall editor is Jean Favier (Paris: Fayard, 1988).

59. Henry Rousso confirms and completes René Rémond's analysis in *The Haunting Past: History, Memory, and Justice in Contemporary France*, trans. Ralph Schoolcraft (Philadelphia: University of Pennsylvania Press, 2002), chap. 2, "For a History of the Present," 25–47. Following Marc Bloch, he recalls that the dialectic between the past and the present is constitutive of the profession of historian, but that "analysis of the present allows us to understand the past" (28). Did not Marc Bloch dare to write *The Strange Defeat* under the influence of events? With the history of the present day, politics and events return in force. The objection regarding the lack of distance pleading in favor of a necessary delay is held to be most often merely an ideological alibi varying according to circumstances. The challenge is considered to be worth taking up on behalf of a dialogue among the living, among contemporaries, and of a questioning directed precisely to the undetermined border that separates the past from the present and, finally, the archives from testimony. It is along this border that the reshaping of the past in collective representations ultimately takes place; it is also here that this obsession must be uncovered and exorcized.

60. Max Weber, *Economy and Society: An Outline of Interpretive Sociology*, ed. Günther Roth and Claus Wittich; trans. Ephraim Fischoff et al. (New York: Bedminster Press, 1968; reprinted Berkeley and Los Angeles: University of California Press, 1978), sect. 1–3; G. H. von Wright, *Explanation and Understanding* (London: Routledge and Kegan Paul, 1971). Von Wright argues on behalf of a mixed model that links together causal segments and teleological segments implied jointly by the intervention of human agents on the social as well as on the physical plane.

61. Jacques Rancière, *The Names of History: On the Poetics of Knowledge*, trans. Hassan Melehy (Minneapolis: University of Minnesota Press, 1994).

62. I, for my part, have called the response of narrative knowledge to the aporias of temporality a "poetics of narrative." See *Time and Narrative*, vol. 3, section 2.

63. Arlette Farges, *Le Goût de l'archive* (Paris: Seuil, 1989).

64. "Such a study falls under what I have chosen to call a *poetics of knowledge*, a study of the set of literary procedures by which a discourse escapes literature, gives itself the status of a science and signifies this status" (*The Names of History*, 8). The word "knowledge" signifies the potential amplitude of the reflective operation.

65. The undecidable, of which I spoke at the end of chapter 2, between memory and history is akin to this poetic indetermination of a principle of "indiscernability" (ibid., 23).

66. We obliquely encountered this third dimension both in discussing the portrait of the king and the discourse of the praise of greatness, and in discussing the great crimes of the twentieth century that have pushed to the forefront the figure of the citizen as third party between the judge and the historian.

67. The discourse on the "dead king" opens another problematic, namely, death in history; I will return in the next chapter to Rancière's contribution to this discussion.

68. Revisionism in general is summed up in a simple formula: "*nothing happened of what was told*" (*The Names of History*, 36). The entire problematic of "standing for" is put to the test here.

## PART THREE, CHAPTER TWO

1. François Dosse places the fourth section of his book, *L'Histoire* (Paris: Armin Colin, 2000), under the sign of the "lacerations of time" (96–136). The author leads the reader from Aristotle and Augustine, passing by way of Husserl and Heidegger, up to the great forms of questioning symbolized by the names of Walter Benjamin, Friedrich Nietzsche, Norbert Elias, and, finally, Michel Foucault.

2. Martin Heidegger, *Sein und Zeit*. This work was published in 1927 in Edmund Husserl's *Jahrbuch für Phänomenologie und phänomenologische Forschung*, vol. 8, and simultaneously in a separate volume. I shall cite the English translation of *Being and Time* by Joan Stambaugh (Albany: SUNY Press, 1996).

3. In this regard, I have nothing to change but only to add to the discussion that I proposed in volume 3 of *Time and Narrative*: that discussion was framed by a question, which is no longer mine here, the question of the relation between a phenomenology of lived time and a cosmology of physical time; then, history was placed under the heading of a "narrative poetics" held to render the "aporetics of time," which initially paralyzed thought, productive.

4. François Dosse reserves for the fifth section of *L'Histoire* the formidable question of the crisis of *telos*: "From Providence to the Progress of Reason" (137–68), the road hesitates between Fortune, the divine hand, reason in history, historical materialism, losing itself in the crisis of historicism.

5. Paul Ricoeur, *Time and Narrative*, 1:42–45, "Included Discordance." The emphasis was placed at that time on the difficult—perhaps unlocatable—relation between the time of the soul and cosmic time; calendar time was proposed as one connector in the transition from one to the other. A different debate is opened here on the border of the ontology of the historical condition and the epistemology of historical knowledge.

6. And again: "If we may speak in these terms, I can see [*video*] three times and I admit [*fateorque*] that they do exist" (Augustine, *Confessions* 11.20).

7. One reason specific to Platonizing Christianity for privileging the present has to do with the reference of the living present to eternity conceived as a *nunc stans*, in other words, as an eternal present. But this eternal present is less a contribution to the constitution of the present of the soul than it serves as a counterpoint and a contrast: our present suffers from not being an eternal present; this is why it requires the dialectic of the other two instances.

8. Henri-Irénée Marrou, *L'Ambivalence de l'histoire chez saint Augustin* (Paris: Vrin, 1950); *La Théologie de l'histoire* (Paris: Seuil, 1968).

9. Françoise Dastur, *Heidegger and the Question of Time*, trans. François Raffoul and David Pettigrew (Atlantic Highlands, N.J.: Humanities Press, 1998).

10. In *Time and Narrative*, I devoted lengthy analyses to preparatory studies concerning, on the one hand, hermeneutical phenomenology (3:61–63) and, on the other, the central position of care in the ontology of Da-sein (3:63–68).

11. Concerning the interpretation of Da-sein as care (focusing on section 41), see Françoise Dastur, *Heidegger and the Question of Time*, 42–55, and Jean Greisch, *Ontologie et temporalité: Esquisse d'une interprétation intégrale de «Sein und Zeit»* (Paris: Presses Universitaires de France, 1994), 236ff.: "Although we might have the impression that with care the existential analysis had arrived at safe harbor, this is not so. Care is much more a starting point than an end point. Thus is proclaimed the necessity . . . for a second great navigation, which occupies the second part of *Sein und Zeit*: the analysis of the relations between *Dasein* and temporality which care allows us to perceive" (241). It is the ahead-of-itself that serves as the effect of the declaration here.

12. Jean Greisch elevates to the place of honor "the recapitulative definition of the authentic possibility of being-toward-death": "anticipation." A more vigorous plea on behalf of an attitude in the face of death close to that articulated in *Sein und*

*Zeit* can be found in Françoise Dastur, *Death: An Essay on Finitude*, trans. John Llewelyn (London: Athlone, 1996).

13. One can mention in this regard the strong comments of Simone Weil on destiny and misfortune. It is always in spite of a contrary destiny that one must live and love. Simone Weil, "Malheur et joie," *Oeuvres* (Paris: Gallimard, 1989), 681–784.

14. One can reread, with the benefit of this wisdom, chapter 20 of book 1 of Montaigne's *Essays*: "To philosophize is to learn how to die." Just like the enemy that cannot be avoided, "we must learn to stand firm and to fight it. To begin depriving death of its greatest advantage over us, let us adopt a way clean contrary to that common one; let us deprive death of its strangeness; let us frequent it, let us get used to it; let us have nothing more often in mind than death. At every instant let us evoke it in our imagination under all its aspects." And again: "A man who has learned how to die has unlearned how to be a slave. Knowing how to die gives us freedom from subjection and constraint" (*The Complete Essays*, trans. M. A. Screech [London: Penguin Books, 1991], 96).

15. Emmanuel Levinas, *Totality and Infinity: An Essay on Exteriority*, trans. Alphonso Lingis (Pittsburgh: Duquesne University Press, 1969), 232–36.

16. "The identifying of death with nothingness befits the death of the other in murder" (ibid., 232).

17. "This nothingness is an interval beyond which lurks a hostile will" (ibid., 236). Indeed we are "exposed to a foreign will" (236).

18. "The Desire into which the threatened will dissolves no longer defends the powers of a will, but, as the goodness whose meaning death cannot efface, has its center outside of itself" (ibid.).

19. Levinas concludes these somber pages by evoking "the other chance that the will seizes upon in the time left it by its being against death: the founding of institutions in which the will ensures a meaningful, but impersonal world beyond death" (ibid., 236). The discussions of justice in *Otherwise than Being or Beyond Essence*, trans. Alphonso Lingis (Dordrecht: Kluwer, 1991), give depth to this rapid sketch of a politics of goodness in the shadow of death.

20. Genesis 35:29; 49:33. Montaigne was not unaware of this wisdom. Earlier we heard him speak of death as the enemy to which we must accustom ourselves. We must also hear him pay justice to it: "The first part of equity is equality. Who can complain of being included when all are included?" (*Essays*, book 1, chap. 20, 104).

21. "Anticipatory resoluteness understands Da-sein in its essential being-in-debt. This understanding means to take over being-in-debt while existing, to *be* the thrown ground of nullity. But to take over thrownness means to authentically *be* Da-sein in the *way that it always already was*. Taking over thrownness, however,

is possible only in such a way that futural Da-sein *can be* its ownmost 'how it already was,' that is, its 'having-been.' Only because Da-sein in general *is* as I *am*-having-been, can it come futurally toward itself in such a way that it comes-*back*. Authentically futural, Da-sein is authentically *having-been*. Anticipation of the most extreme and ownmost possibility comes back understandingly to one's ownmost *having-been*. Da-sein can *be* authentically having-been only because it is futural. In a way, having-been arises from the future" (*Being and Time*, 299, trans. modified).

22. "The concepts of 'future,' 'past,' and 'present' initially grew out of the inauthentic understanding of time" (ibid., 300).

23. "Michel Foucault," in Michel de Certeau, *L'Absent de l'histoire* (Paris: Mame, 1973), 125–32. This outside thinking is held to direct the entire search for meaning toward this "region in which death prowls" (the expression is taken from Foucault in *The Order of Things*). But "to speak of the death which founds all language is not yet to confront but perhaps to evade the death that attacks discourse itself" (132).

24. One cannot too strongly emphasize the influence exerted on the general theory of history by the special history of the mystics in the work of Certeau. Surin is at the center of this history of forms of spirituality apprehended in their language (Certeau, *The Mystic Fable: The Sixteenth and Seventeenth Centuries*, trans. Michael B. Smith [Chicago: University of Chicago Press, 1992]). Besides Surin, Henri Bremond's "philosophy of saints," to which he devotes a substantial review dating from 1966 in *L'Absent de l'histoire*, caught the attention of Certeau. Now this "philosophy of saints" gravitates around nocturnal sentiments such as "desolation," "distress," "emptiness" ("Henri Bremond, historien d'un silence," in *L'Absent de l'histoire*, 73–108). What is remarkable is that, for Certeau, the past is to historical discourse what God is to mystical discourse: absent. What has elapsed is the quasi-"mystical" absent of historical discourse. Certeau indeed says: "That occurred and is no longer." This equation is at the center of the essay, "Histoire et mystique," first published in 1972 in the *Revue d'histoire de la spiritualité* (this essay is contemporaneous with the writing of "L'opération historique," published in *Faire de l'histoire*). It is clearly stated at the end of the study, speaking of the relations between the historical and the mystical, that "this is the hypothesis that little by little formed an itinerary of history in the field of the spiritual literature of the seventeenth century" (*L'Absent de l'histoire*, 167).

25. "The Place of the Dead and the Place of the Reader," in *The Writing of History*, 99–102.

26. "'To mark' a past is to make a place for the dead, but also to redistribute the space of possibility, to determine negatively *what must be done*, and consequently

to use the narrativity that buries the dead as a way of establishing a place for the living" (ibid., 100).

27. Rancière quotes this beautiful passage from Michelet's *Journal*, edited by Pierre Vialaneix: "We must hear words that were never spoken. . . . Only then do the dead accept the sepulcher" (quoted by Rancière, *The Names of History*, 62–63).

28. We also owe to Hegel, for better or for worse, the taste for abstract terms ending in *-heit* and *-keit*. In this regard, the term *Geschichtlichkeit* does not spoil the string of substantivized adjectives, stemming from simple substantives (*Lebendigkeit, Innerlichkeit, Offenbarkeit,* not to mention the astonishing *Steinigkeit*, designating the stoneness of stone!). L. Renthe-Fink supplies an abbreviated list of these in *Geschichtlichkeit: Ihr Terminologie und begrifficher Ursprung bei Hegel, Haym, Dilthey und Yorck* (Göttingen: Vandenhoeck und Ruprecht, 1964), 30–31.

29. The first English translation of Heidegger's *Being and Time*, trans. John Macquarrie and Edward Robinson (New York: Harper and Row, 1962), rendered *Geschichtlichkeit* by "historicality." The more recent translation by Joan Stambaugh, and the one quoted here, uses "historicity" instead.

30. I am grateful for this brief history of the usages of the term *Geschichtlichkeit* to Leonhard von Renthe-Fink's *Geschichtlichkeit.* I would add to it the important monograph of Gerhard Bauer, *Geschichtlichkeit: Wege und Irrwege eines Begriffs* (Berlin: Walter de Gruyter, 1963).

31. A competing usage which has not entirely disappeared designates the factual character of a reported event, in particular, the non-legendary character of evangelical narratives. In this way, exegetes still speak today of the historicity of Jesus, especially after the debate opened by David Friedrich Strauss and the impetus of the *Geschichte der Leben-Jesu-Forschung*, started by Albert Schweitzer at the beginning of the twentieth century. It is in this sense of the true factual character of events that the term "historicity" figures in 1872 as a neologism in the Littré *Dictionnaire*. It will also come to pass that a *geschichtlich* Christ will be opposed to a *historisch* Jesus!

32. Daniel Marguerat and Jean Zumstein, eds., *La Mémoire et le temps: Mélanges offerts à Pierre Bonnard* (Geneva: Labor et Fides, 1991).

33. It is not surprising that Schleiermacher set himself up as the mediator between these two exemplary "moments."

34. The adjective *geschichte* is in competition with *historisch* as early as the announcement of the program of a "critique of historical [*historisch*] reason." See Dilthey's 1875 essay, "Über das Studium des Geschichte der Wissenschaften vom Menschen, der Gesellschaft und dem Staat," in *Gesammelte Schriften* (Stuttgart: B. G. Teubner, 1968), 5:31–73.

35. Wilhelm Dilthey, *Introduction to the Human Sciences*, trans. Michael Neville, ed. Rudolf A. Makkreel and Frithjof Rodi (Princeton: Princeton University Press, 1989).

36. Concerning the term *Geisteswissenschaften* (human sciences), Dilthey admits that he does not have any adequate term available; for lack of anything better, he adopts the term introduced into German in 1849 to translate the expression "moral sciences" found in John Stuart Mill's *Logic*.

37. Wilhelm Dilthey, *The Formation of the Historical World in the Human Sciences*, trans. Rudolf A. Makkreel and John Scanlon (Princeton: Princeton University Press, 2002), 101–209.

38. In her "Translator's Notes" to the French edition, Sylvie Mesure observes: "*Zusammenhang*, a real cross for every translation of Dilthey, is most often translated in French by 'ensemble' but the word also sometimes means 'structure,' 'system,' 'coherence,' or 'context.' *Bedeutungszusammenhang*, 'meaningful whole,' designates a signifying ensemble both as a totality and in its elements." Wilhelm Dilthey, *L'Édification du monde historique dans les sciences de l'esprit*, trans. Sylvie Mesure in Dilthey, *Oeuvres*, vol. 3 (Paris: Cerf, 1988), 27–28. In his French translation of *Being and Time*, E. Martineau translates *Lebenszusammenhang* by "enchaînement de la vie." One can also say "connectedness of life" (Macquarrie and Robinson) or "connection of life" (Stambaugh), reserving the notion of "narrative coherence" for the level of the narrative.

39. Jean Greisch, in *Ontologie et temporalité*, provides two significant statements from *The Formation of the Historical World*: "All the categories of life and of history are forms of expression that . . . receive a universal application in the area of the human sciences. The expressions themselves come from lived experience itself" (quoted by Greisch, 353).

40. Dilthey, "Antrittsrede in der Akademie der Wissenschaften" (1887), in *Gesammelte Schriften*, 5:10–11. "Our century has recognized in the historical school the historicity of man and of social organizations" (11).

41. "Culture is, in the first place, the weaving together of purposeful systems. Each of these—like language, law, myth and religion, poetry, philosophy—possesses an inner lawfulness that conditions its structure, which in turn determines its development. The historical character of culture was first grasped at that time. This was the achievement of Hegel and Schleiermacher. They permeated the abstract systematic structure of culture with the consciousness of its essential historicity. The comparative method and the developmental-historical approach were applied to culture. What a circle of men were at work here!" ("Reminiscences on Historical Studies at the University of Berlin" [1903], trans. Patricia Van Tuyl, in *Selected Works*, vol. 4, *Hermeneutics and the Study of History*, ed. Rudolf A. Makkreel and

Frithjof Rodi [Princeton: Princeton University Press, 1996], 387). This brief discourse nonetheless ends on a troubled note: "The historical world view liberated the human spirit from the last chains that natural science and philosophy have not yet broken. But where are the means to overcome the anarchy of opinions that then threatens to befall us? To the solution of the long series of problems that are connected with this, I have devoted my whole life. I see the goal. If I fall short along the way, then I hope my young traveling companions, my students, will follow it to the end" (389).

42. The correspondence between Dilthey and Yorck can be read in Wilhelm Dilthey, *Briefwechsel zwischen Wilhelm Dilthey und dem Grafen Paul Yorck von Wartenburg, 1877–1897*, ed. Sigrid von der Schulenburg (Halle, 1923).

43. Section 72, which inaugurates the series of analyses concerning historicity-historicality, begins by expressing "a serious reservation": "Has indeed the whole of Da-sein with respect to its authentic *being*-a-whole been captured in the fore-having of our existential analysis? It may be that the line of questioning related to the wholeness of Da-sein possesses a genuinely unequivocal character ontologically. The question itself may even have been answered with regard to *being-toward-the-end*. However, death is, after all, only the 'end' of Da-sein, and formally speaking, it is just *one* of the ends that embraces the totality of Da-sein" (*Being and Time*, 342).

44. What is aimed at here is what I called the third time of history in *Time and Narrative*, the time of traces, of generations, and of the great connectors between cosmic time and phenomenological time.

45. Jean Greisch underscores, in this regard, "the mixture of modesty and pretentiousness that this determination of the task presents." And he adds: "Is it sufficient to do justice to these disciplines [the human sciences], or must one not foresee the possibility of a more positive determination of the relation between the ontology of historicity and an epistemology of the historical sciences?" (*Ontologie et temporalité*, 357–58). This is the proposal that I develop in the pages that follow, in line with my remarks in *Time and Narrative*, vol. 3, in which I spoke of an "enrichment" of the primordial by means of a "innovative derivation" of one from the other (3:73).

46. "Thus the interpretation of the historicity of Da-sein turns out to be basically just a more concrete development of temporality" (*Being and Time*, 350). And later: "*Authentic being-toward-death, that is, the finitude of temporality, is the concealed ground of the historicity of Da-sein*" (353).

47. *Time and Narrative*, 3:78ff.; Jean Greisch, *Ontologie et temporalité*, 369–74.

48. Pierre Legendre, *L'Inestimable Objet de la transmission: Essai sur le principe généalogique en Occident* (Paris: Fayard, 1985), 9.

49. Jules Michelet, *Histoire de France*, présenté par Claude Mettra (Lausanne: Rencontre, 1965, 1967).

50. R. G. Collingwood, *The Idea of History*, a posthumous work first edited by T. M. Knox in 1946 (Oxford: Clarendon Press, 1956) on the basis of lectures delivered at Oxford in 1936, after Collingwood was named to the chair of philosophy and metaphysics, which were revised by the author up to 1940.

51. Jean Greisch (*Ontologie et temporalité*, 374) opportunely compares what Heidegger calls here the "history of transmission" to what Gadamer calls "effective-history [*Wirkungsgeschichte*]" (*Truth and Method*, 267). This important paragraph of *Truth and Method* should not be separated from the one that precedes it, dealing with the hermeneutical signification of "temporal distance": this is not to be understood as an empty space, a separation, but as a productive space of understanding, as a between that completes the hermeneutical circle formed together by interpretation and its vis-à-vis. The temporal distance understood in this way is the condition of "effective-history."

52. In *Oneself as Another*, I underscore the rich meaning of the metaphor of "reckoning," of "counting," which is found in many languages at the base of the idea of imputability ("accountability" in English, *Rechnungsfähigkeit* in German).

53. Jean Greisch evokes the verses of the biblical Qoheleth: "For everything its season, and for every activity under heaven its time: a time to be born and a time to die; a time to plant and a time to uproot" (Ecclesiastes 3:1–3). Greisch opens a discussion at this point (*Ontologie et temporalité*, 394–402) that cannot leave the historian indifferent: does the expression of common or public time offer a choice between two interpretations, the first emphasizing the otherness of the other, after the fashion of Levinas in *Time and the Other*, the second stressing the tie with spatial externality, in relation to the "places" we name along with the dates? Must one choose between these two readings? What we said above, in agreement with Edward Casey, about the "worldly" side of memory (part 1, chap. 1) argues in the second sense; what we said, on the other hand, about the threefold attribution of memory, to oneself, to close relations, and to distant others (part 1, chap. 3) argues in the first sense, in favor of a redistribution of time throughout the entire range of cases of attribution: one's own, close relations, distant others.

54. François Dosse had the fortuitous idea of ending the great inquiry of his work, *L'Histoire*, with the dialogue between history and memory ("Une histoire sociale de la mémoire," 169–93). The sixth course proposed by the author begins in "the national novel" (169ff.), attains its summit with Bergson and "the distinction between two memories," penetrates with Halbwachs into the period of the "history/memory dissociation," to end with the various forms of the mutual problematizing of the two great instances of retrospection. The final word is then

uttered by the instance of the future: from the horizon of expectation comes the invitation to "revisit the areas of shadow," to leave behind "rumination" for "creativity," in short, along with Koselleck, to place memory and history once again under the banner of the "future of the past."

55. See Christian Delacroix, "La Falaise et le rivage: Historie du 'tournant critique,'" *Espaces Temps, Les Cahiers* 59–60–61 (1995): 59–61, 86–111. Under the heading of T.C. (*tournant critique*) the author retraces the path that we followed in the first paragraphs of the chapter "Explanation/Understanding." His route passes by way of many authors that I have also encountered: Bernard Lepetit, the historians of the *microstoria*, Boltanski and Thévenot's sociology of cities. The November-December 1990 issue of *Annales*, on "mobilities," already confirmed this advent of the paradigm of action and of the actor by demanding that "the representations and theoretical and practical legitimations that the actors construct be taken seriously" (1273; quoted by Delacroix, 103).

56. See *Being and Time*, 41, 202, 269, 311–12, 314, 317, 318–19, 324, 337, 357, 374, 376, 377, 388–89; *Index zu Heideggers Sein und Zeit* (Tübingen: Niemeyer, 1961); see also Index to the English translation under the entry, "forgetting."

57. Bernard Lepetit, "Le présent de l'histoire," in *Les Formes de l'expérience*, 273. "It is in the transformation of the value of the present that one finds the origin of the change of situation of the past" (290).

58. Jacques Le Goff, *History and Memory*, trans. Steven Rendall and Elizabeth Claman (New York: Columbia University Press, 1992).

59. André Leroy-Gourhan, *Le Geste et la parole* (Paris: Albin Michel, 1964).

60. Le Goff follows the transition from "simple file cards," to paraphrase Leroy-Gourhan, in the forms of "mechanical writing" and "electronic sequencing" (*History and Memory*, 90). In this way gigantic bibliographical files are constructed, which will prompt the concern of Yerushalmi and Nora.

61. Krzysztof Pomian, "De l'histoire, partie de la mémoire, à la mémoire, objet d'histoire," *Revue de métaphysique et de morale*, no. 1 (1998): 63–110.

62. Richard Terdiman, *Present Past: Modernity and the Memory Crisis* (Ithaca: Cornell University Press, 1993). The work is devoted to "understanding modernity's relationship with memory" (3). The investigation is conducted in the spirit of the history of consciousness taught at the University of California at Santa Cruz and in the French Department of Stanford University, closely related to the thought of Michel de Certeau.

63. Terdiman, "The Mnemonics of Musset's *Confession*," ibid., 75–105.

64. The title of chapter 3 of *The Collective Memory* is "Collective Memory and Historical Memory." In the English translation, chapter 2 is titled "Historical Memory and Collective Memory."

65. These divisions "are imposed from outside upon every individual memory precisely because their source is not in any single one of them" (ibid., 54). This is "also true of those dates on the clockface of history" (54).

66. "The events and dates constituting the very substance of group life can be for the individual only so many external signs, which he can use as reference points only by going outside himself" (ibid.).

67. The first time the word is stated in the text it is prudently evoked as another memory, one termed "historical," "that would be composed only of national events unfamiliar to us as children" (ibid., 57).

68. We have already encountered this question of the generational tie in connection with the Kierkegaardian concept, taken up by Heidegger, of "repetition." At that time we discussed the institutional aspect of this filiation following P. Legendre.

69. *Time and Narrative*, 3:109–16.

70. Alfred Schutz, *The Phenomenology of the Social World*, trans. George Walsh and Frederick Lehnert (Evanston, Ill.: Northwestern University Press, 1967).

71. Elsewhere I stress the fact that birth and death do not constitute personal memories but rely on the memory of close relations who are in a position to celebrate the first and suffer the loss of the second. Collective memory, and even more so historical memory, retain of these "events" only the replacement one by the other of the actors of history following the ordered sequence of the transmission of roles. From the viewpoint of the third-party historian, generations succeed one another in the civil registers.

72. "There is a break in continuity between the society reading this history and the group in the past [*autrefois*] who acted or witnessed the events" (*The Collective Memory*, 79).

73. The very expression "historical memory" is cast into doubt on several occasions (ibid., 57, 62, 68–69, 86).

74. Yosef Hayim Yerushalmi, *Zakhor: Jewish History and Jewish Memory* (Seattle: University of Washington Press, 1982).

75. In my opinion, our author's semantic choice deserves to be extended to the discipline of historians in every cultural context. It signifies that writing and reading constitute, as we demonstrated above, the combined substantive conditions for the operation of the historian.

76. "At the very heart of this book lies an attempt to understand what seemed a paradox to me at the time—that although Judaism throughout the ages was absorbed with the meaning of history, historiography itself played at best an ancillary role among the Jews, and often no role at all; and, concomitantly, that while memory of the past was always a central component of Jewish experience, the historian was not its primary custodian" (*Zakhor*, xiv).

77. "Suddenly, as it were, the crucial encounter between man and the divine shifted away from the realm of nature and the cosmos to the plane of history, conceived now in terms of divine challenge and human response" (*Zakhor*, 8).

78. In this regard, we must be grateful to Yerushalmi for not inflating the opposition between cyclical time and linear time: if the time of history is linear, the return of the seasons, rites, and festivals is cyclical. On this point, read Arnaldo Momigliano, "Time in Ancient Historiography," *Ancient and Modern Historiography* (Middletown, Conn.: Wesleyan University Press, 1977), 179–214. Yerushalmi is correct to note that "memory and modern historiography stand, by their very nature, in radically different relations to the past" (*Zakhor*, 94).

79. "The difficulty in grasping this apparent incongruity lies in a poverty of language that forces us, *faute de mieux*, to apply the term 'history' both to the sort of past with which we are concerned, and to that of Jewish tradition" (ibid., 26). Note the admission: *faute de mieux*.

80. One will note in particular the narratives in the form of *credo*, such as Deuteronomy 26:5–9, on the basis of which the great exegete Gerhard von Rad formerly articulated his theology of the traditions of ancient Israel: *Old Testament Theology*, 2 vols., trans. D. M. G. Stalker (New York: Harper and Row, 1960–65).

81. Holy: that is to say, set apart from the rest of discourse and hence from critical appraisal.

82. This is the title of an article by Hayden White, "The Burden of History," *History and Theory* 5 (1966): 111–34, cited by Yerushalmi, *Zakhor*, 142 n. 14.

83. "The enterprise has become self-generating, the quest—Faustian.... The shadow of Funes the Memorious hovers over us all" (*Zakhor*, 102).

84. "The historian," writes Eugen Rosenstock-Huessy, "is the physician of memory. It is his honor to heal wounds, genuine wounds. As a physician must act, regardless of medical theories, because his patient is ill, so the historian must act under a moral pressure to restore a nation's memory, or that of mankind." *Out of Revolution* (New York: W. Morrow and Company, 1938), 696; quoted by Yerushalmi, *Zakhor*, 93.

85. Pierre Nora, ed., *Les Lieux de mémoire*, vol. 1, *La République* (1984); vol. 2, *La Nation* (1986); vol. 3, *Les France* (1992) (Paris: Gallimard). English translation in three volumes, *Realms of Memory*, ed. Lawrence D. Kritzman, trans. Arthur Goldhammer: vol. 1, *Conflicts and Divisions* (1996); vol. 2, *Traditions* (1997); vol. 3, *Symbols* (1998) (New York: Columbia University Press).

86. Pierre Nora, "Between Memory and History," *Realms of Memory*, 1:1–20.

87. Here, a remark on Jewish memory, for which "history was no concern" (ibid., 2), echoes Yerushalmi.

88. This echoes Halbwachs through the opposition between group memory, which is "by nature multiple yet specific; collective and plural yet individual," and history which "belongs to everyone and to no one and therefore has a universal vocation" (ibid., 3).

89. This statement on history-memory distances Nora from Halbwachs, who drew a clear line between collective memory and historical memory.

90. Quotations that cite roman numerals are not in the English translation, *Realms of Memory*, as many of the texts in that translation are edited and abridged. References are to *Lieux de mémoire*, vol. 1, *La République*, and Nora's lead article, "Entre mémoire et histoire."

91. Second reference to Jewish memory: "The force of this phenomenon is perhaps most evident among nonpracticing Jews, many of whom have felt a need in recent years to explore memories of the Jewish past. In the Jewish tradition, whose history *is* its memory, to be Jewish is to remember being Jewish. If truly internalized, such a memory inexorably asserts its claim over a person's whole being. What kind of a memory is this? In a sense, it is memory of memory itself. The psychologization of memory makes each individual feel that his or her salvation ultimately depends on discharging a debt that can never be repaid" (*Realms of Memory*, 1:11).

92. It is remarkable that the idea of commemoration, mentioned several times, remains caught up in the nostalgia of memory-history. It is not yet denounced as the response of memory to the dominion of history: "Without commemorative vigilance, history would soon sweep them [the places of memory] away" (*Realms of Memory*, 1:7). It is on the basis of its function of refuge that commemorative memory will renew its assault on national history. The sentence from which the final article on the era of commemoration will be launched is worth quoting: "The memorial has swung over into the historical. A world that once contained our ancestors has become a world in which our relation to what made us is merely contingent. Totemic history has become critical history: it is the age of [the places of memory]. We no longer celebrate the nation, we study the nation's celebrations" (7).

93. One hears in this the echo of the criticisms Plato levels against the "memory aid," *hupomnēsis*.

94. Pierre Nora, "La Nation-mémoire," *Les Lieux de mémoire*, vol. 2, *La Nation*, book 3: 647–58.

95. Pierre Nora, "Generation," *Realms of Memory*, vol. 1, *Conflicts and Divisions*, 499–531.

96. "The notion of generation has thus been subverted from within in much the same way as the modern 'mediatized' event" ("Generation," 508). The author refers here to his article, "Le Retour de l'événement" (in *Faire de l'histoire*).

97. Pierre Nora, "The Era of Commemoration," *Realms of Memory*, vol. 3, *Symbols*, 609–37.

98. I discussed this in positive terms in the first part of the present work, in company with Edward Casey. See above, part 1, chap. 1, "A Phenomenological Sketch of Memory."

99. Thus the tricentennial of the Revocation of the Edict of Nantes is held to have done more to nourish the Protestant imagination than the national imagination, devoted to reconciliation and to forgetting the offenses imposed by the sovereign ("The Era of Commemoration," 620).

## PART THREE, CHAPTER THREE

1. J. L. Borges, "Funes the Memorius," *Ficciones*, trans. Anthony Kerrigan (New York: Grove Press, 1962).

2. Harald Weinrich, *Lethe: Kunst und Kritik des Vergessens* (Munich: Ch. Beck, 1997).

3. I am adopting the vocabulary of the neurosciences, which speak of *mnésique* (mnestic) traces with the stipulation that I am limiting the term "mnemonic" to the set of phenomena relating to the phenomenology of memory.

4. Jean-Pierre Changeux and Paul Ricoeur, *What Makes Us Think? A Neuroscientist and a Philosopher Argue about Ethics, Human Nature, and the Brain*, trans. M. B. DeVevoise (Princeton: Princeton University Press, 2000).

5. Straightaway, I stated the following: "My initial thesis is that these discourses represent heterogeneous perspectives, which is to say that they cannot be reduced to each other or derived from each other. In one case it is a question of neurons and their connection in a system; in the other one speaks of knowledge, action, feeling—acts or states characterized by intentions, motivations, and values. I shall therefore combat the sort of semantic amalgamation that one finds summarized in the oxymoronic formula 'The brain thinks'" (ibid., 14).

6. The problem of some notion of an ultimate referent has been encountered several times in this work. Concerning the historiographical operation, I held that the final referent was action in common, through the formation of the social bond and afferent identities. More precisely, on the plane of the literary representation of the historian, I adopted the concept of a reading contract between the writer and the public, by which the expectations, for example, of fiction or reality are marked out, in the case of a told story. A contract of the same nature is tacitly concluded between scientists and the enlightened public.

7. In *What Is Called Thinking?* I raise this as the problem of a third discourse: would it be an absolute discourse, another version of the reflective discourse combated here? Or another kind of discourse, either speculative as in Spinoza or the post-Kantians, or frankly mythical, and open to multiple transpositions?

8. François Azouvi, "La formation de l'individu comme sujet corporel à partir de Descartes," in G. Cazzaniga and C. Zarka, eds., *L'individuo nel pensiero moderno, secoli 16–18* (Pisa: Università degli Studi, 1995).

9. Alain Berthoz, *Le Sens du mouvement* (Paris: Odile Jacob, 1991); Andy Clark, *Being There: Putting Brain, Body and World Together Again* (Cambridge, Mass.: MIT Press, 1997); J. Geanerod, *Cognitive Neuroscience of Action* (Oxford: Blackwell, 1997); Jean-Luc Petit, "Introduction générale," in Jean-Luc Petit, ed., *Les Neurosciences et la philosophie de l'action* (Paris: Vrin, 1997), 1–37. For my part, I became interested in these developments as my approach to the social phenomenon intended by the historiographical operation increasingly coordinated representation and action. At the same time one encounters a thesis dear to George Canguilhem concerning the idea of a milieu. The milieu is not the ready-made world known to lived experience, but the environment that the living being shapes by its exploring activity. See his *La Connaissance de la vie*.

10. D. Schacter, ed., *Memory Distortions* (Cambridge, Mass.: Harvard University Press, 1995).

11. Pierre Buser, *Cerveau de soi, cerveau de l'autre* (Paris: Odile Jacob, 1998).

12. Henri Bergson, *Matter and Memory*, trans. Nancy M. Paul and W. Scott Palmer (New York: Zone Books, 1991).

13. In his book, *Bergsonism*, trans. Hugh Tomlinson and Barbara Habberjam (New York: Zone Books, 1988), chapter 1, "Intuition as Method," Gilles Deleuze observes that, for Bergson, the recourse to intuition does not mean giving free rein to the ineffable: "Intuition is neither a feeling, an aspiration, nor a disorderly sympathy, but a fully developed method, one of the most fully developed methods in philosophy" (13). The method of division, akin to that of Plato in the *Philebus*, is in this respect an important element of this method: not the One in opposition to the Many, posited in the generality, but two types of multiplicity (44–45). A model of multiplicity is proposed in the method of division which outlines a spectrum to examine, opposites to identify, and a mixed nature to reconstruct. It should be noted, again with Deleuze, that the alternation between dualism and monism scattered throughout *Matter and Memory* depends on the sort of multiplicity considered in each case and on the sort of mixed nature constructed. This remark is important, inasmuch as the identification of false problems constitutes another of the maxims dear to Bergson and can be considered a corollary of this distinction applied to the types of multiplicity; now the problem of the union of the soul and the body seems in many respects to be one of these false problems; posing problems well remains philosophy's primary task.

14. A little later, Bergson will observe that in order to preserve images the brain must have the power to preserve itself. "Let us admit for a moment that the past survives in the form of a memory stored in the brain; it is then necessary that the

brain, in order to preserve the memory, should preserve itself. But the brain, insofar as it is an image extended in space, never occupies more than the present moment: it constitutes, with all the rest of the material universe, an ever-renewed section of universal becoming. Either, then, you must suppose that this universe dies and is born again miraculously at each moment of duration, or you must attribute to it that continuity of existence which you deny to consciousness, and make of its past a reality which endures and is prolonged into its present. So that you have gained nothing by depositing the memories in matter, and you find yourself, on the contrary, compelled to extend to the totality of the states of the material world that complete and independent survival of the past which you have just refused to psychical states" (*Matter and Memory*, 149).

15. See above, part 1, chap. 1, "Plato: The Present Representation of an Absent Thing."

16. Here Bergson edges close to the regions of the unconscious visited by Freud. Speaking of the expanding rings that link together in a chain, Bergson notes: "In this epitomized form our previous psychical life exists for us even more than the external world, of which we never perceive more than a very small part, whereas, on the contrary, we use the whole of our lived experience. It is true that we possess merely a digest of it, and that our former perceptions, considered as distinct individualities, seem to us to have completely disappeared or to appear again only at the bidding of their caprice. But this semblance of complete destruction or of capricious revival is due merely to the fact that actual consciousness accepts at each moment the useful and rejects in the same breath the superfluous" (ibid., 146). As far as the relation between the Bergsonian unconscious and the Freudian unconscious is concerned, this is a question we can only touch on in the third section of this chapter. Let us note, however, that Bergson was not unaware of this problem, as this passage from *The Creative Mind*, referred to by Deleuze, indicates: "Even my idea of integral conservation of the past has more and more found its empirical verification in the vast collection of experiments instituted by the disciples of Freud" (*The Creative Mind*, trans. Mabelle L. Andison [Westport, Conn: Greenwood, 1946], 88).

17. If one were to sum up *Matter and Memory* in a single phrase, one would have to say that memory "preserves itself by itself." This declaration is found in Bergson's *The Creative Mind*, 87: I became "aware of the fact that inward experience in the pure state, in giving us a 'substance' whose very essence is to endure and consequently to prolong continually into the present an indestructible past, would have relieved me from seeking and would even have forbidden me to seek, where recollection is preserved. It preserves itself" (quoted by Deleuze, *Bergsonism*, 54).

18. Deleuze underscores this feature of the regressive process required by the path in the direction of the virtual: "We place ourselves *at once* in the past; we leap

into the past as into a proper element. In the same way that we do not perceive things in ourselves, but at the place where they are, we only grasp the past at the place where it is in itself, and not in ourselves, in our present. There is therefore a 'past in general' that is not the particular past of a particular present but that is like an ontological element, a past that is eternal and for all time, the condition of the 'passage' of every particular present. It is the past in general that makes possible all pasts. According to Bergson, we first put ourselves back into the past in general: He describes in this way the *leap into ontology*" (*Bergsonism*, 56–57). On this occasion he cautions against a psychologizing interpretation of the Bergsonian text, as Jean Hyppolite had done before him in "Du bergsonisme à l'existentialisme," *Mercure de France* (July 1949), and in "Aspects divers de la mémoire chez Bergson," *Revue internationale de philosophie* (October 1949). However, for Bergson, the reference to psychology remains a noble one and preserves the distinction between psychology and metaphysics, to which we shall return again.

19. Frédéric Worms, *Introduction à «Matière et Mémoire» de Bergson* (Paris: Presses Universitaires de France, 1997), 187.

20. Deleuze devotes a chapter to the question: "One or Many Durations?" (*Bergsonism*, 37ff.).

21. See *The Voluntary and the Involuntary*, 447–48.

22. Franz Rosenzweig, *The Star of Redemption*, trans. William W. Hallo (New York: Holt, Rinehart and Winston, 1970); Jean-Luc Marion, *Reduction and Givenness. Investigations of Husserl, Heidegger, and Phenomenology*, trans. Thomas A. Carlson (Evanston, Ill.: Northwestern University Press, 1998); *Being Given: Toward a Phenomenology of Givenness*, trans. Jeffrey L. Kosky (Stanford: Stanford University Press, 2002).

23. This paradox is all the more astonishing as it stands apart from the series of occurrences of the term "forgetting" in *Being and Time*; with one exception, the term expresses inauthenticity in the practice of care. Forgetting is not primordially related to memory; as forgetfulness of being, it is constitutive of the condition of inauthenticity. It is the "retreat" in the sense of the Greek *lauthanein*, to which Heidegger opposes the "non-retreat" of *alētheia* which we translate as "truth" (201–2). In a related sense, the chapter on *Gewissen* (conscience) deals with the "forgetfulness of conscience" as evading the summons issuing from the depths of its ownmost potentiality-of-being. It is still in the mode of inauthenticity that forgetting, contemporary with repetition, is revealed as "backing away *from* one's ownmost having-been in a way that is closed off from oneself" (312). It is noted, however, that "this forgetting is not nothing, nor is it just a failure to remember; it is rather a 'positive,' ecstatic mode of having-been; a mode with a character of its own" (312). One can then speak of the "power of forgetting" intertwined with "everyday moods of taking care of what is nearby" (317). With the appearance

of the present incuriosity what comes before is forgotten (319). Those who lose themselves in the world of tools, must forget themselves (324). One can then employ the oxymoron in speaking of "the forgetting that awaits" (337). Forgetting, in this sense, is characteristic of the they, "blind to possibilities," "incapable of retrieving what has been" (357). Caught up in the present of care, forgetting signifies a temporality that "does not await" (374), irresolute, "in the mode of a making present that does not await but forgets" (377). As temporality sinks down into the vulgar conception of so-called "infinite" time, this movement is punctuated by "the self-forgetful 'representation' of the 'infinitude' of public time" (389). To say that "time passes" is to forget the moments as they slip by (389). Against the backdrop of this litany of inauthenticity, the sole allusion in *Being and Time* to the relation of forgetting to memory stands out: "Just as expectation is possible only on the basis of awaiting, *remembering* is possible only on the basis of forgetting, *and not the other way around*. In the mode of forgottenness, having-been primarily 'discloses' the horizon in which Da-sein, lost in the 'superficiality' of what is taken care of, can remember" (312). It is not clear whether the disavowal of forgetting entails the work of memory in its *Verfallen*, or whether the grace of recognition of the past could raise forgetting from this entanglement, this falling-prey, and elevate it to the level of the reserve of forgetting.

24. Henry Rousso, *The Vichy Syndrome: History and Memory in France since 1944*, trans. Arthur Goldhammer (Cambridge, Mass.: Harvard University Press, 1991); *Vichy: An Ever-Present Past*, trans. Nathan Bracher (Hanover, N.H.: University Press of New England, 1998); *The Haunting Past: History, Memory, and Justice in Contemporary France*, trans. Ralph Schoolcraft (Philadelphia: University of Pennsylvania Press, 2002). Let us note that the expression "a past that does not pass," a synonym of obsession, is found in the controversy of the German historians. In this sense, evoking the works of Henry Rousso here should be joined to the discussion of his German colleagues: the difference in the situations in which the French historians and the German historians work could constitute by itself a theme for historians. The works conceived on either side of the Rhine intersect at another sensitive point: the relation between the judge and the historian ("What Court of Judgment for History?" in *The Haunting Past*, 48–83).

25. On the history of memory, see Rousso, *The Vichy Syndrome*, 3. The tie is made here with Pierre Nora's notion of "places of memory."

26. See above, part 3, chap. 1, "The Historian and the Judge." The same sort of evidence is also included in the file of the Franco-German wars and in the file of the great criminal trials: films (*The Sorrow and the Pity*), plays, etc.

27. "What is borrowed from psychoanalysis is simply a metaphor, not an explanatory schema" (*The Vichy Syndrome*, 11).

28. Pierre Vidal-Naquet, *Assassins of Memory: Essays on the Denial of the Holocaust*, trans. Jeffrey Mehlman (New York: Columbia University Press, 1992); Alain Finkielkraut, *The Future of a Negation: Reflections on the Question of Genocide*, trans. Mary Byrd Kelly (Lincoln: University of Nebraska Press, 1988).

29. Immanuel Kant, "The Right to Pardon," *The Metaphysics of Morals*, part 1, *The Metaphysical Elements of Justice*, trans. John Ladd (Indianapolis: Bobbs-Merrill, 1965), Second Part, "Public Law," general remarks E: "The Right to Punish and the Right to Pardon." "The right to pardon a criminal, either by mitigating or by entirely remitting the punishment, is certainly the most slippery of all the rights of the sovereign. By exercising it he can demonstrate the splendor of his majesty and yet thereby wreak injustice to a high degree" (107–8). And Kant adds: "He can make use of this right of pardon only in connection with an injury committed against himself" (108).

30. Nicole Loraux devotes an entire book to this: *La Cité divisée: L'Oubli dans la mémoire d'Athènes* (Paris: Payot, 1997). The path the book takes is significant: it begins with a discussion of the deep connection between "sedition" (*stasis*) and the mythical descendants of the "Children of the Night" in the figure of Eris, Discord ("Eris: The Archaic Form of the Greek Reflection on Politics," ibid., 119). The analysis crosses through the levels of poetry moving toward the prose of the political, assumed and proclaimed. The book ends with the "politics of reconciliation" (195ff.) and attempts to measure the price paid in terms of denial with regard to the repressed ground of Discord. For reasons of personal strategy, I will follow the inverse order, moving from the amnesty decree and the pledge of non-memory in the direction of the invincible ground of "un-forgettable" Anger and Affliction, to borrow the strong language of the author (165).

31. Thierry Wangfleteten, "L'idéal de concorde et d'unanimité: Un rêve brisé de la Renaissance," *Histoire européenne de la tolérance du XVIe au XXe siècle* (Paris: Livre de Poche, 1998).

32. Stéphane Gacon, "L'oubli institutionnel," *Oublier nos crimes: L'Amnésie nationale: Une spécificité française?* (Paris: Autrement, 1994), 98–111. The presentation of the grounds of the proposed law regarding the abolition of certain criminal proceedings at the time of the Dreyfus affair contains the following statement: "We ask parliament to add forgetting to clemency and to approve the legal dispositions which, while safeguarding the interests of third parties, render passions powerless to revive that most painful conflict" (101).

## EPILOGUE

1. The title of this epilogue was suggested to me by Domenico Jervolino's excellent work, *L'Amore difficile* (Rome: Edizioni Studium, 1995).

2. Jean Nabert, *Elements for an Ethic*, trans. William J. Petrek (Evanston, Ill.: Northwestern University Press, 1969), book 1, "The Givens of Reflection," chapter 1, "The Experience of Fault," 3–15. "Feelings nourish reflection, they are its matter: they make reflection, although free, appear as a moment within the history of desire that is constitutive of our being" (4).

3. Karl Jaspers, *Philosophy*, vol. 2, *Existential Elucidation*, trans. E. B. Ashton (Chicago: University of Chicago Press, 1970), part 3, "Existenz as Unconditionality in Situation; Consciousness and Action: Guilt," 215–18.

4. *Freedom and Nature*, general introduction, "Abstraction of the Fault," 20–28.

5. Immanuel Kant, "Attempt to Introduce the Concept of Negative Magnitudes into Philosophy" [1763], *Theoretical Philosophy, 1755–1770*, trans. David Walford, with Ralf Meerbote (Cambridge: Cambridge University Press, 1992), 203–41.

6. Nabert, *Elements for an Ethic*, 5.

7. Jean Nabert, *Essai sur le mal* (Paris: Aubier, 1970).

8. Jean Améry, *Par delà le crime et le châtiment: Essai pour surmonter l'insurmontable* (Paris: Actes Sud, 1995).

9. Myriam Revault d'Allonnes, *Ce que l'homme fait à l'homme: Essai sur le mal politique* (Paris: Seuil, 1995).

10. "Does the absolutely unjustifiable exist? In this question all questions converge, and we have said nothing if it remains unanswered" (Nabert, *Essai sur le mal*, 142).

11. See André LaCocque and Paul Ricoeur, *Thinking Biblically: Exegetical and Hermeneutical Studies*, trans. David Pellauer (Chicago: University of Chicago Press, 1998).

12. Paul Ricoeur, "Evil, a Challenge to Philosophy and Theology," *Figuring the Sacred: Religion, Narrative, and Imagination*, ed. Mark Wallace, trans. David Pellauer (Minneapolis: Fortress Press, 1995), 249–61.

13. Nicolai Hartmann, *Ethics*, trans. Stanton Coit (London: Allen and Unwin, 1932).

14. Quoted by Klaus M. Kodalle, *Verzeihung nach Wendezeiten?* Inaugural lectures given at the Friedrich Schiller University of Jena, June 2, 1994 (Erlangen and Jena: Palm and Enke, 1994).

15. Jacques Derrida, "Le siècle et le pardon," *Le Monde des débats* (December 1999).

16. Karl Jaspers, *Die Schuldfrage* [1946] (Munich: R. Piper, 1979); *The Question of German Guilt*, trans. E. B. Ashton (New York: Dial Press, 1947).

17. Article 2219 of the French Civil Code bluntly states the argument of the effect of time: "Prescription is a means of acquiring or being freed from something

due to a lapse of time, and under the conditions determined by the law." Due to a certain lapse of time? By virtue of time, one person can be robbed at a certain moment and another amnestied with respect to his original violence. G. Bautry-Lacantinerie and Albert Tissier, in their *Traité théorique et pratique de Droit civil: De la prescription* (Paris: Sirey, 1924), cite one of Bourdaloue's Sermons: "I call upon your experience. Look over the houses and the families distinguished by wealth and by the abundance of goods, those who pride themselves on being the most honorably founded, those who would appear to be models of probity and religion. If you were to move back to the source of this opulence, you would find, from the beginning and in the very principle, things that would make you tremble" (25).

18. Crimes against humanity were defined by the charters of the Nuremberg and Tokyo international military tribunals on August 8, 1945 and January 12, 1946. These texts distinguish: inhuman acts committed against the entire civilian population before and during the war, including assassination, extermination, enslavement, and deportation; and persecutions for political, racial, or religious reasons. The United Nations made this notion more precise in the Convention on Genocide of December 10, 1948. The Convention on Imprescriptibility of November 26, 1968 and the resolution of December 13, 1973 recommending international cooperation for the prosecution of criminals placed the seal of international law on the notion. Similarly, the notion of crimes against humanity was included in domestic French law by the December 26, 1964 law that "recognizes" the imprescriptibility of crimes against humanity and of genocide in reference to the 1946 United Nations resolution: these crimes are declared "by their nature imprescriptible." French jurisprudence, as expressed by a series of decisions by the Cour de cassation (the Supreme Court of Appeal) on the occasion of trials in which these accusations were brought (the Touvier and Barbie affairs) has led to recognizing as imprescriptible crimes "the inhuman acts and the persecutions which, practicing a politics of ideological hegemony in the name of the state, were committed in a systematic manner, not only against persons by reason of their membership in a racial or religious community, but also against the adversaries of this politics regardless of the form of their opposition." One initial common element concerns the existence of a concerted plan. A second common element: the victims are persons and never goods, unlike war crimes. The definition of a crime against humanity is henceforth established by Articles 211–1 and following of the new Criminal Code of 1994. Genocide is defined therein as a crime against humanity leading to the destruction of a group, voluntarily threatening life, physical or mental integrity, or submitting the members of a group discriminated against "to conditions of existence of a nature to lead to the total or partial destruction of the group, including abortion, sterilization, separation of adults in condition to procreate, forced transfer of children." All these criminal acts foster the rupture of equality between human

beings affirmed by the first and third Articles of the International Human Rights Charter.

19. It is in this way, I believe, that one can understand the variations on this subject by Vladimir Jankélévitch. In an initial book, titled *L'Imprescriptible*, first published in 1956 (Paris: Seuil, 1986) at the time of the polemics over the prescription of Hitlerian crimes, he argued, by his own admission, against forgiveness. But was this really the question? In any event, that book was, in its tone, more of an imprecation than an argument, in which the other side had no voice. He was right on one point: "All the legal criteria customarily applicable to crimes of law with respect to prescription fall short here" (21): "international" crime, crime against "the human essence," crime against "the right to exist," are all crimes beyond all proportion; "to forget these gigantic crimes against humanity would be a new crime against the human race." This is precisely what I am calling the de facto unforgivable. His study on *Le Pardon* (Paris: Aubier, 1967) takes a different tack, where the time of forgiveness is identified with the time of forgetting. This is, then, the time that wears away ("L'Usure," 30). A third approach followed in 1971 with a title in the form of a question, *Pardonner?* (Paris: Pavillon, reprinted in the 1986 edition of *L'Imprescriptible*). Here, we read the famous exclamation: "Forgiveness! But have they ever asked us for forgiveness?" (50). "It is the distress and the destitution of the guilty that alone would give a sense to and a reason for forgiveness" (50). Here we enter into a different problematic, where in fact a certain reciprocity would be reestablished by the act of seeking forgiveness. Jankélévitch is well aware of the apparent contradiction: "Between the absolute of the law of love and the absolute of wicked freedom there exists a tear that cannot be entirely ripped apart. We have unceasingly attempted to reconcile the irrationality of evil with the all-powerfulness of love. Forgiveness is as strong as evil but evil is as strong as forgiveness" (foreword, 14–15).

20. Kodalle, who is by no means suspected of complacency with regard to cheap exoneration, is nonetheless severe toward "arrogant hypermoralism" (*Verzeihung nach Wendezeiten?* 36) that is paired with it. Confronting the same question after World War I, Max Weber denounced those fellow citizens who, as vanquished, indulged in self-flagellation and in hunting down the guilty: "Everyone with a manly and controlled attitude would tell the enemy: 'We lost the war. You have won it. That is all over. Now let us discuss what conclusions must be drawn according to the objective interests that came into play and what is the main thing in view of the responsibility towards the future which above all burdens the victor.'" "Politics as a Vocation," in *From Max Weber: Essays in Sociology*, ed. H. H. Gerth and C. Wright Mills (New York: Oxford University Press, 1946), 118. Twenty-five years later, Karl Jaspers asks for even greater contrition from his fellow countrymen.

21. Cf. P. Gifford, "Socrates in Amsterdam: The Uses of Irony in 'La Chute,'" *Modern Language Review* 73 (1978): 499–512.

22. Olivier Abel, "Tables du pardon: Géographie des dilemmes et parcours bibliographique," in *Le Pardon: Briser la dette et l'oubli* (Paris: Autrement, 1992), 208–36.

23. Ibid., 211–16.

24. See Walter Schweidler, "Verzeihung und geschichtliche Identität, über die Grenzen der kollektiven Entschuldigung," *Salzburger Jahrbuch für Philosophie* 44–45 (1999–2000).

The author discusses the public excuses of political leaders in America, Australia, Japan, as well as the South African Truth and Reconciliation commission, and even the request for forgiveness formulated by Catholic bishops and the pope himself for the Crusades and the Inquisition. What is in question here is a form of moral responsibility that implies the existence of a "moral memory" on the scale of a community, in other words, the recognition of a moral dimension in collective memory, a moral dimension that would be the source of a "historical identity" for a human community. Memory, the author says, is also something public related to moral judgment. He, too, admits the existence of moral dilemmas relating to the problematic of *perplexio*: the transmission of guilt in the sphere of hyperpolitical human solidarity should not, as a matter of fact, feed the attempts at exoneration of individuals on the plane of what we earlier called moral guilt. Exoneration can indeed be more surreptitious than accusation, which on its own side is in danger of exaggeration. According to Schweidler, the solidarity at issue here belongs to those duties that Kant called "imperfect," and which would be better categorized in terms of Augustine's *ordo amoris*.

25. In "Love and Justice," in *Figuring the Sacred* (315–29), I opposed the logic of superabundance proper to what I termed the economy of the gift to the logic of equivalence proper to the economy of justice, with its weights and measures, even in the application of penalties. Cf. also Luc Boltanski, *L'Amour et la Justice comme compétences.*

26. Marcel Mauss, *The Gift: Forms and Functions of Exchange in Archaic Societies*, trans. Ian Cunnison (New York: Norton, 1967). Mauss's work is contemporary with that of Malinowski in the same field and with the work of the French sociologist Georges Davy in the sociology of law and institutions, on pledging one's word (1922).

27. It is this language that Claude Lévi-Strauss questions in his well-known *Introduction to the Work of Marcel Mauss*, trans. Felicity Baker (London: Routledge and Kegan Paul, 1987): the notions received from the populations studied are not scientific notions. They do not clarify what is to be explained but are a part of

it. Notions like mana represent the surplus of meaning, the free-floating signifier, which is available to man to understand the world. To move beyond mere repetition, tautology, science can see only the pure form of the relation of exchange in one of its prescientific interpretations. Our problem is quite different: it concerns the persistence of this archaic structure on the phenomenological plane of practice and of the understanding we have of the residual forms of nonmarket exchange in the age of science. There is a discussion of Lévi-Strauss's objections in Vincent Descombes, "Les Essais sur le don," in *Les Institutions du sens* (Paris: Minuit, 1996), 237–66. It is framed by a logical analysis of triadic relations and includes the exchange of gifts as a special case (giver, gift, recipient). Descombes holds that Lévi-Strauss's reproach against Mauss for having simply taken the description offered by the participants in the gift transactions in question does not concern the legal character of the obligation presiding over the exchange. To seek the efficient cause of the obligation in an unconscious structure of mind would be to treat obligation as an explanation for which one would have given only an illusory version in terms of "mystical cement." Unlike explanation in terms of the unconscious infrastructures of the mind, "Mauss's *Gift* is written in a descriptive style that cannot help but satisfy philosophers, who, along with Peirce, hold that the relation of the gift includes the infinite and exceeds any possible reduction to brute facts, or yet again, with Wittgenstein, that the rule is not an efficient cause of conduct (a psychological or other sort of mechanism) but that it is a norm that people follow because they want to make use of it to guide themselves in life" (257). It seems to me that the question raised here is that of the relation between the logic of triadic relations (giving something to someone) and the obligation to put it to use in concrete situations of a historical nature. Our problem here then legitimately arises, the persistence of the presumed archaic nature of potlatch in the practice of nonmarket exchange in the age of science and technology.

28. From the start of the investigation conducted among contemporary populations as diverse as North-Western American tribes (from whom the term "potlatch" comes), to tribes from Melanesia, Polynesia, and Australia, the question is raised, for us the readers, regarding the persistence of traces left in our contractual relations by this archaic element in a sphere of exchange prior to the establishment of markets and of their main invention, currency properly speaking. One finds there, Mauss notes, a form of functioning underlying our morality and our economy—"we believe that in them we have discovered one of the bases of social life" (*The Gift*, 2). What this form of exchange between the offering and the counter-offering values is competition in munificence, excessiveness in the gift which gives rise to the gift in return. Such is the archaic form of exchange and its basis. Mauss discerns the relics of this form in ancient laws (very ancient Roman law) and ancient economies (the pledges of Germanic law). It is Mauss's "moral

conclusions" that are therefore of interest to us here: "Our morality is not solely commercial," exclaims the moralist encouraged by the sociologist (63). He adds, "Today the ancient principles are making their influence felt upon the rigors, abstractions, and inhumanities of our codes. . . . This reaction against Roman and Saxon insensibility in our regime is a good thing" (64). And so is joining politeness to hospitality under the aegis of generosity. Note the unsettling movement of the allegedly deadly gift, as is confirmed by the double meaning of the word gift in Germanic languages: a gift on the one hand, a poison on the other. How could we fail to think in this regard of Plato's *pharmakon* in the *Phaedrus*, which has occupied so much of our attention?

29. I will venture to say that I find something of biblical hyperbole even in the political utopia of Kant's "perpetual peace": a utopia that confers on every person the right to be received in a foreign country "as a guest and not as an enemy," universal hospitality constituting in truth a political approximation of the gospel love of enemies.

30. Peter Kemp, *L'Irremplaçable* (Paris: Corti, 1997).

31. Sophie Pons, *Aparteid: L'aveu et le pardon* (Paris: Bayard, 2000), 13. The commission, composed of twenty-nine persons representing religious, political, and civic groups, contained three committees: the Committee on Human Rights Violations, whose mission was to determine the nature, the cause, and the scope of the abuses committed between 1960 and 1994, and which was granted broadened powers of investigation and summons; the Committee on Reparation and Damages, whose mission was to identify victims and to study their grievances in view of indemnification, material aid, and psychological support; the Amnesty Committee, charged with examining requests for pardon, under the condition of complete confessions proving the political motivation of the accused acts.

32. "The greatest innovation of the South Africans had to do with a principle, that of individual and conditional amnesty, in opposition to the general amnesties issued in Latin America under the pressure of the military. It was not a matter of erasing but of revealing, not of covering over crimes but, rather, of uncovering them. The former criminals were obliged to participate in rewriting national history in order to be pardoned: immunity had to be deserved, it implied public recognition of one's crimes and the acceptance of the new democratic rules. . . . From the earliest times, it has been said that every crime deserves punishment. It is at the tip of the African continent, at the initiative of a former political politician and under the guidance of a man of the church, that a country explored a new path, that of forgiveness for those who recognize their offenses" (ibid., 17–18).

33. To the political weight of what was left unsaid must be added the teachings of contempt, the obsession with ancestral fears, the ideological, even theological, justifications of injustice, the geopolitical arguments dating from the cold war

period and the whole set of motivations concerning personal and collective identity. All of this forms an immense mass to lift.

34. Hannah Arendt, *The Human Condition* (Chicago: University of Chicago Press, 1958).

35. A step in this direction was also taken by Jankélévitch in *L'Irréversible et la nostalgie* (Paris: Flammarion, 1974). The irreversible is an expression of the fact that man cannot return to the past, nor can the past return as past. The irrevocable signifies that "having been"—mainly, "having done"—cannot be annihilated: what has been done cannot be undone. This leads to two inverse impossibilities. Nostalgia, the first sentiment explored by Jankélévitch, belongs on the side of the irreversible. It is regret over what is no longer, which one would like to retain, relive. Remorse is something else: it is the desire to efface, to "unlive" (219). Remorse opposes its specifically ethical character to the aestheticizing and intensely felt character of regret. It is no less poignant for this. If "forgetting does not annihilate the irrevocable" (233), if the latter is ineffaceable, one must not count upon temporal erosion to revoke the past but upon the act that unbinds. One must then keep in mind the idea that "revocation leaves behind it an irreducible residue" (237). This is the ineluctable element of mourning. The unpardonable is touched upon here, and with it the irreparable, ultimate vestiges of "having been" and of "having committed." The impossible undone, as Shakespeare says in Macbeth (241). At the end of this chapter Jankélévitch pronounces the phrase printed on the door of his home and placed at the start of this book: "He who has been, henceforth cannot not have been: henceforth this mysterious and profoundly obscure fact of having been is his viaticum for all eternity" (275).

36. The strict polarity between the schemata of binding and unbinding has produced an interesting exploration of its resources of articulation in new areas. François Ost applies to the temporality of law "a four-beat measure": binding the past (memory), unbinding the past (forgiveness), binding the future (promising), unbinding the future (questioning). The time of which the law speaks "is the present, for it is in the present that the four-beat measure of time is played." *Le Temps du droit* (Paris: Odile Jacob, 1999), 333.

37. In Matthew 18:35, we read: "And that is how my heavenly Father will deal with you, unless you each forgive your brother from your hearts." Or, again: "For if you forgive others the wrongs that they have done, your heavenly Father will also forgive you; but if you do not forgive others, then the wrongs you have done will not be forgiven by your Father" (Matthew 6:14–15). Luke 17:3: "If your brother wrongs you, reprove him; and if he repents, forgive him. Even if he wrongs you seven times in a day and comes back to you seven times saying, 'I am sorry,' you are to forgive him."

38. On this point, Hannah Arendt marks a moment of hesitation: "It is therefore quite significant, a structural element in the realm of human affairs, that men are unable to forgive what they cannot punish and that they are unable to punish what has turned out to be unforgivable. This is the true hallmark of those offences which, since Kant, we call 'radical evil' and about whose nature so little is known, even to us who have been exposed to one of their rare outbursts on the public scene. All we know is that we can neither punish nor forgive such offences and that they therefore transcend the realm of human affairs and the potentialities of human power, both of which they radically destroy wherever they make their appearance. Here, where the deed itself dispossesses us of all power, we can indeed only repeat with Jesus: 'It were better for him that a millstone were hanged about his neck, and he cast into the sea'" (*The Human Condition*, 241).

39. Nietzsche opens the Second Essay with a cymbal clash: "To breed an animal *with the right to make promises*—is not this the paradoxical task that nature has set itself in the case of man? Is it not the real problem regarding man? That this problem has been solved to a large extent must seem all the more remarkable to anyone who appreciates the strength of the opposing force, that of *forgetfulness*." Friedrich Nietzsche, *On the Genealogy of Morals and Ecce Homo*, trans. Walter Kaufmann and R. J. Hollingdale (New York: Vintage Books, 1969), 57. And how is it resolved? By the promise set over against such forgetting. Yet forgetting, for its part, is not taken to be a simple force of inertia, but rather as "an active and in the strictest sense positive faculty of repression." Promise-making therefore figures in Nietzsche's genealogy as a second-order conquest, a conquest over forgetting which itself conquers the agitation of life: "That is the purpose of active forgetfulness, which is like a doorkeeper, a preserver of psychic order, repose, and etiquette" (158). Memory works through the encounter with such forgetting, not just or this or that memory, not with memory as the guardian of the past, preserving the past event, the over and done with past, but with that memory that confers on man the power to keep promises, to be constant to himself; the memory of ipseity, I would call it, a memory that, in ordaining the future on the basis of past commitments, makes man "calculable, regular, necessary," hence "able to stand security for his own future" (158). It is against this proud background that unfolds that other "lugubrious affair": debt, fault, guilt. See here a wonderful book, Gilles Deleuze, *Nietzsche and Philosophy*, trans. Hugh Tomlinson (New York: Columbia University Press, 1983).

40. "No other Christian church, no other religion has accorded as much importance as Catholicism to the detailed and repeated confession of sins. We continue to be marked by this incessant invitation and this formidable contribution to self-knowledge." Jean Delumeau, *L'Aveu et le pardon: Les difficultés de la confession*,

*XIII-XVIII siècle* (Paris: Fayard, 1964, 1992). One question is whether granting forgiveness at the price of confession has been more a source of security than of fear and guilt, as Delumeau pondered in the course of his works on *La Peur en Occident* (1978) and *Sin and Fear: The Emergence of a Western Guilt Culture, 13th to 18th Centuries*, trans. Eric Nicholson (New York: St. Martin's, 1990). "To make the sinner confess in order to receive divine forgiveness from the priest and to leave reassured: such has been the aim of the Catholic Church, especially from the time it made private confession obligatory once a year and required in addition of the faithful the detailed confession of all their 'mortal' sins" (*L'Aveu et le pardon*, 9). It is another matter to clarify the presuppositions of a system that confers the "power of the keys" to its clergy, set apart from the community of the faithful, in the triple role of "doctor," "judge," and "father" (27).

41. As the figure of the Anti-Christ—and the jailer of Christ, he who vanquished the three satanic temptations according to the Gospels, but who was vanquished by history—the Grand Inquisitor offers to the multitude a peaceful conscience and the remission of sins in exchange for submission: "Did we not love mankind, so meekly acknowledging their feebleness, lovingly lightening their burden, and permitting their weak nature even sin with our sanction? Why hast Thou come now to hinder us? . . . But with us all will be happy and will no more rebel nor destroy one another as under Thy freedom. . . . We shall tell them that every sin will be expiated, if it is done with our permission, that we will allow them to sin because we love them, and the punishment for these sins we take upon ourselves. And we shall take it upon ourselves, and they will adore us as their saviors who have taken on themselves their sins before God. And they will have no secrets from us" Fyodor Dostoyevsky, *The Brothers Karamozov*, trans. Constance Garnett (New York: Modern Library, 1950), 305–8.

42. "Action is, in fact, the one miracle-working faculty of man, as Jesus of Nazareth, whose insights into this faculty can be compared in their originality and unprecedentedness with Socrates' insights into the possibilities of thought, must have known very well when he likened the power to forgive to the more general power of performing miracles, putting both on the same level and within the reach of man. The miracle that saves the world, the realm of human affairs, from its normal, 'natural' ruin is ultimately the fact of natality, in which the faculty of action is ontologically rooted. . . . It is this faith in and hope for the world that found perhaps its most glorious and most succinct expression in the few words with which the Gospels announced their glad 'tidings': 'A child has been born unto us'" (Arendt, *The Human Condition*, 246–47).

43. Hannah Arendt's union of the pair that forgiveness and promising form together on the basis of their relation to time is not the only possible one. As the

author of *The Human Condition*, she chose the themes of irreversibility and un-predictability, whereas Jankélévitch chose those of irreversibility and irrevocability. Olivier Abel, in unpublished work that I had the opportunity to consult, refers to the temporal sequence constituted by the capacity to begin, to enter into an exchange, to which he joins promising, the capacity of maintaining oneself in the exchange, under the heading of the idea of justice, along with that of moving out-side of the exchange, where this is forgiveness. Between these two poles, he says, stretches the interval of ethics.

44. More precisely, speaking of the conditional forgiveness explicitly requested, Derrida continues: "And who then is no longer through and through the guilty party but already an other, and better than the guilty person. To this extent, and on this condition, it is no longer the guilty person as such whom one forgives" ("Le Siècle et le pardon"). The same, I would say, but potentially other, though not an other.

45. Annick Charles-Saget, ed., *Retour, repentir et constitution de soi* (Paris: Vrin, 1998). The essays from the Centre A. J. Festugière of Paris-X Nanterre which are collected here deal with the interconnections between biblical repentance and the return to the Principle in Neoplatonism. The former takes root in the Hebraic *Teshuvah* as a return to God, to the Covenant, to the straight path, under the sign of the Law. Mark's Gospel, in turn, evokes the baptism of repentance (*metanoia*) of John the Baptist (*metanoia* will be *conversio* in Latin). Christian repentance presents itself, then, less as a "return" than as an inaugural gesture. The Greek of the Septuagint and of the wisdom writings borrows from the figure of the return, of the "Turn," of the *epistropha*. Plotinus' *Enneads*, on the other hand, propose the purely philosophical movement of the *epistrophē*, which is a quest for knowledge at the same time as an affective impetus. With Proclus, the return to the Principle forms a closed circle with itself. It is only with the school of inwardness (see above, part 1, chapter 3) that the question of the contribution of returning or of repentance to the constitution of the self is posed—and, with this question, the series of paradoxes evoked here.

46. Immanuel Kant, *Religion within the Boundaries of Mere Reason*, in *Religion and Rational Theology*, edited by Allen W. Wood and George Di Giovanni, trans-lated by George Di Giovanni (Cambridge: Cambridge University Press, 1966), 39–215.

47. "Granted that some supernatural cooperation is also needed to his becom-ing good or better, yet, whether this cooperation only consist in the diminution of obstacles or be also a positive assistance, the human being must nonetheless make himself antecedently worthy of receiving it; he must *accept* this aid (which is no small matter), i.e., he must incorporate this positive increase of power into his

maxim: in this way alone is it possible that the good be imputed to him, and that he be acknowledged a good human being" (Kant, *Religion within the Boundaries of Mere Reason*, 89–90). A philosophy of religion within the boundaries of mere reason cannot allow itself to choose between the two interpretations that concern personal existentiel commitment, guided by one or another of the traditions of reading and interpretation within the framework of the Religions of the Book. The final section of the "General Observation" exhorts each person to make use of his original predisposition to good in the hope that "what does not lie within his power will be made good by cooperation from above" (95).

48. "How it is possible that a naturally evil human being should make himself into a good human being surpasses every concept of ours. For how can an evil tree bear good fruit? But, since by our previous admission a tree which was (in its predisposition) originally good did bring forth bad fruits, and since the fall from good into evil (if we seriously consider that evil originates from freedom) is no more comprehensible than the ascent from evil back to the good, then the possibility of this last cannot be disputed. For, in spite of that fall, the command that we *ought* to become better human beings still resounds unabated in our souls; consequently, we must also be capable of it, even if what we can do is of itself insufficient and, by virtue of it, we only make ourselves receptive to a higher assistance inscrutable to us" (ibid., 90).

49. André Breton, *L'Amour fou* (Paris: Gallimard, 1937).

50. Walter Benjamin, "Theses on the Philosophy of History," *Illuminations*, trans. Harry Zohn (New York: Schocken Books, 1969), 253–64.

51. This would, in truth, be the case if the future could save the history of the vanquished from oblivion: everything would finally be "recalled." At this future point, revolution and redemption would coincide.

52. Olivier Abel, "Ce que pardon vient faire dans l'histoire," *Esprit*, no. 7 (1993): 60–72. Note the proximity of this problematic to Hegel's in the *Phenomenology of Spirit*, in which forgiveness rests on a reciprocal standing down of the parties, on each side giving up its partiality.

53. Harald Weinrich, *Lethe: Kunst und Kritik des Vergessens* (Munich: Ch. Beck, 1997).

54. Marc Augé, *Les Formes de l'oubli* (Paris: Payot, 1998).

55. Søren Kierkegaard, "What We Learn from the Lilies in the Field and from the Birds of the Air," *Upbuilding Discourses in Various Spirits*, trans. Howard V. Hong and Edna H. Hong (Princeton: Princeton University Press, 1993), 155–212.

# WORKS CITED

Abel, Olivier. "Ce que pardon vient faire dans l'histoire." *Esprit*, no. 7 (1993): 60–72.

———. *Le Pardon: Briser la dette et l'oubli*. Paris: Autrement, 1992.

Améry, Jean. *Par-delà le crime et le châtiment: Essai pour surmonter l'insurmontable*. Paris: Acts Sud, 1995.

Amphoux, Pascal, et al. *Le Sens du lieu*. Paris: Ousia, 1996.

Ankersmit, Frank R. *Narrative Logic: A Semantic Analysis of the Historian's Language*. The Hague: Martinus Nijhoff, 1983.

Anscombe, G. E. M. *Intention*. Oxford: Basil Blackwell, 1957.

Antelme, Robert. *The Human Race*. Translated by Jeffry Haight and Annie Hamler. Marlboro, Vt.: Marlboro Press, 1992.

Arendt, Hannah. *The Human Condition*. Chicago: University of Chicago Press, 1958.

———. *The Origins of Totalitarianism*. New York: Harcourt, Brace and World, 1968.

Ariès, Philippe. *The Hour of Our Death*. Translated by Helen Weaver. New York: Knopf, 1981.

Ariès, Philippe, and Georges Duby, eds. *A History of Private Life*. 5 vols. Cambridge, Mass.: Harvard University Press, 1987–91.

Aristotle. *The Complete Works*. 2 vols. Edited by Jonathan Barnes. Princeton: Princeton University Press, 1984.

———. *De la mémoire et de la réminiscence*. Translated by René Mugnier. Paris: Éditions les "Belles Lettres," 1965.

Aron, Raymond. *Introduction to the Philosophy of History: An Essay on the Limits of Historical Objectivity*. Translated by George J. Irwin. Boston: Beacon Press, 1961.

———. *La Philosophie critique de l'histoire. Essai sur une théorie allemande de l'histoire*. Paris: Vrin, 1938.

———. *La Philosophie critique de l'histoire: Essai sur une théorie allemande de l'histoire*. Revised and edited by Sylvie Mesure. Paris: Gallimard, 1986.

Audard, Catherine, ed. *Anthologie historique et critique de l'utilitarisme*, vol. 1: *Bentham et ses précurseurs (1711–1832)*. Paris: Presses Universitaires de France, 1999.

Auerbach, Erich. *Mimesis: The Representation of Reality in Western Literature*. Translated by Willard Trask. Princeton: Princeton University Press, 1953.

Augé, Marc. *Les Formes de l'oubli*. Paris: Payot, 1998.

Augustine. *The Confessions*. Translated by R. S. Pine-Coffin. New York: Penguin Books, 1961.

Bachelard, Gaston. *The Poetics of Space*. Translated by Maria Jolas. Boston: Beacon Press, 1969.

Bakhtin, Mikhail. *Rabelais and His World*. Translated by Hélène Iswolksy. Bloomington: Indiana University Press, 1984.

Barret-Kriegel, Blandine. *L'Histoire à l'âge classique*. Paris: Presses Universitaires de France, 1988.

Barth, Fredrik. *Selected Essays of Fredrik Barth*, vol. 1: *Process and Form in Social Life*. London: Routledge and Kegan Paul, 1981.

———, ed. *Ethnic Groups and Boundaries: The Social Organization of Culture Difference*. London: Allen and Unwin, 1969.

Barthes, Roland. *The Rustle of Language*. Translated by Richard Howard. New York: Hill and Wang, 1986.

———. "Introduction to the Structural Analysis of Narrative." In *Image, Music, Text*, 79–124. Translated by Stephen Heath. New York: Hill And Wang, 1977.

Bauer, Gerhard. *Geschichtlichkeit: Wege und Irrwege eines Begriffs*. Berlin: Walter de Gruyter, 1963.

Bautry-Lacantinerie, G., and Albert Tissier. *Traité théoretique et pratique de droit civil: De la prescription*. Paris: Sirey, 1924.

Bedarida, François, ed. *L'Histoire et le métier d'historien en France, 1945–1995*. Paris: Éd. de la Maison des Sciences de L'Homme, 1995.

Benjamin, Walter. "Theses on History." In *Illuminations*, 253–64. Translated by Harry Zohn. Edited by Hannah Arendt. New York: Schocken Books, 1969.

Bentham, Jeremy. *Traité des preuves judiciaires*. Paris, 1822.

———. *A Treatise on Judicial Evidence*. London: J. W. Paget, 1825.

Benveniste, Émile. *Problems of General Linguistics*. Translated by Mary Elizabeth Meek. Coral Gables, Fla.: University of Miami Press, 1977.

———. *Indo-European Language and Society*. Translated by Elizabeth Palmer. London: Faber, 1973.

———. *Le Vocabulaire des institutions indo-européens*. Paris: Minuit, 1969.

Bergson, Henri. *The Creative Mind*. Translated by Mabelle L. Andison. Westport, Conn.: Greenwood, 1946.

———. *Matter and Memory*. Translated by Nancy M. Paul and W. Scott Palmer. London: Allen and Unwin, 1950.

———. *Mind-Energy*. Translated by H. Wildon Carr. Westport, Conn.: Greenwood, 1975.

Bernet, Rudolf. "L'Autre du temps." In Jean-Luc Marion, ed., *Emmanuel Levinas: Positivité et transcendance*, 143–63. Paris: Presses Universitaires de France, 2000.

———. "La présence du passé dans la'analyse husserlienne de la conscience du temps." *Revue de métaphysique et de morale* 19 (1983): 178–98.

———. "Die ungegenwärtige Gegenwart: Anwesenheit und Abwesenheit in Husserls Analysis des Zeitbewusstseins." In E. W. Orth, ed., *Phänomenologische Forschungen*, 16–57. Freiburg and Munich: Verlag Karl Alber, 1983.

Berque, Augustin, and P. Nys, eds. *Logique du lieu et oeuvre humaine*. Paris: Ousia, 1997.

Berthoz, Alain. *Le Sens du mouvement*. Paris: Odile Jacob, 1991.

Birnbaum, O. *The Hospitality of Presence: Problems of Otherness in Husserl's Phenomenology*. Stockholm: Almqvist and Wicksell, 1998.

Bloch, Marc. *Feudal Society*. Translated by L. A. Mauyen. Chicago: University of Chicago Press, 1961.

———. *The Historian's Craft*. Translated by Peter Putnam. New York: Vintage Books, 1964.

———. *The Royal Touch: Sacred Monarchy and Scrofula in England and France*. Translated by J. E. Anderson. London: Routledge and Kegan Paul, 1973.

Boltanski, Luc. *L'Amour et la Justice comme compétences: Trois essais de sociologie de l'action*. Paris: Métaillé, 1990.

———. *The Making of a Class: Cadres in French Society*. Translated by Arthur Goldhammer. New York: Cambridge University Press, 1987.

Boltanski, Luc, and Laurent Thévenot. *De la justification: Les économies de la grandeur*. Paris: Gallimard, 1991.

Booth, Wayne. *The Rhetoric of Fiction*. Chicago: University of Chicago Press, 1961.

Borges, J. L. *Ficciones*. Translated by Anthony Kerrigan. New York: Grove Press, 1962.

Bourdieu, Pierre. *Distinction: A Social Critique of the Judgment of Taste.* Translated by Richard Nice. Cambridge, Mass.: Harvard University Press, 1984.

Bourdieu, Pierre, with Loïc J.-D. Wacquant. *Responses.* Paris: Seuil, 1992.

Braudel, Fernand. *Civilization and Capitalism, 15th–18th Century.* 3 vols. Translated by Siân Reynolds. New York: Harper and Row, 1981–84.

———. *The Identity of France.* 2 vols. Translated by Siân Reynolds. New York: Harper and Row, 1988–90.

———. *The Mediterranean and the Mediterranean World in the Age of Philip II.* 2 vols. Translated by Siân Reynolds. New York: Harper and Row, 1972–73.

———. *Writings on History.* Translated by Sarah Matthews. Chicago: University of Chicago Press, 1980.

Breton, André. *L'Amour fou.* Paris: Gallimard, 1937.

Browning, C. R. "German Memory, Judicial Interrogation, and Historical Reconstruction: Writing Perpetrator History from Postwar Testimony." In Saul Friedlander, ed., *Probing the Limits of Representation: Nazism and the "Final Solution,"* 22–36. Cambridge, Mass.: Harvard University Press, 1992.

Burguière, André. "*Les Annales,* 1929–1979." *Annales* 34 (1979): 1344–59.

Burnyeat, Myles. *The Theaetetus of Plato.* Indianapolis: Hackett, 1990.

Buser, Pierre. *Cerveau de soi, cerveau de l'autre.* Paris: Odile Jacob, 1998.

Canguilhem, Georges. *La Connaissance de la vie.* Paris: Hachette, 1952; Vrin, 1965.

Casey, Edward S. *Getting Back into Place: Toward a Renewed Understanding of the Place-World.* Bloomington: Indiana University Press, 1993.

———. *Imagining: A Phemomenological Study.* Bloomington: Indiana University Press, 1976.

———. *Remembering: A Phenomenological Study.* Bloomington: Indiana University Press, 1987.

Cazzaniga, G., and C. Zarka, eds. *L'individuo nel pensiero moderno, secoli 16–18.* Pisa: Università degli Studi, 1995.

Certeau, Michel de. *L'Absent de l'histoire.* Paris: Mame, 1973.

———. *The Mystic Fable: The Sixteenth and Seventeenth Centuries.* 2 vols. Translated by Michael B. Smith. Chicago: University of Chicago Press, 1992.

———. *The Possession at Loudun.* Translated by Michael B. Smith. Chicago: University of Chicago Press, 2000.

———. *The Writing of History.* Translated by Tom Conley. New York: Columbia University Press, 1988.

Cerutti, Simona. "Normes et pratiques, ou de la légitimité de leur opposition." In Jacques Revel, ed., *Jeux d'échelles: La Microanalyse à l'expérience,* 127–51.

Changeux, Jean-Pierre, and Paul Ricoeur. *What Makes Us Think?* Translated by
M. B. DeBevoise. Princeton: Princeton University Press, 2000.

Chapouthier, Georges. *La Biologie de la mémoire*. Paris: Presses Universitaires de
France, 1994.

Charles-Saget, Annick, ed. *Retour, repentir et constitution de soi*. Paris: Vrin 1998.

Chartier, Roger. *On the Edge of the Cliff: History, Language, Practices*. Translated
by Lydia G. Cochrane. Baltimore: Johns Hopkins University Press, 1997.

———. *Au bord de la falaise: L'Histoire entre certitude et inquietude*. Paris: Albin
Michel, 1998.

———. "Formation sociale et économie psychique: La Société de cour dans le
process de civilization." In Norbert Elias, *La Société de cour*, i–xxviii.
Translated by Pierre Kamnitzer and Jeanne Étoré. Paris: Calmann-Lévy, 1974,
1985.

———. *Lecteur et lecteurs dans la France de l'Ancien Régime*. Paris: Seuil, 1987.

Chartier, Roger, ed., *Histoire de la lecture: Un Bilan des recherches*. Paris: IMEC
Éditions and Éd. de la Maison des Sciences de L'Homme, 1995.

Châtelet, François. *La Naissance de l'histoire*. Paris: Seuil, 1996.

Chaunu, Pierre. *Histoire quantitative, histoire sérielle*. Paris: Armand Colin, 1978.

Clark, Andy. *Being There: Putting Brain, Body and World Together Again*.
Cambridge, Mass.: MIT Press, 1997.

Collingwood, R. G. *The Idea of History*. Edited by T. M. Knox. Oxford:
Clarendon Press, 1956.

Corbin, Alain. *The Foul and the Fragrant: Odor and the French Social
Imagination*. Cambridge, Mass.: Harvard University Press, 1986.

Curtius, Ernst Robert. *European Literature and the Latin Middle Ages*.
Translated by Willard Trask. London: Routledge and Kegan Paul, 1953.

Dastur, Françoise. *Heidegger and the Question of Time*. Translated by François
Raffoul and David Pettigrew. Atlantic Highlands, N.J.: Humanities Press,
1998.

———. *Death: An Essay on Finitude*. Translated by John Llewelyn. London:
Athlone, 1996.

Delacroix, Christian. "La Falaise et le rivage: Historie du 'tournant critique.'"
*Espaces Temps, Les Cahiers*, no. 59–60–61 (1955): 86–111.

Deleuze, Gilles. *Bergsonism*. Translated by Hugh Tomlinson and Barbara
Habberjam. New York: Zone Books, 1988.

———. *Nietzsche and Philosophy*. Translated by Hugh Tomlinson. New York:
Columbia University Press, 1983.

Delumeau, Jean. *L'Aveu et le pardon: Les difficultés de la confession, XIII-XVIII
siècle*. Paris: Fayard, 1964, 1992.

———. *La Peur en Occident, XIVe-XVIIIe siècles: La Cité assiégée*. Paris: Fayard, 1978.

———. *Sin and Fear: The Emergence of a Western Guilt Culture, 13th–18th Centuries*. Translated by Eric Nicholson. New York: St. Martin's, 1990.

Derrida, Jacques. *Of Grammatology*. Translated by Gayatri Chakravorty Spivak. Baltimore: Johns Hopkins University Press, 1976.

———. "Plato's Pharmacy." In *Dissemination*, 61–171. Translated by Barbara Johnson. Chicago: University of Chicago Press, 1981

———. "Le siècle et le pardon." *Le Monde des débats*. December 1999.

Descombes, Vincent. "Les essays sur le don." In *Les Institutions du sens*, 237–66. Paris: Minuit, 1996.

———. *Philosophie par gros temps*. Paris: Minuit, 1989.

———. "Une question de chronologie." In Jacques Poulain, ed., *Penser au présent*, 43–79. Paris: L'Harmattan, 1998.

Détienne, Marcel, and Jean-Pierre Vernant. *Cunning Intelligence in Greek Culture and Society*. Translated by Janet Lloyd. Chicago: University of Chicago Press, 1991.

Dilthey, Wilhelm. *Briefwechsel zwischen Wilhelm Dilthey und dem Grafen Paul Yorck von Wartenburg, 1877–1897*. Edited by Sigrid von der Schulenburg. Halle, 1923.

———. *L'Édification du monde de la vie dans les sciences de l'esprit*. Translated by Sylvie Mesure. *Oeuvres*, vol. 3. Paris: Éd. du Cerf, 1988.

———. *The Formation of the Historical World in the Human Sciences*. Translated by Rudolf A. Makkreel and John Scanlon. Princeton: Princeton University Press, 2002.

———. *Gesammelte Schriften*, vol. 5: *Die Geistege Welt*. Stuttgart: B. G. Teubner, 1968.

———. *Introduction to the Human Sciences*. Translated by Michael Neville. Edited by Rudolf A. Makkreel and Frithjof Rodi. Princeton: Princeton University Press, 1989.

Dosse, François. *L'Histoire*. Paris: Armin Colin, 2000.

———. *New History in France: The Triumph of the Annales*. Translated by Peter V. Conroy Jr. Urbana: University of Illinois Press, 1994.

Douglas, Mary. *How Institutions Think*. Syracuse, N.Y.: Syracuse University Press, 1986.

Dulong, Renaud. *Le Témoin oculaire: Les Conditions sociales de l'attestation personnelle*. Paris: EHESS, 1988.

Elias, Norbert. *The Civilizing Process: Sociogenetic and Psychogenetic Investigations*. Translated by Edmund Jephcott with some notes and corrections by the author. Edited by Eric Dunning, Johan Goudsblom, and Stephen Mennell. Malden, Mass.: Blackwell Publishers, 2000.

———. *The Court Society*. Translated by Edmund Jephcott. New York: Pantheon Books, 1983.

———. *La Société de cour*. Translated by Pierre Kamnitzer and Jeanne Étoré. Paris: Calmann-Lévy, 1974.

Farges, Arlette. *Le Goût de l'archive*. Paris: Seuil, 1989.

Favier, Jean, and Danièle Neirinck. "Les Archives." In F. Bedarida, ed., *L'Histoire et le métier d'historien en France, 1945–1995*, 89–110.

Febvre, Lucien. *Amour sacré, amour profane: Autour de l'«Heptameron.»* Paris: Gallimard, 1944, 1971.

———. *Combats pour l'histoire*. Paris: Armand Colin, 1953.

———. *Martin Luther: A Destiny*. Translated by Roberts Tapley. New York: E. P. Dutton and Co., 1929.

———. *The Problem of Unbelief in the Sixteenth Century*. Translated by Beatrice Gottlieb. Cambridge, Mass.: Harvard University Press, 1982.

Feick, Hildegard. *Index zu Heideggers "Sein und Zeit."* Tübingen: Niemeyer, 1961.

Ferry, Jean-Marc. *Les Puissances de l'expérience: Essai sur l'identité contemporaine*. 2 vols. Paris: Éditions du Cerf, 1991.

Finkielkraut, Alain. *The Future of a Negation: Reflections on the Question of Genocide*. Translated by Mary Byrd Kelly. Lincoln: University of Nebraska Press, 1988.

Foucault, Michel. *The Archeology of Knowledge*. Translated by A. M. Sheridan Smith. New York: Harper Torchbooks, 1972.

———. *The Birth of the Clinic: An Archaeology of Medical Perception*. Translated by A. M. Sheridan Smith. New York: Vintage Books, 1975.

———. *Discipline and Punish: The Birth of the Prison*. Translated by Alan Sheridan. New York: Pantheon, 1977.

———. *Madness and Civilization: A History of Insanity in the Age of Reason*. Translated by Richard Howard. New York: Vintage Books, 1988.

———. *The Order of Things: An Archeology of the Human Sciences*. New York: Pantheon, 1970.

Freud, Sigmund. "Erinnern, Wiederholen, Durcharbeiten." *Gesammelte Werke*, vol. 10: 126–36. Frankfurt am Main: S. Fischer Verlag, 1946.

———. *Five Lectures on Psycho-analysis*. *Standard Edition*, vol. 9: 3–55. Translated and edited by James Strachey. London: Hogarth Press, 1957.

———. *The Interpretation of Dreams*. *Standard Edition*, vols. 4 and 5. Translated and edited by James Strachey. London: Hogarth Press, 1953.

————. "Mourning and Melancholia." *Standard Edition*, vol. 14: 243–58. Translated and edited by James Strachey. London: Hogarth Press, 1958.

————. *The Psychopathology of Everyday Life. Standard Edition*, vol. 6. Translated and edited by James Strachey. London: Hogarth Press, 1960.

————. "Remembering, Repeating, and Working Through." *Standard Edition*, vol. 12: 147–56. Translated and edited by James Strachey. London: Hogarth Press, 1958.

————. "Trauer und Melancholie." *Gesammelte Werke*, vol. 10: 428–46. Frankfurt am Main: S. Fischer Verlag, 1946.

Friedlander, Saul, ed. *Probing the Limits of Representation: Nazism and the "Final Solution."* Cambridge, Mass.: Harvard University Press, 1992.

Furet, François. *In the Workshop of History*. Translated by Jonathan Mandelbaum. Chicago: University of Chicago Press, 1984.

Gacon, Stéphane. *Oublier nos crimes: L'Amnésie nationale: Une spécificité française?* Paris: Autrement, 1994.

Gadamer, Hans-Georg. *Truth and Method*. 2nd rev. ed. Translated by Joel Weinsheimer and Donald G. Marshall. New York: Continuum: 1997.

Garapon, Antoine. *Pourquoi se souvenir?* Paris: Grasset, 1999.

Geertz, Clifford. *The Interpretation of Cultures*. New York: Basic Books, 1973.

Geanerod, J. *Cognitive Neuroscience of Action*. Oxford: Blackwell, 1997.

Gifford, P. "Socrates in Amsterdam: The Uses of Irony in *La Chute*." *Modern Language Review* 73 (1978): 499–512.

Ginzburg, Carlo. *Carnival in Romans*. Translated by Mary Feeney. New York: George Braziller, 1979.

————. *Clues, Myths, and the Historical Method*. Translated by John and Anne C. Tedeschi. Baltimore: Johns Hopkins University Press, 1989.

————. *The Cheese and the Worms: The Cosmos of a Sixteenth-Century Miller*. Translated by John and Anne Tedeschi. Baltimore: Johns Hopkins University Press, 1980.

————. *The Judge and the Historian*. Translated by Anthony Shugaar. New York: Verso, 2002.

————. "Représentation: Le Mot, l'idée, la chose." *Annales* (1991): 1219–34.

Gombrich, E. H. *Art and Illusion*. Princeton: Princeton University Press, 1960.

————. *Meditations on a Hobby Horse and Other Essays on the Theory of Art*. London: Phaidon, 1994.

Gouhier, Henri. *Le Théâtre et l'existence*. Paris: Aubier, 1952.

Granger, G. G. *Essai d'une philosophie du style*. Paris: Armand Colin, 1968.

Greisch, Jean. *Ontologie et temporalité: Esquisse d'une interprétation intégrale de «Sein und Zeit.»* Paris: Presses Universitaires de France, 1994.

Grimaudi, Maurizion. "Échelles, pertinence, configuration." In Jacques Revel, ed., *Jeux d'échelles: La Microanalyse à l'expérience*, 113–39.

Guitton, Jean. *Le Temps et l'éternité chez Platon et saint Augustin*. Paris: Vrin, 1933; 4th ed., 1971.

Habermas, Jürgen. *Knowledge and Human Interests*. Translated by Jeremy J. Shapiro. Boston: Beacon Press, 1971.

———. *The New Conservatism: Cultural Criticism and the Historians' Debate*. Edited and translated by Shierry Weber Nicholsen. Cambridge, Mass.: MIT Press, 1989.

Halbwachs, Maurice. *Les Cadres sociaux de la mémoire*. Paris: Alcan, 1925; Albin Michel, 1994.

———. *On Collective Memory*. Edited and translated by Lewis A. Coser. Chicago: University of Chicago Press, 1992.

———. *The Collective Memory*. Translated by Francis J. Ditter and Vida Yazdi Ditter. New York: Harper Colophon, 1950; reprinted 1980.

———. *La Mémoire collective*. Edited by Gérard Namer. Paris: Albin Michel, 1997.

Hart, H. L. A. "The Ascription of Responsibility and Rights." *Proceedings of the Aristotelian Society* 49 (1948): 171–94.

Hartmann, Nicolai. *Ethics*. Translated by Stanton Coit. London: Allen and Unwin, 1932.

Hartog, François. *The Mirror of Herodotus: The Representation of the Other in the Writing of History*. Translated by Janet Lloyd. Berkeley and Los Angeles: University of California Press, 1988.

Hegel, G. W. F. *The Philosophy of History*. Translated by J. Sibree. Buffalo, N.Y.: Prometheus Books, 1991.

———. *Philosophy of Right*. Translated by T. M. Knox. New York: Oxford University Press, 1967.

Heidegger, Martin. *Being and Time*. Translated by John Macquarrie and Edward Robinson. New York: Harper and Row, 1962.

———. *Being and Time*. Translated by Joan Stambaugh. Albany: SUNY Press, 1996.

Henry, Michel. *Marx*. Translated by Kathleen McLaughlin. Bloomington: Indiana University Press, 1983.

Herodotus. *The History*. Translated by David Grene. Chicago: University of Chicago Press, 1987.

Heussi, Karl. *Die Krisis des Historismus*. Tübingen: Mohr, 1932.

Hildesheimer, Françoise. *Les Archives de France: Mémoire de l'histoire*. Paris: Honorée Champion, 1997.

Hillgruber, Andreas. *Zweierlei Untergang: Die Zerschlagung des Deutschen Reiches und das Ende des Europäischen Judentums*. Berlin: Siedler, 1986.

"Histoire et science sociale: Un tournant critique?" *Annales* 43 (1988): 291–93.

Homans, Peter. *The Ability to Mourn*. Chicago: University of Chicago Press, 1989.

Husserl, Edmund. *Cartesian Meditations: An Introduction to Phenomenology*. Translated by Dorion Cairns. The Hague: Martinus Nijhoff, 1969.

———. *Cartesianische Meditationen und Pariser Vorträge*. Vol. 1 of *Husserliana*. Edited by S. Strasser. The Hague: Martinus Nijhoff, 1963.

———. *The Crisis of the European Sciences and Transcendental Philosophy*. Translated by David Carr. Evanston, Ill.: Northwestern University Press, 1970.

———. *Einleitung in die Logik und erkenntnistheorie: Vorlesungen (1906–1907)*. Vol. 24 of *Husserliana*. Edited by U. Melle. Dordrecht: Martinus Nijhoff, 1984.

———. *Erste Philosophie (1923–1924)*. Vol. 8 of *Husserliana*. Edited by R. Boehm. The Hague: Martinus Nijhoff, 1959.

———. *Ideas Pertaining to a Pure Phenomenology and to a Phenomenological Philosophy. First Book: General Introduction to a Pure Phenomenology*. Vol. 2 of the *Collected Works*. Translated by Fred Kersten. The Hague: Martinus Nijhoff, 1982.

———. *Ideen zu einer reinen Phänomenologie und phänomenologischen Philosophie. Erstes Buch: Allgemeine Einführung in die reine Phänomenologie*. Vol. 3 of *Husserliana*. Edited by Walter Biemal. The Hague: Martinus Nijhoff, 1950.

———. *Logical Investigations*. Translated by J. N. Findlay. London: Routledge and Kegan Paul, 1970.

———. *On the Phenomenology of the Consciousness of Internal Time (1893–1917)*. Vol 4. of the *Collected Works*. Translated by John Barnett Brough. The Hague: Martinus Nijhoff, 1991.

———. *Phantasie, Bildbewusstsein, Erinnerung (1898–1925)*. Vol. 23 of *Husserliana*. Edited by Eduard Marbach. The Hague: Martinus Nijhoff, 1980.

———. *Zur Phänomenlogie des innern Zeitbewusstseins (1893–1917)*. Vol. 10 of *Husserliana*. The Hague: Martinus Nijhoff, 1966.

———. *Texte zur Phänomenlogie des innern Zeitbewusstseins (1893–1917)*. Edited by Rudolf Bernet. Hamburg: Meiner, 1985.

Hutton, Patrick H. *History as an Art of Memory*. Burlington: University of Vermont Press, 1993.

Jankélévitch, Vladimir. *L'Imprescriptible*. Paris: Seuil, 1986.

———. *L'Irréversible et la nostalgie*. Paris: Flammarion, 1974.

———. *Le Pardon*. Paris: Aubier, 1967.

———. *Pardoner?* Paris: Pavillon, 1971.

Jaspers, Karl. *Philosophy*, vol. 2: *Existential Elucidation*. Translated by E. B. Ashton. Chicago: University of Chicago Press, 1970.

———. *The Question of German Guilt*. Translated by E. B. Ashton. New York: Dial Press, 1947.

———. *Die Schuldfrage*. Munich: R. Piper, 1979.

Jauss, Hans-Robert. *Pour une esthétique de la reception*. Translated by C. Maillard. Paris: Gallimard, 1978.

Jervolino, Domenico. *L'Amore difficile*. Rome: Edizioni Studium, 1995.

Kant, Immanuel. "Attempt to Introduce the Concept of Negative Magnitudes into Philosophy" [1763]. In *Theoretical Philosophy, 1755–1770*, 203–41. Translated by David Walford, with Ralf Meerbote. Cambridge: Cambridge University Press, 1992.

———. *The Conflict of the Faculties*. Translated by Mary J. Gregor and Robert Anchor. In *Religion and Rational Theology*, 233–327. Edited by Allen W. Wood and George Di Giovanni. Cambridge: Cambridge University Press, 1996.

———. *The Metaphysics of Morals*, part 1, *The Metaphysical Elements of Justice*. Translated by John Ladd. Indianapolis: Bobbs-Merrill, 1965.

———. *Religion within the Boundaries of Mere Reason*. In *Religion and Rational Theology*, 39–215. Edited by Allen W. Wood and George Di Giovanni. Translated by George Di Giovanni. Cambridge: Cambridge University Press, 1966.

Kantorowicz, Ernst H. *The King's Two Bodies: A Study in Medieval Political Theology*. Princeton: Princeton University Press, 1937.

Kellner, Hans. *Language and Historical Representation: Getting the Story Crooked*. Madison: University of Wisconsin Press, 1989.

Kemp, Peter. *L'Irremplaçable*. Paris: Corti, 1997.

Kierkegaard, Søren. *Upbuilding Discourses in Various Spirits*. Translated by Howard V. Hong and Edna H. Hong. Princeton: Princeton University Press, 1993.

Klibansky, Raymond, Erwin Panofsky, and Fritz Saul. *Saturn and Melancholy: Studies in the History of Natural Philosophy, Religion and Art*. New York: Basic Books, 1965.

Kodalle, Klaus M. *Verzeihung nach Wendezeiten?* Erlangen and Jena: Palm and Enke, 1994.

Koselleck, Reinhart. *Futures Past: On the Semantics of Historical Time*. Translated by Keith Tribe. Cambridge, Mass.: MIT Press, 1985.

———. *L'Expérience de l'histoire.* Paris: Gallimard-Seuil-EHESS, 1997.

———. *Geschichtliche Grundbegriffe.* Stuttgart: Klett-Cotta, 1975.

Kreiger, Leonard. *Ranke: The Meaning of History.* Chicago: University of Chicago Press, 1977.

Krell, David Farrell. *Of Memory, Reminiscence, and Writing: On the Verge.* Bloomington: Indiana University Press, 1990.

La Capra, Dominick. "Representing the Holocaust: Reflections on the Historians' Debate." In Saul Friedlander, ed., *Probing the Limits of Representation: Nazism and the "Final Solution,"* 108–27.

LaCocque, André, and Paul Ricoeur. *Thinking Biblically: Exegetical and Hermeneutical Studies.* Translated by David Pellauer. Chicago: University of Chicago Press, 1998.

Lacombe, Paul. *De l'histoire considérée comme science.* Paris: Hachette, 1894.

Langlois, Charles Victor, and Charles Seignobos. *Introduction to the Study of History.* Translated by G. G. Perry. Westport, Conn.: Greenwood, 1979.

Leclerc, Gérard. *Histoire de l'autorité: L'Assignation des énoncés culturels et la généalogie de la croyance.* Paris: Presses Universitaires de France, 1986.

Legendre, Pierre. *L'Inestimable Objet de la transmission. Essai sur le principe généalogique en Occident.* Paris: Fayard, 1985.

Le Goff, Jacques. "Documento/monumento." *Enciclopedia Einaudi*, 5:38–48. Turin: Einaudi, 1978.

———. *History and Memory.* Translated by Steven Rendall and Elizabeth Claman. New York: Columbia University Press, 1992.

Le Goff, Jacques, and Pierre Nora, eds. *Faire de l'histoire*, 3 vols. Paris: Gallimard, 1974. Partially translated as *Constructing the Past: Essays in Historical Methodology.* New York: Cambridge University Press, 1984.

Le Goff, Jacques, Roger Chartier, and Jacques Revel, eds. *La Nouvelle Histoire.* Paris: Retz CEPL, 1978.

Lejeune, Philippe. *On Autobiography.* Translated by Katherine Leary. Minneapolis: University of Minnesota Press, 1989.

Lepetit, Bernard. "De l'échelle en histoire." In Jacques Revel, ed., *Jeux d'échelles: La Microanalyse de l'expérience*, 71–94.

———, ed. *Les Formes de l'expérience: Une autre histoire sociale.* Paris: Albin Michel, 1995.

Leroy-Gourhan, André. *Le Geste et la parole.* Paris: Albin Michel, 1964.

Le Roy Ladurie, Emmanuel. *Carnival in Romans.* Translated by Mary Feeney. New York: George Braziller, 1979.

————. *Montaillou: The Promised Land of Error*. Translated by Barbara Bray. New York: George Braziller, 1978.

————. *Times of Feast, Times of Famine: A History of Climate since the Year 1000*. Translated by Barbara Bray. Garden City, N.Y.: Doubleday, 1971.

Levi, Giovanni. *L'eredità immateriale: Carriera di un esorcista nel Piemonte del seicento*. Turin: Einaudi, 1985.

————. *Le Pouvoir au village: Histoire d'un exorciste dans le Piémont du XVIe siècle*. Translated by Monique Aymard. Paris: Gallimard, 1989.

Levi, Primo. *The Drowned and the Saved*. Translated by Raymond Rosenthal. New York: Vintage Books, 1989.

————. *Survival in Auschwitz*. Translated by Stuart Woolf. New York: Collier, 1961.

Levinas, Emmanuel. *Otherwise than Being or Beyond Essence*. Translated by Alphonso Lingis. Dordrecht: Kluwer, 1991.

————. *Time and the Other*. Translated by Richard A. Cohen. Pittsburgh: Duquesne University Press, 1987.

————. *Totality and Infinity: An Essay on Exteriority*. Translated by Alphonso Lingis. Pittsburgh: Duquesne University Press, 1969.

Lévi-Strauss, Claude. *Introduction to the Work of Marcel Mauss*. Translated by Felicity Baker. London: Routledge and Kegan Paul, 1987.

————. *Race et histoire*. Paris: UNESCO, 1952; Gallimard, 1987.

————. *Structural Anthropology*, vol. 1. Translated by Claire Jacobson and Brooke Grundfest Schoepf. New York: Basic Books, 1963.

————. *Structural Anthropology*, vol. 2. Translated by Monique Layton. New York: Basic Books, 1976.

————. *Tristes Tropiques*. Translated by John and Doreen Weightman. New York: Atheneum, 1981.

Lévy-Bruhl, Lucien. *The Notebooks on Primitive Mentality*. Translated by Peter Rivière. New York: Harper Torchbooks, 1978.

————. *Primitive Mentality*. Translated by Lilian A. Clare. London: Allen and Unwin, 1923; rpt. Boston: Beacon Press, 1966.

Lloyd, Geoffrey E. R. *Demystifying Mentalities*. New York: Cambridge University Press, 1990.

Locke, John. *An Essay concerning Human Understanding*. Edited by Peter H. Nidditch. Oxford: Clarendon Press, 1975.

————. *Identité et différence: L'Invention de la conscience*. Translated by and commentary by Étienne Balibar. Paris: Seuil, 1998.

————. *Second Treatise of Government*. Chicago: Henry Regnery, 1955.

Loraux, Nicole. *La Cité divisée: L'Oubli dans la mémoire d'Athènes*. Paris: Payot, 1997.

Lyotard, Jean-François. *The Differend*. Translated by Georges Van Den Abbeele. Minneapolis: University of Minnesota Press, 1988.

———. *The Postmodern Condition*. Translated by Geoff Bennington and Brian Massumi. Minneapolis: University of Minnesota Press, 1984.

Mandrou, Robert. *De la culture populaire en France aux XVIIe et XVIIIe siècles: La Bibliothèque bleue de Troyes*. Paris: Imago, 1999.

———. *Introduction to Modern France, 1500–1640: An Essay in Historical Psychology*. Translated by R. E. Hallmark. New York: Holmes and Meier, 1975

———. *Magistrats et Sorciers en France au XVIIe siècle: Une analyse de psychologie historique*. Paris: Seuil, 1989.

———. "L'Historie des mentalités." *Encyclopedia Universalis* (1968), 8:436–38.

Marguerat, Daniel, and Jean Zumstein, eds. *La Mémoire et le temps: Mélanges offerts à Pierre Bonnard*. Geneva: Labor et Fides, 1991.

Marin, Louis. *La Critique du discours: Études sur la «Logique de Port-Royal» et les «Pensées» de Pascal*. Paris: Minuit, 1975.

———. *Des pouvoirs de l'image: Gloses*. Paris: Seuil, 1993.

———. *Opacité de la peinture: Essays sur la représentation du Quatrocento*. Paris: Usher, 1989.

———. *Portrait of the King*. Translated by Martha M. Houle. Minneapolis: University of Minnesota Press, 1988.

———. "Une ville, une campagne de loin . . . : Paysage Pascalien." *Littérature*, no. 161 (February 1986): 3–16.

Marion, Jean-Luc. *Being Given: Toward a Phenomenology of Givenness*. Translated by Jeffrey L. Kosky. Stanford: Stanford University Press, 2002.

———. *Reduction and Givenness: Investigations of Husserl, Heidegger, and Phenomenology*. Translated by Thomas A. Carlson. Evanston, Ill.: Northwestern University Press, 1998.

Marrou, Henri I. *L'Ambivalence de l'histoire chez saint Augustin*. Paris: Vrin, 1950.

———. *The Meaning of History*. Translated by Robert J. Olson. Baltimore: Helicon, 1966.

———. *La Théologie de l'histoire*. Paris: Seuil, 1968.

Mauss, Marcel. *The Gift: Forms and Functions of Exchange in Archaic Societies*. Translated by Ian Cunnison. New York: Norton, 1967.

Merleau-Ponty, Maurice. *Phenomenology of Perception*. Translated by Colin Smith. London: Routledge and Kegan Paul, 1962.

———. *The Structure of Behavior*. Translated by Alden L. Fisher. Boston: Beacon Press, 1963.

Michelet, Jules. *Histoire de France*. Présenté par Claude Mettra. Lausanne: Rencontre, 1965, 1967.

Mink, Louis O. *Historical Understanding*. Edited by Brian Fay, Eugene O. Golob, and Richard T. Vann. Ithaca: Cornell University Press, 1987.

Momigliano, A. D. *Ancient and Modern Historiography*. Middletown, Conn.: Wesleyan University Press, 1977.

———. *Studies in Historiography*. New York: Harper Torchbooks, 1966.

Montaigne, Michel de. *The Complete Essays*. Translated by M. A. Screech. London: Penguin Books, 1991.

Nabert, Jean. *Elements for an Ethic*. Translated by William J. Petrek. Evanston, Ill.: Northwestern University Press, 1969.

———. *Essai sur le mal*. Paris: Aubier, 1970.

Nagel, Thomas. *Equality and Partiality*. New York: Oxford University Press, 1991.

Nietzsche, Friedrich. *On the Genealogy of Morals and Ecce Homo*. Translated by Walter Kaufmann and R. J. Hollingdale. New York: Vintage Books, 1969.

———. *Unfashionable Observations*. Translated by Richard Gray. *The Complete Works of Friedrich Nietzsche*, vol. 2. Edited by Ernst Behler. Stanford: Stanford University Press, 1995.

Nora, Pierre. "La Nation sans nationalisme." *Espaces Temps, Les Cahiers*, nos. 59–60–61 (1995).

———, ed. *Les Lieux de mémoire*, vol. 1, *La République* (1984); vol. 2, *La Nation* (1986); vol. 3, *Les France* (1992). Paris: Gallimard. English translation in three volumes, *Realms of Memory*, ed. Lawrence D. Kritzman, trans. Arthur Goldhammer: vol. 1, *Conflicts and Divisions* (1996); vol. 2, *Traditions* (1997); vol. 3, *Symbols* (1998). New York: Columbia University Press.

Osiel, Mark. *Mass Atrocity, Collective Memory, and the Law*. New Brunswick, N.J.: Transaction, 1997.

Ost, François. *Le Temps du droit*. Paris: Odile Jacob, 1999.

Pascal, Blaise. *Pensées*. Translated by A. J. Krailsheimer. Baltimore: Penguin, 1966.

Petit, Jean-Luc. *Du travail vivant au système de l'action: Une discussion de Marx*. Paris: Seuil, 1980.

———, ed. *L'Événement en perspective*. Paris: EHSS, 1991.

———, ed. *Les Neurosciences et la philosophie de l'action*. Paris: Vrin, 1997.

Pharo, Patrick, and Louis Quéré, eds. *Les Formes de l'action*. Paris: EHESS, 1990.

Piper, Ernst Rienhard, ed. *Historikerstreit: Die Dokumentation die Kontroverse um dies Einzigartigkeit der Nationalsozialistischen Judenvernichten.* Munich: Piper, 1987.

———. *Devant l'histoire: Les Documents de la controverse sur la singularité de l'extermination des Juifs par le régime nazi.* Translated by Brigitte Vergne-Cain et al. Paris: Cerf, 1988.

Plato. *Plato: Complete Works.* Edited by John M. Cooper. Indianapolis: Hackett, 1997.

———. *Oeuvres completes.* Translated by Léon Robin. 2 vols. Paris: Gallimard, 1985.

———. *Théétète.* Translated by Michel Narcy. Paris: Flammarion, 1994.

Pollner, Melvin. "Événement et monde commun: Que s'est-il réellement passé?" In Jean-Luc Petit, ed., *L'Événement en perspective*, 75–96. Paris: EHESS, 1991.

Pomian, Krzysztof. "De l'histoire, partie de la mémoire, à la mémoire, objet d'histoire." *Revue de métaphysique et de morale*, no. 1 (1998): 63–110.

———. *L'Ordre du temps*, Paris: Gallimard, 1984.

Pons, Sophie. *Aparteid: L'Aveu et le pardon.* Paris: Bayard, 2000.

Prost, Antoine. *Douze Leçons sur l'histoire.* Paris: Seuil, 1996.

———. "Seignobos revisité." *Vingtième Siècle, revue d'histoire*, no. 43 (July-September 1994): 100–18.

Proust, Marcel. *In Search of Lost Time.* Translated by C. K. Scott Montcrieff and Terrence Kilmartin, rev. by D. J. Enright. 6 vols. New York: Modern Library, 1993.

Rancière, Jacques. *The Names of History: On the Poetics of Knowledge.* Translated by Hassan Melehy. Minneapolis: University of Minnesota Press, 1994.

Rémond, René. *Les Droites en France.* Paris: Aubier, 1982.

———. *Notre siècle, 1918–1988.* Paris: Fayard, 1988.

Renthe-Fink, L. *Geschichtlichkeit: Ihr terminologie und begriffricher Ursprung bei Hegel, Haym, Dilthey und Yorck.* Göttingen: Vandenhoeck und Ruprecht, 1964.

Revault d'Allonnes, Myriam. *Ce que l'homme fait à l'homme: Essai sur le mal politique.* Paris: Seuil, 1995.

Revel, Jacques. "Histoire et science sociale, les paradigms des *Annales*." *Annales* 34 (1979): 1360–76.

———, ed. *Jeux d'échelles: La Microanalyse à l'expérience.* Paris: EHESS-Gallimard-Seuil, 1996.

Ricardou, Jean. *Le Nouveau Roman.* Paris: Seuil, 1973.

Ricoeur, Paul. "Architecture et narrativité." In *Catalogue de la Mostra "Identità e Differenze."* Milan: Triennale de Milan, 1994.

———. *Figuring the Sacred: Religion, Narrative, and Imagination.* Edited by Mark Wallace. Translated by David Pellauer. Minneapolis: Fortress Press, 1995.

———. *Freedom and Nature: The Voluntary and the Involuntary.* Translated by Erzaim V. Kohák. Evanston, Ill.: Northwestern University Press, 1966.

———. *From Text to Action: Essays in Hermeneutics.* Translated by Kathleen Blamey and John B. Thompson. Evanston, Ill.: Northwestern University Press, 1991.

———. *History and Truth.* Translated by Charles A. Kelby. Evanston, Ill.: Northwestern University Press, 1965.

———. *Husserl: An Analysis of His Phenomenology.* Translated by Edward G. Ballard and Lester E. Embree. Evanston, Ill.: Northwestern University Press, 1967.

———. *The Just.* Translated by David Pellauer. Chicago: University of Chicago Press, 2000.

———. *Lectures on Ideology and Utopia.* Edited by George H. Taylor. New York: Columbia University Press, 1986.

———. "Philosophies critiques de l'histoire: Recherche, explication, écriture." In Høistad Guttorm, ed., *Philosophical Problems Today,* vol. 1: 139–201. Dordrecht: Kluwer, 1994.

———. *Oneself as Another.* Translated by Kathleen Blamey. Chicago: University of Chicago Press, 1992.

———. *The Rule of Metaphor: Multi-Disciplinary Studies of the Creation of Meaning in Language.* Translated by Robert Czerny with Kathleen McLaughlin and John Costello, S.J. Toronto and Buffalo: University of Toronto Press, 1977.

———. *Time and Narrative.* 3 vols. Translated by Kathleen McLaughlin and David Pellauer. Chicago: University of Chicago Press, 1984–1988.

Rosenstock-Huessy, Eugen. *Out of Revolution: Autobiography of Modern Man.* New York: W. Morrow and Company, 1938.

Rosental, Paul André. "Construire le 'macro' par le 'micro': Fredrik Barth et la microstoria." In Jacques Revel, ed., *Jeux d'échelles: La Microanalyse à l'expérience,* 141–60.

Rosenzweig, Franz. *The Star of Redemption.* Translated by William W. Hallo. New York: Holt, Rinehart and Winston, 1970.

Rousso, Henry. *The Haunting Past: History, Memory, and Justice in Contemporary France.* Translated by Ralph Schoolcraft. Philadelphia: University of Pennsylvania Press, 2002.

———. *The Vichy Syndrome: History and Memory in France since 1944.* Translated by Arthur Goldhammer. Cambridge, Mass.: Harvard University Press, 1991.

———. *Vichy: An Ever-Present Past.* Translated by Nathan Bracher. Hanover, N.H.: University Press of New England, 1998.

Sartre, Jean-Paul. *The Psychology of Imagination.* New York: Citadel, 1965.

Schacter, D., ed. *Memory Distortions.* Cambridge, Mass.: Harvard University Press, 1995.

Schapp, Wilhelm. *In Geschichten verstrickt.* Wiesbaden: B. Heymann, 1976.

Schutz, Alfred. *Collected Papers.* 3 vols. The Hague: Nijhoff, 1962–1966.

———. *The Phenomenology of the Social World.* Translated by George Walsh and Frederick Lehnert. Evanston, Ill.: Northwestern University Press, 1967.

———. *The Structure of the Life-World.* London: Heineman, 1974.

Schweidler, Walter. "Verzihung und geschichtliche Identität, über die Grenzen der kollektiven Entschuldigung." *Salzburger Jahrbuch für Philosophie* 44–45 (1999/2000).

Seignobos, Charles. *La Méthode historique appliquée aux sciences socials.* Paris: F. Alcan, 1901.

Simiand François. "Méthode historique et science sociale." *Revue de synthèse historique* 6 (1903): 1–22, 129–57; reprinted in *Annales* (1960).

Sorabji, Richard. *Aristotle on Memory.* Providence, R.I.: Brown University Press, 1972.

Spiegelman, Art. *Maus: A Survivor's Tale: My Father Bleeds History.* New York: Pantheon, 1986.

Spinoza, Baruch. *The Collected Works of Spinoza.* Translated by Edwin Curly. Princeton: Princeton University Press, 1985–.

Starobinski, Jean. *La Mélancholie au miroir: Trois Lectures de Baudelaire.* Paris: Julliard, 1989.

Stone, Lawrence. "Retour au récit: Réflexions sur une vieille histoire." *Le Débat*, no. 4 (1980): 116–42.

Strawson, P. F. *Individuals.* London: Methuen, 1959.

Taylor, Charles. *The Ethics of Authenticity.* Cambridge, Mass.: Harvard University Press, 1991.

———. *Sources of the Self: The Making of the Modern Identity.* Cambridge, Mass.: Harvard University Press, 1989.

"Tentons l'expérience." *Annales* 44 (1989): 1317–23.

Terdiman, Richard. *Present Past: Modernity and the Memory Crisis*. Ithaca: Cornell University Press, 1993.

Thévenot, Laurent. "L'action qui convient." In Patrick Pharo and Louis Quéré, eds., *Les Formes de l'action*, 39–69. Paris: EHESS, 1990.

Todorov, Tzvetan. *Les Abus de la mémoire*. Paris: Éditions Arléa, 1995.

Toulmin, Stephen E. *The Uses of Argument*. New York: Cambridge University Press, 1958.

Valla, Lorenzo. *La Donation de Constantin (Sur la «Donation de Constantin», à lui faussement attribuée et mensongère [c. 1440])*. Translated by Jean-Baptiste Giard. Paris: Les Belles Lettres, 1993. [The Treatise of Lorenzo Valla on the Donation of Constantine. Translated by Christopher B. Coleman. Toronto: University of Toronto Press, 1993.]

Vernant, Jean-Pierre. *Myth and Society in Ancient Greece*. Translated by Janet Lloyd. London: Meuthen, 1982.

———. *Myth and Thought among the Greeks*. London: Routledge and Kegan Paul, 1983.

———. *Origins of Greek Thought*. Ithaca: Cornell University Press, 1982.

Vernant Jean-Pierre, and Pierre Vidal-Naquet. *Myth and Tragedy in Ancient Greece*. Translated by Janet Lloyd. New York: Zone Books, 1990.

Veyne, Paul. *Writing History: Essay on Epistemology*. Translated by Mina Moore-Rinvolucri. Middletown, Conn.: Wesleyan University Press, 1984.

———. *L'Inventaire des différences: Leçon inaugurale du Collège de France*. Paris: Seuil, 1976.

Vidal-Naquet, Pierre. *Assassins of Memory: Essays on the Denial of the Holocaust*. Translated by Jeffrey Mehlman. New York: Columbia University Press, 1992.

———. *The Black Hunter: Forms of Thought and Forms of Society in the Greek World*. Translated by Andrew Szegedy-Maszak. Baltimore: Johns Hopkins University Press, 1986.

———. *The Jews: History, Memory, and the Present*. Translated by David Ames Curtis. New York: Columbia University Press, 1996.

Von Rad, Gerhard. *Old Testament Theology*. 2 vols. Translated by D. M. G. Stalker. New York: Harper and Row, 1960–65.

Vovelle, Michel. *Piété baroque et déchristianisation en Provence au XVIIIe siècle: Les Attitudes devant la mort d'après les clauses des testaments*. Paris: Plon, 1973.

Walzer, Michael. *Spheres of Justice: In Defense of Pluralism and Equality*. New York: Basic Books, 1982.

Wangfleteten, Thierry. *Histoire européenne de la tolérance du XVIe au XXe siècle*. Paris: Livre de Poche, 1998.

Weber, Max. *Economy and Society: An Outline of Interpretive Society.* Edited by
Günther Roth and Claus Wittich. Translated by Ephraim Fischoff et al.
New York: Bedminster Press, 1968; rpt. Berkeley and Los Angeles: University
of California Press, 1978.

———. "Politics as a Vocation." In *From Max Weber: Essays in Sociology,* 77–128.
Edited by H. H. Gerth and C. Wright Mills. New York: Oxford University
Press, 1946.

Weil, Eric. *Philosophie politique.* Paris: Vrin, 1956.

Weil, Simone. "Malheur et joie." In *Oeuvres,* 681–784. Paris: Gallimard, 1989.

Weinrich, Harald. *Lethe: Kunst und Kritik des Vergessens.* Munich: Ch. Beck,
1997.

White, Hayden. "The Burden of History." *History and Theory* 5 (1966): 111–34.

———. *The Content of the Form: Narrative Discourse and Historical
Representation.* Baltimore: Johns Hopkins University Press, 1987.

———. "Historical Emplotment and the Problem of Truth." In Saul Friedlander,
ed., *Probing the Limits of Representation: Nazism and the "Final Solution,"*
37–53. Cambridge, Mass.: Harvard University Press, 1992.

———. *Metahistory: The Historical Imagination in Nineteenth-Century Europe.*
Baltimore: Johns Hopkins University Press, 1978.

———. *Tropics of Discourse.* Baltimore: Johns Hopkins University Press, 1978.

Worms, F. *Introduction à «Matière et Mémoire» de Bergson.* Paris: Presses
Universitaires de France, 1997.

Wright, G. H. von. *Explanation and Understanding.* Ithaca: Cornell University
Press, 1971.

———. "On Promises." In *Philosophical Papers,* vol. 1: 83–99. Ithaca: Cornell
University Press, 1983.

Yates, Frances A. *The Art of Memory.* Chicago: University of Chicago Press, 1966.

Yerushalmi, Yosef Hayim. *Zakhor: Jewish History and Jewish Memory.* Seattle:
University of Washington Press, 1982.

# INDEX